Psychology and Law

Psychology and Law
Topics from an International Conference

Edited by
DAVE J. MÜLLER
Preston Polytechnic, UK

DEREK E. BLACKMAN
University College, Cardiff, UK

and

ANTONY J. CHAPMAN
University of Leeds, Leeds, UK

JOHN WILEY AND SONS

Chichester · New York · Brisbane · Toronto · Singapore

Library of Congress Cataloging in Publication Data:
Main entry under title:

Psychology and law.

'Developed from ... the International Conference on Psychology and Law ... held at Swansea in July 1982'—Pref.
   1. Law—Congresses. 2. Law—Psychology—Congresses. 3. Psychology, Forensic—Congresses. I. Müller, Dave J. II. Blackman, Derek E. III. Chapman, Antony J. IV. International Conference on Psychology and Law (1982 : Swansea, West Glamorgan)
K487.P75A55   1982   340″.11   83-21684

ISBN 0 471 90336 1

British Library Cataloguing in Publication Data:

Psychology and law: topics from an international conference.
   1. Law—Great Britain—Psychology—Congresses
   1. Müller, Dave J. II. Blackman, Derek E. III. Chapman, Antony, J.
   344.1′001′9   K487.P75

ISBN 0 471 90336 1

Typeset in Great Britain by
Photo-Graphics, Honiton, Devon, England.
Printed by St Edmundsbury Press, Suffolk.

List of Contributors

J. MAXWELL ATKINSON SSRC Centre for Socio-Legal Studies, Wolfson College, Oxford, UK

MICHAEL ATKINSON Department of Psychology, University of Western Ontario, London, Ontario N6A 5C2, Canada.

DEREK E. BLACKMAN Department of Psychology, University College, PO Box 78, Cardiff CF1 1XL, UK

RONALD BLACKBURN Park Lane Hospital, Maghull, Liverpool L31 1HW, UK

RAY BULL Department of Psychology, North East London Polytechnic, The Green, Stratford, London E15 4LZ, UK

DOUGLAS CARROLL Department of Psychology, University of Birmingham, Birmingham B15 2TT, UK

DAVID CARSON Faculty of Law, University of Southampton, Southampton SO9 5NH, UK

ANTONY J. CHAPMAN Department of Psychology, University of Leeds, Leeds LS2 9JT, UK

DAN COATES Department of Psychology, University of Wisconsin, W. J. Brogden Building, 1202 West Johnson Street, Madison, Wisconsin 53706, USA

HANS F.M. CROMBAG Faculty of Law, University of Leyden, Leyden, The Netherlands.

W. GUY CUMBERBATCH Applied Psychology Department, The University of Aston in Birmingham, College House, Gosta Green, Birmingham B4 7ET, UK

JAMES H. DAVIS Department of Psychology, University of Illinois, 603 East Daniel Street, Champaign, Illinois 61820, USA

STAN DIVORSKI Research Division, Solicitor General Canada, Ottowa, Ontario, Canada

H. J. EYSENCK Institute of Psychiatry, University of London, De Crespigny Park, London SE5 8AF, UK

WILLIAM E. FOOTE 1020 Tijeras NE, Suite M, Albuquerque, New Mexico 87106, USA

M. J. GUNN Department of Law, The University of Nottingham, University Park, Nottingham NG7 2RD, UK

HUGH J. HALEY Corrections Research Ministry of the Solicitor General, Ottawa, Ontario K1A 0P8, Canada

DAVID F. HALL Department of Psychology, University of Washington, Seattle, Washington 98195, USA

CRAIG HANEY Stevenson College, University of California, Santa Cruz, California 95064, USA

OONAGH M. HARTNETT Department of Applied Psychology, Llwyn-y-Grant, Penylan, Cardiff CF3 7UX, UK

BRIAN HAYDEN Walter S. Hunter Laboratory of Psychology, Brown University, Providence, Rhode Island 02912, USA

STEPHEN HERZBERG University of Wisconsin Law School, 975 Bascom Mall, Madison, Wisconsin 53706, USA

LARRY HEUER Department of Psychology, University of Wisconsin, W. J. Brogden Building, 1202 West Johnson Street, Madison, Wisconsin 53706, USA

C. I. HOWARTH Department of Psychology, University of Nottingham, University Park, Nottingham NG7 2RD, UK

KEVIN HOWELLS Department of Psychology, University of Leicester, Leicester LE1 7RH, UK

MICHAEL KING School of Law, University of Warwick, Coventry, UK

JEANETTE LAWRENCE School of Education, Murdoch University, Murdoch, Queensland 6153, Australia

MICHAEL LEVI Department of Social Administration, University College, Cardiff CF1 1XL, UK

ROGER LITTON Bowring Scholfields Ltd, Insurance Brokers, Manchester, UK

DANIEL LINZ Department of Psychology, University of Wisconsin, W. J. Brogden Building, 1202 West Johnson Street, Madison, Wisconsin 53706, USA

ELIZABETH F. LOFTUS Department of Psychology, University of Washington, Seattle, Washington 98195, USA

S. A. LOVEGROVE Criminology Department, University of Melbourne, Parkville, Victoria 3052, Australia

R. J. MENZIES Department of Criminology, Faculty of Interdisciplinary Studies, Simon Fraser University, Burnaby, British Columbia V5H 1S6, Canada

DAVE J. MÜLLER School of Psychology, Preston Polytechnic, Lancs. UK.

MARK A. J. O'CALLAGHAN Department of Psychology, Hollymoor Hospital, Birmingham B31 5EX, UK

CHRISTOPHER ODDIE Circuit Judge, UK

T. S. PALYS Department of Criminology, Simon Fraser University, Burnaby, British Columbia, V5H 1S6, Canada

KEN PEASE School of Sociology and Social Policy, Ulster Polytechnic, Newtown Abbey, County Antrim, Northern Ireland, UK

STEVEN PENROD Department of Psychology, University of Wisconsin, W. J. Brogden Building, 1202 West Johnson Street, Madison, Wisconsin 53706, USA

ANITA POMERANTZ SSRC Centre for Socio-Legal Studies, Wolfson College, Oxford, UK

GIORA RAHAV Department of Sociology, Tel Aviv University, Ramat-Aviv, Tel Aviv 69978, Israel

SOHAIL RASHID Department of Psychology, University of Guelph, Guelph, Ontario N1G 2W1, Canada

SAMUEL ROLL Psychology Department, University of New Mexico, USA

DIANA S. SEPEJAK Metropolitan Toronto Forensic Service, Clarke Institute of Psychiatry, 1001 Queen Street West, Toronto, Ontario M6J 1H4, Canada

JUDITH SHORT Department of Psychology, The University of Western Ontario, London, Canada

GEOFFREY M. STEPHENSON Social Psychology Research Unit, University of Kent at Canterbury, Canterbury, UK

MEIR TEICHMAN Institute of Criminology, Tel Aviv University, Ramat-Aviv, Tel Aviv 69978, Israel

HAZEL P. TRESSILLIAN JONES Department of Psychology, University of Guelph, Guelph, Ontario N1G 2W1, Canada

NORMAN TUTT Department of Social Administration, University of Lancaster, Fylde College, Lancaster LA1 4YF, UK

NEIL VIDMAR Department of Psychology, The University of Western Ontario, London, Canada

CHRISTOPHER D. WEBSTER Metropolitan Toronto Forensic Service, Clarke Institute of Psychiatry, 1001 Queen Street West, Toronto, Ontario M6J 1H4, Canada

A. DANIEL YARMEY Department of Psychology, University of Guelph, Guelph, Ontario N1G 2W1, Canada

Contents

SECTION III: THE SOCIAL CONTEXT OF CRIME

SECTION IV: EYEWITNESS TESTIMONY

SECTION V: EVIDENCE IN COURT

SECTION VI: DECISION-TAKING

SECTION VII: CARE AND REHABILITATION

SECTION VIII: PSYCHO-LEGAL TRAINING

Foreword

Law and Psychology: A Personal View

Christopher Oddie

This book consists of revised versions of papers first presented at the International Conference on Psychology and Law organised by the Welsh Branch of the British Psychological Society. I was fortunate enough to attend the conference, and so it gave me particular pleasure when I was asked if my own contribution to it might become a foreword to the published record of the proceedings. I hope that the personal view of law and psychology which I was asked to give may stimulate readers to enjoy the immensely interesting range of scholarship and research this book contains. Perhaps lawyers may widen their horizons, as I certainly did, by learning of all the ways in which psychological research bears on our everyday work. And the professional psychologist may realize how valuable and relevant the insights of psychology have been to one layperson working in the field.

The first task for anyone expressing a personal view is to describe one's own standpoint. I am neither an academic lawyer nor a member of the senior judiciary with responsibility for policy in the development of the law. My job is to apply the law and take part in the making of legal decisions in the Crown Court and in the County Court. In the former I usually sit with a jury and sometimes with lay magistrates trying criminal cases. In the latter I sit alone trying civil cases, including disputes under family law. My interest in the law and legal processes is therefore a practical one. I will try to give an impression of the way in which psychology bears in the work I do, and try to suggest where and how it might most effectively help other lawyers working in my field. Perhaps my contribution might be seen as a consumer's report on the product, with some comments on future marketing possibilities.

I begin with a short account of my own introduction to psychology. Like many others I began by trying to find out more about other people's behaviour, and ended by examining my own. My first interest was in the contribution of psychology to criminology. I hoped for a better understanding of deviant behaviour with a view to its modification in the criminal justice system. It would be difficult to summarize all the insights shown by psychological research in this field. For my part, I learnt more about the multifactorial origins of crime. It seemed to me that the deviant behaviour was less the symptom of an abnormal personality and more the outcome of different factors upon a normal personality. The opportunities for modifying it within the criminal justice process appeared much less than many people believed. Crime was much more a challenge to society as a whole than a problem which the criminal justice system could be expected to resolve on its own.

The second field on which I found the insights of psychology of great value was in family law. Developmental psychology has much to say to the lawyer about parental relationships and the effect of marriage breakdown upon children. Studies of arbitration processes stimulated my thoughts about the use of the adversarial procedure and the possibility of more effective conciliation and mediation in disputes affecting children.

The third area of my work where psychological research was particularly relevant was in the use of the legal process to reach factual conclusions. I soon came across some of the immense literature upon witness testimony. Of special interest to me were studies of the perceptual limitations of eyewitness evidence in general, of the efficacy of identification by facial features, voice, or other means, of the sorts of factors which are said to enhance recall (such as forensic hypnosis) or interfere with it (such as the verbal techniques used to elicit factual evidence), and of the effect of the adversarial procedure itself. The lessons of this research had an immediate relevance to the way I approached the assessment of witnesses in my everyday work.

The fourth area of interest was the psychologist's perception of the process of legal decision-making itself. Psychological analysis of decision-making has long been a part of graduate business studies, and there can be few lawyers who would not enhance their knowledge of what actually happens in court by an acquaintance with some of the published research on legal decisions. Jury studies are of particular relevance to my own work in the Crown Court.

Lastly, there was the psychologist's analysis of legal concepts. My eyes were opened to the very different view which psychologists have of familiar legal concepts, such as '*mens rea*'. Psychology raises a number of challenging questions about the common-sense assumptions upon which our law is based and our legal decisions are made.

My introduction to psychology had two consequences for me. First, I gained more insight into the practical problems which I encountered in my work. Secondly, I became increasingly aware of the large body of psycho-legal research upon many aspects of the law and legal processes. Anyone to whom this happens in mid-career, as it did to me, must feel a certain unease at the daunting prospect of trying to take in all the academic studies bearing upon one's everyday experience. However, it is an unease which has been considerably allayed since the British Psychological Society's Division of

Criminological and Legal Psychology has set out to interest lawyers in the research which psychologists have done in their studies of law and legal processes, and to encourage discussion of the issues raised by such research. I know that all of us from the law who have been fortunate enough to attend conferences organized by the Division have found them enormously stimulating and enjoyable occasions. At the same time, I think that everyone feels there is much more to be done before the insights of psychology and the limits of its application to law and legal processes can be fully appreciated by all who work in the law and in psychology. I should therefore like to touch upon some topics which arise in any discussion of this central problem.

In considering what psychologists can do to influence the development of the law, I think that one aspect of legal reform can be overlooked. It is easy to think that the law is the sole province of lawyers. Now, of course, lawyers, be they judges, practitioners, or academics, have a crucial part to play in the development and practice of the law. There is a substantial body of what is sometimes called 'judge-made law'. Clearly, those who wish to modify or change the law would be well on the way to their objective if they could muster the combined forces of the academic lawyers, the legal profession, and the judiciary. But some of the questions raised by psychologists could only be resolved by a legislative decision. For example, any substantial change in the law as to the mental element in crime, or any change in the jury system, would require action by Parliament. While there are grey areas in which both statutory provision and judicial interpretation may operate, it is primarily the responsibility of Parliament to change the law. To help it in this task, of course, we have the Law Commission as a permanent review body, and from time to time a Royal Commission is set up by Parliament to report on some particular subject. So, for example, a Royal Commission under the chairmanship of the late Lord Butler was charged with a comprehensive review of the law involving mental disorder, and made a number of recommendations about the liability of mentally disordered persons for criminal offences. More recently, the Law Commission produced a paper on the mental element in crime. The Royal Commission on Criminal Procedure has not only considered a number of areas of the law in which psychologists have shown particular interest: it has commissioned studies by distinguished forensic psychologists to assist in making recommendations to Parliament.

The point I make is obvious, but perhaps needs to be emphasized. If psychologists are to ensure that their views are properly considered in any reform of the law, then the findings of their research must be directed towards those who advise and influence the legislature which has the responsibility for making and changing the law. It seems to me that this may require consideration of two methods of approach. First, to be aware of topics under examination by the Law Commission, any Royal Commission, or Parliament itself, and to prepare detailed and well researched submissions with practical proposals for reform for them to consider. Secondly, like the Law Commission itself, to keep a continuing interest in aspects of the law which psychologists have studied in the course of their research, and, where necessary, to suggest consideration of their findings and future topics for consideration by the Law Commission.

Another question is the scope for legal change in response to the findings of research. One area in which reform has been suggested concerns the participation of the citizen in court decisions. In this country, lay magistrates, sitting in their own courts with a clerk to advise them in the law, decide far more cases than the higher courts. They also sit with circuit judges in the Crown Court to decide on appeals and cases committed for sentence from magistrates' courts. In every contested criminal case committed for trial at the Crown Court, it is a jury of laypeople who decide whether the defendant's guilt is proved or not. I have already referred to the valuable research studies by psychologists into decision-making by juries. There are some people who do not believe in the efficacy of the jury system, and suggest that research findings confirm their view that it should be abolished or substantially changed. They point to the success of the Dutch system, which does without juries, and to the very different form of lay participation in legal processes in Germany and France. I think that the majority of people in Britain would not wish to do away with the jury system, or, indeed, the lay magistracy. If this is right, then it may be because they regard the responsibility placed on the citizen to play his or her part in the administration of justice as one of the fundamental points of our constitution. In short, there are important political considerations, as well as questions of functional efficacy, to be taken into account in any discussion of change. This is true of other areas of the law as well. And so those involved in the law and legal processes may often be more interested in the insights of psychology and more responsive to them in so far as they help us to operate the system we have rather than suggest major changes in it. This is not to say that psychologists should not suggest radical change where they believe it is necessary. It is simply to emphasize that where they have practical suggestions for immediate improvement of the legal system in its day-to-day work, the consideration of these proposals may seem to be the first priority.

Lay participation in legal processes has a significant effect upon the nature and development of the law itself. Just as in Britain we bring the citizen into the process of decision, and eschew the concept of law as a mystery reserved to its priesthood, so we must make it comprehensible for its purpose. Its concepts must not be too abstruse. Its concerns must be practical. It must speak common sense for the common man. Yet it must be comprehensive as well as explicit. These are demanding requirements, and it would be surprising if they were easy to meet. Some legal concepts have been developed to deal with very different problems from others. So, the law may sometimes find itself riding two horses, each intent on pulling in a different direction at the same time. It must find a way, by thorough re-examination of its own propositions and structure, to resolve the contradictions. And, in fact, in the constant review and development of its principles and practice, the law does show a much greater flexibility than it is sometimes given credit for.

The point which I want to emphasize is that the law is a practical system of rules for application by lay as well as professional judges to a wide variety of human behaviour. It is developing all the time, and is much less set in its ways and much more sensitive to change than is sometimes realized. Thus the findings of psychological research, if clear and susceptible to practical application, will not, I believe, be unwelcome to the law. It may not be easy, and it may take time, for their implications to be considered and, where necessary, incorporated in the explicit provisions of substantive law or legal procedure. But, in the meantime, well researched and publicised conclusions will influence those who apply the law as it stands.

As a footnote, I would like to add one further suggestion. Lawyers need to know where their common-sense assumptions are open to criticism by psychologists and why. But they also need to know which of those assumptions are shared if they are to respond to the findings of psychological research. In short, we need to know, not only what psychologists are saying, but how far they think their conclusions go when their practical implementation is considered.

One direct influence of psychology upon the law is through the work of forensic psychologists. There are of course limits upon the extent to which evidence from psychologists is admissible in our courts, particularly where it might be thought to remove from a jury their responsibility for deciding questions of fact for themselves. For example, it may be easier to introduce expert evidence if the issue for decision turns upon the operation of what is seen as an abnormal mind or personality than if it concerns the operation of its normal equivalent. How widely that principle is interpreted in future cases may be open to argument. All I wish to stress here is that, if the law is careful about the admission of expert evidence from other intellectual disciplines, it is by no means closed to it. Lawyers are particularly concerned with the need to assess evidence, and with the best means of doing this so that the right decision is made by those who have to make it. But evidence from all sorts of different specialities is admitted every day in the courts. The range of expert evidence which has to be understood, if necessary challenged, and presented to court by a barrister in common-law practice is wide. For example, in my own professional life I had to argue cases turning on modern obstetrical practice for Friesian cattle, the laws of mechanics affecting the efficiency of a particular car's braking system, and the pharmacological effect and physiological consequences of mixing alcohol with cough mixture. In all these cases the expert witnesses called by the parties went back to first principles, and drew on the findings of research to give their evidence.

Over the years, I think that the medical profession in particular has come to terms with the lawyers' concerns, and has modified the law's approach to issues which are in many ways similar to those raised by psychologists today. I do not wish to minimize the difficulties which forensic psychologists may experience in putting their observations of human nature before the Courts. It is not easy if this questions the assumptions upon which the law and the legal processes are based. Sometimes, I know forensic psychologists have been upset by the response in court to evidence which did not accord with the common-sense assumptions of those to whom it was given. But I am confident that given time, goodwill, and an increasing knowledge by lawyers and psychologists of each other's concerns, these difficulties can be overcome. In particular, when there are more lawyers with a knowledge of psychology, there will be more opportunity for forensic psychologists to be brought into cases where their expertise could assist the court in its decisions.

An indirect influence of psychology upon the law is through the medium of reports by social workers, probation officers, doctors, and others to the courts in cases where the psychological assessment of the person who is the subject of the report is a relevant factor in the decision which has to be taken. Sometimes these reports contain an assessment by personality tests. More often, there is no specifically personal assessment by a psychologist, but the report is either explicitly or implicitly conveying the maker's own perceptions of psychology. Under our adversarial system, there is certainly a risk that an unchallenged report may escape the careful scrutiny which it would otherwise have, particularly if it has a definite recommendation in it. There are occasions when most of us have wondered whether the principles of psychology explicitly or implicitly retailed in a report point quite as conclusively as its author suggests to its assessment of the client. Perhaps one might use an old metaphor and say that the chain of reasoning between the psychologists' research and the decision which is made in reliance upon it is as strong as the weakest link. So we all have a responsibility to see that each person concerned in that process of reasoning is well informed about the nature, extent, and limits of psychology's practical contribution to law and the legal processes. In particular, the more lawyers know about psychology, the better they will be able to recognize and assess the psychological content of reports adduced in evidence by others.

What is the best way of ensuring that all who work in the law and psychology can benefit by a mutual knowledge of each other's concerns? First, and foremost, it seems to me, by occasions at which academic and practising lawyers can meet psychologists to hear the latest contributions to psycho-legal research, and discuss at a formal and an informal level the ways in which that knowledge may be applied to the law and legal processes. Secondly, I believe that psychologists should try and persuade their academic colleagues in the law faculties of universities and polytechnics to encourage an interest in psychology and its relevance to the law. In a very real sense, the law's development depends upon the quality of the legal practitioners who prepare and present cases in the courts. No-one suggests that every lawyer should be a trained psychologist. On the other hand, a knowledge of the basic principles of the science of human behaviour would greatly enhance the professional skills of any practitioner in a profession so concerned with all aspects of human behaviour as the law. Not only will lawyers with such knowledge have a greater understanding of their clients. They will also perceive more of the problems which arise when evidence has to be adduced and assessed in legal proceedings. They will be able to apply the findings of psychology in a practical way to the work of the courts. Whether that is done by the introduction of evidence from forensic psychologists in some cases, or more generally by their own wider knowledge of human behaviour through an acquaintance with the research findings of psychologists, lawyers will have the opportunity to make a greater contribution to the development of the law. Lastly, I hope that psychologists will encourage their own students to emulate the achievement of the contributors to this volume in learning so much about law and legal processes to produce the impressive body of psycho-legal research in the following pages.

Preface

The chapters in this volume are developed from presentations made at the International Conference on Psychology and Law which was organized by the present editors on behalf of the Welsh Branch of The British Psychological Society and was held at Swansea in July 1982. The conference attracted a large number of participants. They came from many countries and were drawn from a wide range of disciplines in addition to psychology and law. The programme consisted of more than 150 papers, the abstracts of which have appeared in the *Bulletin of The British Psychological Society* (1982, **35**, A92–A111). Tape-recordings of most of the presentations are available from Inter-Forum, 2 Park Street, Cirencester, Gloucestershire GL7 2BN, UK.

The chapters have been chosen to illustrate the breadth of common interests in contemporary psychology and law. The book, which may therefore be considered a general introduction to this field, thereby reflects the diversity of topics discussed at the conference. It includes both empirical and theoretical papers, and to some extent efforts have been made to reflect the international participation at the conference.

More specialized sets of papers developed from the conference are to be found in special issues of the following journals:

> *Current Psychological Reviews,* 1982, **2,** 247–358
> *International Review of Applied Psychology,* 1984, in press
> *Journal of Community Psychology,* 1986, in press
> *Medicine and Law: An International Journal,* 1983, in press.

We are indebted to many people who helped in organizing and running the conference as well as in producing this volume. The success of the conference programme owed a great deal to the work of an International Advisory Group:

> Dr A. J. Ashworth (UK)
> Professor S. L. Brodsky (USA)
> Professor N. Christie (Norway)
> Dr R. V. G. Clarke (UK)
> Dr H. F. M. Crombag (The Netherlands)

Professor A. N. Doob (Canada)
Dr D. P. Farrington (UK)
Professor F. Ferracuti (Italy)
Mr J. C. Freeman (UK)
Dr G. K. Laycock (UK)
Dr S. M. Lloyd-Bostock (UK)
Dr A. Lovegrove (Australia)
Professor G. Mikula (Austria)
Professor J. Monahan (USA)
Profesor B. D. Sales (USA)
Dr S. A. Shah (USA)
Mrs M. C. Smith (UK)
Professor G. M. Stephenson (UK)
Professor A. J. W. Taylor (New Zealand)
Professor G. B. Trasler (UK)
Professor D. B. Wexler (USA)

The smooth running of the conference was a reflection of the hard, unobtrusive work of our stewards, Jacqui Eastlake, Sarah Ford, Ken Hughes, Petra Hughes, Mo Roy, Pauline Waldron, and Beverley Watson. Also to be thanked for their generous help are Wendy Sheehy, Gill Fitzgibbon, and Dave Oborne. Finally, special mention must be made of Julia Hawkins for her skilful and tireless administrative and secretarial help during all stages of the planning and running of the conference.

This book, then, has been developed from a memorable international conference. It has been impossible to include papers from more than a fraction of the original participants, but these specially written chapters do reflect the diversity of the programme. We intend that the book should contribute in its own right to a field of interdisciplinary research which is currently vibrant, which addresses questions of social significance, and which in turn casts light on conceptual and methodological issues in its parent disciplines.

August 1983   D. J. Müller, Cardiff
                                         D. E. Blackman, Cardiff
                                         A. J. Chapman, Leeds

SECTION I

Introducing Psychology and Law

Psychology uses systematic empirical methods in an effort to study behaviour objectively and to identify the ways in which behaviour is influenced by other events. Law, on the other hand, serves to regulate human behaviour in a social context, and in so doing it emphasizes autonomy of action and our responsibility for our own conduct. These different perspectives, and the current relationships between the disciplines of psychology and law, are explored in this introductory section.

Blackman, Müller, and Chapman provide a preliminary review of the areas in which psychology and law share common interests. Although they consider in general the potential gains to the two parent disciplines from research on psycho-legal problems, they also consider some tensions which can emerge from the different fundamental perspectives on behaviour and conduct favoured by psychology and by law. These tensions are illustrated by means of a discussion of how legal issues can limit the use of the psychological techniques of behaviour modification. **Hartnett** takes up the question of how the law can be used in an effort to regulate or eliminate prejudice in our society. Her review of recent legislation considers the extent to which anti-discriminatory legislation has been effective. Clearly the need for careful empirical analyses in such a sensitive field cannot be over-emphasized. However, the need for empirical evaluation of the effectiveness of law is discussed more generally by **Howarth and Gunn**, who emphasize that there can be a conflict between the requirements of objective evaluations of the law and the legal insistence on the principles of equity and personalized justice. Howarth and Gunn argue, with support from some striking examples, that adequate empirical evaluations of the effectiveness of a law might serve ultimately to increase public confidence in the legal system.

The following chapters by Haney and by Crombag develop the discussion of how psychology might be used to change the law. **Haney** raises the question of whether in fact psychologists are ever able to dissociate their own values from the empirical evidence which they collect. As a social psychologist, Haney argues that it is impossible to make decisions based only on 'detached'

1

evidence and he therefore suggests that psycho-legal researchers should recognize the values which are involved in using facts to advocate socially or morally desirable legal change. **Crombag**, on the other hand, argues the case for a behavioural analysis of criminal law as a technology of social control. He believes the technology is often ineffective, not because of a confusion between facts and values, but because we are unwilling to rely on clear behavioural criteria of effectiveness. Crombag argues that in this research even the concept of *mens rea*, which is so important in criminal law, is a source of confusion.

In the final chapter of this first section, **King** provides a sceptical lawyer's view of the use of empirical psychology to study the legal system with a view to making it more efficient. He advocates that psychologists should not seek to change the legal system, which has evolved to suit its circumstances and which has its own mechanisms for adjusting to changing requirements. He sees a useful but more limited role for psychologists, that of describing how the legal system operates.

These opening chapters, then, review general questions about the relationships between psychological research in legal contexts and the operation and development of the law itself. While some psychologists may feel their research has implications for more effective or consistent legal processes, the extent to which their facts are in truth value-free has been questioned, and some feel that the law will not (or perhaps should not) prove responsive to the requirements or implications of psychological research. There is a tension here, manifested in all the chapters in this introductory section, and this may serve to temper the optimism apparent in many of the more focused contributions included in subsequent sections.

Psychology and Law
Edited by D.J. Müller, D.E. Blackman, and A.J. Chapman
© 1984 John Wiley & Sons Ltd

Chapter 1

Perspectives in Psychology and Law

Derek E. Blackman, Dave J. Müller, and Antony J. Chapman

Few things in life can be more interesting than what people do and why they do it. Psychologists are therefore fortunate to have marked out the study of human behaviour and experience as their special domain. In the most general terms, contemporary psychology is characterized by the use of systematic empirical methods to obtain valid and reliable data about behaviour and experience on which may be developed adequate accounts which have both predictive and explanatory power. Its data base can sometimes be gained by careful direct observation of what people do in the so-called 'real' world. Usually, however, some form of structure is imposed by investigators, sometimes to the extent of setting up experiments to study the specific influences on behaviour of variables which can be systematically manipulated. In whatever way the facts of psychology are won, however, it has become clear that the gathering of objective accounts of behaviour can be both technically demanding and laborious. For example, the mere act of watching another person's or even one's own behaviour can change it. Such an obvious technique as asking people what they or others do can produce accounts which, though fascinating and potentially important in themselves, may not relate accurately to what they actually do, and people's explanations for their own behaviour are sometimes incoherent or implausible. Despite such problems, psychologists have studied an impressively wide range of conduct, normal and abnormal, of young and old, of individuals and of groups. They have begun to unravel the influences on behaviour and experience of social context, biological disposition, and environmental circumstance. Psychology aims to be an effective scientific discipline, through its objectivity and the power of its explanations.

The discipline of law also focuses on what people do, but it is not normally thought to aspire to any form of scientific status. Instead law is primarily a social system created with a view to regulating the conduct of the members of a community. In general terms, law uses both formal and informal systems to generate and enforce rules which are usually applied to individuals and which express what behaviour is permissible in their community and what is not. These rules are usually said to be designed to ensure that unacceptable behaviour does not occur, but law also incorporates procedures for dealing with any transgressions. In this regard, law too depends on a factual data base, here used for example to establish to some criterion of proof that a behavioural transgression has indeed taken place. The social system of law is a reflection of life in social communities, and it has given rise to a number of professional roles to support its rule, from legislator to crime-prevention and law-enforcement officer, from legal advocate to judge, from supportive counsellor to punitive figure of authority. All these roles are expressed, of course, through the behaviour of individuals appointed officially or unofficially by the community and sustained by general expressions from the community as a whole regarding the appropriate goals to be striven for and the social systems to be operated on its behalf.

It is inevitable then that psychology and law share common interests. The many areas of overlap could provide the ground for hostility and conflict between the professionals of the two disciplines. Fortunately, however, there has in recent years been a constructive surge of interest in the mutual problems of psychology and law. This was reviewed by Tapp (1976), who saw signs that the work then considered was an overture for future research interest. The recent review by Monahan and Loftus (1982) has amply confirmed this prediction. In the intervening period, the American Psychological Association established a new Division of Psychology in Law (Division 41) and The British Psychological Society established its Division of Criminological and Legal Psychology. The Social Science Research Council in Britain has given some of its hard-pressed financial resources to stimulating regular symposia on psychology and law (see Farrington, Hawkins, and Lloyd-Bostock, 1979; Lloyd-Bostock, 1981a,b). Research on psychology and law has flourished, and specialist journals have been established such as *Law and Human Behavior*. Studies in psychology and law have given rise to and are now supported by many excellent analyses and authoritative reviews, both of the field in general and of specific aspects of it, recent examples of which are illustrated by Ellison and Buckout (1981), Feldman (1977), Konečni and Ebbesen (1982), Lipsett and Sales (1980), Loftus (1979), Monahan (1981), Nietzel (1979), Reiser (1982), Sales (1977, 1981), Sprague (1982), Tapp and Levine (1977), and Wexler (1981).

The expansion of academic interest at the interfaces between psychology and law is obvious and has been extensively documented. In the light of an embarrassment of empirical riches to consider, the adequacy of earlier reviews, and the diversity of previous theoretical analyses, this chapter has modest goals. It seeks to indicate in general terms the different kinds of problems in which psychology and law share interests; it considers some of the potential gains for psychologists and for lawyers of the kinds of collaboration which have marked the last decade; and it concludes by briefly considering some sources of tension between psychology and law and the prognosis for the current cross-fertilization of the two disciplines.

SHARED INTERESTS IN PSYCHOLOGY AND LAW

No attempt is offered in this section to review specific programmes. Instead an undocumented discussion is used simply to indicate the breadth of commonality between the disciplines of psychology and law.

A first context in which lawyers might expect to turn to psychologists is in connection with problems related to psychologically abnormal offenders, seeking perhaps psychometric evidence. But more general questions quickly emerge. To what extent is it appropriate to hold criminally responsible for their offences individuals who are either mentally ill or mentally handicapped? What are the appropriate and most effective methods for dealing with psychologically abnormal offenders? These questions in some senses strike at some fundamental general issues in psychology and law which are discussed later. However, they can be expressed here in pragmatic terms with reference to a more limited population.

There is no doubt that some individuals in our community exhibit either consistently unusual patterns of behaviour or unduly limited behavioural repertoires. Psychologists have inevitably been drawn to the study of mental illness and mental handicap both in order to identify general psychological processes, as expressed here in aberrant or limited form, or in the hope of developing effective methods of helping or treating these patients. They have therefore accumulated a considerable amount of empirical information about abnormal behaviour to complement the predominantly medical diagnoses proffered by psychiatrists and others and long considered relevant to judicial processes. One characteristic of much psychological analysis, however, has been a reluctance to diagnose mental illness, for example, as the *cause of* abnormal behaviour. Rather, mental illness is seen by many psychologists as a *label for* aberrant behaviour, a view which emphasizes, along with others, what can be termed the social construction of mental illness. Such an interpretation, based on empirical studies, has gained in influence, and its effect may be to deprive courts of law of easy recourse to diagnoses expounded by experts behind which they may shelter. A specific offence requires to be evaluated in this alternative scheme within the broader context of an individual's *behaviour*. In one sense, responsibility would be absolved to the extent that the offence is *typical* of the accused person's normal behavioural repertoire, and this raises particular problems with respect to judgments (social as well as judicial) about isolated aberrant acts. Psychiatric expertise has almost by tradition appeared to be strained in such cases. Psychologists believe that their systematic studies of abnormal behaviour must be of ultimate benefit in judicial as well as in other contexts.

With respect to the disposal of 'psychologically abnormal' offenders, psychology may again of course have an important role to play. The analyses discussed above blur to some extent fundamental distinctions between bad and mad, with their now traditional association with punishment and treatment respectively. Once more this issue is related to a more general problem, that of appropriate methods of disposal for criminals in general. 'Treatment' for 'psychologically abnormal', or indeed for 'normal', offenders may be desirable, but it demands that appropriate methods of treatment be available, a problem which has itself given rise recently to much litigation in the USA. Psychological research has prompted new forms of treatment for mentally ill and mentally handicapped persons. For example, empirical studies of learning have given rise to the techniques of behaviour modification. These psychological, as opposed to medical, treatments require evaluation in broadly penal contexts. The case of behaviour modification serves to emphasize an important point here, in that its techniques have been used in overtly punitive as well as supposedly therapeutic institutions, that is to say in prisons as well as hospitals. This development immediately limits further the traditional distinctions drawn between punishment and treatment.

It is easy to see how these issues of criminal responsibility and appropriate disposal can be extended to 'psychologically normal' offenders, for example to children. This in turn leads to a second general area in which psychology has great relevance for law, namely the empirical study of individual differences in behaviour. Psychologists have long been interested in why there is variation in behaviour between individuals. They have studied personality characteristics of offenders and found some correlations between these and the different types of offence. Such differences in personality may reflect to some extent genetic influences on behaviour, and psychologists now have techniques for more subtle polygenic analyses of behaviour as well as the single-gene Mendelian model. The epidemiology and aetiology of offending are also surely influenced, however, by environmental factors which interact with an individual's genetic endowment. Thus an individual's exposure to specific environmental milieux may lead to a greater probability of offending. Analyses of genetic and environmental influences on behaviour, and of their interactions, give psychologists an increasing understanding of the provenance of behaviour and in the context of offending thereby identify individuals with higher likelihoods of acting antisocially or criminally. Nowhere do genetic and environmental factors interact to exert greater influence, of course, than in the family context of the growing child. One result of psychologists' studies of genetic, environmental, and developmental influences on behaviour is to extend further questions about the attribution of criminal responsibility for offences even with 'normal' offenders. Such attribution becomes perhaps less easy to the extent that courts are helped to interpret the conduct of an offender in terms of the genetic, environmental, or developmental history of the individual. This question in turn leads again of course to the question of the appropriate disposal of offenders.

The third area in which psychological research has implications for the practices of law is to be found with respect to establishing relevant facts about offences. An excellent example of this is to be found in the extensive literature of eyewitness testimony, which attests lucidly to the selectivity of perception, the structured changes which occur in memories of critical events, the extent to which different methods of investigation can elicit different information from witnesses, and many other problems with practical implications. Such research has amply indicated, for example, that crimes can rarely be replayed in court, but that the incidents which the criminal courts examine are often addressed largely through active but easily overlooked processes of reconstruction on the part not only of witnesses but also of the accused, jurors, or the judiciary. Psychologists have offered general advice to courts with respect to the elucidation and evaluation of such problems, and have also often been in a position to challenge or refute information which stands in danger of becoming the 'facts' of a case.

The judicial and other processes by which the rules of law are related to individual cases have provided a fourth focus of psychological research in legal contexts in which courts are evaluated in terms of the principles of social psychology. For example, it has been shown that different sequences used for conveying information in courts can exert effects on the probability that a defendant will be judged guilty, as can the physical characteristics of the *dramatis personae* in court. Much research has also investigated the effects of the composition of juries on their decision-taking and the social dynamics which may characterize jurors' task of reaching an agreed verdict. The disposal strategies of magistrates and judges have also been considered, sometimes revealing potentially important but unrecognized inconsistencies both within and between individuals. Research in this category again emphasizes that in the process of trial the elucidation of facts is not always a simple matter, and it also indicates that the participants in the process are influenced by more than just the facts of the matter when they make their decisions. Greater awareness of the psychological dynamics of these situations can lead to desirable scepticism and caution and to efforts to control them. Of course it can also be exploited to achieve specific goals, for example by increasing the chances of acquittal by means of the careful, even cynical, manipulation of normally uncontrolled but nevertheless important factors in a trial.

A fifth topic of general interest has been mentioned already, but deserves to be identified in its own right, namely the evaluation of different methods used for dealing with those who are found guilty of crimes. As well as addressing the general issues of punishment rather than treatment noted above, psychological studies have investigated the effects of imprisonment in terms of the mental health of prisoners as well as in terms of its deterrence of further criminal acts by the offender or by others in the community. Psychologists have evaluated in similarly broad terms the effects of alternative methods of dealing with criminals, such as probation and community service. Such evaluations are of course not necessarily carried out only at a global level, for the effects of variations in prison regimes and probation orders, for example, have also been investigated by psychologists, particularly with respect to their effects on the attitudes of offenders and their rate of subsequent offending.

Psychologists have long had an interest in the broad social contexts of legislation and law enforcement, through issues which have received greater prominence generally in recent years. Anti-discrimination laws provide an example of attempts by society to combat social or racial prejudices, topics which psychologists have long studied. Such laws deserve to be evaluated not only in terms of rates of crime but also in terms of the social values of members of the community in general. Psychologists' investigations of the sometimes complex relationships between attitudes and overt behaviour are of particular importance in this connection. It is also interesting that some of the psychometric devices developed by psychologists have themselves been subject to legal scrutiny in recent years. As instruments of educational policy and also in the context of the equal treatment of both sexes, psychometric tests have been challenged with respect to their validity and reliability and in terms of their social impact, thereby exposing the methods and findings of psychology to unusual and surely desirable public scrutiny. The social context of law *enforcement* also provides some important opportunities for psychological research. In Britain the relative merits of low profile community policing and of more prominent and more coercive strategies are being widely debated. The discussion appears at present often to be emotional and lacking in empirical data. It is particularly important, however, that adequate empirical evaluations be carried out with respect both to attitudes and overt behaviour. This problem of maintaining social order may interact malevolently with other social influences in legal contexts, as for example if there are discriminatory attitudes or behaviour on the part of police towards ethnic or other minority groups. Also worthy of mention in these socio-legal aspects of psychology are investigations of how perceptions of the severity or even of the prevalence of crimes can affect crime statistics.

This leads to a seventh important general area of interaction between psychology and law. Applied psychologists in particular have skills in evaluating the demands of jobs and the personal characteristics of those who may fill them. They are therefore in a position to make important contributions to the selection and effective training of professionals throughout the legal system – police, lawyers, magistrates, judges. Some members of these professions are coming increasingly to appreciate the relevance of psychology to their tasks.

Finally, it is worth mentioning that psychology, as a growing element in our social community, is itself becoming more subject to legal control. Legal scrutiny of the use of psychological tests has already been mentioned, but the very discipline of psychology itself is becoming subject to greater legal regulation, especially in its applied roles. Thus psychologists or those who claim to use psychological techniques are already required to be legally registered in some countries, though this is not yet the case in the United Kingdom. Such registration usually allows the profession of psychology to regulate itself, but within a clear legal framework.

A brief account such as this cannot be an authoritative review of psychology and law. It should be noted also that the account is written solely from the perspective of psychologists. This incomplete and idiosyncratic review is therefore designed merely to illustrate that psychology and law do share many common interests, all of course arising from the key fact that behaviour provides the focus of each of the two disciplines.

THE BENEFITS OF SYNTHESIS

The demonstration that psychologists and lawyers share common interests in many fields does not in itself explain the current enthusiasm for research in these areas. It is therefore worth considering briefly the advantages that accrue from emphasizing these mutual interests. What are these advantages for psychologists, and, to a lesser extent, what for lawyers?

The lure of the law for psychologists is readily explained. Of necessity, law has developed in such a way that it is able to deal with a wide range of interesting human behaviour, and this has undoubtedly proved attractive to a generation of psychologists nurtured on detailed studies of rats pressing levers or of people perceiving artificial visual information for brief moments in sterile laboratories. However satisfyingly scientific such studies have proved to be, they do not always capture the richness of human conduct. Not before time, perhaps, psychology is now moving towards a greater emphasis on studies of the 'real' behaviour of 'real' people in their 'real' worlds. Students of memory, to take one example, are currently moving away from the artificial and contrived world of memory drums and nonsense syllables. The problems confronted by courts of eliciting from witnesses memories of events or of faces provide an important and socially relevant field for empirical study, but one which still has some structure imposed upon it by the procedures of law. Many important psychological studies of memory are therefore now conducted either in legal contexts or in situations which simulate crucial aspects of those situations. In general terms experimental psychology is becoming more adventurous in seeking more naturalistic models of human behaviour, and law provides a structured forum for some extremely complex and engaging patterns of human conduct. Social psychologists also find a natural arena for their studies of social dynamics in the structured world of the courtroom, in which the attitudes, expectancies, and conduct of the participants are acted out to some real effect. Similarly the jury room provides a place where social influences on decisions really do occur, and where they really do matter. In general, this wish to extend empirical psychology to the study of behaviour in the real world is greatly to be welcomed, and it is likely to be extremely beneficial to psychology itself. The careful codified world of the law provides a natural focus for psychologists with such aspirations, and has reality for those who play their parts within it.

Arguments such as these can be developed through all the various fields of enquiry discussed in the previous section. In all cases, the processes of law and its methods of social regulation lay before psychologists invitingly real but structured issues, the study of which challenges their prized empirical methods. Methodological issues therefore find ready expression in this field of psychology, where the advantages of field methods and direct observation of structured processes are pitted against the advantages of analogue or simulation studies which attempt to extract the crucial features of the behavioural phenomena, and where the inherent lack of control of the former method is traded off against the problems of extrapolating back to the real world from the latter. Studies in psychology and law also promise to feed back to psychology enriching concepts at the theoretical level, and at the same time to provide useful information which may be of pragmatic benefit to the efficient practice of law. What is more, psychologists have surely noted that the latter outcome provides them with a further potential source of importance or influence through the role of psychologist as expert.

With respect to the law, fields of study such as those reviewed in the previous section hold the promise of a greater awareness of the social dynamics of legal processes. Information which leads to a greater psychological understanding of an offender, to a greater awareness of previously unrecognized influences on judicial decision taking, to more empirical information about the effectiveness of methods of disposal of criminals, or to a deeper appreciation of the social construction of crime, to list but a few possibilities, is to be welcomed by those whose task it is to run an effective, consistent, and sensitive legal system.

Nevertheless it should be recognized that there is sometimes some resistance in legal circles to information which psychological research can bring forward. For example, knowing more about the influences which lead to the commission of offences may help us to feel that we understand offenders better, but it does not necessarily make it easier to decide in law how to deal with them either in their own interests or in the interests of the community as a whole. Psychological information about the fallibility of eyewitnesses, the intrusive influences of 'irrelevant' features of a trial, or the inconsistencies of judges in their decisions about extremely complex sets of circumstances can surely appear negative in its impact to those who must keep legal wheels turning. Similarly, investigations of racial prejudice in police forces or of adverse psychological effects of imprisonment can appear to be little more than attacks on legal authority if they are not presented carefully and sensitively. In particular it should be noted that the adversarial system characteristic of courts is a poor showplace for scientific advances, for in truth most isolated behavioural data are always open to competing interpretations. Some feel that there is a danger of psychologists overselling their prowess in legal contexts or of mounting an apparently destructive attack on procedures arrived at on behalf of the community by custom and precedent.

Some feel that psychologists have produced few unambiguous facts which can be used to contribute to constructive change within the legal system. This conclusion may seem unduly negative, but it should be tempered by the thought that the competent collection of information about psychological aspects of law, coupled with a dispassionate advocacy of their practical relevance, can ultimately only be beneficial to those who have roles to play at the various levels of the legal system. Such benefits may take the form of making them more aware of previously unrecognized influences or of hiatuses in empirical knowledge which can distort the operation of the legal system and prevent it from achieving the goals to which society expects it to aspire. In the conclusion of their recent book, however, Konečni and Ebbesen (1982) are distinctly pessimistic about the possibility of overcoming entrenched professional interests within the legal system by means of psychological information.

CURRENT ISSUES

It should not be thought that the current burgeoning of interest in psychology and law will necessarily assuage any lingering tensions between the two disciplines. Indeed, it could be said that there is at least one major issue between them which will become ever more pressing, to the extent perhaps of deserving the epithet 'paradigm clash'. Put simply, law reflects the predominant views of the members of the society which it regulates. A dominant feature of contemporary Western societies at least is the emphasis on the rights and behaviour of individuals, and these are constructed on an interpretative scheme or philosophy which in general holds individuals *responsible* for their own conduct. Thus the law in general presumes that individuals are conscious of what they are doing and that they are free to conduct themselves as they wish. Thus the very concept of criminal responsibility depends to a large extent on the belief that our intentions and wills exercise hegemony over our behaviour, that 'we' are separable from 'our behaviour'. Much of contemporary psychology on the other hand is built on a model which emphasizes that behaviour is influenced by other events of which it can be described as a dependent variable. This is of course especially true of those parts of psychology constructed on empirical studies of behaviour. Empirical investigations have led to a greater understanding of how behaviour can be explained in terms of biological, social, or environmental influences rather than as a reflection of personal autonomy. Although some psychologists seem to draw back from emphasizing the point, contemporary psychology is built to a great extent on a framework of deterministic analyses of behaviour which sits uneasily with society's predominant attribution of personal responsibility for one's actions.

This fundamental difference between law and psychology is largely philosophical, though a deterministic analysis is of course made more plausible by increasing specific empirical support for its general position. The important general implications of such philosophical differences cannot be considered here. However, it has been seen that they can intrude in the psychologists' approach to the pragmatic use of crucial concepts such as that of criminal responsibility, both with abnormal and normal offenders, and in their analysis of 'appropriate' disposal for offenders. While, as discussed earlier, much psychological research serves to identify influences on the operation of legal process, thereby perhaps helping to make the legal system more consistent and more sensitive, this basic paradigm clash between the two disciplines is an uncomfortable intrusion in their mutual interactions.

The paradigmatic tension between psychology and law is not only confined to such global concepts as criminal responsibility, but can emerge disconcertingly in quite specific contexts. This is illustrated by reference to an important field in which legal process has been used to challenge the legitimacy of a psychological treatment rather than the more frequent cases in which psychology appears to challenge the legitimacy of legal procedures. The issue chosen for discussion here revolves round the use of behaviour modification techniques with institutionalized patients, and has been admirably reviewed and discussed by Wexler (1973). Briefly, one important aspect of behaviour modification is its emphasis on the dynamic effects of the consequences of behaviour on the future probability of its occurrence. Thus efforts are usually made by behaviour modifiers to maximize the pay-offs for any desirable or appropriate behaviour exhibited by patients in the wards of mental hospitals, for example, thereby allowing these environmental influences to exert a desirable therapeutic effect. The litigation in the USA reviewed by Wexler (1973) has had the extremely desirable effect of specifying and expanding the goods and services to which patients in institutions have legal rights. Wexler points out that in widening the range of such rights, however, the law also limits the class of events which can be related to behaviour in programmes of behaviour modification. To take a crass but clear example, if patients have a legal right to nutritionally-adequate meals, then the right is unconditional. Such food cannot, therefore, be made dependent on desirable behaviour, even though the behaviour might invariably occur because of such a programme. A behaviour modification intervention that sought to improve behaviour by using food dependent on behaviour would therefore be illegal.

Although a natural reaction to these developments is to praise the beneficial effects of legal discussions which guarantee a wider range of rights to institutionalized patients, they also prompt concern among some psychologists. Briefly, it can be argued that giving such things as nutritionally adequate meals (to sustain the crude example) independently of behaviour, or regardless of what patients do, does not eliminate the psychological fact that these events will strengthen any behaviour to which they are, now by chance, related. Thus patients may be trapped by accident in a situation in which a legal right determines that food is allowed to relate to and therefore increase the likelihood of *un*desirable or *in*appropriate behaviour! A sensitive programme of behaviour modification which related such things as nutritionally adequate meals to desirable behaviour would be preventing such accidents, would be exploiting the dynamic effects of these environmental events to generate desirable behaviour, and would in any case ensure *both* that desirable behaviour occurred *and* that nutritionally adequate meals were given. It will be appreciated that the controversy is expressed here in extremely crude terms, but it leads to the conclusion that the fundamental assumptions of law and of psychology come into conflict in this specific case.

Monahan and Loftus (1982) conclude their review of recent research in the psychology of law by identifying three recurring issues relating to the aims, the methods and the impact of such research. The first of these is expressed through the distinction, noted earlier in this chapter, between research primarily intended to aid the efficiency of legal procedures and that designed to develop and test psychological theory. Monahan and Loftus argue that these alternative emphases are in fact complementary rather than contradictory, reflecting the more general distinction between scientific prediction and understanding. In urging that both approaches be sustained since both goals are desirable in their own right, Monahan and Loftus argue that they reflect no more than different immediate objectives, and they look to an ultimate synthesis between them. While this is much to be desired, however, it is perhaps possible to suggest that the two approaches of psychologists seen by them as being complementary can have confusing or even adverse effects if they are not clearly differentiated, at least for the purpose of communicating with those from other disciplines. The intellectual excitement of competing theoretical systems in psychology developed by reference to psycho-legal studies can surely seem to be a self-indulgence to those who wish to scrutinize them in the colder light of the pragmatic needs of the law. While Monahan and Loftus are correct to argue that the two approaches are complementary, it will be well to keep the context of specific studies appropriately emphasized.

The second issue identified by Monahan and Loftus (1982) is that of the choice of appropriate empirical methods in psychological research with legal relevance. The analogue or simulation method attempts to identify the effects of possible influences in legal contexts not by studying these settings directly but by setting up models or similar situations in which these variables can be manipulated experimentally. Prominent examples of such an approach are found in the study of decision-taking by simulated juries and of the effects of varying the conditions in which eyewitness 'testimony' is obtained outside actual legal settings. Such a strategy is attractive, especially perhaps to psychologists traditionally trained to regard the experimental approach as *the* scientific method. Yet the importance to law of analogue studies depends of course on extrapolations to the real world, and this is certainly not without its problems. The alternative approach is provided by 'field studies' which gather empirical data by studying real legal situations and procedures directly. Of course, psychologists must take these as they find them. They usually also have to rely on correlations between events in order to infer that some serve as influences on others. Monahan and Loftus discuss this issue sensitively, and relate it to the specific purposes of studies. With respect to psychology, however, field studies in legal settings have made a notable contribution to the welcome growth in the appreciation of non-experimental empirical methods, as the basis of theoretical analysis as well as in relation to the gathering of psychological facts.

The final general issue identified by Monahan and Loftus (1982) relates to the influence of psychological research on the law. Should psychologists seek to assist law to achieve more adequately the goals it sets itself; should they seek to promote alternative values and goals; or should they confine themselves to the more neutral role of fact-gatherers? This is indeed a complex issue which cannot be evaluated here, although it should be emphasized that all three approaches depend on the gathering of relevant psychological information. Without their special role as sophisticated seekers of empirical information, psychologists surely have no special role to play in the context of the law. To emphasize this is not in any way to undervalue the further roles which are potentially open to psychologists.

Monahan and Loftus (1982) also draw attention to the distortion of psycho-legal research with respect to the situations it has addressed. There is a marked imbalance in favour of *criminal* law, perhaps because of its somewhat dramatic confrontations in structured settings with a hierarchy of participants. Law, of course, goes far beyond this aspect of life in our community, and Monahan and Loftus are surely right to alert psychologists to other fields which deserve their attention and skills.

REFERENCES

ELLISON, K.W., and BUCKOUT, R. (1981). *Psychology and Criminal Justice.* New York: Harper and Row.
FARRINGTON, D.P., HAWKINS, K., and LLOYD-BOSTOCK, S. (1979). *Psychology, Law and Legal Processes.* London: Macmillan.
FELDMAN, M.P. (1977). *Criminal Behaviour: a Psychological Analysis.* Chichester: Wiley.
KONEČNI, V.J., and EBBESEN, E.B. (1982). *The Criminal Justice System: A Social-Psychological Analysis.* San Francisco: Freeman.
LIPSETT, P.D., and SALES, B.D. (1980). *New Directions in Psychological Research.* New York: Van Nostrand Reinhold.
LLOYD-BOSTOCK, S. (1981a). *Law and Psychology.* Oxford: SSRC Centre for Socio-Legal Studies.
LLOYD-BOSTOCK, S. (1981b). *Psychology in Legal Contexts: Applications and Limitations.* London: Macmillan.
LOFTUS, E.R. (1979). *Eyewitness Testimony.* Cambridge, Mass.: Harvard University Press.
MONAHAN, J. (1981). *Predicting Violent Behavior.* Beverley Hills, Calif.: Sage Books.
MONAHAN, J. and LOFTUS, E.R. (1982). The psychology of law. *Annual Review of Psychology,* **33,** 441–475.
NIETZEL, M.T. (1979). *Crime and Its Modification.* New York: Pergamon Press.
REISER, M. (1982). *Police Psychology: Collected Papers.* Los Angeles Calif.: Lehi.
SALES, B.D. (1977). *Perspectives in Psychology and Law,* Vol. 1, *The Criminal Justice System.* New York: Plenum.
SALES, B.D. (1981). *Perspectives in Psychology and Law,* Vol. 2, *The Trial Process.* New York: Plenum.
SPRAGUE, R.L. (1982). *Advances in Law and Child Development.* Greenwich, Conn.: JAI.
TAPP, J.L. (1976). Psychology and law: an overture. *Annual Review of Psychology,* **27,** 359–404.
TAPP, J.L. and LEVINE, F.J. (1977). *Law, Justice and the Individual in Society.* New York: Holt, Rinehart and Winston.
WEXLER, D.B. (1973). Token and taboo: behavior modification, token economies and the law. *Californian Law Review,* **61,** 81–107.
WEXLER, D.B. (1981). *Perspectives in Law and Psychology,* Vol. 4, *Mental Health Law; Major Issues.* New York: Plenum.

Psychology and Law
Edited by D.J. Müller, D.E. Blackman, and A.J. Chapman
© 1984 John Wiley & Sons Ltd

Chapter 2

Sex Discrimination Legislation and Psychology

Oonagh M. Hartnett

It is appropriate that the two disciplines of law and psychology should be featured together in a single title since both of them, from their albeit different standpoints, are concerned with the same basic material, that is the behaviour of human beings in all its complexity and variety. The relevance of the topics to each other is particularly clear when, as with sex discrimination legislation, some area of the law attempts to enforce changes in general patterns of behaviour which have, time out of mind, been reinforced and legitimated by cultural norms, beliefs, attitudes, custom, and practice; as well, of course, as being enshrined in previous statutes. Following feminist consciousness raising and campaigns, the 1960s and 1970s saw some form of sex discrimination legislation being entered in the statute books of industrialized nations. The present chapter outlines aspects of this legislation in the USA, the European Community, and Britain.

LEGISLATION

The USA took the lead in passing sex discrimination legislation. Yet even so there was no federal or state law in that country prohibiting such discrimination until the 1960s. Title VII of the Civil Rights Act 1964 (as amended by the Equal Employment Opportunity Act 1972) prohibited discrimination because of race, colour, religion, sex, or national origin in any term, condition, or privilege of employment. The law covered all private employers of 15 or more persons, educational institutions, state and local government, public and private employment agencies, labour unions with 15 or more members, and joint labour management committees for apprenticeships and training. An Equal Employment Opportunities Commission (EEOC) was set up. It had the power to receive and investigate job discrimination complaints and, if conciliation should fail, to go directly to court to enforce the law. Other legislation forbade unfair discrimination in respect of educational opportunity and credit facilities and with regard to the sale or rental of housing.

There is a unique aspect of the US legislation which deserves special mention, namely the 'executive orders'. These orders require what are known as 'affirmative action programs' by all federal contractors and sub-contractors with contracts of over US$50000 and 50 or more employees, or they face the loss of government contracts. These requirements include identifying areas of minority and female under-utilization and taking reasonable action consistent with EEOC guidelines to correct this.

A second aspect of the US legislation also deserves mention. This is the extent to which the government in that country has assumed the burden of enforcing the legislation. Thus a woman in the USA need but make a written statement to the appropriate government agency alleging that she is a victim of job discrimination and the agency will investigate and process her charge, through the Supreme Court if necessary.

Much case law followed the introduction of the legislation. In Griggs v. Duke Power Company,[1] the Supreme Court found it necessary to rule that the 'absence of discriminatory intent does not redeem employment procedures or testing mechanisms that operate as "built in headwinds" for minority groups and are unrelated to measuring job capability' and

'The Act proscribes not only overt discrimination but also practices that are fair in form but discriminatory in practice. ... Nothing in the Act precludes the use of testing or measuring procedures; obviously they are useful. What Congress has forbidden is giving these devices and mechanisms controlling force unless they are demonstrably a reasonable measure of job performance....What Congress had commanded is that any tests used must measure the person for the job and not the person in the abstract.'

Another important decision was that given in Weeks v. Southern Bell Telephone and Telegraph Company.[2] The decision in this case concerned *bona fide* occupational qualifications. Here the court ruled

'that the employer has the burden of proving that he had reasonable cause to believe, that is, a factual basis for believing, that all or subtantially all women would be unable to perform safely and efficiently the duties of the job involved....Southern Bell has clearly not met the burden here. They introduced no evidence concerning the lifting abilities of women. Rather they would have us "assume" on the basis of "a stereotyped characterization" that few or no women can safely lift 30 pounds, while all men are treated as if they can....Moreover, Title VII rejects just this type of paternalism as unduly Victorian and instead vests individual women with the power to decide whether or not to take on unromantic tasks.'

Yet another case (Diaz v. Pan American World Airways Incorporated[3]) dealt with what was adjudged to be discrimination against a male applying for a job as a member of cabin staff on an airline. The dicta reads,

'while we recognize that the public's expectation of finding one sex in a particular role may cause some initial difficulty, it would be totally anomalous if we were to allow the preferences and prejudices of the customers to determine whether the sex discrimination was valid. Indeed, it was, to a large extent, these very prejudices the Act was meant to overcome' (Schaeffer, 1973, p. 33; 1975, p. 37).

A more recent case (Regents of University of California v. Bakke[4]) appeared at first to be a set-back for 'affirmative action programs'. However, in the Bakke case, which involved a white male student being refused a place in medical school whereas black applicants with lesser qualifications were accepted, the university had arbitrarily fixed its quotas of students. Indeed in its defence the university did not rely upon 'any detailed guidance and procedures for crafting an affirmative action plan' (Equal Employment Opportunity Commission, 1978). Since the EEOC Guidelines do not endorse fixed quotas, the Commission considers that the decision does not invalidate either its guidelines or the principle of affirmative action.

Recently the Equal Rights Amendment to the Constitution failed to gain ratification from a sufficient number of states (38). In fact 35 state legislatures ratified the amendment (four of them later changing their minds, the validity of which action has never been determined). Opponents of the amendment undoubtedly made misleading claims: for example, that separate rest-room facilities would not be provided for men and women; that it would sanction homosexual marriage; that alimony would be eliminated. These claims were believed by some people and resulted in their opposing the amendment. So there is evidence of some sort of backlash appearing recently in the USA. However, the non-ratification of the Equal Rights Amendment does not in any way rescind the discrimination legislation previously outlined and it is no small achievement that even as early as 1973 something like US$73 million had been awarded in compensation as a result of sex discrimination cases.

The legislation in the USA influenced opinion in Europe and led to much intensified interest in Article 119 of the Treaty of Rome and promises of equal pay and equal opportunity appeared in the election manifestos of political parties (Commission of the European Communities, 1980). Article 119 of the Treaty of Rome lays down that member states of the European Community shall ensure and maintain 'the principle that men and women shall receive equal pay for equal work'. This article seems to have made little difference to the relative pay of men and women. Indeed it is widely acknowledged that the article was inserted in the treaty not so much to remedy any injustice to women but rather with the object of preventing unfair economic competition between countries which could rely on very cheap female labour and those countries where female labour was somewhat less cheap. It was not until the late 1960s that Article 119 began to have some effect – when the European Court ruled that Article 119 had direct application to the laws of member states. This ruling was followed by a number of community directives each aimed at improving the status of women and all resulting in legal obligations for the member states. The first of these has become known as the Equal Pay Directive (1975). It laid down the principle of equal pay for equal work. It applies to both collective agreements and individual employment contracts. Member states were given one year to comply with this directive. A second directive on equal treatment followed in 1976. This concerned equal treatment for men and women as regards access to employment, vocational training, and promotion and working conditions. A third directive on equal treatment in matters of social security was adopted at the end of 1978. The directive is applicable to the whole working population, including self-employed persons and the unemployed as well as retired and invalided workers. The member states have been given six years to implement this directive and are permitted to exclude some regulations concerned with old age pension schemes, for instance equal retirement ages and benefit entitlements following periods of employment interruption due to bringing up children.

Within the Directorate for Employment and Social Affairs, the Commission has set up a Bureau for Women's Employment Issues. Its main tasks are to promote equality between the sexes in employment matters, to monitor the application of community legislation by member states, to report to the council, and if necessary to take initiative to secure new measures. It does not deal with the problems of individuals. Additionally there is a special information service for women's organizations and press within the General Directorate of Information. Women over 25 years of age are also named specifically as a category of beneficiaries of the Social Fund. The objective is to help women entering or re-entering the labour market as their children reach school age.

Very recently, following a report by the European Parliament's Ad Hoc Committee on Women's Rights, a draft council resolution was drawn up advocating further action on equality. It recommends supplements to the directives already mentioned; for instance, provisions to compel member states to report every two years on how far the objectives of the Equal Treatment Directive had been achieved; and that the Commission should ensure 'that the implementation of the directives on equal pay and equal treatment – and of the Social Security Directive from 1984 onwards – is an essential precondition for the granting of support from the Communities' regional and social funds'. The draft resolution also requests the community not to confine itself to the directives 'but to implement a wider ranging policy' in order, for example, to improve possibilities for 'women (and men) to combine the family and employment roles', women's participation 'in political, social and economic life and in production activities'. The resolution also asks for a reduction in working hours – daily working hours – 'in order to facilitate a better division of efforts between partners in the household, in the raising of children and in active employment' and it asks that hours should be altered in such a way as to enable males and females to choose between a large range of part-time jobs. Other points include the demand that the community must reject all temptation to make women bear the consequences of the present economic crises and should 'promote and support (partly through community funding) an extensive network of social services for children, old people and the handicapped'. Stress was also laid on the need to help women adapt to changes brought about by the new technology. In addition to all this activity, infringement proceedings are being brought against member states, of which Britain is one, for non-compliance with certain aspects of the equal pay and equal treatment directives (Commission of the European Communities, 1980, 1981a,b; European Parliament, 1981).

This leads rather nicely to a discussion of British sex discrimination legislation. The two main pieces of legislation are the Equal Pay Act of 1970 as amended in 1976 and the Sex Discrimination Act of 1975. It is noticeable that implementation of both acts waited upon the European requirement that member states should implement the directives already discussed. This coincidence leads one to suspect, perhaps wrongly, that the major impetus for the implementation of the British legislation stemmed more from a need to comply with commitments as a member of the European Community rather than from any very powerful sense of goodwill on the part of the national government towards equal opportunities. I myself can quite clearly remember that the time-lag between the passing of the Equal Pay Act and its implementation in 1976 was used by employers (supported by some trades unions) to increase segregation of work by sex, so that women would be less able to compare their pay with men doing the same or broadly similar work or work rated equivalent under a job evaluation scheme. The First Annual Report of the Equal Opportunities Commission (1977, p. 25) quoted from a study by the London School of Economics as follows: 'many implementation strategies have served to minimize the effects of the Act rather than to show positive commitment.'

So from its inception the Equal Opportunities Commission has shown itself to be well aware of the inadequacies of the Equal Pay Act and in its Fifth Annual Report (Equal Opportunities Commission, 1981) recommended that the Act should be amended. Unfortunately no notice was taken and the

British Government was taken to the European Court of Justice by the European Commission and found to be in default. The Commission's main complaint was that the Equal Pay Act does not oblige employers to carry out job evaluation schemes and so (particularly given the prearranged job segregation already referred to) many women cannot in British law claim for equal pay (Commission of the European Communities, 1981c). The most recent annual report of the Equal Opportunities Commission (1982) states, 'We take no pleasure at the prospect of a British Government being compelled to comply with European Law as a result of proceedings before a European Court and we urge the government again to give an early indication of their willingness to place our proposals for amendment before Parliament.'

The first British equal pay case to be referred to the European Court of Justice was Smith v. McCarthy Limited.[5] It was backed by the Equal Opportunities Commission. Wendy Smith claimed that her employers were in breach of the Equal Pay Act in that she was being paid $10 per week less than her predecessor in the job, who was a man. Her employers argued the Act did not allow comparison with a man who was no longer employed by the firm. The European Court ruled unequivocally that under Article 119 a woman can legitimately compare her pay with that of a man who was previously doing the same job. This decision is very important and means that the Equal Pay Act will in future have to be applied in the light of this judgment. However, given the inadequacies of this Act, it is hardly surprising that fewer and fewer women are trying to use the legislation. Applications to tribunals have dropped from 1742 in 1976 to 54 in 1981. The Equal Opportunities Commission 'remains of the view that women's relative earnings have reached a plateau and are unlikely to show any significant improvement until the law is altered' (Equal Opportunities Commission, 1982).

Unlike applications connected with the Equal Pay Act, applications concerned with employment matters under the Sex Discrimination Act have remained fairly steady if not numerous. There were 243 applications under this Act in 1976. In 1981 there were 256, of which 59 were on behalf of men. The Sex Discrimination Act applies to employment, education, facilities and services, and the management and disposal of premises. Unlawful discrimination can be of two kinds: direct and indirect.

> 'Direct sex discrimination arises where a person treats a woman (or a man) on the grounds of her sex less favourably than he treats or would treat a man (or a woman)'...Indirect sex discrimination consists of treatment which may be described as equal in a formal sense but is discriminatory in its effect on one sex.'

For example, 'if an employer were to apply a requirement that all his (sic) clerks should be 6 feet tall', it would seem that a woman who was refused a job because of her height would be able to make out a case of sex discrimination (Home Office, 1975). To put it another way, indirect discrimination occurs when a requirement is applied equally to both sexes but is such that the proportion of one sex who can comply with it is considerably smaller than the other and when that requirement is not justifiable in terms of the job being done. The Act also makes direct and indirect discrimination against married persons illegal, but only in the employment field. This inclusion appears to be a result of experience gained in the USA where some employers argued they were not discriminating against women as such but rather against married women. Possibly, also as a result of the American experience, the exemptions allowed for a 'genuine occupational qualification' have been carefully defined. Examples given are modelling clothes and dramatic performances; also considerations of decency and privacy (physical contact, state of undress, use of sanitary facilities). As for separate sleeping accommodation and sanitary facilities, this exemption does not apply if the employer could reasonably be expected to provide the facilities: where the job is in a single sex establishment for persons requiring special care; where the holder of the job provides individuals with personal services (e.g. a woman might respond best to help offered by a female welfare worker); where the job needs to be held by a man because of other laws regulating employment – say the factories legislation; where the job involves work outside the UK in a country whose laws and customs make it impossible for a woman or a man to work effectively; where a job is one of two held by a married couple. The Act also forbids discriminatory advertising, pressure to discriminate, and victimization of a person who has asserted his or her rights under the Act. Sections 47 and 48 of the Act are worth special mention for they permit positive discrimination in training for work for persons of either sex when within the previous 12 months the number of persons doing that work was comparatively small. When these conditions apply employers are also allowed to encourage females only or males only, as the case might be, to take advantage of opportunities for holding such posts.

From its inception there have been inadequacies in the Act. The enforcement procedure is complicated; for instance, employment cases are heard in industrial tribunals whereas non-employment cases go to the county courts; legal aid is not available for tribunal hearings; there is no legal backing for the Equal Opportunities Commission's recommendations following an investigation. Social security and taxation – and in many respects pension schemes – are not covered by the Act, though in time the force of European Community legislation seems likely to remedy these lacunae. The most recent annual report of the Equal Opportunities Commission states that the most significant legal developments of last year 'have highlighted the shortfall between European and domestic legislation' (Equal Opportunities Commission, 1982). The report goes on to discuss some of the obstacles in the way of achieving equal opportunities. In the case of employment, job segregation is a major obstacle. Such segregation is widespread and accepted often by management and unions alike. The Commission regards job segregation as one of its main priorities. Recruitment is another major source of complaints. One big problem here is the difficulty the complainant has of gaining access to relevant information. The Commission believes that it would help greatly were the burden of proof to be 'more equitably distributed between the applicants and the respondent'. At the moment the burden of proof in cases of direct discrimination is totally upon the respondent. Another problem is women being persistently asked at job interviews about their intention to have children and about their family responsibilities instead of about their qualifications for the post. The Commission also warns about sex-biased job evaluation schemes. Its report instances a case in a bank cash centre where heavy lifting was included as a factor whereas mental concentration was not. Selection for redundancy is also causing problems, as is selection for promotion: 'where managerial posts are involved women may not even be considered because of the operation of the "old boy network"'. Unfair discrimination in fringe benefits such as private medical schemes, special mortgage and loan facilities, and car and travel expenses is another source of complaint. There are numerous other problems about occupational pensions and at present complainants must have recourse to Article 119 of the Treaty of Rome rather than to domestic legislation. The inequitable treatment of part-time workers and resistance to job sharing are also causing difficulties.

Problems in respect of education and training also remain. Clashing time-tabling is one very obvious case, in that, for example, craft and design classes clash with home economics. Girls are under-represented in the science subjects and the indications are that cuts in the provision of university education are being directed mainly at arts subjects, these being the very areas in which girls have concentrated. The Commission believes that it is not sufficient for schools to ensure that they simply do not contravene the legislation, but that positive efforts are needed to counter tradition, parental pressure, media and peer group influence, and the attitudes of some teachers (Equal Opportunities Commission, 1982).

From this survey of the law and some of its problems and results it can be seen that there is clearly a long way to go before equal opportunities for men and women are attained.

THE ROLE OF PSYCHOLOGISTS

I wish to suggest that psychologists have it in their power to contribute enormously towards ameliorating many of the problems which confront both the letter and the spirit of equal opportunities legislation. Inherent in this problem are forms of behaviour which are core topics in the discipline of psychology: for example, prejudice; stereotyping; change; allocation of roles, status, and esteem; conflict and altruism; expectations; perceptions; cognitions; achievement; personal abilities and attributes; socialization; and the reinforcement of behaviour. I am prepared to wager that it is impossible to think of a single topic in psychology which is not of relevance to one or more of the problems facing the achievement of equal opportunities for men and women and minority groups in general. This being the case, some people may find it surprising that psychologists have been comparatively slow to take an active interest in the subject. Even when they did start, this did not seem to stem from any positive feeling toward involvement but rather from compulsion when it became clear that whether they liked it or not they were going to be caught up in the testing issue – a matter with some implications for their livelihood as well as for their discipline and profession. It became necessary to ensure that selection tests were not discriminating unfairly. For instance, cultural influences affect test performance and predictive validity is not necessarily equally accurate for different groups.

This comparatively slow build-up of interest in the topic by psychologists is not so surprising when one remembers that psychologists are not free from the cultural biases of their time nor above its prejudices. Analyses of psychology and its applications have shown that psychology also suffers from the effects of sex-role stereotyping – on its theoretical formulations, on its methodology, on the questions which it asks, and on its practice (Brown Parlee, 1975; Chetwynd and Hartnett, 1978; Hartnett, Boden, and Fuller, 1979). In short, before psychologists could become positively involved it was necessary for them to gain some insight into the manner in which their own discipline was flawed. This process naturally took some time, but it is to the credit of psychologists that it did occur and is still occurring. Evidence purporting to show very many sex differences was re-examined and found in the majority of cases to be invalid (Maccoby and Jacklin 1974a,b). Another study showed that clinical psychologists were as subject as any layperson to a belief in sex stereotyping to the disadvantage particularly of their female clients (Anonymous, 1975a; Broverman, Broverman, Clarkson, Rosenkrantz, and Vogel, 1970). Theoretical formulations were scrutinized and were found to be based on an assumption that masculinity and femininity were at opposite ends of a single continuum, which inevitably leads to a belief in the mutual exclusiveness of the attributes associated with these labels; this in turn leads to biased beliefs about men and women (Mednick and Tangri, 1972). Psychological tools, including tests, inevitably reflected these beliefs, as did psychological practice whether in its occupational, educational, counselling, or clinical forms. The very language usage of the discipline was found to be sexist (Anonymous, 1975b); and, of course, as with other professions, women were predominantly in the lower status positions. It was not until the late 1970s that The British Psychological Society, and then only after opposition, decided to set up a working party to consider the matter of unfair discrimination. Since that time psychologists have been taking an accelerated interest in discovering and developing ways in which their expertise might be used to understand the causes of unfair discrimination and contribute to its amelioration. Indeed The British Psychological Society now has a Standing Committee on Equal Oportunities.

At this point it should be made clear that no psychologist worthy of the name would countenance the use of manipulative techniques in this domain or any other. What psychologists are concerned to do is reduce pressures to conform to stereotypes and to expand the freedom to choose for both sexes. Within these self-imposed limitations, and I would argue rightfully self-imposed, the ways in which psychologists can and are beginning to contribute to equal opportunities are numerous.

In research and theory they are countering the bias, already mentioned, of thinking of masculinity and femininity as opposite poles of a single continuum. The work of Bem and Spence on psychological androgyny amply demonstrates this (e.g. Bem, 1975; Spence, Helmreich, and Stapp, 1975). Such work has a very important contribution to make to altering attitudes and in particular to the uncritical acceptance of sex stereotyping. It shows that many males and females possess abilities and attributes which transcend stereotypes. It further indicates that such transcendence seems to lead to more flexible and effective behaviour. Other work has and is being carried out on sex-role socialization which reveals that fiction, the media, and advertising constantly purvey stereotyped messages (Busby, 1975). This work makes people more aware and more critical of such messages and therefore more able to resist them should they choose to do so.

Similar research has been conducted into sex-role stereotyping in schools, a survey of which concluded that both the official and 'hidden' curriculum adopts traditional sex-role stereotyping and very often favours males over females (Lobban, 1978). Other work critically questions the biological and deterministic explanations of stereotypes (Archer, 1978; Griffiths and Saraga, 1979). Yet other work questions belief in the inferior creative capacity of females (Hargreaves, 1979) and links psychological androgyny with better mental health (Williams, 1979). The importance of such basic research and theory formulation cannot be over-emphasized. It informs the attitudes and practices of applied psychologists, all of whom are professionally involved in one or other of the areas covered by the sex discrimination legislation, that is employment, education, and training.

Occupational psychologists are concerned with selection and promotion procedures, with vocational guidance, training, job design, and evaluation, with organization development and design including, as ergonomists, the design of equipment and the physical environment. In particular, they are concerned with the design and validation of selection tests as well as with informal selection procedures such as interviews. Indeed the British Psychological Society Standing Committee on Equal Opportunities, previously mentioned, has already advised employers on some of these matters. Also the Society, together with the Runnymede Trust, has published a booklet covering such topics as job analysis, interviews, and selection tests (Runnymede Trust/British Psychological Society, 1980). The decision of the European Court of Justice on equal pay is likely to result in a growing demand for improved job analysis and especially evaluation techniques. Psychologists know from research studies that work done by women is likely to be undervalued merely because women do the work. Future job evaluation schemes must be informed by this awareness. Occupational psychologists should, in my opinion, be contributing their knowledge and skills to the design of any training scheme (the one area in which positive discrimination is permitted) the object of which is to break down job segregation. It is my considered opinion that such schemes, to be effective, should include a psychological component aimed at ameliorating psychological blocks due to sex-role stereotyping and the under-valuation of work which women do and arising from lack of assertiveness. Furthermore, I would suggest that occupational psychologists involved in organization development and design should try to ensure that tokenism is avoided and that job sharing, part-time work, and flexi-time are integral in any design. Psychologists are aware of the strength of group norms and of the consequent stress likely to be experienced by an unsupported individual whose role runs counter to these norms. Also any psychologist must be aware of the detrimental effect which job segregation is likely to have upon women's aspirations. Social comparison theory indicates that people tend to limit their comparisons to other individuals *within* their own group (Festinger, 1968; Wheeler, 1969). Hence job segregation not only limits what women and men actually do. It also tends to limit what they aspire to. In a heavily job-segregated workforce, such as that in Britain, one would not expect women to be as dissatisfied with their low pay relative to men as they would be in a less segregated situation. In summary, job segregation not only 'gets round' the equal pay legislation, it also tends to result in the victims feeling less dissatisfaction with their lot. The Sixth Annual Report of the Equal Opportunities Commission (1982) was, in my view, justified in giving prominence to this problem of job segregation, and occupational psychologists should be alive to the need for exercising all their skills as agents of change in an attempt to break down this segregation.

Vocational guidance is another aspect of the work of occupational psychologists. There is evidence that career advisers are not free from sex bias and the same accusation can be made of career information literature. Also it is important that vocational interest tests (as well as selection tests) should be free from sex bias. Prediger and Cole (1975) argue that the 'socialization dominance' hypothesis should be replaced by an 'opportunity dominance' one which can facilitate career opportunities which are only just developing.

Educational psychologists obviously have a contribution to make also. This group is much associated with the use of tests – as are occupational psychologists – and they, too, are involved in vocational guidance. Their expertise gives them an influence upon classroom procedures, upon curriculum design, and upon the content of some textbooks.

Both occupational and educational psychologists are influential as teachers. In the case of the former their students include not only psychologists but also management and personnel trainees. The latter are involved in teacher training. Such teaching should include discussion of the means for countering sex-role stereotyping and socialization together with the likely concomitants of such stereotyping at work and in the school.

Counselling is yet another area in which psychologists can exert influence. There is no doubt that considerable psychological stress can attend an individual's attempt to be a role innovator in the context of stereotyping and unfair discrimination. The judicious use of individual counselling can help alleviate such stress.

As I pointed out earlier, it is virtually impossible to think of a topic crucial to the elimination of unfair discrimination with which psychologists are not concerned and indeed in which psychologists are not in key professional positions of influence. It is therefore heartening to feel that they are becoming more alive to their responsibilities, as evidence by their involvement in the publication *Discriminating Fairly: A Guide to Fair Selection* (Runnymede Trust/British Psychological Society, 1980) and by the establishment of The British Psychological Society's Standing Committee on Equality. Also it is now unusual to find a psychology course in which sex-role stereotyping and discrimination does not have a place in the curriculum. Five or so years ago I doubt if more than one module on this topic would have been found in the various curricula.

This, of course, does not mean that psychologists can sit back in a self-congratulatory fashion. We are just beginning to take the topic seriously. In addition to the improvement of techniques in professional practice, much basic research is still required. Unfair discrimination is often very subtle and covert. An analysis needs to be made which will enable what I would call the 'microdots' of discrimination to be recognized, read, and understood. Another area which is in much need of more basic research is the topic of women, leadership, and power. Both women themselves and those whom they would lead have problems accepting women in decision-making positions. Is it that women with power elicit fantasies different from those elicited by men in similar positions – perhaps of the all-powerful, engulfing mother; perhaps of Pandora; perhaps indeed of the all-giving mother? We do not know, but we are no longer so naïve as to believe that the irrational does not enter the so-called rational worlds of work, education, and public life. If equal opportunities are to come about, it is essential that we reduce resistance to women being in decision-making positions alongside men in public life and also weaken the equally strong resistance which there appears to be to men playing a larger role in the fulfilment of home responsibilities.

NOTES

1. Griggs *v.* Duke Power Company, 401 US 424, 1971.
2. Weeks *v.* Southern Bell Telephone and Telegraph Company, 408 F.2d 288, 1969.
3. Diaz *v.* Pan American World Airways Incorporated, 422 F.2d 385, 1971.
4. Regents of University of California *v.* Bakke, 98 S.ct 2733, 1978.
5. Smith *v.* McCarthy Limited, European Court of Justice.

REFERENCES

ANONYMOUS. (1975a). Report of the task force on sex bias and sex role stereotyping in psychotherapeutic practice. *American Psychologist,* **30,** 1169–1175.

ANONYMOUS. (1975b). Guidelines for nonsexist use of language. *American Psychologist,* **30,** 682–684.

ARCHER, J. (1978). Biological explanations of sex-role stereotypes. In J. Chetwynd and O. M. Hartnett (Eds), *The Sex Role System.* London: Routledge and Kegan Paul.

BEM, S. L. (1975). Sex role adaptability: one consequence of psychological androgyny. *Journal of Personality and Social Psychology,* **31,** 634–643.

BROVERMAN, I. K., BROVERMAN, D. M., CLARKSON, F. E., ROSENKRANTZ, P., and VOGEL, S. R. (1970). Sex-role stereotypes and clinical judgments of mental health. *Journal of Consulting and Clinical Psychology,* **34,** 1–7.

BROWN PARLEE, M. (1975). Psychology: review essay. *Signs: Journal of Women in Culture and Society,* **1,** 119–138.

BUSBY, L. (1975). Sex-role research on the mass media. *Journal of Communication,* **25,** 107–131.

CHETWYND, J., and HARTNETT, O. M. (Eds) (1978). *The Sex Role System.* London: Routledge and Kegan Paul.

COMMISSION OF THE EUROPEAN COMMUNITIES (1980). *Women and the European Community.* Brussels: Office for Official Publications of the European Communities.

COMMISSION OF THE EUROPEAN COMMUNITIES (1981a). *Equal Opportunities: Action Programme 1982–85,* Supplement No. 9 to *Women of Europe.* Brussels: Commission of the European Communities.

COMMISSION OF THE EUROPEAN COMMUNITIES (1981b). *Women at Work in the European Community,* Supplement No. 7 to *Women of Europe.* Brussels: Commission of the European Communities.

COMMISSION OF THE EUROPEAN COMMUNITIES (1981c). *Women's Rights: European and UK Law,* Background Report ISEC/B35/81. London: Commission of the European Communities.

EQUAL EMPLOYMENT OPPORTUNITY COMMISSION (1978). *Affirmative Action Appropriate under Title VII of the Civil Rights Act of 1964, as Amended: Interpretative Guidelines* (29 CFR Part 1608). Washington, DC: Equal Employment Opportunities Commission.

EQUAL OPPORTUNITIES COMMISSION (1977). *The First Annual Report 1976.* London: Her Majesty's Stationery Office.

EQUAL OPPORTUNITIES COMMISSION (1981). *The Fifth Annual Report 1980*. London: Her Majesty's Stationery Office.

EQUAL OPPORTUNITIES COMMISSION (1982). *The Sixth Annual Report 1981*. London: Her Majesty's Stationery Office.

EUROPEAN PARLIAMENT (1981). *European Parliament: Working Documents 1980–81*, Documents 1-829/80-I and II. Strasbourg: European Parliament.

FESTINGER, L. (1968). A theory of social comparison processes. In H. Hyman and E. Singer (Eds), *Readings in Group Theory and Research*. New York: Free Press.

GRIFFITHS, D., and SARAGA, S. (1979). Sex differences and cognitive abilities: a sterile field of enquiry. In O. M. Hartnett, G. Boden, and M. Fuller (Eds), *Sex-role Stereotyping*. London: Tavistock.

HARGREAVES, D. J. (1979). Sex roles and creativity. In O. M. Hartnett, G. Boden, and M. Fuller (Eds), *Sex-role Stereotyping*. London: Tavistock.

HARTNETT, O. M., BODEN, G., and FULLER, M. (Eds) (1979). *Sex-role Stereotyping*. London: Tavistock.

HOME OFFICE (1975). *Sex Discrimination: A Guide to the Sex Discrimination Act 1975*. London: Her Majesty's Stationery Office.

LOBBAN, G. (1978). The influence of the school on sex-role stereotyping. In J. Chetwynd and O. M. Hartnett (Eds), *The Sex Role System*. London: Routledge and Kegan Paul.

MACCOBY, E. E., and JACKLIN, C. N. (1974a). *The Psychology of Sex Differences*. Oxford: Oxford University Press.

MACCOBY, E. E., and JACKLIN, C. N. (1974b). Sex differences: myth and reality. *Psychology Today*, **8**, 109–112.

MEDNICK, M. S., and TANGRI, S. S. (1972). New social psychological perspectives on women. *Journal of Social Issues*, **28**, 1–15.

PREDIGER, D. J., and COLE, N. S. (1975). Sex-role socialization and employment realities: implications for vocational interest measures. ACT Research Report No. 68. Iowa City: The Research and Development Division, The American College Testing Program.

SCHAEFFER, R. G. (1973). Nondiscrimination in employment 1963–1972: a research report. New York: The Conference Board.

SCHAEFFER, R. G. (1975). Nondiscrimination in employment 1973–1975: a research report, New York: The Conference Board.

SPENCE, J. T., HELMREICH, R., and STAPP, J. (1975). Ratings of self and peers on sex role attributes and the relation to self-esteem and conceptions of masculinity and femininity. *Journal of Personality and Social Psychology*, **32**, 29–39.

RUNNYMEDE TRUST/BRITISH PSYCHOLOGICAL SOCIETY (1980). *Discriminating Fairly: A Guide to Fair Selection*. London: Runnymede Trust/British Psychological Society.

WHEELER, L. (1969). Factors determining the choice of a comparison other. *Journal of Experimental Social Psychology*, **5**, 219–232.

WILLIAMS, J. A. (1979). Psychological androgyny and mental health. In O. M. Hartnett, G. Boden, and M. Fuller (Eds), *Sex-role Stereotyping*. London: Tavistock.

Psychology and Law
Edited by D.J. Müller, D.E. Blackman, and A.J. Chapman
© 1984 John Wiley & Sons Ltd

Chapter 3

Experimental Legislation

C. I. Howarth and M. J. Gunn

This chapter is an extension of some of the arguments presented earlier (Howarth and Gunn, 1982) about the attribution of responsibility for accidents to child pedestrians. What we have to say can also be regarded as a critical examination of the 'paradigm clash' which occurs whenever lawyers and psychologists address themselves to the same problem.

Both the law and psychology are concerned with the control of human behaviour. The law attempts this by the creation and application of a more or less consistent set of rules, which are derived from those ideals of justice and equity which are the source of all legal decision-making. Psychology attempts, by making use of the techniques of empirical and theoretical science, to discover the causes of behaviour. This contrast between the invention of rules and the discovery of causes is of course an over-simplification. Both lawyers and psychologists are familiar with the use of evidence to clarify our understanding of what happened in the past. But psychologists, like other scientists, use theories to predict the future and then test their theories by experiment. Many psychological theories take the form of rules which prescribe the way the mind works, and which are not totally different in kind from the rules which the law uses to prescribe acceptable social interactions. But it seldom occurs to lawyers to test the operation of their rule systems empirically, and this is the chief limitation on the potential collaboration of lawyers and psychologists.

We wish to consider this limitation in greater detail, to suggest that it is unnecessary, and to propose that a reconciliation of legal and psychological paradigms is not only possible but highly desirable.

The bare bones of our argument can be summarized as follows:

(1) The law is a formalized and institutional agent of social control of great complexity and subtlety. This complexity leads to inconsistencies and

conflicts in the interpretation of the law, and these in turn create a need for experts in its creation, clarification, and implementation. These include Members of Parliament, the judiciary, barristers, solicitors, and the police. They can only be effective when they retain the confidence of the public. This is particularly true of the police, but any general distrust of the law, as in the USA during prohibition, can have disastrous consequences. We rely on consensus to create this confidence, and the creation of consensus is a political process. In the past we have depended on discussion and persuasion, but increasingly people feel a need for opinions to be backed by empirical evidence. This is obvious in relation to economics, but it could be argued it is equally appropriate in relation to the law.

(2) The search for empirical support for the law is hampered by an apparent conflict between the requirements of good experimental design and legal ideals of equity and justice. Good experimental design may require, for example, that people of equal standing in the law should be treated differently, simply in order to discover the effects of the different treatments. In normal legal thinking these different treatments would seem to constitute an injustice. However, these objections have been overcome in some contexts, most notably in studies of sentencing policy. Brody (1976) quotes 29 studies of sentencing policy in which random allocation of treatment has been used. Four of these were in the UK.

We suggest that there are many other areas of the law where objections to the use of empirical evaluation can be overcome. Our own proposal, that drivers should be given, in law, greater responsibility for child pedestrian accidents in residential areas, is one of these (Howarth and Gunn, 1982). In general, the legal objections to experimental testing of the law are weak when we are in a state of genuine uncertainty about the effectiveness or value of two or more forms of legal action. It is only when we are certain that one treatment is more desirable than another that there is any real injustice in allocating treatments in a randomized fashion. This approach to the evaluation of legal processes is similar to the use of clinical trials to evaluate new treatments in medicine, and the ethical problems are also very similar. This similarity suggests that legal experiments should be monitored by ethical committees to ensure that the experimental method is used only when there is genuine uncertainty about the justice or effectiveness of alternative legal processes.

(3) If these arguments were accepted, and if experimental validation of legal processes were to become more widespread, this would in our view increase the effectiveness of the law and increase public confidence in it.

We shall now attempt to put some effective muscle on to this rather skeletal argument.

THE NEED FOR AND CREATION OF PUBLIC CONFIDENCE IN THE LAW

A central feature of our argument is that, if the law is to be effective as an agent of social control, it must retain the confidence of the public. Without that confidence the agents of the law are seen as oppressors, and the majority of people will seek to subvert and to escape the control of law. But to retain public confidence is not easy for the following reasons.

The law is a very finely tuned agent of social control. It is inspired by ideals of equity and justice and human rights about which, fortunately, there is a considerable measure of agreement. The law sets goals to which all are expected to aspire, and provides penalties for those who fail to achieve those goals. By means of legislation, or by case law, it creates a system of rules, the operation of which depends on the effectiveness of the people who administer the law.

But the law is inevitably exceedingly complex, and is full of inconsistencies. The law grows organically so that new inconsistencies are created as others are detected and eliminated. All legal systems have suffered from these inconsistencies, which are partly due to the great complexity of the law which produces inconsistencies inadvertently. But even the ideals of equity and justice can point to opposite conclusions in particular situations, and the continually developing formulations of natural justice and human rights can lead to still more conflict and inconsistency. For example, there may be conflict between the ideals of common justice and equality of treatment, and the ideal of treating each individual in a way which is most appropriate. We must all be conscious, in relation to terrorism for example, of the conflict between human rights and the wish to seek out and punish wrong-doers. Lawyers and legislators try very hard to reconcile these conflicts, and to eliminate the inconsistencies, but no matter how hard they try, the historical evidence suggests that they will not succeed.

These complexities and inconsistencies tend to erode public confidence in the law, and have made it too difficult for the layperson to comprehend the law without the help of experts. These experts are of three kinds. There are politicians who interpret and influence public opinion, which makes it possible for them to create new laws which are acceptable to us, and meet our changing needs. There are solicitors, barristers, and judges who interpret the law in the courts. Finally, there are the police who enforce the criminal law. All three groups depend on public confidence. We need confidence in the integrity and good sense of our politicians, in the impartiality and competence of the police, and in the ability of the courts to determine the justice of the cases which come before them. Without these forms of confidence it would be very much more difficult to achieve a law-abiding society. When confidence is eroded, there is usually an increase in crime and a growth of vigilante groups, private police, and terrorism. Confidence in the law and in the agents of the law depends on public acceptance of its principles and of the rules derived from those principles, and also on public recognition of the effectiveness of the law.

Public acceptance of the principles of the law is determined largely by political pressures. But politics being what they are, the same means can also be used to undermine public acceptance. Politicians wishing, very properly, to change the law or to change institutions based on the law, must run the risk of criticizing the present state of either or both. Various pressure groups do the same thing. Moreover, different groups within society have different needs, and it is in their interests to put different and competing emphases on different aspects of the law.

It is overly optimistic to hope that public confidence in the law can continue to be assured by a consensus achieved by political means. Fortunately most people are prepared to accept the law and its institutions despite their imperfections, for fear that something worse might replace them. Just so long as the law can be seen to be relatively effective, to achieve most of the things we expect from it, then a degree of public confidence can be expected to continue.

EVIDENCE CONCERNING THE EFFECTIVENESS OF THE LAW

But is the law effective, and can we provide evidence that it is? Increasingly, there is a demand for evidence about the effectiveness of the law. Does deterrence work? Are criminals deterred more by the fear of detection or by severity of sentence when caught? If the former then we should spend more money on the police; if the latter then we should spend more money on the prison system. Will the recent law in the UK making the use of seat belts compulsory actually save lives? In relation to these and to many other pertinent questions, the layperson's concept of evidence is closer to that of psychologists and other scientists than it is to that of the lawyer. The difference is due to different conceptions of the nature of a fact.

In law, a 'fact' is largely a matter of opinion. In court, something is accepted as a fact if the 'reasonable man' would accept it. The testimony and beliefs of witnesses are evaluated in these terms; the jury must attempt to represent the opinion of reasonable people; and the judges in summing-up may make their own assessment of what is reasonable. In contrast, psychologists like other scientists attempt to eliminate subjective opinion and seek objective evidence.

Opinions can be a satisfactory guide to social action when there is genuine consensus. But when there is a conflict of opinion, it may be very difficult to resolve. One may attempt to resolve it through debate, but the adversary system of our democratic institutions and of the courts can often accentuate conflict rather than eliminate it. Some people take to the streets, or otherwise try to buy time in the mass media to put their case. Others adopt even more extreme measures, such as disruptive strikes or terrorism. In many cases, where conflict seems irreconcilable, there is a genuine clash of ideology which cannot be resolved by rational means. But in many other cases the conflict might be settled by an appeal to empirical evidence.

As the population becomes more educated, better informed by the media, and less willing to be led by appeals to authority, so the person in the street is also becoming more interested in empirical evidence as a way of settling uncertainty.

In psychology, as in the other sciences, elaborate methods of eliminating human opinions have been developed, in order to obtain evidence which is more objective, in the sense that its nature and significance will be easier for all to accept. These methods include such techniques as the 'double blind' methodology, which ensures, among other things, that the people judging the effect of a treatment are unaware of the nature of the treatment they are judging. Hence their preconceived opinions cannot affect their judgment of it. Another important technique is the assignment of treatments randomly to different people or groups of people, rather than using human judgment in deciding what to do. This ensures that any differences in the effects of treatment are due to it alone, and not to any pre-existing differences between the people who receive it. In these and many other ways, psychologists try to ensure that the evidence they obtain is as objective as possible.

This is not to imply that Parliament and the courts do not make use of scientific evidence. But it is used most easily when the scientific facts are unlikely to conflict with the legal concept of a fact. For example, in the case of lead in petrol, where the government changed, by executive action, the laws about how much lead can be added to petrol, the decision was very much influenced by scientific evidence about the effects of atmospheric lead on the intellectual development of children. The evidence was not very strong, but it was easy to accept because it did not conflict with the views of the 'reasonable man', who seems to have no very strong views about the effects of lead on the development of the brain. But when the scientific evidence conflicts with the legal concept of fact, there is considerably more difficulty.

One excuse which one could give for the comparative distaste which politicans, lawyers, and indeed many intelligent people feel for the social sciences is that the evidence obtained by social scientists tends to be less convincing than that obtained by physical scientists. If the evidence is poor, it is reasonable to be sceptical about the ideas. But the situation is more complicated than that. One reason why the evidence is so poor is because there is strong resistance to the gathering of better evidence. One could, with greater fairness, say that poor evidence is a *result* of the distaste which people feel for the social sciences rather than a cause of it. The paradigm clash which leads people trained in the law to prefer subjective rather than objective evidence is itself one of the causes of the poor quality of the evidence. Lawyers and parliamentarians are so involved in the adversary method of pitting one opinion against another that they do not automatically seek empirical support for their ideas. Furthermore, when they do seek empirical evidence, they may be told that the evidence can only be obtained by techniques which seem to violate the principles which inform their own methods of arriving at a decision.

The most troublesome example of this is the apparent violation of the principles of equity and justice when attempting to set up a properly controlled experiment. We shall now consider this paradigm clash, this clash between legal and scientific ethics, in two concrete instances, sentencing policy and the assessment of responsibility for road accidents.

In relation to sentencing, judges have built up a set of conventions about what is appropriate treatment for different offences, and it is notoriously difficult to change their views, even for the very practical reason that our prisons are overcrowded. To ask them to move to a different set of conventions, even if there were evidence that the new conventions would be more effective, might be very difficult. One would expect it to be even more difficult to persuade them to take part in a properly controlled experiment to acquire evidence about the relative effectiveness of different sentencing policies.

The attribution of responsibility by the courts is an even more jealously guarded enclave of legal thinking. The courts seek to discover where responsibility lies, and regard a particular attribution of responsibility as a *fact* when there is some consensus about it. The consensus may arise from a judge's consideration of precedents, or from the majority verdict of a jury, or both. But the attribution of responsibility is one of the major ways in which the law is used as an agent of social control. Whether the attribution is discovered by the courts or is created by Parliament, there is little doubt that those likely to be considered responsible will take great care to avoid the penalties for failing to exercise proper responsibility.

In this context the scientist may wish to ask what attribution of responsibility would produce a better ordered society rather than to ask, as the lawyer would, what attribution of responsibility would be made by the courts, or would be found acceptable to Parliament. In an earlier discussion (Howarth and Gunn, 1982) we asked, in relation to child pedestrian accidents, whether one might produce a big reduction in these accidents if, contrary to the current practice of the courts, the drivers involved were considered to be to a great extent responsible for them. Instead of regarding responsibility as something to be discovered by the usual legal processes, we suggested that responsibility should be defined in a pragmatic way, in order to save lives, and that the most effective definition should be discovered empirically. Our specific proposal was that responsibility should rest upon the driver in all but the most exceptional circumstances, which the driver would have to establish.

In relation to the apportioning of guilt or blame, the person in the street also has strong opinions, and in many instances these opinions tend to be closer to those of lawyers and legislators than to those of social scientists. In relation to sentencing and to the attribution of responsibility for accidents, neither the person in the street, nor the lawyers, feel comfortable when social scientists discuss them in a dispassionate empirical way.

EMPIRICAL STUDIES OF SENTENCING POLICY

However, the distaste which lawyers feel for the application of the empirical approach to their discipline has been overcome in one notable context. As mentioned earlier, Brody (1976) in a well written and informative Home Office pamphlet, quotes no less than 29 studies in which sentences had been allocated in a random fashion according to the requirements of good experimental design, four of which were in this country. Most of the other studies were done in the USA, some in New Zealand, and some in Australia. They compared the use of different penal institutions, the use of special therapeutic units in these institutions, the development of experimental programmes in the treatment of offenders, the comparison of custodial and non-custodial sentences, and variations within non-custodial treatments. In fact, most of these studies discovered remarkably little difference between the different treatments. This finding need not be seen as discouraging since it is potentially exceedingly important. For example, evidence that shorter sentences lead to the same amount or to slightly less recidivism than longer sentences is not a negligible finding. It almost destroys the justification for longer sentences, and could save a great deal of money.

But not all experiments on sentencing policy have produced small effects. One, not included in Brody's survey, is the Leeds study of the treatment of truancy by magistrates' courts (Berg, Consterdine, Hullin, McGuire, and Tyrer, 1978). Truants were randomly allocated to two treatments. One was the normal treatment provided by truant officers from the Social Services. The other, which was called 'adjournment', simply meant that the offender had to return every month to be quizzed by the magistrates as to how they were conducting themselves. The differences in the effects of these two treatments were surprising, and not at all negligible. School attendance was considerably better in the 'adjourned' group than in the group handled by the truant officers. But even more important was the finding that the subsequent court appearances for other offences from the 'adjourned' group was less than half that of the 'truant officer' group (see Eysenck, Chapter 7, p. 97).

Brody (1976) has a number of interesting comments to make about experiments on sentencing policy. First of all he argues that there is a major political drawback which limits widespread implementation of the experimental approach, this being 'the ethical reluctance to interfere with the course of justice, to send one offender to easy punishment simply at the toss of a coin, while his equally, or less culpable counterpart, receives no such favour' (Brody, 1976, p. 13). However, in an associated footnote Brody also claims that 'their scruples may seem over-fastidious in view of the considerable variations in the frequency with which individual magistrates and judges resort to harsher or more lenient sentences for apparently similar cases'. These 'non-judicial reasons for sentencing disparity' exist for no very good reason. The psychologist, or indeed any social scientist, would argue that to rely on individual opinion, without any evidence that the opinion is competent, is even more ethically objectionable than any apparent inequity produced by the random exigencies of experimental design. This is, in fact, the core of our present argument. It may be ethically objectionable to treat different people differently for no other reason than that you wish to find out something about the effects of treatment. But it is equally objectionable to rely on unsubstantiated opinion, when there is no evidence that the opinion is competent. It is doubly unethical to object to differences in sentencing in an experimental context which could yield useful knowledge, but to accept similar differences based on the whim of individual judges and magistrates.

STUDIES CONCERNING THE ATTRIBUTION OF RESPONSIBILITY FOR ACCIDENTS

In this section we wish to describe some possible experiments which many may consider even more difficult to accept. In our earlier account (Howarth and Gunn, 1982) we suggested that different attributions of responsibility for child pedestrian accidents should be evaluated in terms of their effectiveness in reducing these accidents. At the present time the responsibility for these accidents is put upon the children involved because it is 'well known' that their 'heedless' behaviour is the principal cause of the accidents. We think there is good observational evidence to contradict this common assumption (Howarth and Lightburn, 1980, 1981), and we have suggested that an important element in any attempt to reduce the number of these accidents would be to shift the responsibility for those accidents which occur on residential roads from the children to the drivers (Howarth and Lightburn, 1981).

Our observational evidence conflicts with the evidence of the courts in these cases. The courts almost unanimously accept the plea that 'the child ran heedlessly into the road, and there was nothing the driver could do to prevent the accident'. We have no doubt that our observational evidence is very much better than that presented to the courts, because our evidence is based on direct observation, while the evidence to the courts is based on memories, often distorted by emotion or self-interest. Our colleagues at Nottingham have obtained radar speed meter evidence of the speeds of cars driving past school entrances. They compared the speeds of cars when there was a child waiting to cross the road with the speeds when no children were present. There was no statistically significant difference in the speeds of the cars in the two situations, although the observations were such that we could have detected even a very small change in speed. It seems that drivers do not slow down if a child wishes to cross a road. Not only that, but they do not even swerve. More precisely, we have observed that the mean distance from the kerb was 3.7 feet (1.13 m) in the presence of a child, and 3.5 feet (1.07 m) when no child was present. This difference is neither statistically, nor practically, significant.

Consistent evidence of this kind has now been obtained in three different studies on a large number of sites in the city of Nottingham. We do not suppose that Nottingham drivers are unique, so that the evidence is now very strong that drivers fail to show behavioural evidence that they accept any responsibility for avoiding accidents with child pedestrians. In contrast, the observed behaviour of the children is more cautious and indeed sensible. It is therefore exceedingly unlikely that the drivers who are involved in accidents with child pedestrians are that vanishingly small proportion of drivers who do actually take action in time to avoid such accidents.

So far we have merely cast doubt on the evidence presented to the courts in such cases. The plea that 'the child ran heedlessly into the road so that there was nothing I could do to prevent the accident' is accepted in many cases where a greater degree of caution on the part of the driver could have made it possible to avoid the accident. But that does not prove that any reduction in the willingness of the courts to accept such a plea would in fact reduce the number of accidents.

Unfortunately there is no way in which we can find out whether such a change would reduce the number of accidents except by an appropriate experiment. We therefore suggest that a new attribution of responsibility should be tried in the courts in a limited number of regions, keeping to current practice in the rest of the country and awaiting any effect on the accident rates. There are sufficient numbers of accidents in the different regions that one would not need to wait very long. Any beneficial effect of the new policy would show up very quickly in a comparison of the different regions. Moreover, the information from an experiment of this kind would be much more reliable and sensitive than any information which could be gained from a simultaneous, nationwide implementation of the new policy.

Although the suggestion has aroused some interest, there have also been objections on ethical and legal grounds. Our proposal would attribute a degree of blame where at the present time the courts judge that there is no blame. It would also, at least in the experimental stage, make the degree of blame depend to some extent on the region of the country in which the accident occurred. These are genuine difficulties which should not be faced without good reason. There is enough evidence to suggest that an appreciable number of lives could be saved by the change in the law which we are suggesting. One must therefore decide whether it is ethically more desirable to retain the existing practices of the courts or to change them in an attempt to save children's lives. One must also decide whether it is ethically more desirable to treat everyone by exactly the same rules or to accept some regional variations in the rules, so as to discover what effects the rules are having.

We have little doubt that the saving of lives is more important than the preservation of one particular set of legal practices. We also believe that in a case of genuine uncertainty about the relative effectiveness of different legal procedures, there is a duty to find out which is more effective, even at the expense of a temporary difference in the application of these regimes to different regions.

THE CONTROL OF EXPERIMENTAL LEGISLATION

There is some similarity in the ethical problems posed by experimental legislation and those posed by clinical trials in medicine. When a new form of medical treatment is being developed it should initially be tested on tissue cultures or on animals if necessary until there is good reason to believe it will be better than the best currently available treatment. It should then be compared in a clinical trial with the best currently available treatment. The clinical trial, which is essential to remove any doubts about the efficacy of the treatment, should be conducted as expeditiously as possible. Any inefficiency in the conduct of the trial will only prolong the period of uncertainty and delay the time when an improved treatment can be made generally available.

Changes in sentencing policy intended to reduce recidivism are directly analogous to medical treatments intended to reduce the symptoms of a disease. Our suggestion that a change in the definition of responsibility for accidents could reduce the number of accidents is analogous to some measures in preventive medicine. The same principles as are applied to the evaluation of changes in medical practice could also be applied to possible changes in the law and its application. For example, no change should be contemplated until there is good evidence to believe it will have a beneficial effect, and no change should be universally applied until its effectiveness has been demonstrated in an economical and efficient trial. These are moral imperatives which, in many cases, should over-ride more minor moral scruples.

In the case of sentencing policy, the minor moral and legal scruples have been cast aside many times, and the evidence we have quoted shows what clear conclusions can be drawn from the experimental approach. If the same degree of pragmatism were applied to other aspects of the law and its workings, it seems extremely likely that the effectiveness of the legal process could be improved. As we argued at the beginning of this chapter, this increase in demonstrated effectiveness should also increase public confidence in the law, with consequent beneficial effects.

However, the desirability of any particular change will always be a matter of opinion. There will also be differences of view about the most efficient way to evaluate any change. In medicine clinical trials usually have to be justified to an ethical committee which has a duty to evaluate any proposal. The committee must judge the potential value of the new treatment. It must decide whether there is any genuine uncertainty about its relative value compared with the best of current practice. Only if there is genuine uncertainty is a clinical trial justified. Finally, the committee must assess the design of the trial to see if it will yield the required information with a minimum of risk.

If legislation is to be evaluated as we suggest, then some equivalent of the medical ethical committee will be required to monitor any trials which are done. At present no such machinery exists. But if the principle of experimental legislation is to spread beyond the present limited number of experiments on sentencing policy, then we shall clearly need to think about ways to control it.

CONCLUSIONS

Our central thesis is that public confidence in the law can no longer be left to the vagaries of debate or to the persuasive powers of political movements. Empirical demonstrations of the effectiveness of the law could provide a firmer basis for confidence. Improvements in the law could also follow if changes were made whenever empirical observations found some aspect of the law to be ineffective or counterproductive.

The most informative empirical investigations are those which are properly designed as experiments. There are valid, legal, and ethical objections to an experimental approach to the law when there is no doubt about the relative effectiveness and appropriateness of different formulations and applications of the law. But these objections are invalid when genuine doubt exists. In such cases the over-riding moral imperative is to resolve the uncertainty as quickly and unambiguously as possible, and for this purpose the experimental approach is more efficient and humane than inconclusive debate.

We have given examples of existing and potential applications of the experimental approach, and suggest that it could and should be used much more widely. If this were to happen it would be wise to set up a means of assessing the acceptability of proposed experiments which would be analogous to the ethical committees which monitor clinical trials and other experiments in medicine.

REFERENCES

BERG, I. CONSTERDINE, M., HULLIN, R., McGUIRE, R., and TYRER, S. (1978). The effect of two randomly allocated court procedures on truancy. *British Journal of Criminology*, **18**, 232–244.

BRODY, S. R. (1976). *The Effectiveness of Sentencing – A Review of the Literature*, Home Office Research Study No. 35. London: Her Majesty's Stationery Office.

HOWARTH, C.I., and GUNN, M. J. (1982). Pedestrian safety and the law. In A. J. Chapman, F. M. Wade, and H. C. Foot (Eds), *Pedestrian Accidents*. Chichester: John Wiley.

HOWARTH, C. I., and LIGHTBURN, A. (1980). How drivers respond to pedestrians and vice versa. In D. J. Oborne and J. A. Levis (Eds), *Human Factors in Transport Research*, Vol. II, *User Factors: Comfort, the Environment and Behaviour*. London: Academic Press.

HOWARTH, C. I., and LIGHTBURN, A. (1981). A strategic approach to child pedestrian safety. In H. C. Foot, A. J. Chapman and F. M. Wade (Eds), *Road Safety: Research and Practice*. Eastbourne: Praeger.

Psychology and Law
Edited by D.J. Müller, D.E. Blackman, and A.J. Chapman
© 1984 John Wiley & Sons Ltd

Chapter 4

Social Factfinding and Legal Decision-making: Using Psychology to Change Law

Craig Haney

I imagine that the recent 'surge' of intellectual interest in psychology and law is now apparent to all who work in this hybrid discipline. It has been ably documented (cf. Tapp, 1976; Monahan and Loftus, 1982). The recent success of psychology and law has not been limited to academic circles. In the USA, for example, numerous court decisions over the last 15 years have been based in part or in whole on psychological data. I am thinking primarily of judicial opinions like those that address such diverse topics as the manner in which trial courts should deal with eyewitness identification evidence (e.g. US *v.* Telfaire[1]), the legal rules governing the admissibility of testimony from previously hypnotized witnesses (e.g. People *v.* Shirley[2]), constitutional prohibitions against cruel and unusual punishment in light of psychological evidence on the effects of incarceration (e.g. Pugh *v.* Locke[3]), the biasing effects of certain procedures used in selecting juries in death penalty cases (e.g. Hovey *v.* Superior Court[4]), the unreliability of predictions of dangerousness (e.g. People *v.* Murtishaw[5]), limitations on the use of IQ tests for tracking children in public schools (e.g. Larry P. *v.* Riles[6]), guidelines for the use of employment tests that have a discriminatory impact on minority hiring and promotion (e.g. Albemarle Paper Co. *v.* Moody[7]), and a lower limit on the size of juries that may sit in criminal trials (e.g. Ballew *v.* Georgia[8]).

In addition to enjoying and celebrating this surge of intellectual interest and string of practical successes, however, we might also reflect on these recent events with some degree of caution, even suspicion. 'Why now?' we might ask ourselves. 'Why psychology, and with what eventual consequence?' Particularly because psycho-legal researchers operate in such close contact with a highly charged, combative system like law, it is important that *we* pose the fundamental questions about the manner in which our work will be used and the purposes to which it will ultimately be put. Otherwise I fear that the questions will simply be answered for us, perhaps in ways not much to our liking. Law professors are fond of telling their students that the law is a 'jealous mistress'. She is also a dominant and domineering one. Lawyers and judges are trained from very early in their legal education to see legal forms and categories as primary. All else, including psychological data, tends to be rejected or assimilated into these forms and categories, despite the distortions this process of assimilation may effect (see, for example, Lowy and Haney, 1980).

There is another reason for psychologists to remain cognisant of the broader context in which their work is set. Periods of tremendous productivity in social science are often followed by long spells of inactivity, even disillusionment. As confirmed empiricists, it is easy to become immersed in data-gathering and to lose sight of the purposes to which data are put. Paradigms become stale and seek meaningful application; data sets are rendered useless by a lack of structure and organization. Those familiar with the recent history of my own area – social psychology – will regard this lesson as painfully apparent. One way to avoid this intellectual *anomie* is continually to ask the larger questions, questions made more difficult and complex in psychology and law by the inevitable pressures and accommodations imposed by legalistic imperatives. Contact with another intellectual system like law can act to invigorate tired psychological paradigms, but only if psychologists become more than mere technicians who fill pre-existing legal categories with their data. Success, in the form of huge quantities of data, is not necessarily an unmixed blessing. I believe that psychologists must help to transform legal categories and structures with their data, or their recent success will prove unfulfilling and short-lived.

AN HISTORICAL NOTE ON PSYCHOLOGY AND LAW

Despite talk of the 'unprecedented' growth of psychology and law, there are actually two historical precedents for the extensive intermingling of these disciplines. Both precedents carry a lesson of sorts for current work. The first period began in the last part of the 19th century when psychology, then a fledgling pseudoscience, was used to help legitimize a variety of questionable legal and criminal justice practices. These were the days of eugenic determinism, instinct psychology, and Jamesian will theory, and the law borrowed generously from the semi-respectability of the pseudosciences to help justify policies like punitive segregation, enforced sterilization, and highly restrictive immigration laws (see, for example, Haney, 1982a). In those days, of course, psychology was short on real facts and consisted of little more than social ideology. Not surprisingly, the ideology of this emerging discipline was precisely the one embraced by most of the surrounding society and its legal system. Psychology was employed to add a scientific gloss to the workaday social consensus.

The second precedent is far better known and far less embarrassing. It occurred during the 1930s and 1940s in what was known as the 'legal realist movement'. As part of a generalized concern with the 'realities' of legal process and legal institutions, the Realists were attracted to social science concepts and methods. Psychology was often invoked as one of the central disciplines that legal practitioners and scholars were encouraged to master in order to pierce the myths of law and fashion a more realistic justice. Realist scholars such as Llewellyn and Arnold exhorted the judiciary to look past juridic symbols and legal fictions and to become empiricists sensitive to facts (cf. Rosen, 1972; Twining, 1973).

Notwithstanding the work of judges like Frank, Brandeis, and Frankfurter, however, legal realism was more a movement for the classroom than the courtroom. Its explicit application of data and principles from the social sciences was confined mainly to the law schools, and the judiciary was little affected. More importantly, however, legal realism withered as a movement of legal reform because the Realists had no coherent programme of legal change, nor any substantive theory of value from which such a programme could be generated. They wanted to uncover the myths of legal formalism that had been masquerading pretentiously as legal science, but then what? They offered no theory of justice with which to replace the traditional system that they encouraged each other to analyse 'realistically'.

The earliest use of psychology in the legal system, then, suffered from an absence of facts. Little more was offered than a pseudoscientific dressing for prevailing social ideologies. The second use, legal realism, was limited by an absence of values. Sensitivity to facts, in the absence of substantive goals, was not enough to sustain a programme of legal change. It would be reassuring to think that current work transcends the limitations of these two past attempts at introducing psychology into law. I am not so sure. Psychologists and those concerned with psycho-legal research are still more comfortable with facts than values. Yet the value issues cannot be ignored. In whose interests do we intend to work? Notwithstanding the personal intentions of psychologists, whose interests are likely to be advanced by the legal application of such research? What are the sociological and political blindspots that may be built into research because of who psychologists are and the inevitable limitations that their professional experiences impose? What theory of justice do psychologists hope to advance in their work? I suspect that most of us are uncomfortable with such questions, but I have little doubt that we will be more uncomfortable if the answers come exclusively from the legal system in which this research is applied.

PSYCHOLOGICAL FACTS AND SOCIAL FACTFINDING

What is largely unprecedented about the recent surge of activity in psychology and law is not so much the amount but the kind of psychological data being used by the courts, and the manner in which they employ it. Of course, clinical psychologists have been used extensively in forensic contexts for many years. But much recent activity in psychology and law is not of this sort. In fact, the increased legal use of psychology is occurring at a time when the more traditional forensic applications (in insanity defences and so on) have fallen into widespread disfavour. Instead, psychological data are being employed by courts in what might be called 'social factfinding'. As distinguished from case-specific, *historical* facts that address what did or did not happen in the particular legal conflict or dispute at hand (e.g. who did what to whom, with what state of mind?), *social* facts address the broader factual context in which these specific events occur. Social facts can give meaning and significance to historical facts by placing them in a larger interpretive framework.

Although social facts may profoundly affect the outcome of a legal dispute, their formal status in any single case varies greatly. On occasion, social facts are at the very centre of the legal conflict. That is, in some cases the nature of the broad-based social fact pattern is precisely what is at issue. For example, in Hovey v. Superior Court,[9] the California Supreme Court examined the constitutionality of 'death qualified juries', ones from which persons unequivocally opposed to the death penalty have been excluded. In reaching its decision, the court considered a substantial amount of psychological data about the general effects of this process. (Most of this research appears in Haney, 1984). The *Hovey* opinion is based entirely on a broad pattern of data. But this broad pattern consists of social facts that were neither proven in, nor strictly applied to, the particular case in which the issue was raised. That is, the court did not require proof that the process of death qualification had any specific effect in the case at hand. Instead, it drew reasonable inferences about the likely effects of death qualification in this and similar cases, based on the social facts that were presented. Of course, this is a posture that is more easily assumed by courts that are empowered to 'legislate', namely appellate courts that must fashion rules for later times and subsequent cases.

In other instances, however, the social facts form a background or context against which legal factfinders evaluate case-specific evidence. In criminal cases in which eyewitness testimony is introduced, for example, psychological experts may testify, often in very general terms, about the psychological factors that affect the reliability of such identifications (e.g. Loftus, 1979). Here the social facts are considered and used by the jury in their determination of specific and particularized historical facts in a given case. Similarly, expert testimony about the effects of hypnosis on memory may be permitted by trial courts to assist juries in evaluating the testimony of witnesses who have been hypnotized (e.g. Diamond, 1980). The social facts, psychological studies on the effects of hypnosis, are recognized by courts as relevant to the trier of adjudicative or historical facts. In such cases, experts may rely upon social facts to challenge the assumptions that juries might otherwise make in reaching their conclusions about historical, case-specific facts. Thus such testimony can be used to challenge the common-sense notions that eyewitness testimony is generally highly reliable or that hypnotized persons are more likely to be accurate in their recall of events or descriptions. It should be noted that courts permit such testimony only when, in *their* opinion, there is reason to believe that the actual social facts are different from the ones juries might assume in their decision-making.

In still other cases, the social facts that may affect the decision represent supposedly common knowledge or shared assumptions that are actually unchallenged in particular cases, but which are nonetheless relied upon by the courts in reaching their decisions. In these cases the social facts tend to be more deeply embedded and represent a kind of shared 'common sense'. They embody what is in essence a world view or intellectual framework used by all or most of the participants in the litigation. This shared common sense provides a factual base on which parties build their disputed contentions. Many laws are built on factual premises that consist of 'patterns of human behaviour, assumed to exist on the basis of casual observation, experience, and anecdote, but without systematic or statistical documentation' (Graham, 1981, p. 249). Sometimes formal recognition is taken of these facts by way of judicial notice.

However, often these shared assumptions are so implicit and widely held that they are not formally adverted to or acknowledged in the proceedings at all. Either because they are regarded as unassailable by one or the other party, or because they are simply overlooked by all concerned, these shared assumptions go uncontested. Yet, even uncontested assumptions of social fact can be critically important. For example, in contrast to the notoriety that has surrounded the explicit use of social science by the Supreme Court in Footnote 11 of Brown *v.* Board of Education,[10] consider the crucial but unacknowledged role of prevailing social Darwinist assumptions in the much earlier 'separate-but-equal' decision on race, Plessy *v.* Ferguson.[11] *Plessy* contained the following key assertions:

'If the two races are to meet upon terms of social equality, it must be the result of natural affinities, a mutual appreciation of each other's merits, and a voluntary consent of individuals... Legislation is powerless to eradicate racial instincts, or to abolish distinctions based upon physical differences...' (163 US at 531).

Of course these were assertions of social fact, so much in keeping with popular beliefs that they needed no formal justification. The prevailing social

Darwinist ethic against government intervention in social relations, added to naïve but widespread beliefs about the existence of unmodifiable 'natural instincts' and popular eugenicist theories about innate instinctual differences between races combined to form the intellectal context for the court's opinion. That the court offered no formal citations for its assertions does not make them any less issues of social fact and, therefore, potentially no less subject to empirical analysis, challenge, and critique.

As this last example suggests, the use of broad-based social facts by courts is not of recent origin. Since nobody (not even judges!) can think, comprehend, and analyse in a social and intellectual vacuum, courts have always needed social facts in their decision-making. Use of social facts certainly predates the introduction of the 'Brandeis brief' in 1908, an event commonly regarded as having begun formal use of social science by lawyers.[12] However, Brandeis *did* help to initiate explicit empirical challenges to the courts' unreflective reliance on judicial common sense. By amassing extra-legal facts about the nature of the social world outside the courtroom, and outside the common experience of the judges themselves, attorneys opened legal decision-making to the expertise of outsiders such as social scientists.

Indeed, there are now increasingly fewer cases in which the social facts that may affect the outcome of a case are left implicit and uncontested. Parties are now far more likely to challenge versions of a legal common sense that are not compatible with their own social reality. They are far more likely to anticipate contentious issues of social fact and to address those issues that may frame the context of a decision, and are now more likely to employ the data and methods of social science to do so.

There are numerous reasons for this trend, but let me suggest just two. In the last few decades, American society seems to have become increasingly fragmented and beset with internal conflict. There is no longer an overarching vision to unite diverse groups, and fewer social rules possess unquestioned moral power and force. In matters of fact as well as value, the contested terrain has been expanded. In a society in which life experiences are heterogeneous, in which there is little consensus about values and few widely shared assumptions about the world, conflicts over social reality are much more frequent. Extra-legal facts become more legally important in a pluralistic society in which diverse constituencies contend to have the courts accept *their* version of reality. Social sciences like psychology are used as an authoritative tool for the resolution of such conflict.

Second, and closely related, the civil rights revolution of the last few decades has given legal representation and voice to traditionally disenfranchised groups such as the poor, minorities, women, children, patients, and inmates (see, for example, Haney and Pettigrew, 1986). These groups are unlikely to share the 'common-sense' view of the world held by judges and often incorporated into their legal decisions as implicit and unquestioned assumptions. Social sciences like psychology are being used to challenge these assumptions on behalf of such groups who believe there are more valid patterns of social fact on which to base a decision than judicial common sense. In this context, consider Meehl (1977), who argues that, 'reliance on "what everybody knows" was hardly looked at critically before the experimental and statistical methods of contemporary social science were developed. This historical fact provides a built-in preference for commonsense knowledge of human behavior embodied in positive law' (Meehl, 1977, p. 10).

REFORMS IN SOCIAL FACTFINDING

Not surprisingly, challenges to judicial common sense have not been uniformly welcomed in the legal system. In recent years widespread opposition has developed to the use of social science for purposes of social factfinding in law. Criticisms have been broad and sweeping, and range from the argument that social science data are inherently flawed, the contention that social scientists are invariably biased, the observation that there are perhaps insurmountable incompatibilities in the styles and methods of psychology and law, the belief that courts are institutionally incompetent to process social science facts effectively, and finally to the claim that reliance on psychological data loosens the moral underpinnings of the law.

Much of the criticism has been politically motivated, offered by persons whose interests are threatened or compromised by the introduction of social fact data into law. Legal fictions have usually been employed in the service of the powerful. As they are debunked, powerful enemies are made. Whatever its underlying motivation, however, much of the recent criticism is intellectually serious and reminds those who work in psychology and law about the weaknesses of the enterprise.

However, many of the most vocal critics also concede the growing role for social science in law. Attention thus shifts to possible legal reforms in social factfinding that might control, minimize, or correct for putative weaknesses in data, frictions between the disciplines, and the untoward consequences of injecting large amounts of social science fact into law. These proposals range in focus and scale. For example, procedural safeguards have been suggested that would ensure more complete discovery and more careful scrutiny of social fact evidence. Other reformers have suggested that burdens of proof should be more carefully tailored to the unique contours of social science data. Focusing more on personnel than procedures, others have recommended that judges become more sophisticated in their understanding of social science and that experts be selected by the courts on the basis of their supposed 'neutrality'. A final set of reforms is institutional in scope, calling for the creation of a social science 'institute' where legally relevant social fact questions may be examined systematically, and even a 'science court' where technical factual controversies could be resolved in a special forum. (I have discussed elsewhere, in some greater detail, both the criticisms of social science in law and specific proposals for reform (Haney, 1982b).

Let me suggest, in this concluding section, that several crucial issues will have to be addressed before reforms in social factfinding can succeed and the relationship between psychology and law can be cemented. Although they are largely jurisprudential in nature, these issues are the appropriate subjects for debate and resolution by psychologists as well as the lawyers with whom they collaborate.

Social Science and Social Reality

There is an implicit tension or strain between the use of social science in legal decision-making and the law's fundamental dependency upon common-sense world views and the prevailing social consensus. Courts do at times act against the interests and views of the majority. When they intervene to protect or safeguard the civil liberties of 'discrete and insular minorities', they act undemocratically. In the long run, of course, these actions are thought to legitimize the moral unity and democratic values of society. Repeated use of social science to challenge the legal common sense, however, risks widespread cynicism and animosity towards social science and the courts that rely upon it in decisions that upset social consensus. Social scientists appear to many legal traditionalists and to members of the public as elitist outsiders who occasionally enter the courts to tell society how things *really* are or what *really* needs to be done.

This tension persists despite the widespread popularity of social science in some legal circles. Judge John Minor Wisdom has written, for example, that '[w]hat seemed at first to be antagonism between social science and law has now developed into a love match' (Wisdom, 1975, p. 142). Yet, the affair still seems to be confined primarily to the federal courts. Friedman, Kagan, Cartwright, and Wheeler (1981) report that social science sources were cited in less than 0.6% of the state Supreme Court decisions that they examined. I believe that this fact is due in large part to the greater security and protection that a life tenure appointment gives to federal judges. Especially in recent years, judicial elections in state courts have become intensely political affairs. Often at issue is the fitness of an allegedly 'liberal' judge who, frequently armed with social science data, has intervened to prohibit previously unquestioned traditional practices. Many critics, displeased with particular substantive decisions made by courts that relied on social fact data, have gone on to suggest that the judicial use of such data is unseemly and inappropriate *per se*.

For example, Robinson (1980) has suggested that the empirical data of psychology actually undermine the moral underpinnings of law. He argues that the legal and moral 'ought' has no material reference and cannot be confirmed by empirical methods. Robinson suggests that since universals of right and wrong are not subject to social scientific proof, courts that immerse themselves in social facts must lose sight of the universal principles that should guide them. 'The picture of the modern court', he writes, 'is of an institution increasingly so clouded in its judgment by irrelevant facts and specious theory as to be inaccessible to that body of principle to which it owes its very existence' (Robinson, 1980, p. viii).

Robinson's argument is distinguished by its categorical quality and by his unwillingness to acknowledge the political dimensions of his own objections. Yet, his argument will be echoed by others. Psychology is likely to continue to be criticized on the grounds that it leads legal decision-making away from basic first principles. A way must be found to moderate and modify the ostensibly elitist uses of psychological data by which psychologists seem to impose their visions on others, or else their participation in legal decision-making may be curtailed by apparently 'democratic' yet conservative backlash.

Legal Biases and Scientific Neutrality

The power of psychologists in the legal system derives from the real or apparent truth value of their data. We are nothing in law if not factfinders. But many areas of psychology are still dominated by a natural science model of factfinding that eschews the influence of values and political perspectives. Practitioners in these areas seek or pretend to have no social or political values that guide and direct them. I suggested earlier that this stance would prove ultimately unsatisfying for psycho-legal researchers because it requires them to leave questions of value and purpose exclusively to lawyers. In addition, many psychologists who have embraced the natural science model are likely to be alienated from combative legal arenas where key decisions are made. Ironically, many lawyers share the rigid image of the perfectly neutral and detached scientist, which can intensify the tension between the two disciplines and produce further distortions in the nature and content of psychological data that are introduced into law.

A fascinating example of the friction between legal and scientific conceptions of 'objectivity' is provided in an observation by two psychologists writing about the role of the expert witness. Thorton and Benson suggest that '[i]f the witness has consistently supported either plaintiffs or defendants', then 'it may be difficult to portray a detached, "scientific", and professionally objective demeanor" (Thorton and Benson, 1980, p. 419). They illustrate their point by citing one case where an expert witness had testified on 31 occasions, always on the same side. They note that such a witness may be impeached and certainly can lose credibility with a judge. This observation implies that legal 'objectivity' is more a matter of the expert's identification with one or the other party than his connection to the 'truth'. To be legally 'fair', apparently, one should testify as much for one side as the other. Of course, since one or the other side may be more consistently right or correct, scientific objectivity does not necessarily preclude such legal 'one-sidedness'.

Legal forums are charged with conflicts of values and the clash of partisan perspectives. It is easy for social scientists to be tarred with the brush of bias or politics, especially when their data are used to challenge legal common sense. Indeed, the insights of social science are only regarded as objective and value-free until they contradict or challenge prevailing social norms and ideologies (Kuklick, 1976; see also Furner, 1975, for an historical dimension to this observation). I believe that if psychologists are to succeed in attempts to introduce meaningful applications of social fact data into law, they must re-think the implicit assumptions of 'value-free' science. Otherwise the cutting edge of their role as critics in the legal system will be blunted.

A Jurisprudence of Social Science

Critical reactions to the use of psychology in law often focus on the quality of the data employed. Potential imperfections in the data are used to prohibit or drastically curtail its admissibility. However, the demand for perfection in data is often made by partisans who in other contexts resort unabashedly to untested 'common-sense' explanations, simplistic appeals to the 'obvious', and what one psychologist has called approvingly, 'fireside inductions' (Meehl, 1977). Legal advocates who criticize social science data for failing to achieve perfection rarely offer *any* data on their own behalf. Methodological one-upmanship, when practised by persons uncommitted to social science methods or unsophisticated in the use of social fact data, has a hollow ring to it. As long as they meet prevailing professional standards, social science data are better than no data at all. Courts should be reminded of this.

Indeed, even some critics of heavy judicial reliance on social science concede the power of the trial process to uncover 'soft' or a bad data. Meehl wrote that '[i]f we present a distorted picture even in a good cause, implying that certain technical matters are settled when in fact they are obscure and controversial, the powerful forces of the lawyers' adversary system will sooner or later ferret out the secrets' (Meehl, 1977, p. 19). Moynihan, another critic of the legal use of social science, notes that '*anyone* who brings questionable data or methodology into the various fields can expect to be devastated. And even the most impeccable work will be challenged simply because "it is there"' (Moynihan, 1979, p. 21).

These two comments illustrate another issue that must be resolved before psychology can be used effectively in the legal system. The unique nature of psychological and social scientific data may require special procedures and legal rules of evidence tailored more to the contours of social facts. Changes in the manner in which social facts are received into evidence and evaluated by legal decision-makers, and variations in the allocations of burdens of proof when social science evidence is at issue, may become part of a new jurisprudence of social science. Rather than limiting and constricting the use of psychological social fact data because it does not fit neatly into pre-existing legal forms and procedures, new ways of incorporating, interpreting, and using such data may need to be developed in law. Of course, this does not mean that all psychological data would be uncritically incorporated into law or that seemingly 'expert' psychological opinion would escape careful judicial scrutiny (cf. Haney, 1982c).

In the most sober terms, psychologists who work in the legal system run the risk that the worst parts of their profession will be used to extend and reinforce the least desirable aspects of the legal system. Psychology and law must avoid becoming a rudderless vessel filled with aimlessly collected data. But neither can it allow its course to be charted by legal navigators who orient to legalistic imperatives and little else. To steer clear of these dangers theory is required as well as data, values as well as facts.

Riesman once noted that 'the law has succeeded, as few professions have, in convincing social scientists that it is a formidably difficult affair' (Riesman, 1951, pp. 32–33). Belief in formidable difficulties breeds a kind of timidity that must be transcended. It is necessary to think in terms not only of humanizing the present system but of transforming it, of creating new kinds of institutions and new levels of challenge to the social and economic basis of injustice. It will be necessary to generate proposals for reforming the mechanisms by which courts find facts, and to employ social fact data in ways that will have legal impact beyond the confines of the single case. In so doing, the psychologist's role as critic in the system will have to be balanced against the source of their legitimacy as legal factfinders and their awareness of the political basis on which these dual positions are founded.

NOTES

1 US v. Telfaire, 469 F.2d 552, 1972.
2. People v. Shirley, 31 Cal. 3d 18, 1982.
3. Pugh v. Locke, 406 F. Supp. 318 (MD Ala), 1976, aft'd as modified, 559 F.2d 283 (CA5), 1977.
4. Hovey v. Superior Court, 28 Cal. 3rd 1, 1980.
5. People v. Murtishaw, 29 Cal. 3rd 733, 1981.
6. Larry P. v. Riles, 495 F. Supp. 926, 1979.
7. Albemarle Paper Co. v. Moody, 422 US 321, 1975.
8. Ballew v. Georgia, 435 US 223, 1981.
9. Hovey v. Superior Court, 28 Cal. 3d 1, 1980.
10. Brown v. Board of Education 347 US 483, 1954.
11. Plessy v. Ferguson, 163 US 537, 1896.
12. Muller v. Oregon, 208 US 412, 1908.

REFERENCES

DIAMOND, B. (1980). Inherent problems in the use of pretrial hypnosis on a prospective witness. *California Law Review,* **68,** 317–349.

GRAHAM, M. (1981). Judicial notice of adjudicative and legislative facts. *Criminal Law Bulletin,* **17,** 241–250.

FRIEDMAN, L., KAGAN, R., CARTWRIGHT, B., and WHEELER, S. (1981). State supreme courts: a century of style and citation. *Stanford Law Review,* **33,** 773–818.

FURNER, M. (1975). *Advocacy and Objectivity: A Crisis in the Professionalization of American Social Science, 1865–1905.* Lexington, Kentucky: University of Kentucky Press.

HANEY, C. (1982a). Law and psychology in the 'formative era': the triumph of psychological individualism in criminal justice policy. *Law and Human Behavior,* **6,** 191–235.

HANEY, C. (1982b). Data and decisions: Judicial reform and the use of social science. In P. Dubois (Ed.), *The Analysis of Judicial Reform.* Lexington, Mass.: D. C. Heath.

HANEY, C. (1982c). Employment tests and employment discrimination: a dissenting psychological opinion. *Industrial Relations Law Journal,* **6,** 1–86.

HANEY, C. (Ed.) (1984). Special issue on death qualification: *Hovey v. Superior Court. Law and Human Behavior,* **8,** 1–195.

HANEY, C., and PETTIGREW, T. (1986). Civil rights and institutional law: the role of social psychology in judicial implementation. *Journal of Community Psychology,* in press.

KUKLICK, H. (1976). The organization of social science in the United States. *American Quarterly,* **28,** 124–141.

LOFTUS, E. (1979). *Eyewitness Testimony.* Cambridge, Mass.: Harvard University Press.

LOWY, M., and HANEY, C. (1980). Law school in a nutshell: the creation of legal dependency. In *The People's Law Review.* Reading, Mass.: Addison-Wesley.

MEEHL, P. (1977). Law and the fireside inductions: some reflections of a clinical psychologist. In J. Tapp and F.J. Levine (Eds), *Law, Justice, and the Individual in Society: Psychological and Legal Issues.* New York: Holt, Rinehart and Winston.

MONAHAN, J., and LOFTUS, E. (1982). The psychology of law. *Annual Review of Psychology,* **33,** 441–475.

MOYNIHAN, D. (1979). Social science and the courts. *The Public Interest,* **54,** 312–332.

RIESMAN, D. (1951). Some observations on law and psychology. *University of Chicago Law School,* **19,** 30–44.

ROBINSON, D. (1980). *Psychology and Law: Can Justice Survive the Social Sciences?* New York: Oxford University Press.

ROSEN, P. (1972). *The Supreme Court and Social Science.* Urbana, Ill.: University of Illinois Press.

TAPP, J.L. (1976). Psychology and the law: an overture. *Annual Review of Psychology,* **27,** 359–404.

THORTON, G., and BENSON, P. (1980). Industrial psychologists as expert witnesses: role conflicts in fair employment litigation. *Labor Law Journal,* 417–429.

TWINING, W. (1973). *Karl Llewellyn and the Realist Movement.* London: Weidenfeld and Nicolson.

WISDOM, J. M. (1975). Random remarks on the role of social sciences in the judicial decision-making process in school desegregation cases. *Law and Contemporary Problems,* **39,** 135–149.

Psychology and Law
Edited by D.J. Müller, D.E. Blackman, and A.J. Chapman
© 1984 John Wiley & Sons Ltd

Chapter 5

Some Psychological Observations on Mens Rea[1]

Hans F. M. Crombag

'Most criminal offenses pose a direct physical, material, or social threat to someone' (Vidmar and Miller, 1980, p. 572). It is the purpose of criminal law as much as possible to prevent behaviour which interferes with the interests of others. This is accomplished through the threat of punishment. If such behaviour nonetheless occurs, we actually inflict punishment on offenders. The infliction of punishment is not our primary objective, it is simply the inevitable consequence of our wish to uphold the threat of punishment. Clearly, 'The general object of all law is to prevent mischief' (Bentham, 1973, p. 169). However, in actually inflicting punishment, we create a paradox. Whichever form of punishment we choose, it always implies an interference with the interests of the offender. Thus the criminal justice system achieves precisely what it is supposed to prevent: interference with someone else's interests. This inconsistency can only be solved if there are reasons to believe that the positive effects of punishment will generally exceed its negative effects.

Some authors (e.g. Murphy, 1979) hold that to justify inflicting punishment on offenders it is not necessary to demonstrate that punishment has a deterrent effect; they think retribution is a sufficient justification. However, Walker (1980) has recently argued that all retributive theories of criminal justice are internally inconsistent: they either attribute some utility to retribution, or they assume that retribution justifies itself, which is a *petitio principii* argument.

If a justification for the application of punishment in the criminal justice system is to be sought on utilitarian grounds, its effectiveness is an empirical issue. Skinner (1972) has argued that the system is a technology of behaviour control. The effectiveness of punishment is therefore part of a more general issue of what influences or determines behaviour, and punishment is an example of Skinner's tenet that 'Behavior is shaped and maintained by its consequences' (Skinner, 1972, p. 18).

ON THE DETERMINANTS OF BEHAVIOUR

People behave in the way that they do because the world is arranged in certain ways. If we put our hand in a flame, we burn it. If we walk the streets of a city inattentively, we may be run over by a car. We avoid doing these things because they lead to negative and sometimes even life-threatening consequences. If we treat our fellow human beings in an honest and reliable manner, we may hope to be treated in a similar manner. Since this suits our purposes, most of the time we treat others decently. If we know the physical and social world, we know how to behave in order to elicit positive and to avoid negative consequences for our behaviour, or rather how to behave in such a way that in general the positive consequences of our actions surpass the frequently inevitable negative consequences. To borrow Herrnstein's words: 'action is affected by its consequences to the actor, with reward strengthening, or punishment weakening, the behavior that gives rise to them' (Herrnstein, 1971, p. 399).

If people are not born with such knowledge of the world, it is the result of learning. People learn in various ways: through direct experience, through imitation, and through instruction. Learning presupposes memory. Leaving aside how memory operates, the statement that behaviour is shaped and maintained by its consequences necessarily implies that the organism in some way or other remembers what in the past were the consequences of its actions. Memory here is only a summary name for the organism's knowledge of the world. I do not mean to imply that this knowledge is always 'conscious' (whatever we mean by that word).

The statement that learning implies memory is important. Classical behaviourism maintains that the determinants of behaviour are to be found exclusively in the environment, in the fact that particular actions are followed by certain consequences with a certain regularity (as implied in a schedule of reinforcement). The regular relationships between environment, behaviour, and its consequences are called 'contingencies of reinforcement', which are considered the sole determinants of behaviour (see Skinner, 1969, p. 8). However, since people have to learn these contingencies, they must be remembered, so that one could say with equal justification that the determinants of behaviour are in part located within the organism, in particular in its memory.

While taking this position, I hasten to add that, given the present state of our psychological knowledge, I see no reason to admit among the determinants of behaviour internal states other than knowledge of the contingencies of the environment. The contingencies of the environment and our knowledge of them are sufficient to explain behaviour.

LAW AS AN INSTRUMENT OF AVERSIVE CONTROL

'Law is ... a statement of a contingency of reinforcement maintained by a governmental agency' (Skinner, 1953, p. 339). It specifies behaviours and their consequences as maintained by the judicial system. Since these consequences are almost always punishing, the criminal justice system is essentially a system of aversive control. Aversive control leads to avoidance of punishment, which, however, does not necessarily coincide with rule-conforming behaviour. Aversive control 'has unfortunate by-products. ... The aversive stimuli which are needed generate emotions, including predispositions to escape and retaliate' (Skinner, 1953, p. 183). The likelihood of retaliation in an effort to destroy the source of aversive control will probably increase as the control becomes more repressive. Systems of aversive control are not foolproof, and in using them we should inflict punishment parsimoniously. Such parsimony is required for utilitarian reasons.

Opinions are divided on this issue. The opinion that parsimony of punishment is required for utilitarian reasons is that of Jeremy Bentham. On the other side of the argument one finds such a formidable scholar as Hart (1968), who argues that we should distinguish between two questions: 'What justifies punishment as such?' and 'How are we to distribute punishment, that is whom shall we punish and to what extent?' Hart answers the first of these questions in an utilitarian manner, as does Bentham: we punish to deter. However, if that is so, why do we not punish more severely and why do we punish only offenders and not also their relatives? According to Hart (1968, p. 77) that would be 'unjust' or 'unfair'. According to Bentham, on the other hand, even questions of distribution of punishment can be decided on utilitarian grounds: punishing offenders very·severely and punishing persons other than offenders would be counterproductive (the pertinent arguments can be found in Chapters XIII and XIV of Bentham, 1973). It can be argued that psychological knowledge favours Bentham's side in the controversy. As aversive control becomes stronger, the accompanying emotions likewise become stronger and conforming behaviour may therefore give way to attempts to destroy the source of aversive control (Miller, 1941).

MENS REA

While Bentham and Hart may differ as to why we restrain ourselves in punishing, they nonetheless agree that such restrictions apply. We do not punish every offence or *actus reus*; we restrict punishment to acts that were committed with *mens rea* or a guilty mind. Different levels of *mens rea* may be distinguished. We commonly distinguish between 'intent' and 'negligence'. Within the category of intent we may further distinguish between 'basic intent' and 'specific intent' as defined by Kenny (1978). Within the category of negligence in The Netherlands a further distinction is made between 'conscious' and 'unconscious negligence', which corresponds to the distinction between recklessness and negligence proper as defined by Kenny. Hart (1968, p. 90) defines *mens rea* as 'knowledge of circumstances and foresight of consequences', which fits well with my earlier assertion that behaviour is a function of the contingencies of the environment and our knowledge of these as stored in memory. If individuals with knowledge of circumstances and foresight of consequences nonetheless commit an *actus reus*, it serves a purpose to instruct them through direct experience which contingencies the criminal justice system maintains; in other words, to teach them that, if we can help it, crime does not pay.

However, the distinction between intent and conscious negligence or recklessness is not always clear. To maintain this distinction Kenny (1978) holds that, in addition to knowledge of circumstances and foresight of consequences, a third condition must be met to meet the requirement of intent: there must have been an act of will or a volition. This requirement assumes that every act has both a mental and a physical component. The physical component consists of muscular contractions, whereas volition is supposed to be a mental act. This is, of course, the old mind–body distinction, which one might have expected to have been abandoned long ago (for a critique see Ryle, 1963, or Wynn Reeves, 1958). Should we then avoid using the word 'will' altogether?

Suppose I am driving a car with someone sitting next to me. I stop for a crossing pedestrian, and my companion asks me why I stop. I answer that I do so because I do not want to hit the pedestrian. Suppose my passenger next asks me whether I stopped intentionally; that is, whether my stopping was an act of free will. I might deny this, because in a sense I had no real choice. My behaviour was completely under the control of environmental contingencies. While it is perfectly acceptable to say that drivers stop because they do not want to run over a pedestrian, it would on the other hand be highly unusual to call such an act one of free will.

This example serves to illustrate that 'to stop' and 'to will' belong to different linguistic categories. 'To stop' is behaviour and the word 'stop' is descriptive of behaviour. 'To will' is not behaviour and the word 'will' is not descriptive of behaviour. To use 'will' as a descriptive term implies a category mistake as defined by Ryle (1963). When a judge in court decides whether a defendant has stopped or not, a decision as to fact is made, which may or may not be true. If next the judge decides whether the defendant stopped willfully or intentionally, an evaluation is given. The categories 'true' or 'false' are not applicable to evaluations since there is no empirical test to establish their correctness. This does not imply that evaluations are completely arbitrary, for they must follow conventions. One linguistic convention is that we regard behaviour as more volitional or intentional the more inconspicuous the causes of that behaviour are in that situation (see Skinner, 1972). In common language the convention seems harmless enough for we understand each other well enough. For a judge the decisions about whether an act was intentional and, based upon this, the extent to which a defendant is to be held responsible, are but intermediate steps towards a final decision on the appropriate punishment in order to deter the defendant from future offences. The intermediate steps do not bring any new empirical element to the final decision. Why then not try to decide the final and practical question of appropriate punishment directly in terms of its effectiveness as a deterrent, however difficult that may be, rather than invoke a linguistic issue, which can be confusing? If this were to be done, the distinction between intent and conscious negligence would become problematic, since the distinction rests on the presence or absence of volition. It should be added, however, that the certainty with which people can foresee the consequences of their actions varies, since cause–effect relationships are always probabilistic, and because people vary in their knowledge about the contingencies of the world.

Let us next consider the distinction between conscious negligence or recklessness on the one hand and unconscious negligence or negligence proper on the other. An example may serve to show the difficulty in attempting to distinguish between 'conscious' and 'unconscious'. Suppose a friend and I walk through town while discussing politics. My attention is focused on our discussion, but on which part of it, on the talking or on the subject of our talking? Do I talk consciously? No sooner do I direct my attention to the way I talk than this interferes with my thinking and talking about the subject of our discussion. Does this imply that I talk unconsciously? To say that would be very odd, since talking seems an activity which is by definition conscious.

This problem is related to the problem of volition discussed above. People do not have consciousness in the same way they have hands and feet. Whether we call an act conscious is a matter of linguistic convention. This convention implies that the better we are able to describe verbally the process of an act, the more we are inclined to call that act conscious. How such a convention may develop in a language community is described by Blackman (1981). Under this convention 'to know' equals 'to be able to verbalize'. Of course, we learn more than we are able to reproduce verbally; in that sense we have more foresight of consequence than we can put into words. Learning therefore does not have to coincide with 'conscious' learning. If this is so and if by using punishment we are interested only in its potential effect, then the distinction between conscious and unconscious negligence becomes of little importance.

In practice indeed we do not use the distinction. Defendants will not tell a judge what they thought while committing a crime or, rather, what they now think they thought, for such statements may be used against them. Knowing this, we do not try to establish subjective guilt, we use the fiction of objective guilt: an offender is considered to be responsible for an action of which 'any responsible person in his place and with his knowledge would have known the consequences' (Denning, 1961, p. 17).

There are, however, two restrictions to the use of punishment in this way. The first is that the offender must be able to learn from punishment. The second is that if other people would also not have foreseen the consequences of an action, we do not punish because we consider these consequences as coincidental. We accept both these restrictions, not primarily because it would be immoral or inhumane to do otherwise, as Hart (1968) holds, but because in these cases punishment would serve no practical purpose; that is, we accept these restrictions for utilitarian reasons.

RESTRICTIONS IN PUNISHING

In most criminal systems a person who commits a crime while being mentally disturbed is not punished. Some hold that this is so because to act differently would be inhumane. I submit that it is so because in those cases punishment would be wasteful. Is this controversy not just a matter of words? Am I not saying in utilitarian terms what others say in humanitarian terms? The tension between humanitarian and utilitarian analyses is more complex than that. Excusing mentally disturbed offenders might be anti-utilitarian, because potential offenders may hope to escape responsibility by using a similar excuse. We have to accept this undesirable side-effect, however, for *humanitarian* reasons.

This argument is unconvincing because mentally disturbed offenders do not in fact go free; we commit them to mental institutions. We do not commonly call such a measure punishment, but if punishment means inflicting suffering on someone, then committing someone to a mental institution may in many cases turn out to be punishment. It may indeed prove to be severe punishment, since its duration is uncertain, which, according to Bukstel and Kilmann (1980), adds to the severity of a punishment. If punishment is to be justified on utilitarian grounds, it is difficult to discriminate between a prison sentence and committing someone to a mental institution. The difference might perhaps be one of presumed effectiveness, but this is a subject on which there is no little controversy. In so far as both measures are expected to be effective, they are alternative measures of prevention. This seems to imply that in cases where the mental disturbance of the offender is such that learning must be considered entirely impossible, the offender should be left to go free, for neither commital to prison nor referral to hospital will be effective. With such offenders referral to a mental institution may be for reasons of isolation. In that case, however, the suffering inflicted on the offender through isolation should be weighed in full against the suffering of potential future victims. I see no valid reason to weigh the suffering of potential victims more heavily than the suffering of the mentally disturbed offender. With the exception of potential murderers, I see no instances in which the risk of leaving alone offenders who are unable to learn clearly outweighs the suffering resulting to them from lifelong isolation. It seems to me that in practice we frequently do not live up to the principle stated here.

It is not a sufficient excuse for offenders to say that they did not foresee the consequences of their actions. Offenders must demonstrate that other reasonable persons would not have foreseen them either, in other words that the relation between their action and its consequences was coincidental. Why would that be a valid excuse?

Environmental contingencies are probabilistic in nature. Our knowledge of the world is almost always insufficient to relate effects with certainty to causes. Usually the best we can do is to predict with a certain degree of probability the effect of a given cause. When that probability lies below a certain minimal value, we speak of a coincidence. This linguistic convention is a psychological phenomenon. In the physical world there is no such thing as an uncaused or partially caused phenomenon. Under the postulate of scientific determinism – and this is a postulate because we have no way of knowing otherwise – every event has a sufficient cause. Coincidences only occur in the psychological world. We impose our own subjective structure on the world; we divide it in more or less closed subsystems in order to make it manageable for our limited information processing capacity. Within each subsystem we are able with reasonable accuracy to predict effects given causes, and to infer causes given effects. For this there is, however, one condition: that there be no interference from *other* subsystems. Such interferences do occur, since reality is what it is, undisturbed by our psychological manipulations of it. They are rare, however, since we tend to choose the psychological structure that we impose on reality in such a way that interferences *between* subsystems have a low probability. If they occur nevertheless, we call them coincidences (see Hart and Honoré, 1959; Kohnstamm, 1949; Mackie, 1974).

To call on the *subjective* improbability of the consequence of an action is an insufficient excuse for offenders. On the contrary, if one's subjective estimate of the probability of an effect differs substantially from its objective probability or, as a practical substitute for this, from what reasonable persons would have estimated it to be, then there is reason to assume that the offender has something to learn which other people already know. A corrective measure may serve this purpose while at the same time reminding everybody else what the contingencies are. If, however, the cause–effect relationship had an objectively low probability or, as a practical substitute for this, if reasonable persons would also not have foreseen the consequence, then there is nothing to learn and consequently no purpose in punishing. In that case punishing would even have a detrimental effect, since it would lead to a situation in which, in the eye of the offender, action and punishment would be related in an arbitrary manner. If this happens repeatedly, symptoms of disturbed behaviour may be expected to develop, a syndrome known as 'learned helplessness' (Seligman, 1975). The syndrome is characterized by a general apathy and the inability to learn even in situations where the cause–effect relationships are recognizable.

Those who witness such a system of arbitrary punishment operating, are not more effectively deterred by it, as Hart (1968) seems to think. Rather, their 'just-world hypothesis' (Lerner and Miller, 1978) is destroyed by it. This hypothesis cannot be destroyed without doing considerable damage to the effectiveness of criminal law as a technology of behaviour.

THE JUST-WORLD HYPOTHESIS

If behaviour is shaped and maintained by its consequences, purposive behaviour is only possible if there is a certain degree of stability in the contingencies of reinforcement. Among the contingencies of reinforcement which shape and maintain behaviour we must distinguish between natural and social contingencies. Natural contingencies are those consequences of our actions which are given in nature. If I put my hand in a flame, I burn it. Such is the natural state of affairs. Social contingencies are established and maintained by other people (and by ourselves through mutual reinforcement).

The stability of the environment and its contingencies is an important condition. With natural contingencies there is little problem, since things are what they are and, if they change, we frequently know how they change and at what rate. With social contingencies, however, there is a problem, since frequently we know too little of other people's learning history to make their behaviour sufficiently predictable. In society many of the social contingencies have spontaneously evolved; some, however, have been specifically established for the purpose of behavioural control. To a large extent the latter is the case for law. If law as a technology of behaviour is to serve its purpose, then it is all-important that its contingencies are perceived by all as stable and rational. There has to be a consistent and rational relationship between actions and their consequences, between crimes and punishments. Consistency and rationality are essential to every criminal justice system.

Consistency requires that every crime is followed by punishment and in such a way that similar crimes lead to similar punishments. We therefore require *equal justice* for all. But for practical reasons we cannot always meet this requirement. Our main problem is that we do not succeed in apprehending every offender. If for a particular type of offence the chance of getting caught is low and everybody knows this (as is the case with traffic violations and tax evasion) then the pertinent rules of law lose their potential to regulate behaviour.

Rationality requires that in inflicting punishment we must be *efficient*, which means that we only punish when we have reason to anticipate a specific effect and in such a way that the effect is accomplished at minimal costs. To punish more or less severely than is required for effective behavioural control would destroy this image of rationality. It would create the impression of arbitrariness not only for those who are subjected to it, but also for those who witness it and must fear at one time or other to become victim of such an arbitrary system.

One may summarize the requirements of consistency and rationality as the general requirement of justice. Lerner and Miller (1978, p. 1030) state: 'people have a need to believe that they live in a world where people generally get what they deserve. Without such a belief it would be difficult for the individual to commit himself to the pursuit of long-range goals or even to socially regulate behaviour of day-to-day life'. If this just-world hypothesis is disturbed, people will react strongly. A host of psychological studies, as reviewed by Lerner and Miller, show that, when forced in an experimental situation to witness others being punished undeservedly, subjects act to compensate the victims. If the possibility of compensating the victim in some way or other was excluded from the experimental situation, the experimental subjects choose another way out, by attributing so many negative characteristics to the victims that their suffering becomes justified. Perhaps in criminal law we are doing the same thing. Perhaps we degrade criminal offenders to such an extent that we come to believe that they deserve any punishment the system happens to inflict upon them. Is our tendency to degrade and stigmatize delinquents not an indication that our criminal justice practice may be less consistent and rational than we would wish it to be? Are we not thereby inflicting upon these offenders behaviour patterns which may come close to learned helplessness, which would make them immune to any learning effect due to punishment?

In conclusion, then, I think Bentham was right. We require equal justice and efficiency in the distribution of punishment not for ethical or humanitarian reasons, but for practical, utilitarian reasons. Without at least some adherence to these principles, the criminal justice system becomes ineffective as a technology of behaviour. Those who think this approach cold and inhumane (a reproach made by some to Bentham) should realize that this reproach implies that emotions are more humane than reason. I am of a different opinion: we have in the past all too often been willing to pay for our emotions the price of irrational cruelty.

POSTSCRIPT

The core of the argument in the preceding paragraphs is that the criminal law is a technology of behaviour control. It is supposed to serve this function in two ways. First, by specifying aversive social contingencies as maintained by the community it is supposed to deter citizens from antisocial actions. Second, if individuals nevertheless engage in antisocial behaviour, the criminal justice system tries to teach them to mend their ways.

To many this approach may seem naïve and harsh. They think it naïve since 'everybody knows criminal punishment at best does not work, and at worst has effects opposite to those intended'. I do not wish to deny that in many instances this is what actually happens. The question, however, is why the system does not work out as intended. I submit that the apparent ineffectiveness of the criminal law may be due to the fact that we do not operate the system simply as a teaching technology, but as a way to make people suffer.

The fact that I seem to have little use for a number of subtle distinctions between various degrees of guilt, as traditionally made, may elicit a reproach of harshness on my part. While criticizing these distinctions as unpractical from a psychological point of view, I am not advocating a harsh system of strict liability. Quite to the contrary: instead of looking backward to what unfortunately happened and cannot be changed anymore, I advocate to look forward for possibilities to teach offenders to mend their ways in the future. If there is any hope for this, the criminal law should act; if not, we can only deplore what happened and evidently could not have been avoided. In short, then, I do not want to do away with the various degrees of *mens rea*, I propose to replace them with more practical criteria.

NOTE

1. The author is indebted to Derek Blackman, Job Cohen, Bart Groen, Marilyn Smith, and Joan de Wijkerslooth, who commented on earlier versions. The chapter was first drafted while the author was a visiting Senior Fulbright Scholar with the School of Law at Stanford University, USA.

REFERENCES

BENTHAM, J. (1973). An introduction to the principles of morals and legislation. In *The Utilitarians*. Garden City, N.Y.: Anchor Books. (First published in 1789.)
BLACKMAN, D. E. (1981). On the mental element in crime and behaviourism. In S. Lloyd-Bostock (Ed.), *Law and Psychology*. Oxford: Social Science Research Council Centre for Socio-Legal Studies.
BUKSTEL, L. H., and KILMANN, P. R. (1980). Psychological effects of imprisonment on confined individuals. *Psychological Bulletin*, **88**, 469–493.
DENNING, A. LORD (1961). *Responsibility before the Law*. Jerusalem: The Magnes Press of the Hebrew University.
HART, H. L. A. (1968). *Punishment and Responsibility*. Oxford: Clarendon Press.
HART, H. L. A., and HONORÉ, A. M. (1959). *Causation in the Law*. Oxford: Clarendon Press.

HERRNSTEIN, R. J. (1971). Quantitative hedonism. *Journal of Psychiatric Research*, **8**, 399–412.
KENNY, A. (1978). *Freewill and Responsibility*. London: Routledge and Kegan Paul.
KOHNSTAMM, PH. (1949). Causaliteit en strafrechts-wetenschap. *Tijdschrift voor Strafrecht*, **58**, 201–231.
LERNER, M. J., and MILLER, D. T. (1978). Just world research and the attribution process. *Psychological Bulletin*, **85**, 1030–1051.
MACKIE, J. L. (1974). *The Cement of the Universe: A Study in Causation*. Oxford: Clarendon Press.
MILLER, N. B. (1941). The frustration–aggression hypothesis. *Psychological Review*, **48**, 337–342.
MURPHY, J. G. (1979). *Retribution, Justice, and Therapy*. Dordrecht: Reidel.
RYLE, G. (1963). *The Concept of Mind*. Harmondsworth: Penguin.
SELIGMAN, M. E. P. (1975). *Helplessness*. San Francisco: Freeman.
SKINNER, B. F. (1953). *Science and Human Behavior*. New York: The Free Press.
SKINNER, B. F. (1969). *Contingencies of Reinforcement. A Theoretical Analysis*. Englewood Cliffs, N.J.: Prentice-Hall.
SKINNER, B. F. (1972). *Beyond Freedom and Dignity*. New York: Knopf.
VIDMAR, N., and MILLER, D. T. (1980). Socialpsychological processes underlying attitudes toward legal punishment. *Law and Psychology Review*, **14**, 565–602.
WALKER, N. (1980). *Punishment, Danger and Stigma. The Morality of Criminal Justice*. Oxford: Basil Blackwell.
WYNN REEVES, J. (1958). *Body and Mind in Western Thought*. Harmondsworth: Penguin.

Psychology and Law
Edited by D.J. Müller, D.E. Blackman, and A.J. Chapman
© 1984 John Wiley & Sons Ltd

Chapter 6

Understanding the Legal System: A Job for Psychologists?

Michael King

'SCIENTIFIC' PSYCHOLOGY

Now that psychologists have attached themselves so firmly to the law and legal system that nothing short of a nuclear war or collapse of the Western economy is going to prise them off, it is perhaps timely to ask some fundamental questions about the nature of psycho-legal knowledge and its relation to live legal issues and the 'real world' legal system. Ever since *On the Witness Stand* was published (Münsterburg, 1908), psychologists have not been slow to extol the virtues of their science and stake their claim of expertise over several aspects of behaviour that go on in and around the legal system. The recent growth in psycho-legal research has thrown up a new generation of psychologists who have seen fit to promote psychology as holding the answers to many of the problems and the cure to many of the ills that beset the legal system. These proponents thrive on both sides of the Atlantic. Saks and Hastie, for example, begin their recent book with unrestrained enthusiasm about the powers of psychology: 'Every law and every legal institution is based on assumptions about human nature and the manner in which human behavior is determined. We believe scientific psychology can help us understand these institutions and improve them' (Saks and Hastie, 1978, p. 1).

A similar approach is evident in Haward (1981), although here the author uses the technique of comparing enlightened, progressive, and scientific psychology, with superstitious, anachronistic legal practices. He writes:

'The law is based upon commonly accepted beliefs (not necessarily well founded) and reflects commonly adopted attitudes (however prejudiced).... Modern psychology's attitudes are those of scientific

67

scepticism, its theories derive from the hypothetico-deductive methods of classical science, and its beliefs rely upon public, reproducible facts and the exclusion of at least ninety-five per cent chance' (Haward, 1981, p. 15).

Moreover, it has become common for psychologists (see, for example, Kaplan and Kemmerick, 1974; Landy and Aaronson, 1969) who have carried out experiments on some aspects of behaviour which to a greater or lesser degree resemble what goes on within the legal system, to end their research report with the claim that their results could have practical importance for lawyers, police, judges, and so forth.

A number of assumptions seem to have developed and gained credance among many, if not the majority, of psychologists working in the psycho-legal field. These appear to be (1) that conventional scientific methods of testing and analysis in the hands of psychologists provide powerful tools for revealing the truth about any aspects of behaviour to which they choose to turn their attention; (2) that the truth revealed by psychologists is in some ways superior and more valid than the traditional or 'common-sensical' truths of lawyers, police officers, and others who are not psychologists and who do not apply these methods; and (3) that the substance of the truth revealed by psychologists using these methods has universal significance regardless of the particular social context in which that truth is revealed.

These assumptions cry out for careful critical examination. First, as a point of fact, most of the work carried out by psychologists in connection with the legal system, such as reports in child custody cases, assessments of delinquent children and abnormal offenders, observations of police interrogations, and predictions of the effects of allegedly pornographic literature actually owes little or nothing to scientific method. The experimental method, that most powerful tool of the psychologist's analytical equipment, is in the context of legal psychology, for ethical reasons confined, almost exclusively to simulations. Yet the subject of simulations and what they mean for 'the real world' has generated more controversy than almost any other subject in legal psychology.

In legal psychology, as in other fields of applied psychology, different writers have taken diametrically opposed views on the value of simulations in providing any real advances in understanding behaviour within the legal system. On the one hand there are those who see such studies as incapable of recreating the realities of the legal world in the artificial confines of the controlled experiment and, therefore, rarely able to provide a useful knowledge about behaviour within the legal systems. Konečni and Ebbesen (1979), for example, have demonstrated in their own studies that different research techniques produce different results on the same issue. In one of their studies on bail decisions, these authors found that judges presented with a simulated bail problem offered a 'reasonable decision scheme in setting bail' by requiring people who had little reason to remain in the area (weak community ties) to put up more bail than those with strong community ties. However, when the actual courtroom performance of the same judges was monitored, it was found that community ties played little part in their decisions. Similarly, Kapardis and Farrington (1981) found in a simulated sentencing exercise that English magistrates sentenced male offenders guilty of a serious theft charge more severely than female offenders. However, when Farrington and Morris (1982) analysed 384 actual theft cases from the records of a magistrates' court they found no such disparity in the sentencing of men and women. Even when real judges or magistrates are used, simulations alone are of very limited value in predicting how people will behave when making real decisions in the real legal system. How much more problematic are studies which use students to make judicial decisions?

On the other side of this debate there are those who steadfastly defend simulation studies against attack on their external validity (see, for example, Lind and Walker, 1979). The defenders argue that even when simulation does not replicate precisely the conditions found in police stations, courtrooms, or jury retiring rooms, they are nevertheless valuable in helping to build theories which may have important implications for the legal system and legal issues. They might add, of course, that even given the sophistication of modern statistical methods, it is usually impossible in the real legal world satisfactorily to isolate factors and observe their effects in a way that can be achieved in simulations.

I do not wish to become involved in this particular debate. The first point I wish to make is that both approaches to understanding the legal system depend ultimately upon observations within and about the 'real world legal system'. Devising theoretical models from controlled simulation studies does not avoid this issue, it merely postpones it, for in the final analysis there is no way of establishing the relevance or importance of any theory except by testing it against observations of behaviour within the 'real world'.

My second point is that many psychologists, whether engaging in laboratory simulations, direct observations of courtrooms or analysis of legal archives, give the impression that there is indeed something called 'the legal system' and that this 'legal system' is readily available for psychologists to observe, describe, and use as if it were a discreet entity. Thus Saks and Hastie, as has been noted, write of understanding legal institutions and improving them, while Konečni and Ebbesen (1979, p. 65) go much further in describing the legal system as 'an intact functioning social network' and directing their remarks to 'the researcher who is interested in how the system actually operates'.

It is not surprising that psychologists are in some difficulty here, for the traditional focus of their attentions has always been the individual and not social systems and institutions. More recently, however, psychologists, particularly social and developmental psychologists have increasingly recognized how problematic are general statements about individual human behaviour which fail to recognize the influence of the particular social environment in which people operate. Yet, unlike sociologists, psychologists have not, unfortunately, developed the theoretical models or methods of critical analysis which would enable and entitle them to apply psychological knowledge to the operations of social systems or even to identify the forces operating within these systems.

The way in which most legal psychologists have tended to deal with their deficiencies in this area is to ignore them. Instead of admitting their limitations and perhaps seeking guidance from other disciplines on how they might set about overcoming these problems, the most prolific and influential writers in the field have preferred to go it alone. As has been seen in the earlier quotations from Saks and Hastie (1978) and Haward (1981), they prefer to assert that psychological knowledge is different and indeed superior to other forms of knowledge, simply because it relies upon methods which have proven their worth in the natural sciences.

One might have confidence in this assertion if the phenomena investigated by psychologists within the legal system were essentially similar in nature to those investigated by physical and biological scientists, and if it were possible to apply the experimental method directly to the phenomena under investigation. Unfortunately, the first of these conditions is denied to psychologists by the fact that it is not open to them to assume constancy in the social world they are investigating in the same way that it is open to researchers into physical phenomena to assume constancy in their world. Water is always H_2O; the Sun always produces heat; and the combination of the two creates steam. Legal systems, it is true, 'produce' decisions about people and the conditions that affect their lives. Yet how those decision are reached depends upon the multitude of interlocking variables which are often so subtle and nebulous as to defy quantification or even identification. Moreover, the fact that a court in one place reached a certain decision on a particular day does not mean necessarily that a different court sitting on the same day faced with an identical case would have reached the same decision or even that this decision would have been reached by the same court sitting in a different day. As for the second condition, this too is largely denied to psychologists, for, as we have seen, practical and ethical considerations usually prevent any direct manipulation of variables within the legal system and that prohibits direct investigations through controlled studies.

Clearly, a legal system is not a system in the strict scientific sense of the term. It does not obey rules in the same way that liquid in a cup will respond in predictable ways to forces which are applied to it, such as shaking it or turning it upside down. The legal system, unlike the water in a cup, has no state of equilibrium in which it is possible to identify the forces which act upon it. Moreover, it can never be examined in isolation from the underlying forces, be they political, economic, philosophical, or cultural, which cause it to operate in the way it does. Of course, the fact that the system has no 'inert state' does not in itself necessarily mean that it is not amenable to scientific analysis. The human body is a strict system and the only time it is in an inert state is when it is dead. However, one can at least identify within definable limits the conditions necessary for the efficient operation of the human body and the forces operating to create these conditions. Thus the temperature of the body will be about 37 °C and both the blood pressure level and the blood sugar content will be within definable limits. Furthermore, even though the environment external to the human body may change, we are still able to anticipate that the blood temperature will be about 37 °C and that the blood pressure will not be beyond certain limits. Thus, the human body is a series of self-compensating mechanisms that enable it to neutralize the environment and to this extent it can be said to be a strict system (Holmes, 1976). Moreover, it is possible to identify, simply by looking at the operation of a human body, whether that body is working in an efficient or healthy manner. None of these features is, unfortunately, true of the legal system. It does not operate according to homeostatic rules. It does not react in any predictable ways to environmental forces. It cannot be examined in isolation from the society in which it operates. Its health or efficiency can only be established in relation to predetermined ideological or political criteria.

For these reasons, I believe that the fact must be accepted that 'the legal system' as such is not amenable to scientific investigation by the experimental method or by using the traditional methods of the physical sciences. Understanding the legal system is not the same sort of exercise as understanding the solar system or understanding the limbic system. This does not, of course, mean that legal psychologists should automatically be disqualified from the task which they appear to have set themselves, but simply that their claims to be 'scientific' in the way that biologists or chemists are 'scientific' must be taken with a pinch of salt. Systematic perhaps, painstaking perhaps, but scientific, no.

Psychologists could well plead that, scientific respectability apart, they have other qualities which make them uniquely qualified to investigate social systems. It could be argued that understanding such systems involves a mere extension of the skills and experience they have gained in investigating human and animal behaviour. Up to a point I would go along with this view, but only up to a point. I can best illustrate my reservations by setting out the various levels of knowledge which psychologists would have to assimilate in order to make general statements about the legal system or legal systems. I am assuming here that in order to make predictive or explanatory statements about the legal system, it is necessary to achieve some level of generalization and this in turn necessitates identifying all those factors which might affect behaviour within the system.

GENERALIZATIONS ABOUT THE LEGAL SYSTEM

The six levels of generalization set out in Table 6.1, are representative rather than exhaustive of all possible levels concerning the operation of the legal system. In the USA, for example, one would interpose 'state' between 'region' and 'country'. One might also want to make different demarcations within certain levels, such as drawing a distinction between city courts and rural courts at the level of institutions. In addition to illustrating the problems involved in making any general statements about 'the system' and its 'operation', the purpose of Table 6.1 is to show that these problems increase the further one moves away from statements concerning individual behaviour within a narrowly defined context, such as 'Judges at the Old Bailey...', upwards towards more general statements, such as 'English judges...'.

Let us now examine briefly some of the problems of generalization posed at each of the levels in Table 6.1. Although for brevity's sake I have concentrated in my examples on behaviour in court, there is no reason why the same arguments should not apply to behaviour at prisons, police stations, lawyer's offices, or probation headquarters. First, knowledge about the behaviour of individuals operating within a specifically defined context will be examined. It is known that all the factors set out in column III – personality, social class,

Table 6.1   Levels of generalizations about behaviour within the legal system and their implications

I Level of generalization	II Systematic level	III Confusion factors (cumulative)
1. Individual	Judge; jurors; magistrate; lawyer; policeman/woman	Personality; social class; age; sex; beliefs; race
2. Group	Jury; magistrates' bench; police working together	Group interactions of individual characteristics; group characteristics
3. Institution	Court; police station	Idiosyncratic interpretations of procedures; influence of dominant figure
4. Region	Other courts of similar jurisdiction in the locality; police district	Local attitudes and traditions
5. Country	Jurisdiction	National characteristics; law and procedural rules; political role of legal system
6. The World	All legal systems	All

age, sex, beliefs, and race – may be important as predictors of a person's decision-making or other forms of behaviour, such as the likelihood of a confession under police interrogation. In what circumstances and in what direction these various factors may influence behaviour is not yet entirely certain, but what is clear is that an account of any one person's behaviour may be of limited value in predicting the behaviour of others, unless those others share some salient characteristic or characteristics with that person.

One way of attempting to overcome the problem of human diversity is simply to classify people in terms of the roles they play within the system such as police, jurors, judges, and lawyers. Once classified people are expected to play out their roles according to rules and role expectations, regardless of their individual characteristics. However, generalizing people into roles is likely to lead to gross simplifications in all but the most mechanical aspects of behaviour. Even jurors, whose role is closely defined and circumscribed, are free to choose between verdicts of guilty and not guilty and may reach that choice by a number of different routes. Much so-called role playing within the legal system involves the exercise of discretionary powers which in turn may give scope for the influence of individual personality factors upon behaviour (see, for example, Cicourel, 1968; Davis, 1971; King, 1981).

Moving downwards in Table 6.1 to group behaviour, the first point that needs to be made is that groups incorporate all the variables which may confound generalizations from one individual to another. However, since a group is more than the sum of its individual members, it is necessary to add to these individual factors all those products of group interaction which are not necessarily predictable from knowledge of those individuals who make up the group. Interaction becomes important. Doing different things together often produces different results from the same people doing things separately. Moreover the structure of the group, its cohesiveness, and its history of previous interactions may become significant variables. Conformity, polarization, 'shift-to-risk', and compromise-seeking decision-making are examples of possible group behaviour having no counterpart in individual behaviour which spring readily to mind. Doubtless, there are other, less readily identifiable and less consistent ways in which individuals adapt their decision-making behaviour to accommodate the personalities, attitudes, and values of those with whom they are obliged to share the decision. Even if it is possible to obtain personality and attitudinal profiles of all the members of a jury, predicting how the jury members will respond as a group to a particular defendant and specific items of evidence is an extremely hazardous undertaking. Moreover, attempts to use one jury's decisions as a predictor of the way in which other juries will respond when presented with the same evidence or of the way that first jury will respond if presented with a different set of facts have met with little success (see Saks and Hastie, 1978, Chap. 4).

Generalizations about the decisions of lay magistrates may carry more validity than those concerning juries, as the magistracy in England and Wales is far more homogeneous than juries whose members consist of people chosen more or less at random from the electoral register. Lay magistrates tend to come from similar social backgrounds, and to have similar attitudes in, for example, their support of the police and a belief in the deterrent value of increasingly severe punishments. Nevertheless, as several studies have shown, there are considerable variations in their sentencing, bail, and legal aid decisions (see, for example, King, 1981; Levinson, 1979; Tarling, 1979). No doubt there are complex interactions at work between individual characteristics, role expectations, and group dynamics. What is clear, however, is that, even when dealing with relatively homogeneous groups within small units of the legal system, generalizations about decision-making are perilous undertakings.

Certainly, it is safer to make general statements about magistrates from the same court or police from the same police station or squad than 'the police' or 'the magistrates'. There is ample evidence to suggest that when one starts comparing institutions, such as courts or police stations, differences in policies, in interpretation of rules, and in the acceptability of different forms of behaviour are much more marked than within one single institution. One possible element which might lead to individual courts developing independently their own norms, values, and policies could be the existence of dominant figures, for example The Lord Chief Justice, The Master of the Rolls, the Chair of the Bench, or the Clerk to the Justices, who are able to impose their will on others working within the institutions. However, even without the presence of a dominant figure, groups which meet regularly to perform specific tasks tend to develop their own standard norms. The more independent and autonomous the institution, the more likely it is to operate as a closed system. One study, for example, found that magistrates' courts dispensing justice within a few miles of one another operated very different sentencing policies with no regard whatsoever to what the other was doing (Tarling, 1979).

At level four we encounter 'regional' factors which might confound generalizations. These factors, as has already been suggested, could include the influence of a dominant figure upon policies in an area, which in turn might well affect attitudes and behaviour among the magistrates. The present division among senior police officers in the United Kingdom between community and reactive policing, and the consequent effects upon police policies in different areas of the country, serves as an example of this process. To take another example, there is evidence to suggest that the way in which the criminal courts handled the mass of cases arising from the British street riots of 1981 was far from typical of the 'normal' reaction to crime in terms of the bail/custody decisions, the findings of guilt, and the sentences passed. In the USA Balbus (1973) has documented the varying responses of the criminal justice systems in several cities to the Black riots of the late 1960s. He has shown how these responses differed according to the size of the riot and pre-existing local factors such as the political structure of the city and the availability of civil liberty lawyers. He also demonstrated that, even in the same city, the responses of the courts varied considerably over a relatively short period of time.

Furthermore, it is generally accepted that local attitudes and conditions might well colour the response of juries to a particular defendant or a particular crime. Defence lawyers on both sides of the Atlantic, recognizing the detrimental effect local prejudices can have on the chances of a fair trial, often apply for controversial cases to be tried away from the locality in which the crime took place. To a lesser degree local attitudes may influence jury decisions even in trivial cases. Even if psychologists are able to identify the basic processes by which juries in general reach their decisions, this is a far cry from being able to predict what weight they will place on individual witnesses or particular items of evidence in carrying out those processes. To generalize therefore about the outcome of jury decision-making from jury research confined to one city or one area may be highly speculative.

How much more speculative are generalizations which span countries or continents. For a start, the legal rules and procedures may differ in ways which change important aspects of seemingly identical groups and roles within the legal system. For instance, in direct contrast to American juries, English jurors are rarely challenged, because the rules both limit severely the number of challenges open to the defence and restrict the amount of information available to both sides concerning individual jurors. If there were no difference in the verdicts reached by challenged and random juries, such variations in rules and procedures would be unimportant. Diamond and Zeisel (1974), in a study on admittedly simulated juries, found, however, that randomly selected, unchallenged jurors tended to convict more frequently than jurors challenged by attorneys. Findings such as this cast serious doubt on the validity of general statements made on the basis of studies of 'live' juries operating within the criminal justice system.

While some psychologists, notably Thibaut and Walker (1975), have attempted to investigate and compare different systems of justice, such studies have tended to concern themselves simply with differences in legal rules. There has been hardly any research into differences that might exist between the attitudes of different nations and different cultures to crime, law enforcement, the police, lawyers, judges, punishment, and so forth. Particularly when making trans-Atlantic generalizations, psychologists have been far too ready to assume that because England and America share a common language and a common legal tradition, the attitudes of decision-makers within the legal systems of both countries are also similar, if not identical. Yet, to put it at its simplest, judges in London probably take a very different view of rehabilitative sentences to judges in San Francisco. Police attitudes towards different types of crime may show marked differences between these two cities, and even jurors from the two cities may tend to respond to the same type of evidence in a very dissimilar way.

Cultural differences and cultural changes may also play an important part in confounding generalizations. American researchers have found, for example, that women participate more in jury deliberations today than in the recent past; a result, no doubt of their altered social role and self-image (Saks and Hastie, 1978). It might justifiably be assumed that in countries where most women still perform traditional female roles they will tend to play a secondary part in jury discussions. Yet some psychologists have drawn conclusions from their research which not only ignore cultural factors but which make ethnocentric value judgments on the basis of experiments conducted within a culturally specific setting. Perhaps the most notorious example within psycho-legal research is that of Thibault and Walker (1975). These researchers set out somewhat ambitiously to compare through experimental studies a number of different dispute resolution procedures gleaned from different legal systems. Their conclusion was that the adversary system used in American courts was better than all the others. One problem with this conclusion lies not in the research design or execution, but in the fact that the subjects, and thus the assessors, were all *American* students. It is perhaps not too surprising that they preferred justice which resembled most closely that prevailing in their own culture and with which they were most familiar. Indeed, a subsequent study by LaTour, Houlden, Walker, and Thibaut (1976) of preferences for different judicial procedures among American and West German students found that, while the Americans strongly preferred procedures in which a third party imposes a decision and least preferred those in which the parties at issue control the decision themselves, the German students took an almost directly contrary view.

What this brief review of the various factors which may confound generalizations about the legal system has shown is that the system 'actually operates' in highly complex ways. Moreover, 'understanding the system' is not just a matter of applying a little psychology to what goes on in court. Rather, it may involve the acquisition of knowledge and the application of concepts which are far removed from the subject-matter and training methods of most psychology degree courses. While 'understanding how the system actually operates' may be a useful slogan with which to berate those researchers who make grandiose claims of relevance to the law and legal system based on inadequate simulation studies, as a practical proposition for psychologists interested in pursuing legal issues it has very little value. If this catch-phrase is to be of any use to psychologists who wish to retain the scientific method as the mainstay of their intellectual equipment, much hard work will have to go into defining what precisely is meant by 'system' and what factors affect the system one is attempting to understand.

THE OBJECTIVES OF PSYCHO-LEGAL RESEARCH

The very fact that psychologists should be concerned with how the legal system actually operates and criticize other psychologists for failing to recreate the system accurately in their laboratory simulations suggests some considerable confusion about the objectives of legal psychology. The cause of this confusion seems to lie in the parallel development of the two main approaches or schools. The one springs directly from traditional psychology and is concerned with understanding human behaviour in general and human social behaviour in particular. Those psychologists who take this approach tend to be attracted to the legal system and especially to the criminal justice system, not because of any intrinsic interest in the law or social systems, but because the operation of the law with all its attendant publicity and controversy tends to throw into sharp relief aspects of behaviour which are of enormous interest to psychology, such as recognition and memory, group decision-making, and attitude change. The left-hand side of Figure 6.1 sets out the main features in this approach, and the relationship between these features. The unbroken lines connecting social psychology and psychology indicate that the purpose of such research is to test hypotheses derived from the theoretical concepts of psychology and that the results of such research feed back into the body of psychological knowledge. The broken lines, on the other hand, indicate indirect relationships or non-dependent relationships. This type of research is thus only indirectly connected with the law and the legal system in that the subject-matter of experiments and the conceptual framework within which they are generated appear to have been borrowed from the legal arena. Although there is no direct feedback from the research to the legal system, there may well be some indirect influence on social policy through the medium of psychological knowledge and its effect on 'common-sense' beliefs. This indirect connection is a matter which is considered at a later stage. In the meantime let us turn to the right-hand side of the diagram and the legal-forensic psychology approach.

This second approach takes as its starting point aspects of the law or legal system. Psychologists adopting this approach typically select and investigate some issue of concern to judges, lawyers, legal administrators, or policy makers. Wherever possible their investigations take the form of controlled studies and they submit their results to statistical tests. Where this is not possible, the psychologists will usually make every effort to be systematic and 'objective' in their research methods and the interpretation of results. Although they may invoke psychological theories in their research reports, these researchers are not primarily concerned with testing hypotheses derived from such theories but rather with investigating some policy issue. The investigations might involve the effects or efficiency of some aspects of the system as it operates at present, the likely effects of changes in rules or procedures or suggesting explanations for the behaviour of decision-makers

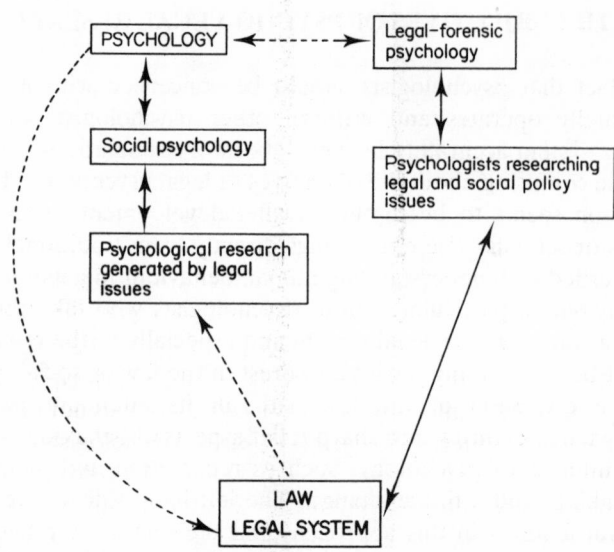

Figure 6.1   The main division in the approach of psychologists researching the aspects of the law and legal system

or others within the legal system. While the results of this research may contribute to a body of knowledge concerning behaviour within the legal system, to which one can give the name 'legal psychology' or 'forensic psychology', their contribution to psychology, the scientific study of behaviour, is likely to be minimal. Moreover, the connection between legal-forensic psychology and the science of psychology may be so tenuous at times as to be almost imperceptible. At other times, it is true, legal psychologists may make use of psychological models and methods developed within mainstream psychology and the findings of legal psychologists may find their way into psychological literature. However, the two disciplines are well able to exist independently of one another. There is certainly no dependency relationship between the two as there is between psychology and social psychology. Hence the broken line between psychology and legal-forensic psychology in Figure 6.1.

The model set out in Figure 6.1 is, of course, a deliberate oversimplification. In practice, it may be extremely difficult to classify people into the left- or right-hand streams, for many psychologists working on aspects of the legal system may at different times be found on either side of the figure. It sets out not to explain the complex relationship between pure and applied psychology nor to provide a comprehensive account of the motivation of legal psychologists, but simply to throw some light on the very confusing claims and counter-claims of psychologists interested in the legal system concerning the efficacy of their work and the work of others in the field. Of course, those researchers who choose to simulate jury discussions in the laboratory should resist the temptation of generalizing from their results to the real world, but the fact that the simulation fails to replicate real world conditions does not in itself render the research invalid as psychology, provided that it has some valid 'psychological' as opposed to 'social policy' purpose.

Similarly, those researchers who choose to study what goes on in particular courts or particular police stations should be prepared to accept the possibility that their work may have parochial value only. They should resist the temptation of claiming universal relevance for their findings in the misguided belief that they are in the business of applying the principles of scientific discovery to something called 'the legal system'. This does not mean that their work is in any way inferior to that of 'pure' psychologists. Rather, it is different both in its motivation and in its objectives. Moreover, the possibility should not be excluded altogether that their results will advance the science of human behaviour in some indirect way. To take a simple example, the fact that Konečni and Ebbesen's (1979) Californian judges tended to ignore community ties in their courtroom bail decisions may have important social policy implications, but from a psychological standpoint far more significant may be the way in which the same judges gave 'ideal' decisions on simulated bail exercises. One could envisage such results making a useful contribution to the literature of role play and also experimenter demands.

THE CONTRIBUTION OF PSYCHOLOGISTS

By now it is clear that I take a sceptical view of the claims of armchair or laboratory-bound psychologists who advocate applying 'the scientific method' to the legal system whether in order 'to understand the system' or to make it more just or more efficient. I am equally sceptical about the claims of scientific respectability of those psychologists actually operating within the legal system. In the long term both the evangelists and the reformers are, I believe, doing psychology and their fellow psychologists a disservice by raising expectations which cannot possibly be fulfilled.

However, I do not wish to end this chapter on a negative note, for I really do believe that both 'mainstream' psychologists and 'forensic-legal' psychologists have important contributions to make to the law and its operation, although perhaps not in the ways they would have us believe. The most important contribution psychology at large can make to the legal system is not by putting that system 'under the microscope', but by making the knowledge they have gained about human cognitive processes readily available and accessible, so that eventually it is taken for granted by everyone as 'common sense'. Take, for example, Loftus' work (e.g. Loftus, 1975; Loftus and

Palmer, 1974) on the effects of interpolating suggestions between perception and memory. One would expect that the more people are aware that the process of 'filling in' does in fact take place, the greater will be their efforts to guard against it occurring in themselves and the greater the caution they will exercise before accepting as true accounts of other people's recollections. As well as developing knowledge about human processes, psychologists can also help to destroy popular myths. Perhaps the most important of these myths for the legal system is the belief that the more confident and unyielding witnesses are in giving their evidence, the greater the likelihood that they are telling the truth. Psychologists, as we know, now have convincing proof that there is no positive relationship between confidence and accuracy.

However, a note of caution is necessary here, for neither of these important psychological findings can readily be translated into rules or procedures which would improve the efficiency of the legal system. It would be possible, of course, to instruct police and lawyers not to suggest answers when questioning witnesses, but this would not prevent suggestions coming from other sources. Moreover, without a detailed profile of the psychological make-up of each witness and a full account of all the information received by the witness between observation of the crime and giving evidence in court, it will be impossible for the judge, magistrate, or jury assessing that witness's evidence to know what to believe simply by applying Loftus' findings. Nor is it possible for the assessor to know whether a display of confidence in the witness box signifies a clear and accurate recollection of events, a strong but mistaken belief in the correctness of the witness's recollection, or a deliberate attempt to deceive the court. Psychologists, as psychologists, may be able to tell us a good deal in general terms about the processes by which human beings perceive, recall, and make decisions, but are they really any better than anyone else in assessing the accuracy of particular perceptions or memories in legal contexts or in predicting the decisions of particular courts?

Psychologists, as people with particular skills and training, working in different parts of particular legal systems on efficiency or social policy issues, may be able to apply their skills and training to good effect. They may, for example, be more capable than others of identifying patterns of behaviour within the courtroom or police station, of suggesting fairer procedures for identification parades, or of applying experimental techniques and statistical tests to determine what factors are important in the decision-making of particular groups at a particular time. What should be clear by now is that, not only do such activities have little to do with psychology as a science, but they are essentially parochial findings, specific to and dependent upon the particular social system and attitudinal and personality factors which prevailed at the time of the findings. They are not the first stage in the creation of universal laws about 'the legal system'.

To conclude, therefore, the headlong pursuit of the scientific understanding of the legal system, far from being a worthy and worthwhile occupation, is a chase which can only lead both psychologists and lawyers alike through the mists of confusion into the marshes of desperation where legal psychology is likely to sink without a trace.

NOTE

(1) The reader is referred by the editors to Chapter 18 for further discussion of this topic.

REFERENCES

BALBUS, I. (1973). *The Dialectics of Legal Repression.* New York: Russell Sage Foundation.

CICOUREL, A. V. (1968). *The Social Organization of Juvenile Justice.* London: Heinemann Education.

DAVIS, K. C. (1971). *Discretionary Justice.* Chicago: University of Illinois Press.

DIAMOND, J. S., and ZEISEL, H. (1974). A courtroom experiment on juror decision-making. *Personality and Social Psychology Bulletin,* 1, 276–277.

FARRINGTON, D. P. and MORRIS, A. (1982). Are male and female offenders sentenced differently? Paper presented at the Annual Meeting of the Social Science Research Council Law and Psychology Group, Oxford.

HAWARD, L. (1981). *Forensic Psychology.* London: Batsford Academic and Educational.

HOLMES, R. (1976). *Legitimacy and the Policies of the Knowable.* London: Routledge and Kegan Paul.

KAPARDIS, A., and FARRINGTON, D. P. (1981). An experimental study of sentencing by magistrates. *Law and Human Behavior,* 5, 107–121.

KAPLAN, M., and KEMMERICK, G. (1974). Juror judgement as information integration. *Journal of Personality and Social Psychology,* 30, 493–499.

KING, M. (1971). *Bail or Custody.* London: Cobden Trust.

KING, M. (1981). *The Framework of Criminal Justice.* London: Croom Helm.

KONEČNI, V. J., and EBBESEN, B. (1979). External validity of research in legal psychology. *Law and Human Behavior,* 3, 36–69.

LATOUR, S., HOULDEN, P., WALKER, L. A., and THIBAUT, J. (1976). Procedure: translational perspectives and preferences. *Yale Law Journal,* 86, 238–290.

LANDY, D., and AARONSON, E. (1969). The influence of the character of the criminal and his victims on the decisions of simulated jurors. *Journal of Experimental Social Psychology,* 5, 141–152.

LEVINSON, H. (1979). Legal Aid in summary proceedings in magistrates' courts revisited. *New Law Journal,* 129, 375.

LIND, E. A., and WALKER, L. A. (1979). Theory testing, theory development and laboratory research on legal issues. *Law and Human Behavior,* 3, 5–19.

LOFTUS, E. F. (1975). Leading questions and the eyewitness report. *Cognitive Psychology,* 7, 560–572.

LOFTUS, E. F., and PALMER, J. C. (1974). Reconstruction of automobile destruction: an example of the interaction between language and memory. *Journal of Verbal Learning and Verbal Behavior,* 13, 585–589.

MÜNSTERBURG, H. (1908). *On the Witness Stand.* London: T. Fisher Unwin.

SAKS, M. J., and HASTIE, R. (1978). *Social Psychology in Court.* New York: Van Nostrand Reinhold.

TARLING, K. (1979). *Sentencing Practice in Magistrates' Courts*. Home Office Research Study No. 56. London: Her Majesty's Stationery Office.
THIBAUT, J., and WALKER, L. A. (1975). *Procedural Justice: A Psychological Analysis*. Hillsdale, N.J.: Lawrence Earlbaum.

SECTION II

The Individual and Crime

This section has chapters on various aspects of the criminal personality. Three broad issues are considered: the development of criminal personality; the ability to predict dangerous behaviour by specified individuals; and the use of personality profiles by defence lawyers.

Eysenck puts forward his theory of crime based on interactions between biological predispositions and social influences. In questioning global socioeconomic and psychoanalytic explanations of criminal behaviour, he argues that personality can be considered as an intervening variable making it possible to assimilate both biological and social influences on criminals. Eysenck's account demonstrates in a contemporary form the traditional interest of psychologists in individual differences in behaviour, here of course focused primarily on criminal behaviour.

The question of when potentially dangerous individuals may be released from constrained environments and returned to a more normal way of life has proved to be an emotive issue, though it is patently of vital humanitarian concern also. **Blackburn** discusses some of the problems inherent in predicting later dangerous behaviour. He suggests that clinicians have achieved more success in this area than is generally believed, but sadly more obvious are the effects of inappropriate judgments to the effect that dangerous behaviour will *not* be exhibited. **Sepejak, Webster, and Menzies** present the results of an empirical study, finding that mental health professionals (including psychiatrists and psychologists) appear to show as much variation within as between disciplines; furthermore, the variable chosen to predict dangerousness has important implications with respect to accuracy.

Finally **Roll and Foote** describe the use of the 'inconsistent personality defence', which focuses defence arguments on incongruencies between the personality of an accused person and the general personality characteristics of different classes of criminals. Their illustrative case study shows clearly the potential efficacy and the general conceptual issues raised by this approach; it is an approach which bridges the traditional gap between idiographic and nomothetic data in psychology.

Many lawyers might expect psychologists to be especially interested in personality variables and individual differences with respect to criminal behaviour. The chapters in this section illustrate that such traditional psychological interests have been sustained, but research is focusing on more limited or specific predictive variables than was once the case.

Psychology and Law
Edited by D.J. Müller, D.E. Blackman, and A.J. Chapman
© 1984 John Wiley & Sons Ltd

Chapter 7

Crime and Personality

H. J. Eysenck

In this chapter a particular theory of the causation of antisocial conduct is discussed, which links it with personality, and hence with physiological and genetic factors. It is not suggested that the theory accounts for *all* the phenomena of antisocial conduct; merely that personality and the inherited propensity of the individual play an important part in the process of socialization. Inevitably personality interacts with a large number of social, economic, educational, and other factors, and these exert some influence on the way in which each person reacts. However, different people react differently to identical situations, and hence both situation and personality must be regarded as important. In concentrating here on the *personality* side of the equation the importance of *situational* factors is not being denied. However, these factors are dealt with in great detail by most writers on the topic, while personality, physiological factors, and genetic factors are largely passed by and ignored; hence the stress upon these latter factors in this chapter.

The term 'antisocial conduct' is used in a more general sense than the term 'crime'. The two are not synonymous. Conduct may be antisocial without being criminal, as defined by the law, for example smoking, alcohol consumption, and adultery. On the other hand, conduct may be criminal without necessarily being antisocial. The so-called 'victimless crimes' (e.g. prostitution) often fall into this category; such conduct may be defined as 'crimes' by people who regard these activities with disfavour, although many might regard them as 'sins', harmless pastimes, or as conduct which, because it occurs between consenting adults, is not within the purview of the law.

In making this differentiation we are paying some attention to those critics (see Wolfgang, Savitz, and Johnston, 1970) who have claimed that the concept of criminal activity is purely subjective, being arbitrarily defined by certain numbers of a given society, and thus having no general validity. It is obviously true that certain activities like smoking, drinking, adultery, prostitution, and homosexuality have been considered criminal at one time, but not others. In the discussion to follow, 'crime' will denote only those types of antisocial activity which have at most times and in most countries been considered as serious breaches of social norms, to such an extent that the state has provided certain types of penalties for such conduct. This concept of crime includes theft and burglary, assault and murder, rape and other sexual crimes, but not the 'sinful' activities listed above.

The problem presented by the existence of criminal and antisocial conduct is twofold. In the first place there is the 'individual differences' problem; how can we explain the fact that in similar or identical situations people brought up in a similar or identical manner in a similar or identical environment react quite differently, some committing criminal acts, others not? The other problem relates to *changes* in the frequency or occurrence of such criminal or antisocial acts, and asks why, say, there has been such a tremendous increase in certain crimes in recent times (Eysenck, 1977). Clearly the two questions are not identical; the population of Great Britain can hardly have changed so drastically as to explain the observed changes in frequency of robbery and violence against the person in terms of genetic change or personality differences.

SOCIOECONOMIC AND PSYCHOANALYTIC PERSPECTIVES

Ideally one would like to be able to answer both questions by recourse to a single theory; we will have to see whether indeed our theory enables us to do this. First, however, two theories which have been advanced in this field should be noted, which although very popular have in fact failed to provide positive evidence for their adequacy. The first of these is sociological or economic and states that criminal behaviour is caused by such socioeconomic factors as poverty, inequality, poor housing, and other similar conditions (Wolfgang *et al.*, 1970). This belief is so widespread, and seems to be so self-evident to many sociologists and economists, that it is hardly ever tested. Yet certain consequences would seem to follow from it which are testable, and which should be looked at in more detail than they have been in the past. One obvious consequence would be that if there is a change in a given population in the direction of less poverty, greater equality, and general improvement in living conditions, then there should be a reduction in criminality. Is this in fact so? In Great Britain over the past 80 years or so, there has been a tremendous reduction in the inequality of possessions, and a great deal of equalization of wealth. At the beginning of the century, 10% of the population owned over 80% of the total wealth of the country; by 1974 this figure had been reduced to approximately 40%. At the beginning of the century, 1% of the population owned about 70% of the total wealth of the country; by 1974 this had been reduced to just over 10% (Eysenck, 1977).

These figures suggest that there should be a considerable decrease in the amount of crime; yet there has been a considerable increase in crime.

There are of course difficulties with this kind of evidence, for it relies on official statistics which are known to be untrustworthy. There are changes in the public's willingness to report certain types of crime to the authorities; there are actual changes in the law, such as anonymity given to victims of rape in court reporting which has probably encouraged more women to go to the police, thus altering the figures; there is plea bargaining, which may alter the type of crime set down in the figures; and there are many more features of the official statistics which make them rather untrustworthy. However, it is unlikely that these changes are entirely responsible for the ever increasing crime rate; for even with crimes which are practically always reported, such as attacks on the police, we find a similar increase.

A proper investigation of deductions to be made from this general theory would require the following steps. First, a separate evaluation is needed of the many hypothetical socioeconomic factors that have been implicated. General levels of well-being, degree of social inequality, housing conditions, and so forth are undoubtedly all correlated, but the correlations are far from perfect, and hence each should be quantified separately. Indeed, it is possible for positive or negative correlations to occur in different countries. For example, in Switzerland there is a very high standard of living, and little inequality; in America there is a high standard of living, but a much greater degree of inequality. Thus one should look at the statistics within and between countries, trying to isolate what are the important variables from the socioeconomic point of view.

An effort should also be made to obtain better statistics for the actual amount of crime, in the hope that the 'grey area' of unreported crime could be reduced by choosing suitable types of criminal behaviour. For example, a more detailed analysis of police proceedings might enable one to obtain a better estimate of the actual amount of criminality in a given area. Admittedly this is much more difficult than simply taking published figures, but unless something of the kind is done, it will never be possible to evaluate the validity of the socioeconomic theory of criminality. It would of course also be necessary to consider relevant variables which might modify these conclusions, such as changing numbers of police, changing probabilities of discovery or changing sentencing procedures. It is safe to say that no existing study has come anywhere near to considering all these factors, and until that is done there is no way of evaluating this hypothesis.

As popular as the socioeconomic model has been the psychoanalytic one (Abrahamsen, 1952; Alexander and Staub, 1956; Hallock, 1967). Psychoanalysts have developed theories linking criminal and antisocial behaviour with traumatic events in the child's infantile sexual history. Unfortunately the theories, though popular, are not usually of a kind which can be tested experimentally, and consequently, as Popper and other philosophers of science have pointed out, they are not scientific theories in any meaningful sense (Popper, 1959). The first task awaiting psychoanalysts, therefore, would be to put these theories into such a form that they can be objectively tested, that is so that falsification is possible. Until that is done very little can be said about this type of theory.

However, there are certain data which clearly are of relevance and interest. Thus, for example, a men's prison has been built in England (Grendon Underwood) in which psychoanalytical principles are used to treat offenders and to facilitate their rehabilitation. This is a very time-consuming and labour-intensive task, involving great public expenditure, and it is obviously of interest to see whether prisoners so treated do in fact show a better rate of rehabilitation (i.e. less recidivism) than do prisoners sent to a more conventional prison. The results of comparing recidivism figures for Grendon Underwood inmates and for inmates for the traditional Oxford prison show that there is in fact no difference, for up to four years after release, between the figures for these two prisons (Eysenck, 1977). The results can hardly be said to encourage belief in the psychoanalytic hypotheses, or the methods of treatment based on them. Of course there are difficulties involved in this comparison. Prisoners are not allocated at random to the two prisons; more neurotic prisoners are more likely to be sent to Grendon Underwood than to Oxford, and vice versa. However, this should lead to a greater success rate in Grendon Underwood, as neuroses tend to remit spontaneously (Rachman and Wilson, 1981), and in so far as neurotic disorders lead to criminal activity, prisoners who exhibit more seriously neurotic behaviour should show an improvement in their crime rate.

What should be noted, in any case, is that the comparison was *ad hoc* and not arranged as an experimental paradigm with proper controls. Grendon Underwood has been functioning for many years now, but we still await a properly conducted experimental trial to demonstrate its effectiveness, if any. Typically, such innovations are introduced on the basis of some theoretical hopes, but are not properly assessed because there is too much official involvement in the success of the enterprise to make objective scrutiny, with possibly negative results, feasible.

More interesting, because of its experimental nature, is the famous Cambridge–Somerville Youth Study (McCord, 1978), instigated by R. C. Cabot in 1936. Several hundred boys from densely populated, factory-dominated areas of Eastern Massachusetts were included in the project, with schools, welfare agencies, churches, and the police recommending both 'difficult' and 'average' youngsters to the programme. These boys and their families were given physical examinations and were interviewed by social workers who then rated each boy in such a way as to allow a selection committee to designate delinquency-prediction scores. In addition the selection committee studied each boy's record in order to identify pairs who were similar in age, delinquency-prone histories, family background, and home environment. By the toss of a coin, one member of each pair was assigned to the group that would receive treatment. The treatment programme began in 1935, when the boys had a median age of 10½ years. Treatment continued for an average of 5 years, and counsellors visited each family on average twice a month. They encouraged families to call on the programme for assistance. Family problems became the focus of attention for approximately one-third of the treatment group. Over half of the boys were tutored in academic subjects, over a hundred received medical or psychiatric attention, one-quarter were sent to summer camp, and most were brought into contact with the Boy Scouts, the YMCA, and other community programmes. The whole programme was based on a combination of psychoanalytic principles and social philosophies of a family-centred kind. The control group participated only through providing information about themselves, and of course both groups contained boys referred to as 'average' and boys considered 'difficult' in equal proportions.

McCord conducted a 30-year follow-up for treatment effects, comparing 253 men who had been in the treatment programme after 1942 with the 253 matched mates assigned to the control group. The results of the study were most disappointing. Almost equal numbers in the treatment and control groups had committed crimes as juveniles – whether measured by official or unofficial records. As adults, equal numbers had been convicted for some crime. Among men who had been in the treatment group, 119 committed only relatively minor crimes, but 49 had committed serious crimes against property (including burglary, larceny, and auto theft) or against persons (including assault, rape, and attempted homicide). Among men from the control group, 126 had committed only relatively minor crimes; 42 had committed serious property crimes or crimes against persons. Twenty-nine men from the treatment group and 25 men from the control group committed serious crimes after the age of 25 years. Not one of the differences was statistically significant; however, a higher proportion of criminals from the treatment group committed more than one crime!

Indeed, not only did the programme fail to prevent its clients from committing crimes, thus corroborating studies of other projects (Craig and Furst, 1965; Empey and Ericson, 1972; Hackler, 1966; Miller, 1962; Robin, 1969), but a number of significant side effects, such as alcoholism, serious mental illness, earlier death, more stress-related diseases, and occupations with lower prestige resulted. These negative aspects of the programme were the only ones to be statistically significant, and no positive effects were found. The results clearly demonstrate the failure of the combination of psychoanalysis, social work, and general 'do-goodism' so characteristic of this type of work. The combination of several features makes it impossible to blame any single one of them for the negative effects produced by the programme, but it is suggested that the failure of any positive effects to occur invalidates all of them.

A BIOSOCIAL THEORY OF CRIME

The particular hypothesis adopted here is fundamentally based on the conception of human beings as biosocial organisms (Eysenck, 1981). It is taken as axiomatic that man as an animal is the product of millions of years of evolution, an evolution which has shaped the brain, developed instincts, affected behavioural responses, and quite generally embodied behavioural predispositions in the morphology of the central nervous system and in genetic constitution. Equally, however, an individual's behaviour is shaped by the social environment, the cultural stimuli to which one is exposed, and the educational messages received. No serious student can doubt the relevance of both the *biological* and the *social* aspects of an individual's behaviour.

Let us begin by considering biological factors which must form a major part in any theory of antisocial and criminal activity. It used to be thought very widely, particularly in the 19th century, that criminals are born and not made. This belief was widespread, although the support for it was anecdotal, and as untrustworthy as that for the socioeconomic hypothesis is nowadays. It should be noted, however, that modern genetics could never demonstrate the proposition that criminals are born and not made. Criminal conduct is clearly a kind of human behaviour, circumscribed and defined by social rules, and as such cannot be directly inherited. All that can be inherited are morphological, physiological, and biochemical characteristics of the nervous system, which, when acted upon by some kind of environment, result in conduct of a certain kind. Thus, even if it should turn out that genetic factors play a part in antisocial and criminal conduct, it would still be necessary to investigate just precisely what it is that is being inherited. In other words, the genetic hypothesis can never be considered sufficient by itself; it merely points the way to a direction in which research may go in order to complement the direct finding of heritability with a more detailed analysis of the nature of the morphological, the physiological, and the biochemical properties which have been inherited, and mediate the conduct in question.

The most direct studies of genetic factors in criminality are of course those dealing with concordance in monozygotic and dizygotic twins. Several investigations have now been done on large numbers of twins, one of whom was known to be criminal; the co-twins were then searched out to determine their zygosity and their criminality or non-criminality. If genetic factors are important, one would expect concordance for criminality in monozygotic twins more frequently than in dizygotic twins. This has in fact been found in practically all the investigations that have been done in Germany, Denmark, Japan, and other countries; on the whole it is found that monozygotic twins are *over four times* as frequently concordant as are dizygotic twins. This is very powerful proof for a genetic factor, although the data do not really enable one to estimate the strength and degree of heritability or to say any more about the genetic architecture involved (Eysenck, 1977).

Twin studies are not the only ones which support a genetic hypothesis, or rather an hypothesis which admits strong genetic components, acting in conjunction, and in interaction, with environmental factors. Equal weight can be given to adoption studies, in which we pitch the environmental connection between children and adopted parents against the genetic connection between children and their natural parents. In the first of the two adoption studies to be mentioned, Schulsinger (1972) in Denmark compared 57 psychopathic adoptees with 57 non-psychopathic controls, equated for sex, age, social class, and in many cases neighbourhood of rearing and age of transfer for the adopting family; carefully defined criteria for psychopathic behaviour were used in this study. Next, the case records of the biological and adoptive relatives of the psychopathic and the control subjects were examined. In spite of the fact that adoption took place at an early age, there were no differences between the adoptive families or the psychopathic and of the control groups; when it came to the biological family members of these groups, however, relatives of the psychopathic group showed an incidence of psychopathy two-and-a-half times as great, and an incidence of mildly psychopathic behaviour also two-and-a-half times as great as was found in relatives of the control group. In other words, the psychopathic group had taken after their biological parents, not their adoptive parents.

In a study by Crowe (1972) in the USA interest was not in diagnosed psychopathy, but rather in the actual record of arrests. Here the investigator started off by locating 41 female offenders who were inmates of a women's prison reformatory, and who had given up their babies for adoption. At the time of the study, they had produced 52 offspring, ranging in age from 15 to 45 years. A properly matched control group of 52 offspring from non-criminal mothers was also studied; these, too, had of course been given up for adoption. It was found that the offspring of the criminal mothers had had more criminal arrests, and had also received a much greater number of convictions; these differences were statistically significant.

Another adoption study has been reported by Hutchings and Mednick (1974). They studied a total sample of 1145 adoptees. Fifty-two adoptees were born to biological fathers who were not known to the police, but with criminal adoptive fathers. A larger group of 219 adoptees had criminal biological fathers, but were adopted by fathers who were not known to the police. This design enables us to answer the question whether having a criminal biological father is more important than having a criminal adoptive father with respect to predicting criminality in the adoptee.

When neither the biological fathers nor the adoptive fathers were known to the police, 10.4% of the adoptees were criminals. When both fathers were criminals, the 36.2% of the adoptees were criminals. The percentages for the two cross-fostered groups are respectively 11.2% and 21.0%. Thus having a criminal biological father is more predictive of criminality than having a criminal adoptive father, in the ratio of about two to one. Clearly, the evidence from adoptive studies agrees well with that from concordance studies, and seems to indicate strongly that genetic factors play a part in antisocial behaviour, although of course it would be grossly inaccurate to say that criminal behaviour is inherited as such.

Genetic evidence tells us that heredity plays a part in the causation of antisocial conduct; it does not tell us what the mechanism is that may be responsible. I have suggested a conditioning theory of antisocial conduct as offering such mediational hypothesis between genetics and behaviour (Eysenck, 1977). Antisocial behaviour, in so far as it is in line with the instinctive proclivities of the individual, and hence useful in accomplishing this end, is a natural type of behaviour for all animals and infants. Socialized behaviour, which often goes against the interest of the individual, although it is in line with the best interests of society, does require an explanation; it is, in a very real sense, 'unnatural'! It is unlikely that socialized behaviour can be acquired through rational means. What is suggested is that punishment meted out by parents, teachers, peers, and others over the years in response to infringements of the social mores acts as a Pavlovian unconditioned stimulus. Through frequent repetition it becomes associated with a conditioned stimulus (e.g. the contemplation or actual perpetration of antisocial or criminal acts). Hence the unconditioned response (pain/fear/anxiety/shame) becomes associated with the conditioned stimulus. In this way 'conscience' is built up over the years which strongly determines the later conduct of the individual. Briefly, this is the conditioning theory of socialization (Eysenck, 1977); it requires certain qualifications, which are presented later, and of course it is here put in far too brief and dogmatic a fashion. This theory, like all theories involving some form of learning or conditioning, starts with the simple fact that what would require explanation is not so much *antisocial* behaviour as *socialized* behaviour.

CRIMINAL PERSONALITY

There would seem to be a link between personality and conditioning. Such a link may be provided by the hypothesis of 'cortical arousal', a property of the cortex mediated by the reticular formation and characteristically involved both in conditioning and in the personality dimension of introversion–extraversion (Eysenck, 1967, 1981). Many studies have been done on the psycho-physiological properties of the nervous system and the cortex of criminals and more particularly psychopaths (Eysenck, 1980); these support the view that psychopaths in particular are characterized by a low level of cortical arousal, which links their behaviour with that of extraverts, who are also characterized by low cortical arousal. This is a prominent and promising line of research which is likely to give us much more important information on the biological side of the equation.

The first point to note is that individuals differ considerably in the degree to which they form conditioned responses, the speed with which they form conditioned responses, the strength of these conditioned responses, and the length of time taken for these conditioned responses to extinguish. Thus if conditioning is really at the basis of the acquisition of socialized responses, the person who acquires conditioned responses easily should be more readily socialized and acquire a stronger 'conscience' than the person who has difficulty in acquiring conditioned responses. Here we may, therefore, have a hint as to the reasons why individuals differ in their behaviour in similar situations, in spite of similar upbringing, socioeconomic status, and so forth.

This hypothesis may seem to be purely biological, and not in accord with the promise to produce a theory which is based on a conception of man as a biosocial animal. However, such an objection would be erroneous. Socialized behaviour, in this analysis, is the outcome of a conditioning process, but this process is determined not only by the conditionability of the individual, but also by two other factors, both of which are socially determined. The first of these is a number of pairings of the conditioned and unconditioned stimulus experienced by the individual. Let us assume that person A is easy to condition, but is only exposed to a few pairings of antisocial behaviour followed by punishment. Compare A with another individual B, who is more difficult to condition, but who encounters large numbers of such pairings. In spite of the relative lack of conditionability of the latter, this person is likely to acquire a stronger 'conscience' because of the much larger number of pairings encountered. This vital point suggests that a general trend of 'permissiveness' (i.e. lack of enforcement of such punishment by parents, teachers, magistrates, and others) will lead to the acquisition of much weaker 'consciences' by individuals than would a determined effort to enforce the rules of society. Thus social features of the conditioning process are required to account for the final product, as much as biological features inherent in the individual.

The second important concern is the *content* of the socialization process. Assume that a group of children is brought up by a modern Fagin; they would become conditioned to steal and behave in antisocial ways. Presumably those children who condition more readily would react to this particular type of training more quickly than would children difficult to condition. Thus the content of the reinforcement and conditioning programme plays an important part in the final behaviour, whether socialized or antisocial.

This prediction is of course susceptible to experimental testing. Raine and Venables (1981) conditioned the galvanic skin response of children of high and low social class using electric shocks as the unconditioned stimulus, and also tested these children on an inventory of antisocial behaviour. The results are shown in Figure 7.1. It will be seen that children in the high social class, presumably receiving rewards for socialized behaviour and punishment for antisocial behaviour, show positive correlation between conditioning (SCR) and pro-social behaviour, whereas children in the low social class, where to some extent it is felt that aggressive and other types of antisocial behaviour are encouraged, showed the opposite. In other words, both the number of replications of the pairings between conditioned and unconditioned stimulus and the particular content of the conditioned stimulus which is being reinforced, play an important part in the final results. It should be noted that it is quite incorrect to regard the theory as being completely deterministic, in the sense that people who condition poorly are doomed to be criminals, and people who condition easily will become law-abiding citizens!

There are other complexities which have to be taken into account in evaluating the theory just proposed. Pavlov drew attention to what he called the 'law of strength', that is the rule that the stronger the unconditioned stimulus, the stronger was the link established between the conditioned stimulus and the conditioned response, broke down at a certain point and had to be supplemented by the law of 'transmarginal inhibition' or 'protective inhibition'. This stated that when the unconditioned stimulus is too strong, inhibition sets in and weakens the response. There is good evidence that this

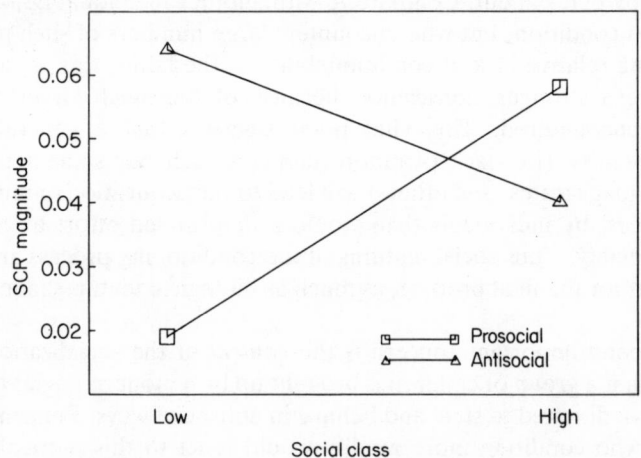

Figure 7.1 Conditioned responses as a function of social class and antisocial conduct in school. From Raine and Venables, 1981, reproduced with permission from the authors and publishers Pergamon

law also applies in human beings, and in conditioning experiments, so that the actual *strength of the unconditioned stimulus* is another feature that would have to be taken into account in any scientific theory of antisocial conduct (Eysenck and Levy, 1972). The fact that the infliction of very painful corporal punishment, such as birching, does not seem to have very beneficial effects on later behaviour of the persons punished suggests that punishments of this type have exceeded the optimal point of unconditioned stimulus strength, and are subject to the law of transmarginal inhibition.

Pavlov noted the marked differences in the formation of conditioned responses in his dogs, and he based a system of personality description on this, which he extended to humans. Research has certainly demonstrated that there are important relations between conditioning and personality, and hence the possibility exists that there might be important relations between personality and antisocial and criminal behaviour. I first suggested specific relationships of this kind (Eysenck, 1960) as a purely theoretical basis, but research since then has amply justified this hypothesis (Eysenck, 1977). There are three major factors in personality research which emerge repeatedly in factor analytic and correlational studies, conducted in many different countries. These factors are extraversion as opposed to introversion; emotional instability or neuroticism as opposed to stability; and psychotism as opposed to superego functioning. Eysenck (1977) has suggested that all three are concerned in antisocial conduct, so that typically the person indulging in such conduct would be extraverted rather than introverted, emotionally unstable rather than stable, and high on psychotism rather than on superego functioning. The evidence from many different sources, including many studies of adult incarcerated criminals, adolescent criminals both incarcerated and not, and children, is fairly conclusive in supporting this hypothesis (cf. Eysenck and Eysenck, 1978)

The evidence is too varied and too numerous to discuss, but Figure 7.2 illustrates the results typically obtained. School-children were administered the Eysenck Personality Questionnaire, which gives measures of psychotism (P), extraversion (E), and neuroticism (N). There are two criteria of antisocial conduct, one provided by ratings made by the teachers (NA) and an antisocial behaviour (ASB) questionnaire filled in by the children themselves. On the abscissa are graphed the number of personality scales on which the children were above the average, in the direction of higher antisocial conduct. In other words, O refers to children who are below the average on P, E, and N; 3 refers to children who were above the average on all three scales. Thus it will be seen that the greater the number of scales on which a child was above the average, the greater was the number of antisocial activities indulged in. All the regressions are linear, and very clear in their indications; other similar studies have given similar results.

It is sometimes suggested that criminality is a purely social concept,

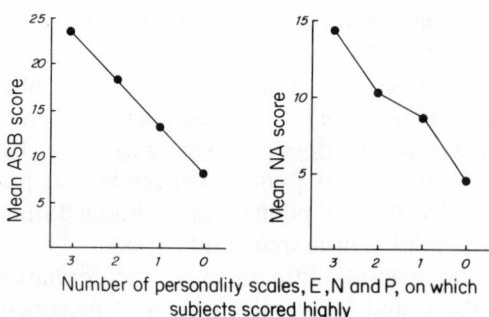

Figure 7.2 Antisocial behaviour as a function of personality traits, P, E and N. From Eysenck, 1977, reproduced with permission from the publishers Routledge and Kegan Paul Ltd

differing from one country to another, and that accordingly no generalizations can be made concerning it. It is further suggested that crime is a function of the political and economic system pertaining to a given country; thus it is suggested that communist, Third World, and capitalist countries are so different that no generalization is possible from one to the other. The position stated here is quite different. It is suggested that all existing societies agree in outlawing a number of different types of conducts which are clearly antisocial, and a tolerance of which would lead to the break up of that society. Murder, unprovoked aggression, stealing, and other similar activities are examples which are considered criminal in any existing society of which there is knowledge. It would therefore be expected, on these grounds, that the same personality traits are involved in antisocial conduct in all types on countries, and the evidence (Eysenck, 1977) does indeed show that similar personality configurations to those found in Great Britain can be observed in criminals in Third World countries like India, or communist countries like Hungary. In all these countries, P, E, and N are personality traits more characteristic of the criminal than of non-criminal, non-offending ordinary citizens. It should be noted finally that there is a strong genetic component to the personality variables involved (Eysenck, 1981). Thus personality traits seem eminently well suited to the task of acting as intermediary between genetic causation and antisocial conduct. The relative contribution of these various personality traits to antisocial and criminal conduct differs from age to age, and may also differ with respect to the type of antisocial activity in question. Extraversion seems to be particularly important in the case of children, less so for adolescents, and least so for adult criminals. Neuroticism seems least important for children, more so for adolescents, and most so for adult criminals. Psychoticism seems important in all ages.

APPLICATIONS OF THE THEORY

This general theory explains to some extent why individuals differ from each other with respect to socialized or antisocial and criminal conduct. Genetic factors predispose them to have certain personality traits, which are connected with the propensity to form weak or strong conditioned responses. Depending on the frequency of pairings between the conditioned and unconditioned stimulus in the field of social behaviour, and on the precise content of the conditioning programme, children will grow up to develop appropriate types of behaviour. Conditionability is a crucial factor on the biological side; permissiveness or morality is a crucial factor on the social or environmental side. In a permissive society where parents, teachers, and magistrates do not take seriously the task of imposing on children a 'conscience' which would lead them to behave in a socialized manner, a large number of individuals with poor or average conditionability will acquire a 'conscience' too weak to prevent them from indulging in criminal activities, although had they been subjected to a stricter regime of conditioning, they might have grown up to be perfectly respectable and law-abiding citizens.

The term 'strict' needs to be defined in this connection; it is too easily equated with demands for excessive and violent punishment. As pointed out above, this is not so: Pavlov's law of 'transmarginal inhibition' suggests that it is the certainty and frequency of conditioned and unconditioned stimulus pairings which are responsible for the formation of strong conditioned responses, rather than any exaggerated strength of the unconditioned stimulus. This suggests that conditioning principles might be able to suggest better and more effective methods of preventing recidivism. This is indeed so.

Consider the experiment reported by Berg, Hullin, and McGuire (1979). Juvenile court magistrates in the Yorkshire city of Leeds assisted with evaluation of two court procedures for the control of truancy by randomly allocating treatments to young offenders appearing before them. One procedure, the more usual one used in Britain in such circumstances, was that of making a *supervision order*. A social worker or probation officer was given supervision of the child, who came back to court only if the appointed welfare officer wanted further action from the magistrate. In the other procedure, referred to as *adjournment*, the court repeatedly adjourned the case and the child came back at varying time intervals at the discretion of the magistrates, depending on progress in school attendance since the last appearance. As a back-up to either procedure an *interim care* order could be made, under which the child went into a residential assessment centre for about three weeks, and if all else failed, a *full care* order would be applied. The Social Services Department would then decide whether the child should be placed in a community home or allowed to remain a while longer on trial. Since both of these procedures had been used for some time with no agreement concerning their relative effectiveness, the magistrates were persuaded that a controlled trial, with random allocation, would be the only way to settle the question.

The results (Figure 7.3) were clear-cut. Before appearing in court both groups had been off school for an average of 75% of the time. In the first six months afterwards, the mean absence of the adjourned cases had fallen to 35% while the supervised children were still away 50% of the time. When the next six month period was looked at in the same way, the superiority of the adjournment procedure was maintained. It did not make any difference whether the child was a boy or a girl. When convictions for criminal offences were considered as a measure of outcome, the results again favoured the adjournment procedure. Before coming to court for truancy, the two groups did not differ significantly in the average number of offences. After the court appearance, the number of criminal convictions dropped markedly in the adjourned group but was hardly reduced at all in the supervised group.

Since adjournment appears to be a non-treatment, and supervision approximates to counselling, it might seem surprising that the former is more effective in getting truants back to school and keeping them out of trouble with the law. Berg *et al.* suggest that the adjournment procedure may be superior because it involves the child's family to a greater extent. The parents may have to accompany the child at each court appearance, which may mean taking time off work, and they are thus actively engaged in treatment rather than being allowed to pass responsibility for the problem on to a welfare officer. Within the current theoretical perspective, however, another possibility is that attendance at court, with the explicit danger of removal from home, is a more anxiety-evoking and motivating force (unconditioned stimulus) than counselling from a sympathetic social worker. If this were true, its success could be accounted for in terms of the conditioning principle. (See Howarth and Gunn, Chapter 3, pp. 37–38).

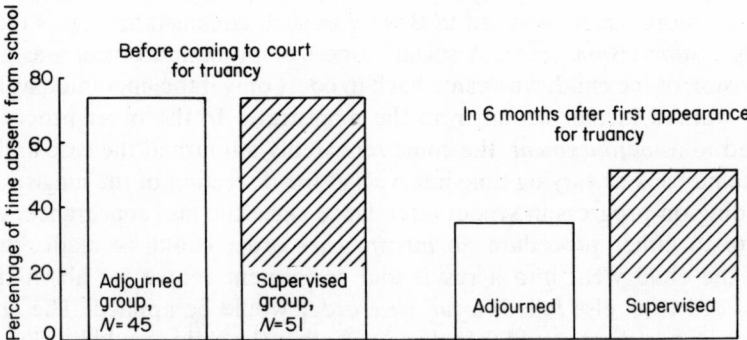

Figure 7.3 Reduction in truancy as a function of adjournment or supervision. From Berg, Hullin and McGuire, 1979, reproduced with permission from the authors and the publishers MacMillan

One final word may be permissible in linking the discussion given so far with the observed increase in crime. As pointed out before, even if there is a strong biolgoical basis for criminal activity, it cannot be argued that this is in any way responsible for the tremendous increase in crime that has taken place over the last 30 or 40 years. Genetic causes take thousands of years to produce any marked changes in the composition of the population, and there simply has not been time for any such change. However, there has been an increase in permissiveness which has preceded and accompanied the increase in crime, and in our hypothesis it is precisely the lack of conditioning contingencies produced by the permissive atmosphere in home, school, and court which would produce such a lessening of the 'conscience' or moral fibre of the population. It can be seen that the theory advocated accounts for the individual differences noted, as well as for the deleterious effects in question. More than that could not be asked of any theory.

It will be obvious to the reader that the theory here developed is indeed just that. There are interesting findings which support the theory, some of which have been discussed in this chapter. However, it will need a great deal more empirical evidence to put the theory on a more adequate footing, and answer some of the obvious objections. Already mentioned has been the necessity of linking more closely personality variables and different types of crime and clearly criminality is not a undimensionable variable. Other weaknesses of the theory have also been touched upon in passing. It should, however, be noted that all other existing theories are equally beset by weaknesses and anomalities, and few of them possess even the limited amount of experimental and factual support that the conditioning–personality theory has. It is confidently hoped that future work along these lines will improve the theory and make it more acceptable to criminologists.

REFERENCES

ABRAHAMSEN, D. (1952). *Who are the Guilty?* New York: Grove.
ALEXANDER, F., and STAUB, H. (1956). *The Criminal, the Judge, and the Public.* New York: Free Press.
BERG, I., HULLIN, R., and McGUIRE, R. (1979). A randomly controlled trial of two court procedures in truancy. In D. P. Farrington, K. Hawkins, and S. M. Lloyd-Bostock (Eds), *Psychology, Law and Legal Processes.* London: Macmillan.
CRAIG, N. M., and FURST, P. W. (1965). What happens after treatment? A study of potentially delinquent boys. *Social Service Review,* **39,** 165–171.
CROWE, R. R. (1972). The adopted offspring of women criminal offenders: a study of their arrest records. *Archives of General Psychiatry,* **27,** 600–603.
EMPEY, L. T., and ERICSON, M. L. (1972). *The Provo Experiment: Evaluating Community-Control of Delinquency.* Lexington, Mass.: Lexington Books.
EYSENCK, H. J. (1960). Symposium: The development of moral values in children. VII. The contribution of learning theory. *British Journal of Educational Psychology,* **30,** 11–21.

EYSENCK, H. J. (1967). *The Biological Basis of Personality*. Springfield, Ill.: Charles C. Thomas.

EYSENCK, H. J. (1977). *Crime and Personality*, 3rd edn. London: Routledge and Kegan Paul.

EYSENCK, H. J. (1980). Psychopathie. In U. Baumann, H. Berbalk, and G. Seidenstucker (Eds), *Klinishce Psychologie. Trends in Forschung und Praxis*, Vol. 3. Wien: Hans Huber.

EYSENCK, H. J. (1981). *A Model for Personality*. New York: Springer.

EYSENCK, H. J., and EYSENCK, S. B. G. (1978). Psychopathy, personality and genetics. In R. D. Hare and D. Schalling (Eds), *Psychopathic Behaviour*. Chichester: Wiley.

EYSENCK, H. J., and LEVY, A. B. (1972). Conditioning, introversion–extraversion and the strength of the nervous system. In V. Nebylitsyn and J. Gray (Eds), *Biological Bases of Individual Behavior*. New York: Academic Press.

HACKLER, J. C. (1966). Boys, blisters and behavior: the impact of a work program in an urban central area. *Journal of Research in Crime and Delinquency*, **12**, 155–164.

HALLOCK, S. (1967). *Psychiatry and the Dilemmas of Crime*. New York: Harper.

HUTCHINGS, B., and MEDNICK, S. A. (1974). Registered criminality in the adoptive and biological parents of registered male adoptees. In S. A. Mednick, F. Schulsinger, J. Higgins, and B. Bell (Eds), *Genetics, Environment and Psychopathology*. Amsterdam: North Holland.

McCORD, J. (1978). A thirty-year follow-up of treatment effects. *American Psychologist*, **33**, 284–289.

MILLER, W. B. (1962). The impact of a 'total community' delinquency control project. *Social Problems*, **10**, 168–191.

POPPER, K. R. (1959). *The Logic of Scientific Discovery*. London: Hutchinson.

RACHMAN, S., and WILSON, T. (1981). *The Effects of Psychological Therapy*. Oxford: Pergamon Press.

RAINE, A., and VENABLES, P. H. (1981). Classical conditioning and socialization – a biosocial interaction. *Personality and Individual Differences*, **2**, 273–283.

ROBIN, G. R. (1969). Anti-poverty programs and delinquency. *Journal of Criminal Law, Criminology, and Police Science*, **60**, 232–331.

SCHULSINGER, F. (1972). Psychopathy, heredity and environment. *International Journal of Mental Health*, **1**, 190–206.

WOLFGANG, M. E., SAVITZ, L., and JOHNSTON, N. (1970). *The Sociology of Crime and Delinquency*. Chichester: Wiley.

Psychology and Law
Edited by D.J. Müller, D.E. Blackman, and A.J. Chapman
© 1984 John Wiley & Sons Ltd

Chapter 8

The Person and Dangerousness

Ronald Blackburn

Rubin (1972) has suggested that claims on the part of psychiatrists to be able to forecast dangerousness are without foundation, and subsequent studies have appeared to endorse this opinion. The evidence is that among offenders incarcerated under mental health legislation, on average less than one in three of those predicted by clinicians as likely to behave dangerously will actually do so if released. The clinician seems only a little less likely to get it wrong when predicting that a released offender will not behave dangerously (Monahan, 1981).

This inability on the part of psychiatrists to demonstrate an acceptable degree of accuracy in this respect has led to clinical predictions of dangerousness being compared to 'the flip of a coin' (Ennis and Litwack, 1974) or characterized as manifestations of 'magic rather than science' (Cocozza and Steadman, 1978). It has also resulted in accusations that psychiatry is acquiescing in a system of repressive social control in which incarceration for treatment serves to ensure punitive detention under the guise of humanitarian concern (Monahan, 1976). Inevitably, it has led to calls for the curtailment of dangerous offender legislation and an end to the involvement of psychiatry in criminal proceedings (Klein, 1976; Monahan, 1973). It has to be noted, however, that psychologists cannot wholly escape these charges. Increasingly, clinical psychologists are involved in making clinical judgments of dangerousness either independently or consensually as members of mental health teams.

The issue is an emotive one, involving as it does the competing claims of society and the individual. Society demands that the clinician minimize false negatives, and thereby ensure that potentially dangerous individuals are not let loose on the public. The principles of civil liberty, on the other hand, demand that clinicians minimize false positives and ensure that individuals are not unjustifiably deprived of their freedom by incorrect decisions. There are, then, questions of value and social policy, summarized in the question 'What represents an acceptable trade-off between the values of public safety and individual liberty?' (Wenk, Robinson, and Smith, 1972, p. 401). This is not a question which we as psychologists are in a better position to answer than anyone else. We do, however, have a professional obligation to ensure that the answer to such a question is fully informed by data as to what is possible in terms of clinical prediction. I argue in this chapter that the data do not yet permit a definitive conclusion.

It is perhaps a reflection of the value-laden nature of the debate that demonstrations of the apparent inaccuracy of clinical judgments of dangerousness have been greeted with indignation. What is frequently overlooked is that such judgments are in principle no different from the judgments of experts made daily in a variety of settings which profoundly influence the course of people's lives. The clinician judging a person's propensity for violence is doing essentially the same as the personnel officer hiring aspiring sales personnel, the university admissions tutor selecting potential academic high-flyers, or the social worker choosing foster-parents. In each case, knowledge of a person, derived from interview and personal history data, is combined to yield an intuitive judgment about that person's dispositions to behave in certain ways. From what we have known for some time from research on clinical prediction, the human judge, no matter what the field of expertise, is typically not very accurate when making such inferences (Goldberg, 1968; Meehl, 1954). We should not, therefore, be very surprised when we learn that the clinician judging dangerousness is also inaccurate. However, in this particular context, two factors are commonly claimed to militate against any improvement in accuracy. The first is the impossibility of predicting such an infrequent event as the commission of a violent crime in the absence of perfect knowledge; that is, the base-rate problem. The second is that there is no such identifiable attribute as a dangerous disposition, because dangerousness is not a property of the person. To the extent that either of these arguments is justified, then there is clearly a case for abandoning attempts to predict dangerousness.

In a moment I question whether they are justified, but first let us consider just how inaccurate clinical predictions of dangerousness really are. If they are totally inaccurate, it would strengthen the argument that dangerousness is not a property of the person.

THE VALIDITY OF CLINICAL PREDICTIONS OF DANGEROUSNESS

As every psychologist knows, though is apt to forget from time to time, the validity of a prediction, represented for example by a correlation coefficient or a percentage accuracy figure, is a function of the reliability of both the predictor and the criterion. (For the moment, I use the term 'predictor' to refer to the clinical judgment itself rather than the input variables on which the judgment is based.) Since we do not usually work with perfectly reliable predictors when attempting to predict behaviour, estimates of validity are typically *under*estimates of what is possible, attenuated by errors in the predictor, and not uncommonly in the criterion as well.

Most of the evidence suggesting that clinical predictions of dangerousness have low validity comes from naturalistic studies of those released from psychiatric institutions directly or indirectly connected with the penal system. In none of the half dozen or so studies summarized by Monahan (1981) was any attempt made to determine the reliability of either predictors or criteria. It is worth considering the sources of error likely to reduce reliability in these cases. First, consider the predictor, usually a dichotomous judgment of dangerous versus non-dangerous. The crucial element here is the cognitive activity of the human judge, usually a psychiatrist. The sources of bias in clinical judgment are beginning to be understood in some detail. They include personal factors such as age, social class, amount of experience, and personal styles, such as dogmatism (Monahan, 1981), but also cognitive factors such as illusory correlations and the 'judgmental heuristics' described by Kahneman and Tversky (1973). Factors such as these appear to be responsible for the mean interjudge reliability of 0.4, which Goldberg (1968) reported to be characteristic of several different kinds of clinical judgment. Such unreliability is not unique to psychiatrists. In Goldberg's research it was found to be similar for nurses, physicians, and clinical psychologists (see also Sepejak *et al.*, Chapter 9). In criticizing the judgment of forensic psychiatrists, it may be salutary to remind ourselves that general practitioners, or for that matter garage mechanics, are probably doing no better.

There is, however, an additional source of unreliability in some of the studies reported, and that is that it is not certain that dangerousness predictions had clearly been made in all cases. Studies such as that of the Baxstrom patients (see Steadman and Cocozza, 1974), in which large numbers of detained mentally disordered offenders have been released from secure institutions by legal injunction, assume that all patients have been predicted to be dangerous to the community. Yet the fact that a person is incarcerated in this kind of institution means that the person *was* diagnosed as dangerous at some time in the past, but not necessarily at the time of release. At least two factors may prolong a person's stay in such a setting. One is uncertainly or difficulty in finding appropriate disposal. Another is sheer institutional inertia. It may be significant that one of the two institutions involved in the Baxstrom case was subsequently closed by the New York State Department of Corrections on the grounds of its lack of clinical policies, conflict between staff, and poor staff morale. In this kind of retrospective study, then, some patients may well be included among the false positives who should more appropriately be assigned to the true negative category.

Turning now to the criterion, this has usually been either re-arrest or conviction for a further violent crime. Yet these two are not themselves equivalent, since an arrest will not necessarily result in a conviction. Moreover, not all violent crimes are reported, and of those that are, by no means all will result in an arrest. Arrest rates cannot therefore be regarded as a reliable criterion of the occurrence of violent behaviour. One recent American estimate is that arrest rates for violence may represent only one out of five actual occurrences (Hall, 1982).

Now, given that the amount of error in both predictor and criterion is probably substantial, it may be that the low levels of predictive validity actually found in practice could well represent a high degree of predictability in principle. For example, if we were to cast such data in correlation terms, with a reliability coefficient of 0.4 in both predictor and criterion, the maximum possible validity coefficient is also 0.4. Yet such a modest coefficient would actually represent perfect prediction if all errors were controlled or corrected for. The point being made here is that recognition of these sources of unreliability means that the appropriate conclusion to be drawn from the available data is that dangerousness *is* probably overpredicted in practice, but not that clinicians are *incapable* of predicting future violence. In the practical situation, there are at least three ways of improving the reliability of clinical judgment. One is simply to pool the judgments of several independent judges, which is equivalent to increasing the reliability of a test by increasing the number of items. Another is to train judges to overcome systematic cognitive biases. Studies of training procedures aimed at debiasing intuitive judgments are now beginning to appear (Wiggins, 1981). A third is to identify the most valid clinical judges and to use a statistical model of their judgmental processes as the predictor (Goldberg, 1970; Wiggins and Cohen, 1971). In the few studies of this so-called 'paramorphic representation' which have been carried out, the models of the judges were invariably superior to the judges themselves, for the simple reason that they are applied more reliably. The difficulty with this approach might lie in persuading the clinician to accept redundancy! Nevertheless, until we pay some attention to the reliability question, our evaluations of the accuracy of clinical judgments of dangerousness will themselves remain inaccurate.

Validity coefficients are not, however, the whole story. An imperfect predictor with a validity of 0.4 may actually be very useful if the base rate of the criterion behaviour is 50%. As Curtis (1971) demonstrated, under these conditions the predictor would reduce misclassification by some 13% when compared with the blanket prediction of calling everyone non-dangerous. It would, however, do no better than the blanket prediction if the base rate were only 10% in the population of interest. At that level, a coefficient of 0.7 would be required to produce any improvement in classification. An argument commonly advanced is that validities of this magnitude are very rare in predictions of behaviour, and that as the base rate of violence in released mentally disordered offenders is extremely low, our overall errors of prediction will always be greater than if we relied solely on the base rate, and called everyone *non*-dangerous. The evidence seems to favour this argument. In none of the studies so far reported have the judgments of clinicians beaten the base rate.

The weakness of the argument is that we do not know for sure what the base rate of further violence is. As argued earlier, the criterion of arrest for further violent offences, which seems to produce base rates of around 10%, represents a considerable underestimate of actual violent behaviour. In the Baxstrom study, the criterion of *any* further assaultive behaviour, which included assaults made in a hospital setting as well as the community, yields a much higher base rate of 20% (Steadman and Cocozza, 1974). It is not inconceivable that attention to the social behaviour of released violent offenders in the context of the family or work would indicate even higher levels of violence. And as the base rate rises, so does our ability to make accurate forecasts with predictors of modest validity.

THE CONTRIBUTION OF THE PERSON TO VIOLENCE

I have argued so far that by reducing errors in both predictor and criterion, we may be able to demonstrate greater accuracy on the part of the clinician judging dangerousness. Perfect reliability, however, would not guarantee high validity of prediction. Several commentators have in fact claimed that future dangerousness is inherently unpredictable. This argument has less to do with the clinical judge than with the input variables on which judgments are based; that is, knowledge of the violent person. Monahan, in 1976, for example, contended that use of a person-oriented model was one reason why dangerousness predictions were 'doomed'. He suggested that '... rather than attempting to identify and modify violence-prone persons, energy could be expended in the attempt to identify and modify situations conducive to violence' (Monahan, 1976, pp. 27–28). Similarly, Klein (1976) proposed that we should give up attempts to forecast dangerous acts because we cannot foresee the social situations which are crucial to their determination.

These arguments are part of the classic 'person–situation' debate. To some extent, however, they miss the point. Few would deny that there are identifiable environmental factors which exert a considerable influence on the level of violence, nor that, in a broad sense, all behaviour is a joint function of the person and the situation, nor that lack of knowledge about future situations imposes an upper limit on the prediction of dangerousness. But none of these is inconsistent with a substantial contribution of the person to violence. The critical question is whether there is sufficient stability in the behaviour of violent people for us to be able to say something about the probability of future violent behaviour without reference to specific situations.

Social learning theorists, such as Mischel (1968) and Bandura (1973) have argued strongly that there is not. In the context of aggressive behaviour, they contend that differences between people are specific to particular kinds of situation, and that the assumption of stability in behaviour implied by traditional concepts of an aggressive disposition or trait is not justified by the evidence. In short, knowledge of violent behaviour in one situation will not enable us to predict violence in another. There are, however, several lines of evidence which favour the notion of stability or consistency in aggressive behaviour.

To take an example from my own work, mentally disordered offenders detained in a maximum security hospital indicated, by means of an 'S-R inventory of hostility', the intensity of each of 12 modes of response (e.g. 'swear', 'feel angry', 'heart beats faster', 'want to hit someone') to 14 situations involving annoyance or thwarting (e.g. 'someone pushes ahead of you in a queue', 'someone turns the television off while you are watching a programme', 'a nurse blames you for something you did not do'). My interest in this approach lay in the fact that much of the debate about person–situation interactions has derived from this kind of data, although for statistical reasons the components of variance approach is now considered to yield results of limited generality (Olweus, 1975). The data were compared with comparable

Table 8.1 Components of variance in an S-R inventory of hostility for male patients at a British Special Hospital. For comparison, data are presented from a study of Canadian students by Endler and Hunt (1968). [Data from Endler and Hunt (1968) are the copyright of the American Psychological Association, 1968, and reproduced with the permission of the authors and the publisher.]

Source	Patients ($N = 81$)		Students ($N = 45$)	
	Variance component	Percentage variance	Variance component	Percentage variance
Persons (P)	0.311	23.16	0.314	19.62
Situations (S)	0.010	0.75	0.079	4.95
Responses (R)	0.044	3.28	0.258	16.14
P × S	0.005	0.37	0.185	11.58
P × R	0.534	39.76	0.180	11.26
S × R	0.032	2.38	0.083	5.19
Residual	0.407	30.31	0.500	31.26

data from the only published study using this format in relation to hostile and aggressive behaviour (Endler and Hunt, 1968), in which an S-R inventory of hostility was given to a Canadian student sample (Table 8.1). There were several clear differences between the two sets of data, notably in the proportion of variance due to response modes and the interactions. The patients seemed to discriminate much less than the students between situations, and this may well be an important feature of aggressive offenders. The main point, however, is that in both samples the persons' variance was substantial, and exceeded that due to the persons × situations interactions. In the patient sample, the largest proportion of variance was that due to the persons × responses interaction, which indicates that patients differ according to preferred modes of responding. There is nothing inconsistent here with a dispositional concept of aggressiveness.

If the major concern, however, is the consistency of the person across situations, the response factor is irrelevant (Olweus, 1975). Re-analysing the data by collapsing across the response factor showed that the percentage of variance due to the persons–situations interaction was clearly substantial for the student sample (35.93%), which indicates that to a considerable extent their reactions vary according to the situations. Again, this was much less the case for patients (9.56%). But for both samples, the largest share of the variance was due to persons (50.77% for students, 87.35% for patients). There is, then, quite considerable stability of behaviour across situations, at least as the subjects perceive it.

Rather stronger evidence for the stability of aggression comes from longitudinal studies which do not rely on self-report. Olweus (1979) has recently reviewed the evidence on the stability of aggression as measured by ratings, peer nominations, and direct observations, periods covered by the studies ranging from 6 months to 21 years. Over 12 investigations, the average correlation between behaviour samples from two occasions of testing, after corrections for measurement error, was 0.79. Given the time spans involved, it is difficult to account for this degree of consistency in terms of situational constancy. The conclusion that aggressiveness is a stable attribute of the person seems inescapable. We have also obtained some data (unpublished) consistent with Olweus' findings. Ratings of ward behaviour by nursing staff were obtained on newly admitted patients to Rampton Hospital, and scored for a factor identified as 'psychopathy' or 'antisocial aggression'. Ratings were repeated two years later for 42 patients, who were by this time in a variety of wards, and who were rated by different nurses. The correlation between the two sets of ratings, without correction, is 0.77. After correction for unreliability, the correlation is actually unity, suggesting that patients retain their rank order in aggressiveness across time, and apparently across situations.

A further line of evidence for stability of aggressive attributes comes from longitudinal studies of the careers of violent offenders. Farrington (1978) reported data from the Cambridge Study on Delinquent Development, which indicated that teacher ratings of aggressiveness made on boys between the ages of eight and 10 years of age identified almost half of those who subsequently became violent delinquents. Wolfgang (1975) has also identified a hard 'core' of violent offenders whose careers of violence begin early in adolescence. In fact, it seems undisputed that past violent behaviour is the best predictor of future violence. Curiously, this point has been used by social learning theorists to attack a dispositional concept of antisocial behaviour, on the grounds that past behaviour is a better predictor than data from measures of personality traits. But if future behaviour is related to past behaviour, this appears to offer *prima facie* evidence for a stable disposition.

PSYCHOLOGICAL MEASUREMENT AND THE PREDICTION OF AGGRESSION

Given, then, that there is empirical justification for regarding the person as a significant contributor to violent behaviour, why have we as yet been largely unsuccessful in identifying dangerous persons? One possibility, as implied earlier, is that clinicians may actually have achieved some success, but that the evidence for this is swamped by unreliability in the research data. However, I now consider whether psychological measurement of person variables holds any promise for improving prediction. Here we move from a consideration of clinical prediction to the prospects for statistical prediction.

The available data are not encouraging. Validity coefficients for self-report trait measures of aggressiveness are usually found to be low. In my own work, for example, a factor analytic scale of aggression which I developed (Blackburn, 1974) has been found to correlate with prior history of aggression and also with ward ratings of aggression, but the correlations fall in the region of 0.3–0.4. These coefficients seem to be typical for this kind of self-report measure. The predictive validity of the scale has not yet been assessed, but, on the face of it, would not appear promising.

There are, however, three possible reasons why our efforts have not shown dividends. The first, as with the clinical prediction data, has to do with the criteria we try to predict. Epstein (1980) has reminded us of the importance of sampling in obtaining reliable criteria. Dispositional or trait descriptions represent average behaviour, and a single observation cannot be taken as a reliable indicator of a disposition. As work evolving from Megargee's concept of the 'overcontrolled aggressor' illustrates (Megargee, 1971), a single act of violence may actually reflect a disposition *not* to behave aggressively. Yet attempts are still made to validate measures of aggressiveness against the criterion of offence immediately preceding admission to a prison or security hospital. Such a criterion cannot be regarded as a reliable measure of a violent disposition.

Related to this is the representativeness of the criterion. Some recent studies have shown that validity coefficients rise when the criterion behaviours are more central to the trait being measured (Buss and Craik, 1980; Olweus, 1980). Some of our failures to demonstrate the validity of measures of aggressiveness may, then, reflect inadequate sampling in the criterion, rather than poor predictor validity.

A second possible reason may lie in the attempt to predict from simple linear aggregates such as the sum of items endorsed on a self-report scale or a rating scale. Such measurement tends to ensure adequate reliability, but it entails prediction from a single variable. Under natural conditions, it seems unlikely that an event such as an act of aggression is a function of a single isolated person variable. Combining variables may improve prediction, and some gains have been made using multiple regression methods (see Monahan, 1981). Such methods, however, fail to capture non-linear effects.

In my own work (Blackburn, 1980), I have been concerned with identifying patterns of personality variables in violent offenders through cluster analysis. Four groups have emerged consistently from this research, and it has become apparent that these represent combinations of extremes on two broad dimensions, labelled 'psychopathy' (PY) and 'social withdrawal' (SW). When criminal records of these four groups were examined, it emerged that a history of sex offences was significantly more likely among those at the 'withdrawn' extreme of the SW dimension, regardless of their position on PY. However, a history of repeated aggressive crimes (i.e. two or more offences) seemed to be related to an additive interaction of PY and SW. The percentages of each group having such a history were as follows: high PY–low SW, 53%; high PY–high SW, 20%; low PY–low SW, 30%; low PY–high SW, 8%. These differences are significant.

I have recently developed scales to measure these two factors. The PY scale correlates slightly better than average with an external variable, a nurse rating scale of 'psychopathy', the correlation after correction for rater unreliability being 0.56 ($N = 57$). However, when the sample was dichotomized at the median of the SW scale, validity increased for the more 'sociable' subjects (corrected $r = 0.81$; $N = 30$), but reduced for 'withdrawn' subjects ($r = 0.24$; $N = 27$). In this case, then, there is a non-linear interaction, or moderator variable effect. In both these sets of data, combined use of two broad personality variables enhances discrimination. Whether it also improves prediction of future aggression remains to be evaluated.

A third reason for our limited success, however, may lie in the kinds of person variable on which we have traditionally relied in predicting aggressive behaviour. As summary descriptions of regularity in behaviour across situations, trait measures may prove quite successful in identifying individuals for whom violent behaviour is more typical. But as Alston (1975) notes, traits are merely a first stab at describing a person. They would explain behaviour only if behaviour were invariant across situations. As it clearly is not, we should be looking more at those person variables which mediate between situation and behaviour, such as beliefs, expectancies, or needs. In this respect, social learning theorists will in the end, I suspect, have their day.

REFERENCES

ALSTON, W. (1975). Traits, consistency, and conceptual alternatives for personality theory. *Journal of the Theory of Social Behaviour*, **5**, 17–45.

BANDURA, A. (1973). *Aggression: A Social Learning Analysis*. Englewood Cliffs, N.J.: Prentice-Hall.

BLACKBURN, R. (1974). *Development and Validation of Scales to Measure Hostility and Aggression*. Special Hospitals Research Reports No. 12. London: Special Hospitals Research Unit.

BLACKBURN, R. (1980). Personality and the criminal psychopath: a logical analysis and some empirical data. In Facolta di Giurisprudenza, Universita di Messina, *Lo Psicopatico Delinquente*. Milan: Giuffre.

BUSS, D. M., and CRAIK, K. H. (1980). The frequency concept of disposition: dominance and proptotypically dominant acts. *Journal of Personality*, **48**, 379–392.

COCOZZA, J. J., and STEADMAN, H. J. (1978). Prediction in psychiatry: an example of misplaced confidence in experts. *Social Problems*, **25**, 265–276.

CURTIS, E. W. (1971). Predictive value compared to predictive validity. *American Psychologist*, **26**, 908–914.

ENDLER, N. S., and HUNT, J. McV. (1968). S-R inventories of hostility and comparisons of the proportions of variance from persons, responses and situations for hostility and anxiousness. *Journal of Personality and Social Psychology*, **9**, 309–315.

ENNIS, B. J., and LITWACK, T. R. (1974). Psychiatry and the presumption of expertise: flipping coins in the courtroom. *California Law Review*, **62**, 694–752.

EPSTEIN, S. (1980). The stability of behavior. II. Implications for psychological research. *American Psychologist*, **35**, 790–806.

FARRINGTON, D. P. (1978). The family backgrounds of aggressive youths. In L. Hersov, M. Berger, and S. Shaffer (Eds), *Aggression and Antisocial Disorder in Children*. Oxford: Pergamon Press.

GOLDBERG, L. R. (1968). Simple models or simple processes? Some research on clinical judgments. *American Psychologist*, **23**, 483–496.

GOLDBERG, L. R. (1970). Man versus model of man: a rationale plus evidence for a method of improving on clinical inferences. *Psychological Bulletin*, **73**, 422–432.

HALL, H. V. (1982). Dangerousness predictions and the maligned forensic profession-al: suggestions for detecting distortion of true basal violence. *Criminal Justice and Behavior*, **9**, 3–12.

KAHNEMAN, D., and TVERSKY, A. (1973). On the psychology of prediction. *Psychological Review*, **80**, 237–251.

KLEIN, J. F. (1976). The dangerousness of dangerous offender legislation: forensic folklore revisited. *Canadian Journal of Criminology and Corrections*, **18**, 109–122.

MEEHL, P. E. (1954). *Clinical versus Statistical Prediction*. Minneapolis: University of Minnesota Press.

MEGARGEE, E. I. (1971). The role of inhibition in the assessment and understanding of violence. In J. L. Singer (Ed.), *The Control of Aggression and Violence*. New York: Academic Press.

MISCHEL, W. (1968). *Personality and Assessment.* New York: Wiley.

MONAHAN, J. (1973). The psychiatrization of criminal behavior. *Hospital and Community Psychiatry,* **24,** 105–107.

MONAHAN, J. (1976). The prevention of violence. In J. Monahan (Ed.), *Community Mental Health and the Criminal Justice System.* New York: Pergamon Press.

MONAHAN, J. (1981). *Predicting Violent Behavior.* London: Sage Publications.

OLWEUS, D. (1975). Modern interactionism in personality psychology and the analysis of variance components approach: a critical examination. Paper presented at the symposium on Interactional Psychology, Saltsjobaden, Sweden.

OLWEUS, D. (1979). Stability of aggressive reaction patterns in males: a review. *Psychological Bulletin,* **86,** 852–875.

OLWEUS, D. (1980). The consistency issue in personality psychology revisited: with special reference to aggression. *British Journal of Social and Clinical Psychology,* **19,** 377–390.

RUBIN, B. (1972). The prediction of dangerousness in mentally ill criminals. *Archives of General Psychiatry,* **27,** 397–407.

STEADMAN, H. J., and COCOZZA, J. J. (1974). *Careers of the Criminally Insane.* Lexington, Mass.: D. C. Heath.

WENK, E. A., ROBINSON, J. O., and SMITH, G. B. (1972). Can violence be predicted? *Crime and Delinquency,* **18,** 393–402.

WIGGINS, J. (1981). Clinical and statistical prediction: where are we and where do we go from here? *Clinical Psychology Review,* **1,** 3–18.

WIGGINS, N., and COHEN, E. S. (1971). Man versus model of man revisited: the forecasting of graduate school success. *Journal of Personality and Social Psychology,* **19,** 100–106.

WOLFGANG, M. (1975). Contemporary perspectives on violence. In D. Chappell and J. Monahan (Eds), *Violence and Criminal Justice.* Lexington, Mass.: D. C. Heath.

Psychology and Law
Edited by D.J. Müller, D.E. Blackman, and A.J. Chapman
© 1984 John Wiley & Sons Ltd

Chapter 9

The Clinical Prediction of Dangerousness: Getting Beyond the Basic Questions[1]

Diana S. Sepejak, Christopher D. Webster, and R. J. Menzies

More often than not researchers in the social sciences find themselves grappling with an empirical problem which suddenly looms much larger and unyielding than originally anticipated. The clinical prediction of dangerousness in persons proceeding through the criminal justice system provides an example of this phenomenon. Before dealing with our own research in this area, it is worthwhile noting the points within the criminal justice process where clinical predictions of dangerousness become a matter of concern. Ordinarily, an individual is charged, convicted, sentenced, and finally terminates his or her involvement with the criminal justice system without ever having been the subject of an assessment for dangerousness. While many avoid psychiatric scrutiny in this regard, there are those for whom the clinical prediction of dangerousness enters into decisions concerning such crucial matters as candidacy for bail, nature of sentence, and, in the case of a finding of 'not guilty by reason of insanity', release from executive detention. Monahan (1981) covers an extensive range of possible situations, both in the criminal and civil spheres, where clinical predictions of dangerousness play a critical role in the decision-making process. We have been concerned mainly with clinical predictions of dangerousness occurring at the pre-trial stage of a criminal case.

In part this interest has been due to the unusual opportunity for observation which we have been afforded by the setting in which we are employed. Before the Metropolitan Toronto Forensic Service (METFORS) was established as a clinical unit in 1977, an itinerant psychiatrist would travel to the various detention centres within Toronto and examine individuals for whom fitness to stand trial was questionable. Since the inception of METFORS, however, these accused individuals are remanded by the court for a brief psychiatric assessment which requires that they be brought from the gaols to the Brief Assessment Unit (BAU) at METFORS. An interdisciplinary team of mental health professionals led by a psychiatrist, including a psychologist, social worker, psychiatric nurse, and very often a correctional officer, interviews each accused person in the BAU. Discussion of the case among team members follows this group interview and the psychiatrist composes a letter based on the findings of the team to accompany the individual back to the gaol. It is at this pre-trial stage of the criminal justice process that we were able to take advantage of a relatively unselected and sizeable sample of subjects in our investigations of the clinical prediction of dangerousness. (For a full description of the BAU population see Webster, Menzies, and Jackson, 1982.) Although all persons seen on the BAU have been charged with a criminal offence, the seriousness of the charge varies from shoplifting to murder. As pointed out earlier, the determination of fitness to stand trial is the primary reason for remanding an accused person to METFORS, though the bulk of individuals leave having been assessed as fit to stand trial. There is also a considerable degree of variability within the BAU population in terms of mental disturbance and future uncertainty depending upon whether or not conviction is forthcoming at trial.

The prospect of being able to employ the BAU population as subjects in an attempt to study the clinical prediction of dangerousness held some cause for optimism. The subject pool was large (approximately 600 persons are assessed annually within the BAU) and relatively unselected. This represented a marked methodological improvement over similar studies previously undertaken in this area (e.g. Cocozza and Steadman, 1974; Steadman and Keveles, 1972; Thornberry and Jacoby, 1979). We were not limited to conclusions based on the use of only those subjects who had expressed some very dangerous form of behaviour, who were assessed to be mentally disordered, and who had already been committed to a facility for the criminally insane. The conclusions reached to date in the literature founded on these types of subject populations are despairing with respect to the ability of mental health professionals to assess dangerousness. (See Ennis and Litwack, 1974, for a well argued criticism of the role of psychiatry in the courtroom.) The availability of a relatively heterogeneous sample, then, provided us with the main impetus for our research.

The basic design of the research was straightforward. When individuals were remanded to the BAU for assessment and interviewed by the clinical team, as a matter of routine all clinicians present at the interview were required to indicate on a simple form whether or not the individual should be considered as dangerous to others on a four-point scale of 'no', 'low', 'medium', and 'high'. Subjects were then followed during a two-year period subsequent to BAU contact and information concerning behaviour they had expressed during this period was collected: (1) further criminal charges; (2) misconducts during incarceration; (3) incidents precipitating contact with psychiatric facilities; and (4) behaviour during psychiatric hospitalization. We then had at our disposal a clinical prediction of dangerousness gathered from practitioners in a number of mental health disciplines for a large sample of subjects (i.e. 598 accused persons). Furthermore, follow-up data gathered over two years allowed us to determine whether or not the original predictions were, in fact, accurate. The research question was a simple one: *How well do forensic mental health professionals predict dangerousness in their patients?*

It was at this point in our research that we realized Pandora's box had been opened and that we were peering into it somewhat bewilderedly. It was clearly incumbent upon us to go beyond the limits of our originally conceived notions in order to re-phrase the nature of the questions we were asking of our data. This meant leaving behind certain assumptions which suggested that the question of prediction accuracy could be answered without attending to possible differences among individual clinicians and among types of subjects or to alternative conclusions heavily dependent upon the definitions of follow-up outcome and the term 'dangerousness' itself. As such, we have attempted to examine the data according to what we think to be a more realistic approach to the problem.

Since the legal responsibility of addressing the issue of a patient's possible dangerousness usually rests with the assessing psychiatrist, inasmuch as he or she writes the letter to the court, we began our analysis of the data by examining the relationship between psychiatric predictions of dangerousness and actual outcome at follow-up. The prediction variable was recorded on a four-point scale, as noted earlier. The outcome variable was developed by the use of the collected follow-up data. A behavioural profile was constructed for each subject in the sample, consisting of the entire set of behaviours discovered at follow-up for that particular subject. Three external raters (all masters degree level students in criminology at the University of Toronto) independently assigned a value from one to eleven per subject designed to reflect the overall dangerousness to others exhibited by each subject in the two-year period subsequent to assessment on the BAU ('one' being extremely low and 'eleven' being extremely high). The mean rating for each subject was used as the outcome measure.

With prediction and outcome measures established it was possible to determine the relationship between the psychiatrists' predictions of dangerousness and actual behaviour at follow-up. When data from the four psychiatrists were pooled, it was found that the Pearson correlation coefficient was 0.20 ($n = 364$, $P < 0.001$). This computation, like all others noted below, was based on cases in which we had at least one item of follow-up data (i.e. all other cases were excluded). The essential point is that, though low, the correlation was in the positive direction and statistically significant. That there was a correspondence between prediction and outcome can be demonstrated in a second and even simpler fashion. The data were divided into low and high dangerousness categories for prediction and outcome (low prediction consisted of choices 'no' and 'low' on the full scale and high prediction consisted of choices 'medium' and 'high'; the outcome scale was split at the median of 4.13, resulting in low and high dangerousness at outcome). Here, too, the relationship between prediction and outcome was a significant one ($\chi^2 = 12.88$, $P < 0.0003$) with larger numbers falling within the cells pertaining to higher accuracy (i.e. 114 and 103 under low prediction/low outcome and high prediction/high outcome respectively). Even though the pattern of data was in the desired direction and statistically significant, as in the case of the Pearson correlation, a large proportion of error is readily apparent. Approximately 40% of the opinions offered by psychiatrists resulted in incorrect predictions (i.e. 81 and 66 under high prediction/low outcome and low prediction/high outcome respectively). If we were to leave the analysis of the data at this point, we would be in a position to answer our simply phrased research question thus: psychiatrists are able to predict the future dangerous behaviour of their patients to a statistically significant degree, allowing for a sizeable margin of error. We have chosen to go beyond the original question and analyse the data according to further lines of inquiry.

WHO IS PREDICTING?

Our original question was answered by the use of pooled psychiatric predictions which, it may be argued, is justified because of the legal implications of psychiatrists' opinions. However, a great deal is to be gained by concentrating attention on who is offering the prediction, both by mental health discipline and by individual clinician. Considering first the discipline and pooling data from individuals within disciplines, we found that psychologists came very close to the psychiatrists ($r = 0.17$, $n = 288$, $P < 0.002$) with correctional officers in third position ($r = 0.12$, $n = 266$, $P < 0.03$). Pearson correlations from pooled nurses and social workers yielded low and non-significant effects ($r = 0.08$, $n = 309$, $P < 0.07$; and $r = 0.03$, $n = 273$, $P < 0.30$, respectively).

Examining predictions made by individual clinicians, rather than pooling the data according to mental health discipline, lends still further refinement to the analysis and places the issue of accuracy in a slightly different light. In Table 9.1, Pearson product moment correlations between prediction and outcome are shown for each individual psychiatrist, psychologist, social worker, nurse, and correctional officer for whom we have a sufficiently larger number of cases (i.e. 10 or more).

Table 9.1   Prediction-by-outcome Pearson correlations for individual clinicians grouped by discipline

	r	n	P
Psychiatrist 1	0.19	160	<0.01
Psychiatrist 2	0.14	75	0.11(NS)
Psychiatrist 3	0.27	86	<0.01
Psychiatrist 4	0.03	43	0.41(NS)
Psychologist 1	0.21	137	<0.01
Psychologist 2	0.21	67	<0.04
Psychologist 3	0.14	68	0.13(NS)
Social worker 1	0.02	224	0.40(NS)
Social worker 2	0.12	16	0.33(NS)
Social worker 3	0.47	16	<0.03
Nurse 1	0.10	264	<0.05
Nurse 2	0.29	23	0.09(NS)
Correctional officer 1	0.21	13	0.24(NS)
Correctional officer 2	0.22	28	0.13(NS)
Correctional officer 3	-0.48	10	0.08(NS)
Correctional officer 4	0.23	31	0.11(NS)
Correctional officer 5	0.21	42	0.09(NS)
Correctional officer 6	0.04	48	0.39(NS)
Correctional officer 7	0.07	38	0.34(NS)

NS = nonsignificant

It is readily apparent that treatment of the data by group is somewhat misleading. For example, although data for psychiatrists yielded a correlation coefficient of 0.20, the individual correlations for psychiatrist 2 and psychiatrist 4 proved not to be statistically significant. Data from all three psychologists result in correlations which are similar, with the possible exception of psychologist 3. Among the three social workers, however, there were marked individual differences. This observation is emphasized by the fact that while social worker 1 had the smallest coefficient found across all of the clinicians, social worker 3 had the largest coefficient. Although nurse 2 obtained a relatively high correlation, she did not see many cases and the relationship was not significant. Her colleague, who examined far more persons, achieved a rather lower correlation which was marginally significant. The correctional officers showed a considerable range with number 3 having a negative correlation approaching significance.

Analysis of the data for individuals indicated that generalizations about prediction accuracy for mental health disciplines may be erroneous, considering the degree of variability which exists among members within any one particular discipline. Furthermore, we have shown that the intuitively obvious statement that some clinicians are likely to be better predictors of dangerousness than others (see Shah, 1978) holds true against empirical testing. Justifiably, the specific question of *who* is offering the prediction must be dealt with in considering the general issue of the clinical prediction of dangerousness.

WHAT IS BEING PREDICTED?

The above analyses were based on outcome measures which represented in numerical form the degree of dangerousness present in the behaviours subjects were discovered to have expressed during the two-year follow-up period. This measure was based on a compilation of all behaviours expressed by any one particular subject subsequent to assessment in the BAU so that both the severity and quantity of the follow-up incidents could be taken into account by our external raters when faced with the task of determining the actual dangerousness of the subject. We had, however, originally carried out an analysis of the data (using approximately one-half of the sample) based on an alternative outcome measure. Since it could be argued that the single most dangerous behaviour that an individual expresses should be the critical focus of any predictions made regarding his or her dangerousness, one might compare predictions of dangerousness with the actual dangerousness inherent in the most dangerous incident during follow-up. Using this rationale, behavioural incidents gathered on all subjects and from all sources were listed individually on a rating form. Five external raters (all masters degree level students in criminology at the University of Toronto) independently assigned each behaviour a score from one to eleven in terms of the degree of dangerousness inherent in the behaviour. A dangerousness value for each behaviour was calculated using the rater mean for that behaviour. The outcome score for each subject, then, consisted of the highest dangerousness value found in his or her follow-up data. Pearson correlation coefficients were calculated for the pooled psychiatric predictions by outcome.

If we compare the correlation for the pooled data derived from this alternative analysis (i.e. $r = 0.16$, $n = 155$, $P < 0.02$) with that in which a composite score was employed as the outcome measure (i.e. $r = 0.27$, $n = 155$, $P < 0.001$), we find that the results show a difference in level of prediction accuracy. Although both correlation coefficients are positive and statistically significant, the analysis based on the composite outcome measure yields a substantially higher correlation than that based on the use of the most dangerous follow-up incident as outcome. It is obvious that the choice of outcome measure has a major effect on the accuracy of predictions of dangerousness. Even though our illustration of this point is restricted to pooled psychiatric data, we would speculate that the same kind of inference could be made from the examination of predictions made by members of the other mental health disciplines involved in the study, and by examining the predictions made by individual clinicians.

ON WHO IS THE PREDICTION BEING MADE?

The above analyses have assumed that the patient sample on whom predictions were made was fairly homogeneous in terms of the degree to which behaviour can be accurately predicted. However, as prediction ability varied from one clinician to another clinician, so too may it be influenced by the type of patient. To examine this, two salient characteristics of the subjects were analysed. The patients seen for assessment at METFORS are known as 'forensic cases', a term which is meant to implicate a possible psychiatric disorder. We divided the sample into three main psychiatric diagnostic categories: psychosis, personality disorder, and other (drug or alcohol abuse, sexual disorder, mental retardation, neurosis, or no diagnosis). For a further analysis, we divided the sample according to whether or not there was violence against persons involved in the criminal charges which precipitated the individual's assessment at METFORS. Since two of the more strikingly observable qualities of the type of individual who passes through the BAU are the presence or absence of violence in the charges and the particular form of psychiatric disorder (especially psychosis as opposed to a personality disorder), we thought it worthwhile to compare the predictive abilities of our clinicians with respect to these specific subsamples of patients. Only the predictions made by psychiatrists were used in the analysis.

A comparison of correlation coefficients indicated that higher and statistically significant correlations were obtained for those patients diagnosed as either psychotic ($r = 0.23$, $n = 90$, $P < 0.01$) or personality disordered ($r = 0.21$, $n = 134$, $P < 0.01$), as opposed to those falling within the other category where the coefficient failed to reach statistical significance ($r = 0.13$, $n = 129$, not significant). Likewise, there appears to be a difference in the level of predictive accuracy with respect to whether or not violence is involved in the criminal charges which the individual is facing at assessment. Surprisingly, psychiatrists seem to be able to obtain a higher degree of predictive accuracy when assessing individuals whose current criminal charges do not involve violence against persons ($r = 0.24$, $n = 215$, $P < 0.01$) rather than when violence is involved ($r = 0.10$, $n = 147$, not significant). We should point out here, however, that neither psychiatric diagnosis nor presence or absence of violence in the charges was found to have any predictive value in itself. Presumably, then, the variation in psychiatric predictive accuracy according to the kind of psychiatric disorder affecting the patient and whether or not the patient is involved in a violent or non-violent offence is not due to any inherent predictive value of these two factors upon which the psychiatrist is either knowingly or unknowingly relying.

Although the analysis of the data in this fashion is not comprehensive, in terms of both alternative predicting clinicians and possible types of patient sub-samples, we offer it in order to lend some support to the basic argument we have been attempting to put forth throughout this discussion; that is, the need for a more specific and refined treatment of the general question concerning the clinical prediction of dangerousness.

WHAT IS THE FORM OF THE PREDICTION?

A final question for which we offer data gathered from our research at METFORS concerns the matter of the form of the prediction used in the analysis of the prediction by outcome relationship. Up to this point, we have employed predictions made on a four-point scale of 'no', 'low', 'medium', and 'high'. In a second study, with a patient sample similar to the one we have been working with so far, we used a 22-item form (Dangerous Behaviour Rating Scheme, or DBRS) for recording the prediction variable. These items were originally recommended and defined by members of the clinical team of the BAU and included personality variables thought to be linked possibly to dangerousness (e.g. hostility, anger, tolerance level) and certain situational variables (e.g. degree of environmental stress, dangerousness influenced by drugs or alcohol). There was also an item, 'degree of dangerousness to others in future', which could serve as the counterpart, in any comparison, to the prediction rating used in the first set of results thus far described. All items in the DBRS were rated on a seven-point scale, rather than a four-point scale, extending from 'extremely low' to 'extremely high'.

The rationale for incorporating a scheme such as the DBRS in a second study of the clinical prediction of dangerousness lies in the possibility of developing a predictive instrument which may result in a greater degree of accuracy when compared to a single rating. Using ratings on the individual items of the DBRS, we constructed a composite prediction rating (CPR) for the assessing psychiatrists. We followed a simple analytical procedure in order to obtain a CPR for each subject in the sample. Of the total of 22 items comprising the DBRS, 10% or more of the data were missing on four items. These items were removed from the analysis and psychiatric ratings on each of the remaining 18 items were correlated individually with composite outcome. Of these items, 11 obtained correlation coefficients of 0.10 or greater. They were the following: passive aggressive, hostility, anger, rage, capacity for guilt, capacity for change, capacity for empathy, tolerance, self-perception as dangerous, dangerous to others at present, dangerous to others in future. These 11 core items of the DBRS were then used to construct a CPR by simply summing the ratings on each of the items for each subject in the sample. In four of the items (i.e. capacity for guilt, capacity for change, capacity for empathy, tolerance) the one to seven scale was reversed since, in these instances, extremely low ratings correspond to extremely high levels of perceived dangerousness. Mean scores were substituted in the case of missing data.

Analysis of the data from this second study produces a finding with respect to the general prediction item of 'dangerous to others in future' which, as we might expect, is almost identical to the psychiatric prediction by outcome correlation presented earlier ($r = 0.19$, $n = 139$, $P < 0.01$). Looking at the analysis we carried out in which the CPR was used as the prediction variable, the results show a marked improvement in the level of accuracy ($r = 0.30$, $n = 230$, $P < 0.00001$). It would appear then that a prediction variable which isolates and combines the opinions of the assessing clinician regarding dangerousness per se with those concerning certain attributes of the patient is a more valid predictor of dangerousness. As in the case of factors we have considered above, what one selects as the actual prediction of dangerousness has important implications with respect to clinical accuracy.

CONCLUSIONS

Returning to our original question of 'can forensic clinicians predict dangerousness?', we have attempted, through presentation of data from our own research, to underline the difficulties in offering simple responses to this complex question. We believe that careful consideration must be given to the various factors which serve to qualify any conclusions regarding this issue if a truly valid account of the clinical prediction of dangerousness is to be obtained. We have shown that both the individual clinician and the type of patient on whom the prediction is being made affect the level of predictive accuracy. Furthermore, an outcome measure which represents the dangerousness inherent in the *total* behaviour expressed by a patient during follow-up, results in a prediction which is stronger than what we obtained using the *single* most dangerous behaviour as outcome. Finally, our research shows that a single statement offered by the clinician concerning the individual's propensity towards dangerousness is not as effective a predictor as is this single statement in *combination* with other opinions held by the clinician regarding certain related characteristics and propensities of the patient.

We would not be so bold as to maintain that we have even scratched the surface of the problem. Indeed, we may only have begged further the question. By this we mean to say that while several individual factors have been examined separately by us, the next step of course is to establish whether or not any of these factors considered in total would lend still further strength to the prediction by outcome relationship. Is it the case, for example, that only certain clinicians are particularly good at predicting dangerousness in only certain types of patients when the CPR, or some such measure, is used as the prediction? It is possible that this kind of inquiry will produce a specific combination of factors which results in a degree of prediction accuracy that surpasses that obtained with the CPR measure for pooled psychiatric data on the entire sample. We think that the rationale underlying such research justifies the time and effort required to proceed. For if forensic practitioners are able to specify more succinctly the conditions in which their predictions of dangerousness are more or less accurate, a major responsibility is being fulfilled, we would argue, both with respect to the enlightenment of the judiciary and the welfare of patients.

A final question we pose here is, 'How well should forensic clinicians be able to predict dangerousness, depending upon the use to which the prediction is being put?'. This question was first brought to our attention by Monahan (1981) who pointed out that the rules of the game, in terms of owed responsibility to individual freedom and protection of society, change depending upon whether we are considering long-term confinement or short-term 'emergency' hospitalization. This question brings to mind the possibility of investigating clinical predictive accuracy within the context of 30-day inpatient assessments. All of the research questions we have been asking and will continue to ask can be related to short-term hospitalization. As such, we plan to transfer much of our thinking and the knowledge we have gained in this area over the past three years to this new setting for inquiry.

NOTE

1. The authors gratefully acknowledge their indebtedness to Dr F. A. S. Jensen, Dr B. T. Butler, Ms D. Slomen, and Mrs J. Pepper, and other staff of the Brief Assessment Unit, Metropolitan Toronto Forensic Service. We also thank the medical record staff at Queen Street Mental Health Centre, Clarke Institute of Psychiatry, St Thomas Psychiatric Hospital, Penetanguishene Mental Health Centre, and Whitby Psychiatric Hospital, and the Research Division of the Ontario Ministry of Correctional Services. Financial support for this study was provided by the Ontario Ministry of Health under Grant DM 395 and by the Department of Justice, Canada, under contract number OIGS 19200-8-0029.

REFERENCES

COCOZZA, J. J., and STEADMAN, H. J. (1974). Some refinements in the measurement and prediction of dangerous behavior. *American Journal of Psychiatry*, **131**, 1012–1014.

ENNIS, B. J., and LITWACK, T. R. (1974). Psychiatry and the presumption of expertise: flipping coins in the courtroom. *California Law Review*, **62**, 693–752.

MONAHAN, J. (1981). *The Clinical Prediction of Violent Behavior,* Crime and Delinquency Issues Monograph, DHHS No. (ADM) 81-921. Bethesda, Md: US Department of Health and Human Services, National Institute of Mental Health.

SHAH, S. A. (1978). Dangerousness and mental illness: some conceptual prediction and policy dilemmas. In C. Frederick (Ed.), *Dangerous Behavior: A Problem in Law and Mental Health,* DHEW Publication No. (ADM) 78-563. Washington, D.C.: US Government Printing Office.

STEADMAN, H. J., and KEVELES, G. (1972). The community adjustment and criminal activity of the Baxstrom patients: 1966–1970. *American Journal of Psychiatry,* **129,** 304–310.

THORNBERRY, T. P., and JACOBY, J. E. (1979). *The Criminally Insane: A Community Follow-up of Mentally Ill Offenders.* Chicago, Illinois: University of Chicago Press.

WEBSTER, C. D., MENZIES, R. J., and JACKSON, M. A. (1982). *Clinical Assessment Before Trial: Legal Issues and Mental Disorder.* Toronto: Butterworth.

Psychology and Law
Edited by D.J. Müller, D.E. Blackman, and A.J. Chapman
© 1984 John Wiley & Sons Ltd

Chapter 10

The Inconsistent Personality Defence

Samuel Roll and William E. Foote

This chapter explores an area in which psychologists can be of service to the criminal justice system, by studying the relationship between personality characteristics and specific crimes. The simplest way of stating our aim is to explore the reasonableness of asking the psychological equivalent of 'Is this the face of a person who could commit such a crime?'; that is, 'Is this the personality of a person who could commit such a crime?' Such a general question can be approached on the basis of a number of assumptions:

(1) Within physical limitations it is *possible* that any person could commit a specific crime.
(2) It is *more probable* that some kinds of persons will be involved in some crimes than others.
(3) By reviewing the data about a particular crime in a particular context, psychologists can develop hypotheses about the kinds of personality variables (or ego structure or habit hierarchies) that are most congruent with the crime.
(4) By reviewing the personal history, psychological development, personality, and situational context of a particular person, a psychologist can develop some hypotheses about the possibility that the person would commit a particular kind of crime.
(5) Psychological research relevant to particular types of crime can help establish the likelihood that a particular kind of person will commit a certain crime in a specified context.

These assumptions are not radical. They are restatements of the working assumptions of most psychologists; that is, that a behaviour results from a person's personality and the environment in which he or she is found. In the present chapter, we use the term 'personality', although others might prefer

125

terms such as 'traits', 'habit hierarchies', or 'ego structures'. A number of general positions can be granted with respect to the relationship between personality and crime:

(1) *Extreme congruence* The personality of the person in question, as we understand it from a personal history, a psychological evaluation, and the situation at the time, is highly congruent with the crime.
(2) *Central position* The personality of the person in question is neither highly congruent nor highly incongruent with the crime.
(3) *Extreme incongruence* The personality of the person in question is highly incongruent with the crime.

It might be helpful here to consider a specific possibility which is not intended to be representative. Given that a man has a long history of being sexually molested as a child, that he has been unable to establish any long-term relationships, that he has low tolerance for frustration, that he has little capacity for compassion or empathy, that he experiences very little guilt, that he is highly impulsive, and that he has extremely negative feelings about women, his personality would be *extremely congruent* with the commission of rape. On the other hand, given that a man has a long history of gratifying interpersonal relationships, that his early history is marked by warm and stable interactions with his parents, that he has a great capacity for compassion and empathy, that he has a well developed sense of morality, that he has adequate control over his impulses, and that he has extremely positive feelings about women, his personality would be *extremely incongruent* with the commission of rape.

The description of any crime can be transformed into a more or less detailed statement about the psychological aspects involved. For example, a crime may require a specific range of intelligence, more or less capacity to plan, greater or lesser control of the impulses, capacity for and kinds of interpersonal relationships, level of reality testing, certain adaptive abilities, and areas of personal conflict and preoccupation. Thus certain crimes (e.g. sustained fraud) directly point to some aspects of the person (capacity to plan, moderately high to high intelligence); crimes of violence, such as rape or murder, may imply high levels of aggression; other crimes may suggest very little about the personality variables likely to be involved.

Useful information can be found in the published reports of the personality variables of those who have committed specific forms of crime. The relevant literature is so voluminous that it cannot be reviewed here, but a few general points can be made. Of the violent crimes, rape has been the most extensively explored, and a number of typologies have been developed. These have been thoroughly summarized by Rada (1978). Cohen, Garofalo, Boucher, and Seghorn (1971) have offered a detailed study of the pattern of paedophiles.

and Hammer and Glueck (1957) give some insight on the personality patterns frequently noted in sex offenders.

Though most psychologists are not familiar with or practised in drawing inferences about likely personality variables from information about a crime, they are familiar with drawing inferences about personality from psychological testing. We are here discussing the use of tests to develop an extensive psychological evaluation of an individual and not to decide on a simple diagnostic label. Such a psychological evaluation is not a list of qualities (high intelligence, low anxiety level, obsessive thoughts) but rather an integrated and elaborate description of at least the following: adequacy of reality testing; capacity for and quality of interpersonal relationships; adaptive strengths (e.g. intelligence); major areas of defences and degree of rigidity; nature, extent, and area of conflict and preoccupation; and degree and style of impulse expression. Such an evaluation might be based on at least a standard battery of tests, but a theoretical focus is also needed to organize this information. A number of levels of inference are possible in this 'profile approach' to assessment in a forensic context.

Least powerful is simple descriptive inference. It is sometimes useful to know that individuals are moderately anxious, that they are of low to moderate intelligence. Indeed, in some forensic cases (those in which the crime requires high levels of intelligence and a very low level of anxiety, such as skilful fraud) a clear finding of low to moderate intelligence and moderate to high anxiety may provide some useful support for a defence. However, of greater power are inferential statements which are based on more subtle observations: for example, though people have only a moderate level of intelligence, they have a keen sense of interpersonal situations and this becomes sharper when they are angry. Of even more power is an inference which integrates statements about situational contingencies as well as describing how several personality variables are related; for example, 'Though a man may have a generally low level of anxiety, he becomes very anxious when approaching women. This anxiety results mostly from a sense of being in only tenuous control of fury about women and the resultant desire to hurt them'. Compare such an evaluation with the following: 'He has a generally low level of anxiety and he becomes very anxious when he approaches women. His anxiety results from his sense that every woman is an important but judgmental figure and he is eager to be judged favourably by them. It is his interest in being "good" that results in his anxiety of women'. In both these cases the man is said to be moderately anxious and his anxiety increases around women. In one case then, anxiety is associated with conflicts over aggression and in the other with a strong desire for approval. The former evaluation is congruent with rape and the latter is incongruent therewith.

To summarize, it is possible to make inferences about the personality characteristics required by characteristics of certain crimes. It is also possible to develop extensive psychological evaluations of particular individuals. Psychologists therefore have a role to play in the criminal justice system by evaluating the extent to which the personality characteristics of defendants 'fit' the personality profiles which are implied by the crimes of which they are accused. The inconsistent personality defence is a presentation of evidence on behalf of a defendant that his or her personality characteristics are in some way(s) inconsistent with the crime of which he or she is accused.

A CASE STUDY

The use of psychological information in an inconsistent personality defence can be illustrated by the specific case of rape reported here. An 18-year-old woman complained to the police that she had been raped. She said that she was walking along a river bank on a warm afternoon and met a man wearing a swimming suit. He covered her mouth with one hand and breast with the other and told her not to scream, because he had a gun concealed in a bag he was carrying. He then took her into some nearby bushes, and had intercourse with her. She reported that he was gentle and considerate of her, and never actually brandished the gun. After she told him that she was using no contraception he withdrew his penis and ejaculated on the ground. They then both dressed and shortly thereafter she reported the events to passers-by, who told the police. Upon being accused of the crime, Mr M. did not deny that he had intercourse with the young woman, but stated that the circumstances had been voluntary rather than coercive. From his point of view, he and the woman met, talked briefly, then decided to have intercourse. They proceeded to the bushes, had intercourse, and parted 'like ships in the night'.

Following his indictment, Mr M. retained an attorney who in turn requested a psychologist to consult on the case. Another psychologist was also asked to participate by performing the interview and testing in the case. The plan was that the psychologists would work together. At the trial one would outline the general characteristics of rapists and establish the groundwork for subsequent testimony. The second psychologist would then present Mr M's data and compare it to the rapist 'profile'.

In preparation for the application of the inconsistent personality defence to this case the psychologists researched typologies of rapists and found a number of them summarized by Rada (1978). Of these, the work on the 'clinical' classification of the rapist appeared most useful, since it delineated five types of rapist. This system was used as a 'checklist', to which the characteristics of Mr M. were compared.

The first, 'the psychotic rapist', is defined by Rada as one who is clinically psychotic according to the criteria of DSM II. This type is seen to commit the rape as a result of a gross disturbance of thinking processes and of behavioural controls. In the evaluation of Mr M. the evidence was clear that he was not psychotic. He had no treatment history and reported no psychotic symptoms. Mr M. showed no signs of thought disorder in that his reality testing was adequate as measured by the Rorschach procedure. Also his Minnesota Multiphasic Personality Inventory (MMPI) scores on the 'psychotic scales' were normal. In short, the interviews and testing record were free of indication of a psychotic disturbance.

Rada's 'situational stress rapist' is an individual who possesses fragile defences. Rape is seen as a means of gaining control of his otherwise chaotic life, especially at a time of extreme stress, such as the loss of loved one or a divorce. Mr M., however, was a person with basically sound defences. He showed adequate defensive flexibility on the Rorschach, and showed no high neurotic scales on the MMPI. His score was congruent with good flexibility in interpersonal relationships. Moreover, at the time of the alleged offence his life was stable: he had a satisfying job at a local corporation, and was happily married. In all, he showed none of the inadequacy seen in the 'situational rapist'.

The 'masculine identity conflict rapist' outlined by Rada is a man who feels great uncertainty about his male role. His sexual assault is usually well planned and may have the violent humiliation of his victim as the aim. In this case, Mr M. appeared to have few concerns about his sexual role. He had some attributes often considered to be feminine, in that he was an extremely gentle person with aesthetic interests in the visual arts, but he accepted those, as part of his personality. In addition, the accusations of the case were not at all in line with this type of rapist since very little force was involved, and no violent humiliation of the victim occurred. The 'victim' described their interaction as gentle and noted that he took care not to ejaculate inside her.

Rada's 'sadistic rapist' is like the 'masculine identity' type in that he derives pleasure from the humiliating aspects of the crime. In addition, he often has a history of sadomasochistic sexual practices. As noted above, the alleged crime had few humiliating or sadistic aspects. Mr M.'s sexual history showed no penchant for perversions, and his testing showed no signs of sadistic or aggressive preoccupation.

The last and largest category outlined by Rada consists of the 'sociopathic rapist' for whom rape is just another antisocial and aggressive act. In the case of Mr M. his overall personality pattern showed few sociopathic trends. In relation to these characteristics outlined by Cleckly (1964) and delineated by Hare (1970), Mr M. fits few of the traits of the 'psychopath'. His MMPI profile showed none of the combinations often seen in this group and his overall life pattern was more organized, deliberate, and adaptively social than that which most psychopaths can accomplish.

Rada noted that

'these five categories of rapists are not mutually exclusive. There is some overlap between the types. It has been suggested that there is a category of rapist who may appear normal in every way.... It is implied with the exception of rape behavior, the rapist does not demonstrate psychopathology.... However, a thorough psychosocial and psychosexual history will usually bring out evidence of a symptomatic or characterological disorder' (Rada, 1978, p. 131).

An exhaustive review of the psychological evidence in Mr M's case indicated no signs of mental disorders and no evidence of a characterological disorder.

Thus the inconsistent personality defence here focuses on the lack of congruence between the personality profiles characteristic of a variety of rapists and the personality of the defendant. Such a defence in the case outlined above could direct a court, therefore, to pay particular attention to evaluating the complaint of the woman and the circumstances of the alleged case.

Since a defence strategy of the kind outlined here is relatively rare, the defence attorney may have to establish clearly the legal basis for the admission of the psychological opinion into evidence (Curran, 1955). Though the admissibility of psychologist's opinion regarding such issues as competence to stand trial, diminished capacity, or sanity has been established for many years, in these cases the expert is considered a 'character witness'. Currently, the admission of psychological testimony may be sought on the basis of a combination of three rules of evidence. In Rule 702, Federal Rules of Evidence states:

'If scientific, technical, or other specialized knowledge will assist the trier of fact to understand the evidence or to determine a fact in issue, a witness qualified as an expert by knowledge, skill, experience, training or education, may testify thereto in the form of an opinion or otherwise' (Moore, 1982, p. 207).

This, of course, is the rule used to allow for expert testimony of any sort. However, in coordination with Rules 404 and 405, the justification is complete. Rule 404 states that character evidence is not admissible to prove conduct except in relation to other crimes. The rule states:

'evidence of a person's character or a trait of his character is not admissible for the purpose of proving that he acted in conformity therewith on a particular occasion, except: (1) character of the accused – evidence of a pertinent trait of his character offered by his accused, or by the prosecution to rebut the same. Rule 405 provides methods of proving character and both of these are germane to the use of this defence. Hence, in all cases in which evidence of character or a trait of character of a person is admissible, proof may be made by testimony as to reputation or by testimony in the form of opinion. On cross-examination, inquiry is allowable into relevant specific instances of conduct. (2) Specific instances of conduct – in cases in which character or trait of character of a person is an essential element of a charge, claim, or defence, proof may also be made of specific instances of his conduct' (Moore, 1982, p. 82).

In the first case, the psychologist's testimony may focus upon the overall assessment of the crime, the person, and the literature to arrive at an opinion of character. The second element may arise when the psychologist cites specific test data to illustrate the case.

All these rules may prove insufficient if the court decides that expert opinion in matters of character carry no more weight than does lay opinion, as it has in some jurisdictions (United States v. Webb[1]). In cases in which such objections are raised, it may be helpful to show that the psychologist's testimony is not based only on the sort of superficial data available to lay witnesses such as friends or neighbours. Rather, the psychologist has a broad base of data from testing and the other sources noted above upon which to base an opinion.

CONCLUSION

As in all cases in which psychology interacts with the legal system, the inconsistent personality defence has pitfalls. To reduce the peril involved in this enterprise, the following caveats are offered.

First, as in other uses of expert testimony, the psychologist is open to cross-examination and to rebuttal of any testimony. Unlike other defence strategies, however, this approach is more vulnerable to contradictory data. This is especially true if there is either documentary evidence or eyewitness testimony (a neighbour who witnessed the violent act) that the client has behaved in a manner incongruent with the psychologist's data. Of course, there is a rare case in which all the data will be entirely in line with the defence approach, so psychologists must use clinical skills to help them arrive at a conclusion based upon the weight of the evidence.

Second, the psychologist should develop test data in great detail. Although this is important in most forensic cases, it requires special emphasis in this defence strategy, as the test data form a foundation stone for the psychologist's contribution to the case. Not only is this the aspect that has the greatest scientific support, but it is the domain of psychologists and is their unique contribution to the legal system. Specific examples from the defendant's data may assist in the exposition of the case to the jury, thereby providing a clear idea of the psychologist's logic and reasoning. Such data provide a basis for resisting cross-examination, especially if the psychologist is able to integrate the information into the answers to prosecutorial questions.

Finally, no matter how consistent, reliable, and unequivocable the data, the inconsistent personality defence shares with other psychological defence strategies essential weaknesses. Juries have difficulty in understanding any psychologist's testimony and, as the testimony is to opinion, it is rebuttable, which often confuses the case greatly. For these reasons, this approach carries a cost to the overall defence strategy which must be weighed against the possible benefits of the approach. In cases in which there is already a good defence (e.g. alibi or self-defence) this cost may be so high as to argue against this approach, as it may detract the jury from the main thrust of the defence case. In cases in which there is a very poor defence, there would probably be insufficient data to constitute the inconsistent personality approach. If there were enough data, the objective facts of the case may make the psychologist's testimony appear at best tortured and at worst speculative. On balance, the most suitable case is one in which a number of facts are open to question, so that the expert's testimony may serve to resolve, rather than augment, the uncertainty of the jury and ultimately to contribute to a fair consideration of the case.

NOTE

1. United States *v* Webb, 625 F.2d 70 9 (CA5), 1980.

REFERENCES

CLECKLY, H. (1964). *The Mask of Sanity*, 4th edn. St Louis: Mosby.
COHEN, M. L., GAROFOLO, R., BOUCHER, R., and SEGHORN, T. (1971). The psychology of rapists. *Seminars in Psychiatry*, **3**, 307–327.
CURRAN, W. J. (1955). Expert-psychiatric evidence of personality traits. *University of Pennsylvania Law Review*, **103**, 999–1019.
HAMMER, E. F., and GLUECK, B. C. (1957). Psychodynamic patterns in sex offenders: a four-factor theory. *Psychiatric Quarterly*, **31**, 325–345.
HARE, R. D. (1970). *Psychopathy: Theory and Research*. New York: John Wiley.
MOORE, J. W. (1982). *Moore's Federal Practice. Federal Rules of Evidence*. New York: Matthew Bender.
RADA, R. T. (1978). *Clinical Aspects of the Rapist*. New York: Grune and Stratton.

SECTION III

The Social Context of Crime

This section focuses on situational influences on criminal behaviour and how such behaviour is perceived and interpreted by the public. **Cumberbatch** provides a challenging critique of the effectiveness of community policing in Britain; and he illustrates clearly the potential conflict between an organizational police structure which rewards the apprehension of criminals rather than the prevention of crime and the pressing need to foster good relations between police and the public. The police may over-estimate public satisfaction with their work, and the concept of 'community policing', which in Britain is currently in vogue, needs to be evaluated carefully and dispassionately.

The two following chapters report studies of how the public make evaluations about mentally ill offenders and the seriousness of deviant acts. **Howells** describes studies designed to investigate how people perceive links between mental illness and dangerous behaviour. Contrary to his expectations, Howells found that there were no clear-cut negative inferences drawn about schizophrenic and depressed offenders in comparison with normal offenders. However, he did find evidence for a greater emphasis on the need for rehabilitation of mentally ill offenders. In Israel it was found by **Rahav and Teichman** that judgments of the seriousness of offences were related to what they describe as the interpersonal resources of the offender and the victim. Their study serves to illustrate the subtleties of appraisal which may be used by the public in evaluating crimes, and these may be used in support of the discretionary powers of the judiciary which are designed to sustain personalized justice.

The chapter by **Levi** provides a discussion of a relatively neglected field of psycho-legal research, that of fraud. Levi reports data gathered from interviews with fraudsters which serve to emphasize the importance of both the social context in which irregularities are committed and the criminals' own perceptions of these irregularities and the probability of their being detected.

Pease and Litton review the effects of attempting to prevent crime. It was noted earlier that crime prevention is often less prominent than crime

133

detection. Pease and Litton consider some of the ways in which the opportunities for crime can be reduced in contemporary society. They emphasize, however, that society must address the question of the extent to which it is prepared to plan for such an outcome, for many potentially effective measures may be unacceptable to the members of the community at large.

The chapters in this section all address, though in different ways, the question of how crime can be said to be constructed in contemporary society. The detection of crime and appropriate methods of disposal for criminals attract much attention in psycho-legal research, as indeed in the community as a whole. These chapters, however, emphasize that other questions also merit scrutiny, and that such questions may impinge directly on the more subtle attitudes and judgments of the public about the social contexts in which crimes are committed.

Psychology and Law
Edited by D.J. Müller, D.E. Blackman, and A.J. Chapman
© 1984 John Wiley & Sons Ltd

Chapter 11

Community Policing in Britain[1]

W. Guy Cumberbatch

Community policing is a polymorphous concept, the close examination of which is akin to probing a hornet's nest: it provokes a whole host of buzzing confusions each with a sting in its tail.

Defining community policing is far from easy. John Stuart Mill once advised that justice, as with other moral attributes, is best defined by its opposites. He might have added 'and stimulated by them too'. Certainly community policing in Britain has in part been defined and certainly stimulated by the riots of 1981. Since the report of Lord Scarman (1982) on these riots, chief constables in almost every one of Britain's 43 separate regional police forces have taken new initiatives in community policing. More than this, most chief constables have succeeded in unearthing dusty community policing projects which they have been able to hold up triumphantly as evidence that community policing always existed. One recent series of interviews with chief constables concluded, 'So chief constables do not so much say that community policing is a fresh answer to their problems, as that it *is* British policing and has been for a century and a half' (Leighton, 1982, p. 50).

In the considerable public debate which has followed the riots and the Scarman report, the above message has been constantly reiterated. The message from chief constables is essentially that all is well with British policing but that the mobile patrol (the 'panda' car) of the unit beat policing system was a mistake; a minor and temporary aberration in fact which isolated our beloved village bobbies from their devoted public. Now that police forces have learned this lesson and foot patrols are being reintroduced all will be well again.

Scarman noted about the police and the riots in Britain's inner cities: 'Their role is critical. If their policing is such as it can be seen to be the application to

135

our new society of the traditional principles of British policing, the role of unrest will diminish...' (Scarman, 1982, p. 135).

Kenneth Oxford of Merseyside Police was one of the first chief constables to recognize that the fast responses offered by police cars was a two-edged sword, distancing the police from their public. He has noted that in the middle of the 1970s 'I banished Land-Rovers from the city and put officers on foot patrol. I got a lot of criticism, but in the last six years, we've contained crime to below the national average' (Oxford, 1982, p. 48).

Unfortunately, this statement is reminiscent of the 13th chime of a clock. It not only casts doubt on itself but on all that has gone before: Merseyside Police in Liverpool 8 suffered some of the worst riots in Britain in 1981. The point of this is hardly that foot patrols created the problem of the poor police community relations in Merseyside (Scraton, 1983; Scraton and Gordon, 1983). The point is rather that foot patrols may not provide the solution so assiduously desired and now so desperately needed.

This review of community policing attempts to cover some of the experiments which have been attempted in Britain. Despite the dearth of social science research here, it seems clear that community policing in Britain is more a rhetoric than a reality. More than this, community policing faces rather serious problems, not the least of which is that it seems incompatible with the organizational philosophy and structure of policing. Finally, police–community relations in Britain have deteriorated so dramatically in the last decade that to suggest Britain faces a 'crisis of policing' (Anonymous, 1982) must be an understatement.

THE HISTORY OF POLICING

The history of British policing has been well documented (e.g. Bunyan, 1976; Critchley, 1978; Manning, 1977; Miller, 1979; Mosse, 1975). There is certainly some truth in the suggestion that community policing has been the essence of British policing for a century and a half – that is, since Sir Robert Peel as Home Secretary established and defined the role of the Metropolitan Police Force in 1829. However, there are unique and very ancient features about British policing and indeed the whole criminal justice system in this country. These have special implications for community policing.

The powers and duties of a police constable are even today essentially derived from the 'common law' of this country and differ little from the powers and duties of every citizen. 'Common law' pervades the British criminal justice system. It is the law of the land which certainly existed long before the Norman conquest. In recent years 'common law' has become overlaid with 'statute law' – that is specific legislation passed by Act of Parliament – and police powers today are more conveniently defined by these statutes. The importance of this is that police officers exercise their powers on their own responsibility and as officers of the Crown and as public servants. They do not do so as agents or employees of the Government, or any one else. Thus police officers can arrest and prosecute regardless of instructions not to do so from senior officers, the Prime Minister or anyone else, as occasionally happens when 'respectable' establishment figures break the law.

Apart from the lack of any state police in Britain (only the Metropolitan Police comes directly under the Home Secretary), there are a few other unique features of British policing. One is the legal discretion not to prosecute but to 'caution' an offender. Another is that police officers act as prosecutors in the courts (with the exception of Scotland which has a 'procurator fiscal' for this).

The regional or community base for policing has perhaps become devalued over time, especially with the recent amalgamation of so many regional forces. However, the structure of British policing can easily be traced back to the Anglo-Saxon system of 'collective pledging' which required every adult male to be enrolled in a group of 10 families ('the tithing'). If any member of the group committed a crime, the others were required to produce the offender for trial. In the 13th century, the head of the tithing became called the 'petty constable' or 'parish constable'. Thus, keeping the peace in Britain remained the responsibility of the community and every citizen in that community.

Very occasionally these days, some bold citizen will demonstrate these ancient powers and duties by arresting some 'felon'. It is rare for fairly obvious reasons. Very early in our history, wealthy people soon paid others to discharge their responsibilities. More recently the growth of police 'professionalization' has served to discourage lay people from doing 'police' work. Nevertheless, the basis for community policing is deeply rooted in Britain's criminal justice system, which is quite unique. Let us examine modern police professionalization and its impact on community policing.

MODERN POLICING

It is difficult to gauge the extent to which policing has changed in the last 150 years. Certainly, many of the current criticisms of the police (e.g. Bunyan, 1976; Cowell, Jones, and Young, 1982) are curiously reminiscent of the fierce debates in Parliament which surrounded Peel's Police Bill. While the County Police Act of 1839 empowered counties to appoint full-time paid police officers, it took until 1856 for an Act of Parliament to make these compulsory. Fears have always been articulated that the police would be more concerned with being an arm of the state than with community protection. This is a crucial issue of course. Everyone seems to agree that a police force is necessary. The debate now, as it was then, relates centrally to the issue of 'what kind of police do the public want and how are the police to be given the mandate to get on with their job?' These questions lay a minefield for social scientists and stretch to the limits their methodological techniques, theoretical tools, and, indeed, diplomatic skills.

On most definitions of the police role, community policing appears to be central and has changed little over time. Thus the Metropolitan Police recruits of 1829, and recruits 150 years later, all learn by heart that:

The primary object of an efficient police force is prevention of crime; the next, that of detection and punishment of offenders if crime is committed. To these ends, all the efforts of Police must be directed. The protection of life and property, the preservation of public tranquillity, and the absence of crime will alone prove whether these efforts have been successful ... much depends on the approval and co-operation of the public, and these have always been determined by the degree of esteem and respect in which the Police are held. Therefore, every member of the Force must remember that it is his duty to help and protect members of the public ... and treat all law abiding citizens, irrespective of race, colour, creed or social position with unfailing patience and courtesy ...' (see, for example, Wegg-Prosser, 1973, p. 212).

Various reports and inquiries on the police have essentially agreed with Peel's formulation of the police role. However, the last inquiry, the Royal Commission on the Police, produced its final report in 1962. Much has changed since then. A new Royal Commission would seem highly desirable to examine policing objectives and methods and provide a new police mandate. The most fundamental changes in British policing have been in a sense almost accidental consequences of fairly trivial technologies in the last two decades, namely telephones, radios, and cars. Until as recently as 15 years ago, policing had involved foot patrol at its primary activity. The accepted method was mainly that of the fixed points system (e.g. Chatterton, 1979) whereby police officers were required to patrol and arrive at fixed locations at set times where supervisory officers could contact them.

In 1966, a Home Office report described various experiments on policing and recommended the now widely adopted 'unit beat' policing system. Under this, 'the constable, preferably living in the area he policed', would provide the ground system. Superimposed on this would be mobile patrols operated day and night.

'The beat man would have a large measure of discretion as to the distribution of his working hours. In this way we should expect to elevate the status of the beat constable in a way that would bring out the best qualities of the beat constable' (Home Office, 1966, p. 118).

Of course it did not work out like this at all. Calls for police assistance routinely got passed to the mobile patrols ('panda' cars) so that the beat officers became somewhat remote from 'real, that is crime related, police work (Cumberbatch and Morgan, 1983).

Today, police work is best described as a telephone call from the public and radio despatch of mobile patrol car (see Ekblom and Heal, 1982; Reiss, 1971). Given that something in the order of 80% of police deployments are *reactive* to public calls for assistance, two important observations can be made. First of all, the prevention of crime can no longer be considered an operational priority of policing. However, secondly, police work is largely defined not by the police but by the public (in the demand that the public makes on the police).

There are problems with the unit beat policing system such as those noted above. Additionally, the information loss between the public and the officers dealing with the incident can be considerable (e.g. Hulbert, 1981). Nevertheless it is potentially, and indeed in practice, a rational and efficient system so that current moves to return to foot patrols in Britain would seem curious. As Sir Philip Knights, Chief Constable of West Midlands Police has noted,

'Not only did the police get into cars, but so did the public. It was only one of the new problems of a society which changed enormously in the sixties. We used to talk to people over the garden fence: now that fence is 20 storeys up in a high-rise building. It was not only the police withdrawing...' (Knights, 1982).

There is little doubt that the general public seems to regret the introduction of 'panda' cars. Over a decade ago, in a large survey of public attitudes to the police in London, Belson (1975) found that 59% of the population agreed with the statement, 'The police have lost touch with people now that police drive around in cars'. More recently, in a survey in Birmingham, Cumberbatch and Walker (1983) found 88% of the public wanting to see more police out on the streets.

Almost everyone seems to cherish fond memories of the village bobby on foot or on his bicycle. Sir Robert Mark (ex-Commissioner of the Metropolitan Police) observed; 'It is part of the English character that we prefer illusion to reality; that we prefer to look in the past rather than to the future' (see Whitaker, 1982, p. 134).

Some imaginative chief constables recognize that community policing cannot involve 'a return to the village bobby' (e.g. Sir Philip Knights, personal communication) and have developed their own concepts of what community policing should be. Let me now review some of the experiments in community policing attempted in Britain.

COMMUNITY POLICING EXPERIMENTS

Holiday makers in Devon and Cornwall are often amused by the legend on a white helicopter that occasionally passes overhead. The legend on its side reads 'community policing'. The humour in this for most people lies in the contrast between modern technology and the old-fashioned ideas of community policing involving avuncular village bobbies. Yet such humour is misplaced. For John Alderson (then Chief Constable of Devon and Cornwall) 'community policing must be a *force* policy' (J. C. Alderson, personal communication). Alderson is perhaps the best known and eloquent of British speakers on community policing. It is difficult to do justice to his ideas in a few brief paragraphs here, but they are well documented elsewhere (e.g. Alderson, 1979). The most important feature of Alderson's approach lay in a comprehensive philosophy or theory of policing which would elevate the role of the police to that of a key institution intimately involved in all aspects of the community, striving to produce constructive social endeavour.

In 1979 he issued 'A Community Police Order' whereby all divisions in his constabulary were to adopt community policing. This was defined: 'Community policing describes a style of day-to-day policing in residential areas in which the public and other social agencies take part by helping prevent crime, and particularly juvenile delinquency, through social as opposed to legal action' (Alderson, 1979). It is difficult to assess how far the policy has become genuine force policy, since neither police ethos nor the police organizational structure is easily changed. Moreover, Alderson himself retired from policing in 1981. However, a number of very interesting experiments were completed during his office. The Crime Prevention Support Unit was a brilliant innovation (see Moore and Brown, 1981). This served as action research unit, most usefully analysing data on local crime and social problems in various divisions. These data were used to encourage inter-agency collaboration to some local problems. A number of such inter-agency schemes were established, for example, the Exeter Community Policing Consultative Group (Blaber, 1979) and a juvenile bureau in collaboration with Devon social services. One other experiment is worth recording, Police Advisory Telephone. This freephone service was introduced to provide assistance, advice, and information easily to the public. Callers were linked to an experienced police officer and this simple method of contacting the police was designed to supplement the 999 system and operate on a 24-hour basis.

Of course similar kinds of community policing projects have been attempted elsewhere. Unfortunately, they are very poorly documented outside the police journals. Schaffer (1980) provides one of the very few listings easily available to date. However, a comprehensive survey is currently being conducted by the Police Foundation (Weatheritt, 1984). Britain compares very unfavourably with the USA in this respect since not only has there been an enormous number of exciting projects well documented in America but some at least have been competently evaluated (see Caiden, 1977; Clarke and Hough, 1980; Radelet and Reed, 1973).

It is possible that all the schemes described by Schaffer (1980) were successful. A juvenile liaison set up by the Chief Constable of Greenock in 1957, for example, apparently led to dramatic environmental improvement through local agencies working together: 'The houses were renovated and restored; the area was landscaped .... a resident's association was set up ... the local police became familiar with the area.... Gradually the area improved and crime fell' (Schaffer, 1980, p. 70). Schaffer describes many such highly imaginative projects, mainly in Scotland. Unfortunately, little evidence is produced that the projects did work or that the considerable effort required in setting them up was rewarded in any tangible way. Of course some measures may be quite misleading. Crime rates, for example, should arguably *increase* in a successful community policing project if more people feel inclined to help the police and society by reporting crimes witnessed or experienced.

It is therefore a little worrying that so many experiments have boasted of drops in crime rates. Local newspapers are a rich source of material on community policing projects and many seem to imply that the police possess mystical powers to control crime. Popular mythology would have us believe that if police officers begin to kick a football on a patch of waste ground, they become Pied Piper figures drawing delinquents from far and wide and occasioning an instant reform in them and slashing the crime figures. Of course this is a nonsense and it is not helpful for anyone to perpetuate this mythology by refusing to acknowledge that most experiments simply do not work in the sense of achieving anything other than a public relations exercise objective (valid though this may be). Thus, in North America in 1974, ABT Associates examined 85000 experiments in crime control but concluded that only 650 could be considered successful and a third of these were questioned (see Caiden, 1977). The reason experiments do not seem to work has much to do with the intractability of crime, rigidity of attitudes, endemic deprivation, and so on. However, the reason why many do not work is probably due more to the stage management of such experiments rather than any intrinsic flaw in the argument.

Social scientists and police officers probably recognize this, but have been very reluctant to admit the fact. Thus in a world of scatterbrained logic, affect and cognition are fused so that virtue must succeed and be shown to succeed. More than this, because community policing experiments reflect on the careers of their architects and principal actors, objective evaluation may be neither possible nor welcome (see, for example, Willmore, 1982). Objectivity is difficult to sustain in police research and poses unusual problems for researchers. On the one hand, heavy involvement must inevitably lead to sympathy for the police while on the other, in research carried out briefly (through self-completed questionnaires and so on) the results are likely to be highly suspect and distorted. The problems arise chiefly from the covert nature of policing and the potential for data rigging (see Falmer, 1980).

It is most unfortunate that in Britain there are numerous projects in community policing being introduced and attempted when they have already been tried and abandoned elsewhere. To date the only serious evaluation research conducted in this country (Cumberbatch and Walker, 1983; Willmore, Hillbard, and Bird, 1983) is not yet generally available. Both studies have been concerned with new and comprehensive community policing projects but have nonetheless produced data of relevance to more conventional schemes.

Thus Cumberbatch and Walker were able to evaluate a school's liaison project. The one which they studied was one of the most intensive (one hour per week over 13 weeks) and extensive (six forms per year) and also carried an unusually good syllabus (of lectures, seminars, quizzes, and visits). Schools liaison programmes, which exist in most police forces, are generally considered to be successful but are rarely evaluated in any objective way. The data from this study were interesting in failing to reveal any effect of the police programme in terms of attitudes to the police but demonstrated clearly that children expected an atypical police officer who was perceived on 17 separate scales to be 'better' than police in general. The authors conclude:

'The majority of police involved seemed to believe that it has enjoyed a degree of success – but judged against modest criteria – such as convincing children that not all police are ogres. Unfortunately, the data reported here would seem to indicate that children knew that already' (Cumberbatch and Walker, 1983, p. 51.).

'... police officers are a very heterogeneous mass and some will perform an excellent service in schools and youth clubs whereas others may undo 6 months' work with a careless comment. The attitudes and intrinsic skills of the police officer provide the dynamics on which the success or failure of an experiment will finally depend' (Cumberbatch and Walker, 1983, p. 106).

This latter point is an important one which is considered in more detail later. For the moment we may note that most police forces consider juvenile liaison to be of some importance and appear to be encouraging initiatives in this direction. One notable development was the Children and Young Persons Act (1969) which gave police the statutory authority to caution juvenile offenders. This encouraged juvenile liaison supervision by the police, but there is little evidence that this discouraged recidivism (Rose and Hamilton, 1970; Taylor, 1971).

It is unfortunate that the vast majority of community policing projects are not even documented, let alone evaluated. Particularly since Scarman (1982) there has been a flurry of activity in this area, with every indication that this will be sustained. Thus Scarman probably merely accelerated a trend which was already under way in British policing. Prior to Scarman, the Home Office Ditchley Conference of 1977 recommended inter-agency collaboration for preventative policing while the Government white paper in the same year on inner-cities essentially urged the same thing (HM Government, 1977). Additionally interest was growing in crime prevention through such things as environmental design (e.g. Clarke and Mayhew, 1980; Ramsay, 1982). Finally, the considerable American literature on police community relations was beginning to penetrate the offices of chief constables, inspectors of constabulary, and the Home Office.

Many of the recent initiatives for community policing projects have come from specialized Community Relations Departments which were established in the mid-1970s (Pope, 1976). Over the years these have grown in size, with full-time community liaison officers attached to them. Their work is not well documented apart from the self-evident one of generally liaising with minority groups and their leaders, statutory and voluntary agencies, and so on. Evaluation research, however, has only just commenced on the work of community liaison officers (Cochran, 1984).

Although more could be written on special community policing projects, the level of documentation and absence of evaluation research detract quite seriously from such an exercise. In any case the assumption usually made (e.g. Leighton, 1982) is that community policing *is* British policing and we now turn to consider how far this is true.

COMMUNITY POLICING IN POLICE WORK

While there is precious little research on British community policing *per se*, a respectable literature has developed on police work. In Britain, Banton (1964) and Cain (1973) were early classics followed by Chatterton (1975) which is often quoted but is not readily available. Since then sound contributions have been made by numerous researchers, notably Holdaway (1977, 1979), Manning (1977), Mawby (1979), and Punch (1975).

The most important finding has been that crime fighting and law enforcement account for a small proportion (probably around 25%) of police work. The largest category of police work is best described as peace-keeping/service work but this is largely hidden from scrutiny and evaluation. An American study by Cumming, Cumming and Edel (1965) was essentially replicated in Britain by Punch and Naylor (1973) who confirmed that over half of the routine calls to the police involved some form of request for help and support for personal or interpersonal problems. The difference between geographic areas was interesting if not surprising – service calls ran to 49% in a new town, 61% in an old town and 73% in a country town. In a later review Punch (1979) shows why the service role should be so high: the police are available 24 hours a day and operate not only as a gatekeeper and referral agency to the social services but also as a safety net to handle cases with which the social services cannot deal. Additionally, 'people involved the police not simply because other services were not available, but because they mistrusted social workers and because they wanted a decisive, authoritative figure to support them in a dispute' (Punch, 1979, p. 107). However, there are other reasons too. Despite the proliferation of service agencies, especially in the voluntary sector, the general public remains fairly ignorant of these. Thus in one recent survey of households in an inner city area well provided by statutory and voluntary agencies, only 52% of people when probed could think of any community agencies at all. More importantly, only 10% knew of the local centres dealing with legal advice (Cumberbatch and Walker, 1983).

Thus, this service role of the police would seem an example of positive community relations. However, few data are available on how things may have changed in recent years. More importantly the police response to this kind of work is ambivalent, as we shall see. Finally, there is no evidence that such work improves police – community relations (though of course it seems reasonable to assume that it might).

The police response to service calls is interesting. It is ambivalent in that while many police officers feel they should help with such problems, this is more as a responsible citizen than as a priority police duty. Indeed, most police officers describe such calls as 'shit' work (e.g. Cain, 1973; Manning, 1977). Additionally, there are few incentives to pursue the spirit of community policing today. Jones (1980) provides an excellently documented argument along these lines. He begins by suggesting that despite the claim made by chief constables that they look on the bobby on the beat as the most valuable resource we have, most evidence suggests the contrary. As we have noted, policing and especially community policing should have as its first priority the prevention of crime rather than its detection. Jones examined commendations given to police officers in one force and concluded, 'whilst not denying the importance of recognising crime detection, it is significant that of 1074 commendations not one recognised crime prevention other than by reference to enforcement statistics' (Jones, 1980, p. 67). Additionally, commendations for 'good police work' all included references to 'good' arrests or 'good' offence reports. Finally, the number of officers commended who were *not* specialized or promoted was a mere 14% of the total (i.e. not typically associated with beat constables' work).

The organizational structure of policing at first sight seems to give priority to the uniformed patrol police officer since this is the largest branch in terms of numbers available. However, in practice uniformed patrol is usually considerably below its establishment strength, with officers creamed off to specialist departments. Thus in Jones' study, uniform was 16% below strength whereas the Criminal Investigation Department was a staggering 68% *above* establishment strength. What this all means is that instead of a 'theoretical' possibility of one uniformed patrol officer for every 366 members of the public, it turned out to be one for every 6038 (in terms of officers on the beat at any one time).

Finally, as Jones shows, the uniformed foot patrol, the police interface with the public, is relatively young and inexperienced with a mean age of 24.6 years compared with 28.8 for mobile patrol, while the specialist departments were older still.

All in all, these figures explain much about police attitudes to community policing. The organizational structure of policing devalues the job to such an extent that 'these constables not only fail to receive any rewards from the organisation but are positively denigrated by their supervisors and colleagues for not conforming' (Jones, 1980, p. 90). The attraction of specialist departments and 'real' police work are very compelling ones.

In the absence of more research data, it is difficult to judge how typical the force studied by Jones was or by how much things have changed over the years. Probably things have got worse over time and all forces reflect the problems identified by Jones to some extent, although few will have witnessed them to the same degree.

The above points on the organizational structure of policing recommend that if community policing is to be encouraged, a systemic view of motivation is needed (e.g. Checkland, 1981). Thus there would seem little point in urging community policing if all the institutional pressures operate against it. Evidently serious consideration will be needed to examine the ways in which community policing can be encouraged by line managers. However, in such a systematic model of policing, a number of other variables would need to be included, not the least of which would be the primary gratifications police officers derive from different types of work. This poses a more serious and intractable problem.

The dramatic image of policing presented in popular fiction of avenging blue angels involved in life and death struggles in their war on crime evidently has considerable appeal to the viewing public for all kinds of reasons. It is unreasonable to expect police officers to be immune from the glamorous appeal of crime detection. Indeed there would seem to be a fundamental asymmetry between prevention and detection. Prevention is slow, has no definite temporal location, is ambiguous about the 'right' approach and so on. Its meaning is blurred by such overtones and the rewards from it thus diminished. Crime detection is far more consensual, tangible, and fixed in time so that the rewards are unambiguously positive, quite apart from the organizational reinforcement noted earlier.

An inescapable fact of police culture, and a hardly surprising one at that, is that crime detection, clever arrests, and dangerous criminals provide the subject of locker room stories and the means to peer status. The experienced police officer

'... often becomes a novelist bent on perpetuating the mystique of detective work. Almost inevitably he will be reluctant to negate that image. The media images of the detective necessarily focus on personalities rather than the slow tedious methodical fact collection of the organisation – for fairly obvious dramatic reasons. Similarly, the police officer in order to demonstrate his *special* skills will be strongly encouraged by the peer culture to produce a script of dramatic success. The shopkeeper who provides crucial information may necessarily become 'my informant' who must be protected by anonymity and possibly rewarded financially from the appropriate police funds!' (Cumberbatch and Morgan, 1983).

The importance of special skills has perhaps been rather neglected in discussions of police work to date. The need to demonstrate special skills is important within the organizational peer culture but is quite vital at another level – that of the professional status of policing as an institution. Manning (1977) has provided a particularly interesting analysis of police work by applying Goffman's dramaturgical metaphor. In this, the public image of policing is one of the *symbols* of effectiveness and these are more important than the reality of them. The approach can be best illustrated by examining medicine as a profession. The symbols of medicine are its high technology, surgical skills, wonder drugs, and sophisticated scientific knowledge. These have the important role of distancing the layperson from the profession. Thus, apart from medical jargon, even parts of the body are pronounced in curious ways to bewilder the layperson. The advantage of the distance created between the profession and the layperson is that the profession can then insist that lay people are not qualified to interfere with the profession's activities. Thus professions are most characteristically self-regulating and self-policing, determining their own training practices, status, and salaries. The medical profession could admit that health has far more to do with prevention than with cure. It could point out that the improvement in health this century has had more to do with hygiene and diet than with drugs. But this is no way to elevate the status, salary, and autonomy of the medical profession. Thus, in an important sense low level community preventive medicine acts against the interests of the profession. Of course, we can see the same problems in psychology which has only generated symbols of effectiveness (the laboratory experiment, statistical analysis, etc.) rather than creating the reality of effectiveness. Consequently it has produced a jargon-riddled vocabulary to confuse the layperson and even deliberately shied away from dealing with practical problems that interest and may therefore be understood by the layperson.

It is hardly surprising therefore that policing has attempted to follow the same route to professionalization. So long as the public believe that forensics is a sophisticated and effective science, that police officers possess special detective skills, and that police work is difficult and dangerous, then salaries and status and autonomy may be commensurate with a profession. Importantly too, policing may be easier if potential offenders are convinced that these special skills and technologies exist in an effective way.

At the beginning of the chapter, it was suggested that community policing is more a rhetoric than a reality. Given the argument offered above, it is difficult to see that community policing can be anything else. It remains fundamentally incompatible with the organizational structure and ambitions of policing as a profession.

CONCLUSION

In this brief chapter, it has been impossible to cover a whole host of issues which are vitally important in policing. Currently, the dynamics of public-police encounters, questions of social skills (and especially race awareness training) are receiving considerable attention (see Bull, Chapter 29). Doubtlessly such initiatives may help to reduce conflict and improve police-community relations, as many have argued (e.g. Grant, Grant, and Toch, 1982).

However, the problems of police-community relations are rather more fundamental than this. Surveys have revealed the growing dissatisfaction of the public with the police and a quite new phenomenon has arisen in that the police no longer underestimate public satisfaction with the police but now overestimate it (see Jones, 1982). This is a very great cause for concern. Evidently, something needs to be done and it is doubtful whether cosmetic surgery is the answer. The dream of John Alderson (1979) that the police could become central agents not just for the prevention of crime but for constructive social endeavour is a fine one. The police are in a unique position to provide the catalyst for community action, to involve themselves in the community for the public good. However, at the end of the day, the debate on the police's future still revolves around the issues raised a decade and a half ago. It is a political debate in many ways. Are the police to be the agents of the state or friends of the community? However, politics disguise a much more fundamental and deeply psychological issue. The debate is more correctly concerned with philosophies of 'human nature' (Wrightsman, 1974). It is a debate primarily about our views of people. Are people to be trusted? Do we believe in the message of *The Lord of the Flies* (Golding, 1959) or that of

The Coral Island (Ballantyne, 1927). These two novels present radically different assumptions about human nature: contemptuous pessimism versus ingenuous faith.

At the end of the day, equity theory and attributional analysis may explain more successfully than anything else just why policing is in such a crisis and why mutual mistrust has grown between the public and the police and why community policing is viewed with some suspicion by some police and some communities. Of course more research is needed, but more than anything a comprehensive theory of policing would seem essential. The police are not uninvited guests but an essential institution to which society must be wedded. Perhaps a new marriage contract is needed, but in the best of traditions, before the honeymoon begins, careful selection will need to be made for that symbolic ritual long enshrined in marriage customs: something old, something new, something borrowed, something blue.

NOTE

1. I wish to thank Doug Sharp for his helpful comments on an earlier draft of this chapter.

REFERENCES

ALDERSON, J. C. (1979). *Policing Freedom*. Plymouth: MacDonald and Evans.

ANONYMOUS (1982). Editorial. *New Society*, 29 July 1982.

BALLANTYNE, R. M. (1927). *The Coral Island*. New York: Dell Paperback.

BANTON, M. (1964). *The Policeman in the Community*. London: Tavistock.

BELSON, W. A. (1975). *Public and Police*. London: Harper and Row.

BLABER, A. (1979). *The Exeter Community Policing Consultative Group*. London: NACRO.

BUNYAN, T. (1976). *The History and Practice of the Political Police in Britain*. London: Julian Friedman.

CAIDEN, G. (1977). *Police Revitalization*. Lexington, Mass: Sage.

CAIN, M. (1973). *Society and the Policeman's Role*. London: Routledge and Kegan Paul.

CHATTERTON, M. (1975). Organisational relationships and processes in police work: a study of urban policing. Doctoral Dissertation, University of Manchester.

CHATTERTON, M. (1979). The supervision of patrol work under the fixed points system. In S. Holdaway (Ed.), *The British Police*. London: Edward Arnold.

CHECKLAND, P. (1981). *Systems Thinking, Systems Practice*. Chichester: Wiley.

CLARKE, R. V. G., and HOUGH, J. M. (1980). *The Effectiveness of Policing*. Farnborough, Hants: Gower.

CLARKE, R.V.G., and MAYHEW, P. (1980). *Designing Out Crime*. London: Her Majesty's Stationery Office.

COCHRAN, R. (1984). *Community Liaison Officers*. London: Home Office Research and Planning Unit, in preparation.

COWELL, D., JONES, T., and YOUNG, J. (1982). *Policing the Riots*. London: Junction Books.

CRITCHLEY, T. A. (1978). *A History of Police in England and Wales*. London: Constable.

CUMBERBATCH, W. G., and MORGAN, J. B. (1983). The police officer. In W. T. Singleton (Ed), *The Study of Real Skills*, Vol. 4. Lancaster: MTP.

CUMBERBATCH, W. G. and WALKER, E. (1983). *The Lozells Community Policing Project*. Birmingham: Applied Psychology Department, University of Aston.

CUMMING, E., CUMMING, I., and EDEL, L. (1965). Policeman as philosopher, guide and friend. *Social Problems*, **17**, 276 – 286.

EKBLOM, P., and HEAL, K. (1982). *The Police Response to Calls from the Public*, Home Office Research and Planning Unit, Paper 9. London: Her Majesty's Stationery Office.

FALMER, D. J. (1980). Out of hugger-mugger: the case of police field services. In R. Clarke and M. Hough, *The Effectiveness of Policing*. Farnborough, Hants: Gower.

GOLDING, W. (1959). *The Lord of the Flies*. New York: Pocket Books.

GRANT, J. D., GRANT, J., and TOCH, H. (1982). Police–citizen encounters and decisions to arrest. In V. J. Konečni and E. E. Ebbesen (Eds), *The Criminal Justice System: A Social Psychological Analysis*. San Francisco: Freeman.

H. M. GOVERNMENT (1977). *Policy for the Inner Cities*. London: Her Majesty's Stationery Office.

HOLDAWAY, S. (1977). Changes in urban policing. *British Journal of Sociology*, **28**, 119–137.

HOLDAWAY, S. (1979). *The British Police*. London: Edward Arnold.

HOME OFFICE (1966). *Unit Beat Policing*, Home Office Research and Planning Branch Report No. 11/67. London: Her Majesty's Stationery Office.

HOME OFFICE (1977). Conference on preventive policing, Ditchley, March 1977 (unpublished).

HULBERT, J. (1981). Human factors in message acquisition for a computer based command and control system. Doctoral Dissertation, University of Aston in Birmingham.

JONES, J. M. (1980). *Organisational Aspects of Police Behaviour*. Farnborough, Hants: Gower.

JONES, S. (1982). Police–public relationship: fact or fiction? Paper presented to the British Psychological Society, Welsh Branch, International Conference on Psychology and Law, Swansea, July.

KNIGHTS, SIR PHILIP (1982). Quoted in M. Leighton, 'The men we have to trust'. *The Sunday Times Magazine*, 26 September 1982, p. 48.

LEIGHTON, M. (1982). The men we have to trust. *The Sunday Times Magazine*, 26 September 1982.

MANNING, P. K. (1977). *Police Work*. Cambridge, Mass: MIT Press.

MAWBY, R. (1979). *Policing the City*. Farnborough, Hants: Saxon House.

MILLER, W. R. (1979). London's police tradition in a changing society. In S. Holdaway (Ed), *The British Police*. London: Edward Arnold.

MOORE, C., and BROWN, J. (1981). *Community Versus Crime*. London: National Council for Voluntary Organizations.

MOSSE, G. L. (1975). *Police Forces in History*. Lexington, Mass: Sage.

OXFORD, K. (1982). Quoted in M. Leighton, 'The men we have to trust'. *The Sunday Times Magazine*, 26 September 1982, p. 48.

POPE, D. W. (1976). *Community Relations: The Police Response*. London: Runneymeade Trust.

PUNCH, M. (1975). Research and the police. In J. Brown and G. Hower (Eds), *The Police and the Community*. Farnborough, Hants: Saxon House.

PUNCH, M. (1979). The secret social service. In S. Holdaway (Ed), *The British Police*. London: Edward Arnold.

PUNCH, M., and NAYLOR, T. (1973). The police: a social service. *New Society*, **24** (554), 358–361.

RADELET, L. A., and REED, H.C. (1973). *The Police and the Community.* Beverly Hills, Calif.: Glencoe Press.

RAMSAY, M. (1982). *City Centre Crime*, Home Office Research and Planning Unit, Paper 10. London: Home Office.

REISS, A. J. (1971). *The Police and the Public.* New Haven, Conn.: Yale University Press.

ROSE, G., and HAMILTON, R. A. (1970). Effects of juvenile liaison scheme. *British Journal of Criminology*, **10**, 15–23.

ROYAL COMMISSION ON THE POLICE (1962). *Royal Commission on the Police, Final Report*, Cmnd 1728. London: Her Majesty's Stationery Office.

SCARMAN, Lord (1982). *The Scarman Report.* Harmondsworth: Penguin.

SCHAFFER, E. B. (1980). *Community Policing.* London: Croom Helm.

SCRATON, P. (1983). *The State of the Police.* London: Pluto.

SCRATON, P., and GORDON, D. (1983). *Causes for Concern: Case Studies in Criminal Justice.* Harmondsworth: Penguin.

TAYLOR, M. (1971). *Study of the Juvenile Liaison Scheme in West Ham.* Home Office Research Unit No. 8. London: Her Majesty's Stationery Office.

WEATHERITT, M. (1984) *Review of Innovations and Experiments in the Police Service.* London: The Police Foundation, in preparation.

WEGG-PROSSER, C. (1973). *The Police and the Law.* London: Oyez.

WHITAKER, B. (1982). *The Police in Society.* London: Sinclair Brown.

WILLMORE, J. (1982). The Police Foundation. *Police Review*, **1982** (6).

WILLMORE, J., HILLBARD M., and BIRD, C. (1983). *Evaluation of Neighbourhood Policing.* London: The Police Foundation.

WRIGHTSMAN, L. S. (1974). *Assumptions about Human Nature: A Social Psychological Approach.* Monterey, Calif.: Brooks-Cole.

Psychology and Law
Edited by D.J. Müller, D.E. Blackman, and A.J. Chapman
© 1984 John Wiley & Sons Ltd

Chapter 12

Public Perceptions of Mentally Ill Offenders[1]

Kevin Howells

This chapter examines whether there is a link perceived by the public between mental illness and 'dangerous' or violent behaviour. Whether mental illness and violence are *objectively* related has been the subject of numerous studies in recent years (for reviews, see Howells, 1982; Rabkin, 1979). Research investigating the association between the two variables has proceeded along two lines:

(1) Attempts have been made to determine whether violent persons have a higher prevalence of mental illness than non-violent persons.
(2) The subsequent criminal histories of patients admitted to mental institutions have been studied to see if such persons are more prone to violent behaviour than the non-mentally ill.

The findings of both types of enquiry have been equivocal (Howells, 1982). It is still unclear whether reliable statistical associations exist between the two classes of social deviance, and where such associations do exist it is far from certain that they reflect a simple causal relationship by which the development of mental illness *causes* a person to act in a violent manner. It is feasible, however, that the tentative and uncertain nature of the links between mental illness and violence is not fully appreciated by the general public and even by professionals involved with patient and offender groups. There are indications from empirical studies that mentally ill people are viewed in stereotyped and prejudiced ways and that an increased propensity for violent and 'dangerous' behaviour forms part of the stereotyped image. Miles (1981) has recently summarized a number of studies which consistently reveal that such images are widespread. A study by Swarte (1969) in the Netherlands, for example, showed that the mentally ill tend to be seen as associated with crime and particularly with violent and sexual crimes against the person.

The sources of such stereotypes are manifold but few would deny that the media play some role in reinforcing traditional ideas of madness and the dangers associated with it. As Miles (1981) points out, it is common to read that a murderer, a rapist, or an escaped prisoner has been treated for mental illness, confirming the image of the dangerousness of the mentally ill. Another study by Swarte (1969) showed that more than one-half of all press reports and articles referring to mental illness in the Netherlands dealt with crime, particularly violent and sexual crime. Even when such reports are accurate they are rarely offset by positive accounts.

It is unlikely that societies are homogeneous with regard to attitudes to the mentally ill. Societies are likely to be 'segmented' rather than 'monolithic' (Quinney, 1970), with different perceptions existing in particular sub-groups. Reliable effects, for example, have been reported for age and for level of education. Younger groups have been consistently found to express opinions and attitudes which are more humanitarian and more sympathetic to the mentally ill (Brockman and D'Arcy, 1978; Miles, 1981; O'Mahoney, 1979). Similarly, the better educated have been found to be less prejudiced and to have less rejecting attitudes than poorly educated groups (Brockman and D'Arcy, 1978).

The ready association of mental illness and dangerous behaviour may pose particular problems for persons who are both criminal *and* mentally abnormal. Such people are *doubly deviant* and seem to be particularly feared by the general public. If such negative perceptions of this group do exist, it is not difficult to see how they might have very negative consequences both for offenders and for professionals involved with them. The stigma of double deviance may, for example, produce difficulties in social acceptance and social integration on leaving institutions for mentally ill offenders which are even more marked than those met by 'normal' criminals. Similarly, psychiatrists have reported marked difficulties in the clinical placement of abnormal offenders and in establishing institutions for them in the community. In a recent paper Hill (1982) attributes such difficulties directly to social attitudes towards abnormal offenders: 'the failure, so far, to implement the medium security units first recommended more than ten years ago is almost certainly due to both public and professional prejudice in the localities where they are proposed' (Hill, 1982, p. 237).

EMPIRICAL STUDIES

The evidence for public and professional prejudice is largely anecdotal and there is a need for objective empirical studies of attitudes towards mentally ill offenders. The only study known to the present author is one reported in the USA by Steadman and Cocozza (1978). These authors looked at public evaluations of a related but slightly different group, the 'criminally insane'. A large sample of subjects applied semantic differential scales to three concepts: (1) 'most people', (2) 'the criminally insane', and (3) 'a mental patient'. The general finding was that the criminally insane were rated in very negative terms, as more 'dangerous, harmful and violent' than control concepts. Steadman and Cocozza concluded that:

> 'public conceptions of the criminally insane are dominated by fear of the extreme danger they are seen as posing, and this danger is substantially greater than that posed by former mental patients who have been shown in previous studies to be highly rejected and feared individuals themselves' (Steadman and Cocozza, 1978, p. 527).

The difficulty in interpreting this study, however, lies in the nature of the comparisons made. The criminally insane were compared with other mental patients. It might be argued that it is quite unsurprising that the criminally insane are viewed as more dangerous than 'ordinary' mental patients. The criminally insane share with mental patients their mental abnormality and are additionally 'criminal'. It is realistic, therefore, to see them as more dangerous. The relevant comparison would be between mentally normal and mentally ill criminals, the important question being: is a person who has engaged in criminal behaviour evaluated more negatively if he or she is *additionally* mentally ill? We have tried to answer this question in a preliminary fashion in two recent studies. Both these studies are small in scale and the groups assessed were not properly representative of the general population. For this reason they are to be regarded as pilot studies for a larger-scale survey.

Study One

The aim of this study was to evaluate the effects of the presence of mental illness on public perceptions of offenders, and in particular to answer the following questions: Would a mentally ill offender be seen as less responsible for judgments about a mentally ill offender be seen as less responsible for criminal behaviour than a normal offender, and would the former be more likely to be seen as requiring treatment rather than punishment? Would a mentally ill offender be seen as more dangerous than a normal offender? Would a mentally ill offender be socially rejected to a greater extent than a normal offender?

The second and third questions flow from the 'doubly deviant' status of mentally ill offenders. Finally, would public judgments about a mentally ill offender be affected by educational level? An affirmative answer to this question would be consistent with findings (above) that higher educated groups are more sympathetic and less hostile towards the mentally ill than are less educated groups. In addition an attempt was made to determine whether the effects of the presence of mental illness would hold for both serious and less serious offences.

Age, a factor known to affect judgments of the non-criminal mentally ill (see above), was held constant in this study. Eighty subjects (40 male, 40 female) aged between 18 and 23 years were recruited. The low education group comprised 40 craft apprentices, clerical trainees, and other students undertaking day-release and other short-term courses at a technical college. Few subjects in this group had educational qualifications beyond a few CSEs or one or two 'O' levels. The high education group comprised 40 undergraduate university students undertaking a variety of courses. The groups did not differ for age and there were equal numbers of males and females for each educational group and each experimental condition.

The procedure was one that has been frequently used in the study of perceptions of deviant behaviour (e.g. Howells, Shaw, Greasley, Robertson, Gloster and Metcalfe, 1984). Subjects were asked to participate in a study of 'what the general public thinks about different kinds of criminal offences'. They were then randomly presented with one of four putative newspaper accounts of a court case. They were told to read the account carefully and to complete the questionnaire when they had finished.

The newspaper accounts described court proceedings involving a male defendant ('Brian Miller') accused of an offence against a casual female acquaintance in a public park. The defendant was described as 'unemployed' and as 'a loner' and background information was provided about him and the circumstances of the offence. The four experimental conditions involved manipulation of the seriousness of the offence and of the mental state of the defendant. In the serious condition the headline for the account was 'Man in Court on Murder Charge' and reported evidence that Miller 'had repeatedly stabbed a 24-year-old woman in a public park'. In the less serious condition the headline was 'Man in Court on Robbery Charge' and evidence was reported that Miller had 'snatched a 24-year-old woman's handbag in a public park'. In the mentally ill condition Miller was described as having a long history of mental illness, as having been admitted to the local psychiatric hospital on several occasions and the account continued: 'he was diagnosed by doctors as a schizophrenic and sometimes "heard voices" and held irrational beliefs'. In the mentally normal condition Miller was described as having no history of mental illness or of being admitted to a psychiatric hospital. In addition 'doctors considered him to be quite normal mentally'. Apart from these experimental manipulations all accounts were identical in content.

The questionnaire comprised nine items with a five-point Likert scale for each item. The items assessed were : Miller's perceived 'responsibility' for the offence; the extent to which he deserved 'blame' for the offence; the severity of punishment deserved; agreement/disagreement with the statement that Miller 'needs medical treatment rather than punishment'; perceived 'dangerousness' of the defendant; perceived likelihood of Miller 'committing a similar offence in the future, when returned to the community'; degree of fear 'at the thought of someone like Miller living in your neighbourhood'; happiness with the idea of Miller 'working in the same place as you work'; strength of anticipated objection to 'an institution for this sort of offender being built in your neighbourhood'.

The first two items were intended to assess perceptions of responsibility and culpability, the next two punitive as opposed to therapeutic evaluations, the fifth and sixth perceived dangerousness, and the last three social distancing and rejection of the defendant.

Each item was subjected to a three-way analysis of variance with mental state of the offender (mentally ill/normal), severity of the offence (serious/less serious), and educational level of respondents (high/low) as factors.

The results showed that the mentally ill offender was perceived as significantly less 'responsible', less deserving of blame, deserving less severe punishment, and as more likely to require treatment than punishment. Subjects objected *less* to the presence of an institution for mentally ill offenders than normal offenders. No significant differences were observed for items five, six, seven, and eight.

In the murder condition Miller was perceived as deserving more severe punishment, as more dangerous, as more likely to re-offend, as more frightening to have in the neighbourhood, and distressing to have in the workplace. Significant effects were not observed for items one, two, four, and nine.

High education subjects objected less to having an institution in their neighbourhood than did low education subjects. No significant effects were observed for other items. Significant three-way interactions were found for perceived responsibility and fear of having the offender in the neighbourhood. The responsibility interaction indicated that the main effect, by which the presence of mental illness reduced perceived responsibility, did not hold equally across seriousness conditions for the high education and low education groups. For the serious crime the high education group took little account of mental illness but did do so for the less serious crime. The reverse was true for the low education group, who took mental illness into account for the serious offence only. The fear interaction indicated that the main effect by which non-serious offences produced lower fear than serious offences did not hold equally across the other two factors. In particular this effect did *not* exist as strongly for low education subjects making judgments about the mentally ill offender. When judging a mentally ill offender, low education subjects were as fearful of the robber as they were of the murderer. This was not true when they judged the mentally normal offender: here they did take account of the seriousness of the offence.

Study Two

The aim of the second study was to assess the replicability of the effects detected in the first. The design and format of the experiment were essentially similar and identical response scales were used. There were, however, important differences in the independent variables. Mental illness/normality were manipulated by describing an offender with a history/no history of depression. The newspaper account included information that the offender 'had been admitted on many occasions to a local mental hospital with a diagnosis of depression'. Doctors had found that he was prone to become deeply depressed in his mood, with feelings of worthlessness and frequent thoughts of suicide'. The serious/less serious variable involved describing an offence either of grievious bodily harm (a non-fatal stabbing) or of criminal damage (smashing the window of a city-centre store). The subjects in this experiment were 96 non-academic university employees. The occupations of the subjects covered the spectrum of social class and they ranged in age from 16 to 65 years. Age itself was included as an independent variable by splitting the group at the median into 'young' and 'old' groups.

The major finding of this study was that the pattern of main effects detected in study one was largely repeated in study two. The mentally ill offender was again seen as less responsible, less deserving of blame, deserving less severe punishment, and more likely to require treatment as opposed to punishment. With minor differences, the effects of the serious/less serious variable were also similar to those in the first study. There were no significant main effects for age though age entered into a number of interactions in a complicated manner.

In both these studies the subjects were asked to write in their own words about the offenders described and how they should be dealt with. Individual perceptions proved to be very diverse and idiosyncratic, and indicated a wide range of evaluations of the mentally ill offender.

The following is a random sample of comments made about the schizophrenic committing the murder offence in study one:'Bring back corporal punishment (*sic*) for all murderers'; 'Prison life would probably ruin the rest of his life and make him violent ... neither would a mental institution help him ... he needs medical attention but not in an institution'; 'With Miller's record of mental illness it is obvious that doctors have to take most of the blame for letting him out to commit a further crime'; 'Should be dealt with very severely – too many get off their sentence due to so-called unfortunate circumstances'.

In the same experiment the following judgments were made about the schizophrenic robber: 'I believe offenders of this type should be treated in the same manner as an ordinary criminal'; 'This sort of person is obviously in need of medical help and putting him in prison would not be adequate and perhaps damage his mental state even further'; 'Obviously need for medical treatment, however punishment should still be enforced because many people get away with crime by blaming illness'.

The tendency in this last example to see punitive *and* therapeutic dispositions as appropriate was unusual. Most subjects appeared to choose one of the two possibilities.

DISCUSSION OF EMPIRICAL STUDIES

The results of these two preliminary experiments provide some tentative answers to some of the questions raised above.

First, it seems clear that the mentally ill offender, whether schizophrenic or depressed, is seen differently even though all other information, including the details of the offence itself, is identical to the normal offender. This finding is consistent with previous research indicating that members of the public *do* use information about the presence of mental illness when making judgments about target persons (Miles, 1981).

The present results seem to contrast starkly with previous studies, and perhaps with the usual predictions of clinicians, in showing an *absence* of clear-cut negative inferences about the mentally ill offender. My own prediction and expectation was that the subjects would be sceptical about reducing the responsibility and blameworthiness of mentally ill offenders and that they would tend to perceive them as deserving treatment similar to the normal offender. This proved not to be the case. The subjects did indeed make allowances for mental illness, seeing the mentally ill offender as less responsible and less blameworthy for the offence committed. In general, this held equally for both serious and less serious offences. It might, perhaps, have been anticipated that where the offence was very serious (e.g. murder) the subjects might choose to ignore the effects of mental illness ('if the offence is really serious then he should not be excused'). This was not the case. Consistent with the perceptions of diminished responsibility were the perceptions that the mentally ill offender deserved less severe punishment and (relative to the normal offender) should be treated rather than punished. Many, though not all subjects clearly supported therapeutic rather than punitive dispositons for the mentally ill offender. This apparent acceptance of psychiatric ideology may reflect changes in the level of psychiatric sophistication amongst the public in recent years.

There is no support in the present results for the hypothesis that the mentally ill offender will be perceived as more dangerous and will be more likely to be socially rejected. In general the mentally ill offender was seen as equally dangerous and as equally likely to re-offend. Subjects were no more unhappy about working or living with an abnormal offender than with a normal offender. Indeed they objected less to having an institution for mentally ill offenders in their neighbourhood (see study one). The difference on this item is perhaps a product of the perceived diminished responsibility of the mentally ill. The latter are, perhaps, more deserving of sympathy and consideration, even though they are no less dangerous than normal offenders. If this finding for institutions could be replicated, it might be of some significance for social policy-makers who would like to persuade communities to accept such institutions. Potential public objections to establishing units for mentally ill offenders might best be countered by *stressing* the abnormal mental status of the patients ('they are sick') rather than by minimizing it.

Perceived dangerousness and social rejection are much more a function of the seriousness of the offence than of the mental state of the offender. In this sense the subjects in the experiments are in agreement with professional researchers who have similarly concluded that the propensity for future dangerous behaviour relates much more strongly to previous serious offending than it does to psychiatric disturbance *per se*.

Socio-demographic variables (level of education in study one and age in study two) had relatively little effect in these studies. The liberalizing effect of education observed in other studies (Miles, 1981) was apparent only on the item assessing acceptability of an institution. The greater acceptability of an institution for educated subjects, however, applied to both the mentally ill offender and the normal offender, indicating that the educated group are generally more tolerant of deviant behaviour rather than tolerant of mental illness in itself. The two interactions in study one suggest some complexity to the effect of educational level. Future research might attempt to disentangle the complex relationship with the other two variables. The failure of age to affect judgments in a clear-cut way (study two) suggests, perhaps, that socio-demographic variables affecting judgments of the non-criminal mentally ill (Brockman and D'Arcy, 1978; O'Mahoney, 1979) may be less potent when mentally ill offenders are the focus of the subjects' attention.

The preliminary nature of these findings should be emphasized. The studies are small in scale and there is a clear need to proceed to the study of a larger, more representative sample drawn, perhaps, from electoral registers. The consistency with which the subjects were more liberal and 'progressive' in their evaluations of the mentally ill offender than might have been expected is nevertheless intriguing. The important question remains of whether progressive *attitudes* predict progressive *behaviour* towards such offenders. Psychologists have long been pessimistic about finding consistent relationships between cognitive beliefs and judgments and behaviour itself. It is also likely that reactions to the mentally ill vary with the immediacy and likelihood of possible contacts with them – prejudices may be far more evident when local residents are presented with actual plans to build an institution for such offenders in their community.

Finally, the extent to which the present results can be generalized is unclear. Although similar results were found for schizophrenia and depression, would similar effects occur if the defendant were described as 'brain damaged', 'mentally handicapped', or 'suffering from a psychopathic disorder'? Would we find interactions between mental illness and the nature of the violence in the incident, such that sexual violence (rape, paedophilic assaults) or arson produced different results to those obtained? Would responses differ significantly to a female offender? The answers to these and many other questions await further empirical researach. It is reasonable to conclude that psychological work in this area of the *social* (as opposed to *psychiatric*) evaluation of dangerousness and social unacceptability in mentally ill offenders is worthwhile and probably overdue.

NOTE

1. I would like to thank Mhairi McEwan, Beverly Jones, and Cindy Mathews for their help in collecting and analysing the data.

REFERENCES

BROCKMAN, J., and D'ARCY, C. (1978). Correlates of attitudinal distance toward the mentally ill: a review and re-survey. *Social Psychiatry*, **13**, 69–77.

HILL, D. (1982). Public attitudes to mentally abnormal offenders. In J. Gunn and D. P. Farrington (Eds), *Abnormal Offenders, Delinquency and the Criminal Justice System*. Chichester: Wiley.

HOWELLS, K. (1982). Mental disorder and violent behaviour. In M. P. Feldman (Ed), *Developments in the Study of Criminal Behaviour*, Vol. II, *Violence*. Chichester: Wiley.

HOWELLS, K., SHAW, F., GREASLEY, M., ROBERTSON, J., GLOSTER, D., and METCALFE, N. (1984). Perceptions of rape in a British sample: effects of relationship, victim status, sex, and attitudes to women. *British Journal of Social Psychology*, **23**, 35–40.

MILES, A. (1981). *The Mentally Ill in Contemporary Society*. Oxford: Martin Robertson.

O'MAHONEY, P. D. (1979). Attitudes to the mentally ill: a trait attribution approach. *Social Psychiatry*, **14**, 95–105.

QUINNEY, R. (1970). *The Social Reality of Crime*. Boston, Mass.: Little, Brown.

RABKIN, J. G. (1979). Criminal behavior of discharged mental patients. *Psychological Bulletin*, **86**, 1–27.

STEADMAN, H., and COCOZZA, J. (1978). Selective reporting and public misconceptions of the criminally insane. *Public Opinion Quarterly*, **41**, 512–533.

SWARTE, J. H. (1969). Stereotypes and attitudes about the mentally ill. In H. Freeman (Ed), *Progress in Mental Health*. London: J. and A. Churchill.

Psychology and Law
Edited by D.J. Müller, D.E. Blackman, and A.J. Chapman
© 1984 John Wiley & Sons Ltd

Chapter 13

Assessing the Seriousness of Deviant Behaviour: The Effects of Interpersonal Resources

Giora Rahav and Meir Teichman

The measurement of seriousness of deviant acts is of interest to a variety of disciplines. Psychologists are interested in it as a problem of perception and attitudes, sociologists as a problem in norm structure; criminologists are concerned with the assessment of offenders by the severity of their crimes, jurists in the equity of crimes and punishments; and so on. Early attempts to assess the seriousness of individual behaviour started in the 19th century, but the problem has been dealt with systematically only since the development of psychological measurement.

One of the earliest methods was developed by Thurstone (1927). He gave his subjects all 171 pairs formed by comparing 19 offences with each other. With the help of a number of plausible statistical assumptions, he was able to construct a scale of seriousness, ranging from 0.0 for vagrancy and 1.03 for bootlegging to 3.28 for rape and 3.16 for homicide. Durea (1933) studied delinquent behaviour using the same method. His scale ranged from 0 for truancy and 0.584 for vagrancy to 3.51 for highway robbery and 5.81 for murder. Thurstone's study was replicated by Coombs (1966) and by Krus, Sherman, and Krus (1977). Both replications observed a trend of declining severity attributed to sex offences, while crimes against the person are considered more serious. In spite of the significant change in values and in attitudes toward their offences, the rank order correlation between Thurstone's and the Krus *et al*'s ratings is 0.48.

The most significant work in this area is unquestionably Sellin and Wolfgang's (1964) *The Measurement of Delinquency*. Following S. S. Steven's work in psychophysics, they asked their subjects to ascribe numbers to various offence descriptions, so that the ratio between any two numbers be similar to the ratio of the seriousness of the respective offences. The scale values obtained by this technique of magnitude estimation closely correlated (after a logarithmic transformation) with the values obtained by a category scaling method. Moreover, including in their offence descriptions simple as well as complex crimes, and various degrees of property loss or bodily injury, they were able to construct a scale of seriousness for various offence components, ranging from 1 for a theft of less than US $10 to 26 for causing a victim's death. Each offence could be characterized by a score based on the sum of its components. These seriousness scores could be used for estimating the total social disutility of the offences committed in a specific geographical area, or to assess the seriousness of a specific act, or of the whole criminal record of an offender.

The Sellin and Wolfgang study has been replicated in several studies which generally confirmed the original findings. (See the symposium on this subject in the *Journal of Criminal Law and Criminology*, **66**, No.2.) However, despite the accumulating confirmation, there is also a growing concern about the deficiencies of this scale and the method underlying it. One point indicated by several critiques is that the marginal improvement attained by weighting offences according to Sellin and Wolfgang's suggestion is negligible (Bloomstein, 1974). Indeed, the very fact that the category and magnitude scales were highly correlated, both in the original study and in its replications (e.g. Walker, 1978) raises the question of the necessity of using the ratio scales. Bloomstein (1974) found that the weighted sums of official crimes were highly correlated with the unweighted values published by the US Federal Bureau of Investigation. Thus, the weighting procedure was unnecessary, since it did not add any significant information to the index of crime. Wellford and Wiatrowski (1975) tried to defend the weighting scheme, arguing that it was intended for individuals rather than for aggregates. It is hard to accept this argument, first, because both Sellin and Wolfgang suggested that their seriousness weights be used for the development of more informative crime statistics. Second, one should remember that all the validations of the seriousness weights were done on the aggregate level, mostly by comparing the mean value of category scales with the means obtained from magnitude scales.

The next problematic issue is that of individual variability. As pointed out above, the high correlation between the logarithms of the magnitude scores and the category scores was always obtained for groups. Lesieur and Lehman (1975) checked this relationship for individuals and found that although the data did show the expected shape and there were similar slopes among groups, no such consistency was apparent among the individual judges. Moreover, even after the most extreme cases were excluded, the ratios between offence seriousness weights varied widely across individuals.

The prevalence of individual differences raises the issue of cultural or sub-cultural differences. As mentioned above, the similarity of results across groups is surprising. Wellford and Wiatrowski (1975), for example, replicated the study 10 years later in Florida. Despite the temporal and geographical distance, the only noteworthy difference between their results and Sellin and Wolfgang's may be explained by the steep rise in crime rates during the decade. Rossi, Waite, Bose, and Berk (1974), also found a surprising similarity across population sub-groups. Normandeau (1970) tried to show that similarity exists even across eight national cultures. His study was seriously criticized by Pease, Ireson, and Thorpe (1975) for ignoring the range of scores within each national sample and the differential meaning (or purchase power) of monetary units across countries. However, even their standardization of Normandeau's weights shows significant similarities among the eight nations represented.

Another controversial issue is the assumption of additivity of offence scores across components, acts, and offenders. This assumption is based on another assumption, that seriousness weights are a form of 'prothetic continuum'; that is to say, that this is a quantitative continuum, like height, weight, and distance, which may allow the summation of components. Steven's psycho-physical law, which is the basis for Sellin and Wolfgang's work, applies only to such prothetic scales. Other continua, such as the pitch of a sound, do not fall under this law. Rose (1966) has pointed out that the only evidence Sellin and Wolfgang had in support of this assumption was that the relationship between the category and the magnitude scales was of the kind predicted by Steven's law, *if* we assume that the category scale represents the 'real' value of seriousness. A number of studies (e.g. Pease, Ireson, and Thorpe, 1974; Wagner and Pease, 1978) have actually shown that the assumption of additivity is not valid; that is, people do not think that an offender who robs two persons is twice as bad as the other who robs only one. Gottfredson, Young and Laufer (1980) have recently found a significant interaction effect, such that the amount of monetary or property loss becomes less important when bodily injury or sexual assault are involved.

Various studies were concerned with the factors that determine the seriousness ascribed to different acts. First, there have been some methodological concerns with regard to the effect of the structure of the questionnaire and the immediate context of each item. While the first of these factors was found to be insignificant (Sheley, 1980; Walker, 1978), Sellin and Wolfgang (1964) and Parducci (1968) found that an act is perceived as more serious if the previous acts were relatively harmless (those evoking only a mild moral indignation) and vice versa.

As noted above, the cultural background of the respondent is known to have some effect upon his answers (Pease *et al.*, 1975; Rossi *et al.*, 1974). An interesting effect, which might be explained by the perceived context, was found by Figlio (1975). In this study, prisoners were more tolerant and more lenient in their assessment of offences than were delinquents who, in turn, were more tolerant than university students.

Another significant factor is criminal intent of the offender. Findings concerning this factor are conflicting. Riedel (1975) found that there is little evidence to support the hypothesis that inferences of intent alter judgment of seriousness. However, Sebba (1978) found that the presumption of intent has a considerable effect on seriousness.

The most significant factor affecting the estimated seriousness of an offence is apparently the extent of injury and loss to the victim. Thus, victimless crimes are typically considered less serious than others. Most studies found that bodily injury is considered a strong aggravating factor. Sellin and Wolfgang (1964) found that the seriousness scores are correlated with a power function of the amount of property loss to the victim. In terms of interpersonal processes, this finding means that severity is perceived as related to the loss, or disutility, experienced by the victim.

These two factors are theoretically important because they represent the two major elements of an offence: *mens rea*, or the culpable state of mind of the offender (see Chapter 5), and *actus reus*, the injurious harm-causing act. These elements have already been found to define an efficient two-dimensional space for the empirical classification of offences (Shoham, Guttman, and Rahav, 1970).

A related issue is that of the dimensionality of the classification of offences. It is usually assumed that the seriousness of offences is uni-dimensional. This assumption has not been tested, and the distinctions between bodily injury and property loss cast some doubt on it. Sherman and Dowdle (1974) asked their subjects to assess the similarity of the members of paired offences. From the similarity scores they were able to extract two dimensions for the classification of each of two subsets of offences. One dimension in each of the subsets has to do with victimization: what happens to the victim. The other dimension is not so clear: in one subset it seems to be whether the offence is openly committed; in the other subset it has to do with the motivation, or planning. In either case, seriousness is not one of the major dimensions. In an unpublished study, Rahav (1980) found that when a population sample was asked to sort offences into groups, the two major dimensions seemed to be (1) intentionality and (2) whether the victim suffers injury or loss. Seriousness emerged only as a projection, or combination of the two dimensions. Thus, it seems that the disservice to the victim, or the kind of transaction that takes place between the participants in the situation, is a major characteristic of the offence.

A classification system of resources which are involved in an interpersonal transaction has been proposed by Foa (1971). The classification, which groups, as well as differentiates, interpersonal resources in a way that reflects similarities and differences in the behaviours associated with them, is based on two characteristics or coordinates, labelled 'particularism' and 'concreteness'. Six resource classes are specified: love, status, information, money, goods and services (See Figure 13.1). 'Love' is defined as an expression of affectionate regard, warmth, or comfort; 'status' is an expression of evaluative judgment which conveys high or low prestige, regard, or esteem; 'information' includes advice, opinions, instruction, or enlightenment but excludes those behaviours which could be classed as love or status; 'money' is any coin, currency, or token which has some standard unit of exchange value; 'goods' are tangible products, objects, or materials; and 'services' involve activities on the body or belongings of a person which often constitute labour for another.

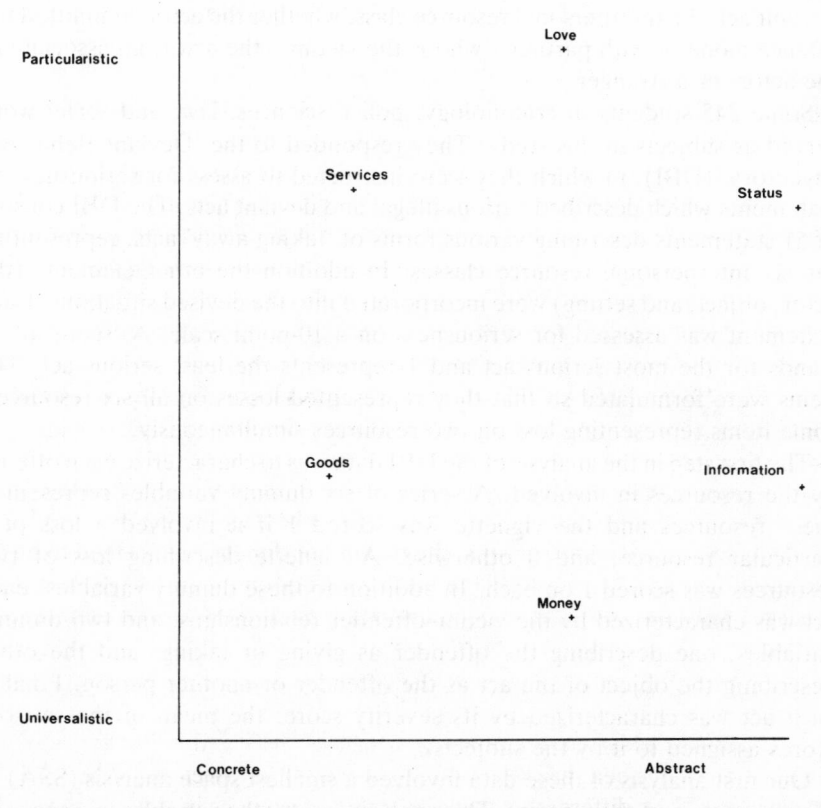

Figure 13.1 The resources in interpersonal exchange and the two major dimensions

The usefulness and applicability of this classification system to diverse problems such as aggression, urban life, racial relationships, labour disputes, etc., have been previously presented and discussed (Foa, 1971; Foa and Donnenwerth, 1971; Foa and Foa, 1972; 1974; Foa, Turner, and Foa, 1972; Teichman and Foa, 1975).

THE PRESENT STUDY

The purpose of the present study is to investigate the effects of the six resource classes upon the perceived seriousness of deviant acts. Most offences and deviant behaviours can be viewed as forms of interpersonal transaction in which one or more persons are taking away from or denying access to one or more of the resources of another person. (Victimless offences, like prostitution, may be described as people taking away from themselves.)

Based on previous studies, particularly Sellin and Wolfgang (1964), we hypothesized that the following elements affect the attributed seriousness of a deviant act: the interpersonal resource class; whether the actor committed the offence alone or with partners; who is the victim – the actor, an associate of the actor, or a stranger.

Some 245 students in criminology, police sciences, law, and social work served as subjects in this study. They responded to the 'Deviant Behaviour Inventory' (DBI), in which they were instructed to assess for seriousness 51 statements which described various illegal and deviant acts. The DBI consists of 51 statements describing various forms of 'taking away' acts, representing the six interpersonal resource classes. In addition the other elements (the actor, object, and setting) were incorporated into the devised situations. Each statement was assessed for seriousness on a 10-point scale. A 'score' of 10 stands for the most serious act and 1 represents the least serious act. The items were formulated so that they represented losses on all six resources, some items representing loss on two resources simultaneously.

The first step in the analysis of the DBI data was to characterize each offence by the resources in involved. A series of six dummy variables represented these resources and the vignette was scored 1 if it involved a loss of a particular resource, and 0 otherwise. A vignette describing loss of two resources was scored 1 on each. In addition to these dummy variables, each act was characterized by the victim–offender relationships, and two dummy variables, one describing the offender as giving or taking, and the other describing the object of the act as the offender or another person. Finally, each act was characterized by its severity score: the mean of the severity scores assigned to it by the subjects.

Our first analysis of these data involved a smallest space analysis (SSA) of the resources and the severity. This analysis locates the variables in a space so that the distances among variables are inversely related to their correlations:

the higher the correlation, the smaller the distance. (For a better description of this method see Bloombaum, 1978).

The results of this analysis are presented in Figure 13.2. This figure reveals a number of things. First, the pattern of the variables is circular. In other words, none is central to the configuration of these variables. Second, an examination of the order of the variables reveals that they reproduce almost perfectly the order suggested by the Foa model. The only exception is the interchange in the locations of 'Love' and 'Status'. As a consequence, it is easy to differentiate between particularistic resources and universalistic ones along one dimension, and between concrete and abstract ones along the other. Finally, it is interesting to note that the 'severity' variable is located in the concrete–universal quadrant of the two-dimensional space.

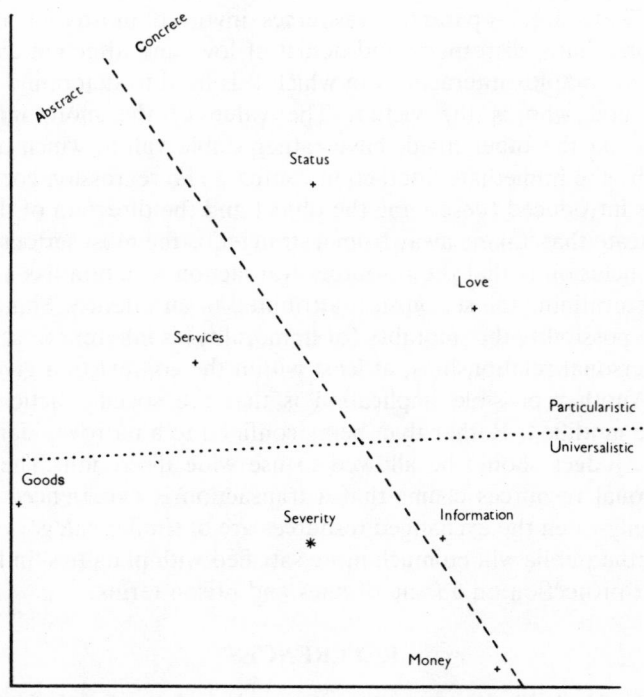

Figure 13.2   A two-dimensional projection of the smallest space analysis

A second mode of analysis was multiple regression with severity as the dependent variable. The regression was run in two steps. First, severity was estimated from the six resource classes. It turned out that the resources alone explained 18% of the variance in seriousness scores. In the second step five terms, describing the offences as acts of giving or taking as well as the object (the offender, an associate, or a stranger), were introduced. The addition of these terms to the regression raised the multiple correlation coefficient, with 40% of the variance being explained. This finding means that while the resource classes may serve as predictors of seriousness, they acquire their full meaning only when the object and direction of the transaction are known. That is to say, the severity of an offence is a function of its elementary descriptors: who takes (or gives) what, from whom?

An examination of the standardized regression coefficients revealed that the more concrete and relatively universalistic resources had the strongest effect (information, money, goods, and services). This corroborates what we have already found by means of the SSA. 'Love' and 'Status' have negative effects. These are, apparently, resources involved mostly in affectionate interactions; hate, disrespect, and denial of love and affection are typically involved in complex interactions in which it is hard to determine who is the offender and who is the victim. The value of the more universalistic resources, on the other hand, have rather stable values which are far less affected by the immediate interaction context. The regression coefficients of the terms introduced (describing the object and the direction of the transaction) indicate that 'taking away from a stranger' is the most serious situation.

Our conclusion is that the resources transaction situation has a significant role in determining the seriousness attributed to an offence. This conclusion raises the possibility that morality (or immorality) is inherent to certain types of interpersonal relationships, at least within the context of a given cultural milieu. Another possible implication is that the social reaction to crime should be modified. Rather than being confined to a narrowly defined set of penalties, judges should be allowed to use wide discretion. The theory of interpersonal resources claims that a transaction is experienced as accomplished only when the exchanged resources are of similar categories. If this is the case, the public will be much more satisfied with penalties 'in kind', than with their projection on a scale of fines and prison terms.

REFERENCES

BLOOMBAUM, M. (1970). Doing smallest space analysis. *Journal of Conflict Resolution*, **14**, 409–416.

BLOOMSTEIN, A, (1974). Seriousness weights in an index of crime. *American Sociological Review*, **39**, 853–864.

COOMBS, C. H. (1966). Thurstone's measurements of social values revisited forty years later. *Journal of Personality and Social Psychology*, **6**, 85–91.

Durea, M. A. (1933). An experimental study of attitudes toward juvenile delinquency. *Journal of Applied Psychology*, **17**, 522–534.

Figlio, R. M. (1975). The seriousness of offenses: an evaluation by offenders and non-offenders. *Journal of Criminal Law and Criminology*, **66**, 189–200.

Foa, U. G. (1971). Interpersonal and economic resources. *Science*, **171**, 345–351.

Foa, U. G., and Donnenwerth, G.V. (1971). Love poverty in modern culture and sensitivity training. *Sociological Inquiry*, **41**, 149–159.

Foa, U. G., and Foa, E. B. (1972). Resource exchange: toward a structural theory of interpersonal communication. In A.W. Siegman and B. Hope (Eds), *Studies in Dyadic Communication.*New York: Pergamon Press.

Foa, U. G., and Foa, E.B. (1974). *Societal Structure of the Mind.* Springfield, Ill.: Charles C. Thomas.

Foa, E. B., Turner, J. L., and Foa, U. G. (1972). Response generalization to aggression. *Human Relations*, **25**, 337–350.

Gottfredson, S. D., Young, K. L., and Laufer, W. S. (1980). Additivity and interactions in offense seriousness scales. *Journal of Research in Crime and Delinquency*, **17**, 26–41.

Krus, D. J., Sherman, J. L., and Krus, P. H. (1977). Changing values over the last half century: the story of Thurstone's crime scales. *Psychological Reports*, **40**, 207–211.

Lesieur, H. R., and Lehman, R. M. (1975). Remeasuring delinquency: a replication and critique. *British Journal of Criminology*, **15**, 69–80.

Normandeau, A. (1970). A comparative study of the weighted crime indices for eight countries. *International Criminal Police Review*, **25**, 15–18.

Parducci, A. (1968). The relativism of absolute judgments. *Scientific American*, **219**, 84–90.

Pease, K., Ireson, J., and Thorpe, J. (1974). Additivity assumption in the measurement of delinquency. *British Journal of Criminology*, **14**, 256–263.

Pease, K., Ireson, J., and Thorpe, J. (1975). Modified crime indices for eight countries. *Journal of Criminal Law and Criminology*, **66**, 209–214.

Rahav, G. (1980). The measurement of crime and delinquency: advances and problems. A paper delivered at the Annual Meeting of the Israeli Society of Criminology.

Riedel, M. (1975). Perceived circumstances, inferences of intent and judgments of offense seriousness. *Journal of Criminal Law and Criminology*, **66**, 201–208.

Rose, G. N. G. (1966). Concerning the measurement of delinquency. *British Journal of Criminology*, **6**, 414–418.

Rossi, P. H., Waite, E., Bose, C. E., and Berk, R. E. (1974). The seriousness of crimes: normative structure and individual differences. *American Sociological Review*, **39**, 224–265.

Sebba L. (1978). Explorations in the scaling of penalties. *Journal of Research in Crime and Delinquency*, **15**, 247–265.

Sellin, T., and Wolfgang, M. E. (1964). *The Measurement of Delinquency.* New York: Wiley.

Sheley, J. F. (1980). Crime seriousness ratings: the impact of survey questionnaire form and item context. *British Journal of Criminology*, **20**, 123–135.

Sherman, R. C., and Dowdle, M. D. (1974). The perception of crime and punishment: a multidimensional scaling analysis. *Social Science Research*, **3**, 109–126.

Shoham, S., Guttman, L., and Rahav, G. (1970). A two-dimensional space for classifying legal offences. *Journal of Research in Crime and Delinquency*, **7**, 219–243.

TEICHMAN, M., and FOA, U. G. (1975). Effect of resources similarity on satisfaction with exchange. *Social Behavior and Personality,* **3**, 213–224.

THURSTONE, L. L. (1927). The method of paired comparisons for social values. *Journal of Abnormal and Social Psychology,* **21**, 384–400.

WAGNER, H., and PEASE, K. (1978). On adding up scores of offence seriousness. *British Journal of Criminology,* **18**, 175–178.

WALKER, M. A. (1978). Measuring the seriousness of crimes. *British Journal of Criminology,* **18**, 348–364.

WELLFORD, C. F., and WIATROWSKI, M. (1975). On the measurement of delinquency. *Journal of Criminal Law and Criminology,* **66**, 175–188.

Psychology and Law
Edited by D.J. Müller, D.E. Blackman, and A.J. Chapman
© 1984 John Wiley & Sons Ltd

Chapter 14

Explaining Commercial Credit Fraud

Michael Levi

The history of psychological explanations of criminality has not been an altogether happy one, inviting as it does the allegation that they utilize stereotypical explanatory models which regard 'criminality' and 'non-criminality' as discrete and internally homogeneous traits rather than as extremes on a series of disparate continua. Even the more recent developments in sociobiology and in learning theory (see Sapsford, 1981) tend to present one-dimensional portraits of the causation of 'criminality', neglecting the important fact that in most spheres of their lives, the great majority of petty, persistent and intermittent criminals are conformist (Matza, 1969).

It would be excessively dogmatic (and false) to argue that behaviourism or sociobiology has no explanatory power in relation to *some* forms of criminality. However, if these theoretical frameworks are to be put forward as explanations for criminality *in general*, they must be tested against all types of criminal behaviour, rather than against the violent and petty, persistent offenders who form the principal targets of research and social concern, as well as the prisons of the state. This chapter examines the motivations of a set of people who have engaged in a form of commercial criminality known as long-firm fraud. A long-firm fraud is a business which orders substantial quantities of goods on credit at a time when the owners of the business either intend not to pay for them or suspect that, *as things stand at present*, they may not be *able* to pay for them. It will be argued that at least for this type of crime, a crucial role is played by verbalization and by socially structured definitions of the situation.

The basis for the sociological conception of motive is to be found in the work of Mills (1940) and Cressey (1962), who argue that motives are not biological drives which 'cause' us to act in certain ways but rather are the words and concepts with which people interpret the meaning of their desires and actions (see also Taylor, 1979). The basic idea is that language is the means by which actors and their audiences are able to assess whether or not a given action is 'deviant', 'conforming', or 'ambiguous'. Other members of society may not honour one's account of one's motives, but that is a separate matter. The principal point is that by depicting our actions to ourselves (whether self-consciously or not) in a favourable light, we are able to redefine 'what might be considered as crime' as either 'no crime' or 'justifiable crime'. This is true irrespective of whether or not we would feel guilty if we *did* define our actions as criminal. By formulating the framework in this way, we are able to divorce the discussion of vocabularies of motive from that of guilt neutralization. We thus side-step the question of whether or not delinquents feel latent guilt, a question that in any event only arises if actors perceive that they are breaking a social or legal rule (which, I argue, is not necessarily the case in frauds).

Cressey (1953, 1965), Ditton (1977), Gerth and Mills (1954), Henry (1978), and Mills (1940) argue that vocabularies of motive are related to general cultural themes which are regarded (at least by the actors themselves) as *justifying* criminal behaviour in certain contexts. They are not just the bizarre *ex post facto* rationalizations of a few distorted intellects. For example, those who conspire unlawfully to fix prices may define this to themselves as seeking to 'stabilize the market' in the long-term interest of the nation. Embezzlers may say that they are only going to use the money temporarily, so they are 'borrowing, not stealing'.

Unfortunately, it is far from clear why some people and not others define their situations in such a way that they turn to law-breaking: a point that is made continually by those who observe that poverty in the 1930s did not 'cause' people to riot as they did in Britain in 1981 (and in the USA in the 1960s). Moreover, there are difficulties in ascertaining the stage at which these verbalizations occur to actors. Unless one does contemporaneous observational work, there is no way of knowing whether reports of motivational accounts are accurate or are lies or are honest but unconscious rationalizations (see Levi, 1981, Appendix A).

Whether or not these issues can be resolved, the study of vocabularies of motive does illuminate criminal behaviour, not least by emphasizing the moral and linguistic links between 'crime' and 'normal behaviour'. One of the best illustrations of this is Cressey's study of the social psychology of embezzlement, which observes that

'Trusted persons become trust violators when they conceive of themselves as having a financial problem which is non-shareable, are aware that this problem can be secretly resolved by violation of the position of financial trust, and are able to apply to their own conduct in that situation verbalizations which enable them to adjust their conceptions of themselves as trusted persons with their conceptions of themselves as users of the entrusted funds or property' (Cressey, 1953, p.30).

If one takes as one's model of human action the non-deterministic one of man as 'self-monitoring agent' (Harré and Secord, 1972), then it is unimportant that one cannot predict trust violation until *after* someone has defined the situation as appropriate for embezzlement, for prediction ceases to become anything more than probabilistic *in principle*. However, the inability to predict does leave us with a gap in what we might *like* to know about why people commit crimes. In particular, we do not know what part 'reflexivity' or active self-awareness plays in the adoption of particular motivational accounts by social actors: somehow, these verbalizations 'just arrive' out of the stock of context-related motives which are on offer in the individual's subculture or in society as a whole at any given historical period.

Bearing in mind these important theoretical difficulties, let us turn to examine the motives of long-firm fraudsters, based on extensive interviewing of convicted and unconvicted fraudsters, both inside and outside prison (see Levi, 1981). I have identified three principal sub-types of long-firm fraud:

(1) *Slippery-slope frauds* occur when those involved in business continue to trade and to obtain goods on credit although there is a high risk that unless their business situation improves greatly, they will be unable to pay for the goods.

(2) *Intermediate frauds* occur when people decide to turn a formerly legitimate business into one which defrauds its creditors.

(3) *Pre-planned frauds* are businesses set up with the intention from the very beginning of defrauding creditors.

Altogether I interviewed nine fraudsters in prison, in two- to three-hour sessions in sight but out of hearing of the prison officers. Having first obtained permission for the interview, I assured the fraudsters that anything they told me would not be attributed to them by name. To guard against any clear tendency to 'second-guess' my desired responses, I told them that unfortunately I was not in any position of influence to help them with parole or with any aspect of their in-prison life: I merely wanted to hear their side of how they saw their work, how they had learned their craft, and why they had chosen this line of activity rather than some other criminal or non-criminal way of making a living. (Conversations did in fact range more broadly than this.) I deliberately chose some minor fraudsters, but most were rated by the police as being towards the top of their 'profession' and had been engaged in major fraud for many years. I became very friendly with one man in particular, and kept up our friendship for several years subsequent to his release. I also talked to several unconvicted people who had been involved directly and indirectly with long-firm fraud, who were introduced to me by businesspeople I had got to know socially, as well as to police officers, lawyers, credit controllers, and others who were involved in the control of fraud. All of these interviews were loosely structured around themes relating to the social and technical organization of fraud, as well as (more indirectly) around their personal reasons for participation.

In reality, it is often difficult to tell whether or not a long-firm was planned as such from the outset. However, that need not concern us here. What is significant is that long-firm fraudsters come from more varied backgrounds than the typical property criminals who come before the courts. They include those in business who have never before committed any substantial property crime as adults (save perhaps tax evasion); those who have intermittently run legitimate businesses as well as frauds (whether simultaneously or consecutively); people who make their living principally from fraud; and people, from small-time 'thieves' to major 'gangsters', who also participate in crime other than fraud.

THE MOTIVES AND CAREERS OF LONG-FIRM FRAUDSTERS

Unlike street criminality, there has been no real attempt to explain business criminality in terms of psychopathology. Eysenck (1977), for example, observes that confidence men are not extrovert neurotics, a fact which is dismissed as explicable because their craft requires normal social relationships. On the assumption that criminology theories ought to seek to build dynamic models which incorporate the way criminality develops over time, we might usefully employ Becker's suggestion (Becker, 1963, p. 23) that we examine separately the processes of (1) how people find themselves in a position to commit crime; (2) how and why they decide to do so; and (3) why they decide to continue or to stop committing crimes. In applying this mode of analysis to long-firm frauds, we must examine the organization of knowledge, opportunity, and social definitions with respect to them.

Knowledge about long firms is obtainable from the underworld, from business associates, and by introspection. These sources are susceptible to changes in the wider society. For instance, the sending to prison of an increasing number of fraudsters during the 1960s may have served to disseminate techniques of fraud (and even the idea of committing it) through the 'alternative old boy network' of convicts; a similar result may be produced by increases in the social mixing of upperworld and underworld in casinos and night clubs. As social barriers become based more on plutocratic than on aristrocratic principles, formal and informal barriers to entry into some kinds of fraud diminish, although intending long-firm fraudsters still require finance to set up the fraud and contacts to dispose of the goods. Even then, however, the equality of opportunity is not unbounded: unless they undergo a period of training as a 'front man' in a fraud, the more proletarian members of the 'underworld' or street culture may not possess the confidence or the flair for commercial life that is required of the competent fraudster. These inhibiting factors should not be underrated. (They may also affect the participation of women in long-firm fraud, since historically, with few exceptions, women do not appear to have been involved either in legitimate or illegitimate sectors of the wholesale trades where those frauds tend to occur.)

Long-firm fraud need not arise from social learning. Like embezzlement (Cressey, 1953) and black marketeering (Clinard, 1952), it can occur as a result of creative introspection. A major 'background operator' expressed the issue to me thus:

> 'What you've got to realize is that in order to be a 'bad' businessman you've got to be a good businessman. The point is that I know what I am doing. I know how to screw someone down while I'm buying and I know where to go for the best price when I'm selling. I'm not one of these gangsters who run an l.f. [long-firm] like it was a toy they had just learned to play with. I'm a businessman, not a thief.'

For non-businesspeople, both knowledge and opportunity may be very restricted. However, almost any trader could carry out a long-firm fraud should he or she desire to do so. It follows, therefore, that any adequate explanation of fraud must also address the issue of why more traders do not engage in long-firm fraud.

THE 'SLIPPERY-SLOPERS'

'Slippery-slope' fraudsters may order goods on credit although they know that as things stand they will be unable to pay for them when their credit period elapses. However, businesspeople genuinely believe and expect that in the interval between the ordering of the goods and the last possible moment for payment, their business cash-flow will have improved sufficiently for them to pay all the bills and continue trading. They make specific false statements to their creditors, such as 'I'll put a cheque in the post tonight', or they may leave a necessary signature off a cheque or put on it non-matching words and figures, in the knowledge that their bank will not pay, thus giving them time. They may even sell some of their goods below cost price in order to get immediate cash. However, when placed in the context of commercial customs and practice, both the immorality and criminality of such conduct are in doubt.

The 'slippery-slopers' are able to make use of what Sykes and Matza (1957) call 'denial of injury'. They believe that no *real* wrong will be caused by their actions: *when* their business recovers, they will repay their creditors, who will be better off than they would have been had they declared insolvency and ceased trading immediately. The fact that they have traded legitimately for some time prior to their lie-telling means that dishonesty is not regarded as a 'master-status' in their character assessment. Indeed, the perception that entry into the 'crime-prone' situation was *not* prompted by dishonest motives is crucial to the way the actions are likely to be defined by policing agencies, juries, and sentencers, as well as by the business person who is being called to account. In a long-firm fraud, evidently, one *can* be 'a little bit pregnant'! 'Slippery-slopers' are able to legitimate their course of conduct by stressing their overall role legitimacy as businesspeople.

It is a criminal offence to continue to incur debts recklessly, that is, neither knowing nor caring whether the debts will be repaid. However, in the abstract, the businessperson *does* care. It is in the context of working and surviving under pressure of living from hand to mouth that many such businesspeople do not perceive themselves as 'putting their creditors as risk'. Furthermore, the individual may carry on as normal, taking out the same money weekly and juggling to pay the most pressing creditors. There is no clear perceptual break between the 'slippery-slopers' and others whose businesses fail or succeed after similar risk-taking behaviour. For 'doing deals' is part of the normal trading ethic. Looked at in this way, the search for early background predictors of commercial deviance seems unlikely to bear fruit. Moreover, given that 'dishonesty' is an essential element in fraud, in what sense can we differentiate the 'slippery-slopers' morally from the businessperson who had traded whilst insolvent but who is lucky or skilful enough to make it back to solvency? We must be careful to define conceptually our universe of 'criminals'.

'INTERMEDIATE' FRAUDSTERS

Most people who go into business on their own account do so in the belief that by owning and running their own business, they can acquire wealth, prestige, and autonomy. They are socialized into a 'normal' orientation towards making profits by buying cheap and selling dear. Occasionally, during the ordinary course of business, someone may be given the opportunity to buy goods particularly cheaply. Provided that little or no risk is believed to be attached to the transaction – either materially, in terms of the perceived chances of criminal prosecution for handling stolen goods, or else psychologically, in terms of one's self-image as a 'respectable person' – the transaction may be entered into. People in business find the purchase of goods from long-firm fraud to be morally and legally relatively safe: morally, because they are buying from 'a businessperson' not from 'a thief'; legally, because the long-firm merchant can transfer title lawfully, and because the purchaser can issue a cheque for the full market value of the goods, getting a kick-back in cash to represent the unofficial 'discount'. This makes the offence of handling stolen goods difficult to prove in long-firm cases.

Sometimes, the purchasers of long-firm goods (or any others in business) may go further. They may feel that they are not getting as much as they require from their businesses, that others of no greater merit are doing better than they, or they may believe that they are going 'bust' anyway. Their sense of commitment to the legal order weakened by these sentiments (and life-problems), they may turn their minds to means of improving their lot. Businesspeople contemplating turning their (relatively) straight business into a long-firm fraud may justify this decision by appealing to higher loyalties (such as the need to support their families). My interviews with fraudsters have led me to regard these justifications as guiltless, rather than apologetic motivational accounts. Unlike the typical burglar, the 'fraudster' has had a prior economic relationship with the victim; from such the victim has benefited, and this makes it particularly easy to take the view that, when considered as a whole, the conduct is morally neutral.

'PRE-PLANNED' LONG-FIRM FRAUDSTERS

Unlike 'intermediate' and 'slippery-slope' fraudsters, the criminal motivations of 'pre-planned' long-firm merchants *precede* the formation of their businesses. However, those whom I interviewed did not appear to view their behaviour as morally problematic. The reason for this was the rather jaundiced view they took of 'legitimate business'. Essentially, they regarded themselves as no different from any successful self-made men, all of whom had committed crimes in the running of their present businesses or had done so on the way to the top. One professional organizer said, 'First, you want to get on. Then, you want honours. And finally, you want to become honest.'

Whereas the 'intermediates' and the 'slippery-slopers' accord legitimacy to the public norms of capitalism, the 'pre-planned' fraudsters treat with cynicism the notion that commercial success is or can be achieved by law-abiding industry. Life is a rat-race in which they are less fortunately placed than others, and their aim is to remedy this by making enough money to be able to afford to be honest. However, the initial motives which lead people to engage in fraud may alter as a result of their experiences. What started out as a banal way of supplementing one's income may become a grand obsession in which the individual comes to require a psychological 'high' from deception. The very risk that this brings for one's social identity as 'respectable' gives added piquancy to the experience, as it does in espionage. And as a result of mixing with 'the chaps' (the underworld), the fraudster may be introduced to a range of novel human experiences, in the areas of sex and gambling, which in the case of men, who are the overwhelming majority, may induce him to discard his dull, workaday self and become a swinger with a taste for 'the good life'. It is so tempting to save from the *next* long-firm!

It would be false to suggest that all first-time fraudsters become enmeshed in a career of fraud. A good many do settle down and, as far as one knows, never return to fraud. However, just as the professional burglar may find it difficult to walk down the street without automatically 'casing' the houses and the shops for potential 'scores', so too is it difficult *not* to think of 'pulling strokes' when one has become skilful at getting goods on credit and disposing of them without paying creditors. The psychological task becomes harder still when former 'colleagues' approach one with tempting suggestions or when one's legitimate business begins to falter. However, if they do not develop the ability to switch off when faced with the opportunity of taking short cuts, they may end their lives as professional fraudsters. The age restrictions on participation in fraud are less pronounced than in other forms of crime, and there have been people who have carried out long-firm frauds while well into their seventh decade.

Labelling theorists emphasize that social control leads to increased deviance by closing off options for rehabilitation to offenders. By contrast, in stressing the economic rationality of motivation for career fraud, the implication is that one would expect the attractiveness of long-firm fraud to *diminish* as social control increased. If the police and allied agencies did not intervene, the long-firm fraudster's only motivation for reform would be the desire for social respectability. And if there were few controls, their social respectability would not be prejudiced unduly by their fraudulent activities! However, there are some aspects of social control which *may* provoke further deviance. First, though I am not recommending solitary confinement or incarceration of fraudsters, imprisoning them can perhaps spread techniques of fraud to members of the underworld who might not otherwise have turned to fraud. And, second, the fact that credit controllers are unwilling to grant credit to known fraudsters forces the latter to employ nominees or 'front men' if they wish to remain in business. Their inability to appear at the business premises in person, combined with the fact that many such 'front men' are not, to put it mildly, 'out of the top drawer', are the basic ingredients of commercial disaster. The fraudsters' problem is that they have been literally dis-credited: experience has shown that one cannot take their surface appearance for what 'they' 'are'. In short, for those fraudsters who *wish* to go straight but who wish to run their own businesses, the organization of social control presents obstacles of a kind which may produce self-fulfilling prophecies. This is an irony which is present throughout crime control (see Erikson, 1964, pp. 15–17).

However, in spite of all these obstacles, like most criminals, nearly all fraudsters give up crime *eventually*, and when they do, they often become straighter than straight. This may be the result of the fact that they remain, in a psychological sense, 'secondary deviants': their heightened awareness of fraud makes the slightest straying from the public norms of capitalism seem like the beginning of the 'slippery-slope' to fraud. Some of them make enough money to be able to retire from fraud completely, a source of dismay to those who had come to rely on them for financing or 'fencing' goods from long firms. Some fade into decent obscurity as the owners of small businesses.

Others go deeper into 'the underworld' and engage in activities such as smuggling gold bullion, passing counterfeit currency, financing lorry hijackings, 'car ringing', international banking frauds involving phoney bills of exchange, and organizing armed robbery. Still others have remained in the twilight world of business, counterfeiting household products or setting up 'offshore investments'. Finally, there are those who ritualistically stick to the trade they know best: long-firm fraud (see Levi, 1981).

Some go into an only partial retirement, returning to long-firm frauds when business is bad or when they become bored with the humdrum routine of small business life. However, I have noted few moral qualms about long-firm fraud among those I have interviewed. This ease of mind is not, in my opinion, merely superficial. To the long-firm merchants I know, their criminality is just one way among others of making a living, neither more nor less immoral than the great majority of lawful (or undetected) commercial activities. Like other ways of making money, long-firm frauds have their peculiar advantages and disadvantages. Among the disadvantages is the fact that fraud is a very high-stress occupation: one's so-called partners may operate on the principle 'Do your friends first, they're easier', and the slightest operational error can lead to an appearance in court.

CONCLUSION: IMPLICATIONS FOR THE CONTROL OF FRAUD

The control of fraud has two principal aspects: (1) people may be prevented from putting into effect their desires to defraud; and (2) people may not *seek* to defraud suppliers of their goods. These dimensions may feed back into one another, for compliance with the law may be a consequence of the perception that lawbreaking will prove unsuccessful. Yet whereas the first dimension is a direct function of the active social control exercised by credit controllers and by police agencies, the second relates to social control in a much wider sense.

There are three main ways in which, in this broad sense, long-firm fraud may be prevented: (1) by socializing people so well that they have no *desire* to defraud; (2) by providing sufficient life-opportunities so that people will not be tempted to resort to fraud by their feelings of 'relative deprivation'; and (3) by giving people a strong and organized system of social control, thereby inducing them to desist from acting upon desires to defraud if and when they experience them. For a more extensive discussion of the problems involved in controlling fraud see Leigh (1982) and Levi (1981, 1983).

Capitalist societies encourage a form of egotistic morality and provide insufficient levels of social opportunity and economic prosperity to generate conditions (1) and (2), though most traders are kept more or less on the 'straight and narrow' by the material and prestige positive reinforcements they receive while so doing. In the final analysis, then, society has to fall back upon (3), or *active* deterrence, which relates to the costs and benefits of different forms of criminal action as perceived by different individuals, and as weighted in terms of the things they value at any given moment.

Apart from opportunity factors, the important influences here are the estimated chances of conviction (and its consequences) and the relatively autonomous sense of right and wrong (affected by socialization). I would not suggest that business people as a whole, or even long-firm fraudsters in particular, are brought up to approve of fraud (though the borderline between 'smart' business and fraud may be a fine one, and behaviourists might question what would happen to the £4000 million lost annually through tax evasion if more middle-class children received avoidance learning in this sphere!). Rather, fraud is not a topic that crops up frequently in discussions of crime and morality in the home, particularly in the early years of life, and this leaves many business people in a state of what one might term 'moral neutrality' towards some fraudulent practices, though not necessarily towards swindling pensioners of their life savings. In other words, for the average businessperson, the morality or even the idea of fraud is not a *gestalt*, a fact that might even reduce fraud, for it may not occur to some temptation-prone businesspeople to commit it.

The low profile of fraud is encouraged by a relative lack of media outcry (though less so today than in the past), a fact that is important because the media are a major source of generalized social sentiment. Moreover, objectively, the amount of policing resources devoted to fraud is trivial, despite the fact that, during 1980, the Metropolitan Police Fraud Squad alone dealt with £400 million in fraud, compared with losses from theft, burglary, and robbery of £550 million for the whole of England and Wales, and despite the fact that fraud is rated more seriously than any other non-violent property crime by the general public in London, Cardiff, Greater Manchester, and Devon and Cornwall (Levi, 1983). And even the minority of frauds that *are* reported to the police or Department of Trade and are 'cleared-up' have a good chance of escaping as a result of prosecutorial discretion, encouraged by the unpredictability of the ordinary juries who try complex frauds (Leigh, 1982; Levi, 1981).

In short, the concatenation of moral neutrality and low risks of detection, prosecution, and imprisonment is conducive to a state of commercial sociopathy. If the chances of conviction were increased considerably, then pre-planned and intermediate fraudsters would be more likely to be deterred. However, it is moot whether any such increase would affect 'slippery-slope' fraud, because individuals become so immersed in the game of staying afloat that broader considerations of whether or not they are continuing to incur debts whilst insolvent may not occur to them consciously. Hence, even if they know that certain detection and heavy sanctions would result from 'naughty' behaviour, they would not perceive the relevance of such sanctions to their own conduct. The only prospects for reducing slippery-slope conduct, then, are to socialize business people in such a way that they are consciously concerned about whether or not they are putting the money of others into jeopardy. That would require a society somewhat different from that of the present, and, even then, the ingenuity exercised by human actors in the verbalization process can be expected to produce 'techniques of neutralization' which would defeat the general moral precepts. Aubert has argued that

'One main obstacle to the development of a fruitful theoretical orientation is to be found in the tendency of treating criminal behavior, on the one hand, and the system of criminal sanctions, on the other, as two separate problems. In our opinion, crime and punishment are most fruitfully handled as two aspects of a group process or two links in a specific type of social interaction (Aubert, 1977, p. 168).

It is hoped that this study of the interaction between language, socialization, and the formal social control process has demonstrated the value of that perspective.

REFERENCES

AUBERT, W. (1977). White-collar crime and social structure. In G. Geis and R. Meier (Eds), *White-Collar Crime*. New York: Free Press.
BECKER, H. (1963). *Outsiders*. New York: Free Press.
CLINARD, M. (1952). *The Black Market*. New York: Holt, Rinehart and Winston.
CRESSEY, D. R. (1953). *Other People's Money*. Glencoe, N.Y.: Free Press.
CRESSEY, D. R. (1962). Role theory, differential association, and compulsive crimes. In A. Rose (Ed), *Human Behavior and Social Processes*. N.Y.: Houghton Miflin.
CRESSEY, D. R. (1965). The respectable criminal. In J. Short (Ed), *Modern Criminals*. New York: Transaction-Aldine.
DITTON, J. (1977). *Part-time Crime*. London: Macmillan.
ERIKSON, K. (1964). Notes on the sociology of deviance. In H. Becker (Ed), *The Other Side*. Glencoe, N.Y.: Free Press.
EYSENCK, H. J. (1977). *Crime and Personality*. London: Paladin.
GERTH, H., and MILLS, C. W. (1954). *Character and Social Structure*. London: Routledge and Kegan Paul.
HARRÉ, R., and SECORD, P. (1972). *The Explanation of Social Behaviour*. Oxford: Basil Blackwell.
HENRY, S. (1978). *The Hidden Economy*. Oxford: Martin Robertson.
LEIGH, L. H. (1982). *The Control of Commercial Fraud*. London: Heinemann.
LEVI, M. (1981). *The Phantom Capitalists: The Organization and Control of Long-Firm Fraud*. London: Heinemann.
LEVI, M. (1983). Controlling company fraud. *The Company Lawyer*, Spring 1983.
MATZA, D. (1969). *Becoming Deviant*. Englewood Cliffs, N. J.: Prentice Hall.
MILLS, C. W. (1940). Situated actions and vocabularies of motive. *American Sociological Review*, 5, 904–913.
SAPSFORD, R. J. (1981). Individual deviance: the search for the criminal personality. In M. Fitzgerald, G. McLennan, and J. Pawson (Eds), *Crime and Society*. London: Routledge and Kegan Paul.

SYKES, G. and MATZA, D. (1957). Techniques of neutralization: a theory of delinquency. *American Sociological Review*, **22**, 664–670.
TAYLOR, L. (1979). Vocabularies, rhetorics, and grammar: problems in the sociology of motivation. In D. Downes and P. Rock (Eds), *Deviant Interpretations*. Oxford: Martin Robertson.

Psychology and Law
Edited by D.J. Müller, D.E. Blackman, and A.J. Chapman
© 1984 John Wiley & Sons Ltd

Chapter 15

Crime Prevention: Practice and Motivation

Ken Pease and Roger Litton

Crime is a type of behaviour. More exactly it comprises a range of behaviours, from soliciting for the purposes of prostitution to murder, from evading a bus fare to large-scale fraud. The range of behaviours is united only by being disapproved of enough to be criminalized. A complex set of interlocking instruments of the state has arisen, having as its major elements police, court, probation and prison services. This set of instruments, known collectively as the criminal justice system, has as a major policy objective the reduction of the incidence of crime through the deterrent, containment, and rehabilitative effect of the criminal justice system (Home Office, 1977). However, the disincentives offered to potential criminals by the criminal justice system may or may not be powerful in relation to other incentives and disincentives to which they may be subject. The purpose of this chapter is to contrast briefly the achievements of crime control through the criminal justice system with crime control achieved, or potentially achievable, through other means, and to speculate on the ways in which public policy may be mobilized in the future for the purpose of crime control. What does the psychologist bring to this enterprise that is distinctive? Perhaps nothing; perhaps the legacy of half a century of work derived from Thorndike's law of effect, which allows a more complete and dispassionate consideration of possible reinforcers than do other discipline bases.

Of the three mechanisms mentioned above whereby crime prevention may occur, deterrence is the first. The police are generally regarded as central in this deterrence process (see, for example, Vader, 1978), yet a recent review of the police role as a deterrent concludes:

'The problem for deterrent policing is that while it is almost certainly true that the existence of the police leads to a reduction in crime, there is no obvious way by which the police effect on crime can be increased. Once the threshold level has been reached, even the most substantial increase in police activity appears to be accompanied by only marginal gains in crime control. To take the example of patrolling – the backbone of routine police work – the best to be hoped for from a large increase in patrol strength (i.e. saturation policing) is that under certain conditions, slight reductions in some aspects of crime taking place in particular places may occur. This is a gloomy prediction but one amply supported by the research evidence' (Heal, 1982, p. 3).

The reason for this is that crime is still a rare event relative to the number of occasions on which it could occur, and much crime takes place in private, where no conceivable patrolling strategy could help (Hough and Clarke, 1980). Additionally, victims often do not directly report crime, so reducing the possibility of apprehension of the offender by the police (Pate, Ferrera, Bowers, and Lawrence, 1976). The picture concerning the effects of other agencies in the criminal justice system in dissuading potential offenders is similarly gloomy: 'Criminologists now seem to be reaching agreement that the scope is limited for improving the system's effectiveness; in particular ... there is considerable doubt about the reductions in crime to be achieved by alternatives in policing or by sentences intended to deter, contain or rehabilitate convicted offenders' (Clarke, 1981, p. 14). Note that Clarke is *not* saying that crime levels are independent of policing or sentencing, merely that crime levels are not sensitive to realistic changes, above a certain threshold level, in policing or sentencing levels. One can make a homely comparison. A car's top speed is only marginally affected by the level of petrol in the tank. However, the folly of concluding that petrol was irrelevant to performance would fairly soon become evident. Similarly, although the effect on crime of realistically conceivable states of the criminal justice system is marginal, the absence of such a system may have dramatic effects. Limited evidence of such effects can be derived from an analysis of police strikes (Meyer, 1976; Reynolds and Judge, 1968).

In short, the research evidence from both sides of the Atlantic suggests that conventional attempts to change the level of crime by changing the disincentives for an offender through the criminal justice system may be less than fruitful in reducing levels of recorded crime. This is a very important conclusion to reach in such cavalier fashion. However, the evidence is substantial and the reader is referred to Clarke (1981) for a masterly and brief review of it. Since the point is only one step in the argument being advanced in this chapter, it cannot be afforded more space here.

SOCIAL FACTORS AS PREDICTORS OF CRIME

Turning to factors outside the criminal justice system, what is the evidence that crime may be responsive to such factors? Levels of recorded crime are associated with other social indices. Brenner (1976a) related known crime statistics for the USA, Canada, England, Wales, and Scotland over a 70 year period to unemployment, gross national product per head, and inflation. He concluded:

'The overall relationships between instabilities in the economy and the major sources of criminal statistics show remarkable correspondence. In general, the rate of unemployment (or declines in employment and in personal income) shows significant and strong relationships to increases in trends of criminal statistical data, for all major categories of crime and sources of criminal statistics' (Brenner, 1976a, p. 42).

Considering the effects of the three economic indicators yields the conclusion that:

'Each one of the three by itself exerts a measurable and statistically significant impact on the criminal data. The combined effect of these three indicators is such that for a great many categories of crime, more than 90% of the variation in trends in criminal statistics can be accounted for' (Brenner 1976a, p. 50).

Brenner (1976b) later showed that the slope of the relationship was such that, for example, a 1% increase in unemployment would be associated with a 5.7% increase in murders. Brenner's work, and that of others like Phillips, Votey, and Maxwell (1972), and Vinson and Hommel (1975), suggests a statistical relationship between unemployment and crime. A study in Northern Ireland (Mulligan, 1982) shows the relationship at an individual level, namely that the commission of crimes could be seen to be more frequent (or in some cases only to occur at all) during periods of joblessness. This information is of particular value because it bypasses many of the criticisms of inferring a relationship from statistical associations between social variables. Specifically, the ecological fallacy is not a possible criticism of Mulligan's data. The ecological fallacy occurs when someone concludes, for example, that differences in murder rates between areas with many Blacks and areas with few Blacks demonstrate the propensity of black people to kill. If areas with many Blacks have high murder rates, it remains possible that all murders are committed by Whites. Conversely, if areas with few Blacks have low murder rates, it remains possible that all murders are committed by Blacks. *Mutatis mutandis,* Brenner's data do not exclude the possibility that most crime is committed by those in employment; they merely do more of it in times of economic hardship (perhaps because each victim yields less). Such an interpretation is not possible with Mulligan's data.

Another interesting example of the relationship between crime and other variables is provided by Lenke (1980), who shows the closeness of the relationship between alcohol consumption and criminal assaults in Scandinavia. He also shows that 'variation in drug availability and price levels markedly influences the frequency of property crimes' (Lenke, 1980, p. 38).

In short, there are relationships between crime and general social factors which are more impressive than relationships between the activities of the criminal justice system and levels of crime. However, it is not particularly helpful to governments to know that joblessness has a cost in crime. (Although they should be made aware that high levels of unemployment are associated with more use being made of prison – over and above the amount that would be appropriate given the extra crime; see, for example, Gladstone (1979).) Politicians intuitively recognize such a relationship but have not elevated crime control to a position in the policy pantheon that would allow it to influence economic policy more positively.

CRIME CONTROL BY OPPORTUNITY REDUCTION

Are there any more modest possibilities for crime control? There are. Collectively they can be referred to as opportunity reduction techniques. The background to the development of the preference for detailed analysis of situations which seem to engender – or at least not hinder – crime, rather than to attempt to change criminal dispositions, is well stated elsewhere (Clarke, 1980). Perhaps the best known opportunity reduction enterprise is the West German finding that since 1963, when certain security requirements came into effect for all cars (old and new), car thefts reduced by 62% relative to 1960, a trend maintained subsequently (Mayhew, Clarke, Sturman, and Hough, 1976). In the United Kingdom, too, the fitting of steering column locks to new cars reduced the percentage of new cars stolen (Mayhew et al., 1976). Van Straelen (1978) reports a reduction in thefts of gramophone records after a reorganization which resulted in customers having no direct access to the records (no listening booths, empty record sleeves). He also reports data from a French supermarket indicating a reduction of 33% in losses following the installation of closed-circuit television cameras. The literature of the Association for the Prevention of Theft in Shops (1979) produces congruent information. Van Straelen (1978) describes Dutch data which show that the legislation in 1975 requiring drivers of motorized bicycles to wear helmets cut the incidence of theft of such cycles to one-third of their previous level, presumably by making helmetless thieves conspicuous. Sturman (1976) shows clearly how patterns of bus vandalism were linked to the lack of surveillance by bus company employees in certain parts of buses. Aircraft hijackings have declined as airport security has improved (Wilkinson, 1977). Thefts of tobacco and wines and spirits in transit in the United Kingdom have plummeted after central organizations concerned with security were established by these industries. In the case of the tobacco industry, the losses in

1978 were reduced to one sixth of the value stolen in 1969, adjusted to 1969 prices (Tobacco Advisory Council Security Liaison Office, personal communication). In the case of wines and spirits the change is, if anything, even more spectacular, from £1 million in 1971 to £48000 in 1978, prices not adjusted. Hauber (1978) showed that the frequency of public transport fraud was highest where a self-service system existed with tickets being sold away from the vehicle, where charges were high, where inspection was infrequent, and where fines were low. Strengthening coin-boxes in telephone kiosks reduces thefts from such kiosks (Mayhew et al., 1976). It was also found that the installation of closed-circuit television in selected stations of the London Underground reduced theft in those stations to one-quarter of its former level (Mayhew, Clarke, Burrows, Hough, and Winchester, 1979).

In Sweden the number of cheque frauds dropped as a result of the tightening of cheque guarantee regulations in 1971 (Kuhlhorn, 1980). Not all the examples cited above are of the highest methodological rigour. Nevertheless, taken together, they provide impressive evidence that opportunity is relevant to incidence of a variety of offences and that manipulation of opportunity will yield lower rates of crime against targets whose vulnerability is reduced.

Not all opportunity reduction tactics appear equally convincing. Notably, the opportunities for intrusion offered by individual houses and estates are not always obviously associated with the probability of falling victim to an intrusion (see, for example, Jackson and Winchester, 1982; Maguire, 1982), but even here there are some suggestions for where opportunity reduction may most profitably be concentrated (Brantingham and Brantingham, 1975; Walsh, 1982; Wilson, 1978, 1982).

However impressive may be the demonstrations of the crime preventive effects of opportunity reduction, they are liable to the criticism that crime is displaced rather than prevented; that is, the notion that crime when prevented simply moves to another place or another time or changes into another type of crime. Discussions of this topic quickly reveal two things: (1) it is impossible to demonstrate that displacement does not occur; and (2) the displacement argument is never used to advocate the reduction of crime prevention measures. To take an example of (1), installing a closed-circuit television in an underground railway station reduced theft in that station. It may be possible (but see Mayhew et al., 1979) to show that crime in other parts of the underground system did not increase in frequency. It may even be possible to show that theft does not spill over to the station's surroundings. The methodological problems become overwhelming, however, if one suggests that, for example, some former station thieves take up shoplifting, others mugging in underpasses, others thefts from cars, and so forth. Thus, realistically, displacement can never be shown *not* to have occurred. However, research such as that of Maguire (1982) and Walsh (1982), interviewing those who committed crimes, together with the experience of others of us who have been tempted to commit crimes, but have been deterred by aspects of the setting, may yield useful service.

The second point is that people only talk about displacement as a reason for not putting on extra locks, never for taking off existing locks. Why do the thorough-going advocates of displacement not suggest that we should leave houses and cars unlocked on the grounds that, if they do not receive the attention of thieves, something equally valuable will? There are perhaps two reasons for this. The first is that intuitively it is more reasonable to conceive of crime as lying at all points on a continuum from the most opportunistic to the most completely premeditated, with the pressure to attack a different target, when the first is protected, varying accordingly. Walsh (1982) interestingly contrasts the apparent permanence of the crime reduction effect of the introduction of steering column locks in West Germany with the continuing need to modify the design of safes in response to changes in techniques used to open them. A plausible inference is that taking motor cars is characterized by a higher element of opportunism than is safe-breaking.

The second possible reason why those who argue for displacement effects lock their own houses and cars is because they specifically recognize that such effects exist and, one presumes, would prefer that it was not their house burgled or their car stolen.

Insurance companies are perhaps prime exponents of the displacement effect. They are not only fully aware of the financial consequences – to their bank balances – of crime directed towards their policyholders, but are also probably more aware than are their policyholders of the actual risks of such crimes occurring. They thus unashamedly attempt to create displacement, by encouraging the fitting of crime-preventive devices, from properties which they insure to properties they do not insure. Similarly, the collective effect of all insurers' acting in this way will be to shift crime from insured to non-insured properties. Acting in this fashion, insurers are behaving perfectly rationally and, as Pease (1979) argues, it is idle to criticize commercial organizations, such as insurance companies, for optimizing their business on the basis of profitability, given the economic environment in which they operate. However, this implied criticism of either insurers or the system leads to speculation about the effects of changes in the contingencies so that it becomes rational (profitable?) for insurers to behave in a more socially desirable fashion. If insurers can displace crime then perhaps, with a little help, they, or their methods, could displace crime to such an extent that the crime becomes a prevented crime rather than merely a displaced crime.

To what points do these musings lead? If one takes the most pessimistic view of displacement, namely that total displacement occurs, does this mean that crime prevention is not worthwhile? The writers would argue that it simply shifts the debate into one about priorities for crime prevention. People express their preference for not, themselves, becoming victims of crime by taking some precautions (often woefully inadequate, but precautions nonetheless). Should there be social priorities expressed in respect of the types and locations of crime towards which preventive efforts should be directed (e.g. the subsidized protection of the homes of the old, or of schools against vandalism)? No doubt there are priorities implicit in patterns of current expenditure. The point is merely that a belief in total displacement by no means ends the debate about the worth of crime prevention.

THE MOTIVATION TO REDUCE CRIME OPPORTUNITY

What strikes an observer generally sympathetic to, and persuaded of the evidence of, the efficacy of opportunity reduction measures as crime preventive, is the chasm between possibility and achievement. For the purposes of the argument it will be assumed that crime displacement is not complete. It is perhaps significant that the thrust of the Home Office Research Unit has moved in recent years from demonstrations of the effectiveness of opportunity reduction to the problems faced by those who would wish to implement such programmes (see, for example, Clarke and Mayhew, 1980; Gladstone, 1981). A similar type of chasm exists elsewhere – for example, in the recognition that smoking is a major cause of death and the triviality of disincentives applied to the smoking habit. Perhaps the causes are analogous ones, although the analysis offered here is specific to crime.

We will draw extensively on Carter's (1974) analysis of property crime which is little known among criminologists. One of Carter's major enabling contributions has been to ascribe economic rationality to the victims of crime. It is noteworthy that in the recent history of criminology the ascription of rationality to the criminal (Becker, 1968) pre-dates the ascription of rationality to the victim.

Crime involves private benefits, private costs, and social costs. It is arguable that it also involves social benefits in asserting a moral consensus (see, for example, Blumstein and Cohen, 1973) but these, if they exist, are difficult to quantify and are in any case irrelevant to the logic of the argument to be presented. Psychological costs and benefits (although an interesting field of study in their own right) will also be ignored as irrelevant to the argument being advanced. Private benefits include the value realized by criminals from stolen goods and money, and more indirectly benefits to manufacturers who sell goods which they might otherwise not have sold, to replace stolen goods. Private costs include the market value of stolen, damaged, or destroyed goods, loss of income due to disruption of business, private payments made to prevent theft, and the cost in income for criminals as a result of the criminal justice process. Social costs of crime include the costs of public services to attempt to prevent and to process crime and criminals – the police, court and penal services and Home Office Departments concerned with crime and criminal justice policy. Perhaps the fundamental question which Carter's analysis invites concerns the relationship between public and private costs of crime. He wrote:

'Ideally when deciding how much to spend on loss prevention the individual should allow for social costs and benefits but, as in other private economic decisions, he will normally be concerned only with items which affect his own pocket. At present after a theft the individual incurs only a little part of the cost of apprehending, convicting and punishing the thief (for example the cost of appearing in court); but neither does he receive a tax or rate rebate for taking precautions which are expected to reduce his demand on public services. Consequently, private decisions are taken without regard to their effect on the total opportunities and costs for thieves, or on the demands for public law enforcement services' (Carter, 1974, p. 32).

In so far as this is true, individuals will take crime prevention measures up to the point at which additional cost on security equals the expected marginal benefit by way of crime prevention. If social costs were incorporated into the calculation, however, the marginal benefits would be higher and more crime prevention would be bought. The failure to incorporate public costs into private calculations applies to the operation as well as to the installation of crime prevention measures. The classic example is perhaps that of the false intruder alarm. Over 95% of intruder alarm calls with which police deal, at public cost, are false alarms (Anonymous, 1977; Carter, 1974; Cross, 1976; Loughborough Consultants Ltd, 1974; Randall, 1976). Crime insurance is also centrally relevant to the choice of level of crime precautions adopted. Litton (1982), in reviewing the relationship between crime prevention and insurance, concluded:

'The influence of an insurance company is potentially critical as it is probably the only agency in a position to offer a property owner financial incentives for crime prevention measures. There is substantial evidence that, when they do choose to act, insurers can function to prevent crime or to change the type of crime which occurs (as witness the apparent displacement of burglaries from commercial to private properties in the 1960s). In fact, insurers are probably uniquely positioned to intervene effectively to influence crime prevention – given that the ability can be recognised and that the incentive can be appreciated and mobilised' (Litton, 1982, p. 20).

Currently the crime reduction effect of insurance is limited by the imprecision of the relationship between crime prevention precautions required and level of risk and by unequal motivations for the fitting of crime-preventive devices. It is probably true to say that the extent of crime-prevention measures taken in an individual case will vary with the perceived risk of crime. A lot depends on who is doing the perceiving, given that many crime-preventive devices are fitted only at the insistence of an insurer, as a condition of granting the insurance, rather than voluntarily by the individual property owner. However, insurers are concerned with making an overall profit and therefore large potential losses are of more importance to them than small ones. They will thus be more concerned to prevent the large loss than the small loss and will direct their priorities accordingly. Insurers are happy to carry out a survey and make recommendations for protections in the case of the large commercial risk, where the potential for a large monetary loss is perceived to exist, but are reluctant to survey the smaller commercial risks or private dwellings where the risk of loss is relatively smaller and where the amount of premium available to fund the survey is also small. The result is that the advice given and the pressure exerted by insurers for their policy-holders to improve their crime prevention measures is either much reduced or is totally absent for cases where insurers perceive the risk of loss to be small (or, on average, smaller than the cost of carrying out a survey).

This conclusion leads to consideration of another factor inhibiting more effective crime prevention in the shape of the different orientation adopted by insurers on the one hand and, on the other hand, by the police, the Home Office, and the victim (Pease, 1979). Insurers, as we have already argued, are more concerned to prevent the large loss than the small loss. To the other parties, however, whether police or victim, a crime is a crime is a crime. Thus the unit of accounting for insurers is the pound sterling, dollar, or whatever, whereas for the police the unit of accounting is the crime (almost irrespective of size). Only if these two viewpoints can be reconciled will the full potentialities for pressure and influence towards better crime-prevention measures be realized.

For his part, Carter (1974) argues that premiums could be varied more to encourage precautions by commercial, government, or private policyholders (although see Litton [1982] for an analysis of some of the difficulties involved in implementing this apparently simple suggestion). An ingenious suggestion by Banton (1978) is that insurance companies should explicitly relate their premiums to the effectiveness of the local authority's criminal policies and publicize the variations in their assessments (although here we must recall our earlier conclusion that scope for improving the effectiveness of the criminal justice system is probably limited).

Thus insurance provides the most obvious dispenser of reinforcements to potential victims of crime. Balch (1980) and Gardiner and Balch (1980) provide useful analyses of how these reinforcers could be applied to victim behaviour. As Heal (1982) remarked:

'There is a decision to be made, both individually and collectively, as to whether we really want to prevent crime and are prepared to pay the social and economic costs of doing so. The costs to be met arise not so much from the development of preventive tactics or their evaluation, but from the process of implementation. It is at this stage that effort is most needed' (Heal, 1982, p. 12).

Although Heal did not explore the point, there is of course the question of whether we really do want to prevent crime. The position that it is the fear of crime rather than crime itself which should be reduced is a perfectly defensible one. Such is the thrust of official publicity in the Netherlands (Fitzmaurice and Pease, 1982). There is also evidence now that the elderly fear becoming victims of crime far more than is justified by the risks they are actually exposed to, and that this fear may be based on the media's presentation of the risks and by pronouncements of politicians (Cook, Fremming, and Tyler, 1981; Home Office, 1982; Mawby, 1982). Some attempts to prevent crime turn out to be at least as concerned with the change of perceptions of crime (Babbs, Dickens, Fitzmaurice, and Stooke, 1978; Hedges, Blaber, and Mostyn, 1980). For those who take this line, the Home Office victim survey will provide an excellent baseline for judgments of the realism of fears of crime.

Given that we do actually wish to prevent crime, it is apparent that practical options for crime prevention do arise from an emphasis upon situational features, especially from a consideration of the direct and immediate relationship between such features and criminal behaviour. By studying the spatial and temporal distribution of specific offences and relating these to measurable aspects of the situation, researchers have begun to demonstrate the possibilities which arise from a manipulation of criminogenic situations in the interests of prevention.

The difficulty posed for measures which reduce opportunity is that of the vast number of potential targets combined with generally low overall level of security. As Clarke (1980) points out, within easy reach of every house with a burglar alarm or car with an anti-theft device are many others without such protection. Van Straelen (1978) states that, in England, in 31% of cases of theft from private cars the theft was possible because the doors or windows were unlocked; similarly, according to police figures, around one-third of burgled dwellings had windows or doors unlocked.

The situational approach might raise fears of a 'fortress society' (Clarke, 1980) in which citizens in perpetual fear of their fellows scuttle from one fortified environment to another. These fears may in some cases be reinforced by the more tangible and sophisticated types of opportunity-reducing measures, especially in their more unattractive forms – barbed wire, heavy padlocks, guard dogs, and private security forces. And, as Bandura put it from a different perspective:

'The notion that human behavior is externally regulated, though amply documented, has not been enthusiastically received. To many people it implies a one-way control process which reduces individuals to passive respondents to the vagaries of whatever influences impinge upon them. Popular accounts of the potentials of psychological control conjure up frightened images of societies in which inhabitants are manipulated at will by occult technocrats' (Bandura, 1977, p. 6).

The situational approach to crime prevention does not go that far, although supporters of the approach must take account of possible public fears of 'Big Brother' forms of state controls, perhaps fuelled by the evidence of some of the more sophisticated forms of preventive device such as television surveillance and electronic intruder alarms. However, as the examples quoted above demonstrate, there are means of reducing opportunities which are not only unobtrusive and relatively cheap but are also not unduly restrictive. Thus, as Clarke (1980) suggests, steel cash compartments in telephone kiosks are indistinguishable from aluminium ones and vandal-resistant polycarbonate looks just like glass. Steering column locks are brought into operation automatically on the removal of the ignition key and many people are unaware that their cars are fitted with them.

Thus, whilst it may not be possible to reduce every category of crime, it seems probable that the situational approach provides the means whereby much crime could be prevented. However, those who would wish to prevent crime in this way need to address themselves to questions of the motivation, not just the mechanics, of the enterprise.

REFERENCES

ANONYMOUS (1977). Alarms and false excursions. *Economist*, 21 May 1977.
ASSOCIATION FOR THE PREVENTION OF THEFT IN SHOPS (1979). Newsletter No. 6.
BABBS, D., DICKENS, R., FITZMAURICE, C., and STOOKE, G. (1978). *Investigation of Vandalism in Residential Areas in Oldham*. Oldham: Oldham Metropolitan Borough Council.
BALCH, G. I. (1980). The stick, the carrot and other strategies. In J. Brigham and D.W. Brown (Eds), *Policy Implementation, Penalties or Incentives?* Beverly Hills, Calif.: Sage.
BANDURA, A. (1977). *Social Learning Theory*. Englewood Cliffs, N. J.: Prentice-Hall.
BANTON, M. (1978). Introductory Address: The police and the prevention of crime. Third Criminological Colloquium of the Council of Europe, Strasbourg, November 1978.
BECKER, G. S. (1968). Crime and punishment: an economic approach. *Journal of Political Economy*, **76**, 168–207.
BLUMSTEIN, A., and COHEN, J. (1973). A theory of the stability of punishment. *Journal of Criminal Law and Criminology*, **64**, 198–207.

BRANTINGHAM, P. J., and BRANTINGHAM, P. L. (1975). Residential burglary and urban forms. *Urban Studies*, **12**, 273–284.

BRENNER, M. H. (1976a). *Time Series Analysis. Effects of the Economy on Criminal Behavior and the Administration of Criminal Justice in Economic Crises and Crime.* New York: UNSDRI.

BRENNER, M. H. (1976b). *Estimating the Social Cost of National Economic Policy Implications for Mental and Physical Health and Criminal Aggression.* Washington, D. C., US Government Printing Office.

CARTER, R. L. (1974). *Theft in the Market,* Hobart Paper 60. London: Institute of Economic Affairs.

CLARKE, R. V. G. (1980). Situational crime prevention: theory and practice. *British Journal of Criminology,* **20**, 136–147.

CLARKE, R. V. G. (1981). The prospects for controlling crime. *Home Office Research Bulletin,* No. 12, 12–19.

CLARKE, R. V. G., and MAYHEW, P. (1980). *Designing out Crime.* London: Her Majesty's Stationery Office.

COOK, T. D., FREMMING, J., and TYLER, T. R. (1981). Criminal victimization of the elderly: validating the policy assumptions. In G. M. Stephenson and J. H. Davis (Eds), *Progress in Applied Social Psychology,* Vol. 1. Chichester: John Wiley.

CROSS, B. (1976). Alarms and response. In P. Young, (Ed), *Major Property Crime in the United Kingdom.* Edinburgh: University of Edinburgh, School of Criminology and Forensic Studies.

FITZMAURICE, C. T., and PEASE, K. (1982). Dutch perspectives on crime prevention. *Crime Prevention News,* No. 2. London: Home Office.

GARDINER, J. A., and BALCH, G. I. (1980). Getting people to protect themselves. In J. Brigham and D. V. Brown (Eds), *Policy Implementation, Penalties or Incentives?* Beverly Hills, Calif.: Sage.

GLADSTONE, F. (1979). Crime and the crystal ball. *Home Office Research Bulletin,* No. 7, 35–39.

GLADSTONE, F. J. (1981). *Co-ordinating Crime Prevention Efforts,* Home Office Research Study No. 62. London: Her Majesty's Stationery Office.

HAUBER, A. R. (1978). *Fraud and Public Transport,* Research Bulletin No. 2. s'Gravenhage: Research and Documentation Centre, Netherlands Ministry of Justice.

HEAL, K. (1982). The police, the public and the prevention of crime. Paper presented to the British Psychological Society, Welsh Branch, International Conference on Psychology and Law, Swansea, July.

HEDGES, A., BLABER, A., and MOSTYN, B. (1980). *Community Planning Project, Cunningham Road Improvement Scheme. Final Report.* Chichester: Barry Rose.

HOME OFFICE (1977). *A Review of Criminal Justice Policy 1976.* London: Her Majesty's Stationery Office.

HOME OFFICE (1982). Elderly not more at risk. *Crime Prevention News,* No. 3. London: Home Office.

HOUGH, J. M., and CLARKE, R. V. G. (1980). *The Effectiveness of Policing.* Farnborough, Hants: Gower.

JACKSON, H., and WINCHESTER, S. (1982). Which houses are burgled and why? *Home Office Research Bulletin,* No. 13, 20–22.

KULHORN, E. (1980). Crime trends and measures against crime in Sweden. Discussion Paper A/CONF/87/9/Sweden, Sixth United Nations Congress on the Prevention of Crime and the Treatment of Offenders, Caracas, August 1980.

LENKE, L. (1980). Drugs and criminality in Scandinavia. In N. Bishop (Ed), *Crime and*

Crime Control in Scandinavia 1976–80. Nordkopung: Scandinavian Research Council for Criminology.

LITTON, R. A. (1982). Crime prevention and insurance. *Howard Journal,* **21**, 6–22.

LOUGHBOROUGH CONSULTANTS LTD (1974). *Investigation of the Ergonomic Aspect of False Alarm Calls from Intruder Alarms,* Project Report DEC/HO/1. Loughborough: Loughborough University of Technology.

MAGUIRE, M. (1982). *Burglary in a Dwelling: The Offence, the Offender and the Victim.* London: Heinemann.

MAWBY, R. I. (1982). Crime and the elderly: A review of British and American research. *Current Psychological Reviews,* **2**, 301–310.

MAYHEW, P., CLARKE, R. V. G., BURROWS, J. N., HOUGH, J. M., and WINCHESTER, S. W. C. (1979). *Crime in Public View,* Home Office Research Study No. 49. London: Her Majesty's Stationery Office.

MAYHEW, P., CLARKE, R. V. G., STURMAN, A., and HOUGH, J. M. (1976). *Crime as Opportunity,* Home Office Research Study No. 34. London: Her Majesty's Stationery Office.

MEYER, J. C. (1976). Discontinuity in the delivery of public service – analysing the police strike. *Human Relations,* **19**, 6–18.

MULLIGAN, G. (1982). Joblessness and crime. Paper presented to the British Psychological Society, Welsh Branch, International Conference on Psychology and Law, Swansea, July.

PATE, T., FERRARA, A., BOWERS, R., and LAWRENCE, J. (1976). *Police Response Time: Its Determinants and Effects.* Washington, D.C.: Police Foundation.

PEASE, K. (1979). Some futures in crime prevention. *Home Office Research Bulletin,* No. 7, 31–35.

PHILLIPS, L., VOTEY, H. L., and MAXWELL, D. (1972). Crime, youth and the labour market. *Journal of Political Economy,* **80**, 491–504.

RANDALL, W. E. (1976). Activities, policies and trends in the security industry. In P. Young (Ed), *Major Property Crime in the United Kingdom.* Edinburgh: University of Edinburgh, School of Criminology and Forensic Studies.

REYNOLDS, G. W. and JUDGE, A. (1968). *The Night the Police went on Strike.* London: Weidenfield and Nicholson.

STURMAN, A. (1976). Damage on buses: the effects of supervision. In P. Mayhew, R. V. G. Clarke, A. Sturman and J. M. Hough, *Crime as Opportunity,* Home Office Research Study No. 34. London: Her Majesty's Stationery Office.

VADER, R. J. (1978). Crime prevention in The Netherlands. In J. Brown (Ed), *The Cranfield Papers.* London: Peel Press.

VAN STRAELEN, F. W. M. (1978). Prevention and technology. In J. Brown (Ed), *The Cranfield Papers.* London: Peel Press.

VINSON, T., and HOMMEL, R. (1975). Crime and disadvantage. *British Journal of Criminology,* **15**, 21–31.

WALSH, D. P. (1982). An appreciation of the quest for vulnerability in victim choice and its consequences for fortification. Paper presented to the British Psychological Society, Welsh Branch, International Conference on Psychology and Law, Swansea, July.

WILKINSON, P. (1977). *Terrorism and the Liberal State.* London: Macmillan.

WILSON, S. (1978). Vandalism and defensible space. In R. V. G. Clarke (Ed), *Tackling Vandalism,* Home Office Research Study No. 47. London: Her Majesty's Stationery Office.

WILSON, S. (1982). Crime and housing: evidence from an investigation of unpopular housing estates. In J. M. Hough and P. Mayhew (Eds), *Crime and Public Housing,* Home Office Research and Planning Unit Paper 6. London: Home Office.

SECTION IV

Eyewitness testimony

Eyewitness testimony is the most extensively investigated topic in psycho-legal research. Studies have provided a rich source of data for contemporary cognitive psychology, with its recently increased emphasis on ecological validity. They have also proved to have some influence on the operation of legal processes.

The chapter by **Hall and Loftus** focuses principally on the roles which psychologists can play in making more valid and reliable legal procedures involving eyewitnesses. They consider the resistance shown by some other professionals to psychological research and expertise in this area, but they argue cogently that jurors and others do need to be made aware of variables which can influence the reports of eyewitnesses, even though these are given in good faith. Hall and Loftus provide an authoritative review which gives both theoretical and empirical support to the claim that psychologists have a role to play in those court processes which are dependent on eyewitness testimony. In more general terms, eyewitness research illustrates how psychologists may be used to make the working of the legal system more consistent and more sensitive.

The following chapter, by **Yarmey, Tressillian Jones, and Rashid,** reports the results of empirical studies of the memory of elderly and of young adults of a simulated crime: they had witnessed it by means of a series of slides. It was found that the old adult witnesses, though more valued by police officers, were less accurate in their descriptions of the criminal assault. Furthermore, the physical demeanour of a suspected criminal can influence subjects' memory of the incident. The perception and interpretation of the *victims* also proved to be a salient variable. This research contributes to our knowledge of the ways in which the accuracy of eyewitness testimony may depend on a multiplicity of variables.

In the final chapter in this section, **Stephenson** re-addresses an important topic, viz. the relationships between the confidence and the accuracy of eyewitness testimony. He questions the prevailing view that there is no reliable relationship between confidence and accuracy. He discusses experimental data which emphasize the importance of individual differences and interpersonal factors, and suggests that advice to the judiciary to disregard the confidence of eyewitnesses would be premature. Stephenson's careful analysis suggests that psychologists should be wary of the effects of prematurely proffering advice to the judiciary.

The chapters in this section provide an overview of a field of enquiry which continues to play an important role in psycho-legal research. They illustrate how the accuracy of eyewitness testimony can be affected by variables which are easily overlooked. They also illustrate the implications of such findings for judicial processes.

sychology and Law
Edited by D.J. Müller, D.E. Blackman, and A.J. Chapman
© 1984 John Wiley & Sons Ltd

Chapter 16

Research on Eyewitness Testimony: Recent Advances and Current Controversy

David F. Hall and Elizabeth F. Loftus

Neisser (1982) has argued that naturalistic investigation promises to add more to the understanding of human memory than does the continued laboratory testing of general theoretical models. Recounting the disastrous usurpment of the domain of comparative psychology by 'biological behaviourists', Neisser has warned that a similar scientific coup could be sprung on overly complacent cognitive psychologists. If psychologists intend to continue their reign over the fields of memory, then they must strengthen their position by giving long overdue attention to the interesting phenomena of remembering in natural contexts.

Miller (1969) suggested in his noted presidential address to the American Psychological Association that the best way to advance psychology is by giving it away. By 'giving psychology away' Miller did not mean to suggest yielding psychology's rightful territory to academic interlopers, although in some instances strategic retreat from indefensible positions might be advisable. Rather, he meant to suggest that psychologists should win allies by making every effort to share their knowledge and their perspective with colleagues in other professions and with non-professionals. Both Miller and Neisser argue convincingly that the questions that are of most interest, or of most practical concern, to non-psychologists are the same questions that will ultimately sustain psychology. Thus, the time may have come to reinforce the long neglected outposts of applied memory research. One such outpost is to be found in the field of eyewitness testimony.

Eyewitness research was pioneered by early forensic psychologists under the leadership of Munsterberg (1908). Münsterburg's contributions helped to forge a small but stable hegemony for psychology in the courtroom. The appearance of psychiatrists and psychologists as expert witnesses in trials, the use of the polygraph and psychological assessment as techniques in investigation, and the introduction of psychological training as a popular elective in law schools and pre-law studies, all stand as tributes to Münsterberg's influential work (Moskowitz, 1977). At times Münsterberg encountered fierce resistance from lawyers, such as Wigmore (1909). However, the impact of Münsterberg's pioneering work was eventually limited not so much by the criticisms of lawyers, as by the lack of interest on the part of succeeding generations of psychologists, who seem to have preferred to taste the lotus of general theory. Fortunately the current generation of researchers has begun to free itself from the general-theory trance; see, for example, Clifford and Bull (1978), Davies, Ellis, and Shepherd (1981), Loftus (1979), and Yarmey (1979).

Controversy about eyewitness testimony continues, in fact, to be intense. The opponents, recalcitrant lawyers and law enforcement professionals, joined by a few from the loyal opposition in the psychology camp, have large numbers, institutional entrenchment, and a capacity to level withering barrages of intransigence and arbitrariness. Psychologists can expect to convince them of their contribution only by demonstrating the practical advantages of scientific empiricism, while at the same time making every effort to disseminate knowledge through a broad range of professional and popular channels.

The present chapter is intended as a report on the current status of psychological research on eyewitness testimony, and some recent controversies that have emerged about the application of this research. The purpose is to highlight some recent advances, rather than to provide a comprehensive review of eyewitness research. Recent eyewitness research has advanced with respect to the following: (1) new findings about the reliability of eyewitness testimony; (2) new findings on the impact of eyewitness testimony on jurors; and (3) increased knowledge about the impact on jurors of expert testimony given by psychologists in the courtroom.

THE RELIABILITY OF EYEWITNESS TESTIMONY

The body of research on eyewitness reliability has become sufficiently large to require the beginnings, at least, of a conceptual framework. We will consider briefly two recent efforts to provide such a framework: Wells' (1978) framework of system variables and estimator variables, and the framework advanced by Hall, Loftus, and Tousignant (1984) for variables affecting alterations in recollection of natural events.

According to Wells' often cited 1978 paper, two mutually exclusive categories, system variables and estimator variables, encompass virtually all recent eyewitness-reliability research. Wells argues that the practical implica tions and utility of any particular finding depend on the category to which the research belongs.

System-variable research includes variables that can be manipulated by police, prosecutors, lawyers, or judges in the course of criminal or civil investigations and trials; for example, the manner of presentation of a photograph montage or of an identification parade. Estimator-variable research includes variables that cannot be controlled in actual investigations and trials; for example, the racial or ethnic identity of suspects and of witnesses.

Wells' framework provides an initial organizational scheme for the burgeoning body of research on eyewitness testimony. It suggests the most appropriate clients for particular eyewitness-research findings, and it provides a coherent way in which to organize information to share with police and lawyers, or even with jurors. It can also provide a meaningful basis for choosing directions in research projects. Much of Wells' research seems to be aimed at elucidation of controllable system variables.

For example, Wells regards the staging of an identification parade as the setting for investigating a number of system variables. In this vein, Wells, Leippe, and Ostrom (1979) have suggested that the functional size of the identification parade is a systematic (i.e. controllable) indicator of the fairness of the parade. The functional size of an identification parade can be defined in terms of choices made by mock witnesses; that is, choices made by witnesses who have never actually seen the suspect but who attempt to make identifications on the basis of a general, cursory description of that suspect. The functional size of the parade is n/D, where n is the number of mock witnesses, and D is the number choosing the defendant. More simply, the functional size of the parade refers to the number of parade members who effectively share the risk of being identified by mock witnesses. A relatively large functional size for an identification parade serves to protect innocent suspects. One reason for such protection is simply the fact that the risk of false identification is shared by a relatively larger number of parade members, thus reducing individual risk. However, there may be another, less obvious, advantage to a larger functional parade.

Lindsay and Wells (1980) offer evidence that a larger functional parade actually confers a greater degree of 'diagnosticity'. Basically, the term 'diagnosticity' refers to the informational value of an attempted identification (Wells and Lindsay, 1980). More precisely, the diagnosticity of a positive identification of any suspect can be defined in terms of Bayesian statistics as the probability that would exist for such an identification if the suspect were actually the criminal, divided by the probability that would exist for an identification if the suspect were not the criminal (i.e. $P(I_{guilty})/P(I_{not\ guilty})$). Similarly, the diagnosticity of a witness's failure to identify a particular suspect can be defined as a ratio of conditional probabilities. Lindsay and

Wells found that the diagnosticity of identifications, and of failures to identify, is greatest when the functional size of the parade is relatively large. On the basis of such results, police and prosecutors who are seeking evidence against a suspect can be advised to include as many similar appearing foils in an identification parade as is practically feasible.

However, the technique suggested by Lindsay and Wells would appear to require a high degree of procedural sophistication, including measurement of the functional size of the parade, and the use of Bayesian analysis to assess the informational value of identifications. Psychologists will have to be highly persuasive if they are to induce the criminal justice system to adopt such unfamiliar techniques. Furthermore, the presumed increase in accuracy depends on fairly subtle assumptions about the extent to which visually similar foils distract a witness's attention from the guilty suspect, as opposed to distracting attention from innocent suspects. Such distraction of attention is likely to be highly dependent on unique characteristics of particular witnesses, suspects, and distractor foils, and, thus, might not be generalizable to all identification parades. Further research could specify the precise circumstances in which increased similarity among identification-parade foils results in greater identification accuracy.

Many variables have been found to affect the fairness, and the diagnosticity, of identification parades (Doob and Kirshenbaum, 1973; Levine and Tapp, 1973; Malpass and Devine, 1981a,b). Although some such variables are systematically controllable by police, others are only partially or marginally controllable. Variables over which police have only partial or marginal control include the suspect's unique appearance and demeanour, as well as the appearance and demeanour of persons who serve as distractors. Also, the effects of witnesses' biases and guessing strategies, the witness's private rehearsal of events, conversational review of details with friends or relatives, or interaction with other witnesses are all difficult to control, or even to estimate, in criminal investigations. Yet all of these variables can influence the extent to which an identification parade is fair or unfair, and diagnostic or uninformative. Thus, the identification parade, which is one of the few procedures that Wells was willing to categorize as a system variable, in fact appears to have the distinctive characteristics of an estimator variable.

It should be noted too that from the perspective of a memory researcher any variable that can be systematically manipulated within an experiment is, within the confines of that particular experiment, a controllable variable. However, if a memory researcher were asked to give expert testimony in court about the potential impact of the same variables, some variables would then have to be regarded as estimator variables. Indeed, any variable might be viewed as manipulable, or as merely estimable, depending on whether one takes the individual perspective of the witness, the police, attorneys, prosecutors, jurors, judges, legislators, or psychological memory researchers. Thus,

he concept of system variables and estimator variables provides a framework
hat is relativistic in nature. Such relativism is perfectly appropriate, however,
ind in fact adds to the potential utility of the framework. It seems reasonable
o categorize research variables not as absolutely manipulable, or as merely
stimable, but rather to specify the circumstances and the manner in which
he variable might be usefully manipulated. Many current efforts provide
examples of this research strategy.

For example, the research reviewed below has been directed at specifying
he circumstances under which a witness's recollection for a crime can be
systematically altered by post-event experiences. Such research has been
supplemented by efforts to specify certain safeguards that can be provided
against memory alteration.

A Framework for Memory Alteration

Hall et al., (1984) offer an alternative conceptual framework for eyewitness
esearch. This is based on the malleability of recollections of natural events.
This recollection-change framework includes an experimental paradigm for
tudying alterations in recollection and two general principles that summarize
he major variables that have been shown to affect changes in recollection.

Scores of experiments show that recollection of details of natural events can
under some circumstances be affected by post-event experiences. The experimental paradigm employed in such studies can be briefly described in
erms of three essential stages:

(1) *Acquisition*–A witness views an initial complex event, such as a
   simulated crime or an autombile accident.

(2) *Retention and change*–A witness encounters new information subsequent to the initial event. The source of new information might include
   biasing suggestions or potentially misleading questions, viewing photographs, a combination of pictures and messages, or even rehearsal of
   the original event. Whatever the source, post-event information is
   added to the original memory, and a process of gradual integration
   occurs between the new information and original memory.

(3) *Retrieval*–At a later time a test of memory for the original event reveals
   that post-event experiences have produced substantial changes in
   recollection. Indeed, the witness reacts as if original memory and
   post-event information have been inextricably integrated. In some
   cases, original memory for the event appears to have been altered or
   even erased by post-event information.

In one typical experiment (Loftus, Miller, and Burns, 1978), subjects
viewed a series of slides depicting an automobile accident. For some subjects,
the slides included a view of a red Datsun stopped at a 'Yield' sign, or, for
other subjects, a view of the same red Datsun stopped at a 'Stop' sign. At

some interval after the slide presentation, subjects were given a set of 2(questions, which for some subjects included one item that contained mislead ing information. For example, the item, 'Did another car pass the red Datsui while.it was stopped at the stop sign?', contained misinformation when aske(of subjects who had actually viewed a yield sign. Finally subjects were teste(for their recollection of the sign. Depending on the time intervals tha occurred between the slides and the intervening questions, and between th(slides and the final recollection, up to 80% of the subjects indicated that thei recollections were influenced by the misinformation. That is, they remem bered a stop sign when a yield sign had been seen, or a yield sign when a sto| sign had actually been seen.

The recollection-change paradigm is intended not only as the blueprint of : typical laboratory experiment, but also as a description of a sequence o events that no doubt occurs with some frequency in natural settings. A crim(is a complex natural event for which a witness acquires and retains a certaii amount of information. Police interviews with witnesses, identificatioi parades, and the presentation of photograph montages are all natura occurrences that are replete with opportunities for the introduction o potentially misleading post-event information. Trials, pre-trial hearings, an(investigations all demand eyewitness recollections that may have been lon; since adulterated by post-event misinformation. When criminal investigation and trials are viewed in this way, it is possible to begin considering variable(that might alter, or even help to conserve, a witness's original memory for : crime. We have previously articulated two general principles that captur(much of what has been learned about the variables that influence memor' alteration:

(1) *Change in recollection for a natural event is more likely to occur i memory for the event has been reactivated by post-event information.*

Lewis (1979) has made a distinction between active memory and inactiv(memory. Inactive memory includes information that has been committed t(storage, but which has not recently been retrieved for active problem solving Active memory, by contrast, includes newly formed memories and memorie(which have been recently retrieved from storage for active problem solving Lewis further contends, with support from animal memory research, tha memory can be altered only if it is raised to an active status. This contentioi supports our own view that post-event experiences evoke from subject incomplete, malleable recollections of an event. Such imperfect or partia recollections can then be altered by adding, deleting, or reworking some o the details. By contrast, it is a commonplace finding that irrelevant filler task assigned during the interval between training and testing do not lead t(changes in recollection. Such filler tasks leave memory relatively unaffected presumably because they do not evoke memory for the event. Thus, onl' fading over time would be expected to occur. In short, there is no indicatioi hat inactive, stored memories undergo spontaneous alteration (Riley, 1962). Rather change occurs because post-event experiences activate memory and render that memory accessible to additions and vulnerable to alterations.

(2) *Change in recollection for a natural event is more likely to occur if discrepancies between the original event and post-event information are not initially detected.*

Scores of experiments have shown that a variety of experimental variables either facilitate or impede alterations in recollection. Such variables include the perceptual prominence or noticeability of details of an event; the time intervals between an event, post-event activities, and testing of recollection; the format of the post-event information; and the presence of warnings to the witness to be wary of potentially misleading information. All these variables appear to have the common feature that they are capable of affecting the likelihood that the witness will detect discrepancies between memory for the original event and details of a post-event message.

It has been shown, for example, that recollections of peripheral details of a complex event are more likely to be altered by post-event experiences than are recollections of salient or central aspects of the original event (Marquis, Marshall, and Oskamp, 1972; Marshall, 1966). In these experiments, subjects viewed a film depicting a crime. The film was, of course, rather complex, and included elements that were judged to be salient (likely to be noticed and recalled with accuracy) and peripheral (likely to be overlooked, difficult to recall). After viewing the film, subjects underwent an interview that included some questions that incorporated potentially misleading information. Marshall and his coworkers found that misleading information reduced accuracy of recall for peripheral elements of the original event, but not for salient elements. Marshall concluded that recollection of salient details is not only more accurate overall, but also less susceptible to alteration, than is recollection of peripheral details.

The results of studies of the effectiveness of warnings also strongly support the second principle of change in recollection. In experiments reported by Greene, Flynn, and Loftus (1982) subjects who had been warned about possible discrepancies between an event and a subsequent misleading message were more resistant to changes in recollection than were subjects who were not warned. Why is such a warning effective? One possibility is that it serves to instruct a witness to search for discrepancies. Forewarned witnesses are likely to find such discrepancies and consequently are more resistant to changes in recollection.

In addition to warnings, another factor, the syntax of a misleading message, also seems to affect the likelihood of a change in recollection (Loftus and Greene, 1980). In particular, misleading information that has been embedded in an auxiliary clause of a complex sentence has been found to be highly effective in changing recollections. By contrast, the same misleading informa-

tion when presented in a simple sentence is less likely to result in th
alteration of recollections. Apparently subjects are capable of assimilatin
information that has been presented in an auxiliary clause of a comple
sentence without giving much direct or careful attention to such information
But information presented in a relatively less oblique manner in a simpl
declarative sentence is given more careful attention. Thus, the detection c
discrepancies and the rejection of false information are more likely wit
simple declarative sentences. Such results strongly suggest that police intei
views of witnesses could be carefully designed to avoid complex an
potentially misleading language.

In summary, experiments which support the second principle of change i
recollection for a natural event include, among others, studies of recollectio
of peripheral as opposed to central details, studies of the effects of warnings
and studies of the syntactic form of misleading messages. To recapitulat
briefly, Hall et al. (1984) have presented an experimental paradigm and tw
general principles that together provide a framework in which to consider th
alteration of memory for complex natural events. This framework may prov
to be useful for laboratory investigations of memory as well as for naturalisti
studies. As was true of Wells' framework, our alternative is offered as
conceptual tool for law enforcement professionals, lawyers, and others. It
basic idea is that recollections are subject to change, but such change ca
probably be minimized by limiting those activities and those circumstance
that are known to facilitate the integration of post-event information witl
original memory for an event.

It was asserted earlier that eyewitness research is a contemporary exampl
of psychology giving itself away. Recent conceptual and empirical develop
ments in eyewitness research suggest some concrete ways in which crimina
justice procedures might be improved. Yet one might nevertheless b
tempted to ask whether the world of justice needs to know about sucl
research. Two other avenues of current eyewitness research bear on thi
question, namely (1) the impact of eyewitness testimony on the verdicts c
jurors and (2) the potential of an expert witness to induce jurors to thinl
more critically about eyewitness testimony.

THE IMPACT OF THE EYEWITNESS ON JURORS

The report of the Devlin Committee (Devlin, 1976) provides wel
documented evidence of the profound impact of eyewitness testimony on jur
decision-making. The Devlin Committee reviewed all identification parade
conducted in England and Wales in the year 1973. The committee noted tha
347 people were prosecuted even though the only evidence against them wa
the testimony of one or more eyewitnesses. Of those 347 cases, 74% resulte
in convictions. It would appear that for many jurors eyewitness testimony i

kely to be regarded as sufficient evidence of guilt. However, as a broad
eview of hundreds of criminal cases, the Devlin report necessarily leaves
nanswered many questions about the circumstances under which jurors'
ecisions are more, or less, likely to be affected by eyewitness testimony.
.ecently, a number of psychological studies have emerged to address these
uestions.

Recent experimental investigation of the impact of eyewitness testimony on
ury decision-making has established a few reliable findings, but has also
ngendered controversy over the interpretation of results. One of the more
eliable, and least contested, findings in the trial-simulation literature is that
ibjects who are exposed to credible, unchallenged eyewitness testimony
ender guilty verdicts more often than do subjects who are not exposed to an
yewitness, even though the only other evidence in the case is ambiguous
rcumstantial evidence (for example, Cavoukian, 1980; Loftus, 1974; Wein-
erg and Baron, 1982). In other words, subjects often regard largely
ncorroborated, or very weakly corroborated, eyewitness testimony as
dequate evidence to convict a defendant.

Thus, the impact of an uncontested eyewitness has been fairly well
emonstrated. By contrast, a smouldering controversy has emerged over the
sue of the vulnerability of the witness to discrediting cross-examination.
ome studies have shown that jurors often persist in believing a witness, even
fter the witness has been manifestly discredited (Cavoukian, 1980; Loftus,
974; Saunders, Hewitt and Vidmar, 1981) while other studies have shown
nat once discredited a witness is no longer believed (Hatvany and Strack,
980; McCloskey, Egeth, Webb, Washburn, and McKenna, 1982; Saunders *et
l.*, 1981, Experiment 1; Weinberg and Baron, 1982). Unfortunately, there
re so many procedural differences between these conflicting studies that it is
ifficult to know why discrediting worked in some cases but not in others.

It seems reasonable to expect that a jury might be impressed by the
itness's overt reaction to a potentially discrediting challenge. Indeed, the
itness's demeanour appears to have been a major variable between experi-
nents. In some experiments, the eyewitness has reacted to a discrediting
hallenge by stubbornly protesting that his version is correct (e.g. Loftus,
974). In stark contrast are other studies in which the witness contritely
cknowledges inaccuracy and apologizes for having taken the stand, or in full
iew of the jury concedes failure on a simple test of perceptual ability (e.g.
latvany and Strack, 1980; McCloskey *et al.*, 1982). Although the witness's
ehaviour appears to be an important variable, it cannot fully account for the
ariety of results in different experiments. For example, Weinberg and Baron
1982, Experiment 2) included a condition in which the eyewitness main-
ained identification of the defendant even after discrediting had occurred. In
pite of such tenacity on the part the witness, Weinberg and Baron's subjects
ere less likely to convict after the witness had been discredited. Thus, it

appears that there are cases in which the witness's composure and consistenc is not sufficient to bolster a sagging credibility. In any case, more research i needed to indicate the circumstances under which the witness's equanimit can overcome the effects of a discrediting challenge.

A number of studies suggest that jurors' decisions are affected by witness's expressed confidence, or lack of confidence, in delivering initia testimony. For example, a set of elegant experimental simulations reporte by Wells, Lindsay, and Ferguson (1979) and by Lindsay, Wells, and Rumpe (1981) indicate that jurors are highly influenced by an eyewitness's confidenc in making an identification, but are rather insensitive to the eyewitness' actual accuracy. The experimental simulations included two phases. In th first phase, subject-witnesses observed a believable enactment of a theft, an later were asked by the experimenter to try to identify the thief. In the secon phase of the study, a group of subject-jurors viewed the cross-examination o one of the earlier witnesses who had attempted to identify the thief. Some o the jurors observed the cross-examination of an accurate witness, whil others observed the cross-examination of an inaccurate witness. Finally jurors were asked to indicate whether or not they believed the witness. I agreement with other studies, jurors were found to be highly influenced b witnesses, and in fact the witness was believed about 80% of the time Furthermore, the witness's actual accuracy or inaccuracy had little effect o whether or not the witness was believed. However, the witness's expresse confidence, which was notably unrelated to accuracy, did affect jurors. I short, jurors tended to confer considerable credibility to most witnesses, an were likely to discriminate between witnesses, if they discriminated at all, o dimensions that are unrelated to reliability. Such findings suggest that th jurors' ability to assess the actual accuracy of a witness is, in man circumstances, minimal.

Are there any circumstances in which jurors are relatively less credulou about a witness's reliability? There is some reason to expect that suc circumstances do in fact exist. Occasionally, they occur spontaneously. Fo example, it has been shown that current news events can affect the likelihoo that jurors will convict in cases involving eyewitness testimony (Loftus, 1982) Apparently the accounts of false identifications and false convictions that no infrequently make news headlines can induce at least a temporary scepticisn about witness reliability in persons called to jury duty. However, such new stories are essentially random events, and their impact on potential jurors i correspondingly unpredictable.

Another, more reliable, variable that seems to induce greater cautiousnes in jurors is the inclusion in the trial procedure of judicial instructions. I criminal cases in the USA, the judge provides the jury with information or the presumption of innocence and on the standard of proof that must be reached in order to render a verdict (e.g. 'beyond a reasonable doubt')

Saunders *et al.* (1981) found that discrediting information about a witness was more effective in reducing juror credulity when judicial instructions were included in the trial procedure than when they were not.

There is another type of event that also promises to improve jurors' critical assessment of eyewitness testimony, namely the appearance in the courtroom of psychologists giving expert testimony about eyewitness reliability, an event which now occurs less randomly than do the dramatic but influential news stories.

EXPERT TESTIMONY IN THE COURTROOM

Why is expert psychological testimony needed? Basically, it is needed because jurors occasionally hold misconceptions regarding many of the factors that affect eyewitness reliability. A number of recent surveys have shown that there exists widespread misunderstanding about eyewitness reliability, both on the part of potential jurors (Deffenbacher and Loftus, 1982; Loftus, 1979; Yarmey and Jones, 1982), as well as on the part of many practising attorneys (Brigham, 1981). Expert psychological testimony may not be adequate to reverse such widespread lack of understanding, but it has been shown that expert testimony can induce subject-jurors to spend more time deliberating the question of an eyewitness's reliability (Loftus, 1980). In two related experiments, subjects read a case against a defendant, including the testimony of an eyewitness. Some subjects were exposed to expert advice about factors that might have affected the witness's testimony, while other subjects were not exposed to such expert advice. Two dependent variables were included in the study: (1) the decision to convict or not to convict; and (2) the amount of time that jurors spent discussing the question of the witness's reliability. Results indicated that the expert advice reduced the number of convictions. However, it is perhaps even more important that subject-jurors who encountered the expert advice spent considerably more time deliberating about the witness's reliability. Such results strongly suggest that admitting expert psychological testimony in the courtroom is one practical way to alert jurors to the possibility that witnesses might be less than totally reliable.

In a related study, Wells, Lindsay, and Tousignant (1980) reported that expert testimony can both reduce subject-jurors' general credulity concerning eyewitness testimony, as well as curbing jurors' typical reliance on the witness's expressed confidence. However, Wells *et al.* tempered their conclusions by noting that expert testimony failed to improve jurors' capacity to discriminate between accurate and inaccurate eyewitnesses.

In short, research suggests that while expert testimony does not instantaneously confer great sophistication on the part of jurors, it can at least increase their general scepticism about eyewitness reliability. In view of the

considerable unreliability that is inherent in eyewitness testimony, suc
heightened scepticism appears to be a reasonable, if modest, goal.

Indeed, to many earnest eyewitness researchers, this may seem too paltry
goal. A more alluring goal is to be able, within the confines of a criminal tria
to teach jurors to be cognisant of those variables that can affect a
eyewitness's accuracy. Wells' two-phased jury simulation paradigm offers
promising methodology for approaching that more distant goal. Whethe
these goals appear modest or alluring, they are often not shared by lawyers
or even by fellow psychologists. It is perhaps not too surprising that th
contributions of eyewitness researchers are being seriously challenged, bot
from within academic psychology and by some individuals in the crimine
justice system. The incursion of any profession into a domain traditionall
dominated by another profession will, perhaps inevitably, create some degre
of distrust. Such inter-professional distrust is likely to be compounded b
mutually alien systems of theory and practice. Just as lawyers may sometime
look askance at expert psychological testimony, so psychologists may some
times view the courtroom with trepidation, or regard it as an inappropriat
arena for deployment of their knowledge.

One of the most vehement recent attacks on eyewitness research, an
especially on the appearance of psychologists as expert witnesses in crimina
cases, has come from within the ranks of academic psychology. McCLoske
and Egeth's (1984) attack includes basically two assertions: (1) that n
evidence exists to support the claim that jurors are too willing to believ
eyewitness testimony; (2) that even if it were possible to demonstrate any sor
of systematic fallibility on the part of jurors, it has not been shown that exper
psychological testimony is capable of correcting such fallibility. Loftus (1984
has responded to these assertions.

It is, of course, true that some people, including a significant number o
judges, lawyers, and law enforcement professionals, may remain unimpresse
by the accumulation of experimental and scholarly evidence that indicate
undue credulity by jurors for eyewitness testimony. It is a fact of life that o
any given issue some people are harder to persuade than others. McCloske
and Egeth's blunt conclusion that the available evidence fails to show tha
jurors are too willing to believe eyewitness testimony probably has to b
respected as an opinion, although many people, both within psychology an
within the law and the criminal justice system, appear to have found th
evidence for juror credulity to be highly convincing.

McCloskey and Egeth's second point, that the effectiveness of exper
witnesses still remains to be demonstrated is, perhaps, more forceful. Indeed
much remains to be learned, through research and through practical experi
ence, about how best to instruct jurors on the factors affecting eyewitnes
reliability. However, that knowledge can hardly be acquired by abandonin
the field at this stage.

CONCLUSIONS

What role can psychologists play to improve legal procedures involving witnesses? A number of influential lawyers, law enforcement professionals, and psychologists either fail to agree with the conclusion that current legal practices often exacerbate the problem of eyewitness unreliability, or they believe that psychologists are ill-equipped to deal with this issue. While not wholly opposed to a certain role for psychologists in this system, such persons might want, at least, to curb psychologists' increasingly frequent courtroom appearances as experts on eyewitness reliability. Some regard the efforts of eyewitness researchers as a potential nuisance or hindrance to their normal professional activities. In response, many eyewitness researchers will wish to be prepared to confront this occasionally impassioned resistance.

How likely is it that eyewitness researchers will be able to overwhelm such resistance? Can they wield new and significant findings to rout a well disciplined and battle-seasoned army of judges, lawyers, legislators, and law enforcement professionals from their position of entrenched disagreement? The history of previous encounters between psychology and the law bodes ill for such a strategy employed in isolation.

Social and professional contacts among the police, lawyers, and the judiciary should also surely be exploited to advantage. Consultation can be offered to attorneys, workshops and classes can be organized, and other services rendered wherever needed. In addition to publishing in journals of academic psychology, issues and ideas can be aired in more popular arenas, in police journals, and in law journals. In short, researchers can make use of many avenues of communication, formal and informal, public and personal, to give away their current knowledge. Equally important, eyewitness researchers should continue to incorporate natural, real-world variables into their experimental designs.

REFERENCES

BRIGHAM, J. C. (1981). The accuracy of eyewitness evidence: how do attorneys see it? *The Florida Bar Journal*, **55**, 714–721.

CAVOUKIAN, A. (1980). Eyewitness testimony: the ineffectiveness of discrediting information. Paper presented at the American Psychological Association Meeting, Montreal.

CLIFFORD, B. R., and BULL, R. (1978). *The Psychology of Person Identification*. London: Routledge and Kegan Paul.

DAVIES, G., ELLIS, H., and SHEPHERD, J. (1981). *Perceiving and Remembering Faces*. London: Academic Press.

DEFFENBACHER, K. A., and LOFTUS, E. F. (1982). Do jurors share a common understanding concerning eyewitness behavior? *Law and Human Behavior*, **6**, 15–30.

DEVLIN, LORD (1976). *Report to the Secretary of State for the Home Office of th Departmental Committee on Evidence of Identification in Criminal Cases.* London Her Majesty's Stationery Office.

DOOB, A. N., and KIRSHEMBAUM, H. M. (1973). Bias in police lineups – Partia remembering. *Journal of Police Science and Administration,* 1, 287–293.

GREENE, E., FLYNN, M. S., and LOFTUS, E. F. (1982). Inducing resistance t misleading information. *Journal of Verbal Learning and Verbal Behavior,* 21 207–219.

HALL, D. F., LOFTUS, E. F., and TOUSIGNANT, J. P. (1984). Post-event informatio and changes in recollection for a natural event. In G. L. Wells and E. F. Loftu (Eds), *Advances in Eyewitness Research.* Cambridge: Cambridge University Press

HATVANY, N., and STRACK, F. (1980). The impact of the discredited witness. *Journal o Applied Social Psychology,* 10, 490–509.

LEVINE, F., and TAPP, J. (1973). The psychology of criminal identification: the ga from Wade to Kirby. *University of Pennsylvania Law Review,* 121, 1079–1131.

LEWIS, D. J. (1979). Psychobiology of active and inactive memory. *Psychologica Bulletin,* 86, 1054–1083.

LINDSAY, R. C. L., and WELLS, G. L. (1980). What price justice? Exploring th relationship of lineup fairness to identification accuracy. *Law and Human Be havior,* 4, 303–314.

LINDSAY, R. C. L., WELLS, G. L., and RUMPEL, C. M. (1981). Jurors' detection o eyewitness-identification accuracy within and across situations. *Journal of Applie Psychology,* 66, 79–89.

LOFTUS, E. F. (1974). The incredible eyewitness. *Psychology Today,* 8, 116–119.

LOFTUS, E. F. (1979). *Eyewitness Testimony.* Cambridge, Mass.: Harvard Universit Press.

LOFTUS, E. F. (1980). Impact of expert psychological testimony on the unreliability o eyewitness identification. *Journal of Applied Psychology,* 65, 9–15.

LOFTUS, E. F. (1982). Current news events can change the results of a psychologica experiment: an example from juror-simulation research. Unpublished manuscript University of Washington.

LOFTUS, E. F. (1984). Silence is not golden. *American Psychologist,* in press.

LOFTUS, E. F., and GREENE, E. (1980). Warning: even memory for faces may b contagious. *Law and Human Behavior,* 4, 323–334.

LOFTUS, E. F., MILLER, D. G., and BURNS, H. J. (1978). Semantic integration o verbal information into visual memory. *Journal of Experimental Psychology Human Learning and Memory,* 4, 19–31.

McCLOSKEY, M., and EGETH, H. (1984). Eyewitness identification: what can psychologist tell a jury? *American Psychologist,* in press.

McCLOSKEY, M., EGETH, H., WEBB, E., WASHBURN, A., and McKENNA, J. (1982) Eyewitnesses, jurors and the issue of overbelief. Unpublished manuscript, Joh Hopkins University.

MALPASS, R. S., and DEVINE, P. G. (1981a). Guided memory in eyewitness identifica tion. *Journal of Applied Psychology,* 66, 343–350.

MALPASS, R. S., and DEVINE, P. G. (1981b). Eyewitness identification: lineu instructions and absence of the offender. *Journal of Applied Psychology,* 66 480–489.

MARQUIS, K. H., MARSHALL, J., and OSKAMP, S. (1972). Testimony validity as function of question form, atmosphere, and item difficulty. *Journal of Applie Social Psychology,* 2, 167–186.

MARSHALL, J. (1966). *Law and Psychology in Conflict.* New York: Bobbs-Merrill.

MILLER, G. A. (1969). Psychology as a means of promoting human welfare. *American Psychologist*, **24**, 1063–1075.

MOSKOWITZ, M. J. (1977). Hugo Münsterburg: a study in the history of applied psychology. *American Psychologist*, **32**, 824–842.

MÜNSTERBURG, H. (1908). *On the Witness Stand*. New York: Doubleday.

NEISSER, U. (1982). *Memory Observed*. San Francisco: Freeman.

RILEY, D. A. (1962). Memory for form. In L. Postman (Ed), *Psychology in the Making*. New York: A. A. Knopf.

SAUNDERS, D. M., HEWITT, E. C., and VIDMAR, N. (1981). Discredited eyewitness testimony, judicial instructions, and juror decisions. Paper presented at Canadian Psychological Association Meeting, Toronto.

WEINBERG, H. I., and BARON, R. S. (1982). The discredible eyewitness. *Personality and Social Psychology Bulletin*, **8**, 60–67.

WELLS, G. L. (1978). Applied eyewitness-testimony research: system variables and estimator variables. *Journal of Personality and Social Psychology*, **36**, 1546–1557.

WELLS, G. L., LEIPPE, M. R., and OSTROM, T. M. (1979). Guidelines for empirically assessing the fairness of a lineup. *Law and Human Behavior*, **3**, 285–294

WELLS, G. L., and LINDSAY, R. C. L. (1980). On estimating the diagnosticity of eyewitness and nonidentifications. *Psychological Bulletin*, **88**, 776–784.

WELLS, G. L., LINDSAY, R. C. L., and FERGUSON, T. (1979). Accuracy, confidence, and juror perceptions in eyewitness testimony. *Journal of Applied Psychology*, **64**, 440-448.

WELLS, G. L., LINDSAY, R. C. L., and TOUSIGNANT, J. P. (1980). Effects of expert psychological advice on human performance in judging the validity of eyewitness testimony. *Law and Human Behavior*, **4**, 275–285.

WIGMORE, J. H. (1909). Professor Münsterburg and the psychology of evidence. *Illinois Law Review*, **3**, 399–445.

YARMEY, A. D. (1979). *The Psychology of Eyewitness Testimony*. New York: Free Press.

YARMEY, A. D., and JONES, H. P. T. (1983). Is the psychology of eyewitness identification a matter of common sense? In S.M.A. Lloyd-Bostock and B.R. Clifford (Eds), Evaluating Witness Evidence: Recent Psychological Research and New Perspectives. Chichester: Wiley.

Psychology and Law
Edited by D.J. Müller, D.E. Blackman, and A.J. Chapman
© 1984 John Wiley & Sons Ltd

Chapter 17

Eyewitness Memory of Elderly and Young Adults[1]

A. Daniel Yarmey, Hazel P. Tressillian Jones, and Sohail Rashid

The relationship between physical appearance and criminality has been studied by social scientists at least since the time of Lombroso in the 19th century. Contemporary researchers of eyewitness identification as well as officers of the court have a particular interest in this relationship, specifically,

'... sterotypic conceptions of what a particular suspect "should" look like, or does not look like, could influence the selection of "the one who did it" by an eyewitness to a crime, particularly when that eyewitness did not have a good, clear look at the offender ...' (Shoemaker, South and Lowe, 1973, p. 432).

Stereotypic beliefs about the appearance of criminals are shared by many people (see Bull and Green, 1980). Observers are predisposed to judge others as being more or less honest because of the presence of certain salient cues, such as the number of facial scars. Whether or not these predispositions actually influence eyewitness identification, however, still needs to be determined.

Research has shown that elderly and young subject-witnesses are not influenced in their identification of an assailant as a function of his 'innocent' or 'guilty' facial demeanour (Yarmey and Kent, 1980). However, elderly subjects, in contrast to young adults, are much more likely to misidentify an innocent bystander to a crime when he or she 'looks like a criminal' (Yarmey, 1982). Simulated criminal scenarios were used in which males were observed assaulting other males and it is possible that memory of eyewitnesses would be more susceptible to stereotypic beliefs about the guilty appearance of a criminal if seen assaulting a woman, particularly if the assault was very complex or ambiguous to the observer.

Age as a factor in eyewitness testimony has received relatively little attention from researchers (see Clifford and Bull, 1978; Loftus, 1979;

Yarmey, 1979, 1984). However, conventional laboratory studies on memory for faces have demonstrated age-related differences (e.g. Brigham and Williamson, 1979; Ferris, Crook, Clark, McCarthy and Rae, 1980; Smith and Winograd, 1978; Warrington and Sanders, 1971). In addition, both Ferris e al. (1980) and Smith and Winograd (1978) found that elderly subjects made significantly more false alarms on facial decoys.

Uematsu (1982) reports that in an investigation he conducted over 40 year ago, elderly Japanese subject-witnesses, in contrast to 17 and 18 year olds, were unreliable both in terms of verbal recall and in their high suggestibility to leading questions. More recently, the superiority of young subjects in recalling details of a criminal event has been shown by Yarmey and Kent (1980), and by Yarmey and Rashid (cited in Yarmey, 1982). These studies also showed that the elderly and the young were equally accurate in recognition memory (hits). Neither of these investigations found significant differences in false alarms. However, the elderly were less confident in their decisions, and, in the Yarmey and Rashid study, made significantly more errors of omission.

The relationship between physical appearance of a suspect and memory of the witness is not independent, of course, from the appearance and actions of the victim. Recently, the phenomenon of rape has generated increasing scientific interest, with particular attention directed to assessing the patterns of attitudes towards both rapists and victims. Rape is a unique crime in so far as, if women are the targets of assault, they may not be perceived with compassion, but instead, may be assigned responsibility for the victimization (Amir, 1971; Curtis, 1974). Attitudes toward rape are also related to attributions of responsibility (Feild, 1978). Males, more so than females, tend to blame victims of rape and hold them responsible for having precipitated their victimization (Calhoun, Selby, and Warring, 1976; Feldman-Summers and Lindner, 1976). However, younger and better educated people are less accepting of rape myths, sex-role stereotyping, and interpersonal violence (Burt, 1980).

Sexual provocativeness of rape victims also has been shown to be related to attribution of responsibilty (Kanekar and Kolsawalla, 1980). It is possible that the extent to which a victim is believed responsible for a sexual assault may be an important determinant of witnesses' memory for that criminal event. Although the relationship between perceptions of subjects and the appearance of a rapist and the victim have not been systematically investigated, it is likely that people would associate a man wearing a black leather jacket and old blue jeans with antisocial tendencies, a man dressed in a business suit with more sociable inclinations, a woman wearing no bra, a shirt, and tight shorts with sexual provocativeness, and a woman clothed in a high buttoned blouse and conventional skirt as unprovocative.

Although not a study of rape, Kanekar, Nanji, Kolsawalla, and Mukerji (1981) found that males were judged as less moral when they attacked females in contrast to attacking males. They concluded that 'a man's aggression against a woman represents atypical behavior which may affect negatively the perceptions of both aggressor and victim' (Kanekar *et al.*, 1981, p. 140). In his review of the literature, Feild (1978) observed that a consistent theme in legal publications is the view that women must show resistance to an assault, and perhaps even be injured before rape is perceived.

In the study to be reported in this chapter we hypothesized that stereotypic assumptions about the criminalistic appearance of a rapist would affect subject-witnesses' memory of a sexual assault. Since a criminal assault is a complex event which often occurs too rapidly for attention to be given to both central and peripheral details, it was predicted that verbal recall for younger subject-witnesses would be more complete and more accurate than that of elderly subject-witnesses. No age-related differences were expected in correct identification (hits) of the rapist. It also was assumed that a sexually provocative victim, especially if she resisted an assault, would be highly memorable. Finally, it was expected that younger subject-witnesses, and especially females, would hold more anti-rape beliefs than older subject-witnesses. Furthermore, since evidence exists that people preferentially learn and recall information consistent with their interests (see Jones and Kohler, 1958; Levine and Murphy, 1943; but also see Brigham and Cook 1969) it was considered possible that subject-witnesses with stronger anti-rape attitudes would be superior in their identification of the rapist.

Our final topic of concern is with the correspondence between accuracy of identification and subject-witnesses' confidence of correctness. Botwinick (1978), in an extensive review of ageing and self-confidence, stated that the assumption that elderly people are generally cautious or have low generalized self-confidence is a myth. It is possible that in some situations the elderly are inhibited and cautious when threatened, and are extra careful in order perhaps to avoid mistakes. Also, they may choose not to respond when questioned since errors of omission may be preferable to responding and being shown wrong. However, Botwinick argues that there is more than one kind of cautiousness and the elderly are not invariably uncertain in all settings and contexts. Yarmey and Kent (1980) found that the elderly are less confident than the young on a facial identification test. Furthermore, Yarmey and Rashid (cited in Yarmey, 1982) found that the elderly made significantly more errors of omission, suggesting increased cautiousness on their part.

In general, the relationship between accuracy of testimony and subjective certainty of response is ambiguous. Some researchers have found a positive correlation between accuracy of testimony and ratings of certainty (Egan, Pittner, and Goldstein, 1977; Lipton, 1977), whereas others have found no relationship (Clifford and Scott, 1978, Deffenbacher, Brown, and Sturgill, 1978), or a negative relationship (Buckhout, Alper, Chern, Silverberg, and Slomovits, 1974; Loftus, Miller, and Burns, 1978). Deffenbacher (1980) has proposed that optimality of observation conditions may be a crucial factor in whether or not confidence will be related to accuracy. If accuracy of identification is shown to be unrelated to subjective certainty in eyewitnesses and in elderly eyewitnesses in particular, it will be important to determine whether or not this is a consequence of general deficits in perceptual-cognitive processes, or to a general lack of self-confidence in eyewitness situations. The present study was designed to examine, among other factors, the influence of subjective confidence on eyewitness accuracy of memory for both elderly and young adults.

EXPERIMENT

Subjects and Procedure

Sixty-four young males and 64 young females ranging in age between 18 and 36 years (mean = 21 years) and an equal number of elderly males and females between 65 and 84 years (mean = 71 years) participated as subject-witnesses. The young adults were chosen randomly from undergraduate psychology classes and elderly subjects were volunteers randomly selected from senior citizen clubs and recreational centres from both urban and rural communities. None of the elderly was resident in hospitals or mental health institutions.

The experiment was divided into six stages: (1) viewing the assault; (2) self-rating regarding personal ability as an eyewitness; (3) free recall test; (4) interrogatory tests; (5) identification tests; and (6) on attitudes toward rape scale.

Subjects were seen individually or in groups ranging in size from two to five persons. They were instructed to watch a series of slides and were told that they would be asked a few questions about the slides.

A sequence of 60 colour slides depicting an assault and implied rape was shown. The slide presentation opened with the instruction that subjects were to imagine they were sitting in a park behind some bushes and could see the events happening a few metres away from them, but no one could see them. The slides began with a view of a parking lot and a young woman seen walking on the footpath toward them. She stops for a short while to talk to a young girl playing with her dog. The woman continues walking and passes a young man who is observed walking from the opposite direction. The man grabs the woman from behind. She is seen either to struggle and fight him off, or meekly accept the assault. The man holds up a knife, places the point against her throat and forces the woman into some dense bushes where they disappear from view. Witnesses again see the child playing with her dog, followed a short time later with a view of the man coming out of the bushes, doing up his trousers, tucking his shirt in, and walking away. Moments later the woman comes out of the bush. Her clothes are very dishevelled. She is crying and obviously upset. The slides end with the little girl coming over to the victim.

Witnesses were shown one of four different scenario combinations of a sexually provocative or unprovocative victim, and an unpleasant- or pleasant-looking assailant. The man and woman who played the roles of rapist and victim were semi-professional actors hired from the local city theatre. The victim was a 21-year-old Caucasian woman, 5 feet 3 inches (1.60 metres) tall, and weighed 130 pounds (59.0 kilograms). She had waist-length, light brown hair. She wore no make-up. In the 'provocative' condition she was barefoot and carried a brown shoulder purse. She wore tight pink shorts and a tight, white sleeveless straptop, with no bra. She walked in a leisurely fashion, swaying her hips, looking around, and smiling. In the unprovocative condition the victim wore a short-sleeved, buttoned-up yellow blouse. Her skirt was mid-calf length, made of blue denim, with buttons to the knee. She wore yellow knee-length socks and flat black ankle-strap shoes. She carried a brown shoulder purse and brown paper lunch bag. She walked in a brisk fashion, looking straight ahead, and not smiling. The assailant was a 22-year-old Caucasian male, 5 feet 7 inches (1.70 metres) in height, and weighed 140 pounds (63.5 kilograms). He had short, mid-blonde hair. In the 'pleasant' condition he wore a light brown two-piece suit, a tie, a dark brown shirt, brown leather shoes, and carried a black attaché case. In the 'unpleasant' condition, the assailant wore a red T-shirt under a waist-length black leather jacket, blue jeans, and blue running shoes. His hair was uncombed, and he walked with a slouching gait. The little girl was an 11-year-old Caucasian child, dressed in a red jacket and blue jeans. She had blonde, waist-length hair, styled in a pony tail.

Each slide was presented for two seconds unaccompanied by any voice narration. The total viewing time for each scenario was 120 seconds. The victim was seen for an average time of 81 seconds, the assailant for 68 seconds, and other environmental information for 22 seconds. Both the rapist and the victim were seen from front, profile, and back views.

After viewing the slides participants were asked to estimate on a four-point scale, ranging from poor to excellent, their general abilities as witnesses for criminal events. Subjects were then instructed to write down as many details as they could remember about the event they had just witnessed. On completion of the free recall test a 30-item multiple-choice questionnaire consisting of 10 questions each on the rapist, the victim, and the environment was given. Each question was a declarative statement requiring a word or a phrase to be completed. For example, one question was 'The victim was wearing: (a) brown dress shoes; (b) no shoes; (c) white running shoes; (d) black dress shoes; (e)'don't know'. Next, participants were asked to identify the assailant, followed by an identification test for the victim. Two nine-person full-face, colour photo line-ups were used for both targets. The photographs did not reveal any clothing. Subjects were given in counter-balanced order a valid line-up containing the suspect and a blank line-up with the suspect absent. Witnesses were told that the suspect's (victim's) picture might or might not be in the line-ups. Three types of identification responses were permitted: (a) 'suspect (victim) is number ...'; (b)'suspect (victim) is not in the line-up'; (c) 'I don't know'. In addition, subjects stated how certain they were of each decision on a four-point scale, ranging from 'I am guessing' to 'I am sure enough to testify in court'. Participants were self-paced and took as much time as needed to make each response. Finally, a 21-item question-naire (Thornton, Robbins, and Johnson, 1981) was the final dependent measure. The scale is comprised of statements reflecting commonly held beliefs or opinions about rape, rapists, and rape victims. For each item witnesses indicated the extent of agreement or disagreement using Likert-type responses. Some of the items included in the scale are as follows: ' "Nice" women do not get raped'; 'in most cases, when a woman was raped, she was asking for it'; 'women provoke rape by their appearance or behaviour'.

Results and Discussion

The first analysis tested the validity of our manipulations of victim provoca-tiveness, victim resistance, and criminalistic appearance of the rapist. A sample of 37 young adults judged each slide scenario. The manipulations proved effective. The victim was rated more sexually provocative when dressed in shorts and a shirt than when dressed in a skirt and blouse. Subjects clearly discriminated between scenarios depicting victim resistance and victim non-resistance. And, as expected, the assailant was perceived as unpleasant (criminalistic) when dressed in blue jeans and black leather jacket in contrast to being seen as pleasant (non-criminalistic) when dressed in a business suit.

Only two elderly and nine young subjects considered themselves excellent witnesses after viewing the crime. Since there were no significant differences in self-ratings as a function of age, and since so few subjects categorized themselves as excellent, no further attention will be given to this characteris-tic except to point out that in this study our subjects were probably inclined to be cautious.

Verbal Memory

The analysis of free recall scores showed that young witnesses were more complete in their memory for the assault than were the elderly. (All reported differences are statistically significant at the 0.05 level of confidence, or higher.) However, young subjects remembered more details of the crime when the pleasant assailant was involved, whereas elderly witnesses remembered more information when the rapist appeared in his criminalistic demeanour. All witnesses reported a more complete account of the assault when the victim was unprovocative in her dress. In other words, the provocative victim was probably highly attended to, whereas other features such as the assailant and the environment were given less attention.

Accuracy of free recall was 95% correct or better over all conditions. When errors were made, young subjects were more inaccurate than the elderly, especially for details regarding the assailant and for the environment. Thus, young adults are more complete in their free recall but completeness of narration appears to increase the probability of error. Free recall descriptions of the provocative victim were less error prone than those for the unprovocative victim, and more errors were made in describing the criminalistic rapist. This latter point is important. If descriptions of an assailant are used by police to construct a photo-display or a line-up, descriptions of an unpleasant suspect, in contrast to a pleasant suspect, may negatively influence the nature of the foils selected for the display.

The qualitative nature of the free recall errors were also interesting. Eighty per cent of the elderly failed to mention that the rapist was carrying a knife in contrast to only 20% of the young. There were many more errors in reporting the correct colour of materials by males than by females. Many witnesses had difficulty in estimating the age of the young girl playing with her dog, and 75% of the elderly, but none of the young, called her a boy. Some of the free recall reports were sensible but very wrong such as, 'the rapist was seen driving up in a car', or 'the rapist was a friend of the victim who was walking with her from the beginning of the scene'.

Once witnesses completed their free reports, specific questions were put to them. Young subjects again were superior to the elderly. More correct information was recalled about the pleasant assailant than the unpleasant rapist, and more information was recalled about the provocative victim than the unprovocative victim. Elderly and young witnesses were similar in recall performance when the victim resisted her attacker, but the elderly showed a slight decrement and the young a slight improvement in recall when the victim was passive.

Is there a relationship between witnesses' completeness of free recall and their accuracy of controlled interrogatory reports? Correlational analyses of young witnesses' two recall scores indicated a statistically significant relationship. When broken down into component parts, reliable correlations were found for assailant characteristics and for environmental details, but not for victim attributes. There were no significant correlations on any of the measures between free and cued recall for elderly witnesses. This latter finding suggests that police should use as many questioning techniques as possible with elderly witnesses, since information attained from one proce-

Table 17.1   Proportions of Subject-Witnesses' Identifications of the Rapist and the Victim from the Valid Photo Line-up as a function of Age and Sex

	Hits	False Alarms	Don't Know	Not Present
Rapist				
Young Males	28	17	4	50
Young Females	22	14	3	61
Elderly Males	20	41	9	30
Elderly Females	16	52	4	28
Victim				
Young Males	26	22	8	44
Young Females	27	9	12	52
Elderly Males	9	39	9	42
Elderly Females	12	53	8	27

dure, such as free reports, is not necessarily related to information gathered from another.

Visual Memory

The final performance measures were the four identification tests with the photo-displays. Table 17.1 presents the proportion of subjects identifying the suspect and victim (hits), foils (false alarms), making no identification (don't know), and stating that the target was not present on the valid line-ups.

Looking first at the identification scores (hits) for the suspects, no reliable differences were found between the two age groups, or between males and females. The only significant main effect was for the appearance of the rapist, with the unpleasant suspect recognized more easily than the pleasant suspect. This result indicates that the physical demeanour of a suspect does influence eyewitness memory. Notice, however, that the nature of this influence is dependent on how memory is tested. Recall of verbal memory descriptions was more accurate for the pleasant suspect, whereas visual identifications were more accurate for the criminalistic-looking suspect. This finding may be similar to traditional verbal learning studies which have compared recall and recognition performance. Words that are rated high in frequency of occurrence in the English language are better recalled than low-frequency words (Hall, 1954). In contrast, recognition is superior for low-frequency words (Gorman, 1961). Perhaps to middle-class people, such as the participants in this study, pleasant males are a more familiar part of their environment while the reverse is true of criminalistic-looking persons. Recent work by Mueller, Heesacker, and Ross (1982) confirms our findings that pleasant suspects are more difficult to recognize in a photo-display than are unlikeable (criminalistic) faces. They propose that likeable people are more difficult to discriminate from one another because their features are more typical. That is, likeable people tend to 'look alike', whereas unpleasant, criminalistic faces are more distinctive and, therefore, more distinguishable (see also, Light, Hollander, and Kayra-Stuart, 1981). These results suggest that pleasant criminals may have an advantage over unpleasant suspects in terms of escaping 'mugshot' or line-up detection.

An understanding of eyewitness identification is incomplete without including the false alarm rate. As Table 17.1 indicates, elderly witnesses made substantially more false alarms. In contrast, the major error for young witnesses was the relatively high proportion of pure misses. That is, young witnesses failed to identify the suspect when he was present, by stating that he was not there.

No significant main effect differences were found for the identification of the victim. However, elderly males and, in particular, elderly females showed a substantial decrement in identification of the provocative victim. Once again, the elderly made reliably more false alarms.

Table 17.2 Proportions of Subject-Witnesses' Identifications on the Blank Photo Line-up as a Function of Age and Sex

	Correct Rejections of Foils	False Alarms	Don't Know
Rapist			
Young Males	70	23	6
Young Females	83	9	8
Elderly Males	36	53	11
Elderly Females	30	63	9
Victim			
Young Males	61	27	12
Young Females	64	28	8
Elderly Males	27	69	4
Elderly Females	36	52	12

Inspection of Table 17.2, which shows the proportion of subjects correctly rejecting the foils, making false alarms, and giving 'don't know' responses on a blank line-up, is consistent with the finding that elderly witnesses have a substantially higher false alarm rate than do young witnesses for both male suspects and female foils. The age groups were similar in their frequency of 'don't know' type of responses.

Subjective Certainty

Young witnesses were consistently more confident in their performance than
the elderly on each of the four identification test situations. Looking only at
the confidence scores given for identification of the suspect on the valid
line-up, young witnesses were most confident in their identification when
victims resisted, and elderly subjects were most confident when the victim was
passive. Similarly, male witnesses were most confident with victim resistance,
and female witnesses were most certain in the non-resistant context. It should
also be emphasized that elderly witnesses were typically reluctant to attach
confidence ratings to their identification responses. Even after encouragement they usually gave low ratings of certainty.

As Table 17.1 indicates, the proportion of correct identifications of the
suspect was low. Consequently, the failure to find positive relationships
between subjective certainty and objective accuracy for young witnesses on
the valid line-ups is not surprising. Analyses of young witnesses' performance
showed a negative correlation between certainty and accuracy of identifying
the suspect in the valid line-up, and no reliable correlation for the victim in
the valid line-up. In contrast, for the elderly, identification was positively
related to subjective certainty for both the rapist and the victim. A different
picture emerges, however, with the blank line-ups. Elderly witnesses showed
negative correlations between certainty and rejection of foils for both male
and female distractors. Young subjects, on the other hand, were relatively
certain and correct in rejecting male foils and victim foils. The fact that the
young and the elderly operated in directly opposite ways from each other
regarding their subjective confidence and accuracy of identifications indicates
the complexity and problematic nature of this relationship. These results
support Botwinick's (1978) hypothesis that elderly people are cautious, but
not necessarily uncertain in all situations and contexts.

Attitudes Toward Rape

Young males and females were reliably more sympathetic to rape victims and
less accepting of rape myths than elderly persons. Furthermore, young
females were much more tolerant of a provocative rape victim than all other
subject-witnesses. For instance, young males who observed a provocative
female were less sympathetic to the issue of rape than were young males who
observed an unprovocative woman. Provocativeness of the victim did not
influence the older persons' attitudes toward rape. In addition, several elderly
males held the opinion that the victim in the non-resistance scenario was *not*
raped because she did not fight back. These findings have implications for
jury trials of sexual assaults. Perhaps defence lawyers should prefer older
persons on a jury, or young males if the victim was provocative when

assaulted, since their attitudes would be more supportive of rape myths, and consequently less positive towards the rape victim.   •

Analyses of verbal and visual memory performance as a function of witnesses' attitudes toward rape were similar to the performance differences revealed by the age factor. Consequently, this discussion need not be repeated again. However, in a recently completed study using only young adults as witnesses to a rape, we found that attitudes toward rape did not influence accuracy of eyewitness memory. Nevertheless, witnesses who held strong anti-rape attitudes were reliably more certain in their ability to identify the suspect (Yarmey and Jones, 1983a). The danger to police investigations and court-room proceedings of relying on subjective certainty to reveal credible testimony is obvious, especially in such emotional circumstances such as rape.

CONCLUSIONS

Young adult witnesses are reliably superior to elderly witnesses in their verbal memory descriptions of a criminal assault. The elderly are not necessarily inaccurate and uncertain about the identity of a suspect if he is present in a line-up, but their substantially higher false alarm rate makes their testimony suspect. Not all elderly persons are poor witnesses relative to the young, as Yarmey and Kent (1980) demonstrated. However, the latter study may have been a special case. The 40 elderly witnesses in the Yarmey and Kent study may have been a 'superior' group since 39 other aged persons withdrew from the study during the testing sessions. These subjects withdrew for many different reasons, unlike the present investigation in which all the subjects tested completed the investigation. Consequently, in the Yarmey and Kent study the 40 elderly witnesses who participated may not represent the average older person in the community. However, this group may not be untypical of those witnesses the police actually use in an investigation. If the police have a choice of elderly witnesses they will choose those who appear to be most co-operative and credible. It may also be concluded that elderly persons are cautious or uncertain about their identifications in eyewitness situations. Nevertheless, the espoused certainty of young adults and some elderly persons in eyewitness identification should be treated with extreme caution.

The physical demeanour of criminal suspects does influence eyewitness memory in certain situations. It is probable that witnesses are more vigilant to the physical appearance of a suspect when he attacks a woman rather than a man. However, high vigilance does not mean memory will be equally good for both verbal descriptions and visual identifications. A criminalistic appearance of a suspect appears to be easier to identify, whereas a pleasant appearance appears to be more accurately and completely described.

The results indicated that the perception and interpretation of a victims's behaviour in a sexual assault does influence witnesses' memory for both the criminal and for other details of the assault. Witnesses observing an unprovocative victim in contrast to a provocative woman attended to more details involving the assailant and the situational context.

Unlike the age factor, which had a significant role in eyewitness memory, the sex of witnesses was not a major determinant of performance. Similarly, whether or not the victim resisted the assault had little effect on memory. Nevertheless, lack of victim resistance did influence some of the interpretations of the elderly male witnesses. These men suggested that women who fail physically to resist an assault are not raped.

Our investigations also demonstrate that police officers, and to a lesser extent lawyers, value the testimony of elderly witnesses. Furthermore, studies by Yarmey and Jones (1982, 1983b) indicate that lawyers, judges, and police are sensitive and protective of the elderly as witnesses. Unfortunately, this protectiveness could be at the cost of justice since the elderly, on the average, are less reliable witnesses to a crime than are young adults. And even young adults are highly fallible eyewitnesses. Although all elderly persons are not necessarily poor eyewitnesses, the courts should treat their testimony with extreme circumspection.

NOTE

(1) This research was supported by a grant from the Social Sciences and Humanities Research Council of Canada.

REFERENCES

AMIR, M. (1971). *Patterns in Forcible Rape.* Chicago: University of Chicago Press.

BOTWINICK, J. (1978). *Aging and Behavior.* New York: Springer.

BRIGHAM, J. C., and COOK, S. W. (1969). The influence of attitude on the recall of controversial material: a failure to confirm. *Journal of Experimental Social Psychology,* **5**, 240–243.

BRIGHAM, J. C., and WILLIAMSON, N. L. (1979). Cross-race recognition and age: when you're over 60, do they still 'all look alike'? *Personality and Social Psychology Bulletin,* **5**, 218–222.

BUCKHOUT, R., ALPER, A., CHERN, S., SILVERBERG, G., and SLOMOVITS, M. (1974). Determinants of eyewitness performance on a lineup. *Bulletin of the Psychonomic Society,* **4**, 191–192.

BULL, R., and GREEN, J. (1980). The relationship between physical appearance and criminality. *Medical Science and Law,* **20**, 79–83.

BURT, M. R. (1980). Cultural myths and supports for rape. *Journal of Personality and Social Psychology,* **38**, 217–230.

CALHOUN, L. G., SELBY, J. W. and WARRING, L. (1976). Social perception of the victim's causal role in rape: exploratory examination of four factors. *Human Relations,* **29**, 517–526.

CLIFFORD, B. R., and BULL, R. (1978). *The Psychology of Person Identification.* London: Routledge and Kegan Paul.

CLIFFORD, B. R., and SCOTT, J. (1978). Individual and situational factors in eyewitness testimony. *Journal of Applied Psychology, 63*, 352–359.

CURTIS, L. A. (1974). Victim precipitation and violent crime. *Social Problems, 21*, 594–605.

DEFFENBACHER, K. A. (1980). Eyewitness accuracy and confidence: can we infer anything about their relationship? *Law and Human Behavior, 4*, 243–260.

DEFFENBACHER, K. A., BROWN, E. L., and STURGILL, W. (1978). Some predictors of eyewitness memory accuracy. In M. M. Gruneberg, P. E. Morris, and R. N. Sykes (Eds), *Practical Aspects of Memory*. London: Academic Press.

EGAN, D., PITTNEY, M., and GOLDSTEIN, A. G. (1977). Eyewitness identification: Photographs vs. live models. *Law and Human Behavior, 1*, 199–206.

FELDMAN-SUMMERS, S., and LINDNER, K. (1976). Perceptions of victims and defendants in criminal assault cases. *Criminal Justice and Behavior, 3*, 135–139.

FERRIS, S. H., CROOK, T., CLARK, E., McCARTHY, M., and RAE, D. (1980). Facial recognition memory deficits in normal aging and senile dementia. *Journal of Gerontology, 35*, 707–714.

FEILD, H. S. (1978). Attitudes toward rape: a comparative analysis of police, rapists, crisis counselors, and citizens. *Journal of Personality and Social Psychology, 36*, 156–179.

GORMAN, A. M. (1961). Recognition memory for nouns as a function of abstractness and frequency. *Journal of Experimental Psychology, 61*, 23–29.

HALL, J. F. (1954). Learning as a function of word frequency. *American Journal of Psychology, 67*, 138–140.

JONES, E., and KOHLER, R. (1958). The effects of plausibility on the learning of controversial statements. *Journal of Abnormal and Social Psychology, 57*, 315–320.

KANEKAR, S., and KOLSAWALLA, M. B. (1980). Responsibility of a rape victim in relation to her respectability, attractiveness, and provocativeness. *Journal of Social Psychology, 112*, 153–154.

KANEKAR, S., NANJI, V. J., KOLSAWALLA, M. B., and MUKERJI, G. S. (1981). Perception of an aggressor and a victim of aggression as a function of sex and retaliation. *Journal of Social Psychology, 114*, 139–140.

LEVINE, J. M., and MURPHY, G. (1943). The learning and forgetting of controversial material. *Journal of Abnormal and Social Psychology, 38*, 507–517.

LIGHT, L. L., HOLLANDER, S., and KAYRA-STUART, F. (1981). Why attractive people are harder to remember. *Personality and Social Psychology Bulletin, 7*, 269–276.

LIPTON, J. P. (1977). On the psychology of eyewitness testimony. *Journal of Applied Psychology, 62*, 90–95.

LOFTUS, E. F. (1979). *Eyewitness Testimony*. Cambridge, Mass.: Harvard University Press.

LOFTUS, E. F., MILLER, D. G., and BURNS, H. J. (1978). Semantic integration of verbal information into a visual memory. *Journal of Experimental Psychology: Human Learning and Memory, 4*, 19–31.

MUELLER, J. H., HEESACKER, M., and ROSS, M. J. (1982). Likeability of targets and distractors in facial recognition. Unpublished paper, Department of Psychology, University of Missouri. Columbia, Missouri.

SHOEMAKER, D. J., SOUTH, D. R., and LOWE, J. (1973). Facial stereotypes of deviants and judgments of guilt or innocence. *Social Forces, 51*, 427–433.

SMITH, A. D., and WINOGRAD, E. (1978). Adult age differences in remembering faces. *Developmental Psychology, 14*, 443–444.

THORNTON, B., ROBBINS, M. A., and JOHNSON, J. A. (1981). Social perception of the rape victim's culpability: the influence of respondents' personal-environmental causal attribution tendencies. *Human Relations, 34*, 225–237.

UEMATSU, T. (1982). The reliability of eyewitness testimony – some results of experimental studies and their practical application. In A. Trankell (Ed), *Reconstructing the Past.* Deventer, The Netherlands: Kluwer.

WARRINGTON, E. K., and SANDERS, H. (1971). The fate of old memories. *Quarterly Journal of Experimental Psychology*, **23**, 432–442.

YARMEY, A. D. (1979). *The Psychology of Eyewitness Testimony.* New York: Free Press.

YARMEY, A. D. (1982). Eyewitness identification and stereotypes of criminals. In A. Trankell (Ed), *Reconstructing the Past.* Deventer, The Netherlands: Kluwer.

YARMEY, A. D. (1984). Age as a factor in eyewitness memory. In G. L. Wells and E. F Loftus (Eds). *Eyewitness Testimony: Psychological Perspectives.* New York: Cambridge University Press.

YARMEY, A. D., and JONES, H. T. (1982). Police awareness of the fallibility of eyewitness identification. *Canadian Police College Journal*, **6**, 113–124.

YARMEY, A. D., and JONES, H. T. (1983a). Accuracy of memory of male and female eyewitnesses to a criminal assault and rape. *Bulletin of the Psychonomic Society*, **21**, 89–92.

YARMEY, A. D., and JONES, H. T. (1983b). Is the psychology of eyewitness identification a matter of common sense? In S.M.A. Lloyd-Bostock and B.R. Clifford (Eds), *Evaluating Witness Evidence: Recent Psychological Research and New Perspectives.* Chichester: Wiley.

YARMEY, A. D., and KENT, J. (1980). Eyewitness identification by elderly and young adults. *Law and Human Behavior*, **4**, 123–137.

Psychology and Law
Edited by D.J. Müller, D.E. Blackman, and A.J. Chapman
© 1984 John Wiley & Sons Ltd

Chapter 18

Accuracy and Confidence in Testimony: A Critical Review and Some Fresh Evidence[1]

Geoffrey M. Stephenson

Testimony – to things heard, seen, felt, or otherwise experienced – is a long-established psycho-legal issue (see Sporer, 1982) going back at least to Münsterberg (1909), and reflected in recent textbooks on 'eyewitness testimony' (e.g. Loftus, 1979; Yarmey, 1979). It is unfortunate that the gist of the message which emerges from a great deal of this work has been pessimistic: identification parades are unreliable, children are very suggestible, adversarial procedures confuse witnesses, and so on. Münsterberg himself established this tradition: 'The confidence in the reliability of evidence ... is a popular illusion against which modern psychology must seriously protest' (Münsterberg, 1909, p. 44). Admittedly, the courts need evidence, but apparently the interrogation of witnesses about their remembrance of past events is not an especially good source.

RELATIONSHIPS BETWEEN CONFIDENCE AND ACCURACY

The issue of the relationship between confidence and accuracy in testimony is a particular example of a topic which currently fuels the purveyors of psycho-legal gloom and doom (e.g. Buckhout, 1974; Yarmey, 1979). It is suggested that there is no positive relationship; or worse, there is a negative relationship. Although there certainly are instances in which the case for pessimism is well founded, I argue that in this instance the case has been overstated, stemming in part from uncritical evaluation of evidence and inadequate analysis of the problem. In particular, definitions of the relationship neglect important conceptual distinctions, and the restriction of experimentation almost exclusively to the laboratory, and largely to the problems of person identification, has proved misleading.

The issue is an important one, and it takes a number of forms. The most frequently illustrated form concerns differences between individuals, and I will call this the question of *objective testimonial validity* (OTV). Is the testimony of a witness who is diffident, cautious, unsure, and uncertain less likely to be accurate than that of a witness who is confident, certain, and has no doubts about the truth of what is said? There can be no doubt that this can be an important and vexing question for the courts; for juror, judge, and counsel, and for the witness. Witnesses may be tempted to feign confidence in order to be more impressive; counsel may refrain from exhibiting too tentative a witness; the judge must advise the jury and the jury must decide between witnesses whose confidence varies and whose evidence conflicts. Certainly, the assumption is frequently made that the level of confidence displayed by any particular witness is an important consideration for all parties, although no psychologist has sought to discover whether the confidence of witnesses is in practice of such importance. What assumptions do the protagonists make? How frequently do judges draw attention to the manner of witnesses, and with what apparent bias? What are the policies of counsel, and how do jurors respond? Evidence is meagre.

We do know that mock jurors, at least, are highly influenced by their perceptions of witness confidence (Wells, Lindsay, and Ferguson, 1979), but we have little idea of how real juries respond to the succession of witnesses who come before them. Jurors, of course, do not themselves interact directly with witnesses, but are prevailed upon to accept the conclusions drawn by advocates from the evidence elicited in examination. Evaluation of testimony may well be influenced by the style of examination, and by the relationship established between the advocate and the jury during the course of the trial. Uncertainty in witnesses certainly seems to be discouraged by the courts, and in particular by advocates, questions being so framed as to encourage an unambiguous answer. Nevertheless, confidence may be turned to disadvantage by a skilled advocate, for confidence is not the only factor testifying to the truth of a witness's evidence. In the proceedings against Jeremy Thorpe, the prominent British politician accused of conspiracy and incitement to murder, it is evident that Peter Bessell gave his testimony with confidence ('firmly'), but this did not impress defending counsel (Sir David Napley):

> 'You have ... succeeded in telling a considerable number of lies over a period of years ... in some cases to experienced journalists ... you yourself have said you now have a credibility problem ... the difficulty is to tell when you are telling the truth and when you are telling lies' (Chippendale and Leigh, 1979, p. 57).

Bessell's acceptance of this accusation may perhaps have rendered his confident manner less than helpful to his cause. Nevertheless, the question of OTV (other things being equal) remains a compelling one: is the more confident witness the more accurate?

Subjective testimonial validity (STV) is a second form of the relationship, and one which has been neglected. The relationship between confidence and accuracy within the individual is then the issue. What happens when an individual's testimony is part confident and part tentative? Is it appropriate to have less faith in an individual's tentative testimony than in testimony delivered with confidence? Whatever merits the testimony of a confident witness may have generally, is it true to say of an individual that those parts of his or her evidence in which greatest confidence is placed will in truth be more accurate than other parts concerning which some doubt is expressed? This issue may not arise explicitly in legal testimony, because degrees of truth are not admitted. Either testimony is regarded as being 'true' or the witness is lying (or at best mistaken). Again, Peter Bessell, who was asked, 'Is your evidence true?' replied, 'It is, sir. I agreed with Sir David that I have told a number of lies over a number of years. I have never lied on oath' (Chippendale and Leigh, 1979, pp. 65–66). Confidence judgments are not called for, expected or desired in courts of law, however indispensable they may be to the experimental psychologist, and even though it may well be that with individuals deemed trustworthy, jurors are influenced differentially by different parts of their evidence, according to the conviction with which it is expressed.

Both forms of the relationship between confidence and accuracy may in practice be of importance, but the recent psychological literature (see Deffenbacher, 1980) emphasizes objective testimonial validity and ignores the question of subjective validity. This is unwise, because it is possible for STV to be high when OTV is low. Some people may generally ooze confidence, others may regularly hesitate: nevertheless, all may be 'subjectively valid' – to the extent that such intra-individual variation in confidence as does exist is consistently related to accuracy (at whatever point on the scale of confidence). Moreover, it is the case that problems of STV are frequently encountered in practice. Testimony from a single witness may extend for many hours, and it is certainly appropriate that one should ask whether the witness's variations in confidence are systematically related to the accuracy of his or her testimony. Here we may note the dangers of basing conclusions about testimonial validity exclusively on studies of identification evidence in line-ups, or from 'photo-spreads'. Much of the recent research evidence comes from studies of confidence in the identification of a single suspect from a simulated line-up. Given that only one identification is required, questions of STV are not raised, and in 'real life' the question of OTV is frequently unreal, since the identification, if made, has to be unambiguous, and most line-ups are in any case subjected to only one (usually key) witness. In fact, a more compelling research question for identification evidence concerns the circumstances in which individuals are prepared to identify someone in the first place, for it may well be that confidence *per se* plays little part in the decision to identify, a point to be considered in relation to the prevalence of laboratory studies of the problem. For the time being, it may be noted that, of course, OTV becomes most important when testimonial accounts conflict. Who is the more confident witness then becomes an important issue. But equally we may note that the problem of STV – which aspects of an individual's account are likely to be accurate – is almost always a vexatious issue in any trial.

There is a third form of the question (suggested to me by D. E. Broadbent, personal communication) which reflects a less obvious problem in courts of law, and this concerns what might be termed *topical validity*. OTV may vary according to the nature of the topic, as may STV. In the first place, individuals' expertise varies, and expressions of confidence in an area of competence may be taken more seriously than expressions of confidence in a less familiar area. Hunter (1972), for example, shows that the 'exceptional' numerical memory of his subject, Professor Aitken, was integrally and functionally related to his competence in mental calculation; his competence both required, and in turn facilitated, his memory. Secondly, it is also likely that individuals generally may operate in certain areas more surely than in others. As we shall see, evidence on the accuracy–confidence relationship stems largely from studies of person identification, and may not be typical of other kinds of 'eyewitness' testimony. It should also be recognized that different meanings may be attached to expressions of doubt or confidence in different topic areas. This could happen for a number of reasons. For example, some amazement is occasionally expressed in court that witnesses can apparently confidently remember the events of 10 – 13 years ago, but be dubious about more recent events (see Chippendale and Leigh, 1979). It is of course true that the events of a particular day 10 years ago may generally be less well recalled than the events of yesterday, but those few outstanding events which *are* recalled may well be endowed with great confidence, perhaps wrongly. On the other hand, considerable doubt may perhaps rightly be expressed about some recollections of yesterday, merely because the amount of generally successful recall is so much higher than in the case of events which occurred a long time ago. OTV, STV, and topical validity are three variations on the theme of the relationship between confidence and accuracy in testimony. Of course they are not independent, and they may not cover all facets of the general issue. Nevertheless, they represent distinctions which we need to bear in mind when evaluating some of the claims which have been made. We now turn to that task.

THE EVIDENCE

Experimental psychologists have demonstrated in a variety of recognition and recall tasks that the 'memory system' can 'evaluate itself' (Groninger, 1976) reasonably effectively, that variations in 'confidence estimates' may be effectively employed as estimates of 'memory strength' (see Broadbent, 1971; McNichol, 1972; Norman, 1969; Norman and Wickelgren, 1965), and that the 'feeling of knowing' has substance (Hauck, Isakson, and Moore, 1978). Such studies have also consistently pointed to the importance of the distinction between OTV and STV, in that, as Wickelgren and Norman (1966) indicated in early studies, it is possible that highly confident persons perform consistently worse than less confident persons. Studies of memory for prose stories have also demonstrated that people can accurately pick out their own errors, and that an accuracy 'set' increases accuracy and confidence (see Gauld and Stephenson, 1967; Kintsch and Greene, 1978).

Deffenbacher's (1980) review of studies of eyewitness testimony makes clear that the evidence for a substantial positive relationship between confidence and accuracy in the testimony is not strong. However, significant correlations between confidence and accuracy, when they occur, are positive, and many of those studies producing non-significant results have serious drawbacks. Very frequently, for example, the level of accuracy is so low that any relationship with confidence is likely to be fortuitous. Deffenbacher's conclusion is that, under optimal conditions, the relationship between confidence and accuracy is usually positive. Another serious problem with previous studies is the tendency to use the term 'eyewitness testimony' inconsistently, and this is a problem not adequately faced in Deffenbacher's review. Some writers restrict the term to identification of a suspect – in vivo or from photographs – whereas others include description of physical features or narration of events. The problem of 'topical validity', in other words, has not been faced, eyewitness identification having been assumed to be representative of eyewitness testimony in general. In the following review of key studies the two topics are separately treated.

Objective Testimonial Validity in Identification Evidence

In another recent review, Yarmey (1979) gave further publicity to Buckhout's (1974) contention that at least in the case of OTV there is a negative correlation between confidence and accuracy: the more confident, the less accurate a witness (see also Buckhout, Alper, Chern, Silverberg, and Slomovitz, 1974; Buckhout, Figueroa, and Hoff, 1975). This claim, if generally true, very seriously undermines common sense views, and is one which should not be made lightly, nor accepted uncritically. Let us, therefore, begin by examining Buckhout's evidence in some detail.

In Buckhout's first reported experiment an incident was staged on campus at Harvard, in which a student 'attacked' a professor in front of 141 witnesses. 'Sworn statements' were taken from witnesses, and each witness rated 'his own confidence in the accuracy of the description' (Buckhout, 1974, p. 29).

Seven weeks later, photographic line-ups (six photographs in each condition) were presented. Instructions were either biased on unbiased, and the photographic spread was either biased or unbiased. The biased instructions hinted strongly that the culprit was in the line-up, and the biased spread showed the culprit smiling and with head, and photograph itself, angled, in contrast to all the others. We are told that, 'The highest proportion of correct identifications, 61 per cent, was achieved with a biased set of photographs and biased instructions. The degree of confidence in picking suspect no. 5, the attacker, was also significantly higher in that condition' (Buckhout, 1974, p. 30). This suggests, not unreasonably, that, when an accusing finger is correctly pointed at a culprit by the experimenter, those who identify the culprit are more confident of their judgments. Unfortunately, these results tell us nothing about the relationship between confidence and accuracy within any one experimental condition or even between subjects in different conditions. To use our terminology, there is no evidence about the level of either OTV or STV.

The report of a second experiment is barely more informative (Buckhout *et al.*, 1974). Of 52 witnesses of a purse-snatching, 14 correctly identified the culprit from a line-up of five people. Seven of these also did not pick out a 'look-alike' in a second line-up which was viewed either before or after the line-up containing the culprit. The seven who picked both were termed 'impeached-successful' witnesses, about whom the authors state: '... the 'impeached-successful' witnesses showed significantly *higher* confidence in their descriptions than the clearly successful witnesses' (Buckhout *et al.*, 1974, p. 192). There are certain factors which render this finding less exciting than it is taken to be by Buckhout:

(1) The ratings of confidence were made *before* subjects made the identification: it is not reported how confident they were after having made the identification. There is no reason to believe that pre-line-up confidence in one's ability to select the right person is the same as post-line-up confidence in one's having selected the right person.
(2) There was no difference overall between the confidence of 'successful' and 'unsuccessful' witnesses.
(3) The figure of 14 correct out of 52 identifications in a line-up of five persons is consistent with the hypothesis that everyone was guessing; that is, the task was so difficult that overall performance was not statistically better than that expected by chance. In that case there is no reason to believe that these witnesses are 'good' and the others are 'poor', because it cannot be said that they had better reason for their judgments than those who were less successful. Buckhout (1974) does also describe the results of a further experiment, in which it was shown that 'good' witnesses who could recall the events of a filmed crime

sequence were also good at picking out the culprit (presumably the one shown on film) from a line-up, but he says nothing about how confident the 'good' and 'poor' witnesses are.

In summary, there is no conclusive evidence from Buckhout's influential published work that either OTV or STV is deficient, and certainly not that an inverse correlation obtains between confidence and accuracy in performance on video-taped line-ups.

Buckhout's scepticism regarding the confidence–accuracy relationship reflects his intention to lower the status of testimony (see Wells, 1978), a job he regards as being long overdue, given that 'the essential findings on the unreliability of eyewitness testimony were made by Hugo Münsterberg nearly 30 years ago' (Buckhout, 1974, p. 31). Part of the problem here derives from the fact that the unreliability is seen at its most dramatic and vivid form in the identification parade. This has received considerable investigation by psychologists, despite its being a rare and untypical form of testimony. Testimony (or 'eyewitness testimony' as it is generally and misleadingly termed) embraces all forms of recall or recognition of events experienced by the witness, from an account of a telephone call to the reporting of a crime itself. Human perception may well be 'sloppy and uneven', to use Buckhout's (1974) phrase, but its manifestation in testimony is not typified in the contrived line-up where, if official guidelines are followed, the conditions are so designed as to render accurate performance unlikely to be adventitious. Nevertheless, it is the (mock) identification parade which has stimulated most of the research on confidence and accuracy, and it is to this research we must now turn.

One reliable piece of relevant experimental evidence comes from Wells et al. (1979). Wells is one of the few to have acknowledged the point that the identification task must not be so difficult that persons can be successful only by guessing. Clearly, if the level of accuracy is no higher than that expected by chance, there is no reason to expect the accurate performers to be more confident of their judgments: all, presumably, have guessed. In the experiment by Wells, following a staged theft, 58% of the witnesses correctly identified the thief from a set of six photographs, a performance higher than that expected by chance. Their confidence was significantly higher than the 20% who made an incorrect identification, the overall correlation of + 0.29 between confidence and accuracy being statistically significant. At least to a limited extent it is appropriate to give more credence to a witness who identifies a suspect more confidently than another. This is a conclusion which receives support from certain other studies. For example, in a recent study Sanders and Warnick (1984) reported a statistically significant correlation of 0.37 between confidence and filmed line-up recognition accuracy. However, this correlation used pooled data from eight different experimental conditions whose effects on accuracy differed significantly (from 14 to 86% of subject making a correct identification), and may mask a more favourable picture ix those conditions that proved more favourable to accuracy. A similar criticism may be made of other studies of confidence and accuracy in identification. For example, Gorenstein and Ellsworth (1980) report a correlation of only 0.1 between accuracy and confidence, as a result of combining subjects from a condition in which performance was close to chance with others from a condition which produced statistically significant results. In fact, combining the conditions, the accuracy was not significantly above that expected by chance, thus vitiating the correlation exercise in the first place. A similar criticism can be made of the reported absence of a significant overall correlation between confidence and accuracy by Lieppe, Wells, and Ostrom (1978), where in three of their four experimental conditions there was no evidence that subjects performed at above chance level.

Brown, Deffenbacher, and Sturgill (1977) also found near zero correlation between confidence and accuracy, but unfortunately their presentation of the results does not make it clear how the component scores were devised. In the 'line-ups', each character was a potential suspect, and subjects knew that a certain number of criminals were present. (This incidentally detracts from its relevance to identification performance in real line-ups.) It would appear that averaged 'accuracy' of identification of all suspects was used together with average confidence ratings to arrive at the correlations 'across subjects' reported by the authors; but this is speculation. Apart from this difficulty there are the following points which detract from the value of these findings (1) confidence was assessed on a relatively crude three-point scale; (2 performance accuracy was exceptionally poor in some conditions. For these various reasons it is difficult to assess the value of their results and, as Wells e al. (1979) pointed out, the relationship between confidence and accuracy was of 'incidental' relevance in this study, being unrelated to any of the investiga tors' formulated hypotheses.

There is then some evidence for statistically significant OTV in the identification parade: that is, those persons who are most sure are most likely to be correct in their identification. Those studies which have set out to examine the relationship directly have obtained evidence for a significant effect (Sanders and Warnick, 1984; Wells et al., 1979), whereas those examining the relationship 'incidentally', in particular Brown et al., (1977) Gorenstein and Ellsworth (1980), and Lieppe et al., (1978), have failed perhaps in some cases because the task was so hard that accuracy was achieved only by accident. All the studies we have reported here neglected to examine the relationship within experimental conditions, even when accuracy of performance was shown to differ significantly between conditions. This is likely to have had the effect of disguising the 'true' level of the correlation in those conditions where the level of accuracy was sufficiently high to suggest at successful performance was not accidental. The suggestion that a *negative* correlation obtains between confidence and accuracy receives no support in the case of OTV in identification parade performance. The best evidence we have is for a statistically significant positive relationship. There are two immediate questions:

(1) How do these conclusions apply to STV in identification parade performance?
(2) What is the position with respect to other kinds of testimony?

Subjective Testimonial Validity in Identification (ID) Performance

Real witnesses are rarely asked to inspect more than one line-up, and within that line-up are asked to pick out no more than one individual. Nevertheless, the question of STV is of more than academic interest, if only because identification procedures can be changed. It would, for example, be feasible in 'real life' to follow the experimental procedure adopted by Brown *et al.*, 1977) and require subjects to assign judgments to their decision about each person in the line-up. If the evidence for STV is strong, then such judgments would yield potentially valuable information concerning the probability that a particular suspect is guilty.

Unfortunately, STV has not been examined in identification performance, although the information was available in Brown *et al.*'s study. In that study, judgments were made of all 'suspects' in one or two line-ups, each line-up containing at least one 'criminal'. Unfortunately, data are presented across all subjects and, as we have seen, it is not quite clear what constituted the accuracy and confidence scores for each subject. In fact, it is common practice for all detailed information regarding confidence ratings to be omitted from published findings. For all the reader is told, in all the studies cited, the variation in the confidence ratings may have been negligible. This lack of concern with detail and with STV as opposed to OTV probably reflects the fact that the question of the validity of confidence ratings has customarily been a subsidiary issue in studies of factors affecting accuracy of performance.

The study by Deffenbacher, Leu, and Brown (1981) on facial recognition does, however, address directly the question of STV, albeit not in a simulated line-up, and it confirms reasonably substantial OTV. In that study two methods of testing were employed, the 'two-alternative forced choice' procedure and the 'yes–no' procedure. The confidence–accuracy relationship was statistically significant at 0.48 across all 72 subjects, with a suggestion that the 'forced choice' procedure yielded a higher correlation than the 'yes–no' procedure. However, the authors also investigated STV by examining the within-individual correlations across trials which certainly indicated consider-

able individual variation, although for no individual did any negative correlation approach statistical significance. At the worst, individuals exhibit zer
STV.

Confidence in Descriptive Recall

Buckhout (1974) was again one of the first to obtain data on confidence an
the recall of past events in legal contexts, but unfortunately he did not repo
any of the raw data he collected, either with respect to OTV or STV
However, he does assert that, 'Our best witnesses had also been among th
best performers in the recall test, that is, they had made significantly fewe
errors of commission (adding incorrect details). They had not given particu
larly complete reports, but at least they had not filled in' (Buckhout, 1974, p
30). Unfortunately, no further details are given.

Subjects in a study by Lipton (1977) were led to believe that the film the
viewed was of a genuine crime. Recall of the events and details was require
in various conditions: witnesses' rating of their confidence of testimony on
seven-point scale on a post-trial questionnaire was also collected. Hence w
have here what appears to be an overall rating of confidence, which Lipto
then correlated with overall accuracy, and with *quantity* of recall. Th
correlation with accuracy was 0.44 and with quantity −0.09. Here, then,
good evidence that the more confident a witness is, the more likely it is tha
the evidence will be accurate (regardless of quantity). Accuracy in th
instance was defined as the ratio of correct items to all those mentionec
Taking into account the crudity of the overall confidence rating (on a singl
scale) of accuracy as applied to approximately 30–110 recalled items, th
correlation of 0.44 may well be a considerable underestimate of the potenti
of witnesses for accurate evaluation of their testimony. Lipton's study woul
certainly have been more useful if each recalled item had been assigned
confidence rating. In that case, a more reliable measure of overall confidenc
would have been obtained, and STV as well as OTV could have bee
examined.

The fact that there was no sizeable relationship between confidence an
quantity rules out one explanation of the observed confidence–accurac
correlation: that the cautious people who produce less are rightly mor
confident of their accuracy. In this respect it is regrettable that Lipton doe
not report the correlations within different experimental conditions. Delay
question bias, and question type all affected both quantity and accuracy c
testimony and it is important to know whether or not the correlation holds u
when a much smaller performance range is under consideration.

A more recent study, Sanders and Warnick (1984), did not find
significant correlation between confidence and accuracy of recall. Recall i
this instance was of the 'features' of an actor seen on video-tape. Specifically

ubjects had to state whether or not the actor wore glasses, a sweater, a moustache, a beard, light or dark hair, and straight or wavy hair. The authors mplied that confidence judgments were required for each item, but no results re presented for STV. The lack of significant results for OTV is not necessarily in conflict with Lipton's findings. In Lipton's study, 144 'items' were identified from a filmed murder, and subjects watched the film believing that the events were real. Hence, Lipton alerted subjects to the criminal importance of the film, and to the events that occurred. Sanders and Warnick's film had no such dramatic quality, and, more importantly, subjects were quizzed about physical features of individuals, not the events portrayed. There is evidence (Dent and Stephenson, 1978, 1979) that physical features or what Dent and Stephenson call 'descriptive' evidence) are much less accurately described than is a sequence of events. In Sanders and Warnick's experiment subjects were not on average scoring above chance level, and the predicted effects of *prior exposure* and *arousal value* on accuracy were not obtained. In other words, we again have the problem of a failure to elicit sufficient variation in successful performances for testimonial validity to be assessed adequately. The important question of topical validity is pertinent here. Maybe for some classes of testimony, 'descriptive' evidence for example, the confidence–accuracy relationship will be intrinsically low because the task is so inadequately performed, yet the willingness to express confidence, for whatever reason, remains undiminished. Wells *et al.*, (1979) suggest that inappropriate feedback is the reason why person recognition is so inadequate. Frequently we may believe we recognize another, and our friendly smile is reciprocated whether or not our belief is genuine. In addition, a genuine belief by one person that he/she has met another 'is practically disconfirmable', even though the other cannot clearly recall the meeting. Moreover, it is perhaps a greater social crime to fail to recognize than to mistakenly 'recognize' another. By the same token, concern with establishing the appropriate relationship with others may lead us to pay little attention to people as objects whose features are a matter of concern: we are more concerned with the role relationship than with how they appear. On all these grounds testimonial validity should be relatively poor for both recognition of people and recall of their features.

Unfortunately for this hypothesis Clifford and Scott (1978), although finding that recall of actions portrayed in film was superior to descriptive recall, did not find that testimonial validity was higher for actions than for physical descriptions. However, Clifford and Scott appear also to have computed their correlation coefficients using a combination of subjects from experimental conditions which produced greatly differing levels of accuracy (e.g. violent versus non-violent episodes), and this may have served to disguise substantial correlations within conditions. A more recent study of undergraduate students' recall of filmed incidents found a statistically non-

significant correlation of −0.06 across conditions (Hollin, 1984) and, surpri
singly, similarly non-significant correlations obtained in each experimentec
condition, despite variations in accuracy between conditions.

Rarely, however, has the accuracy–confidence relationship been examinec
outside the laboratory, one exception being a remembering study by Nickerson and Adams (1979) on adults' recognition of features on the US 'penny'.
When rating their identification responses to 20 different features, in genera
it was found that the higher a subject's confidence in the answer the more
likely was the answer to be correct. More recently, Brigham, Maass, Snyder,
and Spaulding (1982) have assessed the efficacy of eyewitness identification
ingeniously in a naturalistic setting. They make the obvious point that in
laboratory settings the identification of the 'suspect' has no actual consequences either for the suspect or the subject, and that a more cavalier attitude
may be adopted than in naturalistic settings where the evidence provided may
have important consequences for the individuals concerned: appearance and
confrontation in court for the witness; fine or imprisonment for the suspect.
In this study the subjects were 73 shop assistants in 63 different shops. After a
gap of two hours, the assistants were interviewed, and by means of a
photographic line-up assessed as to their ability to pick out the two men who
had earlier, and inconsequentially, visited their shop. The confidence-
accuracy relationship of 0.50 was statistically significant, a relationship which
held even when 'guessing' respones were eliminated. Moreover, there was no
significant evidence – as others have suggested – of a trait of confidence, the
correlation between confidence ratings for the two suspects being positive but
not statistically significant. This study again strongly suggests that the
pessimism generated by laboratory studies of the relationship is indeed
inappropriate, and that the search for factors influencing the strength of the
relationship should continue.

There is a 'strong' interpretation of the concept of OTV which would
demand a literal interpretation of the confidence expressed by an individual.
In theory, it would be possible for OTV to be high even if individuals
reported being either only 'very unsure' or merely 'unsure', as long as
accuracy was consistently related to this limited range of confidence. In the
strong sense of OTV we could, however, demand that, for example, an
'unsure' account would be more likely wrong than correct. Of course, it
would be excellent if when Witness A says he or she is 'sure' that something
occurred this means the same as when B says he or she is 'sure' about
something, and even better if both are right. The courts would have a very
easy job to perform. However, not only may individuals understand different
things by the same word, they may differ in their inherent cautiousness, one
expressing an opinion where another might prefer to keep his or her silence.
Witness A may regard 'very sure' as expressing such a degree of certainty as
could never seriously be entertained by any mere mortal, and may be

repared to limit his or her range to 'maybe' and 'perhaps', whereas B's enchant for the flamboyant may yield a total range from 'sure' to 'certain'. here are then two important points to make:

(1) Each person may be distinguising equally accurately between events, the disagreement between them concerning the precise location of their identical distinctions on the 'scale' of certainty.
(2) Those evaluating the testimony may well make allowance for such individual differences and act quite appropriately not in terms of objective but subjective testimonial validity.

As Wells et al. (1979) say, '... the proper forensic test of the confidence–ccuracy relationship should involve confidence as measured through responses to cross-examination' (Wells et al., 1979, p. 441).

STV has been examined in only one of the investigations so far cited Deffenbacher et al., 1981), although some have obtained information from which estimates of STV could have been derived. STV is an individual measure of the confidence-accuracy correlation, and requires that subjects make confidence judgments about a variety of items such that we can judge whether their variations in confidence are associated reliably with variations in their accuracy. Five more of the studies already described obtained data which are susceptible to analysis in terms of STV, those of Buckhout (1974), Brown et al. (1977), Clifford and Scott (1978), Hollin (1984), and Sanders and Warnick (1984). None examined within-subjects correlations between confidence and accuracy. This is unfortunate, especially as all five reports express dismay at what appears to be poor OTV. The study by Deffenbacher et al. (1981) indicated that perhaps the most important point about STV is individual variation. The confidence of some individuals is to be trusted, and of others to be discounted. As we shall see, this conclusion is echoed in some ecent evidence on long-term memory for different story material.

SOME FRESH EVIDENCE AND NEW ISSUES

It is apparent that concentration on the topic of 'eyewitness identification' has prevented many interesting theoretical issues from being explored; for example, questions concerning the relationship between different forms of the confidence–accuracy issue, problems of individual differences, the effect of social factors on confidence, and other matters which we have seen in principle to be worthy of investigation, but which in practice have been neglected, and may continue to be neglected if the prevailing emphasis continues. In what remains of this chapter, I will describe briefly some findings which impinge strongly on two of these neglected issues – the role of individual differences and of interpersonal factors – and which suggest ways in which future work on the confidence–accuracy relationship might proceed. The results from two experiments will be drawn upon in this discussion. In both experiments the performance of individuals acting alone was contrasted with that of individuals working together in dyads. However, in Experiment 1 subjects (students of the University of Linz in Austria) were recalling the details of an experiment they had read about and discussed together, whereas Experiment 2 (reported in detail in Stephenson, Brandstätter, and Wagner 1983) subjects (men from the city of Linz) were required to recall the details of a story they had been told. In each case, both free recall and answers to a 'cross-examination' questionnaire were required.

Most studies of the confidence–accuracy relationship have examined only OTV and have hence aimed to discern the 'true' level of the correlation to be expected between individuals. Studies of STV on the other hand may be expected to throw light on the question of individual differences in the extent to which degrees of confidence are associated with degrees of accuracy. Deffenbacher et al. (1981) discovered a range of correlations from 0 to +0.6 for individuals in a facial photograph recognition task. In Experiment 1, subjects were required, after having read the background to a psychology experiment, to decide in pairs what they thought the outcome of the experiment had been. Subsequently they were asked to recall details of the experiment, either singly or in dyads, and either immediately after the experiment or after completion of a half-hour filler task. They had not anticipated having to perform the remembering task. Here I wish to describe just the results relating to variation in STV between individuals. From Table 18.1 it is evident, as Deffenbacher et al. (1981) found, that in no individual or dyad do we ever find a negative relationship. In all cases, the bi-serial correlations between accuracy ('right' or 'wrong') and confidence (expressed on a four-point scale) is positive, although approaching zero in some cases. In some individuals, on the other hand, the

Table 18.1 Subjective Testimonial Validity of recall: within individuals (or dyads) bi-serial correlations between accuracy and confidence across 19 items of question-naire (Experiment 1)

		Immediate	Delayed
Individual	X̄	= .48	.46
	Range	= .35 to .61 (.15 to .97)[1]	.16 to .62 (.07 to .79)[1]
	SD	= .11	.16
Dyadic	X̄	= .34	.57
	Range	= .11 to .50	.37 to .84
	SD	= .12	.16

[1] The figures in brackets define the range of individuals comprising averaged pairs. A correlation of .46 or above indicates a statistically significant association (p < .05).

orrelation is near perfect. The picture is one of considerable individual ariation within the positive range, and this was found also in Experiment 2.

We obtained no biographical information about individual subjects, and so annot surmise what underlies the variation. It is possible that interest in the naterial to be recalled played a part, although the relationship between STV ind overall performance did not suggest that task competence was an mportant factor. Clearly, the question to be asked of an individual's or lyad's testimony is not so much how confidently any part is rated, but how ralid a performer is this particular individual. The question of individual onsistency across different tasks and situations is a question of considerable mportance and one on which there is as yet no evidence. We do not know if iTV is a reliable individual measure, or if it varies consistently for an ndividual as we move from one kind of situation to another.

Wells, Ferguson, and Lindsay (1981) point to what they call the 'tractabil-ty' of witness confidence, and to the fact that interpersonal factors (e.g. ehearsal of testimony) may readily increase confidence inappropriately. The omparison between dyads and individuals, incorporated into the design of ixperiments 1 and 2, throws light on the influence of such factors on estimonial validity. In both experiments, an individual ('strong') measure of)TV was produced which measured the extent to which the ratings of onfidence could be taken at face value. This was based on the discrepancy)etween the 'ideal' and 'actual' confidence rating for any one item, regardless)f direction. The ideal rating for a *correct* answer would be 'absolutely :ertain', and would not contribute anything to the *invalidity* score. 'Fairly :ertain' would contribute 1, 'unsure' 2, and 'guessing' 3 points. The same)rocedure was applied in reverse to 'wrong' answers (that is 1 for 'unsure', 2 or 'fairly certain' and 3 for 'absolutely certain'.). Table 18.2 portrays the :orrelations in the four experimental conditions between testimonial *invalid-ty* so defined and STV as defined previously.

It becomes clear from Table 18.2 that individuals more than dyads use the anguage of confidence more validly. Both individuals and dyads make

Table 18.2 Correlations (r) across individuals and dyads between testimonial invalidity and Subjective Testimonial Validity

	Immediate	Delayed
Individuals (averaged pairs)	−.90***(9)	−.95***(9)
Dyads	−.78* (8)	−.62* (9)

*p < .05
***p < .001

subjective distinctions between the confidence of correct and wrong testimony, but in individuals these distinctions are apparently almost perfectly
positioned on the scale of confidence (correlations of −0.90 and −0.95). In
dyads the correlations are significantly lower. The 'tractability' of confidence
does not prevent appropriate distinctions being made between the confidence
of correct and incorrect testimony, but it does reduce the extent to which
these distinctions are appropriately expressed. Results from Experiment 2
clarify these matters.

   Confidence is, indeed, readily induced socially. Both experiments showed
an increase in confidence in dyads, which was fortuitously matched by an
increase in accuracy such that OTV was not adversely affected, and indeed
was enhanced in certain circumstances. Nevertheless, it is the case that social
support may have a general effect on the level of confidence, regardless of the
accuracy of the testimony. Results obtained in Experiment 2 confirm that
although this may inappropriately lead to a raised level of confidence in
erroneous testimony, the subjective validity of testimony may remain unaffected. In this experiment the *individual* measure of testimonial *invalidity*
was again obtained by calculating the scale point discrepancy between the
'ideal' and the 'actual' confidence rating, regardless of direction. Interestingly, although dyads were more accurate and more confident than individuals,
testimonial invalidity did not decrease as a product of social performance.
The highly significant interaction shown in Figure 18.1 indicates why. This

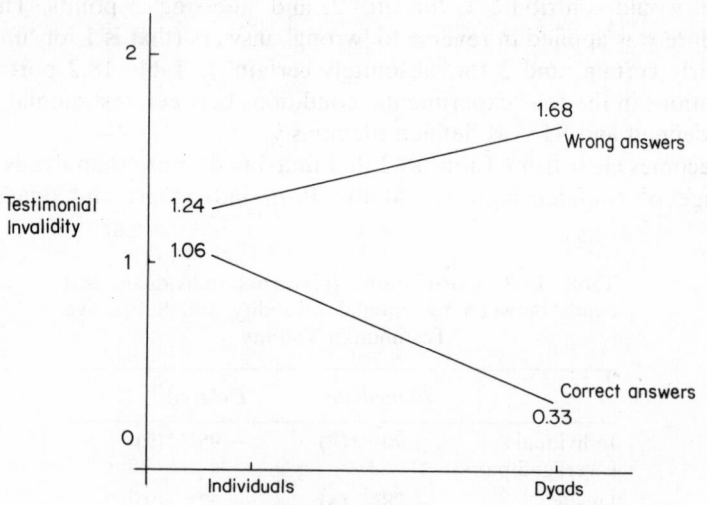

Figure 18.1   Interaction effect for testimonial invalidity. (NB: the higher the
score, the lower the validity.)

portrays testimonial *invalidity* scores for correct and wrong answers. The socially induced increase in confidence levels increased the testimonial invalidity of wrong answers whilst decreasing the testimonial invalidity of correct answers, such that the two effects cancelled one another out.

This does not then mean that the great confidence of the dyads is indiscriminate. Figure 18.2 indicates that although dyads have a higher level of confidence than do individuals, and that this applies equally to wrong answers, nevertheless there remains a comparable distance between their confidence levels for correct and incorrect answers. Whereas dyads tend to be 'fairly certain' of their wrong answers, individuals, more appropriately, are 'unsure' (the German phrase used – *eher unsicher* – implies that the answer was 'probably wrong'). But the one-point gap in confidence for correct and wrong answers is the same for dyads as for individuals. In *objective* terms the performance of dyads is indubitably misleading for wrong answers, and the 'tractability' of confidence is indeed a problem. But in subjective terms they still discriminate effectively between correct and incorrect aspects of their testimony. The 'triers of fact' whom Wells *et al.*, (1981) wish to put on guard against the socially induced increased levels of confidence should be aware that, although the expressed confidence cannot necessarily be taken at face value, witnesses may nonetheless be discriminating effectively between those parts of their testimony that are 'right' and those that are 'wrong'.

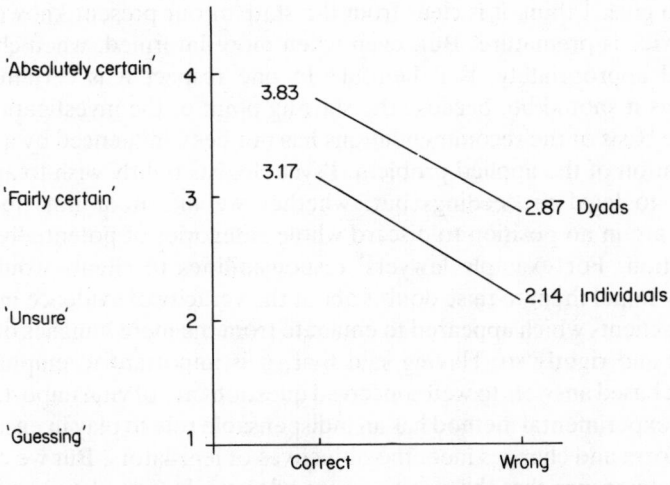

Figure 18.2   Confidence of individuals and dyads for correct and wrong answers

The application of these results from the remembering of written and story material to other aspects of testimony needs to be demonstrated in further work. Certainly the theoretical issues raised are, on the face of it, of considerable importance to issues of what constitutes acceptable evidence. For example, the question of *collaborative* evidence is one which is raised frequently in courts in England and Wales in relation to the evidence of the police. It is now officially permissible for them to collaborate in making notes of an interview, on the grounds that they may thereby 'make sure they have a correct version of what was said' (Court of Criminal Appeal, quoted in McConville and Baldwin, 1981). The results of Experiment 2 give a clear indication that their evidence is likely as a result to increase in confidence, and not always appropriately.

It has become clear from the analysis of the issues and in the review of evidence in this chapter that many important questions concerning testimonial validity remain to be addressed by psychologists – questions of individual differences, of the relationship between different aspects of the confidence–accuracy relationship, and of the particular circumstances in which confidence may or may not be inappropriately enhanced – before we are in a position to instruct the courts and the judiciary on how to assess evidence given with greater or less confidence. We may well ask, however, whether, even given the additional information, the courts or the judiciary would either welcome or be influenced by such informed advice.

Deffenbacher's (1981) earnest advice to the judiciary to ' ... cease and desist from a reliance on eyewitness confidence as an index of eyewitness accuracy' is a good example of the kind of advice which psychologists are prone to give. I think it is clear from the state of our present knowledge that such advice is premature. But, even when more informed, when changed or qualified appropriately, is it helpful? In one respect it is certainly not as helpful as it should be, because the starting point of the investigations which form the basis of the recommendations has not been influenced by a sufficient appreciation of the applied problem. Psychologists rightly wish to apply their findings to legal proceedings but, whether we like it or not, judges and laywers are in no position to discard whole categories of potentially valuable information. For example lawyers' responsibilities to clients would almost certainly impel them to raise doubts about the veracity of evidence incriminating their clients which appeared to emanate from the mere hunches of a hostile witness: and rightly so. Having said that, it is important to emphasize that research based answers to well conceived questions are of vital importance, and that the experimental method has an indispensable role to play in ensuring that legal reform and changes meet the objectives of legislators. But we can surely do more to ensure that the questions are adequately formulated and that our contribution compels their attention.

NOTE

(1) This study was carried out while the author was on study leave in the Institute of Psychology at the University of Linz. Thanks are due to Waltraud Glatz and Sigrid Leitner for their assistance. Financial support is acknowledged from the Social Science Research Council (Grant No. HR5644/1) and the Fonds zur Forderung der Wissenschaftlichen Forschung (Nr 4065). The author is also greatly indebted to Dr. D.E. Broadbent for his helpful correspondence.

REFERENCES

BRIGHAM, J. C., MAASS, A., SNYDER, L. D., and SPAULDING, K. (1982). Accuracy of eyewitness identification in a field setting. *Journal of Personality and Social Psychology*, **42**, 673–681.

BROADBENT, D. E. (1971). *Decision and Stress*. London: Academic Press.

BROWN, E., DEFFENBACHER, K., and STURGILL, W. (1977). Memory for faces and the circumstances of encounter. *Journal of Applied Psychology*, **62**, 311–318.

BUCKHOUT, R. (1974). Eyewitness testimony. *Scientific American*, **231** (6), (December), 23–31.

BUCKHOUT, R., FIGUEROA, D., and HOFF, E. (1975). Eyewitness identification: effects of suggestion and bias in identification from photographs. *Bulletin of the Psychonomic Society*, **6**, 71–74.

BUCKHOUT, R., ALPER, A., CHERN, S., SILVERBERG, G., and SLOMOVITZ, M. (1974). Determinants of eyewitness performance on a line-up. *Bulletin of the Psychonomic Society*, **4**, 191–192.

CHIPPENDALE, P., and LEIGH, D. (1979). *The Thorpe Commital*. London: Arrow Press.

CLIFFORD, B. R., and SCOTT, J. (1978). Individual and situational factors in eyewitness testimony. *Journal of Applied Psychology*, **63**, 352–359.

DEFFENBACHER, K. A. (1980). Eyewitness accuracy and confidence: can we infer anything about their relationship? *Law and Human Behavior*, **4**, 243–260.

DEFFENBACHER, K. A., LEU, J. R., and BROWN, E. L. (1981). Memory for faces: testing method, encoding strategy, and confidence. *American Journal of Psychology*, **94**, 13–26.

DENT, H. R., and STEPHENSON, G. M. (1978). An experimental study of the effectiveness of different techniques of questioning child witnesses. *British Journal of Social and Clinical Psychology*, **18**, 41–51.

DENT, H. R., and STEPHENSON, G. M. (1979). Identification evidence: experimental investigations of factors affecting the reliability of juvenile and adult witnesses. In D. P. Farrington, K. Hawkins, and S. Lloyd-Bostock (Eds), *Psychology, Law and Legal Processes*. London: Macmillan.

GAULD, A., and STEPHENSON, G. M. (1967). Some experiments relating to Bartlett's theory of remembering. *British Journal of Psychology*, **58**, 39–49.

GORENSTEIN, G. W., and ELLSWORTH, P. (1980). Effect of choosing an incorrect photograph on a later identification by an eyewitness. *Journal of Applied Psychology*, **65**, 616–622.

GRONINGER, L. D. (1976). Predicting recognition during storage: the capacity of the memory system to evaluate itself. *Bulletin of the Psychonomic Society*, **7**, 425–428.

HAUCK, W. E., ISAKSON, R., and MOORE, J. N. (1978). Factors influencing the accuracy of the feeling-of-knowing. *Journal of Experimental Education*, **46**, 54–60.

HOLLIN, C. R. (1984). Nature of the witness and incident and status of interview as variables influencing eyewitness recall. *British Journal of Social Psychology*, in press.

HUNTER, I. M. L. (1972). An exceptional memory. *British Journal of Psychology*, **68**, 155–164.

KINTSCH, W., and GREENE, E. (1978). The role of culture-specific schemata in the comprehension and recall of stories. *Discourse Processes*, **1**, 1–13.

LIEPPE, M. R., WELLS, G. L., and OSTROM, T. M. (1978). Crime seriousness as a determinant of accuracy in eyewitness identification. *Journal of Applied Psychology*, **63**, 345–351.

LIPTON, J. P. (1977). On the psychology of eyewitness testimony. *Journal of Applied Psychology*, **62**, 90–95.

LOFTUS, E. (1979). *Eyewitness Testimony*. Cambridge, Mass.: Harvard University Press.

McCONVILLE, M., and BALDWIN, J. (1981). *Courts, Prosecutions, and Convictions*. Oxford: Clarendon Press.

McNICHOLL, D. (1972). *Primary Signal Detection Theory*. London: George Allen and Unwin.

MÜNSTERBERG, H. (1909). *Psychology and Crime*. London: T. Fisher Unwin.

NICKERSON, R. S., and ADAMS, M. J. (1979). Long-term memory for a common object. *Cognitive Psychology*, **11**, 287–307.

NORMAN, D. A. (1969). *Memory and Attention*. New York: Wiley.

NORMAN, D. A., and WICKELGREN, W. A. (1965). Short-term recognition memory for single digits and pairs of digits. *Journal of Experimental Psychology*, **70**, 479–489.

SANDERS, G. S., and WARNICK, D. (1984). Some conditions maximizing eyewitness accuracy: a learning/memory model. *Journal of Criminal Justice*, in press.

SPORER, S. L. (1982). A brief history of the psychology of testimony. *Current Psychological Reviews*, **2**, 323–339.

STEPHENSON, G. M., BRANDSTÄTTER, H., and WAGNER, W. (1983). An experimental study of social performance and delay on the testimonial validity of story recall. *European Journal of Social Psychology*, **13**, 175–191.

WELLS, G. L. (1978). Applied eyewitness testimony research: system variables and estimate variables. *Journal of Personality and Social Psychology*, **36**, 1546–1557.

WELLS, G. L., FERGUSON, T. J., and LINDSAY, R. C. L. (1981). The tractability of eyewitness confidence and its implications for triers of fact. *Journal of Applied Psychology*, **66**, 688–696.

WELLS, G. L., LINDSAY, R. C. L., and FERGUSON, T. (1979). Accuracy, confidence, and juror perceptions in eyewitness identification. *Journal of Applied Psychology*, **64**, 440–448.

WICKELGREN, W. A., and NORMAN, D. A. (1966). Strength models and serial positions in short-term memory. *Journal of Mathematical Psychology*, **3**, 316–347.

YARMEY, A. D. (1979). *The Psychology of Eyewitness Testimony*. London: Macmillan.

SECTION V

Evidence in Court

This section consists of three chapters on the evaluation and interpretation of courtroom evidence. The chapters illustrate several research methodologies which may be used to address this important topic, namely the use of experimentation, the use of observation, interviewing, and content analysis, and the use of ethnomethodological perspectives in conversational analysis.

Davis considers the effects on jurors of the order in which material is presented in court. A number of well designed experiments suggests that order effects are indeed detectable, as are effects of jurors' prior experience and effects of procedural variations such as the joining of charges. Davis concludes his chapter cautiously by emphasizing the need for an integrative theoretical context for such findings, but his results are forceful in suggesting just how tenuous are the constraints of judicial procedure with respect to the dispensing of justice.

Vidmar and Short report the processes of conflict resolution in a small claims court in which a mandatory pre-trial resolution hearing was used with a referee. Their studies of transcripts and outcomes suggest that conflicts often result from a breakdown of communication between the litigants. Vidmar and Short were also able to begin to identify some of the characteristics of cases and litigants which lead to particular outcomes. **Pomerantz and Atkinson** report data from a small claims court in which both parties were bound by an arbitrator's decision. Their detailed conversational analysis of this situation is a demonstration of the ethnomethodological approach; it helps to capture the intricacies of human action.

Psychology and Law
Edited by D.J. Müller, D.E. Blackman, and A.J. Chapman
© 1984 John Wiley & Sons Ltd

Chapter 19

Order In the Courtroom

James H. Davis

Rule-governed interactions for resolving disputes have long been a fixture of civilised societies. The procedural model for determining the type and number of permissible events, the allowable behaviours of participants, the proper order of things, and so on are designed to ensure that whatever ideas of justice are embodied in law are indeed secured in practice. Procedural rules and customs have evolved gradually over time, and while their rationale is sometimes explicit, it is also likely to be a subtle or routine extension of common cultural practices. In either event, justifications of procedure are likely to be widely held truisms about human behaviour – both individual and collective.

However, modern behavioural and social research has increasingly investigated various questions of procedural justice (see general summaries by Bermant, Nemeth, and Vidmar, 1976; Bray and Kerr, 1982; Sales 1978, 1981; Tapp and Levine, 1977). While most procedures and practices seem to fulfil the role for which they have evolved, some do not appear to yield the desired outcomes, and the actual consequences of yet others are unclear. Our attention will here be confined to the courtroom trial, especially jury trials in the USA, and the evaluation of explicit procedural rules as well as the *absence* of definite guidelines. Indeed, the major purpose of this chapter is to consider a rather general procedural question: the influence of *event order* on the verdict preferences of jurors and the verdicts of juries. Although we shall first review briefly empirical findings about the gross order of arguments and testimony from prosecution and defence, the major focus will be on questions of multiple decisions by jurors, and the order in which charges are considered in a joined trial.

PRESENTATION ORDER AND VERDICTS

Perhaps the most obvious object of formalism in a courtroom trial is the presentation of information – opening arguments, presentation of testimony, closing arguments, and instructions to the jury prior to deliberation. It is thus surprising that prior to the incisive investigations of Thibaut, Walker, and their associates (see, for example, Thibaut and Walker, 1975) empirical investigations of various order effects peculiar to courtroom interaction processes were rare. Although studies of attitude change (e.g., Hovland, 1957) had routinely demonstrated various effects from the order of presenting information, the general psychological literature contained remarkably little that directly addressed order effects in complex cognitive and social judgments, such as juror preferences and jury verdicts. However, the potential importance of the order in which evidence is presented had at least been recognized earlier by psychologists (e.g. Lund, 1925) and legal scholars (e.g. Costopoulos, 1972; Lawson, 1969) alike.

The gross order whereby defence always follows prosecution (or plaintiff in civil proceedings) in opening arguments, evidence, witnesses, and closing arguments is fixed by statute and/or judicial practice in US trials. But the *internal* order (scheduling and patterning of testimony) is designed by the attorney presenting the case. Should strong evidence be placed at the beginning or end, or should some more complex plan be used? Such questions have clear practical implications, but it is perhaps less evident that some rather basic questions are also involved. For one thing, all human activity that is complex (several subtasks, stages, or steps) must be performed in *some* order. Yet, most laboratory research on judgment and decision avoids or controls order effects either statistically or by design (e.g. counterbalancing), or attends only to single-task situations. Again, relatively little is known about the cumulative effects of various 'order variables' on *complex* social judgments.

A more regular pattern of order effects is evident from mock trial studies of *gross order* than might have been anticipated from general persuasion and impression formation studies (see Davis, Bray, and Holt, 1977). Mock trial research reports recency effects with some consistency, whereas both recency and primacy effects occur with the latter, depending upon situational variables. In other words, the macro-level conclusion is that the party who presents *last* influences the verdict more. Thus, the defendant in a typical US trial enjoys an advantage in keeping with the desired philosophical bias (a 'defendant protection' norm of sorts) characteristics of the judicial system.

Thibaut and Walker (1975) hypothesized the primacy effect and first impressions are weakened by the clearly two-sided nature of the trial setting. Precisely why early information is discounted remains unclear. In a trial of some length, the earlier information is simply more difficult to recall whereas later information is more readily available to exert an influence. Miller and Campbell (1959) explained communication and persuasion order effects by recall curves, and Anderson (1959) similarly relied on memory phenomena to account for order effects in attitude change.

The variety of possible *internal orders* is very large, but simple monotonic orderings of items of testimony from strong to weak and weak to strong are intuitively compelling arrangements. Remarkably few studies have directly investigated such issues, but Anderson (1959) has reported that weak–strong pairs of arguments were somewhat more effective than strong–weak pairs in persuasion studies. More to the point, Walker, Thibaut, and Andreoli (1972) presented items of carefully scaled testimony to subjects in both strong–weak and weak–strong orders, and found that gross order, internal order, and party (prosecution or defence in an assault case) all interacted to influence mock juror judgments of lawfulness. The climax (weak–strong) order benefited the prosecution, but was a significant factor for the defence only when that side (the defence) was last.

Thibaut and Walker (1975) later hypothesized that these results might be due to jurors weighting differences in the strength of incriminating evidence more than the equally discriminable differences in exonerating evidence. Mock juror responses might therefore be sensitive to the internal order of the prosecution's case but not to that of the defence. (See Kaplan, 1982, and Lind (1982) for further discussions of related issues.)

JURORS AND JURIES

Vollrath (1980) undertook to investigate further the recency effect, using the same procedure and case materials as Walker *et al.*, (1972). However, a major aim was to require jury verdicts as well as to elicit juror preferences as Walker *et al.* had done. (The study of mock juror judgments without accompanying deliberation and verdict has been the more frequent research strategy and sometimes encourages the assumption, usually implicit, that results with the former routinely apply to the latter.) Vollrath reasoned that there are two pieces of evidence to suggest that '... jury verdicts may preserve, and perhaps exaggerate, the recency effect found in juror judgment' (Vollrath, 1980, p. 6). First, Kaplan and Miller (1977) found that the jurors mentioned and discussed a greater variety of facts from later portions of testimony. Second, majority models (of one sort or another) have generally been quite accurate predictors of jury verdicts; and majority models usually (although not always) *exaggerate* the prevailing opinion of individual jurors (e.g. Davis, 1973, 1980; Davis, Kerr, Atkin, Holt, and Meek, 1975; Kalven and Zeisel, 1956; Stasser and Davis, 1981) which, in the case at hand, have typically displayed recency effects.

Vollrath varied the gross order (defence–prosecution or prosecution–defence), internal order (climax or anticlimax), and frequency of judgment (10 periodic judgments or a final judgment). In his first experiment, he found a significant recency effect as expected for lawfulness judgments of mock jurors, whether as responses along a nine-point scale or as a dichotomous (lawful–unlawful) response, but no significant interactions. We will not consider further results from this experiment except to note that order effects in the recall of facts displayed a complex pattern: memory was clearly better for the most recent set of facts and for the side presenting last, but was also better for defence facts despite a tendency to conviction – perhaps casting doubt on order effects explanations relying solely on memory factors (e.g. Miller and Campbell, 1959). All in all, results generally supported and extended the findings of Walker *et al.* (1972).

Vollrath's second experiment held internal order constant (a climax order for both parties), but varied gross order and subjects' judgment (lawfulness) frequency as in the first study. Randomly composed six-person juries received the same set of statements as in the first study, but were instructed in standard fashion to reach unanimous verdicts (guilty or not guilty). The verdict results were similar to those observed with individual subjects; the major finding of interest here is that order again exerted a significant influence on lawfulness judgments (scaled or dichotomous) *and* on the more traditional guilt decisions as well. Previously noted order effects do indeed persist in group decisions following discussion, but with no evident exaggeration. The procedural aim that requires the defendant's case in a criminal trial to be presented last appears justified by the recency results taken as a whole. Any 'biasing' seems likely to benefit the defendant – an outcome consistent with the philosophical disposition that failure to convict the guilty is a more desirable error than conviction of the innocent.

The evidence to date seems clear; the order in which items of testimony are presented, both fairly gross and more detailed, can have a substantial impact upon individual mock jurors *and* the verdicts of mock juries following deliberation. These are procedural events of a rather mundane sort. The empirical demonstrations serve primarily to confirm both our concern for the order of informational input, and in this case, the probable desirability of the order customary in criminal trials.

JUROR EXPERIENCE AND VERDICTS

Somewhat similar to order questions associated with multiple *input* and a single response are order questions associated with multiple *responding* . In other words, we take up the issue of prior experience on verdicts and individual guilt judgments. We consider first the juror hearing multiple cases. Terms of jury service vary by State in the USA; jurors serving in the federal court system may be on call for as long as four months and report for duty for as many as 30 separate court days. Depending upon the length of trial and upon other actors, jurors may sit on more than one case, and occasionally may serve in several. (Multiple case service is more likely in criminal than in civil trials, since the latter are typically longer.)

The problem of how prior jury service influences the juror's subsequent performance is surely a very complicated matter. The few empirical studies of such order effects have rarely employed task materials resembling the complexity of the abstract information characteristic of testimony, arguments, and judicial instructions which must be acquired, stored, and later deliberated prior to a verdict. Moreover, the *kinds* of prior cases, lengths of previous service, and mixtures of the two in a jury of 12 (or perhaps fewer) persons constitute a very large number of possibilities to be considered. Indeed, no relevant study using court records to trace and disentangle the *precise* details (paths) of juror experiences is known to us.

However, the little empirical evidence available (at a somewhat macroscopic level) suggests an *increased* tendency for experienced jurors to vote for a conviction (Dillehay and Nietzel, 1981; Jurow, 1971; Reed, 1965; Skolnick, 1966). For example, Reed (1965) surveyed former jurors in an eastern Louisiana parish and observed that prior experience disposed on them to vote subsequently for conviction; Jurow (1971) reported that subjects with actual trial experience later voted more often for conviction in a mock trial study. Finally, Skolnick (1966) observed that prosecutors typically prefer experienced jurors, believing them disposed to vote guilty, while the defence prefers naive jurors for the opposite reason. Surveys and summaries from court records are rich with *in situ* experience, but offer vexing problems in terms of confounded variables, lack of replication for any one case, aggregations over quite different cases, fallibility of *ex post facto* reconstructions of participants, all serious (and familiar) constraints on inferences from court records and data from actual participants. Mock trial research which often avoids such logical and procedural problems (at the expense of some realism, such as force of actual responsibility for consequences, etc.) typically uses only one case. In something of an exception, Pepitone and DiNubile (1976) reported that the order in which their subjects judged the seriousness of two criminal incidents significantly influenced the average response.

The prior experience question with which we are primarily concerned was addressed most directly by Nagao and Davis (1980), who asked subjects acting as jurors to reach personal verdict preferences after reading two case summaries (rape and vandalism) in one of two orders. Their major results were that respondents were more likely to vote for conviction on a vandalism change when it followed a rape case than when it occurred first; a guilty preference for rape, however, was more probable when that case occurred first rather than when it followed the vandalism case. Consistent with a contrast explanation such as advanced by Pepitone and DiNubile earlier, this result supports the importance of prior experience in such decisions, but not the idea that the experienced juror is only disposed toward conviction – as had been conjectured earlier. The contrast explanation is further supported by a pattern of mean ratings of consequence seriousness upon conviction;

experienced mock jurors perceived the possible consequences to the defendant in the rape (vandalism) case as being more (less) serious than those without such experience and subsequently inclined to conviction at a lower (higher) rate.

In summary, it seems probable that guilt-preferences are at least partly moulded by the kind and order of prior experiences. But a simple unidirectional influence is neither conceptually appealing nor empirically supportable at this point. The combined influence of prior events on verdict preferences is probably not expressible in simple terms, but some kind of contrast explanation seems plausible. In fact, recent studies by Kerr, Harmon, and Graves (1982) not only support the interdependence of a set of verdicts, but also suggest that no simple unidirectional influence is to be expected from what they infer to be a 'contrast phenomenon' of some sort. Immediate implications, if any, for jury service would seem to be toward a *limitation* of jury service. Indeed, two recent recommendations take just this form: The Uniform Jury Selection and Service Act (Administrative Office of US Courts, 1978) limits jury service to 10 court days, and the Model Act prepared for the National Conference of Metropolitan Courts recommends five days (see Van Dyke, 1977). However, the present evidence suggests a service reduction to a single trial – a practice operating in Texas state courts since the early 1970s when legislation provided that jury duty ended with one trial or when excused during *voir dire*.

MULTIPLE CHARGES AND VERDICTS

The possibility of a second kind of order effect in responses arises with the decision to join charges, a common practice in the USA. Indeed, the very question of a joined or severed trial can be the subject of controversy in that joinder is often thought to dispose jurors toward conviction. We will consider this issue briefly, but given both the legal and logical requirements in many instances for a joined trial, along with the pressures of crowded court calendars, it seems likely that joined charges will continue to be a fixture of the judicial system. Thus, the question of the order in which multiple charges are deliberated is an important one.

First, however, we might examine briefly a prior and somewhat simpler question of how judgments about conviction are influenced by joined charges relative to severed charges. Several researchers have examined the possibility of bias resulting from joinder (Greene and Loftus, 1981; Horowitz, Bordens, and Feldman, 1980; Kerr and Sawyers, 1979; Tanford and Penrod, 1982). In principle, charges are to be evaluated independently. On the whole, these investigations showed that mock jurors were more likely to favour conviction on a charge when it was joined with other charges than when it was presented alone – hence the tendency to regard this aggregation effect as a bias. All these studies used case summaries (in written form except for Horowitz *et al.*, who used audio recordings) and solicited the preferences of mock jurors who did not deliberate.

Although investigators have typically used a wide variety of measures, ranging from probability of guilt judgments to the guilty–not guilty verdict preferences similar to criminal trials, we confine our attention to the guilty–not guilty dichotomy, and explore the magnitude of increment in guilty opinion that may be ascribed to joined relative to severed charges. Tanfod and Penrod (1982) addressed precisely such a question by comparing the proportion of guilty preferences relevant to rape and trespass charges when judged alone (severed), or with one, two, or three other charges. (The rape case was always last, and the trespass case first; there was no direct or necessary relation among the alleged offences.) The results showed a significant increase in the proportion of guilty preferences with the number of joined charges. The overall increment in guilty preferences, especially marked between two and three merged charges, represented a striking enhancement of guilt opinion for both rape and trespass. Such enhancement, if at all general, suggests that we are not addressing a matter of minor importance, but an *apparently* minor procedural nuance with major consequences.

A second example of the effect of joined charges may be taken from the study by Greene and Loftus (1981) who required subjects to judge guilt likelihood from case summaries where the charges were murder and rape (Experiment 1). On average, the conviction rate was higher for both charges (significantly only for murder) when merged than when presented alone. Their second experiment differed in several respects from the first, most notably perhaps in the opportunity of subjects to indicate conviction preference to lesser included offences. Again, subjects were more prone to conviction on both charges when joined than when considered alone. Moreover, the differences were quite large. Order of administration, however, produced no significant effect on guilt preferences (or on any other of the several responses) – somewhat surprising in the light of other results noted earlier.

In summary, it seems clear that subject to constraints of situation, procedure, etc., guilt decisions on multiple charges in mock trial contexts are *not* independent, and the direction of judgmental disposition is to *increase* conviction preferences relative to those charges presented alone. Moreover, Tanford and Penrod and Greene and Loftus were careful to use standard instructions to subjects concerning the independence of the charges; the latter investigators even manipulated the instruction variable (given early or later, or absent altogether) without significant effect. Thus, the effect of joinder may not be easily mitigated by judicial instructions alone.

THE ORDER OF MULTIPLE CHARGES

Even though the effect of joinder appears to work preponderantly against the philosophical bias (defendant protection) desired in criminal trials, it is difficult to imagine courts routinely granting motions for severance in view of pressures for efficiency and the absence of compelling evidence of prejudice in the particular case. Our purpose at this point is to explore further the implications of taking up charges in one order or another, *given* a joined trial. It is possible of course that whatever biasing effects develop from joined charges, they are enhanced further or even mitigated by the order in which charges are *deliberated* and decided by a *jury*. Investigations noted above have *all* studied the responses of individual jurors. Of course, the cost in subjects of even small (mock) jury studies is quite considerable. Moreover, there is a large and inviting number of order possibilities (formed by combining logically possible presentation orders with deliberation orders, etc.). Confining our attention only to the deliberation order of a set of charges, there are several bases on which charges may be arranged – seriousness (potential penalty), weight of evidence, similarity of content, and so on. Although offences necessarily vary on several dimensions, the severity of the potential penalty is intuitively the most interesting.

In studies at the University of Illinois (Davis, Tindale, Nagao, Hinsz, and Robertson, in press), 464 mock jurors were presented with a short video-taped trial in which the defendant was charged with reckless homicide (RH), aggravated battery (AB), and criminal damage (CD) to property. Care was taken to balance opening arguments, examination of witnesses, cross-examination, closing arguments, etc., to avoid idiosyncratic events, and to keep the proportion of individual guilt judgments within the ranges established by pilot studies of single offences. The charges were dramatically and logically independent, although they arose out of events contiguous in time and place, such that a joined trial would be in keeping with judicial practice in the State of Illinois.

The trial format conformed to the Illinois State Statutes pertaining to criminal trials; instructions from the judge conformed to the recommended pattern pertinent to charge and independence of multiple charges. A male defendant was alleged to have broken a glass table in a bar during an argument with the current boyfriend of his ex-fiancee, and subsequently to have assaulted him. Upon leaving the bar parking lot in his automobile, and while supposedly driving in a reckless manner, the defendant hit and killed a pedestrian. Testimony was directed at establishing the facts surrounding these events and the character of the defendant.

Subjects were randomly assigned to three conditions in which they were required to deliberate and decide (guilty or not guilty) as six-person juries the charges in order of descending seriousness (RH, AB, CD), in order of ascending seriousness (CD, AB, RH), or in no assigned order. Post-verdict personal judgments of guilt were also assessed in the same order. Various other response measures were also recorded – probability of guilt judgments, testimony remembered, opinion on other-charge influences, testimony believability ratings, and various demographic responses. However, we confine our interest here to the dichotomous judgments, although subject ratings were more common in previous research. Also, the study differed from other investigations dealing with multiple charges in using video-recorded enactment rather than written summaries, and actual deliberation to a group decision.

Only two of the six possible orders were used. We judged the ascending and descending seriousness orders as the most interesting candidates at this initial stage, although non-monotonic orders may hold special interest in terms of certain kinds of content (especially in civil trials); the condition with no assigned order was primarily intended as a baseline or a sample to estimate the relative frequency of subject-chosen orders. (Illinois law provides no official or mandated order, but merely admonishes jurors to consider charges independently – a fairly typical practice.)

Our attention was focused primarily on the AB charge, since we assumed order effects were most likely to appear at this point. Any AB-relevant recall problems (intrusions from other charges), etc., would be relatively constant in both assigned orders, since the AB charge testimony occurred first during the proceedings, and amount of information/testimony was arranged to be relatively constant for the three charges. Although individual subjects can be monitored for compliance with the mandated charge order, and materials (questionnaires, etc.) for both groups and individuals can be suitably arranged, group discussion is largely uncontrollable. However, audio-recordings were sampled and no anomalous departures from assigned orders during discussion were detected. Discussants may develop various debating and voting strategies during deliberation in order to advance their preferred verdict, and the salience of social norms, relatively dormant in the individual, may influence verdicts. Thus, order effects observed with individuals might not be the same as those active within juries.

It was found that the proportion of guilty verdicts on the AB charge was significantly higher in the descending than ascending order for both mock jurors and juries. The control condition (order unassigned) conviction rate fell between the values observed in the two monotonic extremes – perhaps not surprising since six juries chose the descending order and nine followed the ascending order with the remainder scattered over the remaining four possibilities; this result suggests some inclination to take charges in a monotonic order such as those chosen for study. Informal observations suggested very little 'spill-over' from one charge to another during deliberation, although mixed-charge discussion was somewhat more common in the order-uninstructed condition.

Thus, whatever the increment in conviction rate due to the merging of charges, relative to deciding alone, it seems that the sequence or order of consideration can increase (decrease) the conviction rate further. While we found no evidence that actual deliberation would exaggerate an order effect observed with individual jurors, neither did we find that it was much mitigated by group discussion. Although we do not have space here to review additional data on remembering, testimony, other-charge intrusions, feelings about other-charge influences, etc., it is possible to note that we have no evidence suggesting recall failures, testimony confusion, and the like as the basis of the order effect. However, it is more difficult to rule out such explanations as subjects' attributing a criminal disposition to the defendant.

From this perspective, the finding that the (RH, AB, CD) descending order yielded a higher conviction preference rate by jurors on the AB charge deserves further attention. The interesting question is whether the decisive influence is the charge itself or what *happens* in the sequence (i.e. the *particular* preceding decision), or both. Thus, we next examined the *path* to the decision on the AB charge. The relative frequency of guilty judgments was conditioned not only on whether RH or CD preceded, but whether the decision had been guilty or not guilty. For example, we tabulated the guilty preferences on the AB charge, given a guilty (or not guilty) decision on the preceding (i.e. CD or RH), and so on.

For both the RH and the CD preceding the AB decision, there was a statistically significant association between the two guilt judgments. In other words, a guilty decision on the preceding charge significantly increased a guilty decision on the AB charge, *for both types* of preceding charges. Comparison of the decisions on the AB charge by respondents who gave the same previous preference revealed that *among guilty sayers* there was *no significant association* with whether they had decided an RH or a CD charge, whereas *among not guilty sayers* the RH charge occurring first *significantly elevated* guilty judgments over those who had said not guilty to the CD charge earlier.

All in all, *both* the preceding charge and the preceding decision category appear to be associated with mock jurors' decisions, at least under the conditions studied here. Additional analyses including the other charges, especially the third-charge decisions conditioned on the first two, etc., give similar results. Also, mock *jury verdicts* follow a similar pattern and, where the partitioned samples are sufficient for statistical analyses, results are similar.

Our findings suggest that subjects confronted by several charges ostensibly unrelated *do not* decide them separately and independently. A set of charges itself may influence guilt decisions as the studies on joinder and severance discussed earlier suggest; but given joined charges, a later preference is not independent of the previous charge and decision. The simplest explanation, which we cannot disconfirm at this point with ancillary data from question-naires, informal conversations with subjects, or casual observations of mock juries, is that subjects view the trial process as a whole. They may not only infer a criminal disposition on the part of the defendant, but develop more complex causal linkages between the decisions for one charge and those for another, regardless of the apparent lack of logical connections.

In summary, current concerns (e.g. Greene and Loftus, 1981; Horowitz *et al.*, 1980; Kerr and Sawyers 1979; Tanford and Penrod, 1981) about the biasing effects of merged charges are not likely to be mitigated by results from the research reported here. Given a joined trial, the order in which charges are decided exerted an effect on both verdicts and mock juror guilt prefer-ences. Since joinder (for many reasons) is likely to be a fixture of the judicial system, what are the prospects for an ordering that minimizes or at least redirects the effect in a philosophically more acceptable direction? The answer is not at all clear at this point. But, we can point to the influence of previous charge *decisions* as perhaps more important than the particular charge. If defendant protection norms are to be honoured strictly, the weakest (evidentially) and least serious (potential penalty) charges should be taken up first, although such prejudgment of the evidence by a presiding judge would be wholly unacceptable in practice.

Tanford and Penrod (1982) have pointed out that judges currently have little statutory guidance, and must rely on intuition in granting severance. Rule 14 of the Federal Rules of Criminal Procedure recognizes three bases of prejudice and has sometimes been the basis for granting severance motions: jurors may confuse evidence from different charges, may combine or accumulate evidence incorrectly, or may inappropriately infer a criminal disposition in the defendant. (See Tanford and Penrod (1982) for a more comprehensive discussion.) Clearly, one or more of the three may be operating in a given criminal trial; they are not mutually exclusive. However, we would like to support the implications from the reports by Tanford and Penrod and by Greene and Loftus that the inference of a criminal disposition (or some variant thereof) is an especially salient problem. Even with a complete trial enactment (video-recording), full (mock) jury deliberations, and different case material, etc., our findings are essentially compatible with earlier results – and in addition imply charge order to affect decisions further.

SUMMARY

Formal hearings, trials, etc., are concerned with the precise way things are done, and precedence relations have long been recognized as an important component of that process. The research we have reviewed here has supported current practice with regard to presentation order. Although little data exist on the effects of prior experience on jurors' subsequent verdict preferences, it appears that current proposals to limit jury service are prudent. A similar concern for the effects of joining charges *and* the order in which they will be decided seems likewise justified. However, a general strategy to minimize bias, given that a severed trial is not a realistic option, is not obvious; as noted above, charges must be considered in *some* order and a directed (defendant protection) order would itself imply an unacceptable prejudgment of the case by the court. The dilemma, so often the case, is very real.

The typical approach to resolving dilemmas such as the latter is to seek a better explanation for the phenomenon. A good theory of what influences multiple verdicts might imply corrective possibilities not yet entertained. Unfortunately, it seems unlikely that a single cause holds for all classes of cases; the bases of order effects seem likely to shift somewhat with trial content, relevant law, and so on. Thus, a simple theoretical structure seems unlikely. The issue is similar to another procedural controversy about the appropriate (minimum) size for a criminal jury. Precise answers to the jury size question appear to depend in part on various situational parameters. Yet, it has been possible to obtain a rough estimate of verdict implications of different jury sizes from models constructed to summarize statistically the likely effects suggested by various empirical studies as operating across situations. At present, the results of all such theoretical simulations (or thought experiments) show size-dependent verdict differences to be very real, to be occasionally small in magnitude, to reverse in direction for certain parameter values, and generally to favour larger over smaller juries – in response to philosophically preferred biases. (For a more comprehensive discussion see Davis *et al.*, 1977, Tindale and Davis, 1984, and Vollrath and Davis 1980.)

From a similar perspective, we might speculate about the way in which order effects might arise in juries of fixed size (12 persons) when deciding a sequence of charges such as in the study reported earlier. These speculations were organized by assuming that a previous guilty verdict (jury decision) on a more serious charge increased (by 0.15) the probability of a guilty preference in the juror pondering the next decision, and increased it by only 0.10 if a less serious charge preceded. A failure to convict decreased the guilty preference by the same amounts in the same fashion. The jury social decision scheme used in this illustration assumed a two-thirds majority determined the verdict (guilty or not guilty), otherwise no verdict, which was in turn treated as acquittal.

Such a simple system yielded a pronounced order effect over the whole range of juror guilty preferences, although nowhere was this very large. Furthermore, the verdict differences between descending and ascending orders change *direction* – not an intuitively obvious outcome. However, the most notable finding is that the order effect on the middle charge is *absent* –

the very location at which we earlier observed the largest *empirical* effect! Clearly, this simple monotonic incremental model (perhaps the most straight-forward rendering of research findings that remains fairly plausible) is an incorrect account of guilt judgments as studied here. Even if parameter values were altered (e.g. size of increment/decrement or jury size), the magnitudes but not the general *form* of the results would differ from those obtained. Thus, a very much more complex model is apparently needed to accommo-date results observed so far.

Not only is empirical research needed to evaluate particularly interesting (and important) special cases, but some effort must be devoted to building a social judgment theory that is capable of handling the complex decisions of the sort arising in courtroom trials – especially a theory sensitive to the subtle nuances of task and outcome *sequences* that arise in practice. To conclude that jurors might infer a criminal disposition in joined trials, or that event orders can subtly influence trial outcomes may describe empirical findings, but these inferences are not sufficiently developed theoretical notions to sustain the kind of formal models that will predict actual data sets.

REFERENCES

ADMINISTRATIVE OFFICE OF US COURTS (1978). *1977 Juror Utilization in United States Courts.* Washington, D.C.: US Government Printing Office.

ANDERSON, N. H. (1959). Test of a model for opinion change. *Journal of Abnormal and Social Psychology,* **59**, 371–381.

BERMANT, G., NEMETH, C., and VIDMAR, N. (1976). *Psychology and the Law.* Lexington, Mass.: D. C. Heath.

BRAY, R. M., and KERR, N. L. (1982). *The Psychology of the Courtroom.* New York: Academic Press.

COSTOPOULOS, W. C. (1972). Persuasion in the courtroom. *Duquesne Law Review,* **10**, 384–409.

DAVIS, J. H. (1973). Group decision and social interaction: a theory of social decision schemes. *Psychological Review,* **80**, 97–125.

DAVIS, J. H. (1980). Group decision and procedural justice. In M. Fishbein (Ed), *Progress in Social Psychology,* Vol. 1. Hillsdale, N. J.: Lawrence Eribaum.

DAVIS, J. H., BRAY, R. M., and HOLT, R. W. (1977). The empirical study of social decision processes in juries: a critical review. In J. Tapp and F. Levine (Eds), *Law, Justice and the Individual in Society: Psychological and Legal Issues.* New York: Holt.

DAVIS, J. H., KERR, N. L., ATKIN, R. S., HOLT, R., and MEEK, D. (1975). The decision processes of 6- and 12-person juries assigned unanimous and 2/3 majority rules. *Journal of Personality and Social Psychology,* **32**, 1–14.

DAVIS, J. H., TINDALE, R. S., NAGAO, D. H., HINSZ, V. B., and ROBERTSON, B. (In press). Order effects in verdicts from consideration of multiple charges. *Journal of Personality and Social Psychology.*

DILLEHAY, R. C., and NIETZEL, M. T. (1981). Conceptualizing mock jury/juror research: critique and illustrations. In K. S. Larsen (Ed.), *Psychology and Ideology.* Monmouth, Oregon: Institute for Theoretical History.

GREENE, E., and LOFTUS, E. S. (1981). When crimes are joined at trial: institutionalized prejudice? Paper presented at the Biennial Convention of the American Psychology-Law Society, Cambridge, Mass.

HOROWITZ, I. A., BORDENS, K. S., and FELDMAN, M. S. (1980). A comparison of verdicts obtained in separate and joined criminal trials. *Journal of Applied Social Psychology*, **10**, 444–456.

HOVLAND, C. I. (Ed) (1957). *The Order of Presentation and Persuasion*. New Haven, Conn.: Yale University Press.

JUROW, G. L. (1971). New data on the effect of a 'death-qualified' jury on the guilt determination process. *Harvard Law Review*, **83**, 567–611.

KALVEN, H., and ZEISEL, H. (1966). *The American Jury*. Boston: Little, Brown.

KAPLAN, M. F. (1982). Cognitive processes in the individual juror. In R. Bray and N. Kerr (Eds), *The Psychology of the Courtroom*. New York: Academic Press.

KAPLAN, M. F., and MILLER, C. F. (1977). Judgment and group discussion: effect of presentation and memory factors on polarization. *Sociometry*, **40**, 337–343.

KERR, N. L., and SAWYERS, G. W. (1979). Independence of multiple verdicts in a trial by mock jurors. *Representative Research in Social Psychology*, **10**, 16–27.

KERR, N. L., HARMON, D. L., and GRAVES, J. K. (1982). Independence of multiple verdicts by jurors and juries. *Journal of Applied Social Psychology*, **12**, 12–29.

LAWSON, R. G. (1969). The law of primacy in the criminal courtroom. *Journal of Social Psychology*, **77**, 121–131.

LIND, E. A. (1982). The psychology of courtroom procedure. In R. Bray and N. Kerr (Eds), *The Psychology of the Courtroom*. New York: Academic Press.

LUND, F. H. (1925). The psychology of belief. IV. The law of primacy in persuasion. *Journal of Abnormal and Social Psychology*, **20**, 183–191.

MILLER. N., and CAMPBELL, D. (1959). Recency and primacy in persuasion as a function of the timing of speeches and measurement. *Journal of Abnormal and Social Psychology*, **59**, 1–9.

NAGAO, D. H., and DAVIS, J. H. (1980). The effects of prior experience on mock juror case judgments. *Social Psychology Quarterly*, **43**, 190–199.

PEPITONE, A., and DINUBILE, M. (1976). Contrast effects in judgments of crime severity and the punishment of criminal violators. *Journal of Personality and Social Psychology*, **33**, 448–459.

REED, J. P. (1965). Jury deliberations, voting and verdict trends. *The Southwestern Social Science Quarterly*, **45**, 361–370.

SALES, B. D. (1978). *Perspectives in Law and Psychology*, Vol. I, *The Criminal Justice System*. New York: Plenum.

SALES, B. D. (1981). *Perspectives in Law and Psychology*, Vol. II, *The Trial Process*. New York: Plenum.

SKOLNICK, J. H. (1966). *Justice without Trial: Law Enforcement in Democratic Society*. New York: Wiley.

STASSER, G., and DAVIS, J. H. (1981). Group decision making and social influence: a social interaction sequence model. *Psychological Review*, **88**, 523–551.

TANFORD, S., and PENROD, S. (1982). Biases in trials involving defendants involved in multiple offenses. Unpublished manuscript, University of Wisconsin.

TAPP, J., and LEVINE, F. (1977). *Law, Justice, and the Individual in Society: Psychological and Legal Issues*. New York: Holt.

THIBAUT, J., and WALKER, L. (1975). *Procedural Justice: A Psychological Analysis*. Hillsdale, N. J.: Lawrence Erlbaum.

TINDALE, R. S., and DAVIS, J. H. (1984). Group decision making and jury verdicts. In H. Blumberg, P. Hare, V. Kent, and M. Davies (Eds), *Small Groups, Social-Psychological Processes, Social Action and Living Together*. Chichester: Wiley.

VAN DYKE, J. M. (1977). *Jury Selection Procedures*. Cambridge, Mass.: Ballinger.

VOLLRATH, D. A. (1980). Order effects in mock trial presentations: juror judgments and jury verdicts. MA thesis, University of Illinois.

VOLLRATH, D. A., and DAVIS, J. H. (1980). Jury size and decision rule. In R. J. Simon (Ed), *The Jury: Its Role in American Society*. Lexington, Mass.: Lexington Books.

WALKER, L., THIBAUT, J., and ANDREOLI, V. (1972). Order of presentation in an adversary system. *Yale Law Review*, **82**, 216–226.

sychology and Law
.dited by D.J. Müller, D.E. Blackman, and A.J. Chapman
) 1984 John Wiley & Sons Ltd

Chapter 20

Social Psychological Dynamics in the Settlement of Small Claims Court Cases [1]

Neil Vidmar and Judith Short

Disputes between individuals are an inevitable and endemic part of social life. In modern North American societies many of these disputes eventually end up in a small claims court. They may involve a disagreement between two business associates over the carrying out of the terms of a contract, a consumer dispute between an individual and a business, or conflict between two private individuals. The substance of the dispute may centre around an unpaid bill, an automobile accident, a fence dividing property, claims for wages, or in fact any one or more of a myriad issues. While the monetary amount of these disputes, considered individually, may be small, their cumulative totals can be staggering: in the province of Ontario, Canada, alone the small claims courts process claims totalling millions of dollars every year.

In recent years the small claims disputing process has received much attention from legal administrators and practitioners (see Rhunka and Weller, 1978; Sander, 1977) and from scholars in the fields of law, anthropology, and sociology. Considerable effort has been devoted to exploring procedural models other than adjudication for resolving these so-called minor disputes (see McGillis and Mullen, 1977; Nader, 1980). For example, some courts provide the litigants with a choice of arbitration or adjudication (see, for example, Sarat, 1976), others have experimented with mediation (see, for example, McEwen and Maiman, 1981), while others have instituted pre-trial resolution hearings (see, for example, Vidmar, 1981a). The impetus behind these efforts involves both pragmatic and idealistic concerns. On the one hand, court administrators have been concerned with reducing caseloads. To the extent that more efficient procedures to divert cases from trial can be found, the more court dockets will be reduced. On the other hand, some of the reform efforts have arisen from dissatisfaction with adjudication as a

means of resolving disputes. Adjudication, it is argued, has a number c
drawbacks when used for small claims disputes. Adjudication may enhanc
conflict between the parties and ignore core causes of disputes; it is bound b
procedural and substantive rules that inhibit flexible and constructive solu
tions to problems; it is intimidating to many people who as a consequence ar
discouraged from seeking relief for real and pressing problems; it appears t
result in decisions that are biased against defendants (see Nader, 1980
Sander, 1977; Yngvesson and Hennessey, 1975). Yet, many of the assertion
about adjudication or the assumptions favouring alternative procedures ar
without demonstrably solid empirical support.

Indeed, relatively little is known about the small claims disputing process
especially the social psychological factors involved in it. We do know tha
those cases that end up in the courtroom constitute only a small fraction of th
disputes that potentially could have ended up there. Adjudication is the en
of a series of successive choice-points that were reached before and after th
dispute entered the legal system (see Vidmar, 1981b). Felstiner, Abel, an
Sarat (1980–1), Coates and Penrod (1980–1), and Vidmar (1981b) hav
theoretically explored some of the pre-legal stages involved in the disput
process. These include one party perceiving a problem; attributing it to th
fault of another party; voicing it to the other party; the refusal of the othe
party to assume blame; perhaps the involvement of some non-legal thir
party before the dispute eventually ends up in the legal system. At each o
these stages, or choice-points, the parties may settle their dispute or th
initiating party may withdraw his or her claim or just decide to 'lump' th
grievance. Empirical research on the social and psychological factors involvec
in the discretionary behaviour during these pre-legal stages of disput
behaviour is currently under way in several settings in North America
including a Canadian study in our own dispute research project.

There are also, however, a number of choice-points that are reached afte
the dispute formally enters the legal system, allowing other opportunities fo
discretionary behaviour. The defendant may not contest the claim, allowing
the plaintiff to win the case through default. Our research in a Canadian cour
shows that in fact approximately 70% of the small court claims end up ir
default judgments. This figure is similar to findings in studies of United State:
small claims courts. But even for the remaining 30% of cases that are disputec
by the defendant, there is a number of options open to the plaintiff anc
defendant. The plaintiff may then decide to withdraw the claim. The
defendant may decide to pay up. The plaintiff and defendant may ge
together and settle the problem on their own. In fact these appear to be
common outcomes in small claims cases; the filing of the suit acts as a catalys
for settlement (see Sarat, 1976). Even if the parties do not settle on their owr
accord, the legal system may provide the parties with additional options. Fo
example, upon entering the courtroom the judge may give them the choice o

rbitration or adjudication (see Sarat, 1976) or of mediation or adjudication see McEwen and Maiman, 1981). Alternatively, the court may provide a mandatory pre-trial resolution hearing presided over by a referee in an attempt to induce the parties to settle. Thus many of the cases that enter the egal system are diverted without resort to adjudication.

We know only a little about the settlement process for disputes that ormally engage the legal system and are disputed by the defendant. What causes disputes to be settled after they have escalated so far as to involve legal charges and countercharges? Who 'wins' the dispute and how often? The number of systematic empirical studies are few. It has been recognized that he understanding of disputes requires viewing them from the disputants' perspective rather than from a third party or legal perspective, but the studies which have taken this conceptual perspective have involved retrospective interviews of disputants, primarily plaintiffs, and have focused on sociological variables rather than on social psychological ones. It has been speculated, for example, that disputants with a prior or on-going relationship are more likely to settle than disputants without such a relationship. Sarat (1976) found some weak support for this proposition, but McEwan and Maiman (1981) found no support for it. Another hypothesis is that the presence of absence of lawyers for one or for both sides influences settlement, but this hypothesis has not received consistent support (see Rhunka and Weller, 1978). Most studies have shown that the defendant pays the plaintiff something in as many as 90% of the cases, and thus researchers have concluded that the small claims court process is heavily biased in favour of plaintiffs. Working on the assumption that plaintiffs do win, most researchers have then attempted to speculate as to the reasons, such as greater experience and resources on the part of plaintiffs or stronger evidential bases for their claims. However, as we will argue below, based upon an analysis of disputant motives, the assumption that plaintiffs usually win is not a valid assumption.

The remainder of this chapter will examine some dimensions of dispute dynamics on the basis of data derived from a field study of a small claims court that utilizes a mandatory pre-trial resolution hearing. By focusing on the behaviours of the disputants, with particular emphasis on defendants' motives and strategies, as well as on the behaviours of the referee who presides over the hearing, we begin to understand why some cases are settled and others are not. Conceptualizing the dispute from the perspective of the defendant also allows us to take a different perspective in asking 'who wins' in cases that are settled through the hearing or are adjudicated. The data arising from this latter analysis challenge the conventional conclusion that 'plaintiffs usually win'.

The immediately following section of the chapter gives a very brief overview of the small claims court under study, the resolution hearing procedure, and general data on the effectiveness of the hearing in resolving disputes. A following section describes the sources of data for the study. The next simpl describes aspects of dispute behaviour and how the resolution hearing refere acts to attempt to resolve disputes. Based upon these descriptive accounts th subsequent section compares differences between cases that are settled or nc settled and reconceptualizes dispute outcomes in terms of degrees of liabilit conceded by the defendant. A final section summarizes and draws conclu sions.

THE MIDDLESEX COUNTY SMALL CLAIMS COURT

In Ontario small claims courts may deal with claims up to Can$100C Corporations and other businesses, including public utility companies, as wel as individuals, are allowed to be plaintiffs in the court. A lawyer or designated agent may act for the litigants, but many plaintiffs and defendant act for themselves. Claims are limited to civil matters, but the substantiv range of the disputes is extremely broad: for example, automobile damages landlord–tenant disputes; utility, dental, or legal bills; consumer issues business contracts; employer–employee wage disputes. In some cities specia small claims court judges try the cases, but in others, including the Middlese County Small Claims Court, Ontario, regular County Court judges presid over the court on a rotating basis.

Several years ago a pre-trial 'resolution hearing' was instituted in th Middlesex County court. When claims are disputed a resolution hearing i more or less automatically scheduled for a 30 minute session. Attendance a these sessions is not legally mandatory, but through practice directions an the simple fact of scheduling there are strong pressures on the litigants t show up. Only if the resolution hearing fails to get an agreement is the cas scheduled for trial. No evidence brought out at the hearing is admissible i any subsequent trial. The referee who presides at these hearings is not ; lawyer, but has taken special law classes and has substantial practica experience with the small claims court. The referee has no official power t force a settlement. Rather, the referee's task is to bring the parties together, t attempt to ascertain the facts of the dispute, and to suggest settlement options The disputing parties and/or their lawyers or agents meet in a comfortabl private office in the courthouse. Typically, the referee asks the plaintiff to stat his or her case and indicate the nature of the evidence. The defendant i allowed to reply, and then the referee asks additional information and make suggestions. The hearings seldom exceed the scheduled 30 minutes. If th parties agree to a settlement the legal action will be dropped, adjourned sine di pending completion of the settlement, or entered into the court records as ; 'consent' judgment. If the parties do not reach agreement the case is schedule for trial.

The resolution hearing appears to be successful in reducing trial dockets The Middlesex County court was claiming a success rate of approximatel

0% of the cases that went to the hearing. In fact our more systematic data
suggest that the success rate may be higher: up to 62% of cases that go
through the hearing are settled before trial. The claimed success rate of other
Ontario small claims courts that have subsequently adopted the resolution
hearing procedure because of its success is also about 50%, and visits to
several of these courts indicate that the hearings operate in a generally similar
way to the one in Middlesex County.

STUDY METHODOLOGY

The general purpose of our study is to attempt to describe and understand the
social psychological dynamics of minor legal disputes. This includes questions
about how disputes develop, how they are transformed as they proceed
through the legal system, and why cases are settled or require adjudication.
The study also evaluates outcomes according to a number of criteria,
including administrative efficiency and the litigants' perceptions of procedural
and substantive justice.

Several types of methods and data sources have been employed in an
attempt to provide multiple data bases bearing on the dynamics of the dispute
process. First, we have gathered data on 500 disputes cases from the 1980
court records. These archival records allow us to analyse the relationship
between certain legal and sociological characteristics of disputes (e.g. nature
of case, amount, whether plaintiff or defendant is individual or business,
presence or absence of lawyers) on such variables as settlement or judgment
outcomes, compliance rates, and speed of court processing. They also provide
a data base against which the representativeness of our other data can be
compared.

A second set of data involves systematic in-depth interviews with litigants
involved in a randomly selected sample of approximately 200 disputed cases
that came before the court in 1981 and 1982. In these cases we attempted to
interview both the plaintiff and the defendant prior to the resolution hearing
and after the case was either settled, dropped, or adjudicated. These
interviews included both open-ended and structured questions. The substance
of the interviews involved the disputants' description of the nature of the
dispute, how it developed, and why. In the initial interviews we also obtained
data on the disputants' legal strategies, their perceptions and expectations of
the legal system, and their willingness to compromise. The post-interviews
took place some 6–8 weeks after settlement/adjudication.

Another source of data involves systematic observations of the resolution
hearings and the trials of the same sample of cases. In each case a trained
observer sat unobtrusively in the private resolution hearing and took detailed
notes of what transpired, including the behaviour of disputants, the behaviour
of the referee, and changes in the stated nature of the case occurring since the

initial interviews or during the hearing itself. For those cases that went to tria a trained observer took similar systematic notes of the proceedings.

Data collection in the study is not yet complete. The data reported here ar from a subsample of 66 cases where all data have been collected. Th subsample appears representative when compared to the archival data an there is, therefore, good reason to believe that the general conclusions to b drawn are sound, even if the specific figures in the completed study wi eventually vary somewhat.

SUCCESS RATE

'Success' rates of the resolution hearings may be measured by a number o criteria, including legal criteria and litigant satisfaction. This chapter, however deals only with the most straightforward criterion, namely whether the disput was settled or not.

The subsample of cases shows that 62% of them were settled without resor to trial. This figure is similar to the settlement rates in the much larger sampl of cases gleaned from the archival records. A further breakdown of the case is of importance in understanding dispute settlement. Specifically, 36% of th total cases were settled in the hearing itself. For the remaining cases that wer settled (i.e. 26% of the sample) settlement did not occur in the hearing, bu some action by one or both litigants was taken after the hearing that avoidec the necessity of a trial.

While some of these cases would probably have been settled even if resolution hearing had not taken place, there is little question that th resolution hearing had a significant impact on settlement for most of them This will become clearer when we consider differences between cases settlec in the hearing, cases settled after the hearing, and cases proceeding to trial First, however, it is useful to develop a more detailed description of th dynamics of disputes.

DISPUTES AND HEARINGS: A DESCRIPTIVE OVERVIEW

To begin to understand the differences between settled and non-settled case we should first consider why disputes develop. As noted earlier the range o substantive issues involved in small claims disputes is extremely broad anc varied. Moreover, our interviews show an enormous variation in the course and paths of disputes. Unlike the artificial disputes typically created anc studied in the social psychological laboratory, real life disputes are ofter extremely complex. In one sense there is no typical dispute. Some have developed over a long period of time while others are a result of a singlc incident. Some involve friends and others involve strangers. Sometimes prio attempts have been made to settle the dispute and at other times they have not. Often they involve third parties, either as witnesses or as participants to the dispute. Often they involve multiple claims and issues. As many as 20% involve counter-claims by the defendant against the plaintiff.

The motives involved in disputes are equally complex (see Vidmar, 1981a). Some involve a straightforward monetary dispute. Others involve deep and emotional hidden agendas. Retribution, or 'spite', plays an important role in many disputes. In many instances one or both of the parties appear willing to expend far more money and time in the pursuit of 'the principle' or 'justice' than they ever hope to recover even if they win.

Despite this complexity we can begin to make sense of the dispute process and why it is resolved if we look at the basic reasons that are at the core of the dispute, at the role of information in the dispute, and at the behaviour of the referee when the disputants are brought together in the resolution hearing.

All disputes involve a demand by one party on another and the refusal of the second party to comply with that demand. In small claims courts the demand must be phrased in monetary terms even if the dispute involves non-monetary issues: 'You owe me money for X'. When the dispute enters the legal system the first party becomes *the plaintiff* and the second party becomes *the defendant*.

The simplest way to begin to understand the core issues behind the dispute is to ask why the defendant refuses to pay. These reasons fall into five basic categories: (i) the complete denial of legal liability for the debt; (ii) the partial denial of legal liability where some of the debt is acknowledged but not all of it; (iii) an assertion of inability to pay, even though the debt is acknowledged; (iv) unwillingness to pay on the grounds that the defendant's limited resources should be allocated elsewhere; and (v) refusal to pay based upon some other issue, such as spite or some other hidden agenda, or the desire to have a legal rule clarified.

To emphasize the defendant's reasons for disputing the claim does not, of course, suggest that the plaintiff's motives are unimportant (see Vidmar, 1981a). Neither, it should be noted, are these reasons always mutually exclusive. Indeed, many are marked by multiple reasons: for example 'I can't pay, but in any event I wouldn't pay if I could because he insulted me'. Nevertheless, for our purposes here this simplified perspective on the nature of disputes is both helpful and sufficient. We must, however, also consider the role of missing information in the dispute and the role of the resolution hearing as a provider of information and as a facilitator of information exchange.

The interviews and the observations of the hearings clearly indicate that the parties often lack information about the substance of the other party's position or do not believe the information that the other party does convey. One or both of the parties may also lack accurate information about the legal strength of the other party's case, his or her ability to enforce a settlement, and his or her willingness to do so. Finally, one or both parties may be ignorant of collection costs. (Leff 1970 has provided a similar analysis of the information components in disputes – although in a slightly different context.) Consider each of these information gap components separately.

The interviews indicate that in many instances communication between the parties about the substance of the dispute breaks down at an early stage. One party may simply refuse to talk to the other party. The defendant may not even have answered the plaintiff's telephone calls. Alternatively, the parties may have begun to discuss the issues, but an argument ensued and the flow of information stopped. Sometimes the mistrust arising from prior incidents in their relationship or their current behaviour causes them to polarize and exaggerate their own positions and to mistrust the other's intentions and motives and thus mistrust the information that is conveyed.

In other instances the parties may communicate about the facts and issues in the dispute but disagree about the meaning of those facts and issues. Thus, a plaintiff may assert that he or she can legally charge 3% per month on the unpaid balance of an invoice whereas the defendant says this cannot be done. Or a tenant asserts that he or she can break a rental agreement without written notice whereas the landlord asserts that a 60 day written notice is required. In such cases there may be a rather clear and unequivocal external standard by which the dispute can be resolved, but one of the parties refuses to believe it is so. In addition to information about legal rightness or wrongness, one of the parties may also lack information about the other party's legal remedies for collection; for example garnishment of wages or an execution against goods or property, or the secondary consequences of a harmed credit rating.

Finally, the pre-hearing interviews suggest that many persons, especially those involved in the legal system for the first time, do not consider collection costs or, if they do, tend to underestimate them. That is, they do not have accurate perceptions of the amount of time it will take to pursue or dispute the claim and the potential legal and court costs that may be incurred. Nor do they consider the lost wages or income while they take time off work to go to court.

In brief the data show that lack of information or misinformation about various aspects of the dispute is frequent. Examination of the resolution hearings indicates that much of the hearing is in fact devoted to information giving and the facilitation of information flow. In fact the primary activity in the hearings is centred around information.

Sometimes the hearing is the first occasion the parties have had to discuss the actual issues in the dispute, or at least it is the first occasion for a long time. In some of the cases the referee plays a negligible role in the proceedings. The parties, who have finally come together, simply begin to negotiate and resolve their own problems with minimal or no help from the referee.

In most cases, however, the referee plays an active role that facilitates the flow of information between the parties, and more important, provides a third party perspective on the interpretation of facts and issues. The specific behaviours vary with how the referee assesses the issues in the case. But by drawing out the facts from the parties and then interpreting them in the context of other things the referee helps to provide a new perspective on the dispute.

At the substantive level of disputes, one of the most common behaviours of the referee is to play the role of itemizer and accountant. This is especially true in the cases where the defendant admits some liability for a debt but disputes the amount that is owed. In many instances the disputing parties have simply not gone over the bill on an item by item basis, either because the plaintiff would not provide the information or because the defendant refused or did not take the time to look at the specific items. By asking how much each item or service cost the referee can add them up and provide an independant estimate of what the bill should be. In other instances, say a suit arising out of an automobile accident, the referee may sort through the facts and point out inconsistencies in one party's position. In other instances the referee helps one of the parties to bring new information to bear on the dispute, as in one case where the defendant insisted she had not signed a work order for additional services, but the plaintiff produced the order with her signature on it.

In cases where the basic facts are not in dispute but rather the meaning of those facts under the law is the dispute the referee may provide a third party legal perspective. Thus, the referee may point out that the landlord–tenant act requires 60 days written notice before a tenant can vacate or that a landlord may not enter rented premises without the consent of the tenant. With this information one of the parties may see his or her case collapse. In the instances of disputes involving inability to pay or refusal to pay the referee may point out, respectively, the non-utility of pursuing the dispute or the potential negative consequences of not paying. Often these aspects of legal reality are brought home by means of the referee predicting the likely outcome of adjudication if the case goes to trial. The costs of collection are also frequently emphasized by the referee.

This information function is not the only function the resolution hearing plays. The referee may serve as a vehicle for face saving, for example. Rather than admit they are wrong directly to the other party, one of the participants may find it easier to concede to the referee. Attempts may also be made to help an inarticulate party express his or her position, and advice about providing witnesses or documents at trial may also be given. The referee also assists in devising payment schedules when a party has difficulty in making payments and in getting the other party to accept the payment schedule. The referee does engage in some minor mediation and conciliation efforts, but these are primarily in the nature of cajoling one or both of the parties to be a little less rigid. Only very rarely are there attempts to get at hidden agendas underlying disputes, when they occur, or to heal ruptured relationships. The hearing sticks to the legal dispute and seldom digresses to issues which are ancillary to this dispute. In the main, therefore, the principal role of the hearing is to provide information.

OUTCOMES: DIFFERENCES BETWEEN SETTLED AND ADJUDICATED CASES

With this descriptive overview in mind we can now turn to the problem of understanding why disputants settle their cases or instead opt for adjudication. The conceptual basis of our analysis will also allow us to take a fresh look at the question of who 'wins' the dispute.

As noted earlier the data from the archival records suggested that 62% of cases that went to the hearing were settled before trial. Our subsample of interviewed/observed cases also shows a 62% settlement rate but suggests a further categorization of settlement. Some of the cases were settled in the hearing. In others, however, the parties failed to reach agreement in the hearing but were eventually settled before trial. Thus, there are three types of outcome: settled in the hearing; settled after the hearing; proceeding to trial. These three possible settlement types accounted for 36, 26, and 38%, respectively, of the sample of cases under consideration here.

First, we should consider whether there are some obvious legal or sociological characteristics which distinguish the types of cases. The mean amount of the initial claim was somewhat lower for cases settled in the hearing than those settled after or proceeding to trial: Can$567, 702, and 692, respectively. These differences, however, were not statistically significant. It should be noted, moreover, that the archival data, involving over 500 cases, also show no difference in mean claim amount between settled and adjudicated cases, a fact which is consistent with the finding of no significant differences in these interviewed cases. Additional analyses show no differences between type of settlement and the presence/absence of lawyers or whether the parties had a previous/on-going relationship as opposed to no relationship.

It is also useful to compare the three types of case in terms of the commonly used criteria of award outcome. The criterion of award outcome that has been used most frequently in the literature is the percentage of cases where the plaintiff recovers some monetary award from the defendant (see Yngvesson and Hennessey, 1975). The data show that for cases settled in the hearing the plaintiff obtains some monetary award 94% of the time. In cases settled after the hearing the plaintiff received something only 41% of the time. In cases that went to trial the plaintiff was awarded something 70% of the time. These differences are statistically significant. More recently, researchers have used an alternative measure of outcome, namely the percentage of the initial claim that is recovered by the plaintiff (see Sarat, 1976; McEwen and Maiman, 1981). Using this criterion we find that for cases settled in the hearing the mean amount of recovery was 74%, for cases settled after the hearing the amount was 26%, and for adjudicated cases the mean recovery was 59%. These differences are also statistically significant. Further examination of the data show that in 59% of after hearing settlements, the plaintiff withdrew his or her claim. A difference between the 'winning' plaintiffs in cases settled after the hearing and those going to trial should also be noted. In the former case the plaintiff tended to receive only a relatively small fraction of the claim – on average substantially under 50% of it. On the other hand, if the case went to trial and the plaintiff won, he or she was more likely to recover nearly the whole amount of the initial claim.

These findings are generally similar to findings in other studies of small claims courts (see McEwen and Maiman, 1981; Sander, 1977; Sarat, 1976; Yngvesson and Hennessey, 1975). Overall, as measured on these criteria, plaintiffs tend to win. Cases resolved by adjudication tend to be all-or-none decisions whereas cases settled in the hearing tend to be compromise decisions. However, there are unanswered questions. How do we explain the high proportion of withdrawn claims in the cases settled after the hearing? What explains why some cases were settled and others not. Why did plaintiffs 'win' so much more often in cases settled in hearings than in cases settled after hearing or particularly at trial? The presence or absence of lawyers or of a prior relationship between the parties were not related to settlement either.

The pre-trial interviews and hearing observations, particularly with respect to the issue of defendant motives, not only provide a clue but suggest that the traditionally used measures of outcome are totally misleading. Recall from our earlier discussion that defendants' refusals to pay involved five basic reasons: denial of liability; partial denial of liability; inability to pay; unwillingness to pay; denial of liability based upon some other reasons. The first and fifth of these reasons usually involve a total denial of obligation to the plaintiff. The defendant, for example, may assert that he or she did not cause the car accident or contract for services, or may assert that contracted services were not provided, thus voiding the contract. In cases involving other issues, the defendant usually denies liability because of a hidden agenda or because the fact of legal obligation is not clear and no obligation will be assumed until the judge pronounces the legal norms that apply to the case. On the other hand the second, third, and fourth reasons given by plaintiffs involve a condition of at least *some* obligation on the part of the defendant. In the 'cannot pay and do not want to pay' cases the defendant generally admits full obligation. In the partial obligation conditions the defendant concedes that he or she owes something to the plaintiff but not the full amount. For instance, in one case a defendant had contracted to have some electrical wiring installed in his home. He agreed that about two-thirds of the work had been satisfactorily completed but asserted that the plaintiff had not completed other work that had been agreed to. When the electrician sent him a bill for the full amount, he offered to pay for the work that was done, but not for the incompleted work. The electrician asserted that he had provided everything initially agreed to and demanded full payment. The defendant subsequently refused to pay anything. The dispute, therefore, involved disagreement about the facts of what was initially agreed to and what was in fact done. But the important point is that the defendant did concede some obligation and withheld all moneys owing as a legal and psychological strategy. In brief, we can divide the cases into two basic categories: those involving total denial of liability and those involving partial or full acceptance of liability. The latter are more likely to involve breakdown in communications over facts. Further, we should expect that those types of dispute would be more tractable to information facilitating behaviour of the hearing referees.

To test this hypothesis the interview and hearing observation data were used to categorize cases as either total liability denial or admission of (at least some) liability. Then, these categories were compared across type of settlement. The data support our hypothesis. Fully 89% of cases settled in the hearing involved admissions of some liability whereas only 35% and 25%, respectively, of the cases settled after the hearing or at trial involved admissions of some liability. In short, when the defendant admits some obligation or liability to the plaintiff, the resolution hearing is more likely to suceed in obtaining a settlement.

Utilizing this distinction of cases in terms of the defendant's position on liability we can also reconceptualize the nature of the dispute outcome and who 'wins' the dispute. Consider the dispute over the electrical contracting again. The electrician plaintiff claimed Can$500 for the job and the defendant was willing to pay Can$300 of that amount. The dispute, therefore, was not about Can$500 but rather Can$200, albeit the defendant refused to pay anything until the matter was settled. In this particular case the defendant produced evidence about the original agreement and evidence that it was not fully carried out by the electrician's apprentice. The parties had failed to exchange the details about this matter until the hearing but the plaintiff then acknowledged that the defendant's position was legitimate and accepted the Can$300. In brief, although the plaintiff received Can$300, the defendant won the dispute. Again working from the interviews and hearing observation data, it was possible to construct an index for each case of the amount in actual dispute by subtracting the amount the defendant admitted owing from he amount claimed by the plaintiff. The data derived from the index show hat in the cases of admitted liability the amount in actual dispute averaged only 32% of the plaintiff's claim. Of course, in cases of total denial of liability he actual dispute was the full amount of the plaintiff's claim.

Continuing to use this 'actual dispute index' it is now possible to reconsider he question of who 'wins' the dispute. The difference between the plaintiff's claim and the defendant's assertion of what was owed (zero in the instances of denial of total liability) was divided into thirds. If the amount of the settlement award was in the third closest to the plaintiff's claim he or she was considered the 'winner'; if it was in the third closest to the defendant's position the defendant was considered the 'winner'; if the award was in the middle third, the settlement/award was considered a draw.

Looking first at the cases settled in the hearing, some interesting results emerged. First, plaintiffs won in only 42% of cases while defendants won in 40%. The remaining 18% of cases resulted in a draw. In brief, the resolution hearing is not the lopsided affair it appeared to be when we used the index based upon whether the plaintiff recovered something. Defendants 'won' almost as often as plaintiffs. Since the referee seldom engaged in mediation behaviour but rather stuck to narrow legalistic behaviour, it must be assumed that settlement resulted from new information or interpretation of information that was brought forth at the hearing. With this new information the parties agree to settle.

The cases settled after the hearing present an even more favourable 'win' ratio for the defendant. The defendant won in 82% of cases by our criterion. In fact 53% of the time the plaintiff actually withdrew the claim. How are these cases different from those settled in the hearing? One important hint lies in the high percentage of claims that were withdrawn. The hearing often resulted in new information about the facts of the case that were severely damaging to the plaintiff's position. For example, the defendant may have produced documents that essentially destroyed the plaintiff's position. Or, the referee may have produced evidence on the law that indicated that the plaintiff had no case in law: for example 'the Highway Traffic Act clearly states that you and not the defendant should have yielded the right of way'. But why was the case not just dropped in the hearing? Our principal answer seems to be related to an attempt to save face. Plaintiffs who are confronted with this kind of information do not want to admit it to themselves, at least not at first, and certainly not to the other side. They simply refuse to settle. However, away from the hearing and after a few days of thinking about it, the plaintiff can simply decide to not pursue the matter further. In this way a face-to-face admission of failure to the defendant is avoided.

The trial outcomes produce a picture more favourable to the plaintiff. Plaintiffs won in 63% of the cases. As other research has also shown (see, for example, Sarat 1976), adjudicated outcomes tended to be all-or-none. When plaintiffs won they received all or almost all of their initial claim. A further observation is that while it appears valid for both types of settled cases, the hypothesis about the dispute arising simply because the parties do not communicate or because they have misinformation does not appear valid for adjudicated cases.

SUMMARY AND CONCLUSIONS

This chapter has been concerned with the discretionary behaviour of small claims court litigants at the point where the defendant has decided to dispute the claim. Litigants in the court under study have the option of settling in a pre-trial hearing, settling after the hearing, or taking their cases to trial. Pre-hearing interviews with litigants and observations of the resolution hearings suggest that many disputes are characterized by a failure of the parties to communicate information about the dispute or by differing perceptions of the legal issue or facts of the case. The referee at the hearing facilitates information flow and provides a third party perspective on the legal and factual realities of the dispute. However, whether this new perspective on the factual and legal realities in the dispute will result in settlement is also related to the defendant's perception of obligation to the plaintiff. The resolution hearing is most likely to be successful in cases where the defendant admits some obligation, or liability, to the plaintiff. The data also show that, contrary to conclusions reached previously in the literature, defendants may win a substantial portion of small claims court cases.

NOTE

(1) This research was supported by the Donner Canadian Foundation. The authors are indebted to Judge Gordon Killeen, Mr Robert Harris, and Mr Roy Edgecombe for their consent and their active cooperation.

REFERENCES

COATES, D., and PENROD, S. (1980-1). Social psychology and the emergence of disputes. *Law and Society Review,* **15**, 632–680

FELSTINER, W. L. F., ABEL, R. L., and SARAT, A. (1980-1). The emergence and transformation of disputes: naming, blaming, claiming .... *Law and Society Review,* **15**, 631–654.

LEFF, A. (1970). Injury, ignorance, and spite – the dynamics of collective coercion. *The Yale Law Journal,* **80**, 1–46.

McEWEN, C., and MAIMAN, R. (1981). Small claims mediation in Maine: an empirical assessment. *Maine Law Review,* **33**, 237–268.

McGILLIS, D., and MULLEN, J. (1977). *Neighborhood Justice Centers: An Analysis of Potential Models.* Washington, D. C.: US Department of Justice.

NADER, L. (1980). *No Access to Law.* New York: Academic Press.

RHUNKA, J. C., and WELLER, S. (1978). *Small Claims Courts: A National Examination.* Williamsburg, Vancouver: National Center for State Courts.

SANDER, F. (1977). *Report on the National Conference on Minor Disputes Resolution.* Chicago: American Bar Foundation.

SARAT, A. (1976). Alternatives in dispute processing: litigation in a small claims court. *Law and Society Review,* **10**, 339–376.

VIDMAR, N. (1981a). Justice motives and other psychological factors in the development and resolution of disputes. In M. Lerner and S. Lerner (Eds), *The Justice Motive in Social Behavior.* New York: Plenum.

VIDMAR, N. (1981b). Observations on dispute dynamics and resolution hearings outcomes in a small claims court. In S. Lloyd-Bostock (Ed.), *Law and Psychology.* Oxford: SSRC Centre for Socio-legal Studies.

YNGVESSON, B., and HENNESSEY, P. (1975). Small claims, complex disputes: a review of the small claims literature. *Law and Society Review,* **9**, 219–274.

Psychology and Law
Edited by D.J. Müller, D.E. Blackman, and A.J. Chapman
© 1984 John Wiley & Sons Ltd

Chapter 21

Ethnomethodology, Conversation Analysis, and the Study of Courtroom Interaction

Anita Pomerantz and J. Maxwell Atkinson

There is growing interest in applying the approach and findings of ethnomethodology and conversation analysis to the study of interaction in legal settings, and particularly in the analysis of a range of different types of court hearings (e.g. Atkinson and Drew, 1979). The development of such a research programme has been strongly influenced by a number of earlier ethnomethodological studies conducted in legal or bureaucratic settings, including the office of a public defender (Sudnow, 1965), police arrest practices on 'skid row' (Bittner, 1967), a jury room (Garfinkel, 1967, pp. 104–115), agencies concerned with processing delinquents (Cicourel, 1968), a public assistance office (Zimmerman, 1969), police assessments of moral character (Sacks, 1972), a half-way house for ex-convicts (Wieder, 1974), a traffic court (Pollner, 1974, 1979), and a coroner's office (Atkinson, 1978).

Taken together, these studies can be seen as part of the sociological contribution to an evolving and interdisciplinary research effort in the area of law and language, which is reflected in a number of important recent publications (e.g. Danet, 1980; O'Barr, 1982). While the active participation of researchers from different disciplines is in various ways an important and stimulating development, there can sometimes be problems in finding out about what is involved in pursuing research within one or other of the available theoretical and methodological frameworks. The aim of this present chapter is to give a brief outline of some of the main features of research in ethnomethodology and conversation analysis, and to exemplify these by presenting a short research report on a particular study.

THE SUBJECT MATTER FOR ETHNOMETHODOLOGICAL ANALYSES

Although the term 'ethnomethodology' now tends to be used to refer to several related approaches to research, it was not originally intended to denote a social scientific methodology in the same sense that surveys, experiments, or participant observation are methodologies. For in coining the word, its originator, Harold Garfinkel, was concerned to find a shorthand way of describing what he had come to regard as a previously neglected but nonetheless important *topic* for sociological analysis (on the origins of the word 'ethnomethodolgy', see Garfinkel, 1974). For nearly three decades, his own work has reflected a continuing preoccupation with the phenomenon of members' methods of practical reasoning, as too has that of others working within the research tradition he founded. A preliminary appreciation of what is involved by such a topic focus can be obtained by considering the research Garfinkel was carrying out at the time when he was prompted to look for a new word which could be used to characterize the subject matter which interested him.

During the early 1950s Garfinkel became involved in the famous Chicago Jury Project, part of the data for which had been collected by bugging a jury room (Kalven and Zeisel, 1966). In listening to these tapes, Garfinkel found his attention being drawn to various features of the way jurors talked to each other during the course of their deliberations. Although they lacked any formal legal training, they nonetheless seemed to be perfectly well equipped to discuss complicated and highly technical issues in legally relevant ways. And, given that one of the central aims of the research project was to find out how jurors go about reaching their decisions, this apparently simple observation could be seen to have some quite important implications. For it suggested, among other things, that whatever it was that jury work involved might not be as unique, special, or unusual as had been assumed by those who had designed the project. Thus, in the report on his part of the study, Garfinkel makes the following point:

> 'As a person underwent the process of "becoming a juror" the rules of daily life were modified. It is our impression, however, that the person who changed a great deal, changed as much as five per cent in the manner of making his decisions. A person is ninety-five per cent juror before he comes near the court' (Garfinkel, 1967, p. 110).

With this suggestion that the methods of reasoning used in jury decision-making are very similar to those used by ordinary persons in making mundane or routine decisions across various settings in the course of living their everyday lives, two important points about social scientific research begin to emerge. The first is that an understanding of the methods of reasoning used by jurors (or others engaged in any 'specialized' task) will both inform and be informed by our knowledge of the methods of reasoning that are routinely employed by competent members of society in a wide variety of settings. What practices are special or peculiar to any particular setting is therefore to be regarded as an open question that can only be decided in the light of empirical evidence from a range of different interactional contexts. This, of course, might have been insignificant had social scientists already accumulated a considerable amount of knowledge about the methods of reasoning available to and used by human beings for interpreting and producing their everyday activities. However, the second point which became evident from Garfinkel's observations was that researchers had devoted relatively little attention to the question of how ordinary activities are constructed and made sense of in the course of everyday social interaction. Thus, the jurors could be heard to be engaged in the production of analyses of what they had heard, such that Garfinkel (1967, p. 104) found himself characterizing their activities 'as a method of social inquiry'. Furthermore, their immediate practical concerns appeared to be very similar to those of professional social scientific researchers:

> 'In the course of their deliberations, jurors sort alternative depictions made by lawyers, witnesses and jurors of what happened and why between the statuses of relevant or irrelevant, justifiable or unjustifiable, correct or incorrect grounds for the choice of verdict. When jurors address such matters as dates, speeds, the plaintiff's injury and the like, what do the jurors' decisions specifically decide? In something like the jurors' own terms, and trying to capture the jurors' dialectic, jurors decide between what is fact and what is fancy; between what actually happened and what 'merely appeared' to happen; between what is put on and what is truth, regardless of detracting appearances; between what is credible, what is calculated and said by design' (Garfinkel, 1967, p. 105).

Viewed in these terms, it can be seen that jurors have to find ways of reaching, within finite time limits, a series of decisions which are not only very complex, but are also of just the sort that have provided a central and elusive problematic for generations of philosophers and social scientists. And they are also, of course, just the sorts of practical decisions that have to be made by professional researchers in the course of producing orderly descriptions and explanations of some aspect of social reality. As Garfinkel goes on to note:

> 'Jurors come to an agreement among themselves as to what actually happened. They decide "the facts", i.e. among alternative claims about speeds of travel or extent of injury, jurors decide which may be used as

the basis for further inferences and action. They do this by consulting the consistency of alternative claims with common sense models. These common sense models are models jurors use to depict, for example, what culturally known types of persons drive in what culturally known types of ways at what typical speeds at what types of intersections for what typical motives. The test runs that the matter that is meaningfully consistent may be correctly treated as the thing that actually occurred. If the interpretation makes good sense, then that's what happened' (Garfinkel, 1967, p. 106).

Persons involved in legal work, then, cannot enjoy the luxury of speculating about how truth claims can be validated, or whether it would even be possible to specify independent and decontextualized procedures for so doing. The local interactional business at hand is such that, somehow or other, participants have to make decisions about matters of fact and responsibility that are treated as definite 'for all practical purposes'. For the ethnomethodologist, that somehow or other provides the main focus for analytic attention, the challenge being to explicate the taken-for-granted reasoning practices used to produce such decisions and treat them as definite.

In combining the words 'ethno' and 'methodology' to refer to this new domain for investigation, Garfinkel was influenced by the use of terms like 'ethno-botany' and 'ethno-medicine' to refer to folk systems of botanical and medical analysis and classification. For what he had observed and was recommending as a focus for study was a 'folk' methodology comprising a range of 'seen but unnoticed' procedures or practices that make it possible for persons to analyse, make sense of, and produce recognizable social activities, but which have remained largely unexplicated by social researchers. That such an interest has remained central to ethnomethodological investigations will be seen from the analysis presented below. Before proceeding to that, however, it may be useful to note some of the main features involved in pursuing this approach to empirical research.

SOME FEATURES OF THE ANALYTIC APPROACH

Although research in ethnomethodology and conversation analysis has diversified over the years (see, for example, Atkinson and Heritage, 1984; Goodwin, 1981; Psathas, 1979; Schenkein, 1978; Sudnow, 1972), there are at least three central points on which there is a wide consensus among those working within the field, and which have some important implications for the way research is designed and carried out. The first is that the main focus should be on how participants themselves produce and interpret each other's actions. The second is that access to this depends upon the analyst adopting an orientation to interactional data which involves viewing empirical materials as 'anthropologically strange'. In other words, analysts must be willing to treat even the most apparently mundane or ordinary events as puzzling enough to be worthy of serious analytic attention. Otherwise, they too are likely to overlook, or take for granted, the very practices that they are aiming to identify and describe. Third, there is a strong preference for working with naturally occurring interactions, rather than those associated with experimental situations, survey interviews, or other methods involving various sorts of observer intervention or manipulation. And this naturalistic approach to data collection has, of course, been greatly facilitated by the development of audio- and video-recording technology, which enable real-world interactions to be preserved and subjected to repeated and detailed analysis. The use of tape-recordings also means that the data about which analytic claims are being made are openly available for critical inspection by readers or hearers of research reports (within the constraints discussed below).

The emergent research tradition differs from those which have been predominant in the social sciences in at least two important respects. First, the emphasis on describing practices used in the production and interpretation of social behaviour involves a marked shift away from *causal* or *deterministic* theorizing aimed at constructing explanations of behaviour. Thus, whereas social scientists have traditionally been preoccupied with locating the 'causes' of particular types of behaviour, ethnomethodolgists are more interested in what is is about the way people do things that makes them recognizable to others as one particular sort of action rather than another. In other words, ethnomethodological research sets out to describe *how* human behaviour works, rather than to explain *why* some particular type of behaviour occurs.

A second distinctive feature of the approach arises from the insistence on regarding the question of how ordinary activities are produced and interpreted as problematic. The directions any particular analysis will take cannot be anticipated, prejudged or planned in advance of looking at the details of what occurs in the interactional data being studied. In other words, the focus for investigation is dictated by what the participants themselves are doing and how they do it, rather than by *a priori* hypotheses derived from some apparently 'relevant' literature. This is not to say, however, that the findings from such studies will therefore have no theoretical or practical implications, though it does mean that what these may eventually turn out to be cannot be accurately predicted by researchers in advance of empirical analysis.

The following section reports some recent observations from a programme of research in which such an approach is being applied. In addition to describing practices used by persons participating in courtroom interaction, then, it is also intended to provide a more concrete exemplification of the general points outlined above.

A CASE STUDY

The data for this paper are extracts from tape-recordinngs of actual hearings which took place in the London Small Claims Court before its recent closure through lack of financial support. It was one of several independent courts established throughout the UK and operated within the framework of legislation on arbitration procedures. In this particular court, both parties were required to agree beforehand to be bound by the decision of the adjudicator, and neither party was permitted to employ legal counsel to present a case. The hearings were usually conducted around a table in an office at the Polytechnic of Central London.

Though transcriptions of the original tape-recordings have to be used for publication purposes, this does not mean that they are treated as the 'raw data' for analytic purposes. Nor, of course, is it possible for a transcription system to capture and represent the original talk in all its constituent details. The transcripts included here have been simplified from ones prepared by

Table 21.1 Symbology used in transcribing tapes

Symbol	Example	Explanation
::	a::rm,	Colon(s) indicate that the prior syllable is prolonged; the more colons, the longer the sound stretch.
(.) (0.2)	that(.) the (0.2) uh damage	Numbers in parentheses indicate elapsed time in tenths of seconds; a full stop indicates a micro-pause of less than two-tenths of a second
[	A: slee:ve and under P: Yeah	Square brackets indicate points at which talk by one speaker overlaps with that of another
? ?	a little ? (.) there?	Questions marks indicate rising intonation; a question mark with a comma beneath indicates a slight rise

Gail Jefferson using the symbology she has developed over the past 10 years[1] (See Table 21.1).

A central aim of the study was to describe the practices involved in presenting evidence in court. Legal procedure dictates that each of the litigants will have an opportunity to present evidence and counter opponent's evidence. The adjudicator will decide whether adequate grounds have or have not been established to substantiate the plaintiff's claims.

There are a set of 'facts-in-issue' which are directly relevant for establishing the grounds for a judgment in any given case. Is there the damage that the plaintiff claims? What is the extent of the damage? If there is damage, how did it occur? Establishing 'what the facts are' is a large part of what the courtroom interaction is concerned with, and some observations on how this is done are reported in this section.

Various features of the practices involved in presenting evidence are described with reference to illustrative materials. In the interest of brevity the data are drawn from a single case heard in a small claims court. The case is one in which the plaintiff claimed that her dress was damaged while being dry cleaned, and, more particularly, by the pressing machines of the dry cleaning firm. The owner of the firm denied the plaintiff's charge. Independent experts were consulted and had submitted a written report which concluded that the damage was caused by 'friction which appears to be caused by wear and not as a result of solvents used in the cleaning'.

One matter which needed to be established was the extent of the damage to the dress, which was there in the courtroom, and which the parties had already had a chance to examine beforehand as well as in court. A way of describing the extent of the damage is to itemize the damaged areas. This might seem to be a straightforward task, given that the dress was there, and that anyone examining the dress would presumably make a same list of areas where damage can be seen. However, it was not quite that straightforward. The participants in the hearing named different damaged areas on different occasions. For example the plaintiff's description, as read by the ajdudicator, was that 'the braiding round the sleeves, and the belt, and the collar were damaged'. The adjudicator's initial description referred to 'under the sleeve, and under the arm ... and on the inside of the neck'. To that list, the plaintiff added 'round the back there and on the belt'. The question, then, is 'what is involved for the participants in naming areas and in selecting particular descriptions to refer to the areas of damage?'.

Although the areas of damage were described and argued about quite often throughout the proceedings, for present purposes one segment of interaction which is concerned with naming the areas of damage is presented. Below is a highly simplified transcript of the interaction in which the adjudicator is describing the areas of damage that she observed.

ADJUDICATOR: I have? (.) examined the ⌐ dress:::.
                                        └
PLAINTIFF: └ Uh:.

ADJUDICATOR: ˙hh And, (.) uh- (0.2) noted, that (.) the (0.2) uh
                damage appears to be:, (0.4) unde⌐ r
                                                 └
PLAINTIFF: └ There

ADJUDICATOR: the slee::ve, an⌐d under the (.) a::rm,
                                └
PLAINTIFF: └Yeah   Hm=

ADJUDICATOR: =a little? (.) there? ˙hh and o-on the inside

PLAINTIFF: Hm-m,

ADJUDICATOR: of the ne:⌐ck,
                          └
PLAINTIFF: └Round the back there, (.) And on the be:lt.

ADJUDICATOR: The question is w:whe:rre on the belt⌐   is⌐the damage.
                                                     └   └
PLAINTIFF: └Well └'T's all on Look. 'T's
                all round the belt. 'T's all on the back of this, collar? I mean I don't
                wear it like that all day long you know,

The damage on the dress may be viewed through any number of possible
attitudes, interests, or competencies. One attitude which is relevant in court is
to determine or establish the *cause* of damage. That attitude involves viewing
the observables, that is the damaged areas, with one's mind directed toward
answering the question: what process would be most likely to have produced
this particular damage? There are, of course, other attitudes with which a
person may approach the damage on the dress. A seamstress might look to
see what sort of damage it is with respect to the ease or difficulty in repairing
it in order to estimate the time it would take. Its owner, prior to going out for
the evening and hoping to wear it, may view the damage with a mind to
checking its conspicuousness.

In court, however, a decision concerning liability for the damage is
normally the important issue. It is being proposed here that the attitude or
orientation is adoptable by the adjudicator as well as by persons who are
untrained in and unfamiliar with legal thinking, by expert witnesses as well as
by the lay public. When the dress was given to independent experts to

examine and report on to the court, their conclusion also addressed causes of damages.

When the adjudicator named, 'under the sleeve, and under the arm, and on the inside of the neck', participants in the hearing would normally be concerned with how those particular damaged areas stand as evidence in the case. Does that listing constitute evidence for the proposal that the damage was caused by the pressing machines, by normal wear and tear, by the cleaning solvents, or by some other cause?

As the listing proceeded, the areas as named provided progressive support for the proposal that the damage was normal wear damage. It supported the proposal in that the named areas were recognizable as *just* the areas that would suffer from and subsequently show the marks of wear and tear. In other words, if one were looking for threadbare material or fraying, under the armpit and on the inside of the collar would be obvious places to look. Moreover, naming a body part in the location description may work to suggest the cause (armpits perspire and necks move). While other descriptions of the area may have been quite adequate for referring to the damaged area, for example on the sleeve, and on the collar, the particular formulations which were selected, 'under the arm and on the inside of the neck' evoke the image of parts of the garment which are subjected to perspiration and friction. Shortly after the adjudicator named the third area as 'on the inside of the neck', the plaintiff named an area of damage as ' 't's all on the back of this collar':

ADJUDICATOR: And on the inside of the ne:ᵣck

PLAINTIFF: └Round the back there, (.)
And on the be:lt.

ADJUDICATOR: The question is w:whe:rre on the beltᵣ isᵣthe damage

PLAINTIFF: └Well └'T's all on Look. 'T's all round the belt. 'T's all on the back of this, collar? I mean I don't wear it like that all day long you know,

With the naming of the areas, the participants were arguing theory inasmuch as 'on the inside of the neck' is recognizable as a wear area and 'on the back of this collar' is recognizable as a place which does not get friction during normal wear. On most occasions, the cause that an area as named proposes remains unexplicated; on some occasion, however, the implications . of the 'facts' are explicated. With 'I mean I don't w-wear it like tha' all day long you know', the plaintiff proposed the incompatibility of the proposal that the damage was caused by wear with the area named. The particular damaged areas, then, were seen to be damaged in the way that those areas typically get damaged.

In real time, as the listing proceeds, the plaintiff analysed the areas as named by the adjudicator as constituting evidence for a particular cause: the damage was a product of normal wear rather than of negligence by the dry cleaning firm. The plaintiff extended the list of areas in a way which weakened its support for her opponent's proposal. The areas that she added, 'round the back there and on the belt' are not random unmentioned areas but specifically places which would not be subject to friction during normal wear.

ADJUDICATOR: and under the (.) a::rm,

PLAINTIFF: Hm,=

ADJUDICATOR: =a li-ttle? (.) there?`hh and o-on the insi:de

PLAINTIFF: Hm-m

ADJUDICATOR: of the ne:⌐ck,

PLAINTIFF   ⌊Round the back there,
                 (.)

PLAINTIFF: an' on the be:lt.

Thus, the participants in court monitored the descriptions selected and selected their descriptions with respect to how one side's proposals or the other's was being supported or undermined. In the above interactions, the adjudicator's assertions recognizably supported the defendant's position that the damage was caused by normal wear; the plaintiff in such a circumstance was motivated to proffer assertions which attempted to weaken the plausibility of that position by naming instances which are not easily explained in terms of normal wear damage. Given the differing positions and interests of the participants in a hearing, it is not surprising that challenging and refuting, querying and disagreeing are commonly done. In the remainder of this section, one method for challenging an assertion of fact is described.

When an assertion is made which is intended to describe an objective phenomenon, it may be challenged on the grounds that it is not true or on the grounds that it is not the best description for its referent. Both sorts of challenge may be done by proffering an alternative description to the one therein challenged. The interaction which ensued when the plaintiff named 'on the belt' as an area of damage illustrates this device.

PLAINTIFF: Round the back there, (.) And on the be:lt

ADJUDICATOR: ◆ The question is w:whe::rre on the belt⌐   is⌐the da:mage

PLAINTIFF: └Well └'T's all on Loo:k 'T's
all round the belt. 'T's all on the back of this collar? I mean I don't
wear it like that all day long you know,

Just as the adjudicator, in naming 'under the sleeve', 'under the arm', and
'on the inside of the neck', was claiming to describe *actual* verifiable areas of
damage, so the plaintiff, too, intended 'round the back there' and 'on the belt'
to describe actual areas which are there to be verified or confirmed by the
adjudicator. The claim was that the damage was where she says it is, *and* she
was describing it in a way which properly represents it.

The adjudicator, upon hearing the plaintiff's description 'And on the belt',
challenges it. The challenge takes the form of a query:

PLAINTIFF: And on the belt.

ADJUDICATOR: ◆ The question is where on the belt is the damage

In querying, the adjudicator invited the plaintiff to re-characterize the area of
damage, by specifying an area on the belt where the damage is visible.

Parenthetically, it may be noted that this attempt failed. The consequence
was not that the adjudicator abandoned the belief that a specification of belt
area was the right characterization. Later in the hearing the plaintiff again
talked about the damage on the belt. In response, the adjudicator said:

ADJUDICATOR: May I just make (.) one point about the belt.s Miss ____ and that is,
                ˙hhhh the damage on the be:lt, appears to be where it goes through
                the loo(.)ps:::,

Why did the adjudicator, on the first occasion, attempt to have the plaintiff
formulate the area, while on a subsequent occasion proffer the specified
area herself? A possible answer is that in querying, she was not treating the
plaintiff as capable, competent, and open to making the discrimination, but
also as perhaps innocently not discriminating sufficiently. If the query-device
had suceeded and the plaintiff did provide the specification, a long way
toward settlement of the claim would have been travelled. The plaintiff would
have articulated evidence for the opposing side's claims (that the damage was

due to wear) with the plaintiff then having to deal with the implications and hence perhaps modify her initial position.

The two instances, (1) 'The question is where on the belt is the damage' and (2) 'The damage on the belt appears to be where it goes through the loops', were both forms of challenging the plaintiff's assertion that the damage was 'on the belt'. In both, an alternative formulation was being endorsed as valid by the adjudicator. The alternative formulation was a specification of a *part* of an area relative to the plaintiff area formulation, 'on the belt'. In seeking and/or supplying a part of an area formulation, the adjudicator implicitly proposed 'on the belt' as having been too gross. When the adjudicator attempted to have the plaintiff see that the damage was on the part of the belt where it goes through the loops, she is not disputing that the damage is 'on the belt', but that 'on the belt' is not, *for their purposes*, the best way to characterize the damaged area being referenced. There was a tacit assumption that there is one best way of referring to the damaged area. With respect to the formulations 'on the belt' and 'on the belt where it goes through the loops', the more specific was clearly 'better' with respect to the task at hand, that is determining the cause of damage. *This* specificity was in the service of, and relevant to, discriminating between alternative proposals of the cause of the damage.

The finer area formulation ('on the belt ... where it goes through the loops')˙ named just the place on the belt where there would be friction and rubbing. It is with respect to substantiating one of the relevant proposals of cause of damage that that place on the belt was conceived of in terms of friction in the course of wear. If the finer area formulation was valid, the proposal of the cause of damage being wear friction would be supported. The further discrimination of which area on the belt was damaged, then, took on importance by virtue of the concern with determining the cause of damage. Since damage on *that* particular area was arguably caused by friction, the court would treat that discrimination as relevant.

In responding, the plaintiff would have been motivated to refute that assertion which supported damage by wear. Refuting, in this case, was done with a challenge to the *validity* of the part of the area description. The plaintiff challenged it by proposing that it was a *wrong* description of the referent damage:

(1)

ADJUDICATOR: The question is where on the belt⌐   is⌐the da:mage

PLAINTIFF: └Well └'T's all on Loo:k 'T's all
                 r̲ound the belt.

(2)

ADJUDICATOR: ... the damage on the belt, appears to be where it goes through the
loo(.)ps:::.
(0.3)

PLAINTIFF: ◆   It's all over

Whereas in the previous examples the adjudicator used an alternative
formulation to challenge the prior one as not the *best* formulation; in these
examples the plaintiff used an alternative formulation to challenge the prior
as not a *valid* formulation.

CONCLUDING REMARKS

The data considered above illustrate how, in describing the facts in front of
them, the participants in a court hearing do so in a way that is closely oriented
to the immediate local relevances of the interactional business in which they
are engaged. The materials also show how a particular device (proposing an
alternative descriptor) can be used by different participants for different
practical purposes at different points in the course of the same court hearing.
That what counts as relevant for the participants may change during the
course of an unfolding sequence of interaction is not only demonstrably the
case; it is also one of the main reasons why ethnomethodological studies are
centrally concerned with taking the interactional setting, or immediate local
relevances of particular actions, seriously into account.

Such an orientation contrasts somewhat with other approaches to the
'problem of context' that are to be found elsewhere in the social and
behavioural sciences. Thus, the view that the meanings of actions can only be
understood in terms of the context in which they take place is now widely
accepted within various traditions of sociology, social psychology, and social
anthropology. However, when translated into research or theorizing, this
orientation frequently tends to involve the assumption that, for each and
every social context that exists, there is a collection of context-specific rules,
procedures, or practices that is more or less uniquely appropriate for
accomplishing the practical tasks associated with any particular setting.
Relatedly, there is an assumption that this will remain constant throughout
the entire course of a court hearing, a lesson or lecture in a classroom, a
therapy session, or a meeting.

The present study and others like it provide grounds for doubting the
validity of this latter assumption. What would be involved in learning how to
act in different contexts recommends similar scepticism about the view that a

set of contextually specific rules are associated with each social context. For, were this the case, the sheer quantity of 'different rules for different contexts' which individuals would have to learn in order to perform competently within them would be so immense (and perhaps even infinite), that it is difficult to imagine how even a small proportion of them could possibly be learned. By contrast, a central assumption of the ethnomethodological approach is that the analytic methods and practices available to human beings are such that they can be adaptably and transferrably used across a range of settings, as well as within the more temporally localized sequences of interaction that constitute them.

NOTE

(1) While such simplification makes the sequences more accessible to readers unfamiliar with the full range of conventions now used by conversation analysts, a consequence is some loss of detail. Readers interested in obtaining fuller access to the data are therefore invited to write to the authors for copies of the original tape-recording and transcriptions.

REFERENCES

ATKINSON, J. M. (1978). *Discovering Suicide: Studies in the Social Organisation of Sudden Death.* London: Macmillan.
ATKINSON, J. M., and DREW, P. (1979). *Order in Court: the Organisation of Verbal Interaction in Judicial Settings.* London: Macmillan.
ATKINSON, J. M., and HERITAGE, J. C. (1984). *Structures of Social Action. Studies in Conversation Analysis.* Cambridge: Cambridge University Press (in press).
BITTNER, E. (1967). The police on skid row: a study of peace keeping. *American Sociological Review,* **32,** 699–715.
CICOUREL, A. V. (1968). *The Social Organization of Juvenile Justice.* New York: Wiley.
DANET, B. (1980). Language in the legal process. *Law and Society Review,* **14,** 445–564.
GARFINKEL, H.(1967). *Studies in Ethnomethodology,* Englewood Cliffs, N.J.: Prentice Hall.
GARFINKEL, H.(1974). The origin of the term 'ethnomethodology'. In R. Turner (Ed), *Ethnomethodology,* Harmondsworth, Middlesex: Penguin.
GOODWIN, C. (1981). *Conversational Organization: Interaction between Speakers and Hearers.* New York: Academic Press.
KALVEN, H., and ZEISEL, H. (1966). *The American Jury.* Boston: Little Brown.
O'BARR, W. M. (1982). *Linguistic Evidence: Language, Power and Strategy in the Courtroom.* New York: Academic Press.
POLLNER, M. (1974). Mundane reasoning. *Philosophy of the Social Sciences,* **4,** 35–54.
POLLNER, M. (1979). Explicative transactions: making and managing meaning in traffic courts. In G. Psathas (Ed.), *Everyday Language: Studies in Ethnomethodology.* New York: Irvington.

PSATHAS, G. (1979). *Everyday Language: Studies in Ethnomethodology.* New York: Irvington.

SACKS, H. (1972). Notes on police assessment of moral character. In D. Sudnow (Ed.), *Studies in Social Interaction.* New York: Free Press.

SCHENKEIN, J. N. (1978). *Studies in the Organization of Conversational Interaction.* New York: Academic Press.

SUDNOW, D. (1965). Normal crimes: sociological features of the penal code in a public defender's office. *Social Problems,* **12**, 255–270.

SUDNOW, D. (1972). *Studies in Social Interaction.* New York: Free Press.

WIEDER, D. L. (1974). *Language and Social Reality: The Case of Telling the Convict Code.* The Hague: Mouton.

ZIMMERMAN, D. H. (1969). Record-keeping and the intake process in a public welfare agency. In S. Wheeler (Ed.), *On Record.* New York: Sage.

SECTION VI

Decision-taking

Psycho-legal research on how judicial decisions are taken and on the consistency of such judgments has led to considerable debate. The chapters in this section provide an indication of the research which has been carried out and also show why such studies have sometimes seemed controversial.

The thrust of **Lovegrove**'s chapter is to find methods of reducing disparities between judgments. Lovegrove suggests that judges should be enabled to compare a sentence which they have in mind with statistics of judgments made in similar cases. Thus judges would be provided with more information about the general context in which their decision is placed, thereby leading in general to a reduction in disparity of sentencing or at least to a greater awareness of the need for judicial discretion to be exercised.

In the following chapter, **Lawrence** describes how magistrates interpret and construct the decisions which they make, and she emphasizes how relevant information is gathered and evaluated. A model is developed from the self-reports of magistrates, and this model shows the complexity of the processes used. Lawrence's research therefore seeks to describe the cognitive processes used by magistrates in order to make their judgments.

Finally, **Palys and Divorski** provide evidence for disparities of judgments in Canadian Provincial Courts (Criminal Division). However, these authors argue that the reduction or elimination of such disparities is not a question which psychologists should address. Guidelines and other devices for reducing disparity might be said to assume that there is a 'correct' judgment, and moreover that this correctness is defined merely by the central tendency of previous judgments. Palys and Divorski argue that this is essentially a *legal* issue. However, psychologists could play an important role if they were to focus on the consequences of judges' sentencing strategies with a view to evaluating the predictions on which these judgments might be based.

These three chapters offer differing perspectives on judicial decision-taking. Along with other studies, they show that 'disparities' often exist.

However, such disparities may be conceptualized as faults or 'noise' in the system, or of course as results of sensitive discretion with respect to the specific case. Differing attitudes to this issue are displayed in the chapter here. All confirm, however, that judicial decision-taking is a complex task. It is one which could provide a profitable forum for studies of decision-making per se in the growing tradition of an ecologically valid cognitive psychology.

Psychology and Law
Edited by D.J. Müller, D.E. Blackman, and A.J. Chapman
1984 John Wiley & Sons Ltd

Chapter 22

Structuring Judicial Sentencing Discretion

S. A. Lovegrove

The present chapter contributes to current literature on sentencing disparity as it exists or as it is thought to exist in the higher criminal courts and examines the place and style of empirical means of reducing sentencing disparity. The term 'disparity' refers to gross inter-judge variations in sentencing practices. It is held that this phenomenon arises from judicial differences, perhaps temporary, in attitude, skill, and knowledge, and that these differences are manifested through judges' preferences for penal aims, views about the comparative efficacy of penal measures, evaluations of offence seriousness, and the like.

Recently, I completed an empirical study of inter-judge sentencing variation in an Australian state intermediate criminal court. The data base comprised official records for the years 1978, 1979, and 1980 of sentences imposed upon persons whose principal offences were one of the three most common indictable offences heard in the higher courts (viz. robbery, burglary, and theft). Within each of the years there were inter-judge differences in preferred use of imprisonment and, in instances where persons were incarcerated, differences in preferred length of imprisonment. Moreover, the latter disparity was consistent across years (see Lovegrove, 1984).

The significance of these findings is that disparity was found to exist in a jurisdiction which uses the traditional means of curbing inter-judge differences: an active Full Court that hears appeals against sentence from both the Crown and the defence; reported judgments on these appeals; central location of judges so that frequently they are able to consult their brothers about what may be appropriate sentences for particular cases.

Numerous measures have been proposed for the purpose of curbing disparity: mandatory sentences, presumptive sentences, legislatively expressed preferences for or against particular sentences, sentencing councils formed

301

to formulate guidelines, sentencing panels, training conferences, and detaile statistics describing current practice. It is the provision of relevant statistics which this chapter is directed.

CURRENT APPROACHES TO SENTENCING STATISTICS

Official Statistics

In Victoria, Australia, the Law Department prepares annual statistics sentencing practices. The data are classified by principal offence into categories and show the numbers of persons upon whom each of the possib penalties was imposed; sentences of imprisonment are subdivided accordir to length (Victoria Law Department, Research Section, 1981). So now whe judges refer to these statistics they can ascertain the precise range of th sentences imposed for any particular principal offence, but they are left t guess where a particular case lies in relation to that distribution.

The Law Reform Commission (1980) has observed that Australian appe courts are increasingly adopting the practice of requesting the prosecution produce such statistics to help secure uniformity in sentencing. Similarly Rinaldi (1979) cites instances where such statistical schedules have attracte laudatory comments from appellate courts in Australia. Reference to thes statistics when determining sentence has been viewed favourably by membe of the Victorian Court of Criminal Appeal. Adam and Crockett, JJ, upo calling for statistical data relating to sentences imposed in the State for th type of offence before them, said '...a judgment as to what is appropriate b way of sentence must depend upon knowledge of sentences for the same c similar offences ...' (Regina v. Williscroft, Weston, Woodley and Robinson[1] However, Young, CJ, delivering a judgment of the same court, reacted to th present statistical data with greater caution. He commented that statistics tha are not differentiated according to certain offence and offender characteri tics are of little if any use to the courts in their task of determining th quantum of sentence (Regina v. Yuill and Besson [2]).

This chapter addresses the difficulties associated with official statistics: reviews the system of sentencing guidelines and presents a structure whic could be used to develop particularized and readily comprehensible senten ing statistics. Solutions to this problem are likely to attract considerabl attention in the near future. In a recent survey of Australian (Federal an State) judges, 83% of the respondents favoured the provision of detaile sentencing statistics as a means of promoting uniformity; indeed, this was th most popular of the innovative measures canvassed in the survey (La Reform Commission, 1980).

ɛntencing Guidelines

ʔilkins, Kress, Gottfredson, Calpin, and Gelman's (1978) research is an ɾiginal attempt to provide detailed statistics that identify the major offence ɪd offender characteristics, together with their weights, associated with the uantum of sentence. These statistics are compiled by predicting actual ɛntencing decisions from information before judges about cases. The ɛsulting equations represent a mathematical description of sentencing policy. he system proposed by Wilkins et al. (1978) is not just descriptive, but it has prescriptive component. To use this system for a particular case the judge ɪust allot points in terms of the extent to which it is characterized by the ffence and offender characteristics identified in the statistical analyses. The ːores on the dimensions are used to identify the appropriate cell in the table ɪving sentencing data for particular combinations of offence and offender ɪaracteristics. Typically, the statistics cover the percentage imprisoned and, ɔr those imprisoned, an estimate of the length of imprisonment.

This information comprises the guidelines. Judges are expected to impose ɛntences within the guidelines in about 85% of cases. When departing from ɪe guidelines, a judge must provide reasons. The prescriptive element of this pproach rests upon the assumption that like offenders committing like ffences ought to be treated alike. Expressed from another perspective, the uidelines system entails the assumption that as a matter of course the sole ɛterminant in a judgment as to what is appropriate by way of sentence is the uantum of sentence that similar cases have attracted over recent years within ɪe jurisdiction.

In the USA the National Institute of Law Enforcement and Criminal ustice (1978) has produced what amounts to a manual to be followed by ɪose implementing guidelines systems. For the purpose of later evaluation in ɪis chapter it is appropriate to outline some of the major steps in the ɾocedure.

(1) List the variables in the information available to the judge about the offences and the offenders: Wilkins et al. (1978) used about 200 items.

(2) Use stepwise multiple regression to identify a relatively small set of variables (and their weights) that together give the best prediction of actual sentencing decisions.

(3) Establish categories and associated points for each of the variables found to be related to sentence, such that each category marks a substantially different sentence. Wilkins et al.'s most complex variable has six divisions, but binary classifications are not uncommon.

(4) Develop models that show the relationship between the sum of the scores of the offence and offender characteristics and the sentence. Wilkins et al.'s classification of offender characteristics used six items

of information covering past record and employment history. T
differentiate offence, they presented a separate guideline table fo
each of eight State statutory classes of offences. For each table
offences were divided according to estimated seriousness into three o
four groups and assigned rankings determined by project staff mem
bers. Further differentiation was achieved by adding points to this ran
according to the degree of harm or loss suffered by the victim. Eac
table comprised a two-dimensional grid, one axis for the offence an
the second for the offender characteristics. The most complex tabl
comprised 30 (6 × 5) cells.

It is fundamental to the development of guidelines that an advisory boar
comprising judges has the final say on the structure and composition of th
model when their view on the salience of factors differs from the empirica
results.

The approach and techniques devised by Wilkins et al. (1978) appear t
have gained ready acceptance. The guidelines approach has now bee
implemented on a wide scale in the USA (Kress, 1980). In Australia the Lav
Reform Commission (1980) has recommended that guidelines be formulate
for the sentencing of Federal offenders. In doing so they drew attention to th
work of Wilkins and his associates and asserted that these researchers ha
developed a detailed and reliable set of methods. The important question
however, is whether it is a valid strategy. Given the largely uncritica
acceptance of their approach, this is clearly an urgent question. Also, it woul
appear timely for lawyers in the UK to develop an attitude towards thi
system of sentencing guidelines; Wilkins (1980) has urged that it be consi
dered for this country as a solution to the problem of disparity, and th
Advisory Council on the Penal System (1978), while doubting the accepta
bility of these sentencing guidelines in the British context, nevertheles
suggested that it should be watched closely. However, the most recent report
cast doubt on the future of the approach of Wilkins and his associates. In
recent review of sentencing reforms, Tonry (1982) concluded that the earl
enthusiasm is waning.

Before setting up criteria against which one can evaluate attempts t
provide particularized statistics, it is necessary to examine the place o
statistics in the process of sentencing and the purposes of more detaile
statistics.

THE PLACE OF STATISTICS IN THE PROCESS OF SENTENCING

One can discern two elements in the Court of Criminal Appeal's judgment
about what is appropriate by way of sentence. First, there is discussion abou
the principles of sentencing to be applied in particular cases. Second, there i

reference to the Court's view of the quantum of sentence that similar cases have attracted in recent years within the jurisdiction. Through the former component the Court of Criminal Appeal interprets and develops the law of sentencing and provides reasoned decisions in order to guide judges' sentencing in the first instance. This component of the judgment is the heart of the Court's individualizing sentence, and in it one may observe the Court meeting the Victorian Chief Justice's requirement that judges must hold the scales of justice between the offender and the community (Young, 1979). The second dimension, generally referred to as the 'tariff', provides a standard of the quantum of sentence against which the Court can weigh its present response. Together these two aspects of the judgment provide for principled uniformity.

Members of the Victorian Court of Criminal Appeal have attested to the salience of the former component. Adam and Crockett, JJ, said, 'The purposes of punishment are manifold and each element will assume a different significance not only in different crimes but in the individual commission of each crime.' They added that one matter to be considered is whether the crime's contemporary prevalence is a source of considerable disquiet in the community (Regina v. Williscroft, Weston, Woodley and Robinson[1]). Clearly, the Court's resolutions of these questions are not immutable over time. In a judgment (Regina v. Adams, Sharpe and Malm[3]) delivered by Jacobs, P, the New South Wales Court of Criminal Appeal emphasized the significance of the tariff:

'The duty of this Court is to see that there is a consistency in the sentences and it is the duty of all courts to see that some scale is observed. The scale is basically the product of the day to day experience of the many judges ...' (cited by Rinaldi, 1979, p. 120).

In order to understand why some have argued that sentencing cannot be reduced to the mechanical application of a table (Young, 1979), one must appreciate the significance of the former element of the judgment. Tonry and Morris (1978, p. 445) succinctly state the position of those who subscribe to this view: 'Equality in punishment is not an absolute principle. It is a value to be weighed and considered among others. There can be just sentences in which like offenders are not treated alike ...'. They cite the use of exemplary sentences as instances of principled sentencing disparity. Similarly, Thomas (1977, p. 13) concluded that the 'concept of equity in sentencing means more than mechanical quantification of punishment. Equity requires the consistent application of a recognizable and articulated body of principle.'

Such considerations ought not to be taken as undermining the significance of the tariff as a determinant of sentence. Cross and Ashworth, speaking of judges who reject the notion of tariff, stated, 'It cannot be said that they exclude altogether the notion of the appropriate range of sentence, although it may well play its part in determining the final sentence at a later stage in their case than in that of some other judges' (Cross and Ashworth, 1981 p. 169). McKenna, in the course of a lecture delivered while he was a member of the English High Court, imputed a critical role to the tariff in the determination of sentence. After deliberating upon the purposes of punishment, he said,

'In practice the judge escapes these perplexities by pursuing the ideal of equal punishment. If he has no certainty about the right sentence to deter or punish, he can at least try to give the kind of sentence recently given by others for the offence in question .... In his exercise of trying to give the same sentence as others have given he has the help of the Criminal Statistics' (McKenna, 1969, p. 610).

Finally, in this regard, it ought to be noted that in Victoria undue disparity between sentences passed on persons involved in the same and similar offences is a ground for appeal (see Regina v. Tutchell[4]).

The Purposes of Detailed Statistics

In the light of the foregoing discussion one may formulate a role and place for particularized statistics of judges' sentencing practices: namely, to quantify the tariff so as to reduce the degree to which judges must exercise their sentencing discretion without knowledge of how their brothers have acted in similar cases. The aim is deliberately couched in this qualified form so that judicial discretion is left unfettered in relation to the consideration of the purposes of punishment and the uniqueness of the case. Upon accepting this proposition one is forced to eschew prescription.

Several members of the Victorian Court of Criminal Appeal have clearly stated their view on the subjectivity of the determination of sentences. Adam and Crockett, JJ, considering this matter, said,

'... ultimately every sentence imposed represents the sentencing judge's instinctive synthesis of all the various aspects involved in the punitive process ... it is profitless ... to attempt to allot to the various considerations their proper part in the assessment of the particular punishments presently under examination' (Regina v. Williscroft, Weston, Woodley and Robinson [1]).

The Chief Justice has endorsed this view (Young, 1979). While Rinaldi (1980) has condemned, even ridiculed this approach, it seems, given the present lack of quantification of the factors determining sentence, that the Court of Criminal Appeal is correctly and frankly stating the present position. It is submitted that particularized sentencing statistics can meet this need. This issue is taken up later.

EVALUATION OF THE SENTENCING GUIDELINES SYSTEM

Prior to outlining an alternative approach, it is appropriate to evaluate sentencing guidelines in the light of the preceding discussion. Objections to the guidelines system as an empirical solution to the problem of structuring judicial discretion arise because its orientation is prescriptive rather than being merely informative. Not only is this a difficulty *per se*; it appears to have led to the adoption of techniques and solutions that, although perhaps compatible with a presumptive framework, would certainly be unacceptable in a system based on discretionary justice.

A prescriptive system would be inappropriate for several reasons.

(1) It would impoverish the sentencing process. Reference to the appropriate tariff is just one component of the judgment. Deliberations about the purposes of the punitive process are a vital part of sentencing.

(2) There is a danger that the Court of Criminal Appeal would effectively be downgraded to little more than a board of clerks whose duty would be to check the additions of the sentencing judges. Clearly, at the very least the significance of the Court of Criminal Appeal as a source of sentencing policy would be diminished.

(3) Judges would be expected to be discouraged from individualizing sentences. Such pressure might be based on a fear of exceeding the guidelines too frequently, might result from a perceived inferiority of personal judgment against a supposed scientific assessment, or simply have its roots in laziness or expediency. In this light, how can one agree with Wilkins *et al.* (1978) that one advantage of guidelines is that they speed up sentencing? At this point Zalman's (1978) term 'robot sentencing' strikes a chord.

Moreover, the over-riding prescriptive orientation has led its followers to adopt techniques with unfortunate consequences.

(1) The developers of these guidelines rely on sophisticated statistical techniques to identify and weight salient variables and also use complex models to relate sentences to facts about cases. Although Wilkins *et al.*'s two-dimensional model is simpler than some, it imposes scores (corresponding to categories within each variable) between case characteristic and sentence, rather than relating case facts to sentences directly. This latter approach appears to be more consistent with the structure of legal thought (see Thomas, 1979). To be sure, the guidelines models are easy to follow in the 'cookbook' mode. The point is that their representation of the relationship between specific combinations of case variables and the current tariffs would not be comprehensible to judges and barristers without statistical training. This being so, there is the danger that the table would become a master

to be followed blindly, rather than one of a number of reference points against which the judges exercise their discretion.

(2) Although stepwise multiple regression yields the average effect of the case variables that together provide the best linear and additive prediction of sentence, such analyses would be expected to omit and distort the effect of some of the variables that are material to sentence. This consequence might occur for variables that (a) are co-linearly related to a second case variable and sentence, when this second variable is more strongly related to sentence; (b) are not linearly related to sentence; (c) only affect sentence in interaction with certain values of other variables; and (d) have values that are uncommon features of cases and yet exert a salient effect when present. For each of these reasons one would not be surprised if the statistical analysis failed to identify age, for example, as material to sentence.

(3) Where detailed data bases are used the method would not prevent certain variables that ought to be immaterial to sentence from being incorporated indirectly into the guidelines, even if these variables were omitted from the analysis. For example, if race is in fact a determinant of sentence, then for this reason alone factors correlated with race such as unemployment would be found to be associated significantly with sentence.

What are the possible consequences of this? First, the guidelines might unintentionally lead to the creation of new sentencing policies. In these circumstances judges following the guidelines would fail to take into account variables that are material to sentence or would give insufficient or excessive weight to factors. This is a problem that Flaxman (1979) observed in his analysis of the parole guidelines, although the cause of the unintended policy he identified was different. Second, the guidelines might be based on an impoverished set of offence and offender characteristics. One need only compare the limited range of factors to be found in the guidelines solutions outlined above with the richness of the traditional common law approach presented in Thomas' (1979) analysis of the substance of the tariff to appreciate this point. Vining (1979), too, was struck by the contrast.

Wilkins et al. (1978) have argued that the relatively few variables required to predict sentence attest to the simplicity of judicial decision-making. The preceding deliberations point to another explanation. Indeed, it appears that Wilkins et al. may have deceived themselves in their conclusion that they had accounted in 85% of cases for the sentencing decisions, for their criterion of a correct prediction of length of incarceration was indeed generous: for 'felony four' offences (10 years' maximum) a hit was defined as within one year of the specified guideline ranges of between one and two years. This outcome is not unexpected in the light of Wilkins et al.'s pilot analysis using multiple regression. For one sample they found that the six significant offender/offence variables accounted for only 50% of the sentencing variance. Upon increasing the number of variables to 14, they merely accounted for another 3%. For a second sample the explanatory power of their equations was considerably poorer. Even allowing for the fact that later models were refined, the percentage variance left unexplained would appear to have been substantial. A re-analysis of Wilkins *et al*'s study by Hewitt and Little (1981) confirmed two of the original findings, namely there was only a small number of significant variables accounting for past sentencing practice and this set explained only a small percentage of the variance.

Morris (1979) criticized the empirical approach to guidelines on the ground that it gives a sense of false precision. It was for this reason that Morris rejected the empirical approach in favour of the traditional common law form as a basis of guidelines. The alternative empirical solution, presented in the next section, rests on the assumption that the empirical and common law approaches are not necessarily mutually exclusive.

Finally, the guidelines cannot readily incorporate the effect of appellate court decisions, since they are formulated from actual sentencing decisions; so before re-formulating the guidelines one ought to wait until a large number of cases has been sentenced by judges cognizant of the appellate court's new rulings. It is to be expected that there would be many periods during which the guidelines lagged behind current sentencing practices. Clearly, this possibility makes actual sentencing practice an unattractive basis for the guidelines. Wilkins *et al*. suggest that the judges in a jurisdiction ought to meet regularly to review those decisions falling outside the guidelines and, if any of the departures indicate the need for policy revision, then the guidelines should be modified accordingly. One cannot but wonder why the guidelines could not be constructed similarly.

AN ALTERNATIVE EMPIRICAL SOLUTION

The present proposal eschews prescription; it merely attempts to offer more detail than exists currently in the official statistics so that judges would have some idea where a particular case lies in the distribution of principal offence by sentence. Simply, it sets out to be no more than a numerical aid to the common law approach: to quantify some of the principles underlying what Thomas (1979) calls 'the substance of the tariff'. For Thomas (1979) the tariff is a framework to which a sentencer can refer in order to determine what factors in a particular case are relevant and the weight that should be attached to each of them.

The guidelines system is oriented towards prescription and uses prediction (correlation) techniques based on official records. Against this, the present solution is governed by the way judges more or less consciously determine the quantum of sentence. Additionally, it proposes the use of experimental manipulation of fictitious cases (as well as an analysis of official records) to identify how factors affect the sentence. This approach is illustrated by reference to the determination of length of incarceration.

The Judicial Determinant of Sentence

How judges determine sentence has been discussed by both Thomas (1979) and Cross and Ashworth (1981), and their view of judicial thought is adopted here. The present approach proceeds by fitting data to a theory of decision-making, an approach rejected by Gottfredson, Wilkins, and Hoffman (1978) who favour a solution moulded by the data. The difficulty with this latter approach is that it belies the fact that their analysis is really organized around a particular mathematical model of the data. Accepting that one must adopt some model to interpret the data, it is my belief that the one that is most faithful to the structure of judicial decision-making will give lawyers the most accurate, comprehensive, and comprehensible representation of the determination of the tariff.

According to Thomas (1979), the judge, having favoured a sentence of imprisonment, follows three steps to determine the length:

(1) *Defining the range.* The assumption behind the tariff is that within any legal definition a variety of factual situations relating to the offence will recur, and that within each set of actual situations there are upper and lower limits within which the sentence is presumed to fall in the absence of exceptional circumstances relating to the offence and without regard to mitigating circumstances relating to the offender.

(2) *Fixing the ceiling.* Typically, the judge's task is to relate the facts of the case to one of the established patterns of that type of offence, and then to locate the established range of sentence in relation to the particular set of facts. The upper limit of the range is the ceiling.

(3) *Reducing the sentence to allow for mitigating factors.*

Cross and Ashworth's (1981) analysis of the determination of sentence length substantially endorses the model developed by Thomas.

It is now appropriate to examine how Thomas classifies varieties of offences. Take, for example, robbery. Thomas divides robbery into four groups (viz. large-scale organized robbery, violent robbery, robberies of tradespeople and small business premises, and mugging), citing the typical characteristics of each group. One can discern, however, that many of the characteristics (e.g. violence) or their contrasts (no violence) recur across groups. This suggests an alternative way to classify robberies, namely to describe each robbery according to its place on a set of dimensions.

It should be noted that the dimensional classification is more amenable to quantitative analysis with its concomitant benefit of permitting finer discriminations and, hence, greater precision. The imprecision in Thomas' groupings arises from the fact that characteristics comprising his groups are imperfectly correlated. For example, the sentences for mugging reflect the fact that most offenders in this category are young and so receive the benefits of mitigation. However, as Thomas recognizes, a longer sentence may be more appropriate for one with no such claim to mitigation. Without such distinctions the allowance for age is left to the judge's discretion, and without particularized statistics a source of disparity is created.

A second difficulty with Thomas' analysis is that his use of groups imposes a structure on judicial thought that is at variance with their mode of determining the quantum of sentence. Rather, in the illustrative cases Thomas considers, the Court appears to determine length, as it were, by adding (or subtracting) time for aggravating (or extenuating) factors. For example, he cites a case where the Court took 15 years as a starting point and observed that there must be room for differentiation according to factors such as the degree of sophistication in execution, whether firearms were loaded, and the like.

Third, Thomas' analysis faces difficulty, as he acknowledges, for offences for which mitigating factors carry greater weight and where offenders are sentenced on multiple offences. Under these circumstances, his relating of fact and sentence entails substantial guesswork.

The preceding discussion points to a possible solution for presenting more detailed sentencing statistics: for each offence identify a small set of common dimensions, each of two to three categories, and investigate the effect that each factor (or combination of factors) has on the length of sentence. For example, the presence of a firearm may add 12 months to the sentence.

For Thomas' classification of robbery, the following five dimensions appear to provide a comprehensive coverage of his material distinctions: number of offenders, degree of sophistication of planning, amount of violence, presence of a weapon, value of goods sought. From the descriptions appearing in the judgments cited by Thomas one can infer that generally at least three categories are used to make the contrasts. For example, presumably between the categories 'great care and attention to detail' and 'amateurish and spontaneous' there is an intervening category. The numbers of dimensions and categories used would depend on the degree of precision sought in relation to the cost. Mitigating factors would be analysed similarly.

A Data Base of Fictitious Cases

It is proposed that the source of the data base for the particularized statistics should include judges' sentences of fictitious cases. Few would raise opposition to the requirement of judicial independence; the dangers that might arise in its absence are generally regarded as intolerable (see, for example, Alschuler 1978). Certainly, the results of the Law Reform Commission's (1980) survey show that Australian judges view their independence as sacrosanct. Clearly, the sentencing decisions must be of judicial origin.

The choice of fictitious cases over official records is possibly controversial, and so needs defending. Upon reflection, it can be seen to have advantages:

(1) It is necessary to adopt this approach if one is to identify the impact of variables on sentence experimentally.

(2) Cases can be formulated so that it is possible to examine the independent effects of variables that in real life are generally correlated with other factors.

(3) If the Court of Criminal Appeal adopts a new policy, its effect as interpreted by first-instance judges can be determined readily; it is only necessary to compile a set of cases covering a variety of relevant sets of circumstances and then get judges to sentence these cases.

(4) This strategy overcomes the problem of measuring the effect of case factors on the dependent variable for cases in which there are multiple offences. Unless the offences are split, one cannot be sure to what extent a judge's sentence for the principal offence was influenced by an awareness that the offender was to be sentenced for multiple offences.

(5) Variables with values that are uncommon features of real life cases and yet of material relevance to sentence can be incorporated into a sufficient number of fictitious cases so that their effects can be estimated reliably.

(6) Variables that ought not to be material to sentence cannot be incorporated into the guidelines unwittingly through their association with other factors. For, say, race to be included in the guidelines it would have to be written into the fictitious cases. (This must be distinguished from a related problem in which legitimate determinants of sentence may have a disparate impact on certain groups, for example, employment record on race.)

Undoubtedly, critics will liken this to psychological simulation studies in legal settings and question the results on the basis of the apparent artificiality of the method and inconsequential nature of the decisions. But this resemblance is more apparent than real. First, gravity would attend these judgments since the decisions would be a source of reference for sentencing judges. Second, many judges appear to be comfortable with this technique; both in Britain (see Cross and Ashworth, 1981) and in Australia (see Law Reform Commission, 1980) judges attest to the value of sentencing conferences, and yet the source material there comprises fictitious cases. But, more importantly, judges use this approach in the courts. Surely, the use of fictitious cases is analogous to procedures followed by the Court of Criminal

Appeal? There, one of the judges' main sources of information about cases is the trial transcripts, and on this basis they determine and weight material factors. Similarly, reports of cases before the appellate courts rely on abridged versions of the facts of these cases.

Of course, it does not follow that particularized statistics ought to be established by the Full Court. Presumably, the sentences for the fictitious cases would be passed by judges in the jurisdiction in which they were to be used, although under the supervision of the Full Court.

The Experimental Method

The advantage of this method over the correlational technique is that it is possible to determine the presence and magnitude of the effect of causal factors that are material to sentence. Moreover, it can cope with interactions and non-linear relationships between variables.

The first step in implementing this proposal would be to list the factors, or combinations of factors, as well as their salient categories, whose effect on the determination of sentence is of most interest. Given the present approach, the most appropriate sources of guidance for this task are judges and legal analyses of sentencing principles. Vining and Dean (1980), after observing that empirical studies account for relatively small percentages of the sentencing variance, suggest that this is because empiricists have not understood that appellate judgments are a rich source of variables.

The method for examining the magnitude of the effects of the hypothesized material factors can be illustrated simply. One would take a base-grade robbery (e.g. small amount seized, single offender, spontaneous, unarmed, no violence) and compare the sentences for this type of case against one in which the robbery was planned, or planned and in which there were minor injuries to the victim, and so on (i.e. one would add the effects of aggravating factors). The effects of mitigation would be analysed similarly, and these effects would be subtracted from the tariff sentence. This process would be repeated for each specific offence. Thomas has warned that it is not possible to construct a negative tariff of the effects of mitigating factors, since the combination of such factors is normally greater than the sum of the factors considered separately. Nevertheless, the proposed analysis could untangle such interactions.

Two dangers attend this approach. First, certain factorial combinations might be difficult to judge because they rarely occur in real life. Further, the decision-making strategy in other treatments might be affected by these atypical cells (Konečni and Ebbesen, 1979). Second, the use of inappropriate values assigned to factors (Farrington and Knight, 1979) or a context that is impoverished compared to the real world (Bridgeman and Marlowe, 1979) might result in an over- or under-estimate of the significance of factors in real life. These difficulties, however, could be avoided by ensuring that the fictitious cases were faithful reproductions of cases from official records and that the categories and dimensions were of interest to the judiciary.

A Case for Official Records

It would be understandable if some felt uneasiness at the use of fictitious cases: perhaps a sentence imposed where there is face-to-face contact with a particular defendant for whom the sentence has real and immediate consequences would be different? Partridge and Eldridge (1974) have called this the paper defendant problem. Given these doubts, it would seem prudent to analyse official records according to the preceding approach, but using a quasi-experimental design of case-by-case matching to control for extraneous variables. The hazard that attends this approach is that one cannot be sure whether differences in sentence between case factors or combinations of factors are due to those factors rather than their hidden correlates.

The advantage of this bipartite strategy is that many types of cases would be common to the two data bases, such that meaningful comparisons could be made between the sentences passed under both conditions. It would be foolish to dismiss the validity of sentences imposed for the fictitious cases if they were to differ from those relating to the official records; judges sentencing a known offender are open to influence by factors that may be immaterial to sentence, such as the emotional distress of the offender's relatives during the trial. Rather, differences between data bases could be used profitably to formulate hypotheses to account for the disparities.

This strategy can be contrasted with that of treating the real life data as a standard against which one may assess the validity of other methods. Rather, it is related to Konečni and Ebbesen's (1979) view that when studying a social system it is possible to use logical and practical criteria to establish *a priori* grounds for placing greater trust in one method than in others. In the present case it is suggested that one may use comparisons between the data bases to guide decisions on this matter.

If archival data were used, then the sentences passed in the courts of first instance ought to form the data base, except for sentences that had been set aside by the appellate court; in such cases the sentence substituted by the higher court seems more appropriate. The problem with a data base comprising only appellate court decisions is that such courts hear atypical cases and, anyway, only set aside sentences that are manifestly lenient or severe.

CONCLUSION

The purpose of particularized statistics is to reduce inter-judge sentencing disparity. Factors that would limit the effectiveness of this empirical solution arise from the nature of both the sentencing judgment and the empirical methods.

First, the development of detailed statistics would be expected to reduce disparity to the extent that it is due to inter-judge differences in the assessment of the tariff. However, differences between judges in terms of how they determine the purposes of punishment in relation to particular cases would act against particularized statistics promoting uniformity. McKenna, in the lecture to which reference was made earlier, explained the interdependence between the two components of the sentencing judgment:

'A judge, sceptical about the deterrent effect of long sentences and either not believing that it is his duty to punish wickedness or being more imaginative than another about the pains of imprisonment, is likely to choose his sentence at the bottom of the range, or he may find circumstances to justify a lower sentence where another would not. A judge who believes that fear of a longer sentence will more effectively deter, or holds that the wickedness of the crime calls for severer punishment, will choose his at the upper end, and will be less likely than the other to find mitigating circumstances' (McKenna, 1969, p. 610).

In relation to this point, Galligan (1981) has argued that in order to control sentencing discretion it is necessary to give judges guidance as to what factors are to be considered in applying penal goals. If there are significant disparities between judges in the setting of penal objectives in relation to facts about offences and offenders, then it would be expected that these would be manifested in the standard deviations of sentences for the offence/offender categories in the statistics. Should these standard deviations generally be substantial, then the estimates of average or typical sentences would be relatively meaningless and, consequently, the particularized statistics would not be viable at this time. Nevertheless, the analysis would not be without worth, for it would point to the need for greater judicial guidance in determining sentencing policy, assessing offence seriousness, and the like.

Second, there would be sources of disparity in the particularized statistics at points of imprecision. Lack of precision would arise in two ways. One, aspects of cases that could not be described in terms of a manageable set of dimensions and categories. Two, subjectivity in the interpretation of cases in terms of these dimensions, a problem shared with the system of sentencing guidelines (see Hoffman and Stover, 1978). With respect to the first point, its success would rest, along with the analysis of Thomas, on the assumption that 'innovation in crime ... is relatively rare' (Thomas, 1979, p. 29). On the second point, research shows that such scales can be interpreted meaningfully (Moser and Kalton, 1971). In relation to both issues, one must remember that the aim of the study is to quantify the tariff: to provide a reference so that judges can compare the sentences they have in mind against those that would be imposed on similar cases by their brothers. Given the lack of precision inherent in the present qualitative techniques, quantification would be expected to produce improvements. The question is whether the gains warrant the costs.

NOTES

1. Regina v. Williscroft, Weston, Woodley and Robinson, *Victorian Reports* 292, 1975.
2. Regina v. Yuill and Besson, Victorian Court of Criminal Appeal, 10 June 1975, unreported.
3. Regina v. Adams, Sharpe and Malm. New South Wales Court of Criminal Appeal, 1972, unreported.
4. Regina v. Tutchell, *Victorian Reports* 248, 1979.

REFERENCES

ADVISORY COUNCIL ON THE PENAL SYSTEM (1978). *Sentences of Imprisonment: A Review of Maximum Penalties*. London: Her Majestys Stationery Office.
ALSCHULER, A. (1978). Sentencing reform and prosecutorial power: a critique of recent proposals for 'fixed' and 'presumptive' sentencing. *University of Pennsylvania Law Review*, **126**, 550–577.
BRIDGEMAN, D., and MARLOWE, D. (1979). Jury decision making: an empirical study based on actual felony trials. *Journal of Applied Psychology*, **64**, 91–98.
CROSS, R., and ASHWORTH, A. (1981). *The English Sentencing System*, 3rd edn. London: Butterworths.
FARRINGTON, D., and KNIGHT, B. (1979). Two non-reactive field experiments on stealing from a 'lost' letter. *British Journal of Social and Clinical Psychology*, **18**, 277–284.
FLAXMAN, K. (1979). The hidden dangers of sentencing guidelines. *Hofstra Law Review*, **7**, 259–280.
GALLIGAN, D. (1981). Guidelines and just deserts: a critique of recent trends in sentencing reform. *Criminal Law Review*, 297–311.
GOTTFREDSON, D., WILKINS, L., and HOFFMAN, P. (1978). *Guidelines for Parole and Sentencing*. Lexington, Mass.: D.C. Heath.
HEWITT, J., and LITTLE, B. (1981). EXAMINING THE RESEARCH UNDERLYING THE SENTENCING GUIDELINES CONCEPT IN DENVER, COLORADO: A PARTIAL REPLICATION OF A REFORM EFFORT. *Journal of Criminal Justice*, **9**, 51–62.
HOFFMAN, P., and STOVER, M. (1978). Reform in the determination of prison terms: equity, determinacy, and the parole release function. *Hofstra Law Review*, **7**, 89–121.
KONEČNI, V., and EBBESEN, E. (1979). External validity of research in legal psychology. *Law and Human Behavior*, **3**, 39–70.

KRESS, J. (1980). *Prescription for Justice: The Theory and Practice of Sentencing Guidelines.* Cambridge, Mass.: Ballinger.

LAW REFORM COMMISSION (1980). *Sentencing of Federal Offenders.* Canberra: Australian Government Publishing Service.

LOVEGROVE, A. (1984). An empirical study of sentencing disparity among judges in an Australian Criminal Court. *International Review of Applied Psychology,* in press.

McKENNA, B. (1969). The judge and the common man. *Modern Law Review,* **32,** 601–614.

MORRIS, N. (1979). The sentencing disease. *Judges Journal,* **18,** 8–13 and 50.

MOSER, C., and KALTON, G. (1971). *Survey Methods in Social Investigation,* 2nd edn. London: Heinemann.

NATIONAL INSTITUTE OF LAW ENFORCEMENT AND CRIMINAL JUSTICE (1978). *Multijurisdictional Sentencing Guidelines Program Test Design.* Washington, D.C.: US Department of Justice.

PARTRIDGE, A., and ELDRIDGE, W. (1974). *The Second Circuit Sentencing Study.* New York: Federal Judicial Center.

RINALDI, F. (1979). Whitelaw. *Criminal Law Journal,* **3,** 119–120.

RINALDI, F. (1980). Kellow and Townsend. *Criminal Law Journal,* **4,** 55–56.

THOMAS, D.A. (1977). Equity in sentencing. Sixth Annual Pinkerton Lecture, School of Criminal Justice, University of Albany, Albany, N.Y.

THOMAS, D. (1979). *Principles of Sentencing,* 2nd edn. London: Heinemann.

TONRY, M. (1982). More sentencing reform in America. *Criminal Law Review,* 157–167.

TONRY, M., and MORRIS, N. (1978). Sentencing reform in America. In P. Glazebrook (Ed.), *Reshaping the Criminal Law.* London: Stevens.

VICTORIA LAW DEPARTMENT, RESEARCH SECTION (1981). *Sentencing Statistics for Higher Criminal Courts 1980 (Victoria).* Melbourne: Victoria Law Department.

VINING, A. (1979). Reforming Canadian sentencing practices: problems, prospects and lessons. *Osgoode Hall Law Journal,* **17,** 355–414.

VINING, A., and DEAN, C. (1980). Towards sentencing uniformity: integrating the normative and empirical orientation. In B. Grossman (Ed), *New Directions in Sentencing.* Toronto: Butterworths.

WILKINS, L. (1980). Sentencing guidelines to reduce disparity? *Criminal Law Review,* 201–214.

WILKINS, L., KRESS, J., GOTTFREDSON, D., CALPIN, J., and GELMAN, A. (1978). *Sentencing Guidelines: Structuring Judicial Discretion.* Washington, D.C.: US Department of Justice.

YOUNG, J. (1979). Sentencing reference: survey of judges and magistrates. *Justinian,* **1979** (August), 8.

ZALMAN, M. (1978). The rise and fall of the indeterminate sentence. *Wayne Law Review,* **24,** 857–937.

Psychology and Law
Edited by D.J. Müller, D.E. Blackman, and A.J. Chapman
© 1984 John Wiley & Sons Ltd

Chapter 23

Magisterial Decision-making: Cognitive Perspectives and Processes Used in Courtroom Information Processing[1]

Jeanette A. Lawrence

Social scientists studying the courtroom decisions of judges and magistrates have tended to concentrate on *what* and *why* questions, by describing sentencing patterns, and by seeking to explain those patterns by correlation or regression, or multivariate analyses of influential legal and extra-legal variables (Bottomley, 1973; Homel, 1981; Hood and Sparks, 1972). However, little empirical evidence has been available on *how* judicial decisions are made. In this chapter, I report the first phase of the development of a comprehensive description of judicial decision-making, by showing how a group of Australian stipendiary magistrates described their own courtroom deliberations, and I propose a model of magisterial decision-making as cognitive perspectives and information processing.

There is a persistent line of argument in the research on sentencing that greater attention should be paid to the individual judge or magistrate's contribution to sentencing outcomes. Grossman (1966) and Gibson (1978) both argued that judge-related intervening variables were neglected, to their detriment, by researchers who tried to explain sentencing outcomes with simplistic associational models. But most references to judge factors have been expressed in imprecise terms.

Gaudet, Harris, and St John, as far back as 1933, claimed that judges' sentencing tendencies were fairly well determined before they sat on the bench. The determining factor was the judge's environment in its broadest sense, and within that construct they included a group of variables which now would be identified more precisely as the religious, social, and professional influences on an individual's behaviour. For Shoham (1959, p. 335) the individual human factor in sentencing behaviours of his Israeli judges could be described only as 'that indefinable element' which nevertheless served as a significant determinant of case outcomes!

While Shoham's vague conceptualization is by no means unusual in the literature, a few researchers have hinted at a cognitive dimension. Mannheim, Spencer, and Lynch (1957) ascribed differences in juvenile court decisions to subjective and intuitive assessment of individual cases. Green (1961) came closer to a cognitivist position with his significant variable of individual judges' perceptions of offence, offender and facts. Personal perceptions were most influential in cases of intermediate gravity, where greater ambiguity prevailed. He believed that the criteria his judges used were not direct responses to sentencing rules, but were the frames of reference which provided norms for determining case gravity.

Either magistrates' perceptions are to be treated as irrational whims or, as Hood and Sparks (1972) argue, the undifferentiated individual judge element must be broken down into finer descriptive categories. Judges whose sentences exhibit disparity may be following different penal philosophies, as Hogarth (1971) demonstrated; they may work with information of different quality, as Mannheim *et al.* conceded; or they may use different strategies for classifying offences and offenders, as Green (1961) and Shoham (1959) suggested.

What Grossman identified loosely as intervening variables can be more productively viewed as the cognitive processes by which a magistrate assimilates previous experiences and knowledge into a set of working perspectives (Bartlett, 1932). People construct their own realities (Shutz, 1962), and while it is feasible to identify factors contributing to magistrates' constructions, it is not informative to discount an individual's synthesis and differentiation of those factors. Whatever the source of his or her ideas about justice, crime, and culpability, there is formed in the magistrate's memory a set of personal constructs against which new cases can be interpreted (McKnight, 1981).

Once the significance of magistrates' cognitive processes is established, then we need research techniques for obtaining useful and reliable evidence of these essentially covert processes. Hogarth's emphasis on the influence of magistrates' penal philosophies was supported by questionnaire data which cannot yield the kind of sensitive information required to describe how a person makes a sorting and weighing decision. Analyses of cognitive processes have yielded rich data on people's perceptions of their own knowledge and strategies (Brown, 1982). Doubts about people's ability to report on past events, such as those expressed by Nisbett and Wilson (1977), do not necessarily imply that individuals cannot give sensible but assessable accounts of their own perceptions and ideas (Evans, 1980; Harré and Secord, 1973).

There are classes of covert personal thoughts where the best commentator may be the individual whose thoughts they are, and who has privileged access, as Harré and Secord (1973) and Lawrence (1981) have argued. An observer may make inferences about a magistrate's perspectives (Caplan and Le Blanc, 1974), but such inferences are constructed in the observer's mind. It would seem plausible to ask for more direct information about human perceptions from the person concerned.

MAGISTRATES' ACCOUNTS OF THEIR COURTROOM DECISION-MAKING

Fifteen practising stipendiary magistrates were volunteers who responded to an open letter sent via the chief magistrate's office in two major Australian cities. All subjects were males in their middle years. Data were complete transcripts of 14 interviews, and sections of one damaged audio-tape, and comprised responses to specific questions about decision-making procedures used in court, and any other related comments. A cognitive psychologist and an anthropology graduate independently extracted and categorized accounts of decision-making. After initial descriptors were defined, the transcripts were re-analysed.

I have not attempted to describe all responses of each magistrate, nor have I sought to quantify instances of each class of cognitive activity across all subjects. The aim was to abstract initial categories from the accounts, and this abstraction process led to the development of a model which juxtaposed two types of cognitive operation that the magistrates identified.

One aspect of thinking was reported as the general frames of reference or perspectives with which they approached and framed judicial deliberations. The other type involved specific strategies they said they used to process evidence and information. Of course these may be arbitrary and overlapping aspects of cognition, but the division of their descriptions as generalized perspectives and specific information-processing procedures may be the most useful way of developing a comprehensive report of their complex deliberations. Some cognitive psychologists concentrate on describing the generalized and stereotyped schemas, scripts, and frames by which information is represented in memory (Schank and Abelson, 1977). Others, like Newell and Simon (1972), model the sequences of sub-processes by which people solve problems. I am suggesting that the complex accounts given by these magistrates may be usefully modelled as the means by which information is received and evaluated within the mental parameters of particular sets of perspectives, legal philosophies, and frames of reference.

Together with the external parameters which form the operational context of their thinking, these two aspects of thought form the basis of the conceptual model as it stands. The descriptive abstraction traces the development of a case in the magistrates' terms of building and assessing evidence from an inferred starting question of 'What information is available in this case?' to terminal judgment and either imposition of sentence or dismissal of case. Since the magistrates did not differentiate between the two decision tasks of judging and sentencing, the model follows their lead and illustrates each as a decision-making task. The model is presented in Figure 23.1.

Sequencing and linearity have been imposed only for clarity in describing the flow of an hypothetical composite case. In specific cases, sequences and strategies would be determined by offence and offender characteristics, and by contextual effects.

Framing Perspectives

Although introspection on their own thinking was new to the magistrates, each one was able to report something about his courtroom deliberations. Initial statements commonly centred on personal style, and on personal and professional experience. A not atypical comment was made by Magistrate 10 (M10): 'I don't think you can define any of my decision-making cases. It just comes, I suppose, from training and practice over the years'.

While personal experiences figured largely in magistrates' accounts of their decision function, there was a consistent absence of ideas about how their large body of experience and information was annexed and applied to specific cases. Prior material seemed to be held in memory as global abstractions or implicit ideas about judging rather than as more explicit formalized procedures.

They talked about broad guiding principles of fairness and openness, but they did not seem to differentiate those from the working devices by which they applied them to cases. For example, they showed a common commitment to fairness, impartiality, and public accountability but did not distinguish the broad generalized principle from second-order surface rules by which they would achieve them (Cicourel, 1973). There were some clear differences in the frames of reference that some magistrates used in the service of accountability and impartiality. One magistrate (M1) expressed his belief that fairness was an explicit correlate of the public responsibility and accountability of his function: 'My doubt or my position is reasonable when I think it will measure against general and public expectations of what is fair'. He was convinced that he could secure this fairness with consciously attained objectivity: 'I deal with facts'.

In contrast, several other magistrates with similar attachment to fairness and openness expressed different ways of attaining it. One claimed fairness could be achieved by what he called a general principle of openness, although for Cicourel it would be a working surface rule. Another man (M12), aware of the need to prevent his personal values from intruding, adopted a

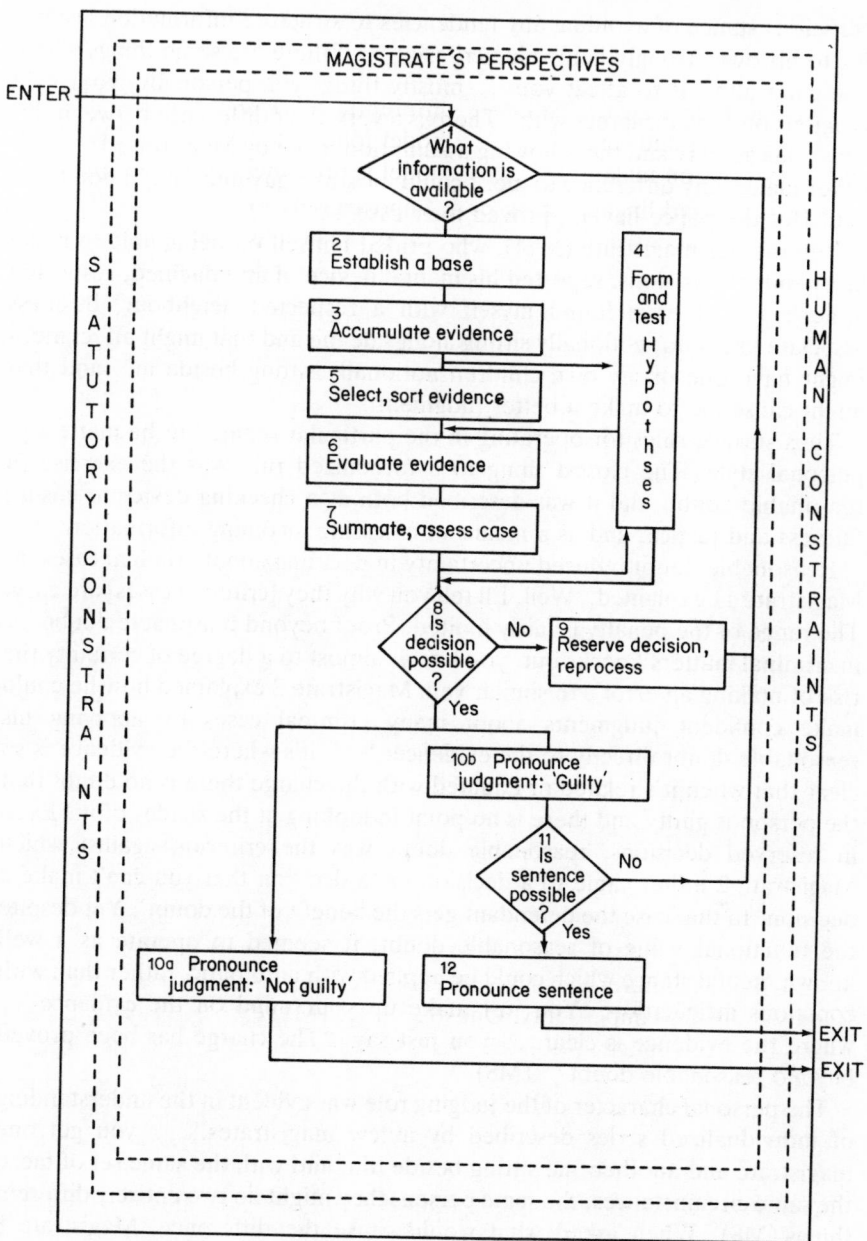

Figure 23.1 Magistrates' decision-making procedures set within framing factors of magistrates' perspectives and external constraints

conscious stance of avoiding any tendencies to structure information according to his own strongly-held value criteria: '. . . there are some things where you can't allow it to affect you . . . mostly things you personally, your own religious outlook disagrees with'. There is a very clear difference between this conscious activity and the following assumption made by Magistrate 1: 'Oh, it never makes any difference to me. I could look at a guy and say, "I don't like you. But the police haven't proved their case". '

Yet another magistrate (M14), who prided himself on being able to make independent decisions, reported his mental device of an imagined, respected 'other': '. . . I have found myself with a respected neighbour, business associate or friend, notionally sitting alongside me and that might affect me. I might have one of my own children notionally sitting beside me, and that might cause me to make a better judgment'.

Thus surface rules for operating in the particular seemed to be matters of personal style. The closest thing to a formalized rule was the exercise of reasonable doubt, and it was described both as a checking device to ensure fairness and justice, and as a means of assessing incoming information.

Reasonable doubt reduced uncertainty in deciding about criminal cases, as Magistrate 11 explained: 'Well, I'll tell you why they [criminal cases] are easy. The range of the penalty is fairly limited. Proof beyond reasonable doubt . . . in criminal matters knocks out, you know, almost to a degree of certainty the risk of making an error'. In similar vein Magistrate 2 explained how he could make confident judgments about many criminal cases by applying his reasonable doubt directly to the evidence: '. . . it's where the evidence is so clear that when it's related or equated with the charge there is no doubt that the person is guilty and there is no point in looking at the shades of it'. Even in reserved decisions, reasonable doubt was the criterion against which Magistrate 2 either came to a decision or 'a decision that you can't make a decision. In that case the defendant gets the benefit of the doubt'. Yet despite the functional value of reasonable doubt, it seemed to operate as a well known mental stance which could be applied with automatic, rather than with conscious articulation: 'You just make up your mind on the evidence . . . where the evidence is clear . . . you just say, "The charge has been proved beyond reasonable doubt" ' (M8).

The personal character of the judging role was evident in the understanding of individualized styles described by a few magistrates:'. . . you get one magistrate and another one sitting beside him and with the same set of facts, the same circumstances, the same person, they might do two entirely different things'(M8). When asked what would cause the difference, Magistrate 8 explained that while some magistrates might be concerned about property matters, others, like himself, regarded them lightly because they did not involve injury to persons, his greater concern.

The development of general reliance on one's own frames and perspectives was described as a sixth sense developed from experience (M13), and as 'taking a punt sometimes' (M7).

Thus while some magistrates considered themselves to be free of framing perspectives, and others worked to nullify their intrusion, still others acknowledged the existence and usefulness of the accumulations of experience and information which gave them working criteria by which to structure their work, cut down on information overload and provide broad directions for sorting details. The qualitative, open-ended technique did not force them to specify all the perspectives that they might use, but showed the importance of including this dimension in more controlled studies.

Information-processing Strategies

In addition to general framing aspects of thought, the model describes explicit strategies which the magistrates said they used in the service of (1) establishing a basis for decision; (2) recognizing and working within constraints; (3) accumulating and evaluating evidence; and (4) summing up evidence in order to pronounce judgment and determine sentence.

Establishing the Basis for a Decision

The point of entry to a hearing and the basis of making a decision was described in terms of (a) treating each case individually and (b) determining the evidential basis of the case.

Treating each case Individually. Magistrates 1 and 4 each expressed an explicit commitment to making a fresh start with each case, but only Magistrate 15 expressed an effective strategy for achieving it, that is, by the laying-aside of accrued patterns: 'I treat each case individually' (M4); 'I try to start afresh every time' (M1); 'I think a good sentencer has to be alive to the unusual. He oughtn't to have everything dragged into his stereotyped patterns' (M15).

Determining the Evidence. A magistrate looks for as much information as possible (M9), and for significant details of factors on which to base a decision. However, the extraction of features is not made in a benign, disinterested context. The magistrate must work with incomplete information gathered within legal and human constraining factors: 'You look for everything that can help you make a decision.... But in every case something comes through predominantly. It is very unusual that there is not one factor that becomes quite important' (M9).

Recognizing and Working within Constraints

The search for leading evidence is set within the legal, and extra-legal parameters of the courtroom context. Laws of evidence, temporal and statutory limitations, and human intentions and abilities all impose particular constraints on the magistrate's search for evidence.

Laws of Evidence. Certain limitations are legally proscribed. Procedural rules lay down what a magistrate may ask, and what other persons are required and not required to reveal (M9). In sentencing, parliamentary acts set the range of penalties which may be imposed: '... you might want to know something. It's not been presented to you by either party, and it either may be calamitous for one side or the other if you ask questions ... you are still restricted at some stage, you are not allowed to find out more' (M9).

Human Intentions and Abilities. The motivations and abilities of other persons in the courtroom set a different kind of parameter on the magistrate's deliberations (M15). The magistrate may be the only person there committed to finding out the truth, and may be the participant most ignorant of the truth (M9, M14): 'The facts are as good as the people who give them' (M15); '... those out of court, and those representing them usually know, oh, at times, 50% more and sometimes 100% more...' (M9); 'The skilled counsellor can lead, they are breaking the rules, so that his client nods his head, and instead of getting the evidence of the witness, you are getting the evidence of the solicitor' (M14).

Time and the System. Indecision and inefficiency are not well regarded by a magistrate's peers, and are not appropriate behaviours in the heavy daily loads of minor courts (M13, M15): 'Certainly in a court like this, you have to make quick decisions' (M13); '... finally the magistrate has got to come to a decision, and he has got to do it straight away' (M15).

Personal Perspectives and Patterning Tendencies. The alert magistrate is aware of continuing temptations to rely on stereotypes and patterns built up in years of practice, but searches for unusual and pattern-breaking features (M15): 'This is a terrible danger in our field, that we grab everything and put it in that kind of circle ... he ought to be helped ... to recognize a situation which requires unusual treatment.... A good sentencer has to be alive to the unusual' (M15).

Once a magistrate recognizes constraining factors, he or she needs to develop the attentional skills which will minimize their influence, and maximize the amount and quality of information on which to form decisions.

Magistrate 9 conceptualized the process as extending the sides of a frame set around fact-finding by other persons 'In a judgement there is definately a frame. All you can do is push the sides out ... but whichever, you are still constricted at some stage'. Magistrate 14 explained how he would use his own notes to verify information: 'Of course sometimes it is plain tht witnesses are lying and you put it to them, "How come you have said that just now? A moment or a couple of pages ago I wrote down that you said something quite dissimilar. Could you explain?"'

Strategies for Accumulating and Evaluating Evidence

The magistrates identified four strategies which they were conscious of using in order to gather and process evidence.

Accruing evidence. Magistrate 2 provided a thumb-nail sketch of the system by which he received and assessed information:

'... if you make fairly comprehensive notes as I do, the facts come out as you go along and you sift the wheat from the chaff and make little notes in the margin, and that by the time you come to the end of the case you look back over your little marginal notes, which are the wheat rather than the chaff, and you have got enough then to make a decision ...' (M2).

Forming early Hypotheses and Opinions. The early generation of opinions and hypotheses discussed by Magistrates 13 and 14 is a mark of the expert problem-solver (Chase and Simon, 1973; de Groot, 1965). Magistrate 13 also was aware of using an automated set of procedures:

'One looks at the file. He forms certain opinions as to what the issues are going to be and how difficult it will be to reach a finding on those issues or facts ... in many cases the decisions are easy to make. You put your judgment-making processing in your mind and you come up with the answer in seconds ...' (M13).

Magistrate 14 commented, '... I form my opinions on the evidence as it comes out'.

Selecting and Sifting Evidence. Selection strategies were described by one magistrate as his own mental classification of data into different boxes. His selection was made in the service of building relevant details into a total body of information and ignoring the irrelevant: '... by putting questions into little boxes, so to speak, and not allowing them to be influenced by outside considerations ...' (M7). Magistrate 8 described how he actively shut out irrelevancies and looked for certain particulars which would influence his decision, e.g. the offender's previous record:

'... decisions seem to flow as a matter of course, because you, in the end, I guess shut out a lot of stuff which you consider is irrelevant, like lawyer's garbage, and you limit yourself to a given set of facts in dealing with matters the only way you can do it' (M8).

Concurrent evaluation of incoming information.   Accumulation of evidence is not value-free absorption. Not all incoming data are given equal importance. As a piece of evidence is sorted into the 'relevant' class, it may also be assigned values and weight: '... I suppose as the case proceeded I was weighing, you know, I was just going backwards and forwards... even while they were talking I was going back to other points of particular interest to me, clearing up lines of thought' (M6). Presented information is assessed according to the magistrates' own criteria: '... as each witness starts to open his mouth you are assessing the evidence... you form tentative opinions as to your problems and how you'll get around them... usually a magistrate knows issues before he goes into court' (M14).

Summation Assessment of Evidence and Judgment

At the conclusion of presentation of evidence, the magistrate is required to give his decision, and penalty, with public rationale. Magistrate 12 described reasonable doubt as a weighing device, and the concept of weighing and differentiating criteria is sustained in this quotation:

'I suppose you would have to have a mental weighing apparatus. This is you know the interesting problem of what is beyond reasonable doubt... there are a number of things that have to be proved... so you listen to the evidence and see whether the prosecution establishes each of those six elements. If they do, and the scales are weighed down heavily in favour of that proposition, then you find the person guilty' (M12).

The notion is of a balancing of scales, or summation of material against criteria by which factors are evaluated. Another two magistrates, M2 and M6, recounted how in reserved decisions note-taking and the act of re-reading the features would clarify thinking, give a fresh lead and a new perspective.

Magistrate 13 gave a classic account of tracing through a sequence of possibilities, and asking a set of critical questions against which to determine the appropriate penalty:

'First you look at the penalty prescribed by Parliament. Then you look at the alternatives you've got by way of probation and parole, dismissal under the section of the code for first offenders. In a serious case, you look at the question . . . is the offence so bad that it merits imprisonment? . . . or you look at whether or not perhaps the matter is fairly trivial and may be dismissed . . . ' (M13).

The process is terminated with a public statement in which covert processing results in a public and justifiable verdict and sentence. Magistrates are aware of the public nature of their function, and the possibility of appeal. In a difficult civil case, Magistrate 6 said that he occasionally would make his findings explicit under duty to the court of appeal.

In summary, the model describes the abstraction of the magistrates' accounts in two types of cognitive activity. Parameters are imposed on information flow by the magistrate's covert general perspectives and by external legal and extra-legal factors.

DISCUSSION

Decision-making analyses have a natural place in a domain where attention to background factors and decision outcomes has not given full account of sentencing trends and disparities, and where the role of judicial discretion has been invoked more often than examined. A pertinent place to begin to develop a description of covert deliberations is with practising professionals' reflections on their own constructions of courtroom decisions.

The study and the model are open to criticisms related to reliance on phenomenal reports, and the value and validity of qualitative analyses of open responses obtained outside their functional context. Yet research on courtroom procedures needs to be grounded in some initial categories. Processes are too delicate and too confidential for heavy-handed investigations and manipulations. Ought not such initial categories and concepts be sought in magistrates' perceptions rather than in the variables which have directed so many psychological studies without due reference to the legal environment? (Konečni and Ebbesen, 1981).

Since the public role of stipendiary magistrate carries with it the concept of a reasonable, legal adjudicator, and since information strategies are the magistrate's working tools, then it is useful to examine how those strategies are exercised in the service of administering law. Thus the study links into Hood and Sparks' proposition that individual differences ought not be considered in isolation from the information available to a judge, nor from his or her personal system for classifying that information.

The initial abstraction of magistrates' accounts of their deliberations has shown the centrality of information in judicial proceedings, and the importance of how a magistrate gathers, sifts, and weighs the information that is available. Without attempting to specify what the effective penal philosophies and purposes of particular decisions might be, the study demonstrates that evidence is actively shaped by underlying frames of reference and strategies of authorized processing agents. Those who think themselves impartial and fair, may not work to discount the influence of personal commitments. If unaware of natural tendencies to stereotype offences and offenders, they may not actively search for the unusual. When the flow of information is hindered by other participants' counter-intentions and inefficiencies, magistrates must engage in perceptive extraction and sifting procedures.

I am not advocating this as an isolated model, but suggesting that it be used in working partnership with quantitative analyses, and whole case descriptions. Work has already begun on applying the model to magistrates' actual courtroom decisions. A major value of the study is that it provides a way of conceptualizing the magistrates' function as the judge of evidence society expects.

NOTE

(1) This research was supported by a grant from the Education Research and Development Committee, Commonwealth of Australia.

REFERENCES

BARTLETT, F. C. (1932). *Remembering*. Cambridge: Cambridge University Press.
BOTTOMLEY, A. K. (1973). *The Penal Process*. London: Martin Robertson.
BROWN, A. L. (1982). Metakognition. Handlungskontrolle, Selbsteurung und andere noch geheimmnisvollere Mechanismen. In F.E. Weinert und R. H. Kluwe (Eds), *Metakognition, Motivation und Lernen*. Stuttgart: Kohlhammer.
CAPLAN, A., and LE BLANC, M. (1974). Sophisticated methodology versus good methodology: a methodological critique of *Sentencing as a Human Process* by J. Hogarth. *Canadian Journal of Criminology and Corrections*, **16**, 77–93.
CHASE, W. G., and SIMON, H. A. (1973). Perception in chess. *Cognitive Psychology*, **4**, 55–81.
CICOUREL, A. V. (1973). *Cognitive Sociology*. Harmondsworth, Middlesex: Penguin.
DE GROOT, A. (1965). *Thought and Choice in Chess*. New York: Basic Books.
EVANS, J. St B. T. (1980). Current issues in the psychology of reasoning. *British Journal of Psychology*, **71**, 227–239.
GAUDET, F. J., HARRIS, G. S., and ST JOHN, C. W. (1933). Individual differences in the sentencing tendencies of judges. *Journal of Criminal Law, Criminology and Penal Studies*, **23**, 811–817.
GIBSON, J. L. (1978). Judge's role orientations, attitudes and decisions: an interactive model. *American Political Science Review*, **72**, 911–924.
GREEN, E. G. (1961). *Judicial Attitudes in Sentencing*. London: Macmillan.
GROSSMAN, J. B. (1966). Social background in judicial decision-making. *Harvard Law Review*, **79**, 1551–1564.
HARRÉ, R., and SECORD, P. F. (1973). *The Explanation of Social Behaviour*. Oxford: Basil Blackwell.
HOGARTH, J. (1971). *Sentencing as a Human Process*. Toronto: University of Toronto Press.

HOMEL, R. (1981). Penalties and the drink-driver: a study of one thousand offenders. *Australian and New Zealand Journal of Criminology*, **14**, 225–241.

HOOD, R., and SPARKS, R. F. (1972). *Key Issues in Criminology*. London: World University Library.

KONEČNI, V. J., and EBBESEN, E. B. (1981). A critique of theory and method in social psychological approaches to legal issues. In B. D. Sales (Ed), *Perspectives in Psychology and Law*, Vol. 2, *The Trial Process*. New York: Plenum.

LAWRENCE, J. A. (1981). A case for the usefulness and plausibility of thinking-aloud verbal data. In M. Lawson (Ed), *Inquiry and Action in Education*, Proceedings of the Annual Meeting of the Australian Association for Research in Education, Adelaide.

MCKNIGHT, C. (1981). Subjectivity in sentencing. *Law and Human Behavior*, **5**, 141–147.

MANNHEIM, H., SPENCER, J., and LYNCH, G. (1957). Magisterial policy in the London juvenile courts. *British Journal of Delinquency*, **8**, 13–33, and 119–138.

NEWELL, A. H., and SIMON, H. A. (1972). *Human Problem-solving*. Englewood Cliffs, N. J.: Prentice-Hall.

NISBETT, R. E., and WILSON, T. D. (1977). Telling more than we can know: verbal reports on mental processes. *Psychological Review*, **84**, 231–259.

SCHANK, R., and ABELSON, R. P. (1977). *Scripts, Plans, Goals and Understanding: An Inquiry into Human Knowledge Structures*. Hillsdale, N. J.: Lawrence Erlbaum.

SHOHAM, S. (1959). Sentencing policy of criminal courts in Israel. *Journal of Criminal Law, Criminology and Public Service*, **50**, 327–337.

SHUTZ, A. (1962). *Collected Papers*, Vol. 1. The Hague: Martinus Nijhoff.

ychology and Law
Edited by D.J. Müller, D.E. Blackman, and A.J. Chapman
© 1984 John Wiley & Sons Ltd

Chapter 24

Judicial Decision-making: An Examination of Sentencing Disparity Among Canadian Provincial Court Judges[1]

T.S. Palys and Stan Divorski

There have been two primary foci in research on judicial decision-making. The first has addressed the question of whether different social groups have received equal treatment before the law, and is evident in the writings of scholars such as Sellin (1928), Johnson (1941), and Green (1961, 1964). The second has addressed the more general questions of how sentencing decisions are made and the extent to which judges are disparate in the sentences they impose. In other words, to what extent are sentences dependent on who hears the case rather than on the 'facts' of the case? It is toward this latter question that our own research was addressed.

ASSESSING SENTENCING DISPARITY

One can differentiate two major approaches to the assessment of sentencing disparity among judges. The first is termed the 'archival' or 'actual cases' approach since it involves the analysis of actual case data.

The Actual Cases Approach

Two of the best studies within this tradition (Hogarth, 1971; Sutton, 1978b) provide grounds for a further distinction within the actual cases approach. Sutton's (1978b) research exemplifies the 'black box' orientation. It gains this title since one's empirical focus is solely on the relationship between 'inputs' (i.e. offence, offender, and contextual variables) and 'outputs' (i.e. sentencing outcomes), while attributes or perceptions of the judges themselves are

333

ignored. In other words, judges are viewed as 'black boxes' who merely process information and about whom nothing need be known since one assumes, initially at least, that all 'black boxes' possess the same qualities and hence are a mere constant in the process.

The 'black box' approach utilized by Sutton (1978b) contrasts with the perceptually augmented approach used by Hogarth (1971) in his classic study of Ontario magistrates. While based upon actual cases, his 'case fact' data were supplemented by inventories which directly assessed judicial attitudes and perceptions. It should be noted that, contrary to the assumptions of the 'black box' orientation, Hogarth's data showed considered variability among judges in their attitudes and penal philosophies. More importantly, Hogarth's study was the first to show that judges' *perceptions* of case facts were substantially more potent predictors of sentence outcomes than the case facts themselves.

As is true of all methodological approaches, the actual cases approach has both strengths and weaknesses. Its strengths lie in the realm of ecological and external validity (see Brunswik, 1955; Campbell and Stanley, 1963; Cook and Campbell, 1979), since one is dealing with the actual sentencing behaviour of real judges with respect to real cases. Internal validity, on the other hand, is frequently compromised in the actual cases approach. An unambiguous demonstration of sentencing disparity would require that many judges be shown to impose different sentences given identical sets of case facts. Regression-based approaches within the archival tradition cannot address the question of disparity *per se*, because they cannot hold cases constant. Rather, disparity must be inferred from unexplained variance. This would not be overly problematic if we could assume that all 'relevant' variables had been included in the analysis, but that assumption is a questionable one. Investigators are typically limited by the data available to them, and it is a mistake to assume that a synonomy exists between 'available' data and 'important' data (see, for example, Vining and Dean, 1980). Note that these comments are not intended to vitiate the utility of the archival approach, but merely to outline its limitations.

The Simulated Cases Approach

The second major approach to the assessment of disparity has been termed the 'simulated cases' approach. This involves presenting a given case or set of cases to groups of judges, who then indicate sentences for the offender. The strengths and weaknesses of this approach are complementary to those of the actual cases approach. Internal validity is maximized in this context, since one is in the optimal situation of presenting *identical* information to many judges. Ecological validity is similarly high, assuming that the respondents are indeed judges rather than some other sample to whom the task of sentencing is unfamiliar (e.g. introductory psychology students). Instead, the simulated cases approach suffers to the extent that external validity is not as well assured as in the archival approach, and must be rationally and/or empirically ascertained (cf. Palys, 1978, 1982; Partridge and Eldridge, 1974).

But while the advantages of the archival approach have been well explored, those of the simulation approach have not. In making this statement, we should note that simulations which utilized introductory psychology students as sentencers (see, for example, Pepitone, 1975) were not considered relevant here. There seems good reason to be sceptical about similarity of decision making processes between judges and undergraduates, although we know of no research which has addressed the question directly (but, for example, see Janis and Mann, 1977). Those which *had* involved judges were either informal sentencing exercises, and hence produced only anecdotal accounts of results (e.g. Remington and Newman, 1971), or seemed too sparse in the amount of information given to judges (e.g. Partridge and Eldridge, 1974).

The research to be reported here utilized a simulated cases methodology. In designing our study, we felt it crucial that the decision-makers be actual sitting judges, and that they be given offender and offence information which would approximate the detail they would receive in court. On the other hand, evidence from Partridge and Eldridge (1974) convinced us that the defendant could be adequately represented on paper, rather than requiring an appearance.

RESEARCH PARTICIPANTS AND PROCEDURES

Our respondents included 206 Canadian judges of the Provincial Courts (Criminal Division) who attended one of eight judicial conferences held in various locations across Canada. Nine of the 10 provinces and one of the two territories were represented, although more than half the judges were from Ontario and Quebec (where more than half the Canadian population resides). All but three of the judges were male. Their experience on the bench ranged from one month to 42 years (the mean was eight years, while the median was six years).

A total of five different cases (involving six accused) were presented in varied order to all judges in the form of a questionnaire. The case descriptions were intended to be as comprehensive as possible and hence included a fairly detailed description of events leading up to the crime, a full pre-sentence report on the accused (including prior record and social history), and information concerning the effects of the crime on the victim. Guilt had already been ascertained. Judges were asked to impose sentence, and then (1) to indicate the facts of the case they perceived to be relevant to sentencing; (2) to assign these facts priority in terms of their importance to deciding sentence; and (3) to indicate the legal objectives they were trying to maximize in imposing sentence. All questions were asked in open-ended fashion, which required the development of appropriate content analytic schemes so that the data might be analysed. A final portion of the questionnaire asked judges questions about themselves and their sentencing environments.

Our first case involved Ray R., a 21-year-old postal worker who had no prior record, but who had a reputation for aggressive behaviour, particularly when drunk. The case information revealed that he attended a bar where music was being played, and, seemingly without provocation, initiated an assault against another male who was merely taking his partner to the dance floor. Part of the assault involved Ray's throwing a glass at the victim. It shattered and caused the victim to lose most of the sight in one eye. Ray felt no remorse for the incident. He was charged with 'assault causing bodily harm' which, in Canada, carries a maximum possible sentence of five years imprisonment.

Our other cases involved (1) Peter R., a recently unemployed 22-year-old who was charged with breaking and entering a dwelling house; (2) Joe J., a successful business person who drove while impaired and accidentally caused the death of two young children; (3) Michael M. and John J., who committed armed robbery and indecent assault in a private home; and (4) Denis D., a 32-year-old employee who embezzled a substantial sum of money in order to support his gambling habit. The complete questionnaire and detailed summary of results from this project may be seen in Palys (1982). Due to limitations of space and the high degree of consistency in findings between cases, detailed results from only one of the cases (Ray R.) are presented here. Summary data across cases are noted where appropriate.

THE IDENTIFICATION OF DISPARITY

As in every other case, our sample judges imposed a disparate array of sentences on the offender. The least severe sentence Ray received was a Can.$500 fine and a six-month probationary period. The most severe called for him to serve five years in prison. On the other hand, there was actually a strong consensus that Ray should spend some time in jail (96% of the sentencing judges felt so), although judges disagreed on the length of time that would be appropriate (periods of incarceration ranged from one week to five years, with a median of six months). There were also disagreements regarding the utility of a probationary period (61% of sentences involved a probation component), or its duration (the range was six to 36 months).

Attention was then focused on the case facts and legal objectives cited by judges. A total of 14 different case facts were cited as 'relevant' to sentencing. One might expect that this list would shrink when judges were asked to identify either the three most important aspects of the case, or the most important, but it did not. Every single case fact that had initially been identified as relevant to sentencing had at least a few judges who cited it as *the* most important aspect of the case. The situation was similar when judges were asked to indicate the legal objectives they were attempting to maximize in their choice of sentence. A total or eight different legal objectives were noted.

THE EXPLANATION OF DISPARITY

In sum, there was wide variety in the sentences judges imposed, in the importance they attached to different case facts, and in the legal objectives they were attempting to maximize. A pessimistic hypothesis at this point would be that these various components came together in random ways like the letters in alphabet soup to form the disparate array of sentences we observed. But the analyses revealed this to be anything but the case. Rather, case facts, legal objectives, and sentences tended to be packaged neatly as a cohesive and rational unit. For illustrative purposes, sentences were segregated into the following groupings: (1) 'out' sentences, that is the disposition involved a fine or suspended sentence which, although it involved punishment, allowed the offender to return to the street; (2) 'short-in' sentences, that is an incarcerative sentence of relatively short duration was assigned – these ranged from one week to six months in jail; and (3) 'long-in' sentences, that is a relatively longer incarcerative sentence was imposed – these ranged from nine months in jail to five years in prison.

Figure 24.1 shows the percentage of judges within each of the three sentence categories who cited each case fact as one of the three most important aspects of the case. A high proportion of judges in all three dispositional categories focused on Ray's lack of remorse. Although this tendency was more pronounced in those groups who imposed more punitive sentences, the salience of this case fact may well explain why Ray received such a high proportion of 'in' sentences. Beyond this attribute, however, it may be seen that those who imposed 'out' sentences more frequently identified Ray's poor social background and lack of prior record as important aspects of the case. In contrast, those who gave incarcerative sentences, and particularly those who gave longer sentences, focused most frequently on the violent nature of the crime, the disastrous consequences of Ray's actions on his victim, and the lack of provocation prior to the assault.

The proportion of judges within each dispositional category identifying particular legal objectives is shown in Figure 24.2. As was the case with the priority attached to different case facts, one can see that punishments of differing severity were indeed tied to different legal objectives. Those who gave 'out' dispositions emphasized Ray's need for rehabilitation and supervision, while general deterrence, specific deterrence, and protection of the public were the highest priorities for those who wanted Ray incarcerated.

338   PSYCHOLOGY AND LAW

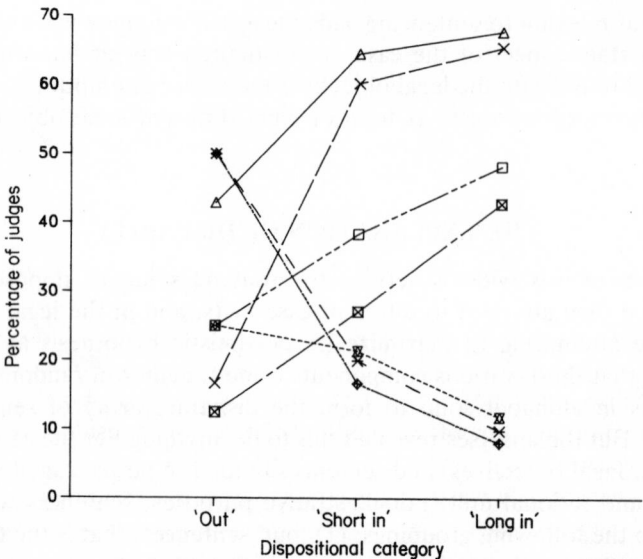

Figure 24.1   Percentage of judges in each outcome category noting factor as one of three most important in sentencing Ray R. Key: △, lack of remorse; ×, violent nature of crime; □, consequence to victim; ⊠, lack of provocation; ⊠, character of offender; ✳, no prior record; ⊕, social background of offender

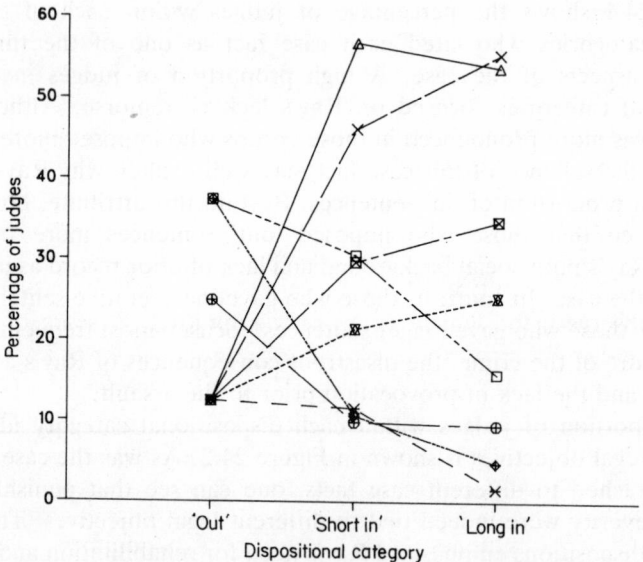

Figure 24.2   Percentage of judges in each outcome category noting specific legal objectives in sentencing Ray R. Key: △, specific deterrence; ×, general deterrence; □, rehabilitation; ⊠, protection of the public; ⊠, deterrence; ✳, maintain employment of offender; ⊕, supervision of offender; ⊕, maintain credibility of court

As these figures show, judges who imposed qualitatively different disposi-tions apparently differed also in their perception of events. At one extreme, we have those who saw a belligerent drunk who, without provocation, initiated an assault and caused permanent injury to his innocent victim. Protection of the public and general deterrence were salient legal objectives, and a substantial term of incarceration was warranted. But, at the other extreme, we have a second group of judges who saw an employed individual, one with no prior record and pitiable social background, who got involved in a fight in a bar. Misguided? Perhaps. Evil? No. The court must show its displeasure regarding this type of activity, but the legal objectives must be supervision and rehabilitation, and they should be accomplished without causing the offender to lose a job. Each of these views is quite rational and internally consistent. The problem, of course, is that they both refer to the same person and the same offence. The same pattern of results was observed in case after case.

A similar consistency was found in the multiple regression analyses which were performed for each case. Legal objectives were typically the major predictor of sentence severity, followed by the importance attached to different case facts. Demographic and contextual variables, incidentally, were a distant third. The total proportion of variance in severity accounted for by these variables ranged from 23 to 55%. We saw this as encouraging, particularly when one considers that an important source of explanatory power – real variability in case facts, charges, and offender characteristics – were held constant in this study.

Given the consistency of these findings, we wondered whether the distribu-tion of judges in terms of leniency–severity was also the same for all cases. In other words, to what extent were particular judges consistent across cases in assigning lenient or severe dispositions? The question was approached by first trichotomizing sentences for each case in terms of lenient, moderate, or severe. 'Natural' breaks in each distribution were sought, although an attempt was made to follow the characteristics of the normal distribution by including approximately 60% of the sentences in the moderate group, and approximately 20% in each of the two extremes. In the one case where a floor effect was observed, the lenient category was omitted. A score of '1' was given to the judge for each case in which a lenient sentence was imposed, '2' for moderate, and '3' for severe. A judge's total score across all six accused could thus range from '7' (all lenient sentences except the one case noted above) to '18' (all severe sentences). The actual distribution of scores is presented in Figure 24.3.

It is noteworthy that the obtained distribution was normal as opposed to flat or bimodal at the extremes. None of the judges was uniformly lenient or punitive, and few were consistently at one extreme or the other. Those who were so, on the other hand, also were consistent in the legal objectives they

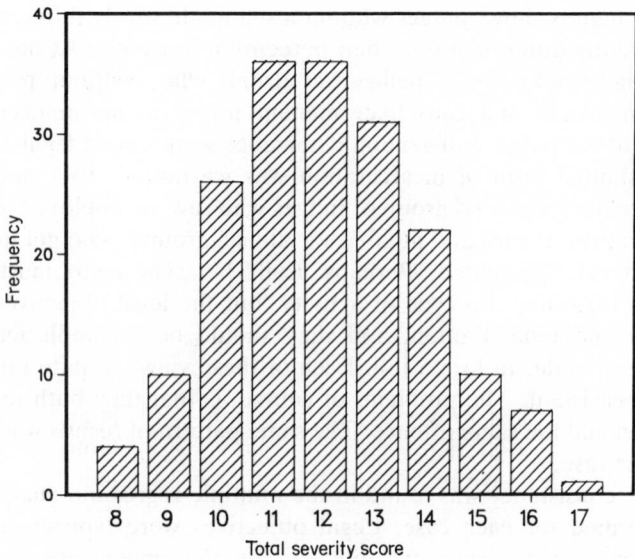

Figure 24.3   Frequency distribution of leniency–severity scores for all judges across all cases

emphasized and in the types of case fact they considered most important. To ascertain this, judges were subdivided into groups of relatively 'lenient' 'moderate', and 'severe' sentencers on the basis of their total sentencing scores (scores for the groups were 8–10, 11–13, and 14–17, respectively). The three groups were then compared in terms of the mean importance rating attached to case facts, and the extent to which different legal objectives were noted, for each case. 'Lenient' judges consistently emphasized mitigating factors and focused on rehabilitative and offender-oriented objectives. Those at the 'severe' end consistently attached great import to aggravating factors and emphasized legal objectives concerned with deterrence, punishment, and protection of the public. The 'moderate' group seemed to achieve a balance between the two, but could sway in either direction depending on the salience of the various attributes.

In sum, our research lends further support to the notion that substantial sentencing disparity exists. Since the information given to judges was held constant, the study also must be seen to undermine the sufficiency of a 'black box' model to judicial decision-making (e.g. Sutton, 1978a). And, finally, our research suggests that a primary locus of sentencing disparity lies in the differential attachment to legal objectives and corresponding emphasis on differing case facts which judges manifest.

WHERE TO FROM HERE?

As empiricists, we are quite comfortable with the notions of individual differences and variability. Consequently, it seems almost paradoxical that a first step in the judicial decision-making area has involved the demonstration that variability among judges exists. One would think that at this point, given the consistency of our own research and that of others before us (who approached the matter with different methodological tools and theoretical orientations), an assertion of the existence of sentencing disparity could be made unequivocally. But given that this can be done and, more importantly, that research such as our own has helped to explain *why* that variability exists, we now come to yet another important question: 'What can be done about sentencing disparity?'

We are not the first to address the question. Wilkins and his colleagues (e.g. Gottfredson, 1981; Kress, 1980; Wilkins, Kress, Gottfredson, Calpin, and Gelman, 1976) have proposed, and, in some jurisdictions, implemented and evaluated a 'sentencing guidelines' model which attempts to 'structure' judicial discretion. Before explaining this process, one must first appreciate that documents such as the Criminal Code of Canada specify only minimum and maximum sentences for specific crimes, which are designed to 'cover' all possible circumstances in which the crime might be committed in all possible ways by all possible offenders. The crime of 'break and enter of a dwelling house', for example, could, theoretically, receive a minimum sentence of a suspended sentence, or a maximum sentence of life imprisonment. The guidelines model attempts to structure and guide choices within this range through the construction of 'sentencing matrices'. These are based on past sentencing behaviour within a jurisdiction, and assert more specific 'appropriate' sentencing ranges given the attributes of the offender (e.g. presence or absence of a prior record) and the offence (e.g. whether a weapon was involved in the commission of the crime). Judges 'score' the case before them on these predetermined attributes, and then refer to the matrix for the suggested appropriate range of sentences which might be imposed. Judges who deviate from this range are required to articulate their justification for so doing. (See Lovegrove, Chapter 22, for a more detailed discussion.)

Other authors have suggested different approaches. Vining and Dean (1980), for example, have asserted a 'courts of appeal' model whereby sentencing principles could be more systematically derived and made salient through decisions made by courts of appeal. Others have advanced the notion of the 'sentencing council' where trial judges would be required to discuss their decisions with other judges before committing themselves to a particular course (see, for example, Smith, 1963).

All these possibilities are united in the sense that they assume that disparity is a pejorative entity which must be reduced. While we would agree to the extent that it is difficult not to consider some of the disparity which we have observed 'excessive', we feel misgivings about the alternatives that have been proposed. First, our contact with the judges leads us to question the pragmatics of such interventions, or at least in how they have been presented, since most judges with whom we spoke perceived these as threats to their independence.

But we also question these possibilities, and the guidelines model in particular, from a more philosophical base. We have no argument with the assertion that the implementation of guidelines would result in more homogeneous judgments. But surely the guidelines model implies that some sentences are more 'right' than others, and we see a grave danger in defining 'rightness' by mere central tendency. An appropriate analogy is evident in Sherif's (1936) classic studies of the autokinetic effect, where individuals and groups developed highly stable group norms concerning the distance a pinpoint of light 'moved' in a totally darkened room. The autokinetic effect 'works' because of natural eye movements coupled with the lack of any visible referents in the blackened room. The light in fact did not move at all, but the research participants saw it as doing so and moved to a consensus on the degree of movement exhibited. Similarly, sentencing guidelines 'work', but it is a mistake to assume that they are 'right' just because they do so. In sum, 'rightness' must be defined not by mere central tendency, but rather by some external criterion. But what?

Consistency with legal objectives seems a reasonable criterion, but the Canadian Criminal Code offers little if any guidance in that domain. To that extent then, virtually all 206 of our sample judges were 'right' in that each tied sentence, legal objectives, and important case facts together in a rational, coherent package. The alternative as we see it is to reconstrue the question.

In our view, judges should not be criticized for sentence disparity *per se* any more than those of us who choose to follow a simulated cases or archival methods approach should be criticized for methodological disparity. Each method contributes its own advantages and limitations, but the quality of knowledge is ultimately enhanced by that diversity. Similarly, we see the heterogeneous legal philosophies judges bring to the bench as one factor which contributes to the overall development of our legal system. We may, as individual citizens, find particular judges' sentencing styles appealing or narrow-minded and misguided, but the 'rightness' of their orientation is not something we as empiricists are equipped to address. As psychologists, we are equipped to deal with empirical questions, not legal ones.

Yet there *are* contributions empiricists can make to the judicial process. In the same way that researchers are accountable for the way their studies are designed and implemented (e.g. for inappropriate or non-existent controls, poor operationalization, and so forth), judges should be accountable for the way in which their legal philosophies are translated into sentencing decisions. Judges may be construed as hypothesis testers in their own right. A judge may state that, 'If I sentence this person (or type of person) to a short term of incarceration for this crime, it will cause him or her to be rehabilitated, learn job skills, appease the victim, and deter this person from committing this particular type of crime in the future.' That statement is an hypothesis that is open to empirical test. It is interesting, however, that judges have virtually no systematic avenues by which they can learn of the veracity of their categorizations or the success of their speculations. They categorize person types (and, according to our informal discussions with them, attach great import to their ability to do so), but we know *nothing* of the constructs they utilize or the accuracy of their impression formation skills. They hypothesize particular 'person X sentence' interactions, but we know *nothing* of what these are. They hypothesize changes on particular dependent variables, but we give them *no* feedback as to the accuracy of their speculations. They make assumptions regarding the current distribution of sentences for particular criminal acts, but we give them no data to allow them to verify or modify their assumptions.

These then, are what we perceive to be the appropriate foci for future research and development. We should not attempt to modify existing legal philosophies or impose one since these are clearly *not* our domain. Rather, we should take this diversity as given and use our empirical techniques to help make judges *better* sentencers in terms of providing the means for them to translate their *own* preferences into actualities. We should not set out to direct the course of legal development, but rather should set out to reduce the error variance which grows in the absence of information. In sum, we should focus on *error* disparity, not *philosophical* disparity. This will, of course, have its own effects, and poses a challenge to us as empiricists as well as to the practitioners. But we should recognize the boundaries of our role, and revel in the challenges it entails.

NOTE

1. This research was funded by the Research Division of the Ministry of the Solicitor General of Canada, while its preparation in written form was facilitated by a Simon Fraser University President's Research Grant to the first author. The authors wish to thank Judge Guy Goulard, currently with the Department of Justice, for his participation and encouragement, and Dr Ronald Roesch, George Tien, Kay Cooper, and Cheryl Schuh for their assistance in bringing this manuscript to fruition. The senior author is grateful to the Social Science and Humanities Research Council for providing the international travel grant which allowed him to present an earlier version of this paper and participate in the conference from which this book was created. The views expressed here are those of the authors, and do not necessarily reflect those of any of the other individuals or institutions noted in these acknowledgments.

PSYCHOLOGY AND LAW

REFERENCES

BRUNSWIK, E. (1955). Representative design and probabilistic theory in a functional psychology. *Psychological Review*, 62, 193–217.

CAMPBELL, D. T., and STANLEY, J. C. (1963). *Experimental and Quasi-experimental Designs for Research*. Chicago: Rand McNally.

COOK, T. D., and CAMPBELL, D. T. (1979). *Quasi-experimentation: Design and Analysis Issues for Field Settings*. Boston: Houghton Mifflin.

GOTTFREDSON, D. M. (1981). Sentencing guidelines. In H. Gross and A. von Hirsch (Eds), *Sentencing*. New York: Oxford University Press.

GREEN, E. (1961). *Judicial Attitudes in Sentencing*. London: Macmillan.

GREEN, E. (1964). Inter- and intra-racial crime relative to sentencing. *Journal of Criminal Law, Criminology, and Police Science*, 55, 348–358.

HOGARTH, J. (1971). *Sentencing as a Human Process*. Toronto: University of Toronto Press.

JANIS, I. L., and MANN, L. (1977). *Decision Making: A Psychological Analysis of Conflict, Choice, and Commitment*. New York: The Free Press.

JOHNSON, E. (1941). The Negro and crime. *Annals*, 271, 93–104.

KRESS, J. M. (1980). Reforming sentencing laws: an American perspective. In B.A. Grosman (Ed.), *New Directions in Sentencing*. Toronto: Butterworth.

PALYS, T. S. (1978). Simulation methods and social psychology. *Journal for the Theory of Social Behaviour*, 8, 341–368.

PALYS, T. S. (1982). *Beyond the Black Box: A Study in Judicial Decision-making*. Research report prepared for the Solicitor General of Canada, Research Devision, Ottawa.

PARTRIDGE, A., and ELDRIDGE, W.B. (1974). *The Second Circuit Sentencing Study*. New York: Federal Judicial Center.

PEPITONE, A. (1975). Social psychological perspectives on crime and punishment. *Journal of Social Issues*, 31, 197–216.

REMINGTON, F. J., and NEWMAN, D. J. (1971). The Highland Park Institute on sentencing disparity. In L. Radzinowicz and M.E. Wolfgang (Eds), *Crime and Justice*, Vol. II; *The Criminal in the Arms of the Law*. New York: Basic Books.

SELLIN, T. (1928). The Negro criminal: a statistical note. *Annals of the American Academy of Political and Social Science*, 140, 52–64.

SHERIF, M. (1936). *The Psychology of Social Norms*. New York: Harper and Row.

SMITH, T. (1963). The sentencing council and the problem of disproportionate sentences. *Federal Probation*, 27, 6–9.

SUTTON, L. P. (1978a). *Federal Criminal Sentencing: Perspectives of Analysis and a Design for Research*, Report SD-AR-16. Washington, D.C.: US Department of Justice.

SUTTON, L. P. (1978b). *Variations in Federal Criminal Sentences: A Statistical Assessment at the National Level*, Report SD-AR-17. Washington, D.C.: US Department of Justice.

VINING, A. R., and DEAN, C. (1980). Towards sentencing uniformity: Integrating the normative and the empirical orientation. In B.A. Grosman (Ed.), *New Directions in Sentencing*. Toronto: Butterworth.

WILKINS, L. T., KRESS, J. M., GOTTFREDSON, D. M., CALPIN, J. C., and GELMAN, A. M. (1976). *Sentencing Guidelines: Structuring Judicial Discretion*. Washington, D.C.: Criminal Justice Research Center.

SECTION VII

Care and Rehabilitation

The first two chapters in this section examine the provisions for the care and rehabilitation of children within a legal setting. **Hayden** examines the role of the psychologist in deciding how the best interests of a child may be served during parental separation or divorce. The psychologist's role as seen by **Hayden** is the contribution of empirical and evaluative skills in collecting information from the child at this stressful time, so that courts may recognize and consider the child's own views. **Tutt** considers the historical context of how juveniles can be diverted from custodial sentences in England and Wales. He notes that, while there has been a relative reduction in the use of custodial sentences with adults, there has been a substantial increase in such sentences for children. Tutt concludes that this is not in the best interests of the young offender, and he considers alternative approaches.

Carroll and O'Callaghan examine the case for the external regulation of psychosurgery, particularly with prisoners, children, and institutionalized psychiatric patients. With reference to case law in the USA, it is suggested that there is a strong argument for the regulation of psychosurgery. On the basis of their review, Carroll and O'Callaghan advocate broad-based review committees to regulate psychosurgery in the interests of maximal patient care.

Finally, **Haley** considers the theoretical and empirical bases for a policy of sentencing based on a model of retribution rather than on the currently more dominant model of rehabilitation. He argues that a major problem for such an approach is in the measurement of the psychological effects of different periods of imprisonment. Such problems, particularly as they affect the individual, might lead to only a marginal effect on the discretionary powers of the judiciary. While the simple model of retribution may therefore be neither desirable nor possible, Haley argues that some concept of retribution is a vital component for what he terms a 'just criminal system'.

Psychology and Law
Edited by D.J. Müller, D.E. Blackman, and A.J. Chapman
© 1984 John Wiley & Sons Ltd

Chapter 25

In the Best Interests of the Child: The Psychologist as Child Expert and Child Advocate

Brian Hayden

Legal considerations and psychological sensibilities, or even ambiguities, become enmeshed when the query of 'What is in the best interests of the child?' arises. In a variety of domestic litigations involving a child, typically divorce, a major concern is which parent or environment is most suitable and emotionally constructive for a particular child. The question of 'best interests' is seemingly straightforward. But often the meaning and implications of the question are unclear. Determining the child's best interests must not be confused with parental rights or with the adjustment problems both child and parents may be experiencing as a result of divorce. More often than not neither parent is demonstrably bad nor reliably or meaningfully assessed as being a more loving parent. And so legal considerations can supercede the child's interests. To prevent this, the complex and far-ranging psychological interests of the child need to be articulated and presented to the court. In other words, within the context of the emotionally charged situation of divorce or battling parents a reasonable approach to determine the child's interests must be developed.

FAMILY IN CRISIS: CHILD AND PARENT

Within the disintegrating emotional climate of a family in crisis conflicts inevitably arise. Various responses to conflict or existing tensions are aggravated by the fact that each family member's adjustment to the processes of separation, divorce, and post-divorce are complex and involve multiple transitions. So tensions do not at a discrete moment rise and recede. Quite often there are prolonged, chronic tensions with episodic flare-ups. Regard-

347

less of the nature and content of the conflicts, children's emotional responses are powerful and predictable: anger, fear, depression, and guilt (Hetherington, 1979; Kurdek, 1981; Wallerstein and Kelly, 1980; Westman, 1971). Nevertheless, children's emotional responses to the various dynamic processes vary; they may fester, they may be encouraged implicitly or explicitly, or they may be aggravated and manipulated by one parent (or extended family member). How these are expressed and during which one of the processes of separation, divorce, and post-divorce vary among children and among differing ages of children. Since parental conflict is the single best predictor of social nonconformity among children (Schwartz and Getter, 1980), it is not surprising that children from dissolving families are likely to have behavioural problems (Hetherington, 1979; Kurdek, 1981; Wallerstein and Kelly, 1980).

One reason for these behavioural problems is that the child is often placed in a situation of conflicting loyalties; therein, the stage is set for one parent by means of coercion or gentle persuasion to urge a child to reject (by actions or statements) the other parent. The child's naturally occurring emotions of fear, anger, sadness, and sense of loss are compounded by these conflicting loyalties. The child feels an implicit sense of abandonment or emotional hiatus with one or both of the parents. Over time the child may in response to parental quarrels develop exploitative and manipulative skills designed to draw guilt, gifts, or favours from parents. The resulting behaviours of the child may cause further child–parent or parent–parent conflicts. One common result of the child's exposure to parental conflict is that the mutual demeaning and criticism of parents lead to some emotional dissonance. That is, the child feels it necessary to 'side' with one parent as a way to remove tension. In so choosing, the child de-idealizes to some extent one parent (in extreme family conflicts both parents are de-idealized). As a parent is de-idealized, that parent no longer exercises the same degree or quality of influence on that child. The parent has diminished control and constructive impact on this angry, guilty, sad child. This lack of constructive influence on the child further compounds anger with that parent, the child's guilt over behaviour, and the child's growing sense of having lost a sense of order, security, and structure to life. The child's sense of losing control in an increasingly confusing situation is aggravated further. And a child's poor adjustment to divorce is directly associated with his perception that no one has much control over what is happening to family members (Kurdek, Blisk, and Siesky, 1981). Once again the stage is set for a family member to attempt to resolve the conflicts in order to alleviate or totally remove the trauma, the emotional pain, and both child and adults sensing a loss of some or most control over what is happening. For instance, a child may attempt to stop parental conflicts over visitation by a statement to mother (e.g. 'I hate Daddy...I don't want to see him') or some action (e.g. severe behavioural problems while on visits to or from the non-custodial parent) which effectively justifies cessation of visitation, thus, from the child's perspective, making the conflicts stop. The child's behaviour serves two functions: to make sense and give more order to the child's life and to reduce or remove further emotional trauma and tension. The child assumes the mission of self-sacrifice. And the child may clearly state things or act in a way that on one level appears to clarify what the child wants, prefers, or wishes. But the action or statement, in fact, causes legitimate and serious concern as to 'what is in the child's best interests?' This is not to suggest that a child's stated preference is discounted. Rather, the preference gives a most vital insight into determining what may serve that child's needs. Any stated preference must be clearly understood in its proper context. This understanding is most complete when one can discount the possibility that the preference reflects the child's temporary behaviour difficulties with a parent (e.g. anger with a disciplining mother), or coercion by one parent (e.g. one parent is experiencing difficulty in dealing with loss), or the child's attempt to reduce or eliminate tensions between parents or even within a parent (e.g. a child has taken upon him- or herself some sacrifice in a relationship).

While the child often assumes that the divorce decree will bring an end to the family turmoil, unfortunately the types of quarrels and tensions between parents increase, rather than decrease, during the year following divorce. The tensions persist for two years, or even longer, following the actual divorce (Kurdek, 1981; Kurdek et al., 1981). More often than not these disputes are over children and they linger or erupt over prolonged periods (Wallerstein and Kelly, 1980). The majority of divorcees continue some kind of emotional involvement at least two years after their divorce, and some 30% have repeated interactions and extremely bitter ones indeed (Westman, Cline, Swift, and Kramer, 1970). Emotional strain of parents results in less effective parenting skills, as well as their being less able to cope in general (Wallerstein and Kelly, 1980). Divorcing parents, for example, are often more inconsistent, less sensitive, less affectionate, and less able to control their children than non-divorcing parents (Hetherington, Cox, and Cox, 1978; Robinson, 1980). The majority of children are adversely affected by divorce (Wallerstein and Kelly, 1980; Westman et al., 1970), by the decline in parenting skills, and, no doubt, by the intensified negative interactions between their parents.

In the divorce and post-divorce situations, the emotional climate is less than optimal to meet a child's psychological or emotional needs; it is often detrimental. Typically, the child becomes embroiled in the mutually destructive and reciprocal cycle of negative parental interactions, and this is just when the parents are less adequately coping as parents. Moreover, the child of a divorcing or divorced couple encounters specific kinds of adjustment, is asked to make (or at least participate in) decisions, to deal with complex issues of loyalty and allegiances, and to consider alternatives (e.g. living arrangements) that no child from a non-divorced family typically encounters. Consequently, there is one loser: the child. It is within this context that a child's best interests are considered. And very few guidelines exist (Watson, 1969). An approach, therefore, is proposed for how to approach or gather relevant information for the determination of a child's best interests.

WHAT ARE THE CHILD'S BEST INTERESTS?

Until recently, one biological parent, unless proven otherwise, was viewed as the only charge to raise a child. Thus, child custody battles were resolved with a simple formula. This formula created, however, conceptual problems. In the abstract, the focus is on who is the better person, a concern that both denigrates a parent and weakens an adult's parental skills and confidence at a time in the child's life when both parents are, in fact, faltering in their abilities to cope as parents and often as adults. Inadvertently, the possibilities increase for a parent's manipulation in order to 'win' the child. In effect, these practical consequences are a disservice to the child's psychological development. But the most fundamental flaw is on a more general level – the emphasis is on what kind of *person* rather than on what kind of *parent* is the mother and father of the child.

More recently a major position defining 'best interest' was put forth by Goldstein, Freud, and Solnit (1979). They argued that the best interest of a child involved more than only a child's physical well-being. Rather the focus must be placed on the child's psychological needs. They specifically suggested that a child's best interests rested with the least detrimental available alternative. For determining that alternative they emphasized the child's need for continuity with the psychological parent who had day-to-day interaction, companionship, and shared experiences with the child. They felt that this need for continuity over-rode all other considerations, even if the application of this guideline denied visits to or from a non-custodial parent. In effect, the parameter of continuity or stability in relationship served as the guide to determine what was the least detrimental alternative. And this single guide had been used implicitly or explicitly to favour the continuity and stability in relationship offered by the biological *mother*. Thus, one person's impact on the child was valued over that of another. While this position helped to shift focus on to the quality of an adult's parenting, the position articulated only a small and partial view both of parenting and of a child's full array of psychological needs.

What has to be derived is a more comprehensive definition of 'best interests'. The emphasis has to be on the child's psychological needs and the parent most likely to meet these uniquely expressed needs of the particular child. Inclusively this position must consider the child's (1) full array of psychological needs (not just the need of continuity) as they unfold and are expressed within the context of the family and parents of the child, (2) adjustment level, and (3) developmental status. These three considerations acquire greater specificity and simultaneously make salient certain types of behaviours (e.g. mother–son conflicts, stated preferences, accusations of abuse, visitation refusals) when viewed in the light of two critical factors: the various childhood behavioural difficulties associated with separation and divorce, and the child's perception of each parent. These latter perceptions often reveal (1) to whom the child is emotionally responsive and thus most likely to have his or her needs constructively met, and (2) how, often single-handedly, a child's behaviour or statements are efforts to resolve or reduce the emotional tensions impinging on the child and/or the parents.

To provide a more comprehensive framework of a child's psychological needs, the rights of the child as delineated by the Joint Commission on the Mental Health of Children (1969) of the United States will be cited. This Commission noted as a child's rights: (1) the right to be wanted; (2) the right to live in a healthy environment (physical and psychological); (3) the right to obtain satisfaction of basic needs; (4) the right to receive continuous loving care; (5) the right to acquire the intellectual and emotional skills necessary both to achieve individual applications and to cope effectively in society; and (6) the right to receive care and treatment. These rights or needs, in conjunction with the child's need for continuity and stability in relationships (cf. Goldstein *et al.*, 1979), are proposed as seven specific guidelines both to articulate a child's psychological needs and to focus attention on which parent may most effectively meet them. Each of these guidelines acquires meaning only when viewed within the reciprocal interpersonal emotional climate created by a child's parents and siblings; that is, the child's development must be considered within an interpersonal context (Erikson, 1950; Sullivan, 1953). What makes the reciprocal interpersonal situation constructive, that is workable, for a child depends on that child's perception of and way of responding to the available social and emotional environment created by the parent–child interactions.

Another major consideration of 'best interests' is a child's present adjustment level. This second parameter serves as an important foundation with which to determine 'best interests'. The issue of adjustment level takes on two aspects. First, the child's level of adjustment is viewed in terms of the degree to which the child has prospered from the impact of the emotional climate created by the parents prior to the divorce. Hence, adjustment can be viewed in the traditional terms of personality structure or characteristics (Rutter, 1975). Despite a reasonably healthy personality, a child may manifest a variety of behavioural difficulties which relate to his or her specific level of adjustment to the present turmoil within the family. Thus, what must be assessed separately are the child's general personality functioning and how that child is specifically coping with the processes of separation, divorce, or post-divorce. Otherwise a child's common behavioural responses to divorce may be cited as evidence of, or misconstrued as, one parent's inability to provide adequate parenting.

Empirical research has highlighted several factors associated with a child's good adjustment to separation/divorce (Hetherington *et al.*, 1978; Hetherington, 1979; Kudek *et al.*, 1981; Parke, 1981). When assessing a child's psychological needs and personality adjustment consideration of these factors could permit determination of 'best interests' which minimizes disruptions in a child's cognitive, emotional, and social development. In effect, the presence of some factors, or the absence of others, may maximize the opportunity to meet a child's needs, and thus help to justify a determination of issues, such as joint custody versus sole custody or type of visitation arrangements. At least theoretically, there could be greater prospects for the child's psychological needs being safeguarded.

Two clusters can be gleaned from among these factors identified from the research: (1) a cluster highlighting the child's psychological status and personality qualities; and (2) a second cluster which makes salient some environmental and situational characteristics. First, a child's good adjustment is most likely to occur when the child was well adjusted prior to the marital crisis, is older (over 10 years of age), can engage in good social reasoning, has an internal locus of control (i.e. individuals feel in control by means of their own actions, intentions), and, perhaps most importantly, experiences a minimal degree of change in financial status or in geographical location or any other dramatic environmental alterations. Second, good adjustment to divorce can be best ensured when there is a low degree of conflict between parents before and after divorce; when the parents jointly focus on being parents, and hence they more clearly express approval and love to the child; and when they agree on child-rearing practices which tend to be firm and not permissive. A working mother and frequent visits to or from the non-custodial parent help minimize the degree of disruption to children.

These two clusters of factors highlight issues that must be considered, and assessed, when determining what will best serve the psychological needs of a particular child. Nevertheless, behavioural problems often may exist simply as a result of the child trying to adjust to the divorce process. Thus, it is essential to appreciate what types of common behavioural difficulties may arise and to discern when these behaviours are manifestations of the reactions to the separation, or divorce, or post-divorce phenomenon; or to ineffectual parental skills; or to dysfunctional relationships or psychopathology (in child, parent, or family).

Some commonly occurring behaviours can be expected of a child in a divorcing family. Children respond to divorce with feelings of sadness, fear, anger, and hostility. These potentially intense emotions are expressed in a variety of ways at home, school, and with peers. Children may become despondent and weepy; they may become increasingly fearful and withdraw socially from a wide range of situations.

A second type of reaction which affects a child's adjustment to parents' divorce stems from some of the fantasies and thoughts a child entertains. First, children tend to blame themselves for a divorce; that is, they maximize their contributions to the demise of the intact family structure (Westman *et al.*, 1970). Children also persist in fantasies of the family re-uniting (Westman *et al.*, 1970), despite elapsing years or the arrival of step-parents. In effect, children remain loyal to the pre-divorce family structure (Kurdek *et al.*, 1981) and, thus, often react inappropriately and disruptively to a parent (especially a mother) dating. Additionally, children are unaware of just how problematic was the parents' relationship prior to a divorce (Kurdek *et al.*, 1981). Indeed, their faulty and incomplete perceptions and thoughts are both persistent (over four years) and remarkably stable (Kurdek *et al.*, 1981). As Wallerstein and Kelly (1980) noted, children of divorced families remain dissatisfied and unhappy about their life and what has happened. Children's understanding of the divorce is confused, limited, and not articulated. Such confusion affects the child's reactions to divorce. Moreover, the confusion and limited or restricted understanding makes the child particularly vulnerable to parents or relatives attempting to sway a child to one perspective; that is, without sufficient understanding, it is difficult for a child to counter systematic denigration of one parent.

In summary, the consideration of a child's psychological needs include assessing general personality adjustment; and how the child specifically adjusts to the divorce, inclusive of the detection of factors associated with good or poor adjustment to divorce, as well as the discernment of the common behavioural difficulties and fantasies which complicate the child's functioning in the home, school, playground, and neighbourhood.

Parents affect the impact of divorce on the child by their actions and the resulting change in emotional climate. Poorer adjustment by the child is intensified when the parents are more distraught before and during the divorce (Hetherington, 1979; Westman *et al.*, 1971), when the parents place expectations on a child which are far too high (Hetherington, 1979), when parents fail to understand how their child feels and thinks about the divorce (Kurdek, 1981), and when parents fail to provide a sense of security, safety, continuity, and stability for the child. In turn, the child's expectations about the custodial parent may increase dramatically: one parent must now provide all the emotional support and discipline once supplied by two adults. If changes occur in financial status or geographical location, then even greater pressures are placed on the child, and adjustment to divorce is more difficult (Kurdek, 1981). The situation is aggravated when a child engages in a variety of ineffectual ways to handle, or ignore, the divorce. Left to his or her own devices, the child's behaviours, fantasies, perceptions, and thoughts in response to separation and divorce can leave the child floundering in the past, unreceptive to the social and psychological demands of the present, and ill-equipped for the future. Psychological adjustment exists when parents assist in creating an emotional climate which fosters the child's growth and increases the child's efforts to make sense of the world (Hayden, 1982).

The third parameter of 'best interests' includes the child's age, the child's sex, and the developmental task (e.g. sex identity, moral reasoning, autonomy) confronting the child. These factors interplay in how a child copes with the trauma of divorce.

For the infant the single greatest variable determining the magnitude of impact of divorce will be the nature of the parents' personalities and their relationship with the infant. The more disturbed the parent, the more probable it becomes that the infant will be affected through the emotional state of the caregiver (Rutter, 1975). For instance, the parent may displace on to the infant some of the rage or sadness generated by the divorce.

The most vulnerable children may be those of pre-school age (Hetherington, 1979), for it is at this age that the child is most likely to develop faulty perceptions of why parents are separated or divorced. These children are, therefore, quite susceptible to self-blame and adult manipulations. During the pre-school period, children are likely to show an increase in depression, to experience eating and sleeping disturbances, nightmares, occurrences of bed-wetting, and some problems in sexual identity (e.g. a boy 'playing' with his mother's clothes or cosmetics), and to express feelings of guilt and hurt for the non-custodial parent (Hetherington, 1979). Any or all of these behavioural difficulties will arise and may persist as a function of the degree of tension between the parents. In one sense, the degree and persistence of the child's reaction to the divorce serve as indicators of the parents' ability to cope with their own emotional crisis, as well as how they manage as parents.

The most dramatic and explosive reaction will come from the school-aged child. Deterioration in attitude, performance, and behaviour can be dramatic. Some children show deterioration in cognition and motivational and emotional functioning at home and/or school. Furthermore, at this age children often view the departure of the non-custodial parent as a profound personal loss. This loss may be expressed in the form of depression, marked social withdrawal, acute problems with one or two members of the family, or marked deterioration in school performance and/or behaviour. Moreover, the child may become increasingly aggressive, easily angered (often with the custodial parent), and emotionally labile.

Presumably, the adolescent is less affected by divorce since many of the issues of competency, sex identity, and sex typing have been handled to some extent (Kurdek, 1981). However, the adolescent, in contrast to the pre-adolescent, may be affected in a less obvious fashion. For instance, some adolescents make a clear preference with regard to whom they will live or with whom and when they will visit. Often their decision is based on a sense of outrage felt toward one parent: for being disloyal, for having had an affair, for having remarried, for hurting the other parent.This anger is justified with a self-righteous explanation.

A child's sex also affects different adjustment problems. A boy tends to express his behavioural difficulties towards his mother. Indeed, mother–son conflicts are extremely common (Hetherington, 1979) and often only fade two years after the divorce (Kurdek et al., 1981). It appears to be far more stressful for boys than for girls to sustain the loss of their father and sense of togetherness (Robinson, 1980). In part this may be because boys, unlike girls, are exposed to more of the stress, frustration, and aggression within the family as it begins to fall apart. As the processes of separation and divorce unfold, boys receive less of the emotional support which mother, teachers, and friends seem to provide unsolicited and more spontaneously to girls (Hetherington, 1979).

A final consideration of developmental needs is the timing of a person's impact on the child. One of the most critical psychological needs or rights cited earlier is the acquisition of intellectual and emotional skills. These skills are necessary to achieve individual aspirations and to cope in society. These skills develop within an interpersonal context, but the content of that context varies in importance depending on the task facing the child. For instance, a child's developing aspirations are most influenced by adults (Hartup, 1979), whereas peers have the greater impact on developing a child's coping skills (e.g. developing and incorporating status, norms, identity). And it may not be until the age of eight years that the child is most receptive to peers. Another right or need mentioned earlier is that of being wanted. This right is maximized in a particular environment. Young children raised within families providing warmth and security have self-confidence and high levels of competence, and are socially successful throughout their childhood (Hartup, 1979; Lieberman, 1977). In contrast, in an environment in which a mother (who 'wants' the child dearly) is hostile and critical of a father, psychological harm will occur. The impact of such a mother varies, however, on her child. Her son will suffer most in pre-adolescence when he tries to cope with his masculinity (Hetherington, 1979). Her daughter's scars will be most damaging when inflicted in childhood and pre-adolescence (Biller, 1974), yet go unseen until she tries to develop a sense of her own femininity and engages in heterosexual relationships (Hetherington, 1979). In other words, each of the seven needs noted earlier interact with one another, as well as within the emotional context created by each parent. And it is this context which, in effect, the child perceives and interprets.

The major parameters of the seven psychological needs, the adjustment to pre- and post-divorce, and the child's developmental status hold together only when a child's perceptions of and feelings towards each parent are known. A child's perceptions and feelings towards particular persons may or may not match with what the adult as a *parent* attempts to provide that child. In terms of the seven earlier cited rights/needs of a child, the child, for example, must be wanted by a parent and that child must perceive that parent as wanting him or her. Love, stability, and continuity certainly must be provided to children. But these needs are met by that person or persons to whom the child has positive, loving, and caring feelings and perceptions. Otherwise, no matter what degree of wanting or loving is given that child, the critical and determining factor of that wanting is whether the child perceives, and therein experiences, the parent as such. If a child does not perceive and experience the parent as wanting and loving, then the child will be unresponsive and unreceptive to that parent's best intentions. By default, the child relegates that parent to a position of relative psychological irrelevance. What the parent emotionally offers and tries to provide to meet a child's best interests goes uninterpreted. That child's best interests are not being served by that parent. In contrast, the child who is responsive and receptive to a parent's emotional offerings will thrive in such an emotional climate and develop confidence, competency, and friendships (Lieberman, 1977), the cornerstones to living effectively. In effect, the child's needs and best interest are being served by exposure to such a parent or parents.

The child's perceptions of each parent relate to the child's psychological needs, for these perceptions determine to whom the child is receptive and responsive. A child's interpretations of other people and of self determine personality adjustment and many important behaviours (Adams-Webber, 1979; Hayden, Nasby, and Davids, 1977; Hayden, 1979; Hayden, 1982). In effect, knowledge of these perceptions is essential to understand fully and adequately how the child is adjusting to the divorce and how the child may be attempting to resolve or eliminate emotional hurt and trauma. These considerations articulate the child's best interests and provide a guide to answering the thorny questions which pertain to custody, living arrangements, visiting, and need for treatment.

THE PSYCHOLOGIST'S ROLE

This framework for articulating the various parameters with which to approach a determination of a child's best interests, in turn, defines a new and active role for the psychologist. The psychologist's contribution is to assist the court in its final determination of a child's best interests. This assistance is ensured if the psychologist provides to the court an awareness and understanding of how a child perceives itself and others, and the child's situation; and, most significantly, of how a child's possibly problematic behaviours fit within a larger developmental context. For it is the psychologist's unique contribution to represent as fully as possible to the court the child's perspective on issues and concerns which effectively define each particular child's best interests. In doing so, a child's behaviours (e.g. a preference to live with one parent, refusal to visit a parent, behavioural problems with a parent, or an accusation of abuse against one parent) become more understandable.

To assess the child's psychological interests and unique perspective, the psychologist should have training and experience in the assessment and treatment of children. That training and experience are invaluable when synthesizing the multifaceted information base necessary to address a child's best interests. Part of this synthesis might include the rather traditional concerns of the quality of love and affection between each parent and child; the potential of each parent to continue expressing love, affection, and guidance; the general mental health of each parent so as to appraise the relative permanence of the emotional climate created by each parent (Schwitzgebel and Schwitzgebel, 1980; Woody, 1977). These concerns, however, are only helpful in those situations of rather gross parental deficiencies. In litigation cases involving issues of custody or other related concerns, typically the differences between two parents are a matter of degree. More often than not the consideration of best interests, instead, focuses most extensively on good parenting in the sense of to whom the child is most emotionally responsive. And it is for such purposes that the present comprehensive framework is suggested.

In essence, the psychologist actively articulates the child's psychological needs within the developmental and familial contexts and this will clarify which environment may facilitate or impede the meeting of needs. To achieve the goal of providing this kind of understanding of a child's unique perceptions and perspectives, the psychologist must be viewed exclusively as the child's advocate, thereby maximizing accessibility to the child's view of the world. The psychologist can only be perceived as the child's advocate if the confidence of the child is gained. Then, the psychologist can assess, using a wide variety of psychological tests and techniques and strategies (Lanyon and Goldstein, 1982), each of the proposed parameters to define a particular child's best interests. Thereafter, the real benefit from this process is that the parents can be helped in their general understanding of how their child views them as parents, the divorce process, and its impact on the family members. The parents in turn, may better recognize how to co-operate as parenting partners so that the child has the opportunity to continue to develop an active and constructive relationship with each parent.

SUMMARY

While the final determination of a child's best interests is based on psychological and non-psychological factors, it is the psychological ones that are critical. These factors go beyond what kind of person a child's parent is. The focus is on the psychological factors which make that child unique: the perspective of the world and the parents. When the four parameters of psychological needs, adjustment level (inclusive of the existence of features associated with a child or parent's adjustment of divorce which facilitate divorce adjustment), developmental status, and the child's perceptions and interpretations of each parent and respective custodial environments are considered, then the child's view acquires a richness in substance and meaning, as well as providing a framework within which to answer specific questions. Moreover, statements or actions or behavioural difficulties or fantasies can be envisaged at one level, at least, as the child's attempt to adjust to the divorce and/or resolve or eliminate the emotional hurt and confusion created by the process of parental separation and divorce.

The proposed comprehensive and developmental vantage point of best interest consists of piecing together the many elements of an assessment puzzle. The pieces do not fit together simply by having available a presumably well-meaning adult, but the puzzle is completed when an assessment of the child's personality and adjustment and developmental status and perception of each parent help to make understandable certain behaviours, even seemingly perplexing ones. Even in apparently straightforward situations, a child's unique view helps to make apparent a course of action which may ensure the child perceiving and experiencing the availability of certain opportunities to develop emotionally, intellectually, and socially. The proposed approach need not be used to shape and guide an answer in those situations involving grossly deficient parenting, but even in such situations it can help to shape and guide a deeper, or more profound, answer to the question, 'What is in this child's best interests?'

The answer to this question must incorporate a broad spectrum of concerns, not merely that of in which custodial environment should the child live. The seven rights or needs and the proposed parameters serve as guidelines in shaping the perspective of 'best interests' and helping the psychologist to articulate the child's world so as to contribute uniquely to the court's final determination.

The adults' rights should not be considered with the child's rights and psychological interests. Because of the fury of divorcing parents, the perspectives of adult and child must not become enmeshed, even when a parent is attempting to do what is best for the child. At issue is not a parent, but the child. Hence, the psychologist must present him- or herself as the child's advocate. In order to understand fully that child and the child's psychological interests, an assessment needs to be made in accordance with the approach delineated. The psychologist, thereafter, truly becomes that child's advocate.

REFERENCES

ADAMS-WEBBER, J. R. (1979). *Personal Construct Theory: Concepts and Applications.* Toronto: Wiley.

BILLER, H. (1974). *Paternal Deprivation.* Lexington, Mass.: D. C. Heath.

ERIKSON, E. H. (1950). *Childhood and Society.* New York: Norton.

GOLDSTEIN, J., FREUD, A., and SOLNIT, A. (1979). *Beyond the Best Interests of the Child.* New York: Free Press.

HARTUP, W. W. (1979). The social worlds of childhood. *American Psychologist.* **34**, 944–950.

HAYDEN, B. (1979). The self and its possibilities for change. *Journal of Personality*, **47**, 546–556.

HAYDEN, B. (1982). Experience: a case for possible change. In J. Mancuso and J. R. Adams-Webber (Eds), *The Construing Person.* New York: Praeger.

HAYDEN, B., NASBY, W., and DAVIDS, A. (1977). Interpersonal conceptual structures, predictive accuracy and social adjustment of emotionally disturbed boys. *Journal of Abnormal Psychology*, **86**, 315–320.

HETHERINGTON, E. M. (1979). Divorce: a child's perspective. *American Psychologist*, **34**, 851–858.

HETHERINGTON, E. M., COX, M., and COX, R. (1978). The aftermath of divorce. In J.H. Stevens, Jr, and M. Matthews (Eds), *Mother–Child, Father–Child Relations.* Washington, D.C.: National Association for the Education of Young Children.

JOINT COMMISSION ON THE MENTAL HEATH OF CHILDREN (1969). *Crisis in Child Mental Health: Challenge for the 70's.* New York: Harper and Row.

KURDEK, L. A. (1981). An integrative perspective on children's divorce adjustment. *American Psychologist*, **36**. 856–866.

KURDEK, L. A., BLISK, D., and SIESKY, A., JR (1981). Correlates of children's long-term adjustment to their parents' divorce. *Developmental Psychology*, **17**, 565–579.

LANYON, R. I., and GOLSTEIN, L. D. (1982). *Personality Assessment.* New York: Wiley.

LIEBERMAN, A. F. (1977). Preschoolers' competence with a peer: relations with attachment and peer experience. *Child Development*, **48**, 1277–1287.

PARKE, R. (1981). *Fathers.* Cambridge: Harvard University Press.

ROBINSON, R. (1980). *My Parents are Divorced Too.* New York: Everset House.

RUTTER, M. (1975). *Helping Troubled Children.* Harmondsworth: Penguin.

SCHWARTZ, J. C., and GETTER, H. (1980). Parental conflict and dominance in late adolescent maladjustment: a triple interaction model. *Journal of Abnormal Psychology*, **89**, 573–580.

SCHWITZGEBEL, R. L., and SCHWITZGEBEL, R. K. (1980). *Law and Psychological Practice.* New York: Spectrum.

SULLIVAN, H. S. (1953). *The Interpersonal Theory of Psychiatry.* New York: Norton.

WALLERSTEIN, J. S., and KELLY, J. B. (1980). *Surviving the Breakup: How Children and Parents Cope with Divorce.* New York: Basic Books.

WATSON, A. S. (1969). Child custody following divorce. *Syracuse Law Review*, **21**, 55–86.

WESTMAN, J. C. (1971). The psychiatrist and child custody contests. *American Journal of Psychiatry.* **127**, 123–124.

WESTMAN, J. C., CLINE, D., SWIFT, W., and KRAMER, D. (1970). Role of child psychiatry in divorce. *Archives of General Psychiatry*, **23**, 416–420.

WOODY, R. H. (1977). Psychologist in child custody. In B. D. Sales (Eds), *Psychology in the Legal Process.* New York: Wiley.

Psychology and Law
Edited by D.J. Müller, D.E. Blackman, and A.J. Chapman
© 1984 John Wiley & Sons Ltd

Chapter 26

Diverting Children from Custody

Norman Tutt

The Children and Young Persons Act, 1969, the major legislation under which juvenile offenders aged between 10 and 17 years are processed in England and Wales, was intended to be a diversionary statute. The diversionary intent was most clearly illustrated in Section 4 of the Act, which would have raised the age at which a young person could be prosecuted from 10 years of age to 12, and ultimately to 14 years, over a phased period; Section 5 of the Act made consultations between the police and social services a statutory requirement prior to the decision to prosecute any child or young person; Section 7(1) was concerned with the diversion of young people, after a court hearing, away from custodial establishments which are staffed and administered by the Prison Department. This diversion from custody was to be achieved by raising the age at which a young person could be sentenced by the Crown Court for borstal training from 15 years to 17 years of age. Section 7(3) of the Act underlined the intent to divert from custody by raising the age at which a young person could be sentenced to junior detention centre by the Magistrates Court from 14 years to 17 years; this section also envisaged that the expansion of 'intermediate treatment' facilities by social services departments would replace the need for attendance centres.

Between the passage of the Act through Parliament and its date for implementation, 1 January 1971, a general election took place and the incoming Conservative government decided not to implement the Act in full. Consequently, not one of the sections referred to above was implemented. Despite later changes in government in the 1970s neither Labour nor Conservative administrations have shown any intent to implement these sections. In fact the Criminal Justice Bill introduced in 1982 makes it clear that these sections have little likelihood of being anything other than interesting historical references on the statute book.

It is of considerable interest that public and political attitudes should have hardened so much against the possibilities of diversion, since in the mid-1960s both formal government opinion and public attitudes were strongly in favour of a much more radical diversionary policy than even that represented in the Children and Young Persons Act 1969. In 1965 the Home Office for England and Wales published a White Paper entitled *The Child, the Family and the Young Offender* to provide 'New arrangements... for determining and providing treatment for young offenders under 21'. The radical nature of these new arrangements, in particular the proposal to abolish the magistrates court, now appears almost beyond belief, but they are nevertheless worth quoting at length since the White Paper clearly articulated the argument for diversion, and moreover the White Paper illustrates the history of the argument for diversion and the extent to which at one time it gained widespread official recognition:

'There has been an increasing weight of informed opinion over the last ten years in favour of changes in our methods of dealing with children and young persons under 16 who now come before the juvenile courts. These courts were created in 1908. They have their own simplified procedures and they are served by selected magistrates. But though care is taken to avoid the characteristics of a criminal court, their procedures naturally derive from the criminal courts. We believe that these arrangements (namely the juvenile courts) should be radically changed because:

(1) Children should be spared the stigma of criminality.
(2) In the great majority of cases of offenders brought before the juvenile courts, the facts are not in dispute. The problem is to decide the appropriate treatment, and the court procedures, designed essentially for testing evidence, do not provide the best means for directing social inquiries and discussing possibilities with the child's parents and the social services that might be concerned with treatment.
(3) Although when children appear in the juvenile courts their parents attend whenever possible, the present arrangements do not provide the best means of getting parents to assume more personal responsibility for their children's behaviour.
(4) Decisions as to treatment are made in the form of a court order. This does not allow sufficient flexibility in developing the child's treatment according to his response and changing needs.

We therefore propose to remove young people so far as possible from the jurisdiction of the court, and to empower each local authority, through its children's committee, to appoint local family councils to deal with each case as far as possible in consultation and agreement with the parents' (Home Office, 1965, p. 5).

It should be remembered that these proposals were for England and Wales. In Scotland, which had never had a well established system of magistrates courts, a reform similar to that proposed in the White Paper did in fact take place. Scotland's experience over nearly 15 years of existence of the 'children's hearings' clearly illustrates that alternative methods of social control of juvenile offenders can be established, do maintain public credibility, and have different outcomes in terms of sentencing patterns (Martin, Fox, and Murray, 1981).

It is important to note that the White Paper envisaged increased diversion as part of the establishment of a 'welfare'-based system for dealing with juvenile offenders, that is a system aimed at developing children's treatment according to their responses and changing needs. This particular approach has been much criticized by those who believe a more 'justice'-based system would be both more effective and more humane (Morris and Giller, 1980). These critics argue that a 'justice'-based approach would limit discretion in the system, produce punishment proportional to the trivial nature of most juvenile crime, and provide determinate sentences which are understood by juveniles. Although there are apparently wide and irreconcilable divisions between the proponents of 'welfare' and 'justice', both agree that diversion away from formalized court hearings by means of police cautioning and reductions in the levels of use of custody are desirable objectives to pursue, despite the fact that an increase in police cautioning could be seen as a contradiction of the 'justice' model in that the child and the family are unrepresented and quite possibly encouraged to accept a finding of guilt in order to gain a caution rather than contest the case in court.

Agreement on the desirability of diversion of juvenile offenders from formal court proceedings has persisted despite other changes in policy. This consensus was clearly illustrated in 1980 with the publication by the Government of a White Paper entitled *The Young Offender* (Home Office, 1980a) which, although promising a tougher policy on juvenile crime, at the time stated:

'All the available evidence suggests that juvenile offenders who can be diverted from the criminal justice system at an early stage in their offending are less likely to re-offend than those who become involved in judicial proceedings. The now wide-spread police practice of giving a formal caution instead of instituting proceedings is therefore of particular importance, especially when the youngsters concerned can also be encouraged to participate in intermediate treatment programmes on a voluntary basis. The practice of cautioning is an aspect of the chief officer's discretion to prosecute and the whole question of police prosecution policy is currently under consideration by the Royal Commission on Criminal Procedure. Whatever the Commission recom-

mends on cautioning, however, it will clearly be important that all the
relevant local agencies work together with the police to ensure that the
juvenile concerned receives whatever help and, if necessary, support he
needs' (Home Office, 1980a, p. 12).

The All Party Penal Affairs Group (1981) produced a strategy document
which encouraged further expansion of police cautioning policy:

'1. The use of the caution should be sanctioned in legislation and
   attention should be given to achieving greater consistency in cautioning
   practice throughout the country.
2. All first-time minor offenders under seventeen who admit guilt
   should be cautioned, and this should also be the normal practice in
   regard to those who commit a second minor offence.
3. Formal cautions should not be administered where there is insufficient evidence for prosecution.
4. Cautioning should be used more often for young adult offenders.'

This further encouragement occurred in the face of growing research
criticism of the real effect of increased cautioning. Ditchfield (1976) suggested
that at least part of the reason for the national phenomenon of an apparent
vast increase in juvenile crime was that the pool of officially labelled juvenile
offenders has increased as a direct result of changes in police practice since
1969. This view has been supported by Farrington and Bennett (1981), who
examined the impact of changes in police policy as opposed to the impact of
legislation. They examined the effect of the establishment of a Juvenile
Bureau within the Metropolitan Police Force. The setting up and operation of
the Juvenile Bureau predated the implementation of the Children and Young
Persons Act 1969. The researchers argued that between 1968 and 1970, the
year in which the Bureau was fully operational, arrests increased 97% for
10–13 year olds, 88% for 14–16 year olds and yet only 52% for 17–20 year
olds, who were beyond the scope of the Bureau. The researchers suggest that
it is 'implausible' that these figures represent a 'real' increase in juvenile crime
but instead reflect the 'net-widening' effect of a change in police policy. They
continue by arguing that the change in police policy had a more profound
effect on arrests and findings of guilt than the later introduction of new
legislation.

Analysis of data for later years (1976–9) for the same police force area
currently being carried out by the author (unpublished) supports some of the
findings of Farrington and Bennett, most notably that it is the seriousness of
the offence which is most closely related to the disposition decision, but it also
illustrates clearly that the massive increase in arrests described by the
previous researchers did not persist into the latter half of the decade. In fact
the number of arrests for 10/17 year olds dropped back consistently from a

peak in 1977 over the following two years, although the proportion cautioned remained surprisingly constant: in 1976 some 32% were cautioned; in 1977, 1978, and 1979 some 34% were cautioned. Over this period the national average for police forces in England and Wales rose to over 50%.

The true cautioning figures are notoriously difficult to establish since there are differential rates of cautioning for boys and girls and for younger and older children, generally younger girls (10–14 years) are more likely to receive a caution than all other groups; the cautioning rate for this sex and age group is over 80% nationally. For younger boys it drops to approximately 55%; for older girls (14–16 years) it falls to approximately 55%; and for older boys it declines to about 35%. There are equally marked variations by offence committed and between police force areas. Moreover, as Parker, Casburn, and Turnbull (1981) have shown, in some police force areas referral to a juvenile bureau is 'by-passed' in favour of a rapid decision to prosecute. This procedure ensures that substantial numbers of juvenile offenders, normally older boys, are not even considered for a caution. A study of Northampton Juvenile Court (Redmond Pyle and Stevens, 1982) supports Parker et al's finding and shows that over 40% of juveniles appearing in court during the period studied had no known previous offence, nor had they received a caution.

The difficulties in establishing true cautioning rates; in ensuring that the real effect of cautioning is diversionary; in reducing wide variations in police practice; and in ensuring that certain groups of offenders receive equal opportunity for a caution has supported the arguments of the 'justice' proponents for less discretion to be allowed. Consequently research to date on cautioning practice would suggest that the greatest diversionary impact could be achieved by changing police practice rather than by legislation, and the change required would make a presumption for a caution on all first offenders with the rare exception of those charged with extremely serious offences, the definition of which has proved problematic in the past. Moreover, there should also be a presumption of a caution for all second offenders for whom the rate of cautioning currently drops very rapidly. These proposals are in line with those suggested by the All Party Penal Affairs Group and would seem, if introduced, to have some possibility of increasing diversion from the court.

There may be other strategies for increasing cautioning which involve social services departments. If the aim of social workers, as apparently envisaged in legislation, is to increase diversion, they should set about influencing police practice to increase cautioning rates. However, they need to ensure that they are increasing the rate of cautions on children who would otherwise be prosecuted rather than on those children on whom 'no further action' would otherwise have been the outcome of police discretion. Therefore the social worker, through contact with the local juvenile bureau, should seek to establish the local cautioning rate and the rate at which 'no further action decisions are made. Having determined these local rates, the social worker's aim should be to ensure that the 'no further action' numbers at least remain static and preferably increase, thereby increasing diversion, and that the cautioning rate increases.

The type of action a social worker might adopt to ensure this outcome will vary according to local circumstances, but some possibilities are as follows: First, to give priority and emphasis to the consultation procedures adopted by the local juvenile bureau. Although Section 5 of the Children and Young Persons Act 1969 has never been implemented, its spirit is alive, in some areas at least. This section would have made consultation between the police and social services a statutory obligation prior to prosecution in the juvenile court. Although not implemented, nearly all juvenile bureaux have implemented some form of informal consultation with social services departments and probation offices. Normally this means that the police send a written enquiry on each referral they receive in the bureau. The enquiry, usually in a standard form, asks both if the child is known to the social work agency and for any advice on action to be taken in terms of a caution or prosecution. Many local authorities deal with those enquiries in a routine and superficial fashion. However, if the social worker's aim is to increase diversion, greater emphasis on responding helpfully to the police enquiry, and a policy of recommending cautioning more frequently, could prove effective.

The second course of action is linked with the above. The social worker might be prepared and able to offer a child voluntary involvement in an existing intermediate treatment programme or some form of voluntary supervision, either by the social worker or by volunteer adults recruited specifically to work with juvenile offenders. An offer of this kind could be made to the police on the understanding that the child would be involved in an activity following a formal caution. It is likely that an increase in cautioning would result, since the police often prosecute not because they are seeking punishment, but because prosecution is at present the only route whereby the offender can gain access to the 'welfare system'. The offer of a specified voluntary programme would effectively increase the cautioning rates for offences for which prosecution is normally routine. Many of the offences which involve motor vehicles, and particularly those contrary to the Road Traffic Acts, are normally prosecuted by the police. The development of a range of 'motor projects' (whether motorbike maintenance groups or 'banger' racing clubs) has been linked with increased formal cautioning for this specific group of offenders. A number of the projects involve staff from the police, probation, and social services, working in the project together. An example of the kind of activity envisaged here is described as follows in the Home Office circular on co-operation between the police and other agencies:

'Youth Motorcycle Club: complaints about youths causing nuisance with motorcycles and complaints of "nothing to do" led to setting up of the club, mainly consisting of youngsters with previous convictions or referred by the probation or social services. Club members organised to raise money to buy motorcycles (sponsored walks, rubbish collecting, etc.) which are overhauled and repaired by members under supervision. Training in riding and display formation riding and the club now gives displays in public. 120 youngsters between 11–19 involved (Cambridgeshire)' (Home Office, 1980b, Appendix).

The third course of action is to increase police awareness of the possibilities which exist for increased cautioning. A number of children and young people taken before the juvenile court have their cases dismissed or receive conditional or absolute discharges. In those cases it can be argued that the court, after due consideration, decided that no further action against (or for) the child was required. In those cases (if the child originally pleaded guilty) the social worker could reasonably return with the file to the police and ask why the child had not been cautioned, assuming that the requisite criteria had been met; that guilt had been accepted; that parents and the victim agreed to a caution; and that there was no question of compensation. If the social worker were to return with these cases (on a regular basis) to the juvenile bureau, it might have the effect of increasing the cautioning rate, since officers of the bureau might feel safer in being prepared to take greater risks in cautioning.

The implementation of these strategies must be closely monitored to ensure that the overall impact on the juvenile justice system is diversionary rather than creating the net-widening effect as outlined by Thorpe (1984).

If a substantial diversion from the juvenile courts could be established, it would presumably have a knock-on effect on the number of custodial sentences passed on juvenile offenders since the numbers of young people available for such sentencing would be decreased. However, it would also appear necessary to implement specific strategies aimed at diverting young people after a finding of guilt away from a custodial sentence. Such strategies are imperative since there is increasing evidence that the sentencing policy in England and Wales is operating in contradiction to that of other countries.

A report of the Department of Health and Social Security shows that the proportion of convicted juveniles given some form of custodial sentence has been roughly constant in Sweden (which makes little use of custody), in the Netherlands and Italy, and in Germany (which makes comparatively frequent use of it). The proportion has risen in France, though not as fast as in England and Wales. Sweden and Scotland are examples of countries where a welfare-based judicial system seems to have succeeded without extensive use of custody for the more difficult children.

Moreover, there is clear evidence that within England and Wales, whilst major reductions in proportionate use of custody are occurring for adults, it is increasing substantially for juveniles. Thus whereas 30 years ago 25% of all adult offenders convicted of serious offences were sent to prison, today only 14% receive an immediate custodial sentence. The overcrowding of adults' prisons had not been caused by an increase in the proportion of offenders being sent to prison, it has remained at 14% for the last decade, but by an increase in the numbers convicted of serious offences and, therefore, receiving long sentences. The reverse trend can be observed for juveniles; despite the intention of the Children and Young Persons Act 1969 to phase out the use of borstal training and detention centre as sentences for persons under 17 years of age, it is precisely these sentences that have shown the greatest growth since 1969. In 1969 there were 2750 detention centre and borstal sentences passed on young people aged 14–16 years, by 1979 the number had risen to 6876. Part, but not all, of this increase can be explained by the overall increase in juvenile offending which in 1969, in round figures, was 118,000 indictable offences for juveniles between 10 and 17 years of age; it reached a peak in 1977 of 198,000 and dropped back in 1978 and 1979, in which it was nearer 160,000. The increase in juvenile crime amongst 14/16 year-old-boys, those for whom detention centre and borstal sentences are possible, would account for a 40% rise in the use of these sentences for the period 1969–79; in reality the rise has been over 150%. This sharp rise in the proportionate use of custody has been succinctly described by a Home Office Minister:

'Let me start by putting the problem into perspective. There is no doubt that recorded crime among juveniles has increased substantially during the past twenty years. But, contrary to the impression normally given, it has not increased more than adult crime. The proportionate increase in the number of offences by juveniles has been about the same as for adults; both have approximately tripled. Nevertheless, serious crime and offences by girls have risen disproportionately and this must give cause for concern. Where the greatest difference has been is not in the commission of offences but in what happens to the serious offender. During the past twenty years the proportion of convicted adults received into custody has been more than halved. During the same period the proportion of juveniles receiving custodial sentences, and I do not include Care Orders, has more than tripled. In 1955 an adult was twenty times more likely than a juvenile to get a custodial sentence for an indictable offence. Now he is only twice as likely' (Brittan, 1979).

However, such custodial sentences are not by virtue of their age available for children between the ages of 10 and 14 years; for them and for those between 14 and 16 years, in addition to the custodial order, the magistrates are empowered to make a 'care order'. The effect of such an order under the

Children and Young Persons Act 1969 is to remove all parental rights from the parents to the local authority, which is empowered thereby to determine where the child shall reside. Such care orders, normally made under Section 7(7) of the Act, require only proof of the child having committed an offence, and would be in force, unless revoked, until the child's 18th birthday, or until the 19th birthday if the young person is over the age of 16 when the order is made. Zander (1975) and Cawson (1981) have clearly demonstrated that the making of such an order under normal circumstances leads to the removal of the child from home and placement into a residential establishment. Studies available from the Centre of Youth, Crime and Community, University of Lancaster, have shown that a child is likely to be in a residential institution for a substantial period, that is on average for a period in excess of 12 months. Although such residential establishments are not technically custodial, the boundaries between them and a purely custodial institution are highly permeable. A Department of Health and Social Security report (DHSS, 1981) has discussed the growth of secure accomodation within the local authority child care sector, a growth of more than 300 places in a decade: in 1969 there were approximately 150 secure places for children, by 1980 this had risen to over 500 such places. The Children's Legal Centre (1982) carried out a survey of the use of secure accommodation by local authorities and was concerned by its increasing use; the confused state of the law; the way in which major research findings have been ignored by politicians and practitioners in the child care system; and the lack of publicly available information and statistics. They found the restriction of children's liberty without speedy judicial review contrary to the principles of natural justice, reflected in articles in the European Convention on Human Rights.

Moreover, it is now increasingly obvious that care orders may be made on children with very short criminal careers rather than being seen as the 'last resort' of the tariff system. Redmond Pyle and Stevens (1982) recorded 10 care orders out of a court sample of 242 cases. Of the 10 care orders made, three were 'repeats' (that is, the child was currently on a care order and had re-offended), two had no known previous offence, two had only a previous caution, and three had previously been on a 'supervision order'. Thus in this small sample four of the 10 were in court on their first court appearance. This small sample study is in keeping with those of Cawson (1981), 31% of a sample size of 71, and Giller and Morris (1981), 45% of a sample of 99. The significance of the care order appearing low on the tariff is increased since it appears to lead to later custodial sentences. Tutt (1975) showed that children in residential care on care orders exhibited high levels of absconding behaviour accompanied by offences which led to further reconviction. The reconviction is very likely to lead to a higher tariff disposal which, given that the child is of the appropriate age, is a custodial sentence. The permeability of the boundary between the 'welfare' system and the criminal justice system is illustrated clearly by the finding that 54% of 15-year-olds admitted to borstal had an operative care order; 44% and 29% of 16- and 17-year-olds respectively had operative care orders (DHSS, 1981). No national figures exist for young people in detention centres, but Fludger (1976), in a study in the South West Region of the Prison Department, showed that about half the 14/16-year-old boys were, or had been, subject to care orders; of the boys subject to current care orders, 80% had been in community homes at the time of the sentence. These figures are compatible with the reconviction rates of boys in community homes reported by the Centre of Youth, Crime and Community in its work with local authorities.

Given this evidence a possible initial strategy for diversion from custody is to begin to erode the numbers of young people receiving care orders. Such a move would seem to be an essential step in attenuating the tariff system for the more persistent juvenile offender. The Centre of Youth, Crime and Community, University of Lancaster, has conducted a number of projects within local juvenile justice systems aimed at reducing the numbers of care orders. In general these projects follow the pattern of first identifying the files of all young people placed into the care of the local authority under Section 7(7) of the Children and Young Persons Act 1969. Second, a panel of local authority staff is established with representatives from both management and 'front-line' field and residential social workers. The panel, with the addition of research staff, is usually some eight people. Third, the panel is asked to agree criteria, the existence of which would signify that the young person should be in residential care. Briefly, these criteria are similar to those outlined by the Government for the guidance of courts when making 'certificates of unruliness'. These are as follows:

(1) The child or young person is a danger to themselves or to the community. This would include those young people who indulge in a range of self-destructive behaviour, self-mutilation, or serious drug abuse, as well as those who are charged with serious acts of violence or arson, and thereby pose a threat and proven danger to the community.

(2) The child has no identifiable home which can, with appropriate support, provide an adequate degree of care and control. The panel is encouraged to consider not merely the parental home as existing, but the possibilities either that the parental home could be supplemented by specific social work or other services to support the parents, that is by adequate provision of welfare rights or home help service, to cope with their children. Moreover, the panel would be asked to consider the possibilities of other members of the family accepting some responsibility for the child during what may be a relatively temporary crisis.

(3) The child has specific medical, educational, vocational, or psychiatric requirements which can only be met within a residential setting. This

criterion is concerned with severe disabilities, which are also relatively rare, such as psychosis, brain damage, epilepsy, or physical illness or handicap which require forms of containment or specialized treatment that could not be effected in the community. The panel is urged to employ this criterion rigorously and not consider those children who require specialist facilities but which could be provided by means other than admission to care. For example, a child may reasonably require remedial education, but that can be met on a daily basis in a community-based centre; whilst the child remains living at home it does not require placement in a residential institution.

With these three criteria in front of them the panel is asked to sort the files of all those children currently on care orders. If from the file the case meets any one of the criteria, then there is assumed to be a *prima facie* case for the child to be in residential care. If the panel fails to agree on any one case file, then the child is deemed to require residential care. If the members of the panel are agreed unanimously that the case files meet none of the criteria, it is indicated the child does not need to be in an institution.

There are obvious drawbacks to this exercise. First, the panel is examining case files in retrospect. The recording on the file may well omit crucial evidence or pressure on courts at the time of the child's admission into care. Second, the exercise is by its nature hypothetical and the panel is not open to public pressure or the responsibility to the public that the juvenile court may experience at the time of sentencing. In spite of these reservations the findings are quite extraordinary.

Table 26.1 The number of Section 7(7) care orders and the percentages rated as inappropriate within six local authorities studied

Local authority	No. of Section 7(7) care orders	Percentage inappropriate
1	132	90
2	28	89
3	44	70.5
4	112	89
5	165	75.5
6	66	93

Table 26.1 illustrates the numbers and the rates at which panels determined care orders as inappropriate. These figures appear extreme and yet gain some support from an unpublished study using the same methodology but carried out independently in a London Borough Social Services Department. From a

sample of 84 Section 7(7) care order cases, 54 cases (64%) were found to be inappropriately subject to such orders and not in demonstrable need of residential care (N. Patrick, personal communication).

These figures are also supported by the analysis of the background factors of children on care orders; for example, an analysis of the 66 Section 7(7) care orders held by Stockport Metropolitan Social Services Department on 31 March 1980 showed that 33% had no previous conviction prior to the making of the care order. The 66 children were charged with a total of 357 offences; over 97% of these were concerned with offences against or attempted against property, while those involving violence or threatened violence against persons amounted to only 0.8%. Some 50% involved theft or damage of property of less than £50.00; only 23% involved property valued at over £200.00. These figures clearly illustrate the trivial nature of most juvenile crime and society's dramatic reaction to those crimes.

This analysis indicates that the children and young people subject to such care orders are not persistent or dangerous offenders and it would therefore seem inappropriate for them to be placed in a residential institution.

The studies of the Centre of Youth, Crime and Community clearly indicate that wide scope exists for a further reduction of the placement of young people in institutions. It is predicted that this reduction would eventually lead to a reduction of young people entering custodial establishments merely by attenuating the tariff system operated by juvenile courts.

REFERENCES

ALL PARTY PENAL AFFAIRS GROUP (1981). *Young Offenders – A Strategy for the Future.* London: Barry Rose.

BRITTAN, L. (1979). In *Getting on with Intermediate Treatment.* London: Department of Health and Social Security.

CAWSON, P. (1981). *Young Offenders in Care.* London: Her Majesty's Stationery Office.

CHILDREN'S LEGAL CENTRE LTD (1982). *Locked up in Care.* London: Children's Legal Centre.

DHSS (1981). *Report of a Working Party on Legal and Professional Aspects of the Use of Secure Accommodation for Children in Care.* London: Department of Health and Social Security.

DITCHFIELD, J. (1976). *Police Cautioning in England and Wales,* Home Office Research Study No. 37. London: Department of Health and Social Security.

FARRINGTON, D. P., and BENNETT, T. (1981). Police cautioning of juveniles in London. *British Journal of Criminology,* **21**, 123–136.

FLUDGER, N. (1976). *A Survey of the Characteristics of Junior Detention Centre Trainees whose Home Areas are in the Prison Department South West Region.* London: Home Office. Reprinted in Department of Health and Social Security (1981). *Offending by Young People. A Survey of Recent Trends.* London: Department of Health and Social Security.

GILLER, H., and MORRIS, A. (1981). *Care and Discretion. Social Workers' Decisions with Delinquents.* London: Burnett Books.

HOME OFFICE (1965). *The Child, the Family and the Young Offender.* London: Her Majesty's Stationery Office.
HOME OFFICE (1980a). *Young Offender.* London: Her Majesty's Stationery Office.
HOME OFFICE (1980b). Home Office Circular No. 83/1980, 29 August 1980.
MARTIN, F., FOX, S. J., and MURRAY, K. (1981). *Children out of Court.* Glasgow: Scottish Academic Press.
MORRIS, A., and GILLER, H. (1980). *Juvenile Justice.* Lancaster: University of Lancaster Centre of Youth, Crime and Community.
PARKER, H., CASBURN, M., and TURNBULL, D. (1981). *Receiving Juvenile Justice: Adolescents and State Care and Control.* Oxford: Basil Blackwell.
REDMOND PYLE, D., and STEVENS, M. (1982). *Report on the Northampton Juvenile Criminal Justice System.* Lancaster: University of Lancaster Centre of Youth, Crime and Community.
THORPE, D. H. (1984). The justice model and intermediate treatment. In A. Morris and H. Giller (Eds), *Providing Justice for Children.* London: Edward Arnold.
TUTT, N. S. (1975). Recommittals of juvenile offenders. *British Journal of Criminology,* **16**, 355–388.
ZANDER, M. (1975). What happens to young offenders in care? *New Society,* 24 July 1975, 185–187.

Psychology and Law
Edited by D.J. Müller, D.E. Blackman, and A.J. Chapman
© 1984 John Wiley & Sons Ltd

Chapter 27

Controlling Psychosurgery

Douglas Carroll and Mark A. J. O'Callaghan

Psychosurgery can be defined briefly as brain surgery where histologically normal tissue is destroyed for the explicit purpose of modifying some aspect of human behaviour or some psychiatric disorder. Following Stone (1975), we would exclude from the rubric procedures designed to treat intractable pain or epilepsy, where these conditions are clearly demonstrable. Nor would we include procedures used to treat organic brain conditions, even though such procedures may also involve the interruption of normal brain tissue. These latter interventions are more properly regarded as neurosurgical. It is important to stress, though, that it is not the techniques and anatomical foci of surgical exercises that qualify them as examples of psychosurgery; the same techniques and foci can characterize neurosurgery. It is the explicit intention of the surgery to promote behavioural change that is crucial.

Few therapeutic enterprises have proved as consistently contentious as psychosurgery. Indeed controversy has pursued the practice since the initial upsurge of operations in the 1940s, and, although a reduction in psychosurgical activity in the 1960s afforded some respite, recent initiatives have once again rekindled the debate.

Our present concern is with the issue of regulation. A variety of prescriptions have now been offered for policing and controlling psychosurgery. It is our intention to review and assess these. At the outset, though, it is worth noting that clinical practice has rarely been subject to formal external regulation. Certainly, early psychosurgical operations encountered no formal regulatory obstacles. Addressing the problems involved in drafting a statute to police the use of lobotomy, an editorial in the *Stanford Law Review* concluded as follows: '... the greater good will be achieved by avoiding legislative fetters and relying for protection on the high standards of the medical profession and the individuals who compose it' (Anonymous, 1949, p. 474). This *laissez-faire* ethic prevailed for the next two decades. As Annas

375

and Glantz (1974, p. 251) commented: 'Throughout the 1950s and 1960s. psychosurgery was ignored by the legal community.' It is an arrangement that continues to attract wide support from within the medical profession. In an editorial in *Biological Psychiatry*, Wortis contested the wisdom of legislating against contemporary psychosurgery. His comments are reminiscent of the 1949 submission: There is room in our society for some mandatory laws for health and sanitation, but they should be few and cautious. It is simply not possible to settle our scientific differences through legislation, or to insure good medical practice or judgment by laws' (Wortis, 1972, p. 100).

In the face of such persistent opposition, are there persuasive arguments in favour of regulation? There are, in fact, several good reasons for submitting that psychosurgery deserves regulatory attention.

First of all, recent analyses indicate that psychosurgery still lacks an adequate scientific rationale and possesses at best only the most superficial and precarious empirical support (Carroll and O'Callaghan, 1981; O'Callaghan and Carroll, 1982; Valenstein, 1973). Given that the efficacy and validity of psychosurgery are still in doubt, regulation would seem quite appropriate. Second, only in a regulated milieu will it be possible to insist on the experimental control and assessment procedures necessary to evaluate properly the therapeutic status and utility of psychosurgery. The absence of systematic regulations certainly licences haphazard and shoddy conduct. Third, there is now substantial public concern and even alarm about psychosurgery, particularly in the United States. Admittedly, some of this is based on the fairly unlikely proposition that psychosurgery offers the potential for unlimited social control and the somewhat metaphysical construct that the brain is inviolable. Nevertheless, widespread and intensely held views, whether grounded in logic or not, demand formal recognition; the regulation of psychosurgery would seem the appropriate response.

Finally, in spite of protestations to the contrary, psychosurgery is not simply a medical concern. It is a matter of social ethics. In fact, it is difficult to contest the case that all medical treatment and experimentation embodies issues of morality. This is emphatically so when the treatment or experiment is aimed specifically at altering behaviour. (The failure of some psychosurgeons to recognize even the existence of fundamental ethical problems is, in itself, a powerful argument for external regulation.) When confronted with far-reaching ethical questions, it has usually proved propitious to formulate regulations for the purpose of guidance and arbitration.

Having established that external control is warranted, let us consider what style of regulation would be appropriate. Several models have been put forward.

PEER REVIEW

The least radical and intrusive model for regulation involves the scrutiny of proposals for psychosurgery by peer review committees. As Offir (1974, p.

59) wryly commented, these are 'the physician's peers, not the patient's'. Since 1966, such committees have been an integral part of federally funded American hospitals. Further, some legislations have placed great emphasis on peer review committees. For example, in Australia, the New South Wales Mental Health Act of 1959 (see Maddison, 1977) made provisions for the establishment of a leucotomy committee to deal with proposals for psychosurgery on involuntary committed patients. Several Australian commentators have been critical of this review system. Winkler (1977), for example, contended that, since most psychosurgery in Australia is conducted in private practice, any review procedure should be widened to include voluntary patients. The legislation recently enacted in California does, in fact, make this sort of provision for voluntary patients.

The rationale underlying the peer review system is straightforward. It is presumed that the issues are essentially esoteric, susceptible only to special medical expertise which in turn is available only to those bearing the appropriate professional credentials. Several commentators have harboured doubts about the validity of this rationale. As Edgar (1975, p. 131) pointed out it 'may be grounded more on monopoly than in reason'. Certainly, the issues transcend specialized considerations of medicine and embrace the concerns and skills of other professional groups – behavioural and social scientists for example. In addition, they are much more generally accessible than a peer review system credits. Finally, and most importantly, there is evidence that peer review offers less than optimal protection to patients in this context.

BROAD-BASED REVIEW

Winkler's proposal (1977) for a mandatory review by a committee comprised of both physicians and non-physicians would seem to overcome some of the problems associated with peer reviews. Many American hospitals already possess broad-based review bodies of this sort. In fact, in October 1973, the Department of Health, Education and Welfare in the USA proposed that all institutional review committees should consist of individuals of varying backgrounds and contain at least five persons in all.

The first comprehensive American state legislation specifically aimed at psychosurgery gives the onus for decision-making to such a broad-based review board. The Oregon Statute was enacted in 1973 and reflected the initiative of two neuroscientists (a neurologist and a neurophysiologist). The statute provides that psychosurgery may be performed only with the approval of at least six members of a nine-member review board. The review board operates on a state-wide basis and its nine members are appointed by the Governor of Oregon from specified medical, psychological, neuroscientific, and lay backgrounds.

The function of the Oregon board is twofold. First of all, it is charged with determining, according to statutory guidelines, whether the consent of the patient or proxy is properly informed and voluntary. Second, having satisfied itself about consent, the board has to decide whether the operation has clinical merit and is an appropriate treatment for the patient.

In England and Wales, a government review of the Mental Health Act of 1959, published in 1978, places similar emphasis on review by a broad-based committee or panel. In its recommendation it is argued of certain treatments including psychosurgery: 'Treatment which is irreversible, hazardous or not fully established should not be imposed without the patient's consent (except to save life), and, even if the patient (whether informal or detained) does give consent treatment, should not be administered with a concurring second opinion' (DHSS, 1978, pp. 141–142).

Three modes of second opinion were considered by the White Paper: an independent psychiatrist's opinion; a committee in each hospital charged with oversight of the rights and responsibilities of staff and patients (essentially, a peer review committee); a multidisciplinary panel especially established for the purpose. The British government clearly favoured the final option.[1]

While it is clear that such committees are likely to afford the patient much more protection from equivocal treatments than a peer review arrangement, the systems outlined above have attracted criticism. Annas and Glantz pointed to what they regarded as weaknesses with the Oregon legislation:

'At least a majority and as many as seven members of the nine-member board may be physicians. Only one need be an attorney and only one is designated as a 'member of the general public'. The board is thus heavily biased toward the scientific research community and may approve the performance of psychosurgery even against the dissent of the "lay" members' (Annas and Glantz, 1974, p. 263).

The British White Paper does not offer much guidance regarding committee membership. However, it is clear that here, too, only one lay member is envisaged. Annas and Glantz were also critical of the Oregon consent hearing. They indicated that the hearing, as presently structured, could permit surgery against a patient's wishes.

Let us consider these two criticisms in turn. First, while lay membership of such committees might reasonably be strengthened, minority lay opinion is always likely to bow to majority professional opinion. For example, one of the lay members of the consent committee in the celebrated Detroit psycho-surgery case (reviewed later) declared his own lack of competence and explicitly acknowledged the heavy reliance he placed on the good intentions and technical competence of the medical assessors. Annas and Glantz seem to imply that it is lay domination in review committees that is required to provide optimal patient protection. However, there is no reason for believing that lay members possess better judgment and greater moral integrity than their professional co-members. It is not the exact composition of the panel that would seem to be crucial, save that it must be broad based, but its independence.

The second problem cited by Annas and Glantz stems to a large extent from Oregon's failure to distinguish between legal competence and the capacity to give informed consent. Involuntary status should not *per se* render a patient incompetent to consent or dissent from psychosurgery. It is noteworthy in this context that the Californian legislation recognizes that an individual judged to be legally incompetent as a general matter may nevertheless retain the specific capacity for informed consent to psychosurgery.

Ervin (1977) indicated what is perhaps a more fundamental difficulty with the Oregon Statute. It is a problem Oregon shares with other prescriptions relating to psychosurgery: 'The one thing that the committee has not established – and I hope it will – is a mechanism for systematized preoperative plus post-operative clinical and psychological evaluation' (Ervin, 1977, p. 126). Edgar (1975) also stressed the importance of regulating not simply whether or not an operation is performed in a particular case but also the manner in which psychosurgical experiments are generally conducted.

TWO-TIER SYSTEM

Several commentators have proposed a two-tier committee system; usually a peer review followed by a broader-based assessment. For example, Ervin (1977) strongly recommended this system to the Australians. The Massachusetts Task Force Report (Stone, 1975) also advocated the two-tier approach in hospitals considering psychosurgery. Further, unless a hospital's submitted protocol satisfied the Department of Mental Health that it possesses such facilities, psychosurgery would not be permitted there. The report also stressed the importance of appropriate pre- and post-operative assessment and acceptable experimental design. A central state registry was proposed to enable the collation of data from past and future psychosurgical exercises so that the effectiveness of the procedures could be accurately evaluated. The recent report, from the USA, of the National Commission for the Protection of Human Subjects of Biomedial and Behavioral Research (1977) also advocated a central monitoring agency for psychosurgical procedures.

While the two-tier system has gained wide acceptance in the USA, in general it would seem to offer little, if any, advantage over a single broad-based committee: especially where the membership of one of the two tiers has close links with the physicians proposing the treatment. In addition, it is questionable logic that separates the issues surrounding psychosurgery, as some proposals do, into scientific/medical and ethical/social, where the former are deemed the prerogative of a peer review and the latter the concern of a 'community' committee. These concerns would seem to be intimately interwoven. In determining the scientific status of a proposal for psychosurgery, a peer review body necessarily establishes the framework for subsequent ethical deliberations in the community committee. Finally, committees are somewhat cumbersome and unwieldly instruments; given that no sources of information are lost, one is always better than two.

With regard to the National Commission recommendations, the establishment of a national apparatus for the on-going evaluation of psychosurgical procedures would seem a genuine advance. However, the weakness of the National Commission's submission is that it places too much reliance on local, institutional peer review. As we indicated previously, there are strong precedents for doubting the appropriateness of peer reviews in matters of patient protection. Further, given that the national Psychosurgery Advisory Board also amounts to peer review, the whole regulatory system appears somewhat 'incestuous'.

COURT REVIEW

Court review offers an alternative to peer review or review by a broad-based committee. An example of this alternative is provided by California's penal legislation. Enacted in 1976 and addressed to involuntarily institutionalized individuals (pursuant to Californian penal code), the Californian Statute provides for mandatory court review of any proposed psychosurgery. The confining institution is required to petition for a court order authorizing the operation. Before issuing an order, the court, having appointed both an independent medical expert and a public defender for the indigent, must be satisfied that the patient has the capacity for informed consent, and has, in fact, consented, and that the operation has clinical merit. Here the court must determine that the psychosurgery proposed is beneficial; that there is compelling interest justifying the operation; that there are no less onerous options available; and that the operation is in accordance with sound medical and psychiatric practice.

A similar provision for involuntary patients has been recommended by the National Commission: that in addition to the assessment of the Psychosurgery Advisory Board and institutional peer review, proposals for psychosurgery on involuntary patients should satisfy court review. In addition, according to the Commission, proposals for psychosurgery on children should be subject to the same sort of regulation.

It is important to note at the outset that these schemes make no distinction between involuntary institutionalized psychiatric patients, where the grounds for confinement are psychiatric, and prisoners, where the motives for confinement are social rather than psychiatric. However, it is submitted that these two classes of involuntarily institutionalized individuals merit independent consideration. We shall return to this matter later and, in particular, to the thesis that psychosurgery on prisoners should be prohibited.

For the moment, though, let us focus on the appropriateness of court review for the involuntarily institutionalized mental patients. We would submit that the grounds for treating involuntary and voluntary patients in a qualitatively different manner are rather weak. Either the nature of psychosurgical procedures necessitates close control of these procedures or it does not. The manner of regulation should be determined by the status of the treatment and not by the status of the patient. It is a point emphasized by King (1977) in her dissenting statement in the National Commission's report.

Both the National Commission's recommendations and the Californian legislature embody noticeable inconsistencies in their approach to the involuntarily institutionalized patients. While both submissions take care to distinguish between the legal status (voluntary or involuntary) and the psychological status of and individual in the matter of capacity to give informed consent, legal status is deemed of major significance in establishing the clinical merit of a psychosurgical procedure, by describing the manner in which such a determination is made. However, clinical merit would seem markedly less likely to interact with the legal status of the patient than the capacity to consent.

One solution here is to require all proposals for psychosurgery, whether aimed at voluntary or involuntary patients, to be subject to court review. However, we are not convinced that this is the optimal means of affording patient protection. There seems little reason for trusting that a lay judge and jury, exposed to fairly limited expert testimony, are capable of better judgment than a broad-based committee, serviced by centrally collated data, evaluations, and guidelines. The judgments of courts in matters relating to psychosurgery have not, to date, been noticeably consistent. Further, court review as a matter of course for all psychosurgery proposals is likely to prove an awkward and protracted business.

PROHIBITION

Several critics have called for a ban on psychosurgery. Breggin's has undoubtedly been the most insistent and uncompromising voice. In his submission in the US *Congressional Record*, Breggin (1972) declared: '... I believe that all forms of psychosurgery should be outlawed in America as they were in Russia' (Breggin, 1972, E1611). (Psychosurgery has been prohibited in the Soviet Union since 1951.)

Breggin's views, however, are not widely shared. It is more usual to find the abolition case expressed in terms of partial or selective, rather than total, prohibition. Psychosurgery would be allowed but only, for example, in specific classes of institution or psychiatric facility; or, alternatively, psychosurgery might be permitted only for certain categories of patient; or, finally, only certain psychosurgical procedures might be allowed. Let us consider each of these in turn.

Undoubtedly the most far-reaching and prohibitive proposal for institutional regulation was drafted by United States Representative Louis Stokes, in 1973. The Stokes' bill would have outlawed psychosurgery in federally connected health care facilities. The practice of psychosurgery in violation of this bill would result in institutions and/or individual physicians being barred from federal government support. Further, the bill envisaged fines of up of US $10,000 per operation. A watchdog committee would be established to investigate whether psychosurgery was taking place and what penalties would be levied against those practising it. In addition, the bill would have opened the district courts to civil actions by patients.

There are, however, major weaknesses with the Stokes' bill. First, the parameters of the bill were not allied in any systematic manner to the scientific, clinical, and social status of psychosurgery. Meister's (1975) assertion, that if psychosurgery is to be performed anywhere it should be in the most sophisticated and most accountable facilities, is in accord with the spirit of several of the formal submissions for regulating psychosurgery discussed previously in this chapter. The National Commission's (1977) recommendations serve to illustrate:

'Until the safety and efficacy of any psychosurgical procedure have been demonstrated, such procedures should be performed only at an institution with an institutional review board (IRB) approved by the DHEW [Department of Health, Education and Welfare] specifically for reviewing proposed psychosurgery, and only after such IRB has determined that:

(A) the surgeon has the competence to perform the procedure;

(B) it is appropriate, based upon sufficient assessment of the patient, to perform the procedure on that patient;

(C) adequate pre- and post-operative evaluations will be performed; and

(D) the patient has given informed consent'

(National Commission for the Protection of Human Subjects of Biomedical and Behavioral Research, 1977, p. 57).

By demanding that an institution proposing to perform psychosurgical operations must conform to certain regulations regarding evaluation and review, the National Commission clearly intends to channel psychosurgery away from facilities that accommodate casual and poorly controlled practices.

Various authorities have proposed outlawing psychosurgery for particular classes of patient (e.g. Annas and Glantz, 1974; Chorover, 1974). Usually, it is argued that psychosurgery should not be permitted for involuntarily institutionalized individuals. By far the most influential advocacy for this style of selective ban arises from the ruling of the Wayne County Court, Detroit, in the 1973 case of Kaimowitz v. The Department of Mental Health.[2] While the decision of a lower court in the United States establishes only weak precedent, the ruling of the three judges in Wayne County is of some consequence. As Annas and Glantz (1974, p. 261) testify, 'Although this lower court opinion has no binding precedential effect in Michigan or any other jurisdiction, it is likely to influence future judicial and legislative activity if only because it is the first judicial pronouncement in this area.' For a detailed and critical account of the case and its implications, the reader is referred to Shuman's (1977) scholarly critique. The present treatment is necessarily brief.

The case arose from an application by Drs Robin and Gottlieb to examine the comparative efficacy of amygdalotomy and the drug cyproterome acetate in controlling violent and aggressive behaviour. Initially, it had been hoped that 24 subjects would be recruited, but only one person was deemed suitable. This candidate had been confined for 17 years in a Michigan State Hospital as a criminal sexual psychopath. Following the acquisition of consent, the subject was scheduled for electrode implantation as a diagnostic preliminary to surgery. However, before the researchers could proceed, Gabe Kaimowitz, a senior attorney for the Michigan medical Committee for Human Rights, brought suit to prevent the experiment. Although the subject subsequently recanted his consent and was discharged from hospital, and the Department of Health withdrew its approval for the project, the Wayne County Court considered that the case raised questions of permanent sigificance. Consequently, the three judges heard testimony from a variety of expert witnesses and set themselves the task of determining whether involuntarily confined patients could legally consent to participate in this sort of experiment.

The court ruled that psychosurgery for the amelioration of aggressive behaviour should be regarded as highly experimental. Having established the status of the operation, the court then ruled on the matter of consent, and concluded that the inherently coercive atmosphere of lengthy institutionalization reduces the involuntarily confined individual's independence and hence his or her competence to give rational and voluntary consent to a highly experimental venture. The experimental status of the procedure was viewed as undermining the knowledgeability requirement of consent.

It is important to appreciate that, in the court's determination, it is the combined or interactive effects of institutionalization and a highly experimental procedure that mitigated adequate consent. The court noted that its ruling did not prevent involuntarily confined individuals from giving adequate consent to neurological procedures or even amygdalotomy should it become an accepted, non-experimental treatment. This ruling that patient status and treatment status interact in the matter of consent has clearly puzzled a number of commentators. Annas and Glantz (1974, p. 262) exemplify: '... the court's reasoning seems contradictory. On the one hand, the court emphasized the effects of institutionalization on the capacity of the patient to give informed and voluntary consent. On the other hand, however, it limited its holding to experimental situations.' Shuman (1977) was equally critical of the court's ruling. There would seem to be a great deal of merit in the contention that a procedure is either sufficiently unpredictable and risky to suggest prohibition or it is not. The status of the patient would not seem to interact with this. Further, if consent is deemed a requirement for a particular treatment (emergency treatments may be exempted from the consent requirement), either the patient's status prevents adequate consent or it does not. In addition, as we argued earlier, it is important to distinguish between the patient's legal status as involuntary and his incompetence to consent. The two are not inevitably dependent. Rada (1974) indicated the reactionary nature of the Kaimowitz ruling in this respect: '... the progressive trend in mental health law has been to refute the concept of legal incompetence based solely on mental patient status (voluntary or involuntary), but the logical extension of the Kaimowitz ruling runs counter to that progressive trend' (Rada, 1974, p. 98). It is an ironic aspect of the Kaimowitz case that when the constitutionality of the subject's detention was challenged, he was released on the basis of expert testimony that he was competent to return to society. Thus the patient was ruled competent to leave hospital by one court while incompetent to give consent by another.

The Wayne County Court also ruled that proxy consent was legally inadequate in the matter of amygdalotomy. While it considered that proxy consent may be legally adequate when arising out of traditional therapeutic circumstances, it is legally ineffective in the case of psychosurgery. Stated simply, the court ruled that a proxy cannot do what the patient is legally unable to do.

The Kaimowitz ruling would seem fraught with difficulties. If a procedure mitigates adequate knowledgeability, it is difficult to see how the matter of proxy consent arises anyway. It should only arise when, given knowledgeability, patients' circumstances mitigate rationality, either through their intrinsic incapacities or through the coercive character of their surroundings. It is important to emphasize, however, that an adequately informed and sensitive proxy consent should never be permitted to over-rule patient dissent in instances where the patient's competence is compromised by a coercive environment.

The Wayne County Court also presented constitutional reasons for not permitting the subject's consent. The court argued that the First Amendment of the American Constitution, which guarantees freedom of speech, necessarily protects freedom of thought and mental processes and that psychosurgery, by interfering with mental processes, infringes on this constitutional freedom. The subject's consent was therefore seen as unacceptable. The constitutional barriers to consent established by the Kaimowitz case have been treated with notable scepticism (see Shuman, 1977, for a detailed discussion). As the National Commission (1977, p. 19) emphasized, 'A "conclusive or irrebuttable presumption" of incompetency would appear to conflict with First Amendment and privacy cases which require that individual rulings must be made on claims which involve infringement of fundamental rights.' In summary, then, this 'no consent' ruling would seem an unfortunate further infringement on those already poorly endowed with civil liberties.

As we indicated previously, it is important to distinguish between involuntarily confined mental patients and individuals institutionalized for other reasons, that is prisoners. While psychosurgery might be considered a legitimate part of the treatment package available to involuntary patients, it would seem entirely inappropriate for criminal, social, or political 'deviance'. Several psychosurgeons have, in fact, registered their disapproval of psychosurgery in these areas. Scoville (1973, p. 35) has undoubtedly been the most persistently explicit: 'I am alarmed by the present trend of questions asked us by both politicians and news reporters as to whether mental surgery will benefit criminals, rebels and social misfits. Mental surgery will never restore social conscience, character defects or infantile sexual arrest.'

Let us consider the case against psychosurgery on prisoners. First, it is worth emphasizing that psychosurgery is sustained by the assumption that some concealed cerebral dysfunction underlies particular patterns of disturbed behaviour. While inferences of cerebral pathology could constitute legitimate speculation when dealing with grossly disturbed psychotic behaviour, they are entirely unjustified in the area of criminal behaviour, where there now exists a convincing body of evidence demonstrating the overriding importance of complex social learning processes and the pervasive influence of social and cultural context (see Feldman, 1977).

Second, there is now a large backlog of experience (negative as well as positive) in the area of treating mental patients with psychosurgery. Substantial data have been gathered over the years. While much of these are suspect, they at least offer clues to effectiveness and risk. The use of psychosurgery on prison inmates can boast no such tradition. It possesses no data base to intimate effectiveness and risk. In addition, issues regarding experimental control and design, and evaluation, have at least received occasional rehearsal in the context of traditional psychosurgery. No such discussion has attended the matter of psychosurgery on prisoners. As Valenstein (1973, p. 349) indicated:

'There has been almost no discussion of the problem of evaluating the effectiveness of the psychosurgery within the limits of the confining institution. If a prisoner were to be subjected to brain surgery, how should he be tested before it is decided that the operation has been successful and it is safe to release the person into society?'

In conclusion, these two considerations, the existence of contrary theoretical indications and the absence of pertinent empirical data, reveal that psychosurgical operations on prisoners represent a highly experimental activity. Purely experimental psychosurgery is clearly deplorable. Prohibition would appear the appropriate recourse. It is important to appreciate that, in contrast to the Wayne County ruling, prohibition would be based solely on the highly experimental nature of procedures as they relate to this class of individual, that is prisoners. It is not premised on the issue of coercion. As such, our present submission is without implications regarding the matter of consent.

In view of current alarm, one particular subgroup of prisoners deserves special mention. These are political 'deviants' (revolutionaries and 'terrorists' are subsumed here). Given the prevailing political climates in countries such as the United States and Britain, this subgroup would at present appear an unlikely target for psychosurgical intervention. However, well reported practices in the Soviet Union demonstrate how readily psychiatric diagnosis and treatment can become instruments of political repression. The activities of Soviet psychiatrists should caution us against complacency. It was clearly with sociopolitical abuse in mind that the National Commission (1977, p. 58) stated, 'The Commission affirms that the use of psychosurgery for any purpose other than to provide treatment to individual patients would be inappropriate and should be prohibited.' The difficulty with this sort of pronouncement is that it affords the political dissident only marginal protection and does not, in fact, counter the more pernicious Soviet-style practices. By simply attributing politically inspired deviant behaviour to individual psychiatric pathology, treatment (including psychosurgery) is rendered acceptable. A more explicit formulation, prohibiting psychiatric intervention in cases of political deviance, would seem appropriate.

Children comprise another class of patient frequently deemed appropriate for special protection. Both Chorover (1974) and Older (1974), for example, have advocated that psychosurgery on children should be outlawed. While few formal submissions have explicitly addressed the issue of psychosurgery and children, the National Commission (1977) argued that patients under the legal age of consent be subject to regulations analogous to those proposed for involuntary patients; that is, psychosurgery may be performed but only after a favourable determination by the national Psychosurgery Advisory Board, a recommendation by an Institutional Review Board, and the approval of a court in which the patient had legal representation. The informed consent of both parents was considered necessary. However, the Commission conceded that it did not, in fact, review data relating to psychosurgery and children.

This certainly moderates their submission that psychosurgery should be permitted on children.

Had the Commission undertaken such a study, it might have uncovered two fairly persuasive arguments in favour of prohibiting psychosurgery on children. The first relates to differences in neural organization between children and adults; the second to behavioural differences.

Various authorities now attest that the functional organization of the brain is not static, but dynamic. In particular, neural organization changes dramatically during the course of development. The effects of brain damage on psychological processes is demonstrably dependent on the age of the brain damaged. Luria (1973) presented impressive evidence that the disruption of the same cerebral structures in chidren and adults has markedly different consequences. For example, while damage to primary sensory areas in adults has fairly circumscribed consequences for sensory processes, damage in the same region in children can result in the failure to elaborate the higher intellectual capacities that depend for their evolution on the early integrity of these primary processes. The general implications are clear enough. Because of the changing significance of cerebral structures during development, identical surgical lesions in adults and children can have markedly different consequences. As we have already seen, the behavioural effects of psychosurgical interventions in adults are far from perfectly predictable. The dynamic character of cerebral organization makes prediction even more difficult for children. In addition, the nature of the interdependence of cerebral structures in children intimates the very real possibility of stifling later higher development through psychosurgery, by excising its anatomical prerequisites.

The second argument against psychosurgery in the case of children concerns behavioural rather than neural fluidity. Stated simply, children have a far greater capacity for behavioural change and recovery than adults in the areas of emotional instability and social maladjustment. Highly disruptive children frequently emerge as competent and responsible adults, with no or only minimal formal therapeutic intervention. The distribution of 'hyperactivity' in children attests to this. 'Hyperactivity' is disproportionately frequent before the age of eight, becomes less frequent thereafter and is almost totally absent in children during their middle teens. Yet 'hyperactivity' is one of the main behavioural indications for psychosurgery in children. In summary, there appears to be a strong case for excluding children from psychosurgery.

The final style of partial ban mentioned involves the selective prohibition of particular psychosurgical procedures. Thus some psychosurgical procedures would be permitted, while others would be banned. Overall, this approach has much to commend it. It embodies an acknowledgment that psychosurgery comprises a collection of procedures of varying scientific status. It is a point missed by most of the prescriptions for regulating psychosurgery. The National Commission (1977) proposal, however, is a noteworthy exception.

Here, a national Psychosurgery Advisory Board would be charged with determining whether any 'specific psychosurgical procedure has demonstrable benefit for the treatment of an individual with the psychiatric symptom of disorder of the patient'. It is clearly implied that the Advisory Board might find some procedures acceptable, that is having demonstrable benefit, and others not. A list of those not, at present, meeting even the least stringent requirements is likely to include, for example, amygdalotomy, thalamotomy, prefrontal leucotomy, and rostral leucotomy (see O'Callaghan and Carroll, 1982).

CONCLUSION

Our present analysis strongly favours the vigilant and assiduous regulation of psychosurgery. Of the models considered a broad-based review committee, servicing a group of hospitals, rather than anchored at one institution, would seem to provide maximum patient protection without unduly stultifying research. The committee would deliberate on both the ethical and scientific merits of any psychosurgical proposal, as well as assuring that less drastic therapeutic intervention had already been exhausted. However, by itself, in the absence of back-up in the form of firm and unambiguous guidelines, a broad-based committee is likely to prove inadequate. Thus some additional and superordinate regulatory medium is required. As Annas and Glantz (1974, p. 267) indicated,

'Our experience with multidisciplinary committees, however, is so limited that we must guard against their becoming a mechanism merely serving a legitimizing function on the basis of inadequate consideration. The criteria they employ and the decisions they reach should receive constant scrutiny to assure that the rights of patients are being protected.'

The prior provision of criteria to the review committee would seem preferable to *post hoc* monitoring. Two mechanisms suggest themselves here.

First of all, legislation could be enacted to curtail certain practices. Psychosurgery on children and prisoners would seem appropriate areas for legislative prohibition. Similarly, psychosurgery could be prohibited in institutions that fail to conform to the highest standards in terms of surgical skill and evaluative expertise.

A national Psychosurgery Advisory Board offers a second mechanism for guiding the deliberations of broad-based review committees. Elaborating the National Commission's proposal, an advisory board would concern itself with the following: collating and evaluating data from psychosurgical studies; advising review committees on the theoretical and empirical status of any particular psychosurgical procedure; providing pertinent research summaries and bibliographies; indicating the types of alternative treatments available; establishing firm guidelines regarding the conduct of proposed psychosurgery (particularly in matters of design and pre- and post-operative assessment), in order to maximize the quality of the advisory board's data base. This last matter should be nationally directed and not, as the National Commission proposes, left to local wisdom. Thus the status of psychosurgical procedures would attract continuous and co-ordinated review with guidelines modified accordingly. The facility for on-going amendment embodied in this mechanism is not readily available with formal legislative control. It should be stressed that a national Psychosurgery Advisory Board would not determine the merits of individual proposals. The onus for such decision-making would rest with the broad-based review committees.

Finally, broad-based review would also be charged with establishing the validity of consent. Again it should proceed from explicit guidelines. Here, however, a national Psychosurgery Advisory Board would seem an inappropriate mechanism, since the issues surrounding consent are of general significance and not simply matters pertaining to psychosurgery. A special commission to establish principles governing consent would seem worthwhile, given that there is little existing consensus.

In the absence of such a body, however, the following guidance might be offered. The broad-based review committee must ensure that consent is both knowledgeable and rational. If it is deemed irrational, then a proxy should be appointed; the capacity for proxy consent would normally rest with the next of kin. Involuntarily committed patients should not be excluded from the consent process simply because of their involuntary legal status. The review committee must determine in a particular case whether the patient's psychological condition is sufficiently disordered or the prevailing environmental circumstances are sufficiently coercive to undermine rationality. In the event of such a determination, proxy consent would again seem the appropriate recourse. Finally, in such cases, therapy should never proceed against the patient's wishes; that is proxy consent should never be allowed to override patient dissent.

NOTES

1. The Mental Health (Amendment) Bill (November, 1981), which stemmed from this White Paper, restricts its consideration to involuntary patients. At the time of writing, the Bill is in the committee stage and as such is itself liable to amendment. As it stands, however, the Bill recognizes three categories of treatment which vary in their requirements regarding regulation. Its provisions for psychosurgery depend on the category to which psychosurgery is allocated. The Bill is unfortunately far from explicit in this respect. If psychosurgery is to be accorded only mid-category status,

treatment can proceed either with the patient's consent, where only the treating physician need verify that the patient is capable of consent and that consent has been given, or without consent, where a physician appointed for the purpose by the Secretary of State has certified that the patient is not capable of consenting or has not consented but that treatment should be given nonetheless. If, however, psychosurgery is to be formally specified as an instance of the 'most serious treatments', and it is possible that when the Bill emerges from committee this will be the case, then more stringent provisions would apply. In essence, treatments in this category would only be permitted on involuntarily detained patients where an independent physician, again appointed for the purpose, has certified that the patient is capable of consenting (and has, in fact, consented) and that the treatment should be given. A press release (DHSS 1982) hints at a change here; a three-person review panel, of whom only one is a medical doctor, may replace the appointed physician as second opinion in such matters. It should be noted that this is certainly more in line with the spirit of the White Paper.

2. Kaimowitz v. Department of Mental Health for the State of Michigan, *Prison Law Reporter*, **2**, 433–480, 1973.

REFERENCES

ANONYMOUS, (1949). Editorial. *Stanford Law Review*, **1**, 474.

ANNAS, G. J., and GLANTZ, L. H. (1974). Psychosurgery: the law's response. *Boston University Law Review*, **54**, 249–267.

BREGGIN, P. R. (1972). The return of lobotomy and psychosurgery. *Congressional Record*, **118** (24 February), E1602–E1612.

CARROLL, D., and O'CALLAGHAN, M. A. J. (1981). Psychosurgery and the control of aggression. In P. F. Brown and D. Benton (Eds), *The Biology of Aggression*. Alphen an den Rijn, Netherlands: Sijthoff and Noordhoff.

CHOROVER, S. L. (1974). Psychosurgery: a neuropsychological perspective. *Boston University Law Review*, **54**, 231–248.

DHSS (1978). *Government Review of the Mental Health Act 1959*. London: Her Majesty's Stationery Office.

DHSS (1982). Consent to treatment by detained mentally disordered patients. Press release, May 1982.

EDGAR, H. (1975). Regulating psychosurgery: issues of public policy and law. In W. M. Gaylin, J. S. Meister, and R. C. Neville (Eds), *Operating on the Mind*. New York: Basic Books.

ERVIN, F. R. (1977). The American experience. In J. S. Smith and L. G. Kiloh (Eds), *Psychosurgery and Society*. Oxford: Pergamon Press.

FELDMAN, M. P. (1977). *Criminal Behaviour: A Psychological Analysis*. Chichester: Wiley.

KING, P. A. (1977). Dissenting statement of Commissioner Patricia A. King. In National Commission for the Protection of Human Subjects of Biological and

Behavioral Research, *Psychosurgery.* Washington, D.C.: US Department of Health, Education and Welfare.

LURIA, A. R. (1973). *The Working Brain.* Harmondsworth: Penguin.

MADDISON, J. C. (1977). The legal aspects of psychosurgery in New South Wales. In J. S. Smith and L. G. Kiloh (Eds), *Psychosurgery and Society.* Oxford: Pergamon Press.

MEISTER, J. S. (1975). The need for policy. In W. M. Gaylin, J. S. Meister, and R. C. Neville (Eds), *Operating on the Mind.* New York: Basic Books.

NATIONAL COMMISSION FOR THE PROTECTION OF HUMAN SUBJECTS OF BIOMEDICAL AND BEHAVIORAL RESEARCH (1977). *Psychosurgery.* Washington, D.C.: Department of Health, Education and Welfare.

O'CALLAGHAN, M. A. J., and CARROLL, D. (1982). *Psychosurgery: A Scientific Analysis.* Lancaster: Medical and Technical Press.

OFFIR, C. W. (1974). Psychosurgery and the law. *Psychology Today, 7,* 69–70.

OLDER, J. (1974). Psychosurgery: ethical issues and a proposal for control. *American Journal of Orthopsychiatry, 44,* 661–674.

RADA, R. T. (1974). Psychosurgery and the psychiatric implications of the Kaimowitz case. *Bulletin of the American Academy of Psychiatry and the Law, 11,* 96–100.

SCOVILLE, W. B. (1973). Surgical locations for psychiatric surgery with special reference to orbital and cingulate operations. In L. V. Laitinen and K. E. Livingston (Eds), *Surgical Approaches in Psychiatry.* Lancaster: Medical and Technical Press.

SHUMAN, S. I. (1977). *Psychosurgery and the Medical Control of Violence: Autonomy and Deviance.* Detroit: Wayne State University Press.

STONE, A. A. (1975). Psychosurgery in Massachusetts: a task force report. *Massachusetts Journal of Mental Health, 5,* 25–46.

VALENSTEIN, E. S. (1973). *Brain Control: A Critical Examination of Brain Stimulation and Psychosurgery.* New York: Wiley.

WINKLER, R. (1977). Current psychosurgery in Australia: local concerns. In J. S. Smith and L. G. Kiloh (Eds), *Psychosurgery and Society.* Oxford: Pergamon Press.

WORTIS, J. (1972). Lobotomy and the law. *Biological Psychiatry, 5,* 99–100.

Psychology and Law
Edited by D.J. Müller, D.E. Blackman, and A.J. Chapman
© 1984 John Wiley & Sons Ltd

Chapter 28

Retribution and the Definition of a Just Measure of Pain

Hugh J. Haley

The concept of rehabilitation has been increasingly emphasized by the criminal justice system for the last 20 – 30 years. More recently the centrality of this idea in correctional and sentencing policy has been strongly criticized, not only for failing to meet its lofty aspirations (Bailey, 1966; Brody, 1976; Greenberg, 1977; Lipton, Martinson, and Wilks, 1975; Martinson, 1974; Robinson and Smith, 1971), but, perhaps more importantly, for the perceived injustices derived from its enthusiastic implementation (American Friends Service Committee, 1971; Fogel, 1975, 1978; Morris, 1974; Von Hirsch, 1976). This rejection has resulted in the re-examination of sentencing policy with an accompanying re-emphasis on the more traditional models of retribution (Von Hirsch, 1976), general deterrence (Andenaes, 1966, 1974, 1975), denunciation (Law Reform Commission of Canada, 1974), and incapacitation (Van den Haag, 1975; Wilson, 1975). Because of a complete reversal from a dependence on rehabilitation towards these more traditional sentencing models, an examination of the logical implications and empirical support for each of these models in a modern criminal justice system now appears warranted. The growing tendency within North America to adopt a retributive model for determining the length of prison terms makes a detailed assessment of this model particularly important. This chapter will therefore undertake an analysis of the retributive model, not only to clarify the ramifications of its adoption, but also to illustrate how similar analyses can be applied to other proposed sentencing rationales.

Historically, one of the earliest forms of criminal sanctions was a defined amount of corporal punishment that was to be administered according to the harm caused by the offence. These sanctions, which were most often justified by retribution, were eventually rejected because of their cruelty, and prison terms, which appeared to be more humane, gradually replaced physical punishment as the principal criminal sanction. The use of prison, however, evolved in parallel to the development of the rehabilitative model, and changing the offender's behaviour was increasingly emphasized as the primary correctional objective (Fogel, 1975; Foucault, 1977; Ignatieff, 1978; King, Morgan, Martin, and Thomas, 1980). With such an emphasis on the offender's personality, rather than the offence, the length of time needed for behavioural change began to be increasingly important in the determination of the length of prison sentences. This resulted in cases, noticeably in the USA, in which relatively minor offences received longer sentences than more serious crimes because of the perceived need to contain the offender long enough to receive necessary treatment. In extreme cases, the length of imprisonment was no longer determined by the courts but by the discretionary decisions of correctional personnel who decided when the offender had received the required amount of treatment and could be safely released.

A retributive model has been advocated as an alternative means to determine the length of prison terms for serious offences without apparent injustice or administrative difficulties (American Friends Service Committee, 1971; Von Hirsch, 1976). The adoption of this suggestion would result in retribution providing the reasons for the amount of punishment, with the form of the punishment itself being the sanction that evolved within the rehabilitative era. Through this proposal, different aspects of two apparently opposing models have re-emerged as a rationale for modern criminal sanctions. A test of this new model's adequacy would necessitate an assessment of the ramifications of its adoption on all levels of the criminal justice system, including not only criminal legislation and the judiciary but also the correctional system. While it is probably unrealistic to expect that this or any opposing model will be completely adopted, the use of such models to simplify extremely complex social policy and programme issues should have broad-ranging practical ramifications in demonstrating the importance of issues or concerns that might otherwise be overlooked.

THE RETRIBUTIVE SENTENCING MODEL

Advocates of a retributive sentencing structure argue that punishment should be determined solely by the seriousness of the offence. In their view, when the period of time necessary to change an offender's behaviour is emphasized, similar crimes are responded to differently on the assumption of future events which can never be positively validated. In contrast, when there is a clear connection between an offence and its punishment, apparently arbitrary judicial and correctional discretion is eliminated. Historically, the clearest example of this was in the law of Talion, where the punishment was a settling of accounts and was therefore equivalent to the harm done to the victim. The extent to which the offender could be punished, as well as the limit to which the state was justified in imposing punishment, was thereby determined by an equation between harm and punishment. Under this rationale, a sentencing strategy whereby the amount of punishment is determined solely by the offence is seen to be more just than one that considers the personality of the offender. It is argued, therefore, that modern sentencing and correctional practice should determine the length of imprisonment on the basis of the seriousness of the offence rather than by the likelihood of the offender committing further crimes.

In order to examine the logical conclusions of this retributive model of sentencing, each side of the equation between harm done and length of imprisonment must be examined. While neither of these issues has been adequately explored, the determination of guilt has received relatively more attention through the development of criminal codes and traditional procedures and practices (Sherman and Hawkins, 1981). In this way, reasonably satisfactory normative definitions have developed as to the seriousness of various criminal behaviours. For this reason, the proposed model might require few major modifications to this side of the equation. In contrast, the rehabilitation model was often perceived to be incompatible with the infliction of punishment, with the result that there has been very little attention to the question of what type and degree of sanction would reflect the harm done by different types of criminal behaviour. The resulting shift in emphasis away from punishment to effective behavioural change made it unnecessary to consider the appropriate amount of pain that would result from imprisonment. In reintroducing the issue of a just amount of pain or discomfort, as the consequence of an offence, a retributive model requires that society establish a scale of punishment proportionate to the amount of blame or harm done by the offender. A logical connection between the crime and the punishment, such as theoretically existed in *lex talionis*, is not readily available to a modern criminal justice system. The adequacy of a retributive sentencing structure will then largely depend upon the extent to which it is able to define the sentence of imprisonment as a just punishment.

Von Hirsch (1976) suggests that the punishment side of the equation can be completed by defining the maximum sentence that would be required to attain the utilitarian goal of general deterrence for the most severe offences. Less severe sentences could be graduated accordingly. In this way, equitable sentences could be determined by legislation with the result that there would be little if any requirement for discretionary judgment by the judiciary in the determination of culpability, or by the correctional authorities in the administration of the prison term. This suggestion rests on several assumptions which have little empirical support. One of these is that more serious crimes, such as murder, can be deterred by severe sanctions. In fact, little is known about the effect of increasing the severity of sanctions on the rate of crime (Fattah, 1976; Tittle, 1973; Zimring and Hawkins, 1973) and this limited understanding suggests that deterrence is relatively ineffective for many of our serious offences (Baxter and Nuttall, 1975). Another assumption is that equal units of time in prison are perceived by the general public to be equivalent to equal degrees of pain or discomfort. Knowledge in this area is, if anything, more limited than in the area of deterrence, but it is generally accepted that the public's knowledge of incarceration is severly limited. While additional empirical work is warranted, the possibility of calculating the effectiveness of different lengths of imprisonment on general deterrence appears limited, which suggests that this is not a practical measurement of just punishment.

Von Hirsch's solution is not only impractical because of lack of support of a clear relationship between punishment for serious crimes and general deterrence, it can also be challenged because it reintroduces the possibility of abuse that the retributive model attempts to eliminate. The removal of inequity does not eliminate injustice if the system might still impose extremely severe sentences for all offences, or even at one extreme of the offence-seriousness scale. Sentencing structures would still be unjust if they imposed punishments that were perceived to be disproportionally harsh in relation to the crime committed. Ideally, retribution would establish limits to the pursuit of utilitarian objectives, such as general deterrence, by restricting the severity of the punishment by the seriousness of the criminal offence (Morris, 1974; Packer, 1968; Ruby, 1968; Thomas, 1979; Weiler, 1974). The determination of a just amount of punishment cannot, therefore, be ultimately dependent upon an utilitarian objective, but must be determined by the severity of the offence itself. Since it is doubtful that a logical connection could be made between many of the offences in the criminal code and their punishment, it appears that the punishment side of a retributive equation will be ultimately dependent upon a normative process similar to that which provided society's definition of the relative seriousness of offences. Information on the deterrent effect of imprisonment will, no doubt, influence such a normative process, but a more important aspect will be the effect of various lengths of imprisonment as perceived by society and as experienced by the inmate. This suggests that social policy makers will have to define the appropriate degree of pain for different degrees of harm performed by the offender. The ramifications of a modern retributive sentencing model will therefore be largely dependent upon our social system's understanding and tolerance of the amount of punishment inflicted on offenders by modern criminal sanctions.

DEFINING THE PAIN OF IMPRISONMENT

The return to a consideration of the just amount of pain to be inflicted on offenders is a major shift from more recent criminal justice thought. Under the rehabilitative ideal, criminal sanctions consisted of the removal of those rights and liberties for the period of time that was necessary to contain offenders temporarily while changing their behaviour. Since pain was both unnecessary and incompatible with these objectives, its importance gradually declined as these sanctions developed. A de-emphasis of punishment in criminal sanctions was also assisted by a progressive recognition that the conviction and sentencing of offenders does not involve a complete denial of their citizenship status. These combined influences have culminated in defining the punitive aspects of imprisonment as the deprivation of free movement and in obliging correctional authorities to avoid any aggravation of the prisoner's suffering beyond what is implicitly or explicitly derived from that deprivation (Jobson, 1978; United Nations, 1958). The result is that any negative effects from prison environments are seen as an unjust infringement of an offender's remaining rights, much in the same way that earlier corporal punishments were viewed as excessively harsh. Inmate rights codes and advocated improvements of prison environments have stressed these negative effects and prison programmes have been implemented to remove them. Acknowledgments of such effects, or even their possibility, have led to the search for alternatives to prison, with the result that imprisonment is now advocated only for selected types of offender. However, in implicitly rejecting all negative effects of the sanction, this orientation is inconsistent with a retributive rationale which advocates that the inmate deserves a just amount of punishment and, as such, is meant to suffer some pain or discomfort. A retributive model would acknowledge that some of the unpleasant effects of prison are, at the very least, an accepted consequence of imprisonment.

A return to a strictly retributive model would have particularly broad ramifications for correctional practice. Because modern criminal sanctions involve holding offenders for long periods of time, it has been necessary to develop complex correctional bureaucracies to administer these sanctions. Until recently relatively, little attention has been given to the manner in which the sanction is to be administered. This was not a major issue while containment and rehabilitation were valid sentencing objectives because administrative discretion on such issues as the appropriate type of prison environment for different types of inmates and their placement in particular institutional programmes were determined by the combined needs to contain offenders temporarily while permanently redirecting their criminal behaviours. If a retributive model is to replace containment and rehabilitation, it will be necessary to re-examine the manner in which correctional authorities are to enforce the punitive sanction of imprisonment (Haley, 1982; Haley and Lerette, 1981; King et al., 1980).

If correctional authorities were not to consider containment or rehabilitation, administration of the sanction would simply consist of the enforcement of an imposed deprivation of free movement. Such principles as Rule 57 of the UN Standard Minimum Rules for the Treatment of Prisoners (United

Nations, 1958), as well as common law interpretations (Jobson, 1978), hold that this restriction of liberty is sufficiently afflictive to meet the punitive ends of imprisonment. Lacking any other direction, the removal of self-determination will therefore require holding the offender in either the prison environment, or under some form of control, for a specific period of time in a manner prescribed by law. Any additional negative effects caused by the prison environment might then be considered as unjustified punishment which correctional authorities would be obliged to remove. There would appear to be a point, however, when the removal of the negative consequences of imprisonment would lead to the establishment of a prison environment incompatible with the punitive intent of the sanction. Social policy makers would therefore have to define more clearly the conditions under which offenders are to be contained in order to ensure that the punitive intent of the sanction is maintained.

It is commonly acknowledged that prison environments do involve negative consequences for the inmate. Some of these, such as extreme threats to personal safety (Bailey and Cohen, 1976) or greater exposure to suicide (Burch and Ericson 1979; Ross and McKay, 1979), are clearly unintended, but their documentation is often inconclusive, so that the extent to which they might be a tolerable consequence of imprisonment is not clearly understood. For example, research demonstrating that assaults are actually lower within prison environments than among citizens of similar sex and age (Sylvester, Reed, and Nelson, 1977) does not necessarily remove the responsibility for correctional officers to improve inmates safety. The fear of assault (Hamburger, 1967; Toch, 1975), as well as the potential for unique forms of injury such as occur in riots or hostage taking, still exist in the prison environment. Since the total removal of the possibility of injury is impractical even in free society, what degree of restriction is justified to reduce the incidence of such events within a prison environment? If it is acknowledged that prisoners should not be exposed to physical danger, when does the need to prevent offenders from harming one another conflict with the right of the general inmate population, or individual members of it, to have social contacts and freedom of movement within the institution? This need to balance the general good with the individual's freedom is the same issue as exists for the general criminal justice system (Packer, 1968), but what is that particular balance within an institutional setting for a population of individuals who have lost the right to free association as punishment for their criminal conduct? The recognition of the need to protect the inmate from extreme security restrictions has led to advocacy for just procedures within institutions to control discretion (Fogel, 1978), but due process procedures developed for society are not necessarily transferable to the institutional environment. Before policy makers can define the appropriate balance between institutional control and the individual offender's rights, the dynamics of the prison and behaviour within it must be better understood.

Physical safety, while perhaps most dramatic, is not the only negative effect of imprisonment that requires a greater understanding. Even if it was acknowledged that prison environments should and could be physically safe and comfortable, the same issues arise in considering the effect on offenders of removing them from the general society. For example, while there is little empirical evidence that such deterioration actually occurs (Bukstel and Kilmann, 1980; McKay, Jayewardene, and Reedie, 1979), there is striking anecdotal evidence that long-term offenders will retain strong fears that the social isolation of imprisonment will cause psychological deterioration (Cohen and Taylor, 1972). There is also empirical evidence indicating that adaptation to the prison environment (Clemmer, 1940) disrupts the normal maturational processes characteristic of Western culture such as career development, accumulation of economic benefits, establishment of family units, and preparation for retirement. This, combined with the destruction of normal social ties (Cohen and Taylor, 1972; Schneller, 1975), not only causes psychological pain but also places a released inmate in a disadvantageous position. However, maintaining such social ties with families, who themselves are experiencing considerable difficulty in coping with the experience of one of their member's imprisonment (Freidman and Esselstyn, 1965; Morris, 1965) may be as much, if not more painful, than breaking them. The establishment, or maintenance, of non-familial social contacts is probably more difficult. Furthermore, these obvious concrete consequences of imprisonment may not be as painful as the more subtle psychological pains of living in custodial environments. A considerable amount of recent psychological research indicates that the perception of freedom is central to human functioning (Harvey, 1976; Lefcourt, 1976; Rotter, 1966; Wortman and Brehm, 1975). This suggests that the removal of freedom may be the most painful part of prison experience. However, research under the general topic of freedom represents several unrelated theoretical orientations and our understanding of the experience of freedom, as well as the psychological effects of its loss, remains limited (Ferguson, Katzko, and Rule, 1979; Westcott, 1977, 1978, 1980).

These examples demonstrate that, while we do not understand the full effects of imprisonment, the need to measure the just amount of pain for a retributive sentencing model raises serious policy issues that were less salient under the containment–rehabilitative paradigm. The subjective nature of the experience of living in a modern penitentiary (Toch, 1977), makes it extremely difficult to determine the amount of pain inflicted by a number of years in prison. Modern societies have rejected the use of the extreme physical suffering of various forms of torture, as well as the humiliation of public ridicule, but it is almost impossible for someone who has never lived a comparable experience to understand the psychological pain of years of imprisonment. This difficulty is greatest for those social groups who have limited first-hand exposure to the experience. This is particularly relevant because inmates tend to be from lower socioeconomic segments of society, while middle and upper income groups are the major contributors to social policy. Since these latter groups have restricted contact with both offenders and their families, their attitudes may easily be distorted toward a perception of imprisonment as either too harsh or too lenient. Without any stable criteria of what happens to offenders as a consequence of punishment, there is a danger of either extreme positions or vacillation in social policy of what constitutes a just amount of punishment. If this is to be counteracted, it will be necessary to neutralize adversarial conflict between concerns for the welfare of convicted offenders and the need that they be justly punished. In the ideal, this would be most effectively accomplished by an objective scientific assessment documenting the effects on the offender of our modern sanctions. To the degree that this can be practically attained, social policy will be better able to enunciate the appropriate kind and amount of pain for particular types and conditions of criminal conduct.

In order to determine a just amount of punishment, criminal justice policy would have to stipulate the number of years of imprisonment appropriate for specific types of crime and for particular incidents of criminal behaviour. This is difficult because the responsibility for determining the just amount of punishment is shared by several jurisdictions. The number of years of imprisonment appropriate for different types of criminal conduct is broadly defined in legislation. The judiciary is then responsible for not only determining the guilt of the offender, but also for interpreting the legislation by stipulating a sentence according to the details of the particular offence and individual offender. The appropriate amount of punishment is therefore defined by these two jurisdictions and corrections is responsible for enforcing the prescribed sanction. This will require that the appropriate punishment be clearly defined by legislation or the judiciary. Corrections, however, because of responsibility to administer the sanction is the criminal justice agency that is best able effectively to monitor over time the effects of that punishment (Haley and Lerette, 1981). These differences between jurisdictions, in both their responsibility for determining the punishment and their understanding of the effects of the sanction, may explain why some legal authorities have believed that the punishment of imprisonment might be simply and consistently measured by the number of years of confinement. If the legislative and judicial functions of the criminal justice system are to be able to define explicitly both the length and the conditions of the sentence, they will need to have as complete an understanding of the effects of these punishments as do those individuals who are responsible for administrating them.

The currently limited understanding of the consequences to the offender of spending different lengths of time in confinement makes it difficult for correctional authorities, let alone legislators or jurors, to define the length of imprisonment that would be a just punishment for different types of crime. Further research documenting the effect of various lengths of imprisonment might allow social policy makers to define sentence lengths that more closely approximate the just amount of punishment. It is doubtful, however, that there is any clear relationship between length of confinement and its effects, without considering the various conditions under which convicted offenders are retained. To the extent that the effect of various lengths of confinement may be influenced by different types of prison environment, it will be necessary to consider the conditions of confinement in the pronouncement of the sentence. This will require legislative and judicial decisions that define not only the length of imprisonment but also the conditions under which they expect correctional authorities to enforce the retributive intention of the sanction. They cannot effectively do this unless they are better informed about the effects of these sanctions. It therefore appears that to the extent that the criminal justice system moves towards a strictly retributive sentencing structure, corrections will have an obligation to monitor the effects of various lengths and conditions of confinement. Since, however, the present restrictions on their administration of punishment forbids their modification of the punitive intent of the sanction, they would not be able to adjust the terms of the sentence unilaterally. This would require that the discretionary enforcement of the punitive intent of the sanction be retained either by the sentencing authorities or by some other semi-judicial authority other than those who administer the punishment.

In North America advocates of a retributive model of sentencing, such as Von Hirsch, have argued that this model would eliminate many abuses caused by the discretionary modification of the punitive intent of the sanction. This argument, however, overlooks the fact that a retributive model requires that the punishment experienced by offenders be proportional to their crime, so that any individual differences in the pain experienced under similar conditions of imprisonment would have to be somehow neutralized (Fattah, 1982). The limited amount of research which indicates that inmates perceive various lengths and conditions of confinement differently (Bukstel and Kilmann, 1980; Toch 1977), makes this individual enforcement of punishment particularly difficult. If the subjective dimension of the pain of imprisonment is to be considered, as a truly retributive model would require, it would be necessary to take it into consideration at the time of sentencing. This might require correctional experts to advise the judiciary of the likely consequences of various sentences. It is highly unlikely, however, than an individual's response to a term of imprisonment will be fully known until it is actually experienced. Procedures would then be required to monitor and then adapt the punishment as the offender passes through the term of imprisonment. This might be accomplished by a judicial or semi-judicial body, but, although it might result in greater visibility and control of discretion, it would not eliminate it. In carrying a retributive sentencing structure to its logical conclusions, therefore, discretion would still remain, and the procedural complexities of the administration of punishment would be increased. The actual extent of that increased complexity will not be known until there is a greater undertanding of the effects of our punishments.

CONCLUSION

The extent to which definitive lengths of incarceration would be appropriate punishments for different types and degrees of criminal behaviour depends upon the actual effects of different lengths and conditions of imprisonment. Although the knowledge of what happens to offenders when they are placed in prison environments for various lengths of time is limited, there are strong indications that adoption of various lengths of imprisonment as just punishment for different degrees of serious criminal behaviour will not be as administratively simple as proponents of this model appear to suggest. Adoption of a truly retributive model will require closer monitoring of the consequences of placing offenders in a prison environment and the development of procedures to establish norms of what would be considered appropriate punishment within the prison model for different types of criminal conduct. Furthermore, since an individual's response to imprisonment will probably be unique and variable over time, an adjustment mechanism throughout the term of the sentence to ensure a just application of punishment will be required. Acknowledgment of these facts would require the retention of administrative arrangements similar to existing pre-sentence reporting and parole release. A retributive model carried to its logical conclusion, therefore, will not be likely to have the expected effect on the discretionary determination of individual sentences, and it is doubtful that efforts to change administrative procedures as presently exist in sentencing and parole practices can be justified.

If a retributive rationale was carried to its ultimate conclusions, there might not only be minimal impact on the discretionary administration of the sanction, but it could also have long-term social and moral consequences. While the impact to a social system of a preoccupation with punishment is unknown, the ethical issues raised by the practical ramifications of adopting a purely retributive paradigm should be evident. The administration of physical pain is no longer accepted as justified punishment for wrong doing, but it is doubtful that a comparable degree of suffering cannot result from the psychological experience of imprisonment. If corrections becomes primarily concerned with ensuring that it delivers a just amount of punishment, this would probably result in a major reorientation on the part of correctional practitioners away from the concern for the needs of the offender that was at least sometimes evident under the rehabilitative model. One might expect a similar result from the research on the effects of imprisonment if the documentation of pain becomes an end in itself. The negative consequences of a society developing an insensitivity to inflicting physical pain have been emphasized in arguments to eliminate sanctions such as flogging or capital punishment. There is no reason to believe that insensitivities to psychological suffering could not develop as easily as expected for physical pain. Any social system which is concerned for the development of humane sanctions must be careful not to substitute visible pain for a more subtle but equally cruel sanction. The return to a strictly retributive model could result in the criminal justice system unintentionally adopting policies that are substantially similar to those which were rejected in very early attempts to humanize criminal sanctions.

A careful assessment of any simple sentencing model has to acknowledge that sanctions serve a multitude of purposes, all of which must be carefully balanced (Packer, 1968; Ruby, 1968). A simplistic retributive model clearly does not acknowledge the complexity of true justice (Fattah, 1982), but it does demonstrate needs and objectives that were de-emphasized under a rehabilitative/containment paradigm. A recognition that criminal sanctions are ultimately punitive provides an appropriate limitation on the rights of society to punish. The extent of this right cannot be enunciated, however, unless the real consequences of modern sanctions are clearly understood. Before policy makers could determine a balance between the needs of the individual offender and the rights of society to incarcerate offenders, the psychological suffering caused by the imposition of imprisonment must be documented. A similar argument could be made for less severe sanctions such as probation or community service orders. A careful assessment of the theoretical sentencing model of retribution not only sets limits on society's right to punish but requires society to understand what actually happens to offenders when different types and degrees of punishment are inflicted upon them. It must therefore be acknowledged that while retribution may be inadequate as a model of sentencing, it is a vital concept for a just criminal system.

REFERENCES

AMERICAN FRIENDS SERVICE COMMITTEE (1971). *Struggle for Justice*. New York: Hill and Wang.

ANDENAES, J. (1966). The general preventative effects of punishment. *University of Pennsylvania Law Review*, **114**, 949–983.

ANDENAES, J. (1974). *Punishment and Deterrence*. Ann Arbor, Mich.: University of Michigan Press.

ANDENAES, J. (1975). General prevention revisited: research and policy implications. *Journal of Criminal Law and Criminology*, **66**, 338–365.

BAILEY, R. S., and COHEN, A. K. (1976). *Prison Violence*. Lexington Mass.: D. C. Heath.

BAILEY, W. C. (1966). Correctional outcome: an evaluation of 100 reports. *Journal of Criminal Law, Criminology and Police Science*, **57**, 153–160.

BAXTER, R., and NUTTALL, C. (1975). Severe sentences: no deterrent to crime? *New Society*, **31**, 11–13.

BRODY, S. R. (1976). *The Effectiveness of Sentencing – A Review of the Literature.* London: Home Office Research Unit.

BUKSTEL, L. H., and KILMANN, P. R. (1980). Psychological effects of imprisonment on confined individuals. *Psychological Bulletin,* **88,** 469–493.

BURCH, B. E., and ERICSON, R. V. (1979). *The Silent System: An Inquiry into Prisoners who Suicide and Annotated Bibliography.* Toronto: University of Toronto Centre of Criminology.

CLEMMER, D. (1940). *The Prison Community.* Boston, Mass.: Christopher Publishing House.

COHEN S., and TAYLOR, L. (1972). *Psychological Survival: The Experience of Long Term Imprisonment.* Harmondsworth: Penguin.

FATTAH, E. A. (1976). Deterrence: a review of the literature. In Law Reform Commission of Canada, *Fear of Punishment.* Ottawa: Ministry of Supply and Services.

FATTAH, E. A. (1982). Making the punishment fit the crime – the case of imprisonment. Problems inherent in the use of imprisonment as a retributive sanction. *Canadian Journal of Criminology,* **24,** 1–12.

FERGUSON, T. J., and KATZKO, M. W., and RULE, B. G. (1979). The influence of the perception of control on the correctional experience: a literature review. Unpublished manuscript, Ministry of the Solicitor General, Ottawa.

FOGEL, D. (1975). *We Are the Living Proof: The Justice Model for Corrections.* Cincinnati: Anderson.

FOGEL, D. (1978). The justice model of corrections. In J. C. Freeman (Ed), *Prisons, Past and Future.* London: Heinemann.

FOUCAULT, M. (1977). *Discipline and Punishment: The Birth of the Prison.* New York: Pantheon Books.

FREIDMAN, S., and ESSELSTYN, C. T. (1965). The adjustment of children of jail inmates. *Federal Probation,* **28,** 55–59.

GREENBERG, D. F. (1977). The correctional effects of corrections: a survey of evaluation. In D. F. Greenberg (Ed), *Corrections and Punishment.* Beverly Hills, Calif.: Sage.

HALEY, H. J. (1982). Correctional effectiveness: an elusive concept. *Canadian Journal of Criminology,* **24,** 205–219.

HALEY, H. J., and LERETTE, P. (1981). *Correctional Objectives: A Set of Canadian Options.* Ottawa: Ministry of the Solicitor General.

HAMBURGER, E. (1967). The penitentiary and paranoia. *Correctional Psychiatry and Journal of Social Therapy,* **13,** 225–230.

HARVEY, J. H. (1976). Attribution of freedom. In J. H. Harvey, W. J. Ickes, and R. F. Kidd (Eds), *New Directions in Attribution Research I.* Hillsdale, N. J.: Lawrence Erlbaum.

IGNATIEFF, M. (1978). *A Just Measure of Pain: The Penitentiary in the Industrial Revolution 1750–1850.* New York: Partheon Books.

JOBSON, R. B. (1978). The inmate as a citizen. *International Journal of Offender Therapy and Comparative Criminology,* **22,** 164–178.

KING, R. D., MORGAN, R., MARTIN, J. P., and THOMAS, J. E. (1980). *The Future of the Prison System.* Farnborough, Hampshire: Gower Press.

LAW REFORM COMMISSION OF CANADA (1974). The principles of sentencing and dispositions. In Law Reform Commission of Canada, *Studies on Sentencing,* Working Paper No. 3. Ottawa: Information Canada.

LEFCOURT, H. M. (1976). *Locus of Control: Current Trends in Theory and Research.* Hillsdale, N. J.: Lawrence Erlbaum.

LIPTON, D., MARTINSON, R. M., and WILKS, J. (1975). *The Effectiveness of Correctional Treatment*. New York: Praeger.

MCKAY, H. B., JAYEWARDENE, C. H. S., and REEDIE, P. B. (1979). *The Effects of Long-term Incarceration*. Ottawa: Ministry of Supply and Services.

MARTINSON, R. (1974). What works? – Questions and answers about prison reform. *The Public Interest*, **35**, 22–54.

MORRIS, P. (1965). *Prisoners and Their Families*. London: Allen and Unwin.

MORRIS, N. (1974). *The Future of Imprisonment*. Chicago: University of Chicago Press.

PACKER, J. P. (1968). *Limits of the Criminal Sanctions*. Stanford, Calif.: Stanford University Press.

ROBINSON, J., and SMITH, G. (1971). The effectiveness of correctional programs. *Crime and Delinquency*, **17**, 67–80.

ROSS, R. R., and MCKAY, H. B. (1979). *Self Mutilation*. Toronto; D. C. Heath.

ROTTER, J. B. (1966). Generalized expectancies for internal versus external control of reinforcement. *Psychological Monographs*, **80** (whole no. 609).

RUBY, C. C. (1968). *Sentencing*. Toronto: Butterworth.

SCHNELLER, D. P. (1975). Prisoners' families: a study of some social and psychological effects on the families of Negro prisoners. *Criminology*, **12**, 402–412.

SHERMAN, M., and HAWKINS, G. (1981). *Imprisonment in America: Choosing the Future*. Chicago: University of Chicago Press.

SYLVESTER, S. F., REED, J. H., and NELSON, D. O. (1977). *Prison Homicide*. New York: Spectrum Publications.

THOMAS, D. A. (1979). *Principles of Sentencing*, 2nd edn, London: Heinemann.

TITTLE, C. R. (1973). Punishment and deterrence of deviance. In S. Rottenberg (Ed), *The Economics of Crime and Punishment*. Washington, D. C.: American Enterprise Institute.

TOCH, H. (1975). *Men in Crises: Human Breakdowns in Prisons*. Chicago: Achine.

TOCH, H. (1977). *Living in Prison: The Ecology of Survival*. New York: Free Press.

UNITED NATIONS (1958). *Standard Minimum Rules for the Treatment of Prisoners and Related Recommendations*. New York: United Nations.

VAN DEN HAAG, E. (1975). *Punishing Criminals: Concerning a Very Old and Painful Question*. New York: Basic Books.

VON HIRSCH, A. (1976). *Doing Justice: The Choice of Punishment*. New York: Hill and Wang.

WEILER, P. C. (1974).The reform of punishment. In Law Reform Commission of Canada, *Studies on Sentencing*. Ottawa: Information Canada.

WESTCOTT, M. R. (1977). Free will: an exercise in metaphysical truth or psychological consequences. *Canadian Psychological Review*, **18**, 249–263.

WESTCOTT, M. R. (1978). Toward psychological studies of human freedom. *Canadian Psychological Review*, **19**, 277–290.

WESTCOTT, M. R. (1980). Quantitive and qualitative aspects of experienced freedom. Department of Psychology Reports No. 89, York University, Toronto.

WILSON, J. Q. (1975). *Thinking about Crime*. New York: Basic Books.

WORTMAN, C. G., and BREHM, J. W. (1975). Responses to uncontrollable outcomes: an integration of reactance theory and the learned helplessness model. In L. Berkowitz (Ed), *Advances in Experimental Social Psychology*, Vol. 8. New York: Academic Press.

ZIMRING, F. E., and HAWKINS, G. J. (1973). *Deterrence: The Legal Threat in Crime Control*. Chicago: University of Chicago Press.

SECTION VIII

Psycho-legal Training

This final section considers different aspects of training in a psycho-legal context. **Bull** examines how psychology can contribute in a practical way to the training of more sensitive and effective police officers. Four main areas are examined: social skills in dealing with the public; methods of detecting deception; organizational principles; and strategies for improving memory of relevant information. The chapter suggests there is a clear case for including psychology in police training.

The following chapter identifies variables which seem to influence the effectiveness of expert witnesses. **Carson** argues that it is important for witnesses to become as skilled as possible, even if it appears that they are thereby acquiring 'tricks' to suit the requirements of the court rather than simply presenting evidence to be evaluated objectively. This chapter suggests for the structured world of the court that *how* information is presented can be as important as *what* information is presented.

A similar viewpoint is presented with respect to improving advocates' skills by **Penrod** and his colleagues in the final chapter. A review of literature on topics such as bargaining, non-verbal behaviour, human memory, eyewitness reliability, and persuasive communication leads the authors to argue that careful use of empirical research findings can help attorneys, the courts, and juries to attain a higher quality of justice.

Psychology and Law
Edited by D.J. Müller, D.E. Blackman, and A.J. Chapman
© 1984 John Wiley & Sons Ltd

Chapter 29

Psychology's Contribution to Policing

Ray Bull

Even though the discipline of psychology ranges across all human experience, its contribution to date to improving many aspects of life has been somewhat limited. Many non-psychologists believe that this limitation is due to the inability of psychology to produce much that is of practical value. On the other hand, many psychologists believe that psychology can make important contributions but that non-psychologists fail to appreciate their significance. Within the last decade these two contrasting views have both been shown to be short-sighted regarding psychology's recent contribution to criminological and legal practices and procedures. One area in which psychology's contribution appears limited but where, in fact, psychology *does* have much to offer is that of policing. Although in North America some improvements in policing have come about, in part, due to the involvement of psychologists (who may themselves also be police officers), in the rest of the world, and particularly in Britain, the effective contribution of psychology has been slight. Perhaps the police feel threatened and therefore ignore a discipline which suggests improvements by pointing out their human weaknesses. This may also be reinforced by the nature of the psychology texts produced for police officers (e.g. Dudycha, 1976; Reiser, 1982; Steinberg and McEvoy, 1974).

The 1980s may well be seen as the decade in which the relationship between the police and psychology changed from insularity to interdependence. This development will require fresh thinking not only on the part of the police and psychologists, but also on the part of the media, who typically portray the police not so much as peace officers but as law enforcers rushing from one major crisis to the next. As Kelling (1978) noted, 'Training will have to focus less on legal and crime-related matters and more on conflicting management and social relations. Less organizational emphasis need be placed on command and control . . . and more can be placed on developing quality relations with citizens' (Kelling, 1978, p. 175). Kelling also believes that, 'If police critics are correct the strategy of preventive patrol has not only failed to demonstrate its effectiveness but also has created the worst possible situation: an ineffectiveness which alientates citizens' (Kelling, 1978, p. 177).

Social scientists must not be seen solely as critics of the police; they should also suggest improvements. Some progress is being made here by Goldstein (1979), who suggested that

'The police seem to have reached a plateau of which the highest objective to which they aspire is administrative competence. And, with some scattered exceptions, they seem reluctant to move beyond this plateau – toward creating a more systematic concern for the end products of their efforts. But strong pressures generated by several new developments may now force them to do so' (Goldstein, 1979, p. 239).

Goldstein underlines his point by claiming that

'as citizens press for improvement in police service, improvement will increasingly be measured in terms of results. Those concerned about battered wives, for example, could not care less whether the police who respond to such calls operate with one or two officers in a car, whether the officers are short or tall, or whether they have a college education. Their attention is on what the police do for the battered wife' (Goldstein, 1979, p. 240).

One new development that Goldstein (1979) did not mention is one to which Stratton (1980) draws attention. This is concerned with recent legal decisions in the USA which 'have held police organizations responsible for the behaviour of their employees who had not, in the eyes of the courts, been adequately prepared for their assignments' (Stratton, 1980, p. 75). Stratton delineates three important areas in this regard. The first concerns the acceptance of individuals into police forces who are not fit (physically, psychologically, or otherwise) for the job. The second focuses on inadequate and inappropriate training – 'some training in the areas of understanding human dynamics and diverse behaviors appears not only important but necessary' (Stratton, 1980, p. 75). The third area concerns the retaining of officers in posts in which they are no longer functioning adequately. In each of these three areas a substantial contribution from psychology is not only desirable but essential, and before too long it may be forced upon outmoded police forces by the law itself.

This chapter is divided into four sections. The first deals with the topic of police interactions with the public. The second is concerned with the detection of deception on the part of people being questioned by the police. The third covers personnel management, selection and training, stress, and counselling. The final section deals with memory and its relationship to policing.

INTERACTING WITH THE PUBLIC

Many surveys of police work have consistently revealed that up to 90% of police time is *not* spent on catching criminals (Keller, 1978; Stratton, 1980). By far the largest proportion of police time is spent by officers on patrol interacting with members of the general public. Although in the past work on improving this aspect of policing has been ignored in favour of costly, even gimmicky, electronic gadgetry, fast-response police cars, and the like (Kelling, 1978), in recent years a greater awareness of the role of police–public relations in the prevention and detection of crime has led to attempts by the police to make their personnel more skilled in interacting with citizens. Cumberbatch (Chapter 11) refers to work in Birmingham, England, in which police–public relations were examined. Another example of psychology's contribution on this topic is Bull's (1982–4) evaluation of the London Metropolitan Police's new recruit training programme in 'human awareness'. The fact that the police (and related bodies) are prepared to spend substantial sums of money on psychology's contribution in this area of policing suggests that here, at least, a useful dialogue has been established.

Psychology can make a contribution to police interaction with the general public and with certain specified groups; for example, rape victims, persons suffering from the effects of drugs or alcohol, people who are psychologically disturbed or 'mentally ill', aggressive persons, and those who attempt suicide (see Bull, Bustin, Evans, and Gahagan, 1983). All of these aspects of policing require police officers to have as full and as valid an understanding of human behaviour as possible.

Understanding Human Behaviour

Many people, including police officers, may believe that the knowledge which they have informally acquired is sufficient for successful performance in their job and that since they can interact well with colleagues and friends, they have little to learn concerning the social skills and levels of human awareness that some training programmes attempt to impart. They may also feel that the expectancies or stereotypes they have of people (e.g. because of their physical appearance, demeanour, and race) are reliable and valid.

There now exists quite a lot of evidence that the police share society's view of the relationship between physical appearance and criminality (Bull, 1982;

Bull and Green, 1980; Clifford and Bull, 1978; Piliavin and Briar, 1964) and that these stereotypes have a considerable influence on police practices, especially on the street. Psychologists must constantly remind the police of how set, expectancy, and other biases in perception may affect their behaviour. Sometimes stereotypes are of use (e.g. when a 'suspicious-looking' person is therefore stopped and is found to be in possession of incriminating items) but often they are misleading or potentially very harmful (e.g. in race relations). Psychologists can also contribute to police interpersonal skills training. However, as Keller (1978, p. 24) notes, follow-up to this aspect of initial training is 'frequently minimal and not taken seriously once the officer has started working. Ironically, the more seasoned personnel may instruct the newly trained recruit to forget his formal human relationships training. For these reasons the police organization often sabotages the introduction of effective interpersonal skills training'. The police should now ensure that they use effectively what psychology has to offer and that appropriate rewards are given to officers who display the high level of social skill required. Psychologists themselves are not, of course, free from blame for the lack of widespread and effective social skills training within police forces. Every time the media sensationalize psychological trivia or psychologists publicly criticize each other's work, opportunities arise for those who wish to denigrate psychology.

It is not only with respect to understanding other people that psychology is of value to policing. It can also help police officers to understand themselves and their own feelings and behaviour. It may be that many police officers are injured or even killed because they had little insight into their own over-reactions. Similarly, a large proportion of the complaints that citizens lodge against their police forces relate to alleged poor self-control on the part of the officers concerned. Even though 'rather extensive personality testing of police has not confirmed that police are in any way different from the average citizen' (Sykes and Clark, 1975, p. 585), and notwithstanding Colman and Gorman's (1982) finding suggesting some differences, it may well be that the experience of being a police officer leads such individuals not to look within themselves for explanations of why conflict between police and public occurs. Even though law enforcement agencies may rightly feel that they have little control over the circumstances that lead people into anti-social behaviour, this should be no excuse for failing to train police personnel effectively in social and self awareness.

Badalmente, George, Hatterlein, Jackson, Moore, Rio (1973) have persuasively argued that police forces need to 'Broaden the coverage of subjects pertaining to the policeman's social role in training programs, to include law enforcement orientation to the behavioral and social sciences, human behavior, civil rights and minority culture patterns' (Badalmente et al.,

1973, p. 453). Not all major police forces have instituted effective training in interacting with citizens and therefore much remains to be achieved concerning this aspect of psychology's contribution to policing.

Dealing with Aggression

Aggression is one of the ever increasing problems that the police encounter. Such research and advice as is available to the police on this topic has focused not only on how to deal with aggression from citizens but also on how police officers can control the urges towards aggression that they experience within themselves. To enable a police officer to be able to cope with his or her aggression should be part of basic recruit training. Psychologists have studied this topic for decades in considerable depth and breadth, yet useful, direct applications to policing of these research efforts are still awaited.

One situation where, at least in parts of the USA, the police are as likely to be seriously injured (or killed) trying to help the public rather than apprehend criminals is that concerning domestic violence. Several studies (e.g. Driscoll, Meyer, and Schanie, 1973) have pointed out that police officers may wish to adopt less force than they do at present when called to a home in which, for example, a man and a woman are having a violent quarrel. Psychologists should attempt to provide the police with a greater understanding of why a fiercely quarrelling couple often combine and turn violently on a police officer who is trying to help. Not only may this serve to reduce the frequency and severity of police and public injuries, it may also serve a useful community relations role in that (perhaps paradoxically) domestic crisis intervention is often requested (Bayley and Mendelsohn, 1969) by citizens who are naïvely thought to hold the police in the lowest regard.

However, such a possible contribution from psychology serves to highlight a problem in police training on interacting with citizens, namely that the officers undergoing such training believe it is more suited to social workers than to law enforcers. It is for the police (especially senior officers) to dispel the myth that their success will come from technological developments and physical fitness rather than from a fuller understanding of human behaviour. Nevertheless, psychologists must assist the police to up-date their views on what is crucial for efficient policing in today's societies.

Evaluation

A serious weakness in the social sciences' contribution to policing is the very frequent and serious omission of any satisfactory evaluation of the approaches and training derived from this perspective. After special training in, for example, crisis intervention the officers are usually informally reported as having enjoyed it, feeling better equipped, and so forth, but only rarely, if ever, has proper evaluation been undertaken. Thus there exists scant evidence with which to deny the view still held by many police officers that psychology's contribution to police interaction with citizens is of no value. Of course, not all police officers are of this view all of the time, and in certain areas of policing there may exist a belief that psychology has been of some use (e.g. in crowd control and hostage negotiations). Yet in these very areas it appears that common sense and police experience have contributed more than has academic psychology. This is not to say that common sense, police experience, and psychology offer different perspectives on the same problems, but for psychology to make a meaningful contribution to policing it has to do more than be seen as common sense.

THE DETECTION OF DECEPTION

Another important part of policing is concerned with questioning persons who are detained or arrested because it is believed that they have been involved in committing an offence. During such interrogations the police try to sift the truth from any deception. It is very commonly and perhaps naïvely believed that if a person is purposefully being deceitful then this will be accompanied by some sort of 'tell-tale' signs and that if only these signs could be noted then the deception would fail. These signs have been searched for in the external behaviour and in the physiological activity of the deceiver.

Psychophysiological Signs of Deceit

The use of apparently sophisticated electrical hardware has possibly led the general public and the police to believe that polygraphic lie-detectors and the psychological stress evaluator (which monitors aspects of the voice) are infallible detectors of deception. What is rarely discussed outside psychology is whether these procedures can do more than merely react to general stress on the part of the person being monitored (Brenner, Branscomb, and Schwartz, 1979). Rice (1978) points out that the claims made by the manufacturers of voice analysis machines of over 95% deception detection rates differ markedly from the success rates found with criminal suspects (which are hardly better than chance level). Yarmey has concluded that the psychological stress evaluator is not effective in detecting deception (Yarmey, 1979), yet these machines are still being widely advertised in police journals and magazines.

Some psychologists, however, do claim that polygraphic lie-detectors can accurately determine if a person is lying. Commonly these machines monitor palmar sweating, although other forms of physiological activity (e.g. heart rate, blood pressure) may sometimes be measured. One of the foremost supporters of the accuracy of these procedures is Raskin (e.g. Podlesny and Raskin, 1977), but it must be pointed out that he believes polygraphic lie-detection to be a valid and reliable procedure if, and only if, it is conducted by a properly qualified and fully competent person. Yarmey points out that in the USA polygraph tests have become big business (Yarmey, 1979), and several training centres of varying quality have been set up. These training centres make some attempts to make the human aspect of polygraphic lie-detecting (the framing of the questions to be asked, the interpreting of the activity charts, etc.) as reliable as are the machines employed to monitor and quantify the suspect's physiological responses. However, since the human examiner contributes as much to the final decision of 'lying' or 'truthful' as does the machine, there is considerable room for human error. Yarmey points out that 'very few professional polygraphers have more than a minimal training in physiological psychology and even fewer are qualified psychologists' (Yarmey, 1979, p. 171) and this may well account for the fact, noted by Raskin (1981), that often polygraph examiners may arrive at different conclusions when examining the *same* printout from a machine.

Raskin notes that in the USA virtually all major law enforcement agencies utilize polygraph techniques for screening out innocent subjects (Raskin, 1981) and he has presented quite a strong case for this being done *if* the polygraph examiner is qualified and *if* another examiner independently arrives at the same conclusion. Courts in 36 states have admitted polygraph evidence and in New Mexico Raskin reports that 'they are routinely admissible over objection' (Raskin, 1981, p. 12). The objections to the use of polygraphic lie-detectors have taken several forms and many psychologists believe them (e.g. Lykken, 1979) to be too unreliable to be used in judicial proceedings, especially if used by the prosecution. In response to this it has been pointed out that evidence gained from well conducted polygraph tests may be no more unreliable than that gained from eyewitnesses which, until recently, was a readily accepted form of evidence in most courts. However, there still remains the problem of how much faith a jury may put in polygraphic lie-detection procedures unless steps are taken (Cavoukian and Heslegrave, 1980) to make them aware of the machine's and the human examiner's limitations.

External Behaviour as a Sign of Deceit

The detection of deception based on a person's overt behaviour is not clouded by any belief in the infallibility of machines. Several psychologists have investigated in somewhat artificial research circumstances whether people behave differently when lying than when telling the truth. It has been reported that these studies have found 'only minimal differences between deceivers and non-deceivers in these behavioral displays' (Miller, Bauchner,

Hocking, Fontes, Kaminski, Brandt, 1981, p. 147). Of course it could be the case that when lying people do give off tell-tale cues and that these studies failed to monitor them. In contrast to the claim by Miller et al., some psychologists have claimed that 'We know, for example, that when a person lies, he or she gesticulates less and displays few positive head nods' and that 'The feet and legs frequently shift in agitation when deceitful messages are being controlled through facial expressions. Liars also . . . have higher-pitched voices' (Yarmey, 1979, p. 169). However, Yarmey does point out that 'In spite of the confidence that the average person has in his or her ability to detect liars by their non-verbal behaviors, there is little justification in the research literature to support such belief' (Yarmey, 1979, p. 169). Thus present research could be taken as suggesting that untrained police officers are unlikely to be able to detect deception from non-verbal behaviour. But since psychologists' studies of this topic have to date been somewhat artifical in terms of the liars' belief concerning the consequences of the detection of their deception, it could be that lying in the police setting is easier to detect, notwithstanding psychologists' attempts to make their studies of deception as ecologically valid as possible. Perhaps trained and experienced police officers are more likely to detect deception from non-verbal cues. Miller et al. point out that whether their 'findings would hold for trained investigators – for example, police officers – is a question for future research' (Miller et al., 1981, p. 146).

Few studies of the detection of deception have looked at the question of whether more useful cues can be gained from merely listening to or reading a person's story. Maier and Thurber (1968) had their subjects view live interviews, hear tape-recordings of them, or just read transcripts of the interviews. The audio-tape and written modes produced greater levels of detection of deception (77%) than did the live mode (58%), which itself hardly differed from a chance level of performance. This, and part of the work of Miller et al. (1981), suggests that in the detection of deception visual cues may distract attention from possible verbal and paralinguistic cues to lying. Thus the current police practice of examining what is said and how it is said rather than how the speaker otherwise behaves may be the least error-prone way to attempt to detect deception. Inconsistencies in stories, whether detected by the police themselves or by psychologists, may be more useful to policing than a constant and perhaps naïve search for clues from non-verbal behaviour as to whether someone is lying or not. Psychologists could have a role to play in the training of police officers in the skills of interviewing as they are now having in training other groups (such as lawyers and doctors).

THE POLICE FORCE AS AN ORGANIZATION

Psychologists have contributed in many ways to the successful running of many organizations. Even though there exist some significant dissimilarities between police forces and the organizations which have successfully employed psychology, the similarities suggest that considerable benefit may arise.[1] For example, police organizations depend on efficient leadership and decision-making at all levels and, although these two topics are not discussed here, psychology is able to offer considerable advice on these matters (Bull *et al.*, 1983) and on other areas relating to organizational behaviour.

Psychologists, perhaps more than police officers, can see considerable similarity between a police force and other large organizations. For example, the roles of middle or senior managers in industry can be equated with those of senior police officers in terms of the manpower and of the capital equipment and maintenance costs for which they are responsible. A chief superintendent in London may often have a manpower, equipment, and building annual budget of over £3 million. The problems and stresses found to be associated with such responsibilities in industry are also likely to occur within police forces and therefore psychology's contributions on these matters in the industrial setting may be relevant to policing. However, this similarity may not be so apparent to senior police officers, some of whom may have been promoted or believe that they have been promoted because they have a good record as police officers in the detection and prevention of crime rather than as managers.

Another important dissimilarity between police forces and other large organizations is that within police forces (at least in the UK) the managers, however senior they may be, began their employment at the most junior level in the organization. Such policies of internal promotion must have their benefits, but they do place upon police managers the problems of role change and role strain. Further, an exclusive reliance upon a policy of internal promotion should, but does not always, have an effect upon the selection of new recruits. The fact that senior police officers are required to demonstrate skills for which they may not initially have been recruited argues that appropriate training is very necessary. This is especially so in the light of another dissimilarity between police forces and other organizations. This difference is concerned with the disciplined and strictly hierarchical nature of police forces and here direct extrapolations from psychologists' work in other organizations on such topics as performance appraisal, leadership style, and information dissemination may be made invalid by police official codes of conduct and the like. However, this is not to say that an occupational/industrial psychologist cannot be of benefit to police forces.

Recruitment, Selection, and Training

The methods psychologists have developed in other organizations may be relevant to police recruitment and selection. Not only have attempts been made to assess applicants' intellectual powers but also information concerning their personalities and attitudes has been thought to be relevant. When the number of applicants wishing to join a police force has been few compared to the number of vacancies, little selection research has been undertaken. Recently, however, in many countries the ratio of applicants to places has grown considerably. Police recruitment and selection has largely been conducted without the assistance of psychologists outside the police service and little research work has been published on the reliability and validity of the procedures used. However, some attempts have been made to screen out maladjusted individuals (Fenster and Schlossberg, 1979). Some studies have claimed that police officers are authoritarian, power conscious, conservative, or prejudiced (for a full bibliography see Fenster and Schlossberg, 1979), but few of these have made valid comparisons with members of the public. Furthermore, these studies have frequently failed to distinguish between new recruits and those police officers who have been within the organization for some time. Those studies which have made this distinction have often come to the conclusion that the main aspects of 'the police personality' are acquired on the job rather than being present from the start (Butler and Cochrane, 1977). However, Colman and Gorman (1982) claim to have found evidence that police recruits are more conservative and authoritarian than a *somewhat* socioeconomically, academically, and age-matched group of non-police. They noted that recruit training had a liberalizing effect but claimed to have found data to support the contention that continued police service may wipe out these effects of initial training on police personality.

Psychologists have also been involved in the designing and running of a variety of police training courses (mainly in North America). These courses have largely been concerned with parts of the human relations aspects of policing. Other areas of police training have rarely directly had a psychological input. In very few cases have these or any other police training courses ever been properly evaluated for their effectiveness. Few police forces have any data on how successful their training really is, nor how valid their promotion examinations are (Shimberg, 1974); and here policing may benefit from an evaluative contribution from psychologists.

Stress and Counselling

One area in which some evaluation has taken place is that concerning stress reduction in police officers. A small number of forces in the USA now employ psychologists (some full-time) to assist officers in coping with stress and to offer counselling to them and their families. Sometimes these psychologists have attempted to evaluate the usefulness of their contributions.

Somodevilla (1978) claims that policing is the most emotionally dangerous of all professions and he notes (in the USA, at least) that

> Police officers have one of the highest rates of divorce of all professions (75%); problem drinking (20%); and suicide (six and a half times higher

than the average of the population). Cardiovascular disorders and other health problems are also very frequent and psychosomatic illnesses in general are rampant in police work (Somodevilla, 1978, p. 21).

Stratton (1978) presents an overview of police stress and, being a psychologist, he details the ways in which psychology can help police officers deal with the stress that their jobs entail (both inside and outside working hours). He also suggests various ways in which psychological counselling can be of assistance.

Schilling (1978), a senior police officer, points out that the few psychological counselling programmes that have been established (almost all of them in the USA) to help police officers may considerably reduce the present practice of secreting away officers suffering from stress, alcoholism, and so forth, into low visibility, low responsibility posts. He points out that police officers' employment is rarely terminated on psychological grounds even though 'Some recent civil liability cases have resulted in police agencies being held liable for damages resulting from the actions of officers known by the agencies to be behaviorally marginal who were not afforded rehabilitative care' (Schilling, 1978, p. 30).

Psychology seems to be the profession best equipped to assist police agencies in providing not only rehabilitative care but also preventive advice, yet, as noted by Schilling (1978, p. 32), 'Most agencies are not yet making maximum use of behavioral sciences in this regard.' Wherever the fault for this lies, police forces are coming to realize that psychological counselling can be very cost effective. Stratton (1977) suggests that many experienced officers leave the police service because they had nowhere to turn when job-related emotional problems overcame them and Schilling (1978, p. 30) notes that 'It is frequently much less costly to rehabilitate an employee than to replace him.' Thus it seems that in several ways organizational, occupational, and industrial psychology can contribute to the cost effectiveness and efficiency of police forces.

MEMORY

Effective policing is often dependent upon the efficient memorizing of relevant information. This is so not only regarding police officers' daily reception of information (Bull and Reid, 1975), but also regarding members of the public who have witnessed a crime.

Eyewitnessing

In recent years, following a number of notorious wrongful convictions (especially in Britain), psychologists have provided a number of insights concerning the accuracy or fallibility of eyewitnesses. This topic is fully reviewed in Clifford and Bull (1978), Loftus (1979), and Yarmey (1979), and recent perspectives are considered in Section IV of this volume. However, the level of understanding that psychology presently has of eyewitnessing is not sufficient to enable the police to decide whether any one witness is more likely to be correct than any other witness, although improvements in general procedures, such as the nature of the questioning of witnesses (Bull and Clifford, 1979) are now possible. Thus psychology could be seen by the police to have limited the strength of one of their methods of having criminals convicted without providing them, as yet, with many ways of improving this state of affairs. Some positive advice and guidance to the police is now becoming available, for example on the efficient construction of identification parades (Lindsay and Wells, 1980) but much more is still to be done. Yarmey and Jones (1982) have found that there are some important differences between the concensus view of some psychologists who were deemed to be experts on eyewitness performance and the beliefs of the police. Thus, it may still be the case that some police officers are making considerable errors of judgment concerning eyewitness testimony.

Note-taking

A topic related to that of eyewitnessing concerns the efficiency with which the police can take notes either when an eyewitness is being questioned or in the many other aspects of policing in which the taking of notes is deemed to be important. In several countries, including England, a police officer is often permitted to consult a notebook whilst giving evidence in court. This suggests that police note-taking is an efficient procedure. Although this is a topic which to date has received little research attention within police forces, Yuille's report (1984) of a survey conducted at the British Columbia Police Academy in Vancouver and the larger body of research conducted on student note-taking (e.g. Hartley, 1983) suggests that police note-taking would benefit from psychological research.

Police Accuracy

The suggestion made in the previous sentence may well not be readily accepted by the police, and one reason for this is that the greatest proportion of research on note-taking has been conducted using students. Often the police claim that because of their special training (and selection) they possess levels of skill over and above that of members of the public. This may well be the case concerning some attributes (e.g. physical fitness, self-defence) but time and again psychologists have shown that the police are usually as limited as are other human beings. Although this whole chapter serves to illustrate how policing is limited in its efficiency because it employs human beings, one area in which the police have been shown repeatedly to be only as efficient as the general public is in their accurate remembering of people and events. Even though police recruitment advertisments suggest that officers are selected and/or trained to be efficient observers and recorders of information, the considerable body of research on this topic (Bull *et al.* 1983) has consistently found that police officers are as inaccurate as are members of the general public.

Hypnosis

Some police officers still seem to believe that during remembering the eyes act like a camera and the ears like a tape-recorder and that any problems in subsequent recall are merely due to retrieval failure. At least one police department psychologist also shares this belief: 'Although the mind is like a camera and sees and records all aspects of a situation, it may not be able to recall every detail of information' (Stratton, 1977, p. 72). Such erroneous beliefs as this (Clifford and Bull, 1978) have led police officers to imagine that under hypnosis accurate recall of 'what really happened' will occur. This simplistic view of hypnosis is in need of rectification by psychologists and, although at present many courts wisely do not permit information gained under hypnosis to act as direct evidence, much more research on the benefits and drawbacks of this technique is needed (Loftus, 1979; Yarmey, 1979). A few outstanding examples of the usefulness of information gathered from a witness under hypnosis should not blind the police to the pitfalls inherent in using this procedure (Gibson, 1982).

CONCLUSION

This chapter has briefly examined some aspects of policing to which psychology could make a meaningful contribution. In only a few of these areas is there at present a real dialogue between psychologists and police officers and almost all of this is taking place in North America. In Britain police officers seem largely ignorant of what psychology is and how it could relate to policing. This ignorance may be due in part to the closed minds of many police officers but much of the blame should be apportioned to the kind of psychologist to whom Sir Desmond Pond referred in his 1982 Myers Lecture to The British Psychological Society, in which he said 'Let us hope you can get more quickly out of closed institutions like laboratories to where it is all happening' (Pond, 1982, p. 54). Policing is an important aspect of life and gives scope for psychology to justify to society why money should be invested in this discipline.

NOTE

1. I am grateful to C. Lewis for sharing his thoughts with me on this matter. He is involved in the training of newly promoted superintendents in a large police force in the UK.

REFERENCES

BADALMENTE, R. V., GEORGE, C. E., HATTERLEIN, P. J., JACKSON, T. T., MOORE, S. A., and RIO, R. (1973). Training police for their social role. *Journal of Police Science and Administration*, 1, 440–453.

BAYLEY, D. W., and MENDELSOHN, H. (1969). *Minorities and the Police*. New York: The Free Press.

BRENNER, M., BRANSCOMB, H. H., and SCHWARTZ, G. E. (1979). Psychological stress evaluator – two tests of a vocal measure. *Psychophysiology*, 16, 351–357.

BULL, R. (1982). Physical appearance and criminality. *Current Psychological Reviews*, 2, 269–282.

BULL, R., and CLIFFORD, B. R. (1979). Eyewitness memory. In M. M. Gruneberg and P. E. Morris (Eds), *Applied Problems in Memory*. London: Academic Press.

BULL, R., and GREEN, J. (1980). The relationship between physical appearance and criminality. *Medicine, Science and Law*, 20, 79–83.

BULL, R., and REID, R. L. (1975). Police officers' recall of information. *Journal of Occupational Psychology*, 48, 73–78.

BULL, R., BUSTIN, B., EVANS, P., and GAHAGAN, D. (1983). *Psychology for Police Officers*. Chichester: John Wiley.

BUTLER, A. J. P., and COCHRANE, R. (1977). An examination of some elements of the personality of police officers and their implications. *Journal of Police Science and Administration*, 5, 441–450.

CAVOUKIAN, A., and HESLEGRAVE, R. J. (1980). The admissibility of polygraph evidence in court. *Law and Human Behavior*, 4, 117–131.

CLIFFORD, B. R., and BULL, R. (1978). *The Psychology of Person Identification*. London: Routledge and Kegan Paul.

COLMAN, A. M., and GORMAN, L. P. (1982). Conservatism, dogmatism and authoritarianism in British police officers. *Sociology*, 16, 1–11.

DRISCOLL, J. M., MEYER, R. G. and SCHANIE, C. F. (1973). Training police in family crisis intervention. *Journal of Applied Behavioral Science*, 9, 62–82.

DUDYCHA, G. (1976). *Psychology for Law Enforcement Officers*. Springfield, Ill.: Charles C. Thomas.

FENSTER, C. A., and SCHLOSSBERG, H. (1979). The psychologist as police department consultant. In J. Platt and R. Wicks (Eds), *The Psychological Consultant*. New York: Grune and Stratton.

GIBSON, H. B. (1982). The use of hypnosis in police investigations. *Bulletin of The British Psychological Society*, 35, 138–142.

GOLDSTEIN, H. (1979). Improving policing: a problem-oriented approach. *Crime and Delinquency*, 1979, 236–258.

HARTLEY, J. (1983). Note-taking research: re-setting the scoreboard. *Bulletin of The British Psychological Society*, 36, 13–14.

KELLER, P. A. (1978). A psychological view of the police officer paradox. *The Police Chief*, 45, 24–25.

KELLING, G. L. (1978). Police field services and crime: the presumed effects of capacity. *Crime and Delinquency*, **1978**, 173–184.

LINDSAY, R. C. L., and WELLS, G. L. (1980). What price justice? Exploring the relationship of lineup fairness to identification accuracy. *Law and Human Behavior*, **4**, 303–313.

LOFTUS, E. F. (1979). *Eyewitness Testimony*. Cambridge, Mass.: Harvard University Press.

LYKKEN, D. T. (1979). The detection of deception. *Psychological Bulletin*, **86**, 47–53.

MAIER, N., and THURBER, J. (1968). Accuracy of judgments of deception when an interview is watched, heard and read. *Personnel Psychology*, **21**, 23–30.

MILLER, G. R., BAUCHNER, J. E., HOCKING, J. E., FONTES, N. E., KAMINSKI, E. P., and BRANDT, D. R. (1981). How well can observers detect deceptive testimony? In B. D. Sales (Ed), *The Trial Process*. New York: Plenum.

PILIAVIN, I., and BRIAR, S. (1964). Police encounters with juveniles. *American Journal of Sociology*, **70**, 206–214

PODLESNY, J. A., and RASKIN, D. G. (1977). Physiological measures and the detection of deception. *Psychological Bulletin*, **84**, 782–799.

POND, D. (1982). Psychology – prop or profession. *Bulletin of The British Psychological Society*, **35**, 49–55.

RASKIN, D. G. (1981). Science, competence and polygraph techniques. *Criminal Defense*, **8**, 11–18.

REISER, M. (1982). *Police Psychology*. Los Angeles: Lehi.

RICE, B. (1978). The new truth machines. *Psychology Today*, **12**, 61–78.

SCHILLING, C. (1978). Behavioral science services for police. *The Police Chief*, **45**, 28–32.

SHIMBERG, B. (1974). The role of the behavioral scientist in police recruit testing. In J. L. Standing and D. McEvoy (Eds), *The Police and the Behavioral Sciences*, Springfield, Ill.: Charles C. Thomas.

SOMODEVILLA, S. A. (1978). The psychologist's role in the police department. *The Police Chief*, **45**, 21–23.

STEINBERG, J. L., and McEVOY, D. (1974). *The Police and the Behavioral Sciences*. Springfield, Ill.: Charles C. Thomas.

STRATTON, J. G. (1977). The department psychologist. *The Police Chief*, **44**, 70–73.

STRATTON, J. G. (1978). Police stress: an overview. *The Police Chief*, **45**, 58–62.

STRATTON, J. C. (1980). Psychological services for police. *Journal of Police Science and Administration*, **8**, 31–39.

SYKES, R. E., and CLARK, J. P. (1975). A theory of deference exchange in police–civilian encounters. *American Journal of Sociology*, **81**, 584–600.

YARMEY, A. D. (1979). *The Psychology of Eyewitness Testimony*. New York: The Free Press.

YARMEY, A. D. and JONES, H. T. (1982). Police awareness of the fallibility of eyewitness identification. *Canadian Police College Journal*, **6**, 113–124.

YUILLE, J. (1984). Research and teaching with police – a Canadian example. *International Review of Applied Psychology*, in press.

Psychology and Law
Edited by D.J. Müller, D.E. Blackman, and A.J. Chapman
© 1984 John Wiley & Sons Ltd

Chapter 30

Putting the Expert in Expert Witness

David Carson

Unlike other witnesses, 'expert' witnesses are allowed to state their own opinions (Cross, 1979). Being an expert witness is a matter of status and not necessarily of quality. This chapter is concerned with the quality of expert witnesses. Its principal object is to indicate those variables that affect witness quality, for, by controlling those variables and changing their behaviour, expert witnesses should become more expert.

The central premises of the present approach are first that the court or tribunal's decision is not exclusively a decision on the facts of the case but involves interpretation and assessment, and second that the source of the information upon which the judges, magistrates, or juries must make these interpretations and assessments are to be found in the witnesses' appearance, behaviour in the witness box, and written or oral statements. It is recognized that courts and tribunals, judges, magistrates, and juries vary considerably, and this is one of the problems facing witnesses. But the points mentioned below may be applicable and relevant to different degrees. Particular attention is paid to criminal trials and juvenile court proceedings in England and Wales. For convenience reference is made simply to courts and to judges or magistrates as appears most appropriate at the time.

THE CONTEXT

The role played by expert witnesses will vary according to both the court involved and the type of proceedings. A trial in a Crown Court differs considerably from one in a magistrates' court. Several studies have indicated that there is a considerable gap between the ideology of the courts and daily reality. It is clearly important that expert witnesses should be alive to these differences if they are to achieve their objectives in the courts and to retain as much control over the content and use of their testimony as is possible. Glib statements about courts and trials, such as the rule that everyone is presumed

425

innocent until proved guilty, should be placed in an appropriate context: magistrates' courts process guilty people. Well over 90% of defendants in magistrates' courts plead or are found guilty. Three-quarters of those pleading not guilty are found guilty.

Magistrates are frequently faced with trained police officers or prosecuting solicitors and unrepresented defendants. They know that thought is given before the decision to prosecute is made and that therefore several people have assessed the likelihood of and need for conviction. 'Common-sense knowledge' like the expression that 'there is no smoke without a fire' will affect magistrates as much as anyone else. There may be an expression that 'everyone is equal before the law', but magistrates are sometimes faced with a straight conflict of evidence between a police officer or someone else in an authoritative position, such as a psychologist, and the defendant. They must consider the implications of disbelieving the police officer or psychologist. To disbelieve such a person can easily be seen as a criticism or denial of their professional competence possibly justifying disciplinary action. It is of course required of the prosecution that a case be proved beyond all reasonable doubt, although in civil juvenile court proceedings proof rests on a balance of probabilities. But if a defendant simply denies the prosecution's story and does not offer an alternative (e.g. 'I do not know what speed I was going at but it was not 73 m.p.h.') the courts will often be suspicious and indeed may use the defendant's reliance on the rule about proof as evidence that he or she has no answer to the charge. These and similar points have been developed by McBarnett (1981a).

Some writers have seen the courtroom proceedings as a status degradation ceremony (Garfinkel, 1956). Others have looked at it in terms of status passage (Glaser and Strauss, 1971; King, 1978). Both approaches concentrate upon the defendant and the way that the procedures lead to the defendant being perceived differently over time. But the points about the artificiality of the setting and the dependence on oral statements and ritual are also relevant for witnesses. Evidence must be given from the witness box. Formal qualifications must be stated but qualities such as experience, respect, and leadership cannot be so easily communicated. The oath must be taken.

Other writers have analysed courtroom proceedings in terms of games or as dramas (Carlen, 1975). Carlen's work in this framework is particularly illuminating. For example, she has studied ways in which defendants' statements, particularly those that question the appropriateness of the proceedings, are neutralized and ignored (Carlen, 1974). A number of other writers have concentrated on the content of the questions or answers in courts (Atkinson and Drew, 1979; Danet and Bogoch, 1980; Dunstan, 1980). Some have studied the use of courts to de-politicize certain issues (Bankowski and Mungham, 1976, 1980). And a developing interest in 'the reality' of court-room proceedings was indicated by the publication in 1981 of an empirical study of child care cases and the relationships between solicitors and social workers (Hilgendorf, 1981). But relatively little seems to have been written on desirable skills for witnesses in this country. That may be related to the fact that the principal books on advocacy in this country are short and practical but substantially anecdotal (Du Cann, 1964; Napley, 1975) or consist of a few passing comments in what is otherwise a textbook on forms and procedures (Barnard, 1979; Clitheroe, 1980).

THE SETTING

While courtrooms differ considerably in size, arrangements, and facilities, they have common features. Witnesses should note the arrangements before they give evidence, as certain barriers are involved. Height and space are used to set apart both the judge or magistrates and the defendant (Carlen, 1976). Many witnesses find the distance from the other participants somewhat daunting. They must project their voices not just to their questioner but to the farthest magistrate or juror, taking into account the possibilities of deafness and, especially in magistrates' courts, a continual noise of activity from people not involved in that case. Both volume and pitch have to be considered, and some pitches can 'get lost' in some buildings and with some furnishings. It is easy to become disconcerted by being asked to speak up, particularly if there is over- or under-compensation or a marked change of pitch. Some actors and lecturers notionally pick upon someone at the back of the room and project to that person in particular. There are, however, problems with this in courts as all answers have to be addressed to the judge or magistrates.

The lawyer elicits information from the witness on behalf of the court. The witness has to give that information, and can be interrupted and told to give that information, directly to the judge or magistrates. This breaks the rules of normal conversation and discussion for we normally look at our questioners when aswering, indeed we regard it bad manners not to look at them. Witnesses should first note that giving evidence is not simply a formal conversation. The witness does not control the subject matter. At times it is more like giving a series of short lectures. The confusion that arises from not knowing how to regard the process of evidence-giving or where to look can utilized by the lawyer. Conversations have a degree of informality and involve both parties working together to develop and interpret the subject matter. Lecturing is much more formal; the lecturer is in some senses alone. The lawyer can move between these two forms, causing further confusion. The lawyer could, for example, provide alternative words for the witness to choose from when having a difficulty in answering. But the lawyer can quite suddenly stop this co-operation, leaving the witness floundering.

Witnesses must address the judge or magistrates. But there is no requirement on the judge or magistrates to look at the witness, indeed they may be looking around the room or at their papers, since they are not involved in any conversation with the witness. The situation is unusual in that the witness is forbidden to reply to the questioning lawyer but required to address other people. This has caused problems for many witnesses. It can be helpful for them to think of it as lecturing to the magistrates, especially if they make an effort to 'teach' the magistrates about the case. For example, lecturers can learn not to depend upon visual contact and to regulate the speed of delivery of information to maximize comprehension and note-taking and they can learn the value of enumerating their points. Numbering points has an almost magical quality in leading audiences to write down a summary of each point which aids comprehension and retention, and the numbers can be used when the magistrates discuss their decision amongst themselves.

Witnesses can use the rule about addressing the magistrates to their own advantage. The more they look at the lawyer the more visual cues they will give about any problems in answering or being about to finish. Looking at the lawyer will also lead to their being more receptive to the lawyer's cues about when the lawyer wishes to intervene. By facing the judge and looking away from the lawyer these problems are minimized. Further, by a demonstrative turning gesture the witness can turn back from looking at the judge to looking at the lawyer thereby signalling preparedness for another question. In this way the witness can influence the speed of questioning.

THE CAST

Many points mentioned above were described and developed by Carlen in her study of a London magistrates' court (Carlen, 1976). She also noted a series of alliances between pairs of people who regularly worked in the court. For example, lawyers needed to have good relationships with the police in order to negotiate about any charges that might be dropped. Expert witnesses, such as social workers and educational psychologists, could become involved in these alliances and should be aware of the power and influence it can give them. Particularly in magistrates' and juvenile courts, lawyers do not have much time or funds to make extensive inquiries for themselves. Lawyers are heavily dependent, in such cases, on the expert witness's report (Hilgendorf, 1981). They will frequently use the report to re-present their client, simply changing the value-loaded words in the report. They have a limited range of mitigation tactics (Williamson, 1980) and the expert's report is a valuable way to 'flesh out' the mitigation plea. As lawyers want the reports as early as possible, the authors have a power over them which they could use to negotiate easy cross-examinations. Such negotiation occurs in other alliances (Bankowski and Mungham, 1976).

Those who work in the courts regularly come to recognize familiar arguments and people. They are as prone to categorizing and stereotyping as others (Carlen, 1976). Expert witnesses should appreciate this, for their testimony may simply have the effect of putting someone into a pigeon hole. If a lawyer or anyone else wants to indicate that a particular case is special and different, then this has to be clearly signalled to the court. And it needs to be appreciated that not every case can be special. So the participants have to accept and present most of their cases as falling within the 'typical kind of case'. As Williamson writes, ' . . . it is important to reinforce the idea that solicitors representing defendants in the juvenile court are continually trying to seek a balance between a powerful (and possibly successful) defence and mitigation, and losing credibility in front of the magistrates' (Williamson, 1980, p. 48).

One of the sets of stereotypes that magistrates seem to have is of the quality of different kinds of expert witnesses. They seem to have a high regard for probation officers, perhaps because of greater familiarity with them, but they seem to have a low opinion of social workers. A study of Scottish magistrates' attitudes to social workers revealed a marked preference for the 'elderly motherly type' and distaste for younger social workers perceived as being 'left-wing' and opinionated (May, 1978–9) and there are good grounds for believing that similar attitudes are held by English magistrates.

Amongst the variables affecting an individual witness's performance are such matters as clothes and stance. However trivial and unimportant these ought to be regarded as, it needs to be remembered both that we all use such cues when we assess other people and that judges and magistrates have little else to use.

Magistrates are advised to wear clothes that are 'discreet and according to accepted usage', and this is to deflect attention from the person to the office (Young and Clarke, 1976). Solicitors are advised to be neat and tidy for 'It is simple psychology . . . that people are predisposed to accept the opinions of those whom they like and to reject those put forward by persons whom they dislike' (Napley, 1975, p. 80).

THE REPORTS

Expert witnesses often have to speak to a written report that they have prepared. Obviously it would be wise for them to avoid problems by preparing their reports appropriately. Social inquiry reports are frequently presented. Whilst there is no prescribed format for them, a number of publications discuss what they should contain (Herbert and Mathieson, 1975; Wright, 1979). Clearly reports should be efficient in giving a lot of information in a small space.

Reports have to be understood by their readers, so the use of jargon and technical expressions can cause problems. If a lawyer has to have an expression explained, the court will want to know why it was not explained that way initially. Some technical terms, such as 'diagnoses' or perhaps 'intelligence quotient' figures, might be necessary, although it is sometimes difficult to see the relevance of the latter. The witness should clearly distinguish between that material which is factual and that which is based upon opinion, including all the inferences drawn from the facts. The lawyer will be making that distinction, as the following quotation illustrates:

> 'The fact remains, however, that expert witnesses in general and medical witnesses in particular, provide, if the advocate is properly prepared, the most useful and easily assailable material for successful cross-examination. Witnesses as to facts speak to matters of positive recollection within their own experience. . . . Doctors, by comparison, are dealing, within the realm of informed opinion, with the subject matter of an art, which is neither exact nor necessarily scientific' (Napley, 1975, p. 31).

The quotation actually reveals an ignorance of psychology and of the selection and interpretation processes in recall which will often involve opinions about causal connections, but it emphasizes the importance of the distinction between fact and opinion. Reports should contain as high a proportion of fact to opinion as is possible. It is often claimed that facts speak for themselves, and witnesses can utilize this. Witnesses can use the facts to show that a certain conclusion or opinion is not just theirs but is the only reasonable one in the light of the weight of the data.

Reports should refer to the witness's qualifications, but not just in a formal manner. Courts will often look beyond formal qualifications to experience which can be general, such as working with deaf children, or specific, such as working with a particular deaf child. This sort of information can give a depth to the witness's qualifications. Magistrates are often suspicious of qualifications per se and of theories, so practical experience is valued (May, 1978–9). They can be suspicious if their common-sense approach to the world, which has been satisfactory for them, is dressed in technical terms, for example in references to bonding of parents and children rather than just care and affection.

Reports are requested for a particular purpose. Social inquiry reports are designed to help the court make a wise decision as to sentence or placement. Thus the courts are making decisions for the future. Many reports provide no information about the future even when a specific recommendation is made. The court is surely more likely to follow a particular recommendation if it knows what will happen. The witness could, if appropriate, tell the court about the services that would be provided and the responsibilities the witness would undertake. That could count as fact. The court could also be told the witness's opinions as to what the client or defendant is likely to do if the particular recommendation is not followed. The judges and magistrates have difficult decisions to make and the more that expert witnesses can supply reasons and rationalizations for them the better.

Lawyers will read reports looking for weak spots such as vague expressions. Witnesses would do well to adopt Mager's (1973) distinction between 'fuzzies' and 'performances'. A 'performance' is a clear statement open to empirical verification whilst a 'fuzzy' is a vague and ambiguous statement. Mager developed a 'Hey Dad' sentence completion test whereby a statement like 'Hey Dad, look at me being phobic' or 'aggressive' is seen to be a fuzzy in contrast with 'Hey Dad, look at me sweating and not breathing when I see spiders' or 'Hey Dad, look at me hitting people of my own age without warning or provocation'. Expert witnesses could perhaps develop a 'Hey Judge' test. It would be a good way of avoiding both vague expressions and opinions, leaving the lawyer faced with mere fact which, it is hoped, the witness can prove.

THE QUESTIONS

Although advocacy and cross-examination skills are now taught to barristers and solicitors, they are still principally regarded as arts developed through experiences and not as tricks or devices. Certainly high standards of professional conduct are expected and lawyers have a duty to the court (Boulton, 1975; Napley, 1975). But it is part of the lawyer's job to probe and test the witnesses' evidence and their credibility and authority.

It is possible to outline certain tactics adopted by lawyers. As argued above, lawyers look for weak spots in a report and in answers: 'Professional cross-examination proceeds ... by indirect approaches, by a series of questions on apparently peripheral matters, with a crucial issue casually dropped in en route, by a series of questions leading the witness to an accusation which the witness cannot logically deny without discrediting his previous answers' (McBarnett, 1981b, p. 185). Witnesses should not have over-dramatic expectations of cross examination based on films and television. Most daily cross-examination is subtle and suggestive rather than dramatic and destructive. Lawyers, particularly in criminal cases, rely upon the burden and onus of proof. They do not try to prove that the prosecution is totally misconceived but rather that it is not proved satisfactorily beyond all reasonable doubt. By presenting enough doubt, either about the evidence or the witnesses, they try to get the court to decide that although the prosecution were probably right enough doubt has been introduced to make a guilty verdict too risky. So they may try to discomfort witnesses and shake them:

'Approach the witness on the areas peripheral to the client's account, testing the witness on the areas peripheral to the essential facts first. If doubt can be sown, either in his mind or the mind of the court, as to the accuracy of his recollection on peripheral facts, it will make more effective the suggestion that his account of the central issue may also be mistaken' (Clitheroe, 1980, p. 93).

Results are often achieved indirectly, by apparently agreeing with the witness:

'Moreover if you can present your arguments on the basis that you accept the evidence which your opponent has adduced but that you are able to place a different interpretation on it, you are immeasurably nearer to a favourable result than in presenting a case involving facts which the court must first determine by reconciling or rejecting the version of one side or the other. Elimination and selection are the two keys to effective practical examination' (Napley, 1975, pp. 104–105).

An effective way of introducing doubt into a witness's evidence is to question certain words. For example, if it is said that there is a 'danger' of a child being hit again, then it is sensible to discuss what exactly is meant. (If a 'Hey Judge' test had been used the witness might not have given the lawyer this opening.) Witnesses must accept some alternative words if they are not to appear foolish. But the lawyer could get a witness to accept that there is a risk of the child being hit again and then comment that there are risks in crossing roads. Witnesses need to be on guard against this happening to them and at an appropriate stage indicate that the words being used have become inappropriate.

Lawyers are not supposed to use questions as opportunities for making speeches but can start to do so through prefatory remarks. These remarks could include a statement that the witness does not accept but the question that follows may not provide an opportunity to refute this. For example, a question in a disputed child custody case could be, 'I am sure that you will agree with major text-books that boys need a strong father-figure in their lives if they are to develop properly, so could you, please, explain to me the basis of your developmental tests relating to attachment?' Witnesses must anticipate these questions and learn to dissent from any prefatory remarks that they disagree with before they answer the question. If they answer the question first the lawyer may have proceeded to the next question before there is an opportunity to dissent.

The lawyer controls the tempo and subject-matter of the questioning, and can jump from one subject to another. Whilst the lawyer has an excuse for confusion about details and dates, any confusion by the witness gives a bad impression. The lawyer may try to establish a rhythm with a series of questions requiring a short 'yes' or 'no' answer. But soon afterwards a question may not be so easily answered and a reply that begins 'No, but . . .' can sound suspicious and defensive. The witness can also try short prefatory remarks like 'Now that is a different kind of question'.

If the lawyer's client has an alternative explanation for some event, then the lawyer needs to put that explanation to witnesses on the other side. Social workers are encouraged to indicate their willingness to put points in favour of the opposite view (Wright, 1979). This indicates an openness and objectivity. Dismissal of alternative explanations can appear to indicate a closed mind. Highly implausible explanations can be rendered plausible as, it can be argued, they would not be offered if they were not true and we all know that sometimes strange things do happen. The witness who assesses rather than declares, or who states that the explanation is unlikely or unreasonable in all the circumstances rather than impossible or untrue, can appear more authoritative.

Problems can arise when a witness gives an explanation which the lawyer regards as unspectacular and is thereby able to use to suggest incompetence in the witness. For example a parent who has been deprived of a child may be described as depressed and consequently unfit to have the care of the child. The lawyer can suggest that the depression is only natural, indeed there would be grounds for concern if the parent was not, in the circumstances, depressed. In the heat of the moment the witness may be unable to think of the additional information, if there is some, to separate the link the lawyer has suggested between the removal of the child and the depression. Witnesses can apply a 'So what?' test to their own evidence, inquiring whether they are saying anything remarkable at all. Frequently they may find that they have simply omitted certain facts.

If a lawyer leads a witness to say or imply things that he or she did not mean, a quick statement to the judge or magistrates to the effect that incorrect evidence has been given should lead them to allow a restatement. The lawyer for the witness's side has a right to go through the testimony again with the witness and this may sometimes be sufficient.

SUMMARY

Many might argue that it is wrong to teach or encourage 'tricks' or skills, like the above, for use in courts as witnesses. They might argue that it could lead to a different statement of the evidence or assessment of the witness. But, as has been indicated, witnesses can be subjected to experiences and 'tricks' that will lead them to mis-state their evidence or create poor impressions. Allowing witnesses to become skilled as such can, at least, allow a greater concentration on the evidence than the person. It may also contribute towards a thorough scientific assessment of courts and court processes.

NOTE
(1) Since this chapter was written Evans (1983) became available and presents a different perspective.

REFERENCES

ATKINSON, J. M., and DREW, P. (1979). *Order in Court.* London: Macmillan.

BANKOWSKI, Z., and MUNGHAM, G. (1976). *Images of Law.* London:Routledge and Kegan Paul.

BANKOWSKI, Z., and MUNGHAM, G. (1980). Political trials in contemporary Wales: causes and methods. In Z. Bankowski and G. Mungham (Eds), *Essays in Law and Society.* London: Routledge and Kegan Paul.

BARNARD, D. (1979). *The Criminal Court in Action.* London: Butterworth.

BOULTON, SIR W. (1975). *A Guide to Conduct and Etiquette at the Bar,* 6th edn. London: Butterworth.

CARLEN, P. (1974). Remedial routines for the maintenance of control in magistrates' courts. *British Journal of Law and Society,* **1,** 101–117.

CARLEN, P. (1975). Magistrates' courts – a game theory analysis. *Sociological Review,* **1975,** 347–379.

CARLEN, P. (1976). *Magistrates' Justice.* London: Martin Robertson.

CLITHEROE, J. (1980). *A Guide to Conducting a Criminal Defence.* London: Oyez.

CROSS, SIR R. (1979). *Evidence.* London: Butterworth.

DU CANN, R. (1964). *The Art of the Advocate.* Harmondsworth: Penguin.

DANET, B., and BOGOCH, B. (1980). Combativeness in the adversary system of justice. *British Journal of Law and Society,* **7,** 36–60.

DUNSTAN, R. (1980). Context for coercion: analysing properties of courtroom questions. *British Journal of Law and Society,* **7,** 61–77.

EVANS, K. (1983). *Advocacy at the Bar.* London: Financial Training Publications Ltd.

GARFINKEL, H. (1956). Conditions of successful degradation ceremonies. *American Journal of Sociology,* **6,** 420–424.

GLASER, B., and STRAUSS, A. (1971). *Status Passage.* London: Routledge and Kegan Paul.

HERBERT, L., and MATHIESON, A. (1975). *Reports for Courts.* London: National Association of Probation Officers.

HILGENDORF, L. (1981). *Social Workers and Solicitors in Child Care Cases.* London: Her Majesty's Stationery Office.

KING, M. (1978). A status passage analysis of the defendant's progress through the magistrates' court. *Law and Human Behavior,* **2,** 183–221.

MCBARNETT, D. (1981a). *Conviction: Law, the State and the Construction of Justice.* London: Macmillan.

MCBARNETT, D. (1981b). Magistrates' courts and the ideology of justice. *British Journal of Law and Society,* **8,** 181–197.

MAGER, R. F. (1973). *Goal Analysis.* San Francisco: Fearon.

MAY, D. (1978–9). The children's hearing system; the limits to social work influence. *Journal of Social Welfare Law,* **1,** 86.

NAPLEY, SIR D. (1975). *The Technique of Persuasion.* London: Sweet and Maxwell.

WILLIAMSON, H. (1980). Defence and mitigation in the juvenile court: the role of the solicitor in juvenile justice. In Z. Bankowski and G. Mungham (Eds), *Essays in Law and Society.* London: Routledge and Kegan Paul.

WRIGHT, D. (1979). *The Social Worker and the Courts.* London: Heinemann.

YOUNG, A. F. and CLARKE, K. C. (1976). *Chairmanship in Magistrates' Courts.* London: Barry Rose.

Psychology and Law
Edited by D.J. Müller, D.E. Blackman, and A.J. Chapman
© 1984 John Wiley & Sons Ltd

Chapter 31

The Implications of Social Psychological Research for Trial Practice Attorneys[1]

Steven Penrod, Daniel Linz, Harry Heuer, Dan Coates, Michael Atkinson, and Stephen Herzberg

This chapter is concerned with psychological resources that typical attorneys, working with limited resources, might employ to assist them in their trial work. These resources may be contrasted to the traditional trial materials employed by attorneys. We have found that traditional trial advocacy materials contain many myths and stereotypes and common-sense suggestions that have not been subjected to empirical scrutiny (Bailey and Rothblatt, 1971; Bergman, 1979; Hegland, 1978; Keeton, 1973; Mauet, 1980; Morrill, 1972). What these volumes overlook is the fact that there are substantial bodies of research on topics such as bargaining and negotiation, non-verbal behaviour, presentation of victims, human memory and eyewitness reliability, and persuasive communication that can be used to improve the quality of trial advocacy. While there may be questions about the generalizability of psychological findings to the courtroom (Bray and Kerr, 1982), we believe that, in most instances, empirically-based solutions to trial practice problems will out-perform those suggested in traditional trial advocacy text-books. We would go one step further and assert that with careful use of the empirical research findings, attorneys, the courts, and juries can attain a higher quality of justice. In the next few pages we give several examples of how existing research may be used to provide answers to some of the common problems that confront practitioners.

HOW CAN I BE A MORE EFFECTIVE NEGOTIATOR?

Negotiating and bargaining is one area of research which is often overlooked by practising attorneys and legal scholars alike. This oversight is most important when one realizes that the vast majority of an average lawyer's cases are resolved before going to trial. Most estimates are that approximately 90% of all criminal cases in the USA are settled through plea bargaining. Given the popularity of negotiated settlements, the relative inattention to negotiating skills is surprising. Perhaps one explanation for the lack of attention to this research is an implicit theory on the part of legal scholars and practitioners that skilful negotiators are born rather than made. But much of the research that has attempted to relate personality variables to bargaining skills has been disappointing (Donohue, 1978; Hermann and Kogan 1977). One important question, then, that a legal practitioner could ask of research in this area is 'What will increase my effectiveness at bargaining?' We can point to four aspects of negotiation that an attorney can consider before they make contact with opposing counsel.

What are my Goals?

Consider the negotiating style that is appropriate to the situation. Deutsch (1973) defines 'constructive conflict' as that which results in the greatest benefit to both the conflicting parties. According to Deutsch the most important suggestion for resolving conflict constructively is for the parties to approach the conflict co-operatively and to view their tasks as problem-solving rather than as a competitive struggle. Rubin and Brown (1975) address similar concerns, and, based upon their extensive review of the literature, they make the following suggestions for increasing bargaining effectiveness: (1) whenever possible, intangible issues should be converted into more tangible ones; (2) the disputed issues should be formulated so as to avoid 'winner take all' (zero sum) outcomes; (3) variables such as the number of issues to be dealt with, their sequencing, format, abstractions, manner of presentation, and the display or arrangement of alternative solutions should be consciously formulated, whenever possible.

While constructive plea bargaining settlements are ultimately desirable, the adversarial system clearly serves as a substantial barrier to the development of co-operative negotiation. To the extent that attorneys define their conflict as a contest which will be either won or lost, they are likely to engage in competitive rather than co-operative bargaining. This seems especially likely when one considers the American Bar Association's code of professional responsibility which requires zealous representation in seeking the lawful objectives of a client (Canon 7, ABA Code of Professional Responsibility). Osgood (1959, 1962, 1966) outlined a strategy for reducing tensions in strained negotiations by increasing the trust between the negotiators. According to Osgood's graduated reciprocation in tension reduction (GRIT) strategy, one party can initiate tension reduction by making a series of unilateral concessions and inviting reciprocation from the opponent with each conciliatory act. Despite the pressures imposed by the adversarial system, negotiation is rarely reduced to purely competitive terms. Most attorneys find themselves negotiating with the same opposing counsel at some point in the future. Under these conditions any given client's outcomes are likely to be considered against the backdrop of future negotiations, and this imposes some pressures toward constructive negotiation.

What Opening Offer and Concession Strategies Should I Consider?

There is an abundance of research directed at finding the combination of opening offer and concession strategy which will evoke the most concessions from one's opponent. Different theories have suggested diverse strategies ranging from extremely tough bargaining behaviour to extremely generous concession strategies. More moderate concession strategies have been proposed, such as reciprocating exactly an opponent's concessions or making the first offer a fair one and not making any subsequent concessions. Hamner and Yuki (1977) review the various offer strategies in some detail and conclude that a tough strategy is effective when a negotiator has ample time, and is interested in reaching a larger outcome than his or her opponent. However, a soft concession strategy is more effective when a bargainer wishes to reach an agreement which is satisfying to both parties. Lawler and MacMurray (1980) present some evidence that the most effective strategy for eliciting concessions from one's opponent is to start out with a tough opening offer followed by a more generous concession strategy. They suggest, as do Chertkoff and Esser (1976), that a bargainer should foster the impression of being 'firm but reasonable'.

Where Should Negotiations be Conducted?

Most of the research on the physical setting has not used bargaining paradigms, but research from other areas indicates that the physical arrangements can play an important role in the course of the negotiations. For example, Martindale (1971) provides evidence that bargaining on one's home turf can be advantageous. Negotiating at home, in addition to the obvious advantage it provides in access to resources, can also increase the host's assertiveness and produce better outcomes (Rubin and Brown, 1975).

What Role Should my Client Play?

Whether representing a criminal defendant, prosecuting on behalf of a crime victim, or representing civil clients, attorneys must remember that they are ultimately working to achieve satisfaction for the client: goals, for instance, ought to be formulated in the best (and probably realistic) interest of the client. What role should the client play in the negotiating process? This question of constituency surveillance is probably best considered in the light of research relevant to discussion of plea bargaining reform. A common suggestion for reform is to include the judge or defendant in the negotiating process (Morris, 1974). One line of research indicates that such a reform might not be in the defendant's best interest. Negotiators become increasingly concerned with their appearance as tough or competent representatives when they are being observed by an audience (Brown, 1968). This concern with one's appearance has been shown to lead to more competitive bargaining than would otherwise occur: marked by more threats, greater positional commitments, and reduced outcomes (Carnevale, Pruitt, and Britton, 1979). However, there is also research which is more supportive of increased defendant participation in the bargaining process. Results of a study by LaTour (1978) revealed that subjects preferred those adjudication procedures which allowed them to choose their own attorneys. Research by Houlden (1981) showed that actual defendants preferred plea bargaining procedures which allowed their participation, or at least the participation of a community volunteer who would be present to guard a defendant's rights. Thus, it would seem that if the attorney can maintain a flexible negotiating style, there may be benefits, particularly to the client, to keeping clients well informed about negotiations and perhaps fostering direct involvement.

HOW CAN I SELECT AN UNBIASED JURY TO HEAR MY CASE?

In the USA attorneys have a unique opportunity to shape the composition of the jury that ultimately hears a case. Psychologists and other social scientists sometimes play a role in this selection process.

How Should I Select Jurors at the Trial?

The stage at which the attorney has the greatest opportunity to affect the make-up of the final jury is at what is called the *voir dire* or jury selection stage. Although jury selection procedures vary from one state to another (Van Dyke, 1977), the general procedure involves an examination of prospective jurors (via questions addressed by the two trial attorneys or by the judge) for the purpose of detecting potential juror biases. The trial attorneys may excuse 'biased' jurors through the use of two types of challenge. An unlimited number of the challenges for 'cause' may be exercised by either attorney if the attorney can convince the trial judge that the prospective juror's responses indicate predispositions in the case. If the judge is unconvinced on this point, the attorney may exercise one of a limited number of 'peremptory' challenges (which generally range between three challenges in minor cases to as many as 20 challenges in major felony cases).

The availability of peremptory challenges has fostered the development of a number of jury selection strategies offered with great aplomb in traditional trial practice handbooks (e.g. Bailey and Rothblatt, 1971; Keeton, 1973; Morrill, 1972). One of the long-standing beliefs about trial practice is that it is possible with careful forethought to select a jury that will be maximally disposed to hear a case in its most favourable light. This traditional lore on jury selection consists largely of ethnic, occupational, sexual, and other stereotypes presumably adduced from the expert practitioner's own experiences. In fact, there is virtually no empirical support for these strategies (Feild, 1978; Hepburn 1980). But the ambiguities of the jury selection process, particularly the exercise of peremptory challenges, has opened the door to the use of 'experts' in jury selection. Although critics such as Saks (1976) and existing research on attitude–behaviour relationships (Petty and Cacioppo, 1980) indicate that the method has extremely limited value, expensive public opinion survey techniques have been used to aid juror selection in a number of widely publicized cases (ranging from the Harrisburg draft resistance trial in the early 1970s to the Watergate era trial of former US Attorney General, John Mitchell).

Since survey methods are simply not available to most attorneys for changes of venue and jury composition challenges, and since selection of jurors based on trial stereotypes is unreliable, what can psychologists say to attorneys to aid them in jury selection?

(1) *Following personal intuitions.* Although this advice is far from scientifically based, there is little reason to think that any strategy based on stereotypes or personality traits or attitudes is likely to predict how jurors will vote after hearing the evidence. There are several layers of inference of dubious validity involved: first, an assumption that juror attitudes or characteristics are related to voting patterns; second, that the attorney or psychologist knows these relationships; and, third, that the jurors can accurately report their relevant attitudes or that attorneys can accurately detect personality traits. However, there may well be a beneficial 'placebo effect' for attorneys that exclude jurors who would make them or their client feel uncomfortable. The presence of a disquieting juror in the jury box may well adversely affect an attorney's performance throughout the trial even if there are no grounds for discomfort.

(2) *Use the* voir dire *to begin educating jurors about the case, about the evidence, and about the law.* If an attorney has substantial latitude in questioning during *voir dire*, it may be possible to sensitize jurors to the evidence and the law that they will have to consider during the course of the trial. By way of illustration, it is clearly desirable for the defence attorney in a criminal case to ensure that jurors understand that the burden of proof is on the prosecution, that they must acquit the

defendant unless the prosecution proves every element of the offence beyond reasonable doubt, and that the defendant has the benefit of a presumption of innocence. Research on the impact of decision criteria on legal judgments (Nagel and Neef, 1979; Thomas and Hogue, 1976) clearly demonstrates that an informed application of these standards can affect the likelihood a juror will vote for conviction.

(3) *Secure commitments from jurors that they will perform certain important behaviours during the trial.* For example, it might be beneficial to secure commitments that they will maintain an open mind during the trial, that they will search their own minds for reasonable doubt, and that they will hold out for acquittal if they are not convinced beyond a reasonable doubt. Classic social psychological research (Kiesler, 1971; Sherif, 1976) indicates that public commitments to behaviour help to assure that the behaviours will be enacted. It is sometimes even possible to secure individual oral commitments from each juror that they will perform the requested behaviour: 'Ms Jones, can you assure me that you will . . . ?'

MY CLIENT OR WITNESS PERFORMS POORLY IN COURT – WHAT CAN I DO TO ASSURE THAT THE JURY LISTENS TO HIS OR HER STORY?

What this complaint frequently signals is the fact that the client witness may look untrustworthy or sound untrustworthy, even when the attorney is convinced that the witness is telling the truth. If jurors form the same impression, it is possible that the defendant's testimony will be given little weight. Why does the client look or sound bad? What is he or she doing that undermines his or her credibility?

What Factors Influence Perceptions of Credibility?

Non-verbal behaviours are extremely important in impression formation, particularly with respect to perceptions of credibility. Mehrabian and Weiner (1967) found that as much as 93% of the variance in impressions about other people was accounted for by non-verbal information alone. Although other researchers (e.g. Ekman, Friesen, O'Sullivan, and Scherer, 1980) have suggested that the actual level of influence is much lower, the fact remains that these non-content aspects of communication do influence our perceptions of other individuals and their role may be even more acute in courtroom settings where jurors may intentionally make judgments about witness credibility.

What Non-verbal Behaviours are Actually Associated with Honesty and Credibility?

Studies have attempted to identify the non-verbal behaviours actually associated with both credibility and deception. Miller and Burgoon (1982) conclude in their review that, in general, a dissembling individual tends to use a low level of eye contact, has a relatively high-pitched tone of voice (compared to his or her normal pitch), hesitates and pauses when speaking and appears nervous and fidgety. On the other hand, credibility or honesty is indexed by increased eye contact, closer interaction distances, a moderate speech rate with few hesitations or pauses, lower voice pitch, and illustrative gestures. The honest person's behaviour appears spontaneous and natural, in contrast to the liar's behaviour, which often appears deliberate and exaggerated.

How Accurately do People Make Judgments of Credibility and Honesty?

Although the particular patterns of non-verbal behaviour described above are associated with people who are actually lying or actually telling the truth, research results suggest that, even though people are aware of the non-verbal cues that signal deception, they are not very good at the detection and identification of deceptive behaviour. For example, Ekman and Friesen (1974) found that their observers were about 64% accurate (only 14% better than expected by chance) in detecting deception from visual cues (stimulus tapes were shown without sound). But this was only the case when the observers had viewed a prior sample of the target individual's honest behaviour, and only when they attended to body, rather than facial cues. A field study by Kraut and Poe (1980) illustrates how difficult it is to detect a dissembling individual. These researchers recruited airline passengers to participate in a customs inspection. Half of the passengers were given 'contraband' and all were questioned by actual customs officials. The interactions were video-taped and later shown to student observers. The task for both the customs officials and the student observers was to decide which passengers should be stopped and searched for contraband. Results indicated that neither the customs officials nor the student observers could identify accurately those passengers who were lying when asked about contraband.

Considering the literature on the detection of deception, one point is quite clear. Even though they know which non-verbal cues are indicators of deception, people are simply not very good at detecting deception when it occurs and this is particularly true when we are considering the behaviour of strangers. Indeed, Miller and Burgoon (1982) report that the mean accuracy level across a number of studies is about 55%, just 5% above chance. The grave problem for the attorney with a client who performs poorly is that jurors may use behaviours associated with deception as an indicator of deception when, in fact, they are only an indication of nervousness and anxiety. For example, in situations where we believe that deception may occur and we observe someone hesitating or fidgeting there is a strong tendency to assume that the individual must be lying. It may well be the case that the person is only anxious and is actually telling the truth. Kraut and Poe (1980) reported that observers were consistent in their misidentification of deceivers, and were confident that their decisions were correct. Unfortunately, most of the cues to deception are also associated with simple nervousness and people who are inexperienced with courtroom testimony are likely to *be* nervous.

How can a Witness Avoid Giving a Bad Courtroom Impression?

In the courtroom, a witness may lose credibility simply because he or she displays non-verbal behaviours that have been associated with deception. A study by Hemsley and Doob (1978), for example, indicated that a defendant who looked downward while testifying was seen as less credible and was rated as more guilty than a defendant who looked directly at the jurors.

From a practical standpoint, there are several things that an attorney might do to avoid biased inferences of dishonesty generated by inappropriate demeanour. For most people, the courtroom is a very formal and somewhat frightening place. Thus, it is important for attorneys to talk to witnesses and familiarize them with the courtroom and court procedure. Knowing what to expect, perhaps through rehearsal of testimony, should help to reduce stiffness, anxiety, and nervousness on the witness stand. Witnesses and, in particular, defendants are seen as less credible if they fail to make eye contact with the jurors and the attorney. Consequently, witnesses should look at the jury members and the attorney when listening to and when answering questions. To avoid the problem of shifting gaze between the attorney who is asking questions and the jurors, the attorney might conduct the direct examination from behind the far corner of the jury box. In this way, a witness can gaze at both the attorney and the jurors without any postural shifts, and with a minimal shift in the exact focus of eye contact. If possible, the attorney can even arrange to pre-try the examination and cross-examination of witnesses and video-tape the proceedings.

A caveat must, however, be sounded. Deliberate behaviour often appears intentional and exaggerated. It is a bad idea to prepare a 'script' for a particular witness's testimony – this will probably result in more rather than less bias. It is much better for the attorney to elicit demeanour from a witness by making full use of the courtroom (e.g. asking questions from behind the jury box). Identifying and correcting these potential sources of bias can reduce the chance that the attorney will undermine his or her own credibility.

THE VICTIM HAS JUST TESTIFIED – THE STORY WAS A 'TEAR-JERKER' – WHAT CAN I DO TO COUNTER THIS HIGHLY SYMPATHETIC PRESENTATION?

It may surprise most attorneys to learn that 'tear-jerking', emotional testimony by a victim, may produce jury sympathy but undermine the credibility of and liking for the victim. In the 1960s, two theories were proposed to explain at least part of the process underlying the judgments and impressions of victims. Both of these theories, Lerner's 'just world' model (Lerner and Simmons, 1966) and Walster's 'theory of defensive attribution' (Walster, 1966), indicate that we may often blame and derogate victims in order to maintain our own sense of security. We do not like to face the fact that tragedy can strike us, so we try to convince ourselves that victims are different from us, more stupid, more careless or just not as good, and thereby explain the victim's misfortune in a way that enables us to believe that we can escape a similar fate. There is substantial empirical support for the general notion that most of us do form rather negative and biased impressions of victim's personal characteristics and responsibility (Coates, Wortman, and Abbey, 1979; Lerner and Miller, 1978; Sadow and Laird, 1981).

In criminal trials, the victim's testimony is often crucial to the prosecution's case. From a common-sense point of view, it might seem that the best way to elicit sympathy and understanding for the victim would be to emphasize the pain and suffering that he or she has been through. But, if the processes described by the 'just world' and 'defensive attribution' theories operate among jurors in the courtroom, the tactic of stressing the victim's suffering may well backfire. Jurors may be all the more inclined to derogate and blame victim-witnesses, and perhaps doubt their credibility, when the severity of their victimization is made more evident.

There are probably many cues we use in determining how severely a crime victim has suffered. One obvious indicator would be the extent of physical injury. But for many types of crimes, such as burglary, robbery, or even some types of sexual assault, the victim may exhibit no apparent physical injury. A more general indicator of the condition of victims is their apparent emotional state. To the extent that victims seem more distressed or upset, they are also likely to be seen as suffering more severely.

Previous laboratory studies have examined how a victim's emotional state influences others' judgments of him or her. In one of these experiments (Coates *et al.*, 1979) some subjects just heard about a victim's background and her story of a sexual assault. Others also heard the victim explain that while she had been very depressed at first, in the months since the attack she had regained her positive attitudes toward life and her interests in the world. Still others were told the story and also heard the victim explain that she was doing better than she had been at first, but still felt unhappy, apathetic, and unable to forget the rape. The subjects rated the positive effect victim as more attractive and more likeable, while they rated the negative effect victim as less attractive and less likeable than the control victim. The subjects tended to form more negative impressions of victims who seemed depressed and upset.

Calhoun, Cann, Selby, and Magee (1981) reported a similar study that yielded somewhat different results. In their study, subjects read or watched parts of a rape victim's interview with a clinical psychologist the day after the sexual assault had occurred. Half the subjects were exposed to an emotionally distressed victim and the other half were exposed to a victim who demonstrated 'blunted affect' in which the victim appeared calm and described herself as emotionally detached from the immediate situation. In this experiment, unlike the earlier one, subjects rated the victim who seemed distressed and anxious as more likeable. They also rated the more obviously disturbed victim as more innocent and credible.

The findings from these two studies are not really in conflict, for the time that had elapsed since the assault varied considerably in the two studies. In the Coates *et al.* study it was six months, while in the Calhoun *et al.* experiment it was only one day. A victim who is still upset six months after the attack is likely to be seen as suffering more severely than one who is upset a day later, and therefore may be more likely to elicit negative judgments from observers. Since several months are likely to pass before a victim makes it to trial, this reasoning would suggest that emphasizing a victim's unpleasant emotional state would work against him or her in the courtroom.

THE CRITICAL WITNESS IN THE PROSECUTION'S CASE IS AN EYEWITNESS – I AM WORRIED THAT THE JURORS WILL GIVE THE TESTIMONY MORE WEIGHT THAN IT DESERVES

Many times the sole evidence against a defendant may be the testimony of an eyewitness or victim who has identified the defendant from a line-up of photographs. There have been so many instances of false arrests and convictions on the basis of eyewitness identifications and testimony that one British committee (Devlin, 1976) has gone so far as to suggest that prosecutions ought to be halted if the only evidence against a defendant is from eyewitness testimony. Notorious cases such as the Father Pagano prosecution in the USA, in which at least seven robbery victims had made positive identifications of the defendant, only to have another man step forward during Pagano's trial and confess to the crimes (Ellison and Buckhout, 1981), underscore the problems posed by well intentioned but unreliable eyewitnesses.

Why do Problems such as these Arise and what can the Attorney do in Response?

As a starting point, it is clear that attorneys need to know something about how human perception and memory work and to be sensitive to sources of bias or distortion in the witnessing process. There are several discussions of the problems of eyewitness reliability and selected topics are reviewed in this volume (see Section IV), so we will do little more than highlight some of the most important threats to witness reliability.

There is some evidence that police procedures may heighten witness confidence without affecting accuracy (Wells, Ferguson, and Lindsay, 1981), and that jurors are inclined to over-estimate eyewitness accuracy (Wells, Lindsay, and Ferguson, 1979) and to give it too much weight (Loftus, 1980). This problem is compounded when a witness testifies and expresses great confidence in the accuracy of his or her testimony. Particularly in situations in which witnesses have had a poor opportunity to observe what they are reporting on, there is evidence that accuracy and confidence are only very weakly related (Deffenbacher, 1980).[2]

Is the Witness Reporting about Phenomena that are Difficult to Judge?

Grether and Baker (1972) note that people have difficulty in making judgments of size, distances, and speeds in unfamiliar situations or under conditions which have few contextual cues (e.g. it is easier to judge the size of an aeroplane when it is on the ground and can be compared to other objects than to make the same judgment when the plane is airborne). There are many demonstrations of the difficulty people have in estimating the duration of events (e.g. Schiffman and Bobko, 1974).

If the Witness was Attending the Event, did he or she have a good Opportunity to Observe?

Repeated exposures to an event or person improves witness memory (Sanders and Warnick, 1984), as does a longer period of observation that allows witnesses to study and 'rehearse' what they have seen (Graefe and Watkins, 1980).

Was the Witness Under Stress at the Time of Observation?

Research in field (Kuehn, 1974) and laboratory settings (Clifford and Scott, 1978) indicates that higher levels of stress or arousal can, contrary to popular conceptions, undermine witness performance.

How Long has it been Since the Events the Witness is Reporting about?

What is perhaps most interesting about the research on 'forgetting' is that there is apparently relatively little or no degradation or loss of information from memory; rather it appears that memory is non-permanent in the sense that it undergoes change over time as a result of new or incoming information (Loftus and Loftus, 1980). This means the attorney should be alert to post-event behaviours.

Has anything Happened since the Original Event that would Alter the Witness's Memory for the Original Event?

Various studies have shown that 'original' memories can be changed. In a series of inventive studies, Loftus and her colleageus (Loftus, 1977) have shown that investigatory procedures that presuppose the existence of objects or events have the effect of 'planting' a memory for these non-existent objects and events. Simple changes in question wording (Loftus and Palmer, 1974) will affect witness's characterizations of what they have seen. As Malpass and Devine (1981) have demonstrated, in a line-up it is possible, through even a weak suggestion by police that 'the suspect is in the line-up', to increase false identifications of innocent people rather dramatically (from 33% to 78% of identifications in their study).

If the Witness is Reporting an Identification from a Line-up, what are the Potential Sources of bias?

In addition to the type of problem suggested by the Malpass and Devine study, there is a growing body of research demonstrating that the 'functional size' of a line-up plays an important role in reducing identification errors. It is generally recommended that a line-up contains six to eight people who look similar to the suspect. The reasoning behind this is that if a suspect is not the actual perpetrator, the presence of a number of 'foils' will reduce the chance that the suspect will be identified by chance. Thus, it is important to assess the functional size of line-ups in order to determine whether they have been fairly constructed. If only one other person in the line-up actually resembles the suspect, the functional size of the line-up may be only two persons, because only the suspect and the person who resembles the suspect have a chance of being selected by a witness (Malpass, 1981; Wells, Leippe, and Ostrom 1979).

Just how Accurate are Eyewitnesses?

Perhaps the best answer to this question is supplied by examining a variety of eyewitness experiments conducted under realistic circumstances. In one of the most realistic studies (Brigham, Maass, Snyder, and Spaulding, 1982) the 'suspects' made purchases at 24-hour stores, taking care to interact with the clerks for several minutes. When an 'investigator' showed the clerks a photo-spread two hours later, only 34% of the 73 clerks could make an accurate identification. In a pre-test of the procedures used in this study, Brigham *et al.* found that only one out of 15 clerks tested 24 hours after the original purchase could make an accurate identification. Although higher accuracy rates have been reported in 'staged crime' studies (nearly 100% in a live line-up study by Egan, Pittner, and Goldstein, 1977; 58% in a study by Wells, Lindsay, and Ferguson, 1979; and 81% in Lindsay, Wells, and Rumpel, 1981, even lower rates have been reported in other studies (31% in Leippe, Wells, and Ostrom, 1978, and 14% in a study by Buckhout, 1975, in which over 2000 television viewers tried to identify the perpetrator of a televised handbag snatch). The point is that eyewitness accuracy can sometimes be very good, particularly if identifications are made from live line-ups immediately after witnessing events, but they can also be no better than chance, as in the Buckhout study.

How can the Unreliability of Eyewitness Reports be Brought Home to Jurors?

Some commentators have recommended or considered the use of expert psychological testimony (e.g. Loftus, 1979; Woocher, 1977) and Loftus (1980) has shown that communicating information about eyewitness research findings does make mock jurors more sceptical of eyewitnesses. An unevaluated method of bringing eyewitness problems before the jury is for attorneys to raise critical questions during the cross-examination of witnesses and reiterate those questions in closing arguments while also pointing out the threats to eyewitness accuracy noted above.

HOW CAN I BE MORE PERSUASIVE IN THE COURTROOM?

As we noted earlier, there are many trial practice 'handbooks' designed to improve the attorney's in-court performance. Nearly all of these include sections on how to make an 'effective' opening statement and a 'persuasive' closing argument. Some of the advice in these handbooks is quite sound, but virtually none grounds its suggestions in relevant psychological research on persuasive communication.

How can I use the Opening Statement to Facilitate Information Processing?

To be persuaded the juror must first comprehend and recall the facts of the case and the attorney's arguments. One way to facilitate information processing throughout the trial is to provide the jury with a theme, story, or schema which it can use to integrate the facts of the case and the testimony of the witnesses. Bower (e.g. Bower, 1978) has conducted experiments on how people understand and remember coherent prose which demonstrate how a theme can increase comprehension and recall of a set of facts. It is argued that we come to understand a person's actions by identifying goals and plans which imply certain actions. Actions comprehended in the light of a goal are remembered best and recalled most accurately since comprehension is nearly always highly correlated with recall. Other research (Bower, Black, and Turner, 1979; Minsky, 1975; Schank and Abelson, 1977) on 'themes', 'frames', and 'schema' has suggested that they influence memory performance in three major ways: (1) they determine what we will attend to in a message and what we encode into memory; (2) they act as a framework for organizing new information; and (3) they guide the retrieval of information from memory.

Jurors unaware of the goals, plans, and motives of defendants, victims, or other witnesses called to the stand during a trial will have difficulty remembering these characters' actions, and reconstructing the sequence of events as they allegedly transpired. The attorney can facilitate comprehension and recall of testimony by providing the jurors with a 'theme' or 'schema' in the opening statement with which to integrate and understand the testimony of witnesses who will be called to the stand throughout the trial. Recently it has also been suggested that story telling is a powerful organizing device spontaneously used by jurors during deliberation (Bennett, 1978, 1979; Pennington and Hastie, 1981). If the attorney can provide the jurors with a coherent story constructed around a specific theme at the beginning of the trial, he or she may aid this naturally occurring fact-reconstruction process.

Should I Forewarn the Jury about my Opponent's Arguments and Intentions?

While it is not legal for the prosecution directly to allude to evidence that the defence is expected to produce, and probably not advisable for the defence to anticipate too many of the prosecution's points for fear of making the prosecution's case seem more formidable than it is, both sides should anticipate the other side's positions and try to refute them in the opening statement. Social psychological research has demonstrated that refuting an argument or appeal even before an opponent presents it is an effective way to (1) forewarn the audience of impending persuasion attempts by an opponent; (2) facilitate the generation of counter-arguments to your opponent's position; and (3) 'innoculate' the audience against your opponent's future persuasion attempts. Underlying most of this research is the assumption that people are active information processors, not just passive recipients of communications (Petty, Ostrom, and Brock, 1981). From this perspective, it is important that the attorney assist the juror in rehearsing 'counter-arguments' to persuasive appeals made by an opponent. The assumption, of course, is that if each juror were actively to process the communications received during the course of the trial, juror decision-making *biases* which stem from inadequately thinking about the *content* of arguments and testimony would be eliminated (e.g. being convinced by a message simply because it comes from an expert, or listening only to the prosecution's arguments because the defence attorney is personally unappealing, Kaplan and Miller, 1978).

The social psychological research on forewarning, counterarguing, and 'innoculation' has revealed why these strategies work. First, giving people a general warning that they are about to hear a communication designed to make them change their minds about a particular issue causes them to generate counter-arguments *during* the subsequent persuasive appeal (Hass and Grady, 1975). Forewarnings concerning the specific content of an appeal are also effective in motivating subjects to generate counter-arguments if there is a sufficient time delay between the forewarning and the subsequent appeal (Petty and Cacioppo, 1979a,b). Second, if people generate these counter-arguments on their own, or even if they are provided with counter-arguments they have not thought of themselves (Brock, 1967; Petty and Brock, 1976; Petty, Brock, and Brock, 1978) before hearing a persuasive message, they will be less persuaded by the appeal when it comes (Adams and Beatty, 1977; McGuire and Papageorgis, 1961; Pryor and Steinfatt, 1978). Third, a forewarning is *not* effective because it causes the listener to attend selectively to the persuasive appeal (screening out what they do not agree with) or forget what they have heard (Petty and Cacioppo, 1979a). Instead, it is effective because it facilitates more *thought* about the message. Fourth, there are two factors which affect a person's motivation to counter-argue: who will be delivering the appeal and whether or not the topic of the message is a personally involving one. A message coming from a low credibility speaker will produce more thinking and counter-arguing (Gillig and Greenwald, 1974). A message that is of personal importance to the listener will stimulate more counter-arguments (Petty and Cacioppo, 1979b). Finally, enduring attitude change is most likely to occur when people have thoroughly processed the information contained in a communication and generated cognitions that are either favourable or unfavourable to the position advocated (Petty, 1977).

What Persuasive Strategies are Available?

A trial strategy for openings and closings based on each of the above findings might look like the following:

(1) Above all else the attorney should be assisting the juror in trying actively to assimilate arguments. The more the attorney can stimulate or motivate the juror actively to process the information at trial, the better the chances that the truth of the case and arguments will be realized. The juror must be 'drawn in' as a 'cognitively active' participant in the courtroom proceedings. The attorney's goal should be to make the juror a more competent information processor.

(2) After the attorney has made the important points in the opening statement or closing argument, it is important to anticipate the opponent's points (in opening if prosecuting; in closing if defending) and refute them. This may entail making an explicit statement about the fact that the opponent has every intention of persuading the jury to his or her side or the case. State the important points your opponent may make (in a weakened form) and ask jurors to generate their own counter-arguments to the position, as well as think about an explicit list of counter-arguments that the attorney has provided them. This will help them defend against the opponent's persuasion attempts. The attorney's opponent will be attacking your assumptions and arguments and the jurors will have had little practice defending your point of view. The more arguments counter to the opponent's position the attorney can get the jury members to rehearse mentally, the better the chances that they will resist the opponent's appeal.

CONCLUSION

We have discussed only a few of the areas of social scientific research applicable to trial practice. There are many others that could have been included here. For example, we have discussed only a small portion of the rapidly growing field of memory and cognition which suggests strategies for increasing juror understanding and retention of evidence presented in a criminal trial. Other domains of research on persuasive communication have been neglected; for example, variables related to source credibility and message and situation factors such as intelligence which may affect jury understanding of trial events and attorney arguments. We have also had to neglect a large body of research on small group processes and jury decision-making (e.g. Davis, 1980; Penrod and Hastie, 1979; Saks, 1977) which may assist the attorney in preparing for a criminal trial. There are also studies that have examined the influence of rules procedure and evidence on jury decision-making, e.g. the influence of inadmissable evidence (Sue, Smith, and Caldwell, 1973), adversary versus non-adversary proceedings (Thibaut, Walker, and Lind, 1972), comprehension of jury instructions (Sales, Elwork, and Alfini, 1977), studies of severance (Tanford and Penrod, 1984), and many others. It should be clear from what has been presented here that there is a great deal of social psychological research that is very responsive to the practical problems confronted by trial attorneys.

NOTES

(1) This research was supported by a grant from the National Institute of Justice, Grant 80-IJ-CX-0034, to Steven Penrod and Dan Coates.
(2) The reader is referred by the editors to Chapter 18 for further discussion of this topic.

REFERENCES

ADAMS, W. C., and BEATTY, J. J. (1977). Dogmatism, need for social approval, and the resistance to persuasion. *Communication Monographs*, **44**, 321–325.
BAILEY, F. L., and ROTHBLATT, H. B. (1971). *Successful Techniques for Criminal Trials*. New York: Lawyers Cooperative.
BENNETT, W. L. (1978). Storytelling in criminal trials: a model of social judgment. *Quarterly Journal of Speech*, **64**, 1–22.
BENNETT, W. L. (1979). Rhetorical transformation of evidence in criminal trials: creating grounds for legal judgment. *Quarterly Journal of Speech*, **65**, 311–323.
BERGMAN, P. (1979). *Trial Advocacy in a Nutshell*. St Paul, Minn.: West.
BOWER, G. H. (1978). Experiments on story comprehension and recall. *Discourse Processes*, **1**, 211–231.
BOWER, G. H., BLACK, J. B., and TURNER, T. J. (1979). Scripts in memory for text comprehension. *Cognitive Psychology*, **11**, 177–220.
BRAY, R. M., and KERR, N. L. (1982). Methodological considerations in the study of the psychology of the courtroom. In N. R. Kerr and R. M. Bray (Eds), *The Psychology of the Courtroom*. New York: Academic Press.
BRIGHAM, J. C., MAASS, S., SNYDER, L. D., and SPAULDING, K. (1982). Accuracy of eyewitness identification in a field setting. *Journal of Personality and Social Psychology*, **42**, 673–681.
BROCK, T. C. (1967). Communication discrepancy and intent to persuade as determinants of counterargument production. *Journal of Experimental Social Psychology*, **3**, 269–309.
BROWN, B. R. (1968). The effects of need to maintain face on interpersonal bargaining. *Journal of Experimental Social Psychology*, **4**, 107–122.
BUCKHOUT, R. (1975). Nearly 2000 witnesses can be wrong. *Social Action and the Law*, **2**, 7.
CALHOUN, L. G., CANN, A., SELBY, J. W., and MAGEE, D. L. (1981). Victim emotional response: effects on social reactions to victims of rape. *British Journal of Social Psychology*, **20**, 17–21.
CARNEVALE, J. D., PRUITT, D. G., and BRITTON, S. D. (1979). Looking tough: the negotiator under constituent surveillance. *Personality and Social Psychology Bulletin*, **5**, 118–121.
CHERTKOFF, J. M., and ESSER, J. K. (1976). A review of experiments in explicit bargaining. *Journal of Experimental Social Psychology*, **12**, 464–486.
CLIFFORD, B. R., and SCOTT, J. (1978). Individual and situational factors in eyewitness testimony. *Journal of Applied Psychology*, **63**, 352–359.
COATES, D., WORTMAN, C. B., and ABBEY, A. (1979). Reactions to victims. In I. H. Frieze, D. Bar-Tal, and J. S. Carroll (Eds), *New Approaches to Social Problems*. San Francisco, Calif.: Jossey-Bass.

DAVIS, J. H. (1980). Group decision procedural justice. In M. Fishbein (Ed), *Progress in Social Psychology*, Vol. 1. Hillsdale, N. J.: Lawrence Erlbaum.

DEFFENBACHER, K. A. (1980). Eyewitness accuracy and confidence: can we infer anything about their relationship? *Law and Human Behavior*, **4**, 243–260.

DEUTSCH, M. (1973). *The Resolution of Conflict*. New Haven, Conn.: Yale University Press.

DEVLIN, LORD (1976). *Report to the Secretary of State for the Home Office of the Departmental Committee on Evidence of Identification in Criminal Cases*. London: Her Majesty's Stationery Office.

DONOHUE, W. A. (1978). An empirical framework for examining negotiation processes and outcomes. *Communication Monographs*, **45**, 247–257.

EGAN, D., PITTNER, M., and GOLDSTEIN, A. G. (1977). Eyewitness identification: photographs versus live models. *Law and Human Behavior*, **1**, 199–206.

EKMAN P., and FRIESEN, W. V. (1974). Detecting deception from the body or face. *Journal of Personality and Social Psychology*, **29**, 288–298.

EKMAN, P., FRIESEN, W. V., O'SULLIVAN, M., and SCHERER, K. (1980). Relative importance of face, body and speech judgments of personality and affect. *Journal of Personality and Social Psychology*, **38**, 270–277.

ELLISON, K. W., and BUCKHOUT, R. (1981). *Psychology and Criminal Justice*. New York: Harper and Row.

FEILD, H. S. (1978). Juror background characteristics and attitudes toward rape: correlates of jurors' decisions in rape trials. *Law and Human Behavior*, **2**, 73–93.

GILLIG, P. M., and GREENWALD, A. G. (1974). Is it time to lay the sleeper effect to rest? *Journal of Personality and Social Psychology*, **29**, 132–139.

GRAEFE, T. M., and WATKINS, M. J. (1980). Picture rehearsal: an effect of selectively attending to pictures no longer in view. *Journal of Experimental Psychology*, **6**, 156–162.

GRETHER, W. F., and BAKER, C. A. (1972). Visual presentation of information. In H. P. VanCott and R. G. Kinkade (Eds), *Human Engineering Guide to Equipment Design*. Washington D.C.: US Government Printing Office.

HAMNER, C. W., and YUKI, G. A. (1977). The effectiveness of different offer strategies in bargaining. In D. Druckman (Ed), *Negotiations: Social-Psychological Perspectives*. London: Sage.

HASS, R. G., and GRADY, K. (1975). Temporal delay, type of forewarning and resistance to influence. *Journal of Experimental Social Psychology*, **11**, 459–469.

HEGLAND, K. F. (1978). *Trial and Practice Skills in a Nutshell*. St Paul, Minn.: West.

HEMSLEY, G. D., and DOOB, A. N. (1978). The effect of looking behavior on perceptions of a communicator's credibility. *Journal of Applied Social Psychology*, **8**, 136–144.

HEPBURN, J. R. (1980). The objective reality of evidence and the utility of systematic jury selection. *Law and Human Behavior*, **4**, 89–102.

HERMANN, M. G., and KOGAN, N. (1977). Effects of negotiator's personalities on negotiating behavior. In D. Druckman (Ed), *Negotiations: Social-Psychological Perspectives*. Beverly Hills, Calif.: Sage.

HOULDEN, P. (1981). Impact of procedural modifications on evaluations of plea bargaining. *Law and Society Review*, **15**, 267–291.

KAPLAN, M. F., and MILLER, L. E. (1978). Reducing the effects of juror bias. *Journal of Personality and Social Psychology*, **36**, 1443–1455.

KEETON, R. E. (1973). *Trial Tactics and Methods*. Toronto: Little, Brown.

KIESLER, C. A. (1971). *The Psychology of Commitment*. New York: Academic Press.

KRAUT, R. E., and POE, D. (1980). Behavioral roots of person perception: the deception judgments of customs inspectors and laymen. *Journal of Personality and Social Psychology*, **39**, 784–798.

KUEHN, L. L. (1974). Looking down a gun barrel: person perception and violent crime. *Perceptual and Motor Skills*, **39**, 1159–1164.

LATOUR, S. (1978). Determinants of participant and observer satisfaction with adversary and inquisitorial modes of adjudication. *Journal of Personality and Social Psychology*, **36**, 1531–1545.

LAWLER, E. J., and MACMURRAY, B. K. (1980). Bargaining toughness: a qualification of level-of-aspiration and reciprocity hypotheses. *Journal of Applied Social Psychology*, **10**, 416–430.

LEIPPE, M. R., WELLS, G. L., and OSTROM, T. M. (1978). Crime seriousness as a determinant of accuracy in eyewitness identification. *Journal of Applied Psychology*, **63**, 345–351.

LERNER, M. J., and MILLER, D. T. (1978). 'Just world' research and the attribution process: looking back and ahead. *Psychological Bulletin*, **85**, 1030–1049.

LERNER, M. J., and SIMMONS, C. H. (1966). Observers' reactions to the 'innocent victim': compassion or rejection? *Journal of Personality and Social Psychology*, **4**, 203–210.

LINDSAY, R. C. L., WELLS, G. L., and RUMPEL, C. M. (1981). Can people detect eyewitness-identification accuracy within and across situations? *Journal of Applied Psychology*, **66**, 79–89.

LOFTUS, E. F. (1977). Shifting human color memory. *Memory and Cognition*, **5**, 696–699.

LOFTUS, E. F. (1979). *Eyewitness Testimony*. Cambridge, Mass.: Harvard University Press.

LOFTUS, E. F. (1980). Impact of expert psychological testimony on the unreliability of eyewitness identification. *Journal of Applied Psychology*, **65**, 9–15.

LOFTUS, E. F., and LOFTUS, G. R. (1980). On the permanence of stored information in the human brain. *American Psychologist*, **35**, 409–420.

LOFTUS, E. F., and PALMER, J. P. (1974). Reconstruction of automobile destruction: an example of the intersection between language and memory. *Journal of Verbal Learning and Verbal Behavior*, **13**, 585–589.

McGUIRE, W. J., and PAPAGEORGIS, D. (1961). The relative efficacy of various types of prior belief-defense in producing immunity against persuasion. *Journal of Abnormal and Social Psychology*, **62**, 327–337.

MALPASS, R. S. (1981). Effective size and defendant bias in eyewitness identification line-ups. *Law and Human Behavior*, **5**, 299–309.

MALPASS, R. S., and DEVINE, P. G. (1981). Eyewitness identification: line-up instructions and the absence of the offender. *Journal of Applied Psychology*, **66**, 482–489.

MARTINDALE, D. A. (1971). Territorial dominance behavior in dyadic verbal interactions. In *Proceedings of the 76th Annual Convention of the American Psychological Association*. New York: American Psychological Association.

MAUET, T. A. (1980). *Fundamentals of Trial Techniques*. Boston: Little, Brown.

MEHRABIAN, A., and WIENER, M. (1967). Decoding of inconsistent communications. *Journal of Personality and Social Psychology*, **6**, 108–114.

MILLER, G. R., and BURGOON, J. K. (1982). Factors affecting assessments of witness credibility. In N. L. Kerr and R. M. Bray (Eds), *The Psychology of the Courtroom*. New York: Academic Press.

MINSKY, M. (1975). A framework for representing knowledge. In P. Winston (Ed), *The Psychology of Computer Vision*. New York: McGraw-Hill.

MORRILL, A. E. (1972). *Trial Diplomacy*. Chicago: Court Practice Institute.

MORRIS, N. (1974). *The Future of Imprisonment*. Chicago: University of Chicago Press.

NAGEL, S., and NEEF, M. (1979). *Decision Theory and the Legal Process*. Lexington, Mass.: Lexington Books.

OSGOOD, C. (1959). Suggestions for winning the real war with communism. *Journal of Conflict Resolution*, **3**, 295–325.

OSGOOD, C. (1962). *An Alternative to War or Surrender*. Urbana, Ill.: University of Illinois Press.

OSGOOD, C. (1966). *Perspective in Foreign Policy*. Palo Alto, Calif.: Pacific Books.

PENNINGTON, N., and HASTIE, R. (1981). Juror decision-making models: the generalization gap. *Psychological Bulletin*, **89**, 246–287.

PENROD, S., and HASTIE, R. (1979). Models of jury decision making: a critical review. *Psychological Bulletin*, **86**, 462–492.

PETTY, R. E. (1977). The importance of cognitive responses in persuasion. *Advances in Consumer Research*, **4**, 357–362.

PETTY, R. E., and BROCK, T. C. (1976). Effects of responding or not responding to hecklers on audience agreement with a speaker. *Journal of Applied Social Psychology*, **6**, 1–17.

PETTY, R. E., and CACIOPPO, J. T. (1979a). The effects of forewarning of persuasive intent and involvement on cognitive responses and persuasion. *Personality and Social Psychology Bulletin*, **5**, 173–176.

PETTY, R. E., and CACIOPPO, J. T. (1979b). Issue involvement can increase or decrease persuasion by enhancing message-relevant cognitive responses. *Journal of Personality and Social Psychology*, **37**, 1915–1926.

PETTY, R. E., and CACIOPPO, J. T. (1980). *Attitudes and Persuasion: Classic and Contemporary Approaches*. Dubuque, Iowa: W. C. Brown.

PETTY, R. E., BROCK, T. C., and BROCK, S. (1978). Hecklers: boon or bust for speakers? *Public Relations Journal*, **34**, 10–12.

PETTY, R. E., OSTROM, T. M., and BROCK, T. C. (1981). Historical foundations of the cognitive response approach to attitudes and persuasion. In R. E. Petty, T. M. Ostrom, and T. C. Brock (eds), *Cognitive Responses in Persuasion*. Hillsdale, N. J.: Lawrence Erlbaum.

PRYOR, B., and STEINFATT, T. M. (1978). The effects of initial belief level on innoculation theory and its proposed mechanisms. *Human Communication Research*, **4**, 217–230.

RUBIN, J., and BROWN, B. (1975). *The Social Psychology of Bargaining and Negotiation*. New York: Academic Press.

SADOW, D. C., and LAIRD, J. D. (1981). Irrational attributions of responsibility: who's to blame for them? *European Journal of Social Psychology*, **11**, 427–430.

SAKS, M. J. (1976). Scientific jury selection. *Psychology Today*, Jan., 48–57.

SAKS, M. J. (1977). *Jury Verdicts*. Lexington, Mass.: D. C. Heath.

SALES, B. D., ELWORK, A., and ALFINI, J. J. (1977). Improving comprehension for jury instructions. In B. D. Sales (Ed), *Perspectives in Law and Psychology*, Vol. 1, *The Criminal Justice System*. New York: Plenum.

SANDERS, G. S., and WARNICK, D. (1984). Some conditions maximizing eyewitness accuracy: a learning/memory model. *Journal of Criminal Justice*, in press.

SCHANK, R. C., and ABELSON, R. P. (1977). *Scripts, Plans, Goals, and Understanding*. Hillsdale, N. J.: Lawrence Erlbaum.

SCHIFFMAN, H. R., and BOBKO, D. J. (1974). Effects of stimulus complexity on the perception of brief temporal intervals. *Journal of Experimental Psychology*, **103**, 156–159.

SHERIF, C. W. (1976). *Orientations in Social Psychology*. New York: Harper and Row.

SUE, S., SMITH, R., and CALDWELL, C. (1973). Effects of inadmissible evidence on the decision of simulated jurors: a moral dilemma. *Journal of Applied Social Psychology*, **3**, 345–353.

TANFORD, S., and PENROD, S. (1984). Biases in trials involving defendants charged with multiple offenses. *Journal of Applied Social Psychology*, in press.

THIBAUT, J., WALKER, L., and LIND, E. A. (1972). Adversary presentation of bias in legal decisionmaking. *Harvard Law Review*, **86**, 386–401.

THOMAS, E. A. C., and HOGUE, A. (1976). Apparent weight of evidence, decision criteria, and confidence ratings in juror decision making. *Psychological Review*, **83**, 442–465.

VAN DYKE, J. M. (1977). *Jury Selection Procedures: Our Uncertain Commitment to Representative Panels*. Cambridge, Mass.: Ballinger.

WALSTER, E. H. (1966). Assignment of responsibility for an accident. *Journal of Personality and Social Psychology*, **3**, 73–79.

WELLS, G. L., FERGUSON, T. J., and LINDSAY, R. C. L. (1981). The tractibility of eyewitness confidence and its implications for triers of fact. *Journal of Applied Psychology*, **66**, 688–696.

WELLS, G. L., LEIPPE, M. R., and OSTROM, T. M. (1979). Guidelines for empirically assessing the fairness of a line-up. *Law and Human Behavior*, **3**, 285–293.

WELLS, G. L., LINDSAY, R. C. L., and FERGUSON, T. J. (1979). Accuracy, confidence, and juror perceptions in eyewitness identification. *Journal of Applied Psychology*, **64**, 440–448.

WOOCHER, F. D. (1977). Did your eyes deceive you? Expert psychological testimony on the unreliability of eyewitness identification. *Stanford Law Review*, **29**, 969–1030.

Index

457